Phil Edmonston

LEMON-AID

2013

NEW CARS

and TRUCKS

Phil Edmonston

LEMON-AID

2013

NEW CARS and TRUCKS

DUNDURN

TORONTO

Editing: Jade Colbert, Andrea Douglas, Lisa Sparks
Layout and production: Jane Goodwin, Jack Steiner
Illustrations: Rachel Rosen
Design: Ingrid Paulson
Printer: Webcom

1   2   3   4   5   16   15   14   13   12

 Conseil des Arts   Canada Council
du Canada   for the Arts    Canadä   ONTARIO ARTS COUNCIL
                                                        CONSEIL DES ARTS DE L'ONTARIO

We acknowledge the support of the **Canada Council for the Arts** and the **Ontario Arts Council** for our publishing program. We also acknowledge the financial support of the **Government of Canada** through the **Canada Book Fund** and **Livres Canada Books**, and the **Government of Ontario** through the **Ontario Book Publishing Tax Credit program**, and the **Ontario Media Development Corporation**.

Care has been taken to trace the ownership of copyright material used in this book. The author and the publisher welcome any information enabling them to rectify any references or credits in subsequent editions.
J. Kirk Howard, President

Printed and bound in Canada.
www.dundurn.com

Dundurn Press
3 Church Street, Suite 500
Toronto, Ontario, Canada
M5E 1M2

Gazelle Book Services Limited
White Cross Mills
High Town, Lancaster, England
LA1 4XS

Dundurn Press
2250 Military Road
Tonawanda, NY
U.S.A. 14150

MIX
Paper from
responsible sources
FSC® C004071

CONTENTS

KEY DOCUMENTS

Introduction

BETTER CARS, BAD DEALS

A $1,199 "Administration" Fee

Although I usually negotiate no "administration" fee or a reduced fee, I do track what dealers normally charge as an indication to my customers of what I can save them. I just did a small search of administration fees charged over the last year and the results may surprise you.

The administration fees have ranged mostly between $199–$499, however, there have been some charges of $600–$700, and one dealer even billed $1,199.

This does not surprise me, because as the profit margins for the dealers have been falling (excluding holdback; obvious or hidden) and as some manufacturers do not allow the dealers to charge an administration fee, the administration fees that are levied have been going up (if allowed) and a cornucopia of other fees are often added (etching, nitrogen in the tires, etc.). These additional fees have also been going up and cover a lot more items.

BOB PREST
PRESIDENT, DEALFINDER
DEALFINDER@MAGMA.CA
MAY 29, 2012

I don't write *Lemon-Aid*. My readers do.

I transcribe what I learn each year from my readers and whistle-blowers throughout Canada who send me their complaints, compliments, questions, and insider tips. Other sources of information that give *Lemon-Aid* validity no other auto consumer guide can match include lawsuits, court judgments, government reports, and confidential service bulletins detailing "secret warranties," like this one, below.

SPECIAL COVERAGE ADJUSTMENT–CATALYTIC CONVERTER WARRANTY EXTENSION
BULLETIN NO.: 10134 — DATE: NOVEMBER 17, 2010

2006–07 Chevrolet Malibu equipped with 2.2L Engine (L61)
2006–07 Pontiac G6 equipped with 2.4L Engine (LE5)

CONDITION: Some customers of 2006–07 model year Chevrolet Malibu vehicles with a 2.2L engine (L61) and Pontiac G6 vehicles equipped with a 2.4L engine (LE5) may comment about the illumination of the indicator lamp. This may be due to erosion of the mat within the catalytic converter.

SPECIAL COVERAGE ADJUSTMENT: This special coverage covers the condition described for a period of 10 years or 120,000 miles (193,000 km), whichever occurs first, from the date the vehicle was originally placed in service, regardless of ownership. The repairs will be made at no charge to the customer.

Using this secret warranty could save you $600.

When *Lemon-Aid* was first published 42 years ago, it focused on crooked Esso diagnostic clinics, complaints relative to Allstate insurance claims payouts, and Ford's secret J67 warranty covering that company's prematurely rusted cars and trucks. Since then, the book has been a Canadian bestseller with almost 2 million copies sold and a target of two lawsuits filed by Nissan and Honda for $5 million (both cases were thrown out of court).

Over the years, *Lemon-Aid* has successfully advocated for tougher consumer protection laws for auto buyers, more effective small claims courts with higher claim limits, class-action legislation (remember the failure-prone 1971–72 Vauxhall Firenza?), and no-fault insurance. This advocacy has resulted in bedrock jurisprudence that today protects Canadian motorists from unsafe and unreliable automobile "lemons" (see *Kravitz vs. GM*), and dealer/automaker misrepresentation (*Pelletier vs. Nissan*).

But holding Canada's auto industry accountable for its mistakes and false advertising is an ongoing battle. Just when you thought you had seen it all after four decades of research and advocacy, along comes Toyota with millions of cars that suddenly accelerate and lose their braking ability; radioactive vehicles exported from Japan following a series of nuclear reactor meltdowns last year; front head restraints that are literally a pain in the neck; and fuel-saving hybrids and electric vehicles that cost more money than they save (see next page).

Nevertheless, this year's crop of new cars, trucks, and minivans is considerably improved when compared with previous years' models. Crashworthiness standards now include roof strength, Toyota's lineup now has a standard brake override of the throttle, and most vehicles are more fuel frugal thanks to engine improvements like Ford's EcoBoost and Mazda's Skyactiv. For the most part (there are notable exceptions listed in Part Three), reliability is better than ever, with *Consumer Reports* giving even the much-maligned Kia models a "Recommended" rating this year.

Ford's Fiesta, top-ranked for crashworthiness, starts at $12,999, but the more versatile hatchback costs $3,800 more. Why? Less Japanese competition.

On the other hand, automakers are still overcharging Canadians for vehicles that sell for 10–20 percent less in the States, as they continue boosting delivery fees in Canada by more than 100 percent. Also, better quality control at the factory level hasn't been applied evenly for all models. Ford's 2011 Fiesta and Honda's 2012 Civic are just two examples of new models that don't perform as well as expected.

Ford's 2012–13 Fiesta delivers good fuel economy, but reliability has been worse than average, a common trait of vehicles new to the market. Engine, transmission, and electrical malfunctions are the main culprits.

2011 FORD FIESTA FACTORY-RELATED DEFECTS

Technical Service Bulletins

NUMBER	DATE	TITLE
11-10-20	10/20/2011	M/T - Pops Out Of Reverse At High RPM's
11-10-19	10/20/2011	Interior - Rust Colored Stains On Headliner
11-10-13	10/10/2011	A/T, Engine Controls - MIL ON/DTC's Set/TCS Lamp ON
11-9-2	09/07/2011	ASMT Controls - Hesitation/Harsh 1-2 Shifts
11-8-20	08/30/2011	A/T - Grind/Rattle in 2nd/4th/Reverse Gears
11-8-15	08/30/2011	A/T - Grind/Rattle Noise In 2nd, 3rd, 4th/5th Gear
11-8-6	08/18/2011	Emissions/Engine Controls - MIL ON/DTC P0456 Set
11-7-6	07/07/2011	Fuel System - Slow Fuel Fill/Nozzle Shuts Off
11-6-9	06/15/2011	SYNC(R) System - Intermittent Voice Recognition
11-6-8	06/15/2011	A/T - Fluid Leak From Clutch Housing
10B19S1	06/01/2011	Campaign - Engine Block Heater Replacement
11-5-24	05/31/2011	Engine Controls - Starting/A/T Engagement Issue/MIL/DTCs
11-5-23	05/31/2011	Electrical - Starting/A/T Engagement Issues
11-5-22	05/31/2011	Electrical - ABS/TCS Lamps ON/Multiple DTC's Set
11-5-21	05/31/2011	Electrical - MIL ON/DTC U029F/No Crank Condition
11-5-4	05/10/2011	Locks - Autolock(R) Function Non Operational
11-4-5	04/27/2011	Engine, A/T Controls - Harsh 1-2 Shifts
11-3-34	03/31/2011	Body - Window Glass Drops While Driving
11-3-33	03/31/2011	A/T - Rattle/Grinding Noise In Reverse
11-3-21	03/15/2011	Instruments - Clock Loses Time
11-3-6	03/15/2011	Engine - Oil Leak At Cylinder Head Behind Exh Cam Phaser
11-2-17	02/28/2011	Body - Rear Door Weatherstrip Is Loose
11-2-16	02/28/2011	Starting System - Ign. Chime Stays ON With Key Removed
11-2-1	02/07/2011	Wipers/Washers - Rear Washer Fluid Leak
11-1-2	01/25/2011	Instruments - Fuel Gauge Reads 1 Gallon Less Than Actual
10-25-9	12/23/2010	Fuel System - Thumping Noise From Fuel Filler Neck Area
10-25-2	12/23/2010	A/T - Sticky Grease Like Residue In Bell Housing
10-22-5	11/22/2010	A/C - Condensation On Passenger Front Floor
10-22-7	11/22/2010	A/T - Fluid Leak From R./H Axle Seal
10-21-12	11/08/2010	Engine - Slow Return To Idle
10-20-5	10/25/2010	Cooling System - Block Heater Coolant Leak
10-19-5	10/11/2010	Cooling System - Coolant Leak Into Spark Plug Wells
10-17-5	09/13/2010	Engine Controls - Rolling Idle At High Altitude/Temps.

Green, Not So Green

As gas prices continue their upward climb, motorists are investing in hybrid cars that use some battery power to cut driving costs. Yet a study published in April 2012 by *TrueCar.com* has found that even if gas were to reach $5 (U.S.) per gallon, the average driver's lower fuel bills wouldn't offset the higher cost of the vehicle.

The study, commissioned by the *New York Times*, concludes that "it would take the average American consumer more than a decade to realize enough return on investment (ROI) savings to make their high value car purchase worth the acquisition…"

Three vehicles that paid off their higher initial cost the quickest (less than two years) were the Toyota Prius and Lincoln MKZ hybrids and the diesel-powered Volkswagen TDI. Chevrolet's Volt electric car would need to be kept 26.6 years before any savings would occur (see page 15 for True Car's ROI chart that lists other cars, trucks, and SUVs).

2013 Buying Tips

Detroit has bounced back this year after Chrysler and GM emerged from bankruptcy in 2009 following federal and provincial bailouts, Fiat's purchase of Chrysler, and three natural disasters last year that temporarily shut down Japanese auto production and weakened the supply line.

New and used car prices have risen due to the weakened competition and pent up demand for new cars. These prices are expected to remain firm until late 2012 as European makes struggle with a continent-wide recession. By late winter, Chrysler, Ford, and GM will have built up hefty cash reserves to feed new rounds of rebates and discounts to keep their sales momentum going and drive prices downward.

What should the savvy buyer do?

1. Don't buy a new vehicle until the end of the year or early in 2013 when prices will be more competitive, dealer sales incentives and manufacturer rebates will be sweetened, and factory defects will be fewer.
2. If leasing a new vehicle, make sure you have the option to purchase the vehicle at a reasonable price when the lease expires.
3. Buy a discounted 2012 truck or SUV while fuel prices continue their downward trend this winter.
4. Shop in the States for fully loaded trucks, SUVs, vans, and sports cars.
5. Consider only vehicles recommended by *Lemon-Aid*, and steer clear of imported Japanese new cars and trucks until their radiation levels have been verified.

Forget Japanese car bargains in the short term. There won't be any. Instead, consider the South Korean makes. They will continue to rake in big sales numbers by retailing their 2013 vehicles with about half the increase predicted for Detroit-based automakers. Take note that Hyundai and Kia models have become even more popular as a result of the *Consumer Reports* 2012 Annual Auto Issue, which gives a "Recommended" green light to most of Hyundai's 2012 lineup and to a few Kia offerings.

Urgent: A Canadian "Lemon Law"

After a decade of runaway, brakeless Toyotas, "death wobble" Chrysler Ram trucks, computer-controlled cars that go berserk, and record recall campaigns, Canadian car owners need a Lemon Law now more than ever.

It makes no sense that Canadian consumers don't have the same protection that Americans have had in every state for over three decades. Canadians need a code of conduct that all automakers in Canada must follow when their products are unreliable, unsafe, or unfit for their intended use. A Lemon Law does just that.

With a Lemon Law, Canadian consumers can leave their protest signs at home and use the courts, without adding to government bureaucracy and regulations.

In the past, aggrieved car owners could go to court, picket, decorate their cars with lemons, or use independent garages to prove a mechanical failure was factory- or design-related.

Unfortunately, with today's high-cost ($31,000 average transaction price) and high-tech vehicles, only the automaker or dealer has the diagnostic tools and software needed to discover what went wrong and this information is rarely shared with a complaining customer.

Car owners are too often told their vehicle is operating "normally," or that they are driving too fast or too slow, or that all cars of that model behave the same. Other times owners are bounced back and forth between dealer and carmaker, or simply told that the failure couldn't be duplicated.

A Lemon Law would end this ping-pong run-around by telling both the dealer and the automaker "Fix it within three tries, replace it, or refund the purchase price." Instead of hiring a costly expert to find out the cause of the car's stalling, sudden acceleration, loss of brakes, water leaks, paint peeling, etc., the plaintiff need only show the car was out of service more than a certain number of days, or that the dealer failed to fix the vehicle after several attempts.

This is a very simple legal requirement that sends a clear message to buyers and sellers as to their rights and obligations. A Lemon Law evens the playing field because dealers will know their third unsuccessful "fix" could be their last chance and auto owners would see a "lemon" defined legally, thereby encouraging them to file suit, without waiting for government help.

Lemon-Aid has successfully lobbied over the past 42 years for class actions, no-fault auto insurance, strong small claims courts, and effective provincial consumer protection legislation. Hopefully, lemon laws will soon be adopted by all Canadian provinces.

Lemon Law Background Information

Just over a decade ago the province of Ontario came within a whisker of adopting its own Lemon Law.

In 1992, Mississauga Tory MPP Rob Sampson proposed a bill that allowed buyers to take back to the automaker any vehicle that hadn't been successfully repaired under the manufacturer's warranty after three attempts to correct the same problem, or that would cost more than $1,000 to repair. The Bill, if approved by the legislature, would have been Canada's first Lemon Law.

Under Sampson's bi-partisan bill, the consumer had the option to make the automaker repurchase the motor vehicle or provide a free replacement.

Unfortunately, a provincial election was called before the proposed legislation could be passed at Queen's Park.

What's New in *Lemon-Aid 2013*?

We know that car-buying attitudes have changed dramatically. At one time, you were judged by what you drove, and what you drove was traded in every three to five years. That's no longer the case. We are now more environmentally sensitive and cost-conscious. Buyers expect their new cars to burn less fuel, and they want their vehicles to last much longer than the finance payments. To this end, we have made the following changes to the 2013 *Lemon-Aid New Car and Truck Guide*:

- There are more vehicles rated, and we have made some surprising downgrades and upgrades relative to some redesigned models.
- We have included more roof crashworthiness ratings and updated our cross-border shopping guide, so you can buy for less in the States or ask your Canadian dealer to match the *Lemon-Aid*-listed price.
- Revised summaries of safety- and performance-related defects that are likely to affect 2012 and 2013 vehicles. This information is gleaned from internal service bulletins, government-posted consumer complaints, and *Lemon-Aid* reader feedback.
- In Appendix I, "Mini-Reviews and 2014 Previews," we rate vehicles that have been on the market for only a short time or are sold in small numbers, as well as give previews of some 2014 models that may be better choices.

Better yet, *Lemon-Aid* lists websites you can use on the dealer's lot to compare prices and owner complaints for particular models. Additionally, you will know

SAMPLE LEMON LAWS IN STATES BORDERING CANADA

LOCATION	LEMON LAW COVERAGE	REPAIR INTERVAL AND COVERAGE PERIOD
All States	Consumers everywhere are protected by the Federal Lemon Law, which applies to all consumer products, including automobile, trucks, motorcycles, RVs, boats, and all other ordinary consumer products including computers and household appliances.	3 to 4 repairs for the same problem, or 6 to 8 repairs to the entire product during the warranty period.
		Warranty period + up to 4 additional years.
		1 year or 12,000 miles.
Alaska	Any land vehicle having four or more wheels, that is self-propelled by a motor, is normally used for personal, family, or household purposes, and is required to be registered. Does not include a tractor, farm vehicle, or a vehicle designed primarily for off-road use.	3 repair attempts or 30 business days out of service.
		Warranty period or 1 year.
		Warranty period, 2 years, or 24,000 miles.
		2 years or 24,000 miles.
		18 months or 18,000 miles.
		Warranty period, 2 years, or 24,000 miles.
		Warranty period, 2 years, or 24,000 miles.
Illinois	New cars. Light trucks and vans under 8,000 pounds. Recreational vehicles excluding trailers. Excludes motorcycles.	4 repair attempts or 30 business days out of service.
		1 year or 12,000 miles.
		18 months or 18,000 miles.
		Warranty period or 1 year.
		Warranty period or 1 year.
Maine	Any vehicle purchased or leased. Excludes commercial vehicles over 8,000 pounds.	3 repair attempts or 15 business days out of service.
		2 years or 18,000 miles.
		1 year or 15,000 miles.
Michigan	Any new car, van, or truck bought by a resident of Michigan for personal or family use.	4 repair attempts or 30 business days out of service.
		Warranty period or 1 year.
		Warranty period or 1 year.
		Warranty period or 1 year.
		2 years or 18,000 miles.
		Warranty period or 1 year.
New York	Any non-commercial motor vehicle purchased or leased, except for motorcycles, certain motor homes, and off-road vehicles.	4 repair attempts or 30 calendar days out of service.
		2 years or 18,000 miles.
		1 year or 18,000 miles.
		Warranty period, 1 year, or 12,000 miles.
		Warranty period or 1 year.

LOCATION	LEMON LAW COVERAGE	REPAIR INTERVAL AND COVERAGE PERIOD
Vermont	Passenger motor vehicles and trucks under 10,000 pounds GVW. Does not include snowmobiles, motorcycles, mopeds, or the living portion of recreational vehicles.	3 repair attempts or 30 calendar days out of service.
		Warranty period.
		18 months.
Washington	Any new self-propelled vehicle, including a new motorcycle, primarily designed for the transportation of persons or property over the public highways. Does not include living portions of motor homes or trucks with 19,000 or more GVW.	4 repair attempts or 30 calendar days out of service. 2 attempts for a serious safety defect.
		2 years or 24,000 miles.
Wisconsin	All vehicles except mopeds, semi-trailers, or trailers designed for use in combination with a truck or truck tractor.	4 repair attempts or 30 days out of service.
		Warranty period or 1 year.

Source: *www.carlemon.com/lemons.html*

the wholesale and retail value of your trade-in and see a projection of its value over three and five years.

"A Tough Customer"

Yes, *Lemon-Aid* is tough.

As always, this year's guide combines test results with owner feedback to provide a critical comparison of 2012 and 2013 vehicles as to their real fuel-economy and crashworthiness.

Head restraints "styled by sadists."

If new features are "more show than go," or improvements and additional safety features don't justify the higher costs of newer models (like run-flat tires and Marquis de Sade head restraints), we say so and suggest you buy the less-loaded, safer, more reliable, better-designed, and cheaper alternative. Front, offset, side, rear, rollover, and roof strength crash test results are also included, along with an exhaustive list of accessories and optional safety features; we'll tell you which are useful and which are useless. We show how much profit dealers make on each vehicle, and what should be considered a fair price on both sides of the border. We are also carefully watching cross-border prices. We know many new- and used-car prices in the States beat the Canadian MSRP by 10–25 percent.

Essentially, *Lemon-Aid* endorses fair prices, safety features that work, reliable products, and respectful, honest dealings.

Is that too tough?

Phil Edmonston

October 2012

Volvo's Driverless Cars

The future of fully automated driving just got a whole lot closer as Volvo successfully led a road train—consisting of a Volvo XC60, a Volvo V60, and a Volvo S60, and one truck—at 85 km/h for 200 kilometers through Spain. The event was part of Volvo's "Safe Road Trains for the Environment" in which cars were outfitted with cameras, radars, and laser sensors to monitor and mimic the lead vehicle and other vehicles in their immediate vicinity. The wireless communication system allowed the vehicles to accelerate, brake, and make turns the same way as the leader. Throughout the test the vehicles were about 20 feet apart.

MARC CARTER
HTTP://INHABITAT.COM/VOLVOS-SARTRE-FULLY-AUTOMATED-ROAD-
TRAIN-TRAVELS-124-MILES-THROUGH-SPAIN

Volvo's Brakeless Cars

The exhibition was supposed to show off the vaunted "city safety" feature on Volvo's S60 sedan, which applies brakes automatically in the event of an imminent crash. Instead, a dais full of journalists was treated to the spectacle of the shiny, orange sedan plowing headlong into the back of a strategically placed transport trailer, then bouncing back after impact with its windshield wipers flapping ridiculously. Erik Coelingh, technical leader of Volvo's so-called "active safety" program, recently told Maclean's that the braking system had failed due to lack of power from an improperly charged battery. But there was no avoiding the tsunami of ridicule this sort of footage tends to elicit. "What's the problem here?" snickered one Web commenter. "It came to a complete stop, no?"

CHARLES GILLIS
WWW2.MACLEANS.CA/2011/11/03/DRIVING-AMBITION

Detroit: Profit from Disaster

In a desperate effort to cut costs, a lot of makes have been culled from the Detroit herd within the last few years, much to the relief of *Lemon-Aid* staff who said their purchase was a huge mistake in the first place. Those divisions that weren't shut down like Pontiac, Mercury, and Saturn, were sold to other auto manufacturers for barely one-third of their original acquisition cost (Jaguar, Land Rover, Saab, and Volvo). Saab later declared bankruptcy.

Nevertheless, Chrysler, Ford, and General Motors are now making more profits from selling fewer cars. Ford, the only automaker that didn't take a bailout from the feds (except for part of a $25 million "green car" campaign), is leading the pack with its popular Fusion, Escape SUV, and Mustang sports car.

Ford's 2013 Mustang is powerful, fuel efficient, and fun to drive. Too bad it has major powertrain failings highlighted by frequent transmission failures. The revised 2011s have three times the normal number of safety failures; the 2012 model has double the failures one would expect. Here's one NHTSA post from *safercar.org*:

My 2012 Mustang GT was most likely totaled tonight when the transmission did not allow a shift into 5th gear. It slid into 3rd gear and caused the wheels to spin resulting in the car fishtailing and hitting a tree in the median. It had just started to rain which was a factor in this as the road was slicker than normal, but transmission problems [had] been reported to the local Ford dealership this past week. They were too busy to check the car when reported and ironically, the car was supposed to be looked at in the morning. We had reported to Ford an issue with shifting into 5th gear. They told us there was a common issue with this but there was no recall. All airbags deployed and luckily there were no deaths.

Chrysler: Fiat's Saviour?

GM's extensive restructuring accomplishments make Chrysler's roll of the dice with a Fiat partnership look extremely risky, especially considering the debt crisis putting many European countries one election away from bankruptcy. Ironically, after rescuing a bankrupt Chrysler, Fiat now needs Chrysler cash to avoid bankruptcy itself.

Detroit's smallest automaker posted a $225 million profit in 2011 to complete its first profitable year since its bankruptcy and bailout in 2009. The profit came on the back of $15.1 billion in revenues, up a whopping 41 percent from 2010. Chrysler promptly withdrew an application for a U.S. government loan worth more than $3 billion to help it make cars and trucks that are more fuel efficient. The company said it was confident in its ability to adopt new technologies and make competitive products without new government assistance.

And, Fiat? Not so good. The Italian new car market contracted by 18 percent last April, and Fiat, Italy's largest carmaker, has sustained even bigger losses. Fiat is presently offering to pay half the cost of fuel to buyers of its cars for the first three years of ownership. This harkens back to the '70s when bankruptcy-bound American Motors Canada offered free television sets to Gremlin buyers (the TVs lasted longer than the cars).

CANADA'S TOP 30 BESTSELLERS

PLACE	MODEL	APRIL 2012	APRIL 2011	%
1	Ford F-Series	31,669	29,669	+6.7
2	Dodge Ram	22,234	18,575	+19.7
3	Honda Civic	20,288	17,181	+18.1
4	Dodge Grand Caravan	16,957	18,895	-10.3
5	Hyundai Elantra	16,236	14,528	+11.8
6	Toyota Corolla	13,230	13,480	-1.9
7	GMC Sierra	13,218	13,194	+0.2
8	Mazda 3	11,894	10,720	+11.0
9	Honda CR-V	11,775	9,406	+25.2
10	Ford Escape	11,527	13,031	-11.5
11	Chevrolet Silverado	11,050	11,623	-5.0
12	Chevrolet Cruze	9,599	11,528	-16.7
13	Dodge Journey	9,014	11,123	-19.0
14	Ford Focus	7,814	6,444	+21.3
15	Volkswagen Jetta	7,393	8,522	-13.2
16	Hyundai Accent	7,298	6,781	+7.6
17	Toyota RAV4	7,231	8,698	-16.9
18	Hyundai Santa Fe	6,896	7,565	-8.8
19	Chevrolet Equinox	6,846	7,240	-5.4
20	Toyota Camry	6,551	2,878	+128.0
21	Jeep Wrangler	5,824	4,246	+37.2
22	Nissan Rogue	5,778	4,094	+41.1
23	Hyundai Sonata	5,609	6,263	-10.4
24	Ford Fusion	5,230	5,339	-2.0
25	Chrysler 200	5,087	1,879	+171.0
26	Ford Edge	4,715	4,306	+9.5
27	Kia Forte	4,561	4,311	+5.8

CANADA'S TOP 30 BESTSELLERS continued

PLACE	MODEL	APRIL 2012	APRIL 2011	%
28	Nissan Altima	4,502	3,588	+25.5
29	Hyundai Tucson	4,422	5,014	-11.8
30	Toyota Matrix	4,195	5,418	-22.6

Source: Automakers and *Automotive News*

Note: Canadians aren't hybrid or electric car fans. The Chevrolet Volt, Mitsubishi i, and Nissan LEAF posted a total of 372 sales in the first four months of 2012. Toyota's Prius registered 864 sales, without counting the just-released Prius C or Prius V. Listed as number 10 in sales in the States, the Prius lineup holds 48th place in Canada.

MODELS SELLING THE FEWEST CARS IN CANADA

PLACE	MODEL	APRIL 2012	APRIL 2011	%
1	Lexus HS250h	77	136	-43.4
2	Mitsubishi i MiEV	68	—	—
3	Jaguar XJ	62	73	-15.1
4	Volvo C70	58	52	+11.5
5	Audi A8	57	76	-25.0
6	Acura ZDX	55	39	+41.0
7	Porsche Cayman	54	30	+80.0
8	Dodge Nitro	53	143	-62.9
9	Audi R8	46	46	0.0
10	Mercedes-Benz SLS AMG	41	54	-24.1
11	Honda Insight	39	142	72.6
12	Hyundai Equus	37	27	+37.0
13	Nissan GT R	36	6	+500.0
14	Dodge Dakota	31	570	-94.6
15	Ford Crown Victoria	30	1,020	-97.1
16	Mazda RX-8	25	33	-24.2
17	Jaguar XK	25	47	-46.8
18	Mercedes-Benz SL-Class	25	63	-60.3
19	Lexus LS	24	53	-54.7
20	Acura CSX	20	571	-96.5
21	Saab 9-3	14	26	-46.2
22	Porsche Boxster	13	48	-72.9
23	Acura RL	8	25	-68.0
24	Saab 9-5	5	15	-66.7
25	Dodge Viper	4	13	-69.2
26	Kia Borrego	4	44	-90.9
27	Honda Element	3	121	-97.5
28	Lexus LFA	2	4	-50.0
29	Cadillac STS	2	6	-66.7
30	Cadillac DTS	2	131	-98.5

Note: Saab declared bankruptcy on December 11, 2011; GM Canada will honour the warranty on all Saabs it sold.

Buying Strategies

The global economic slowdown has pushed down oil prices. The resulting cheaper fuel is boosting the prices of large, fully loaded trucks, vans, and SUVs while small and mid-sized vehicles are discounted. Savings of 20 percent or more are commonplace and will probably increase as we go into the winter months.

With that in mind, here are 10 strategies for buying in 2013:

1. Don't let fuel economy stampede you into buying a vehicle that's underpowered or too small. Instead, look for a new or used vehicle that is relatively uncomplicated to drive and service, has been on the market for some time, and has been sold in large numbers. This will ensure that cheaper, independent garages can provide service and parts.

2. Look for a discounted 2013 model that's finishing its model run or is scheduled to be revised next year. But steer clear of models that will be dropped because of poor reliability or mediocre performance (see Part Three).

3. Stay away from heavily discounted European offerings, especially SUVs. Dealership networks are weak, parts are inordinately expensive and hard to find, and with all the economic turmoil, few garages will invest in the expensive equipment needed to service complicated emissions and fuel-delivery systems. The old axiom that there is a right way, a wrong way, and a European way to troubleshoot a car still holds true.

4. Don't buy a hybrid, electric, or high-end diesel model. Hybrids are complicated to service, are dealer-dependent, and they don't provide the fuel economy or return on investment they hype. The recent Fukushima earthquake destroyed many of the hybrid component suppliers and has forced automakers to cut back hybrid production, resulting in long waits for some replacement parts. Electric cars have different drawbacks: a lack of recharging infrastructure; poor performance in cold weather or when running over hilly terrain; and you don't get a decent return on investment before 26.6 years. Small diesels are your best choice for maximum savings, but their complexity has increased due to more stringent emissions regulations and they require frequent, expensive urea fill-ups. This said, the VW TDI is your best diesel choice, providing a favourable ROI in just over a year.

5. Don't buy Chrysler, Dodge, Jeep, or Fiat models. Chrysler is the weakest of the Detroit Three, its lineup has a sad history of serious safety- and performance-related defects, and its automatic transmissions, brakes, and air conditioners are particularly troublesome. This may all change by next year if this year's new powertrains and assorted other improvements correct two decades of design deficiencies. The Dodge 200 and Grand Cherokee refinements will tell us if Chrysler quality has improved. The same holds true for the recently arrived, overpriced Fiat 500.

6. Don't buy vehicles imported from China. Crash test ratings for many China-made vehicles are listed as "Poor," and their assembly quality is crude, at best. Jacob George, vice-president of China operations for J.D. Power Asia Pacific, says China-built vehicles won't match U.S. average initial quality before 2016.

	MODEL	AVERAGE PRICE	M.P.G.	ANNUAL FUEL SAVINGS	YEARS TO BREAK EVEN
Ford	Fiesta	$15,557	33.5	$23	
	Fiesta SFE	$16,170	34.0		26.8
Chevrolet	Cruze Eco	$19,925	34.3	$446	
	Volt*	$31,767	—		26.6
Honda	Civic	$18,675	33.0	$440	
	Civic Hybrid	$23,999	44.0		12.1
Ford	Escape	$23,048	24.2	$623	
	Escape Hybrid	$30,204	32.7		11.5
Toyota	Highlander	$35,746	19.3	$938	
	Highlander Hybrid	$44,623	28.0		9.5
Ford	Focus	$16,874	32.5	$48	
	Focus SE SFE	$17,305	33.4		9.0
Nissan	Versa	$18,640	33.6	$1,119	
	Leaf*	$28,421	—		8.7
Ford	Fusion	$22,924	27.5	$610	
	Fusion Hybrid	$28,080	38.8		8.5
Porsche	Cayenne	$64,917	18.7	$470	
	Cayenne Hybrid	$68,843	21.8		8.4
Toyota	Camry	$24,253	29.5	$481	
	Camry Hybrid	$27,124	39.1		6.0
Hyundai	Sonata	$23,110	29.0	$444	
	Sonata Hybrid	$25,664	37.3		5.8
Kia	Optima	$23,543	29.0	$444	
	Optima Hybrid	$25,994	37.3		5.5
Ford	F-150	$28,878	17.7	$181	
	F-150 EcoBoost	$29,731	18.7		4.7
Chevrolet	Cruze	$19,231	31.4	$156	
	Cruze Eco	$19,925	34.3		4.4
Lexus	IS 250	$34,137	25.1	$796	
	HS 250h	$36,040	34.6		2.4
Toyota	Camry	$22,097	29.5	$794	
	Prius	$23,537	49.7		1.8
Lincoln	MKZ	$32,493	22.1	$1,129	
	MKZ Hybrid	$33,887	38.8		1.2
Volkswagen	Jetta	$24,816	27.2	$373	
	Jetta TDI	$25,242	35.4		1.1

Hybrid price **includes federal tax credit** when applicable.

Fuel savings are based on a price of **$3.85 per gallon** of regular gas, **$4.14 per gallon** of diesel.

The m.p.g. includes **both city and highway.**

*The Volt's m.p.g. takes into account both battery use and gas mileage; the Leaf's energy cost is based on the cost of electricity alone.

Source: *www.truecar.com*

In fact, last May three people died when a China-built electric car burned to the ground.

7. Consider Honda: the automaker has offered more reliable and better-performing buys since it started cutting costs and selling off large chunks of the company several years ago. The added cash was invested in new models

and better quality control that has made some Below Average models (such as the 2012 Honda Civic) into Average (2013 Civic) buys.

8. Don't buy from dual dealerships. Parts inventories at many dealerships may have been depleted due to slow sales, and qualified mechanics may be in short supply. The auto companies represented by a dual dealership see the dealership as less than loyal and will cut the dealership little slack in vehicle deliveries and warranty assistance.

9. Don't buy any vehicle that requires an extended warranty due to a reputation for past failures. Choose a better car instead.

10. Use your credit card for the down payment, and put down as little money as possible. Use credit instead of cash to pay for repairs and maintenance charges. If you want to cancel a sales contract or work order, it's easier to do with a credit card than with cash.

Trustworthy Advice

Current, independent, and reliable car-buying advice is hard to find, especially as it relates to the Canadian market. Although most of your friends and relatives will have something to say, don't believe everything they tell you. One study carried out by the Sauder School of Business at the University of British Columbia says that friends with expertise in a certain field may provide inaccurate advice when recalling complex or nuanced facts relating to another matter.

Check facts out with several other independent sources. There's always *www.thetruthaboutcars.com*, *www.jalopnik.com*, and the National Highway Traffic and Safety Administration's (NHTSA) complaint website, *www.safercar.gov*. On the following page is a screenshot of the latter—pay particular attention to the tabs running down the left side of the page. They link you to other key sites that include relevant service bulletins, safety-related recalls, past and present defect investigations, and crashworthiness rankings.

NHTSA info is useful when dealer service managers lie and say your problem isn't safety-related or hasn't been seen before.

> I entered into a parking lot behind a cluster of homes, a car was behind me and the driver indicated that I was going at less than 3-5 miles per hour. I parked the car and all of the sudden the car accelerated, went over the parking bump and over a wood safety wall, over some bushes and landed 2 feet down, damaging the homes and a couple of heating units. I pressed the brake, but the car kept on accelerating. This car should not be on the market.

Publications you can trust are *Consumer Reports* and the British Consumers Association's *Which?* In Canada, the *Toronto Star*'s long-time consumer columnist Ellen Roseman is a tough advocate for consumer rights and often scoops the motoring press in exposing scams and defects.

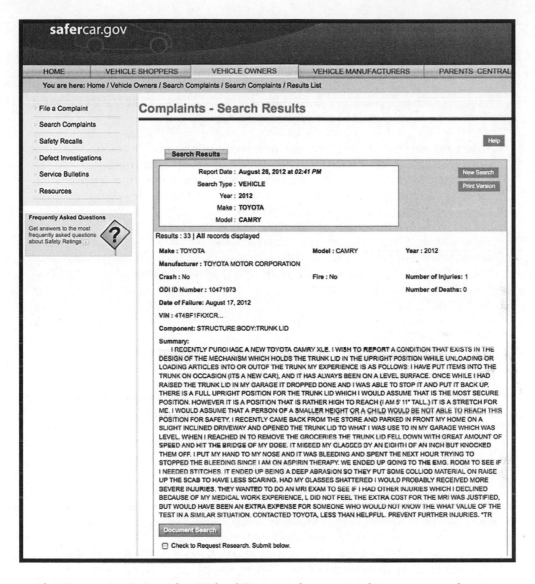

The *Toronto Star*'s Saturday "Wheels" section has come a long way over the past three decades. It no longer relies so much on auto industry puff pieces, free press junkets, and the free product "souvenirs" that garnish automaker press conferences. Originally an apologist for the automakers with kissy-kissy car reviews and a weekly "say nothing" column from the president of the Toronto Automobile Dealers Association (TADA), "Wheels" has been improved by its increased use of young freelance journalists and female writers. Yes—female writers! They sweat the details more, are less likely to be intimidated by Oshawa and Oakville suits, and take into account (when necessary) what families need in terms of vehicle performance.

I particularly like the practical articles written by Mark Toljagic (such as "If the warranty runs out, who ya gonna call?"—an article about good places to repair Hondas, Saabs, and Volvos in Toronto, which can be found at *www.wheels.ca/if-the-warranty-runs-out-who-ya-gonna-call-1230*) and independent-minded Jil McIntosh, an antique car and hot rod hobbyist with knowledge of custom cars and restored vehicles (such as "Prius-like Lexus hardly worth premium," which can be found at *www.wheels.ca/prius-like-lexus-hardly-worth-premium*).

An example of the "Wheels" section's new tough reporting style is John LeBlanc's May 15, 2010, exposé of the Automobile Journalists Association of Canada (AJAC) and that group's annual Canadian Car of the Year awards. In a large header, LeBlanc asks a simple question: "Should Automakers Pay for Awards?"

His article begins by rehashing the *Wall Street Journal*'s report blasting *Consumers Digest* magazine (not to be confused with *Consumer Reports*) for asking automakers to pay them $35,000 for the right to advertise that they've received *CD*'s "Best Buy" rating, and $25,000 for each lower rating ("Auto Awards Clouded by Fees," *Wall Street Journal*, May 10, 2010).

Before the entry was rewritten with an advertorial slant, Wikipedia had this to say about *Consumers Digest*:

> Founded in 1960 and published by Consumers Digest Communications, LLC, *Consumers Digest* is an American for-profit magazine that allows companies to use its reviews for marketing purposes for a fee. Many car makers have financial ties to the publication. The magazine chose 15 General Motors vehicles for its 2010 "Best Buy" awards—and then GM paid the magazine for the right to mention those awards. According to *Consumers Digest*, the magazine awards its Consumers Digest Best Buy seal to products its staff judges to be of the best quality for the most reasonable price.
>
> The magazine charges a $35,000 annual fee for use of its green and gold Consumers Digest Best Buy seal. Some of the brands that have licensed the seal include Cal Spas hot tubs, Bridgestone Tires, Brinks Home Security, Multi-Pure Drinking Water Systems, McKleinUSA Business Cases and Mercury Automobiles....The magazine is sold at newsstands only and does not reveal its sales figures. In 2001, when it ceased subscription distribution, it listed 700,000 subscribers....
>
> The publication has no connection to the *Consumers Digest* magazine published by Consumers Union (which, unlike *Consumers Digest*, is an independent non-profit organization). It also has no relationship to the defunct *Consumers Digest* published by the pioneering Consumers' Research, Inc., 1910–1983, from which Consumers Union sprang.

But how's this for an example of Canadian car columnists' ingenuity: LeBlanc discovered that AJAC doesn't charge a fee for publicizing its 56 or so annual vehicle ratings (hurray!). Instead, AJAC demands that the automakers simply pay the Association $6,900 for each of the 56 vehicles tested, after supplying the vehicle gratis.

Writes LeBlanc:

> Although AJAC says on its site the purpose of its event is to "provide consumers with sound, comparative information on vehicles that are new to the market," not all "new" cars are evaluated....Brands like Aston Martin, Bentley, Chrysler Group, Ferrari, Maserati, Maybach, Lamborghini, Lotus and Rolls-Royce did not participate at all.
>
> So, the question is: Should there be a clear separation of church (automotive award organizers) and state (automaker PR departments) when it comes to automotive awards?

Lemon-Aid says the real question to ask should be this one: If you take bribes (money, trips, computers, clothes, etc.) from companies to extol their products, are you a journalist or a prostitute with a keyboard?

We first answered that question in the 1995 edition of *Lemon-Aid* when we denounced the AJAC and car columnists for taking money from the industry whose cars they were testing.

The "Wheels" article alleges that AJAC is possibly charging automakers 56 times $6,900 annually, or $386,400, not counting the 125 or so individual journalist memberships at $320 each, $3,000 corporate dues, $935 associate corporate dues, and $175 affiliate dues. That's a lot of gas money, and it certainly merits investigation as to where the money goes, who pays what, how elections are carried out, and what family relationships the directors and employees have with the auto writers.

I assume everything is on the up and up with AJAC, but then, when dealing with the auto industry and its apologists, keep in mind that their credibility is only a notch or so above that of British Petroleum (BP) in Louisiana.

For an exceptionally well-written and thoroughly researched update on "Wheels" junkets and more, go to Joe Clark's personal blog at *http://blog.fawny. org/2008/05/18/wheels-ethics*.

The American "Car of the Year" (COTY) Scam

After nearly 42 years writing *Lemon-Aid*, I know that car manufacturers run from the truth and look upon independent critics with hostile suspicion. That's why independent car critics have such a difficult time rating new and used vehicles without selling out to the car industry.

Yet the road to "auto-censorship" is so subtle that few writers or broadcasters can resist compromising their integrity: The kids need private schooling; the mortgage must be paid. The smooth-talking executive car pimps are always there to say how much the company admires your work, but then they tell your editor or program director how much better your stories would be with more "balance." And then these hustlers invite you on their trips to Asia and Europe, where they give you free food and drink, hats, jackets, laptop computers, specially prepared vehicles, and interviews with the top brass. They even sponsor annual journalism awards to make sure their coterie of friendly scribes spouts the party line.

Once you've established a budget and selected some vehicles that interest you, the next step is to ascertain which ones have high safety and reliability ratings. Be wary of the "Car of the Year" ratings found in car enthusiast magazines and on most websites; their supposedly independent tests are a lot of baloney.

Imagine: *Car and Driver* rated the Ford Focus as a "Best Buy" during its first three model years, while government and consumer groups decried the car's dozen or so recall campaigns and the huge number of owners' safety and reliability complaints.

Motor Trend, another American car buff magazine, has been giving out annual COTY awards since the late 1940s. At first the publication recognized automakers only, and then branched out to individual models. Most of the models were heavily publicized in *MT's* text and ads. Also, many of the highly rated vehicles became infamous for poor reliability and mediocre performance.

Through the years an entire lemon orchard has grown in *Motor Trend's* Car of the Year lists. Can you see someone trying to sell their AMC/Renault Alliance, Chrysler Omni, Volare, or Aspen, Ford Taurus/Sable, or GM Vega/Astre as COTY "classics"?

In the final analysis, new car buyers would be better served by a Ouija board's buying recommendation than a "Car of the Year" designation put out by any publication.

Credible Auto Info

Most investigative stories done on the auto industry in Canada (such as exposés on secret car warranties, dangerous airbags, and car company shenanigans) have been written by business columnists, freelancers, or "action line" troubleshooters rather than by reporters on the auto beat. Also, many full-time auto writers have been fired as ad revenues have dried up over the past few years. Most media outlets are now using syndicated, homogenized articles from the States or Toronto that may be only marginally relevant to the rest of Canada.

Again, it bears repeating that those auto reporters who still have a job are regularly beaten into submission by myopic, "kiss-butt" editors and greedy publishers who don't give them the time or the encouragement to do hard-hitting investigative exposés. In fact, it's quite impressive that we do have a small cadre of reporters who won't be cowed.

Canada also has a number of auto experts and consumer advocates who aren't afraid to take on the auto industry and follow good stories, no matter where they lead. Here are some of my favourites:

- Jeremy Cato and Michael Vaughan are two of Canada's best-known automotive and business journalists. This duo is the epitome of auto journalism and business reporting excellence because they ask the tough questions automakers hate to answer. They appear regularly on the Canadian television Business News Network and freelance for a number of national newspapers, including the Toronto *Globe and Mail*.
- Mohamed Bouchama, president of Car Help Canada, shakes up the auto industry by rating new and used cars, providing legal advice, and teaching consumers the art of complaining on his *Auto Shop* television program shown every Sunday at 8:00 p.m. on Toronto's CP24.
- I have known and respected the *Toronto Star*'s Ellen Roseman for more than 30 years. She is one of Canada's foremost consumer advocates and business columnists, and never pulls back from an important story—no matter how loudly advertisers squeal. She teaches, does TV and radio, and maintains a blog to give her readers current information on all types of consumer issues.
- Phil Bailey is a Lachine, Quebec, garage owner with almost five decades of experience with European, Japanese, and American cars. In his insightful comments on the car industry, he's as skillful with his pen as he is with a wrench, and he's got the everyday garage experience to make him and Toronto AM740 Zoomer Radio broadcaster and garage owner Alan Gelman such unimpeachable auto industry critics. Alan co-hosts Dave Redinger's *Dave's Corner Garage* on Saturdays at 10:00 a.m.

These reporters and consumer advocates represent the exception, not the rule. Even the most ardent reporters frequently have to jump through hoops to get their stories out, simply because their editors or station managers have bought into many of the fraudulent practices so common to the auto industry. Haranguing staff for more "balance" is the pretext du jour for squelching hard-hitting stories that implicate dealers and automakers. News editors don't want truth; they want copy and comfort. They'll spend weeks sifting through Prime Minister Stephen Harper's trash bins looking for conflicts of interest while ignoring the auto industry scams threaded throughout their own advertisers' ads and commercials.

Want proof? Try to decipher the fine print in *The Globe and Mail*'s or the *Toronto Star*'s new car ads, or better yet, tell me what the fine print scrolled at breakneck speeds on television car commercials really says. Where is the investigative reporter who will submit these ads to an optometrists' group to confirm that the message is unreadable?

Think about this: Dealers posing as private parties and selling used cars from residences ("curbsiders") are periodically exposed by dealer associations and "crusading" auto journalists. Yet these scam artists place dozens or more ads every week in the classified sections of local newspapers that employ these same muck-raking reporters. The same phone numbers and billing addresses reappear in the ads, sometimes days after the scam has been featured in local news reports. The ad order-takers know who these crooks are. News editors know that their own papers are promoting these scammers. Why isn't there an ad exposé by reporters working for these papers? Why don't they publish the fact that it's mostly new-vehicle dealers who supply curbsiders with their cars? That's what I'd call balanced reporting.

Two of my favourite auto journalists—Dan Neil, automotive writer for the liberal *Los Angeles Times*, and Robert Farago, a long-time columnist, auto critic, and creator of *The Truth About Cars* (a UK-based website)—were both punished for writing the truth.

Neil's paper was hit with a $10 million (U.S.) loss after General Motors and its dealers pulled their ads in response to his sharp criticism of GM for a series of poor management decisions that lead to the flop of its 2005 G6 model:

> GM is a morass of a business case, but one thing seems clear enough, and Lutz's mistake was to state the obvious and then recant: The company's multiplicity of divisions and models is turning into a circular firing squad, someone's head ought to roll, and the most likely candidate would be the luminous white noggin of Lutz. [The G6] is not an awful car. It's entirely adequate. But plainly, adequate is not nearly enough.

> *LOS ANGELES TIMES*, APRIL 6, 2005

The *Times* stood by Neil, a Pulitzer Prize–winning automobile columnist. GM's ads eventually returned after a hiatus of several months.

Farago didn't fare as well. In late August 2005, he was canned and stayed canned. His column was permanently axed, without explanation, by the uber-liberal *San Francisco Chronicle* after his criticism of Subaru's Tribeca, as an SUV wannabe.

Other Information Sources

Funny, as soon as they hear that you're shopping for a new car, all your relatives, co-workers, and friends want to tell you what to buy.

After a while, you'll get so many conflicting opinions that it'll seem as if any choice you make will be wrong. Before making your decision, remember that you should invest a month of research into your project of buying a $15,000–$30,000 new car. This includes two weeks for basic research and another two weeks to bargain with dealers to get the right price and equipment. The following sources provide useful information that will help you ferret out what vehicle best suits your needs and budget.

Auto shows

Auto shows are held from January through March across Canada, starting in Montreal and ending in Vancouver. Although you can't drive or buy a car at the show, you can easily compare prices and the interior and exterior styling of different vehicles. In fact, show officials estimate that about 20 percent of auto show visitors are actively seeking info for an upcoming new-car purchase. Interestingly, while the shows are open, dealer traffic nosedives, making for much more generous deals in showrooms. Business usually picks up following the auto shows.

Shopping on the Internet

The key word here is "shopping," because *Consumer Reports* magazine has found that barely 2 percent of Internet users actually buy a new or used car online. Yet over 80 percent of buyers admit to using the Internet to get prices and specifications before visiting the dealership. Apparently, few buyers want to purchase a new or used vehicle without first seeing what's offered and knowing all money paid will be accounted for.

New-vehicle shopping through automaker and independent websites is a quick and easy way to compare prices and model specifications, but you will have to be careful. Many so-called independent sites are merely fronts for dealers and automakers, tailoring their information to steer you into their showroom or convince you to buy a certain brand of car.

Shoppers now have access to information they were once routinely denied or had trouble finding, such as dealers' price markups and incentive programs, the book value for trade-ins, and considerable safety data. Canadian shoppers can get Canadian invoice prices and specs by visiting the Automobile Protection Agency (APA) at *www.apa.ca*.

Other advantages to online shopping? Some dealers offer a lower price to online shoppers; the entire transaction, including financing, can be done on the Internet; and buyers don't have to haggle—they merely electronically post their best offers to a number of dealers in their area code (for more convenient servicing of the vehicle) and then await counteroffers. But here are three caveats: (1) You will have to go to a dealer to finalize the contract, and be preyed upon by the financing and insurance sales agents; (2) as far as bargains are concerned, *Consumer Reports* says its test shoppers obtained lower prices more frequently by visiting the dealer's showroom and concluding the sale there; and (3) only one-third of online dealers respond to customer queries.

Auto Quality Rankings

Consumer groups and non-profit auto associations like APA (*www.apa.ca*) and Car Help Canada (*www.carhelpcanada.com*) are your best bets for the least biased auto ratings for Canadians. They're not perfect, though, so it's a good idea to consult both groups and look for ratings that agree with each other.

Consumer Reports (CR) is an American publication that once had a tenuous affiliation with the Consumers' Association of Canada before their relationship went sour in the '80s.

CR's ratings mostly reflect the Consumers Union's annual U.S. member survey; the responses don't quite mirror the Canadian experience. Components that are particularly vulnerable to our harsh climate usually don't perform as well as the *CR* reliability ratings indicate, and poor servicing caused by a weak dealer body in Canada can make some service-dependent vehicles a nightmare to own here, whereas the American experience may be less problematic.

Based on more than one million responses from subscribers to *Consumer Reports* and *ConsumerReports.org*, *CR*'s annual auto reliability findings are impressively comprehensive, though they may not always be correct. Statisticians agree that *CR*'s sampling method leaves some room for error, but, with a few notable exceptions, the ratings are fair, conservative, and consistent guidelines for buying a reliable vehicle. Not so for child safety seats. A January 2007 *CR* report said that 10 out of 12 seats it tested failed disastrously at impact speeds of 56–61 km/h. NHTSA checked *CR*'s findings and discovered that the side-impact speeds actually exceeded 112 km/h. *CR* admitted it made a mistake.

My only criticism of the *CR* auto ratings is that many Asian models, like ones by Toyota and Honda, haven't always been as harshly scrutinized as their American counterparts, yet service bulletins and extended "goodwill" warranties have shown for years that they also have serious engine, transmission, brake, and electrical problems. *Consumer Reports* confirmed this anomaly in its April 2006 edition, where it admitted that Asian vehicle quality improvement has "slowed" since 2002—one incredible understatement when one considers that Toyota especially has been coasting on its reputation for quality since the mid-'90s. Toyota owner reports of sudden, unintended acceleration incidents started to climb in 2002.

When and Where to Buy

When to Buy

Shop in the first quarter of 2013 to get a reasonable price and find a good supply of vehicles already on the dealer's lot (cars on the lot usually get the best rebates). Shoppers who wait until next summer or early fall can double-dip from additional automakers' dealer incentive and buyer rebate programs. Honda, Nissan, and Toyota will likely pour the most money into sales incentives in an effort to recapture market shares lost through reduced production in 2011. Remember, too, that vehicles made between March and August offer the most factory upgrades and fewer factory-related glitches.

Visit the showroom at the end of the month, just before closing, when the salesperson will want to make that one last sale to meet the month's quota. If sales have been terrible, the sales manager may be willing to do some extra negotiating in order to boost sales staff morale.

Where to Buy

Large cities have greater selection, and dealers offer a variety of payment plans that will likely suit your budget. Prices in cities are also very competitive as dealers use sales volume to make most of their profit.

Finding a Good Dealer

But price isn't everything, and good dealers aren't always the ones with the lowest prices. Buying from someone who you know gives honest and reliable service is just as important as getting a low price. Check a dealer's honesty and reliability by talking with motorists in your community who drive vehicles purchased from the local dealer (identified by the nameplate on the vehicle's trunk). If these customers have been treated fairly, they'll be glad to recommend their dealer. You can also check the dealer's thoroughness in new-vehicle preparation and servicing by renting a dealership vehicle for a weekend, or by getting your trade-in serviced.

How can you tell which dealers are the most honest and competent? Well, judging from the thousands of reports I receive each year, dealerships in small suburban and rural communities are often fairer than big-city dealers because they're more vulnerable to negative word-of-mouth testimonials and to poor sales—when their vehicles aren't selling, good service picks up the slack. Their prices may also be more competitive, but don't count on it. Unfortunately, as part of their bankruptcy restructuring, Chrysler and General Motors closed down many dealerships in suburban and rural areas because the dealers couldn't generate sufficient sales volume to meet the automakers' profit targets.

Dealers that sell more than one manufacturer's product line present special problems. Their overhead can be quite high, and the cancellation of a dual dealership by an automaker in favour of setting up an exclusive franchise elsewhere is an ever-present threat. Parts availability may also be a problem because dealers with two separate vehicle lines must split their inventory and may, therefore, have an inadequate supply on hand (read: Smart/Mercedes and the former Mitsubishi/Chrysler partnership).

Despite these drawbacks, you can always get better treatment by going to dealerships that are accredited by auto clubs, such as the Canadian Automobile Association (CAA), or consumer groups like the Automobile Protection Association (APA) and Car Help Canada. Auto club accreditation is no ironclad guarantee that a dealership will be honest or competent; however, if you're insulted, cheated, or given bad service by one of their recommended garages (look for the accreditation symbol in a dealer's phone book ad, on the Internet, or on their shop windows), the accrediting agency is one more place to take your complaint to apply additional mediation pressure. And, as you'll see in Part Two, plaintiffs have won substantial refunds by pleading that an auto club is legally responsible for the actions of a garage it recommends.

The quality of new-vehicle service is directly linked to the number and competence of dealerships within the network. If the network is weak, some parts will likely be unavailable, repair costs can go through the roof, and the skill level of the mechanics may be subpar, since better mechanics command higher salaries. Among foreign manufacturers, Asian automakers have the best overall dealer representation across Canada, except for Mitsubishi and Suzuki.

Kia's dealer network is adequate and growing through strong sales after having been left by its former owner, Hyundai, to fend on its own for many years. Mitsubishi, on the other hand, was floundering last year, despite having a good array of quality products. Its major problems have always been an insufficient product and a weak dealer network paired with outlets that sold other makes. After many dealers closed their doors when Chrysler and GM went bankrupt, Mitsubishi had to scurry around looking for new dealers who hadn't been gobbled up by Hyundai, Kia, and Mazda. Nevertheless, last year's surge in small car sales has helped Mitsu's bottom line tremendously, forcing the automaker to bolster its North American dealer body.

European automaker profits are expected to stagnate throughout 2012 and into early 2013 as the recession continues to hammer new car sales in Europe. The poor economy has already forced European auto manufacturers to offer attractive dealer sales incentives and customer rebates geared to move the large stock of cars on dealers' lots before the 2013s arrive. So don't be surprised to see BMW, Fiat, Mercedes, Smart, and Volkswagen put up sizeable cash discounts and low-interest financing plans to keep their small cars selling. European luxury cars are less vulnerable to a souring economy, but they may also need some sales incentives if Chinese and European sales erode.

Automobile Brokers and Vehicle-Buying Services

Brokers are independent agents who act as intermediaries to find the new or used vehicle you want at a price below what you'd normally pay. They have their Rolodex of contacts, speak the sales lingo, know all the angles and scams, and generally cut through the bull to find a fair price—usually within days. Their services may cost a few hundred dollars, but you may save a few thousand. Additionally, you save the stress and hassle associated with the dealership experience, which for many people is like a trip to the dentist.

Brokers get new vehicles through dealers, while used vehicles may come from dealers, auctions, private sellers, and leasing companies. The broker's job is to find a vehicle that meets a client's expressed needs and then to negotiate its purchase (or lease) on behalf of that client. The majority of brokers tend to deal exclusively in new vehicles, with a small percentage dealing in both new and used vehicles.

Ancillary services vary among brokers and may include such things as comparative vehicle analysis and price research.

The cost of hiring a broker can be charged either as a flat fee of a few hundred dollars or as a percentage of the value of the vehicle (usually 1–2 percent). The flat fee is usually best because it encourages the broker to keep the selling price low. Reputable brokers are not beholden to any particular dealership or make, and they'll disclose their flat fee up front or tell you the percentage amount they'll charge on a specific vehicle. Brokers used to purchasing cars in the States may charge a few thousand dollars, seriously cutting into the savings you may get from a lower purchase price. Seriously consider doing the transaction without a broker. It's that easy.

Finding the right broker

Good brokers are hard to find, particularly in western Canada. Buyers who are looking for a broker should first ask friends and acquaintances if they can recommend one. Word-of-mouth referrals are often the best because people won't refer others to a service with which they were dissatisfied.

Dealfinder

For most buyers, going into a dealer showroom to negotiate a fair price is intimidating and confusing. Numbers are thrown at you, promises are made and broken, and after getting the "lowest price possible," you realize your neighbour paid a couple thousand dollars less for the same vehicle.

No wonder smart consumers are turning away from the "showroom shakedown" and letting professional buyers, like Ottawa-based Dealfinder Inc. separate the steak from the sizzle and real prices from "come-ons." In fact, simply by dealing with the dealership directly, Dealfinder can automatically save you the $200+ sales agent's commission before negotiations even begin.

For a $159 (plus tax) flat fee, Dealfinder acts as a price consultant after you have chosen the vehicle you want. The agency then shops dealers for the new car or truck of your choice in any geographic area you indicate. It gets no kickbacks from retailers or manufacturers, and if you can negotiate and document a lower price than Dealfinder gets, the fee will be refunded. What's more, you're under no obligation to buy the vehicle they recommend, since there is absolutely no collusion between Dealfinder and any manufacturer or dealership.

Dealfinder is a small Ontario-based operation that has been run by Bob Prest for over 20 years. He knows the ins and outs of new car price negotiation and has an impressive list of clients. His reputation is spread by word-of-mouth recommendations and the occasional media report. He can be reached by phone at 1-800-331-2044, or by email at *www.dealfinder.org/index.htm* and *dealfinder@ magma.ca*.

Is Dealfinder worth its cost? *Lemon-Aid* thinks so, and so do many of the buyers using the service, judging by the following testimonials:

> I was excited when I first contacted Bob Prest of DEALFINDER Inc. and learned of his innovative vehicle-consulting program. I wondered why I had not heard about his service earlier. He quickly explained that advertising-driven publications would not permit him to advertise his service. Therefore, he relied on personal endorsement for his growth.
>
> I immediately offered to notify *Canadian MoneySaver* about his (then Ontario-only) program.
>
> A SATISFIED CLIENT

•

> I bought a new car in October, using the services of DEALFINDER. I found them to be pleasant and extremely efficient. They saved me several thousand dollars and renewed my subscription to your magazine which I continue to enjoy and profit from.
>
> JOHN THATCHER, MISSISSAUGA, ONTARIO

•

> This is a note to tell you how thoroughly satisfied with the "shopping" Bob Prest did for me. I leased a new Honda Civic LX for $202.01/month...this compares with Honda's ads (without any of my options) for $218.00/month. Bob was very open and thorough in developing cost and mark-up information for me, and never pressed me in any way.
>
> TED BJERKELUND, OTTAWA, ONTARIO

•

> Great service. Great deal. What can I say except—How great thou is!
>
> JOHN MCEWEN, DALHOUSIE, NEW BRUNSWICK
> (JOHN SAVED $2,983 ON HIS NEW DODGE CARAVAN PURCHASE)

•

> Mr. Prest listed our requirements...We were pleasantly surprised to hear (from Bob) the next day with a very attractive quote. No Pressure, no signing and a great price. He held our hands throughout with total understanding.
>
> NEIL THOMPSON, WEST VANCOUVER, BRITISH COLUMBIA

Buying a New Car, Truck, SUV, or Van

I remember in the '70s, American Motors gave away free TVs with each new car purchase, just before shutting its doors. In the past decade, GM gave away free Dell computers and VW hawked free guitars with its cars. The Detroit Three auto-makers continue to build poor-quality cars and trucks, although it appears there have been some improvements over the past several years. The gap between Asian and American automobile quality has narrowed; however, this may reflect only a lowered benchmark following recent glitches with Honda, Nissan, and Toyota powertrains, electrical systems, and body fits. Nevertheless, Japanese and South Korean makes continue to dominate J.D. Power and Associates' dependability surveys, while American and European makes are mostly ranked below the industry average, but are trending upward.

Toyota has done extraordinarily well, even in light of its sudden, unintended acceleration and brake failure safety problems that resulted in a $48.8 million government-imposed fine and $10 billion spent in recall campaigns and investigations. Although profits plummeted 77 percent during the first quarter of 2011, principally due to the March 2011 earthquake, the company has now recaptured most of its market share.

Step 1: Keep It Simple

First, keep in mind that you are going to spend much more money than you may have anticipated—almost $31,000 for the average vehicle transaction, according to Dennis DesRosiers, a Toronto-based auto consultant. This is because of the many hidden fees, like freight charges and so-called administrative costs, that are added to the bottom line. But, with cut-throat discounts and armed with tips from this guide, you can bring that amount down considerably.

According to the Canadian Automobile Association (CAA), the average household owns two vehicles, which are each driven about 20,000 km annually and cost an average of $800 a year for maintenance; DesRosiers estimates $1,100.

Do Toyota hybrids really save you money over a similar gasoline-powered small car? Not according to CAA. In its 2010 *Driving Costs* brochure the auto association says Toyota's Prius hybrid costs more to drive than an equivalent Chevrolet Cobalt. The total cost of driving 32,000 kilometres in a 2010 Toyota Prius is $10,783, while the 2010 Chevrolet Cobalt LT would cost slightly less at $10,694. The cost rises to $14,363 for a 2010 Dodge Grand Caravan. With fuel costs plummeting by over 20 percent during the first half of 2012, the Cobalt advantage would likely be more today.

Keep in mind that it's practically impossible to buy a bare-bones car or truck, because automakers know this is a seller's market until early 2013, so they cram new cars with costly, non-essential performance and convenience features in order to maximize their profits. Nevertheless, money-wasting features like electronic navigation, self-parking, camera vision, digital screens, and voice-command capability can easily be passed up with little impact on safety or convenience. In fact, voice command and in-dash computer screens can be very distracting while driving—producing a negative safety effect. Full-torso side curtain airbags and electronic stability control, however, are important safety options that are well worth the extra expense.

Our driving needs are influenced by where we live, our lifestyle, and our age (see pages 48–49 for a discussion of vehicles best suited to mature drivers). The ideal car should be crashworthy and easy to drive, have minimal high-tech features to distract and annoy, and not cost much to maintain.

In the city, a small wagon or hatchback is more practical and less expensive than a mid-sized car like the Honda Accord or Toyota Camry. Furthermore, have you seen the newer Civic and Elantra? What once were small cars are now quite large, relatively fuel-efficient, and equipped with more horsepower than you'll ever likely need. Nevertheless, if you're going to be doing a lot of highway driving, transporting small groups of people, or loading up on accessories, a medium-sized sedan, wagon, or small sport-utility could be the best choice for price, comfort, and reliability.

Don't let spikes in fuel prices frighten you into buying a vehicle unsuitable to your driving needs. If you travel less than 20,000 km per year, mostly in the city, choose a small car or SUV equipped with a 4-cylinder engine that produces about 140 hp to get the best fuel economy without sacrificing performance. Anything more powerful is just a waste, unless you intend to load the vehicle with a lot of extra equipment, or carry a heavy load of passengers. Extensive highway driving may also be safer and more comfortable with a slightly larger 6-cylinder engine.

Be especially wary of the towing capabilities bandied about by automakers. They routinely exaggerate towing capability and seldom mention the need for expensive optional equipment, or that the top safe towing speed may be only 72 km/h (45 mph). Generally, 3.0L to 3.8L V6 engines will safely accommodate most towing needs. The 4-cylinder engines may handle light loads but will likely offer a white-knuckle experience when merging with highway traffic or travelling over hilly terrain.

Remember, you may have to change your driving habits to accommodate the type of vehicle you purchase. Front-drive braking is quite different from braking with a rear-drive, and braking efficiency on ABS-equipped vehicles is compromised if you pump the brakes. Also, rear-drive vans handle like trucks, and you may scrub the right rear tire during sharp right-hand turns until you get the hang of making wider turns. Limited rear visibility is another problem with larger vans, forcing drivers to carefully survey side and rear traffic before changing lanes or merging.

Step 2: Be Realistic

Don't confuse styling with needs (do you have a bucket bottom to conform to those bucket seats?) or trendy with essential (will a cheaper downsized SUV like a Hyundai Tucson or Subaru Forester suit you as well as, or better than, a mid-sized car?). Visiting the showroom with your spouse or a sensible friend will help you steer a truer course through all the non-essential options you'll be offered.

Women ask the important questions. Men, take your mother, wife, or sister along next time!

Oftentimes, getting a female perspective can be really helpful. Women don't generally receive the same welcome at auto showrooms as men do, but that's because they make the salesmen (yes, usually less than 10 percent of the sales staff are women) work too hard to make a sale. Most sales agents admit that female shoppers are far more knowledgeable about what they want and more patient in negotiating the contract's details than men, who tend to be mesmerized by many of the techno-toys available.

In increasing numbers, women have discovered that minivans, SUVs, and small pickups are more versatile than passenger cars and station wagons. And, having spotted a profitable trend, automakers are offering increased versatility combined with unconventional styling in so-called "crossover" vehicles. These blended cars are part sedan and part station wagon, with a touch of sport-utility added for function and fun. For example, the 2012 Ford Flex is a smaller, sporty crossover vehicle that looks like a miniature SUV.

Ford's $29,999 ($29,355 in the States) Flex is somewhat pricey, but it does offer car-like performance, SUV versatility, and excellent crashworthiness. A perusal of Ford service bulletins shows long-term reliability is still a question mark.

Step 3: What Can I Afford?

Determine how much money you can spend, and then decide which vehicles in that price range interest you. Have several models in mind so that the overpriced one won't tempt you too much. As your benchmarks, use the ratings, alternative models, estimated purchase costs, and residual value figures shown in Part Three of this guide. Remember, logic and prudence are the first casualties of showroom hype, so carefully consider what you actually need and how these things will fit into your budget before you compare models and prices at a dealership. Write down your first, second, and third choices relative to each model and the equipment offered. Browse the automaker websites both in Canada and in the States to find the manufacturer's suggested retail price (MSRP), promotions, and package discounts. Look for special low prices that may apply only to Internet-generated referrals. Once you get a good idea of the price variations, get out the fax machine or computer at home or work (a company letterhead is always impressive) and then make the dealers bid against each other (see page 79). Call the lowest-bidding dealership, ask for an appointment to be assured of getting a sales agent's complete attention, and take along the downloaded price info from the Canadian and American automaker websites to prevent arguments.

Sometimes a cheaper "twin" will fit the bill. Twins are nameplates made by different auto manufacturers, or by different divisions of the same company, that are virtually identical in body design and mechanical components, like the Chevrolet Silverado and GMC Sierra pickups; Chrysler minivans; and the 2012 turbocharged Hyundai Sonata and Kia Optima—both cars have practically the same equipment.

Let's look at the savings possible with "twinned" Chrysler minivans. A 2006 Grand Caravan SXT that was originally listed for $35,735 is now worth about $5,000. An upscale 2006 Town & Country Limited that performs similarly to the Grand Caravan, with just a few additional gizmos, first sold for $47,905 and is now worth about $8,500 Where once almost $12,000 separated the two minivans, the price difference is now only $3,500—and you can expect the gap to close to almost nil over the next few years. Did the little extras really justify the Town & Country's higher price, or make it a better buy than the Grand Caravan? Obviously, the marketplace thinks not.

And don't get taken in by the "Buy Canadian!" chanting from Chrysler, Ford, General Motors, and the Canadian Auto Workers. It's pure hokum. While Detroit-based automakers are beating their chests over the need to buy American, they buy Japanese and South Korean companies and then market the foreign imports from Asian factories as their own. This practice has resulted in bastardized nameplates whose parentage isn't always easy to nail down. For example, is Chrysler American or Italian? Is an Aveo a Chevy or a Daewoo? (For the record, it's a Daewoo, and not that reliable, to boot.)

Vehicles that are produced through co-ventures between Detroit automakers and Asian manufacturers have better quality control than vehicles manufactured by companies that were bought outright, and this looks like one of the factors that may save the American auto industry. For example, Toyota and Pontiac churned out identical Matrix and Vibe compacts in Ontario and the United States; however, the cheaper, Ontario-built Matrix has the better reputation for quality. On the other hand, Jaguar and Volvo quality declined after Ford bought the companies, and GM-owned Saab didn't do much better. As for Daimler's takeover of Chrysler, what innovative, high-quality products did we see as a result? Very few, and the jury's still out as to whether Chrysler or Fiat has benefited the most from Fiat's takeover of Chrysler.

Sometimes choosing a higher trim line that packages many options as standard features will cost you less when you take all the features into account separately. In Canada, it's hard to compare these bundled prices with the manufacturer's base price and added options, though U.S. automaker websites often provide more details. All of the separate prices are inflated and must be individually negotiated down, while fully equipped vehicles don't allow for options to be deleted or priced separately. Furthermore, many of the bundled options are superfluous, and you probably wouldn't have chosen them to begin with.

Minivans and full-sized vans, for example, often come in two versions: a base commercial (or cargo) version and a more luxurious model for private use. The commercial version doesn't have as many bells and whistles, but it's more likely to be in stock and will probably cost much less. And if you're planning to convert it, there's a wide choice of independent customizers that will likely do a better—and less expensive—job than the dealer. Of course, you will want a written guarantee from the dealer or customizer, or sometimes both, that no changes will invalidate the manufacturer's warranty. Also, look on the lot for a low-mileage (less than 10,000 km) 2012 demonstrator that is carried over unchanged as a 2013 version. You will get an end-of-model-year rebate, a lower price for the extra mileage, and sundry other sales incentives that apply. Remember, if the vehicle has been registered to another company or individual, it is not a demo and should be considered used and be discounted accordingly (by at least 25 percent). You will also want to carry out a CarProof VIN search and get a complete printout of the vehicle's service history.

Fraud by Freight

Lemon-Aid has always cautioned new-car buyers against paying transportation and PDI (pre-delivery inspection) fees, or suggested that these fees can be whittled down by about half. This advice worked well up until last year, when charges ballooned to $1,400–$2,000 and automakers started making them part of the MSRP instead of listing the item separately or not at all. This impacts the final price in two ways—one bad, the other good. As part of the MSRP, this extra charge is hidden from the customer and is seen as part of the vehicle's overall cost. On the other hand, when rolled into the MSRP the freight charge/PDI can be more easily negotiated downward with the car's price, since they are no longer touted as sacrosanct "must pay" items.

Leasing without Losing

Why Leasing Costs More

There are many reasons why leasing is a bad idea. It's often touted as an alternative that can make high-cost vehicles more affordable, but for most people it's really more expensive than buying outright. Lessees usually pay the full MSRP on a vehicle loaded with costly options plus hidden fees and interest charges that wouldn't be included if the vehicle was purchased instead of leased. Researchers have found that some fully loaded entry-level cars leased with high interest rates and deceptive "special fees" could cost more than what some luxury models would cost to buy. A useful website that takes the mystery out of leasing is *www.federal-reserve.gov/pubs/leasing* (Keys to Vehicle Leasing), run by the U.S. Federal Reserve Board. It goes into incredible detail comparing leasing versus buying, and has a handy dictionary of the terms you're most likely to encounter.

Decoding "Lease-Talk"

Take a close look at all the figures found in the leasing contract. Be especially on the lookout for items that have been included twice in the monthly amount. For example, if the agreed to figure is $30,000 plus a $300 administration fee and $80 lien registration charge, sometimes these figures are already built into the dealer's computer program (as an automatic charge) and therefore the customer is actually double-billed $399 plus $80. Divided by, say, 48 months, that equals $9.98 plus tax a month. The only way to ensure this does not happen is to do the calculations yourself, making sure the monthly amount is correct.

Pay particular attention to specific words and phrases relating to the model year, condition of the vehicle ("demonstration" or "used"), equipment, warranty, interest rate, buy-back amount, down payment, security payment, monthly payment, transportation and preparation charges, administration fees, "acquisition" and "disposal" fees, insurance premiums, the number of free kilometres, excess-kilometre charges, and what constitutes "excess wear and tear."

Leasing Advantages

Leasing once made up almost 35 percent of all motor vehicle sales transactions in Canada because of then-rising interest rates and prices. Now, hard-to-find credit and the economic recession have driven leasing down to about 20 percent of all auto transactions. Detroit automakers have backed away from leases, leaving the market to the Asians and Europeans. But leasing is still a fairly popular option, leading to 60-month leases and a proliferation of leasing deals on luxury models. Insiders say that almost all vehicles costing $60,000 or more are leased vehicles.

Experts agree: If you must lease, keep your costs to a minimum by leasing for the shortest time possible, and by making sure that the lease is close-ended (meaning that you walk away from the vehicle when the lease period ends)—this last option is used by 75 percent of lessees, according to CAA.

Leasing does have a few advantages, though. First, it saves some of your capital, which you can invest to get a return greater than the leasing interest charges. Second, if you are taking a chance on a new model that hasn't been proven, you know that yours can be dumped at the dealer when the lease expires.

But taking a chance on an unproven model raises several questions: What are you doing choosing such a risky venture in the first place? And will you have the patience to wait in the service bay while your luxury lemon waits for parts or a mechanic who's ahead of the learning curve?

Some Precautions and an Alternative

On both new and used purchases and leases, be wary of unjustified hidden costs, like a $1,100 "administrative" or "disposal" fee, an "acquisition" charge, or boosted transport and freight costs that can collectively add several thousand dollars to a vehicle's retail price. Also, look at the lease transfer fee charged by the leasing company, the dealer, or both. This fee can vary considerably.

Instead of leasing, consider purchasing used. Look for a three- to five-year-old off-lease vehicle with 60,000–100,000 km on the clock and some of the original warranty left. Such a vehicle will be just as reliable for less than half the cost of one bought new or leased. Parts will be easier to find, independent servicing should be a breeze, insurance premiums will come down from the stratosphere, and your financial risk will be lessened considerably if you end up with a lemon.

Breaking a Lease

It's not an easy thing to do, and you may wind up paying $3,000–$8,000 in cancellation fees.

The last thing you want to do is stop your payments, especially if you've leased a lemon: The dealer can easily sue you for the remaining money owed, and you will have to pay the legal fees for both sides. You won't be able to prove the vehicle was defective or unreliable, because it will have been seized after the lease payments stopped. So there you are, without the vehicle to make your proof and on the receiving end of a costly lawsuit.

There are several ways a lease can be broken. First, you can ask for free Canadian Motor Vehicle Arbitration Plan (CAMVAP) arbitration (see page 112) if you believe you have leased a lemon. A second recourse, if there's a huge debt remaining, is to send a lawyer's letter cancelling the contract by putting the leasing agency and automaker on notice that the vehicle is unacceptable. This should lead to some negotiation. If this fails, inspect the vehicle, have it legally tendered back to the dealer, and then sue for what you owe plus your inconvenience and assorted sundry expenses. You can use the small claims court on your own if the amount in litigation is less than the court's $10,000–$25,000 claim limit.

The leasing agency or dealer may claim extra money when the lease expires, because the vehicle may miss some original equipment or show "unreasonable" wear and tear (dings, paint problems, and excessive tire wear are the most common reasons for extra charges). Protect yourself from these dubious claims by having the vehicle inspected by an independent retailer and taking pictures of the vehicle prior to returning it.

Buying the Right Car or Truck

Front-Drives

Front-drives direct engine power to the front wheels, which pull the vehicle forward while the rear wheels simply support the rear. The biggest benefit of front-drives is foul-weather traction. With the engine and transmission up front, there's lots of extra weight pressing down on the front-drive wheels, increasing tire grip in snow and on wet pavement. But when you drive up a steep hill, or tow a boat or trailer, the weight shifts and you lose the traction advantage.

Although I recommend a number of front-drive vehicles in this guide, I don't like them as much as rear-drives. Granted, front-drives provide a bit more interior room (no transmission hump), more car-like handling, and better fuel economy than do rear-drives. But damage from potholes and fender-benders is usually more extensive, and maintenance costs (especially premature suspension, tire, and brake wear) are much higher than with rear-drives.

Rear-Drives

Rear-drives direct engine power to the rear wheels, which push the vehicle forward. The front wheels steer and also support the front of the vehicle. With the engine up front, the transmission in the middle, and the drive axle in the rear, there's plenty of room for larger and more durable drivetrain components. This makes for less crash damage, lower maintenance costs, and higher towing capacities than with front-drives.

On the downside, rear-drives don't have as much weight over the front wheels as do the front-drives, and therefore can't provide as much traction on wet or icy roads and tend to fishtail unless they're equipped with an expensive traction-control system.

Four-Wheel Drive (4×4)

Four-wheel drive (4×4) directs engine power through a transfer case to all four wheels, which pull and push the vehicle forward, giving you twice as much traction. The vehicle reverts to rear-drive when four-wheel drive isn't engaged. The large transfer-case housing makes the vehicle sit higher, giving you additional ground clearance.

Keep in mind that extended driving over dry pavement with 4×4 engaged will cause the driveline to bind and result in serious damage. Some buyers are turning instead to rear-drive pickups equipped with winches and large, deep-lugged rear tires.

Many 4×4 customers driving SUVs set on truck platforms have been turned off by the typically rough and noisy driveline, a tendency for the vehicle to tip over when cornering at moderate speeds, vague or truck-like handling, high repair costs, and poor fuel economy.

All-Wheel Drive (AWD)

A standard feature on all Subarus beginning with the 1999 lineup, AWD is four-wheel drive that's on all the time. Used mostly in sedans and minivans, AWD never needs to be deactivated when running over dry pavement and doesn't require the heavy transfer case that raises ground clearance and cuts fuel economy. AWD-equipped vehicles aren't recommended for off-roading because of their lower ground clearance and fragile driveline parts, which aren't as rugged as 4×4 components. But anyhow, you shouldn't be off-roading in a car or minivan in the first place.

Safety and Comfort

First the good news: Every year, fewer people are dying and suffering injuries on Canadian roads, according to Transport Canada statistics that confirm a dramatic decline in severe road collisions. Furthermore, safety researchers expect the injuries and deaths to continue dropping as more Canadians use mass transit and economic pressures keep an aging population at home.

Transport Canada's *Canadian Motor Vehicle Traffic Collision Statistics*, found at *www.tc.gc.ca/eng/roadsafety/tp-tp3322-2009-1173.htm*, reveals that there were 12 percent fewer deaths (a decrease of 2,182) in 2008 than in the year before—the lowest death toll on Canadian roads in almost 60 years. About 54 percent of those who died were motor vehicle drivers, 20 percent were passengers and 12 percent were pedestrians. The dramatic decline positions Canada to achieve its goal of reducing fatalities by 30 percent from the baseline period of 1996–2001, to the average for the years 1998–2010. Preliminary data for 2009 show the decline is continuing: Fatalities were down by 172 and there were 3,600 fewer injuries (172,883).

Active safety

Advocates of active safety stress that accidents are caused by the proverbial "nut behind the wheel" and believe that safe driving can be best taught through schools or private driving courses. Active safety components are generally those mechanical systems—such as anti-lock brake systems (ABS), high-performance tires, and traction control—that may help a driver to avoid accidents if they're skillful and mature.

ABS is no auto safety panacea. Alone, it is often ineffective, failure-prone, and expensive to service. Yet combined with electronic stability control (ESC), it is a proven lifesaver. Essentially, ABS prevents a vehicle's wheels from locking when the brakes are applied in an emergency situation, thus reducing skidding and loss of directional control. When braking on wet or dry roads, your stopping distance will be about the same as with conventional braking systems. But in gravel, slush, or snow, your stopping distance will be greater.

The theory of active safety has several drawbacks. First, a study of seriously injured drivers at the Shock Trauma Center in Maryland showed that 51 percent of the sample tested positive for illegal drugs while 34 percent tested positive for alcohol (*www.druggeddriving.org/ddp.html*). Drivers who are under the influence of alcohol or drugs cause about 40 percent of all fatal accidents. All the high-performance options and specialized driving courses in the world will not provide much protection from impaired drivers who draw a bead on your vehicle. And because active safety components get a lot of use—you're likely to need anti-lock brakes 99 times more often than you'll need an airbag—they have to be well designed and well maintained to remain effective. Finally, consider that independent studies show that safe driving taught to young drivers doesn't necessarily reduce the number of driving-related deaths and injuries, as was shown in this DeKalb County, Georgia study (*The Lancet*, July 2001):

> The DeKalb Study compared the accident records of 9,000 teens that had taken driver education in the county's high schools with 9,000 teens that had no formal driver training. The final results showed no significant difference between the two groups. In other words, DeKalb County, Georgia, paid a large amount of money for absolutely no value.

Passive safety

Passive safety assumes that you will be involved in life-threatening situations and should be either warned in time to avoid a collision or automatically protected from rolling over, losing traction, or bearing the brunt of collision forces. Head-protecting side airbags, electronic stability control, brake override systems, daytime running lights, and a centre-mounted third brake light are four passive safety features that have paid off handsomely in lives saved and fewer injuries.

Passive safety features also assume that some accidents aren't avoidable and that, when those accidents occur, vehicles should provide as much protection as possible to drivers, passengers, and other vehicles that may be struck—without depending on the driver's reactions. Passive safety components that have consistently been proven to reduce vehicular deaths and injuries are seat belts, laminated windshields, and vehicle structures that enhance crashworthiness by absorbing or deflecting crash forces away from the vehicle's occupants.

The Best Safety Features

Automakers have loaded vehicles with features that wouldn't have been imagined several decades ago, because safety devices appeal to families and some features, like airbags, can be marked up by hundreds of dollars. Yet some safety innovations, like adaptive cruise control (ACC), don't deliver the safety payoffs promised by automakers and may create additional dangers. For example, ACC may slow the vehicle down when passing another car on the highway, not maintain the proper speed when traversing hilly terrain, or suddenly engage or disengage without warning.

Some of the most effective safety features are a crashworthy vehicle, seatbelt pretensioners, head-protecting side airbags, electronic stability control, adjustable brake and accelerator pedals, standard integrated child safety seats, adjustable head restraints, and sophisticated navigation and communication systems.

Seat belts provide the best means of reducing the severity of injury arising from both low- and high-speed frontal collisions. In order to be effective, though, seat belts must be adjusted properly and feel comfortably tight without undue slack. Owners often complain that seat belts don't retract enough for a snug fit, are too tight, chafe the neck, or don't fit children properly. Some automakers have corrected these problems with adjustable shoulder-belt anchors that allow both tall and short drivers to raise or lower the belt for a snug, more comfortable fit. Another important seat belt innovation is the pretensioner, which is part of the airbag system. It is a tiny explosive charge housed in a small cylinder which when triggered yanks your belt down to hold you snug against the seat.

Crashworthiness

A vehicle with a high crash protection rating is a lifesaver. In fact, crashworthiness is the one safety improvement over the past 40 years that everyone agrees has paid off handsomely without presenting any additional risks to drivers or passengers. By surrounding occupants with a protective cocoon and deflecting crash forces away from the interior, auto engineers have successfully created safer vehicles without increasing vehicle size or cost. And it is not unreasonable to assume that you'll be involved in an accident someday. According to IIHS, the average car will likely have two accidents before ending up as scrap, and it's twice as likely to be in a severe front-impact crash as a side-impact crash.

Since some vehicles are more crashworthy than others, and since size doesn't always guarantee crash safety, it's important to buy a vehicle that gives you the best protection from frontal, frontal offset, side, and rear collisions while keeping its rollover and roof-collapse potential to a minimum.

Two Washington-based agencies monitor how vehicle design affects crash safety: the National Highway Traffic Safety Administration (NHTSA) and the Insurance Institute for Highway Safety (IIHS). Crash information from these two groups doesn't always correspond because tests and testing methods vary. NHTSA's crash tests performed on 2011 models are much tougher than the tests previously performed, resulting in dropped star ratings for many vehicles. For example, in the first batch of 30 cars retested under the more severe regulations, only BMW's 5 Series and the Hyundai Sonata kept their five-star safety ratings. Two surprising losers: the Toyota Camry, which went from five stars to three, and the Nissan Versa, which earned an overall rating of only two stars while the previous model had earned four stars.

NHTSA crash-test results for 1990–2012 vehicles and tires are available at *www.safercar.gov/Safety+Ratings*. Information relating to safety complaints, recalls, defect investigations, and service bulletins can be found at *www.safercar.gov/Vehicle+Owners*. IIHS results may be found at *www.iihs.org/ratings*.

Don't get taken in by the five-star crash rating hoopla touted by automakers. There isn't any one vehicle that can claim a prize for being the safest. Vehicles that do well in NHTSA side and front crash tests may not do very well in IIHS offset crash tests, or may have poorly designed head restraints that can increase the severity of neck injuries. Or a vehicle may have a high number of airbag failures, such as the bags deploying when they shouldn't or not deploying when they should.

Before making a final decision on the vehicle you want, look up its crashworthiness and overall safety profile in Part Three.

Cars versus trucks

Occupants of large vehicles have fewer severe injury claims than do occupants of small vehicles. This was proven conclusively in a 1996 NHTSA study that showed that collisions between light trucks or vans and small cars resulted in car occupants having an 81 percent higher fatality rate than the occupants of the light trucks or vans did.

Vehicle weight offers the most protection in two-vehicle crashes. In a head-on crash, for example, the heavier vehicle drives the lighter one backward, which decreases forces inside the heavy vehicle and increases forces in the lighter one. All heavy vehicles, even poorly designed ones, offer this advantage in two-vehicle collisions. However, they may not offer good protection in single-vehicle crashes.

Crash test figures show that SUVs, vans, and trucks also offer more protection to adult occupants than do passenger cars in most crashes because their higher set-up allows them to ride over other vehicles (Ford's 2002 Explorer lowered its bumper height to prevent this hazard). Conversely, because of their high centre of gravity, easily overloaded tires, and unforgiving suspensions, these vehicles, when not equipped with electronic stability control, have a disproportionate number of single-vehicle rollovers, which are far deadlier than frontal or side collisions.

Standard electronic stability control and more-stable designs make SUVs like the Honda CR-V (above) much safer than the average-sized car. Which vehicles had the highest and lowest driver fatality rates in the IIHS study? The Nissan 350Z was the most dangerous, and several minivans were least likely flip over.

Interestingly, a vehicle's past crashworthiness rating doesn't always guarantee that subsequent model years will be just as safe or safer. Take Ford's Escort as an example. It earned five stars for front-passenger collision protection in 1991 and then earned fewer stars every year thereafter, until the model was discontinued in 2002. The Dodge Caravan is another example. It was given five stars for driver-side protection in 2000, but got only four stars through the 2007 model year.

Rollover ratings

Although rollovers represent only 3 percent of crashes (out of 10,000 annual U.S. road accidents), they cause one-third of all traffic deaths from what are usually single-vehicle accidents.

Rollovers occur less frequently with passenger cars and minivans than with SUVs, trucks, and full-sized vans (especially the 15-passenger variety). That's why electronic vehicle stability systems aren't as important a safety feature on passenger cars as on minivans, vans, pickups, and SUVs.

Auto safety experts once thought that SUVs were safer to drive than cars because sport utility vehicles were heavier, larger, and generally sat higher off of the ground. But the Ford Explorer changed that thinking forever.

It all started in the late '90s with a stream of reports from Saudi Arabia, Venezuela, and the southern United States regarding deadly rollovers involving Ford Explorers equipped with faulty Firestone tires. Product liability lawyers made millions in secret settlements, Ford and Firestone accused each other of negligence and paid millions in compensation to victims, and automobile engineers, while denying they were ever at fault, quietly set out to install safety features that would make SUV rollovers less likely.

The engineers succeeded. From the 1999 to 2002 model years, SUVs recorded an average of 82 driver deaths per million registered vehicle years. For model years

2005 to 2008, that rate had plummeted to just 28 per million. Since 2006, SUVs are much less likely to be involved in rollover crashes than are ordinary cars.

In fact, someone driving a 2009 model year car is almost twice as likely to die in a rollover accident as someone driving a 2009 model year SUV, says the Insurance Institute for Highway Safety in its June report comparing real-world auto accident death rates for various types of 2006–09 vehicles.

Broken down into vehicle classes, the IIHS picked minivans as the safest (25 fatalities per million registered vehicle years), followed by SUVs (28 per million), then pickup trucks (52 per million), with the "cars" class rated most deadly (56 deaths per million).

The Institute credits the increased use of electronic stability control and more-stable car-based designs for the overall declining frequency of SUV rollover accidents. Starting with the 2012 model year all passenger vehicles sold in North America must be equipped with ESC.

More Safety Considerations

Although there has been a dramatic reduction in automobile accident fatalities and injuries over the past three decades, safety experts feel that additional safety features will henceforth pay small dividends, and they expect the highway death and injury rate to start trending upward. They say it's time to target the driver. NHTSA believes that automobile accident fatalities would be cut by half if everyone wore a seat belt and we had fewer drunk drivers on the road.

Safety programs that concentrate primarily on motor vehicle standards won't be as effective in the future as measures that target both the driver and the vehicle—such as more-sophisticated "black box" data recorders; more-stringent licensing requirements, including graduated licensing and de-licensing programs directed at teens and seniors; and stricter law enforcement.

Incidentally, police studies have identified an important benefit to arresting traffic-safety scofflaws: netting dangerous career criminals or seriously impaired drivers before they have the chance to harm others. Apparently, sociopaths and substance abusers don't care which laws they break.

Beware of unsafe designs

Although it is hard to believe, automakers will deliberately manufacture a vehicle that will kill or maim simply because, in the long run, it costs less to stonewall complaints and pay off victims than to make a safer vehicle. I learned this lesson after listening to the court testimony of GM engineers who deliberately placed fire-prone "sidesaddle" gas tanks in millions of pickups to save $3 per vehicle and after reading the court transcripts of *Grimshaw v. Ford* (fire-prone Pintos) from 1981. Reporter Anthony Prince wrote the following assessment of Ford's indifference in an article titled "Lessons of the Ford/Firestone scandal: Profit motive turns

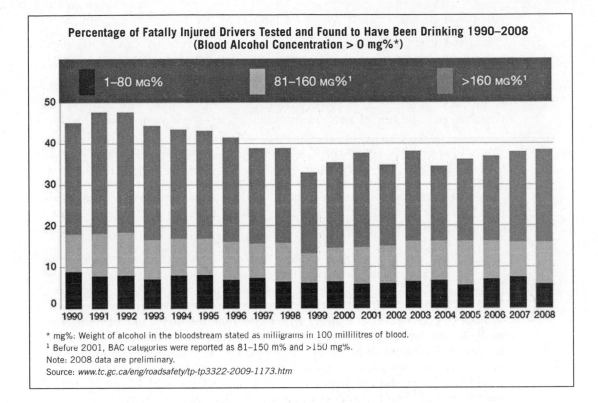

Percentage of Fatally Injured Drivers Tested and Found to Have Been Drinking 1990–2008
(Blood Alcohol Concentration > 0 mg%*)

1–80 MG%   81–160 MG%[1]   >160 MG%[1]

* mg%: Weight of alcohol in the bloodstream stated as milligrams in 100 millilitres of blood.
[1] Before 2001, BAC categories were reported as 81–150 m% and >150 mg%.
Note: 2008 data are preliminary.
Source: *www.tc.gc.ca/eng/roadsafety/tp-tp3322-2009-1173.htm*

consumers into road kill," (*People's Tribune* [Online Edition]; Vol. 26, No. 11, November 2000):

> Rejecting safety designs costing between only $1.80 and $15.30 per Pinto, Ford had calculated the damages it would likely pay in wrongful death and injury cases and pocketed the difference. In a cold and calculating "costs/benefits" analysis, Ford projected that the Pinto would probably cause 180 burn deaths, 180 serious burn injuries, [and] 2,100 burned vehicles each year. Also, Ford estimated civil suits of $200,000 per death, $67,000 per injury, [and] $700 per vehicle for a grand total of $49.5 million. The costs for installing safety features would cost approximately $137 million per year. As a result, the Pinto became a moving target, its unguarded fuel tank subject to rupture by exposed differential bolts shoved into it by rear-end collisions at speeds of as little as 21 miles per hour [34 km/h]. Spewing gasoline into the passenger compartment, the car and its passengers became engulfed in a raging inferno.

And here are more recent examples of corporate greed triumphing over public safety: "exploding" pre-1997 airbag designs that maim or kill women, children, and seniors; anti-lock brake systems that don't brake; flimsy front seats and seatbacks; fire-prone Ford cruise-control deactivation switches; and minivan sliding doors that trap children or suddenly fly open.

Distracted driving

Distracted driving is a major cause of automobile accidents that can be prevented by drivers using common sense (active safety). The danger of distracted driving is real. For example, a driver talking with other passengers in the car is said to be the cause of 81 percent of auto crashes. Auto accident statistics show that other significant causes of car accidents are listening to or changing radio stations (involved in 66 percent of all accidents) and talking on cell phones (25 percent).

Interestingly, a 2006 University of Utah study compared cell phone use to drunk driving (*www.distraction.gov/research/PDF-Files/Comparison-of-CellPhone-Driver-Drunk-Driver.pdf*). Researchers found impairments associated with using a cell phone while driving can be as significant as those associated with driving with a blood alcohol content of 0.08% (the legal limit in many countries, including Canada and the U.S.).

What about stricter laws? Don't get your hopes up—research shows tougher laws have no effect if they aren't enforced rigorously. A 2010 study carried out by the Highway Loss Data Institute reviewed insurance claims in New York, Connecticut, California, and the District of Columbia and compared the data to other areas without cell phone bans. Conclusion: laws banning the use of hand-held devices while driving did not reduce the rate of accidents (*www.cnn.com/2010/US/01/29/cellphone.study/index.html*).

Safety Features That Kill

In the late '60s, Washington forced automakers to include essential safety features like collapsing steering columns and safety windshields in their cars. As the years have passed, the number of mandatory safety features increased to include seat belts, airbags, and crashworthy construction. These improvements met with public approval until quite recently, when reports of deaths and injuries caused by ABS and airbag failures showed that defective components and poor engineering negated the potential life-saving benefits associated with having these devices.

For example, one out of every five ongoing NHTSA defect investigations concerns inadvertent airbag deployment, deactivation of the front passenger airbag, failure of the airbag to deploy, or injuries suffered when the bag did go off. In fact, airbags are the agency's single-largest cause of current investigations, exceeding even the full range of brake problems, which runs second.

Side Airbags—Good and Bad

Side and side curtain airbags are designed to protect drivers and passengers in rollovers and side-impact crashes, which are estimated to account for almost one-third of vehicular deaths. They have also been shown to help keep unbelted occupants from being ejected in rollovers. Head-protecting side airbags can reduce serious crash injuries by 45 percent. Side airbags without head protection reduce injuries by only 10 percent. Ideally, you want a side airbag system that protects both the torso and head.

Because side airbags were not originally subject to federal regulation in Canada or the States, neither government has developed any tests to measure their safety for children or small adults. However, new rules are now in place that force auto-makers to comply with a government-imposed "performance standard."

There's a downside to increased side airbag protection: Sit properly in your seat, or face serious injury from the deploying side airbag. Preliminary safety studies show that side airbags may be deadly to children or to any occupant sitting too close to the airbag, resting his or her head on the side pillar, or holding onto the roof-mounted assist handle. Research carried out in 1998 by safety researchers Anil Khadikar of Biodynamics Engineering Inc. and Lonney Pauls of Springwater Micro Data Systems (*Assessment of Injury Protection Performance of Side Impact Airbags*) shows there are four hazards pertaining to most airbag systems:

1. Inadvertent airbag firing (short circuits, faulty hardware or software)
2. Unnecessary airbag firing (sometimes the opposite-side airbag will fire; the airbag may deploy when a low-speed side-swipe wouldn't have endangered occupant safety)
3. A small child, say, a three-year-old, restrained in a booster seat could be seriously injured
4. Out-of-position restrained occupants could be seriously injured

The researchers conclude with the following observation: "Even properly restrained vehicle occupants can have their upper or lower extremities in harm's way in the path of an exploding [side] airbag."

The 1998 study and dozens of other scientific papers confirm that small or tall restrained drivers face death or severe injury from frontal and side airbag deployments for the simple reason that they are outside of the norm of the 5'8", 180-pound, male test dummy.

And don't forget NHTSA's side airbag warning issued on October 14, 1999:

> Side impact airbags can provide significant supplemental safety benefits to adults in side impact crashes. However, children who are seated in close proximity to a side airbag may be at risk of serious or fatal injury, especially if the child's head, neck, or chest is in close proximity to the airbag at the time of deployment.

Protecting yourself

Because not all airbags function, or malfunction, the same way, *Lemon-Aid* has done an exhaustive analysis of U.S. and Canadian recalls, crash data, and owner complaints to determine which vehicles and which model years use airbags that may seriously injure occupants or deploy inadvertently. That data can be found in Part Three's model ratings.

Additionally, you should take the following steps to reduce the danger from airbag deployment:

- Buy a vehicle with head-protecting side curtain airbags for front and rear passengers.
- Make sure that seat belts are buckled and all head restraints are properly adjusted (to about ear level).
- Choose vehicles with head restraints that are rated "Good" by IIHS (see Part Three).
- Insist that passengers who are frail, short, or have recently had surgery sit in the back and properly position themselves away from side airbags.
- Ensure that the driver's seat can be adjusted for height and has tracks with sufficient rearward travel to allow short drivers to remain at a safe distance (over 25 cm) away from the bag's deployment and still be able to reach the accelerator and brake.
- Consider buying pedal extensions to keep you at a safe distance away from a deploying airbag if you are short-statured.

Top 25 Safety Defects

The U.S. federal government's online safety complaints database contains well over 100,000 entries, going back to vehicles made in the late '70s. Although the database was originally intended to record only incidents of component failures that relate to safety, you will find every problem imaginable dutifully recorded by clerks working for NHTSA and posted at *www.safercar.org*.

A perusal of the listed complaints shows that some safety-related failures occur more frequently than others and often affect one manufacturer more than another. It is also evident that some safety features like head restraints and tire pressure sensors are poorly designed for real-world driving. Here is a summary of the most commonly reported complaints:

1. Sudden, unintended acceleration
2. ABS total brake failure; wheel lock-up
3. Airbags not deploying when they should, or deploying when they shouldn't
4. Tire-tread separation
5. Electrical or fuel-system fires
6. Stalling
7. Electrical failures
8. Transmission failing to engage, or suddenly disengaging
9. Adaptive cruise control malfunctions
10. Transmission jumping from Park to Reverse or Neutral; vehicle rolling away when parked
11. Steering or suspension failures; uneven terrain "death wobble"
12. Seat belt failures
13. Collapsing seatbacks in collisions
14. Head restraint forces driver's chin to chest

15. Defective sliding door, door locks, and latches
16. Poor headlight illumination; glare
17. Dash reflecting onto windshield
18. Gauges cannot be seen in sunlight
19. Hood flying up
20. Falling trunk lid
21. Wheel falling away
22. Tire pressure sensor (TPS) malfunctions
23. Steering wheel lifting off
24. Transmission lever pulling out
25. Exploding windshields

Are you Comfortable?

The advantages of many sports cars and minivans pale in direct proportion to your tolerance for a harsh ride, noise, a claustrophobic interior, and limited visibility. Minivan and truck owners often have to deal with a high step-up and lots of buffeting from wind and passing trucks. With these drawbacks, many buyers find that after falling in love with the showroom image, they end up hating their purchase—all the more reason to test drive your choice over a period of several days to get a real feel for its positive and negative characteristics.

Check to see if the vehicle's interior is user-friendly. For example, can you reach the sound system and AC controls without straining or taking your eyes off the road? Are the controls just as easy to operate by feel as by sight? What about dash glare onto the front windshield, head restraint comfort, and headlight aim and brightness? Can you drive with the window or sunroof open and not be subjected to an ear-splitting roar? Do rear-seat passengers have to be contortionists to enter or exit, as is the case with many two-door vehicles?

To answer these questions, you need to drive the vehicle over a period of time to test how well it responds to the diversity of your driving needs, without having some impatient sales agent yapping in your ear. If this isn't possible, you may find out too late that the handling is less responsive than you'd wanted.

You can conduct the following showroom tests: Adjust the seat to a comfortable setting, buckle up, and settle in. Can you sit 25 cm away from the steering wheel and still reach the accelerator and brake pedals? Do the head restraints force your chin into your chest? When you look out the windshield and use the rear- and side-view mirrors, do you detect any serious blind spots? Will optional mirrors give you an unobstructed view? Does the seat feel comfortable enough for long trips? Can you reach important controls without moving your back from the seat-back, or taking your eyes off the road? If not, shop for something that better suits your needs.

Vehicles for Older Drivers

Drivers over 80 are the fastest-growing segment of the driving population. According to Candrive, the Canadian Driving Research Initiative for Vehicular Safety in the Elderly, there are currently more than 3 million senior drivers in Canada, and their numbers are expected to double by 2040. By 2030, it's estimated that there will be roughly 15,000 centenarians driving in Canada—approximately three times as many as there are today. Surveys show that husbands do the bulk of family driving, which usually involves short trips (11–17 km per day, on average) for medical appointments and visits to family, friends, and shopping malls. This puts older women, who tend to outlive their husbands, in a serious bind because of their lack of driving experience—particularly in rural areas, where driving is a necessity rather than a choice.

I'm 68, so I know that older drivers, like most other drivers, want cars that are reliable, relatively inexpensive, and fuel efficient. Additionally, we require vehicles that compensate for some of the physical challenges associated with aging (I'm getting fatter, slower, and much more taciturn, I'm told) and provide protection for accidents more common with mature drivers (side impacts, for example). Furthermore, as drivers get older, they find that the very act of getting into a car (sitting down while moving sideways, without bumping their heads or twisting their necks) demands considerable acrobatic skill. And don't even ask about shoulder pain when reaching up and over for the shoulder belt!

Safety Features

The driver's seat should be mounted high enough to give a commanding view of the road (with slower reaction times, seniors need earlier warnings). The driver's seat must also offer enough rearward travel to attenuate the force of an exploding airbag, which can be particularly hazardous to older or small-statured occupants, children, or anyone recovering from surgery. Adjustable gas and brake pedals are a must for short-legged drivers.

And while we're discussing airbags, remember that they are calibrated to explode during low-speed collisions (at less than 10 km/h) and that reports of injuries caused by their deployment are commonplace. Therefore, always put at least 25 cm between your upper torso and the steering wheel.

Look for handles near the door frame that can be gripped for support when entering or leaving the vehicle, bright dashboard gauges that can be seen in sunlight, and instruments with large-sized controls.

Remote-controlled mirrors are a must, along with adjustable, unobtrusive head restraints and a non-reflective front windshield (many drivers put a cloth on the dash-top to cut the distraction). Make sure that the brake and accelerator pedals aren't mounted too close together.

As far as safety features are concerned, a superior crashworthiness rating is essential, as well as torso- and head-protecting side airbags, since most intersection collisions involving mature drivers occur when drivers are making a turn into oncoming traffic. The extra head protection can make a critical difference in side impacts. For example, with its $680 head-protecting side airbags, Toyota's 2004 RAV4 earned a "Best Pick" designation from IIHS. When tested without the head protection, it received a "Poor" rating in the side test.

Don't be overly impressed by anti-lock brakes, since their proper operation (no tapping on the brakes) runs counter to everything you have been taught, plus they aren't that reliable. Look for headlights that give you a comfortable view at night, as well as turn signal indicators that are easy to see and hear. Ensure that the vehicle's knobs and switches are large and easy to identify and that the gauges are sufficiently backlit that they don't wash out in daylight. Also, be sure to check that the dash doesn't cause windshield glare (a common problem with light-coloured dash panels). Having an easily accessed, full-sized spare tire and a user-friendly lug wrench and jack stand is also important.

Access and Comfort

I've been told that some drivers with arthritic hands have to insert a pencil into their key ring to twist the key in the ignition. Make sure your ignition lock doesn't require that much effort. Power locks and windows are a must, especially if the vehicle will be operated with hand controls. A remote keyless entry will allow entry without having to twist a key in the door lock. A vehicle equipped with a buttonless shifter will be less difficult to activate for arthritis sufferers and drivers with limited upper-body mobility. Cruise control can be helpful for those with lower-body mobility challenges.

Get a vehicle that's easy to enter and exit. Check for door openings that are wide enough to get into and out of easily, both for you and for any wheelchairs or scooters that may need to be loaded. Make sure the door catches when opened on a slight incline so that it doesn't close as you are exiting. If necessary, your trunk or rear cargo area should have a low liftover and room to stow your wheelchair or scooter. Bench seats are preferable because they're roomier and easier to access; getting a power-adjustable driver's seat with memory is also a good idea. Make sure the seat is comfortable and has plenty of side bolstering.

Forget minivans, unless you invest in a step-up and choose one with an easily reached inside-grip handle—and you don't mind bumping the left-side steering-column stalk with your knee each time you slide into the driver's seat. Incidentally, some General Motors minivans come with a useful Sit-N-Lift option: a motorized, rotating lift-and-lower passenger seat that's accessed through the middle door and can be taken out when not needed.

Drivers with limited mobility, or those who are recovering from hip surgery, give kudos to the Cadillac Escalade SUV and GM Venture/Montana minivans; Toyota's Echo, Yaris, Matrix, and Avalon; and small SUVs such as the Honda CR-V, Hyundai Tucson, and Toyota RAV4. Of this group, only the recently discontinued GM minivans give me cause for concern, because of their poor reliability.

Other Buying Considerations

When "New" Isn't New

Nothing will cause you to lose money faster than buying a new car that's older than advertised, has previously been sold and then taken back, has accident damage, or has had the odometer disconnected or turned back.

Even if the vehicle hasn't been used, it may have been left outdoors for a considerable length of time, causing the deterioration of rubber components, premature body and chassis rusting, or severe rusting of internal mechanical parts, which leads to brake malfunction, fuel line contamination, hard starting, and stalling.

You can check a vehicle's age by looking at the date-of-manufacture plate usually found on the driver-side door pillar. If the date of manufacture is 7/12 or earlier, your vehicle was probably one of the last 2012 models made before the September changeover to the 2013s. Redesigned vehicles or those new to the market are exceptions to this rule. They may arrive at dealerships in early spring or mid-summer and are considered to be next year's models. They also depreciate more quickly owing to their earlier launching, but this difference narrows over time.

Sometimes a vehicle can be too new and cost you more in maintenance because its redesign glitches haven't been worked out yet. As Honda's North American manufacturing chief, Koki Hirashima, so ably put it, carryover models generally have fewer problems than vehicles that have been significantly reworked or just introduced to the market. Newly redesigned vehicles get quality scores that are, on average, 2 percent worse than vehicles that have been around for a while, says J.D. Power. Some surprising poor performers of recent vintage are the 2012 Ford Explorer and Mustang, Honda Civic, and Hyundai Sonata.

Because they were the first off the assembly line for that model year, most vehicles assembled between September and February are called "first-series" cars. "Second-series" vehicles, made between March and August, incorporate more assembly-line fixes and are better built than the earlier models, which may depend on ineffective "field fixes" to mask problems until the warranty expires. Second-series vehicles will sell for the same price or less, but they will be far better buys because of their assembly-line upgrades and more generous rebates. Service bulletins for Chrysler's Caliber and Charger; the Ford Fusion, Zephyr, and Milan; and GM's Solstice, Torrent, and Sky roadsters show these vehicles all had serious quality shortcomings during their first year on the market. It usually takes a couple of years for the factory to get most of the quality glitches corrected.

There's also the very real possibility that the new vehicle you've just purchased was damaged while being shipped to the dealer and was later fixed in the service bay during the pre-delivery inspection. It's estimated that this happens to about 10 percent of all new vehicles. Although there's no specific Canadian legislation allowing buyers of vehicles damaged in transit to cancel their contracts, B.C. legislation says that dealers must disclose damages of $2,000 or more. In a more general sense, Canadian common-law jurisprudence does allow for cancellation or compensation whenever the delivered product differs markedly from what the buyer expected to receive. Ontario's revised *Consumer Protection Act* is particularly hard-nosed in prohibiting this kind of misrepresentation.

Fuel Economy Follies

Poor gas mileage is one of the top complaints among owners of new cars and minivans. Drivers say gas mileage is seldom as high as it's hyped to be; in fact, it's likely to be 10–20 percent less than advertised with most vehicles. (Gas mileage, measured in mpg, is the opposite of metric fuel consumption, measured in L/100 km. In other words, you want gas mileage to be high and consumption to be low.) *Consumer Reports* magazine once estimated that 90 percent of vehicles sold don't get the gas mileage advertised.

Why such a contradiction between promise and performance?

It's simple: Automakers cheat on their tests. They submit their own test results to the government after testing under optimum conditions. Transport Canada then publishes these self-serving "cooked" figures as its own research. One Ford service bulletin is remarkably frank in discounting the validity of these tests:

> Very few people will drive in a way that is identical to the EPA [sanctioned] tests. These [fuel economy] numbers are the result of test procedures that were originally developed to test emissions, not fuel economy.

Stephen Akehurst, a senior manager at Natural Resources Canada, which tests vehicles and publishes the annual *Fuel Consumption Guide*, admits that his lab tests vehicles under ideal conditions. He says that actual driving may burn about 25 percent more fuel than what the government tests show. Too bad we never see this fact hyped in the automakers' fuel economy ads.

The Automobile Protection Association (APA) backs up that observation. It says the Canadian government does not publish accurate numbers in its *Fuel Consumption Guide*. In fact, identical vehicles sold in Canada and the U.S. have government-approved fuel consumption ratings that are 15–20 percent apart. The Canadian figures consistently promise better mileage than the vehicle is able to deliver in real-world driving. For example, in Canada, Toyota's smallest car, the

Yaris hatchback, is rated at 5.5 L/100 km for highway driving, but is rated significantly higher—22 percent (6.7 L/100 km)—in the United States. That works out to about seven miles per Canadian gallon less using the U.S. rating, which is much closer to what Yaris owners report their vehicles actually consume.

Fuel consumption ratings are derived by driving the vehicle in a laboratory setting on a "rolling road" under ideal conditions. The air temperature is comfortable and a cooling breeze soothes the engine. Acceleration is leisurely, and the highway speed of 90 km/h is about 20 percent slower than the average on Canadian highways. The result is an optimistic projection, with a theoretical range in highway driving of 700–800 km on a tank of gas. Most vehicles tested by the APA manage 500–650 km, so the consumer is being "shorted" about 100 km per tank compared to the numbers in car ads. Dealers and the carmakers know this, but they hide behind the veneer of approval from Transport Canada when using their numbers to make their pitch.

Canada and the United States used the same test procedure to calculate City and Highway fuel consumption ratings. In 2007, the Americans modified their calculation to take into account more realistic driving speeds, temperatures, and the use of air conditioning. As a consequence, posted consumption rates increased by 15–25 percent for most vehicles, and consumer complaints about the ratings abated in the U.S.

CBC's *Go Public* recently discovered there is no government testing in Canada. It's performed by the carmaker for the North American market and then two numbers are supplied: a rosy one to Canadian authorities, and a more accurate one to U.S. authorities. A comparison chart can be seen at *www.cbc.ca/news/canada/story/2011/11/27/f-fuel-efficiency-compare.html*).

Canada relies exclusively on the Americans to spot check the carmakers' fuel consumption ratings—but Canada doesn't use the more realistic American fuel consumption figures. Canada needs to bring its fuel consumption ratings closer to reality. The easiest and least expensive solution would be to apply a metric version of the U.S. fuel consumption rating.

For provinces with green levies, APA recommends accepting the current, optimistic number for gas-guzzler penalties, so that the change is taxation neutral. Alternatively, the provincial guidelines could be modified to reflect the new, more realistic numbers, so that the public is not penalized when several vehicles move into higher consumption brackets.

What you can do: The APA advises motorists to use the City rating as a prediction of what you will get in mixed driving. The City figure is optimistic compared to actual fuel consumption in real urban driving, but it's a helpful average for overall fuel consumption in city and highway driving. The APA has been using only the City number for years in its vehicle ratings.

When shopping for a vehicle, use the U.S. fuel consumption figures, which are also listed in metric form in the *U.S. Fuel Economy Guide*.

Keep in mind that although good fuel economy is important, it's hardly worth a harsh ride, excessive highway noise, side-wind buffeting, anemic acceleration, and a cramped interior. You may end up with much worse gas mileage than advertised and a vehicle that's underpowered for your needs.

If you never quite got the hang of metric fuel economy measurements, click on the fuel conversion tool found at *www.euronet.nl/users/grantm/frans/fuel.html* to see how many miles to a U.S. gallon of gas your vehicle provides. A listing of the fuel consumption of all vehicles sold in Canada since 1995 written in miles per gallon and the metric equivalent can be found at *http://oee.nrcan.gc.ca/transportation/tools/fuelratings/ratings-search.cfm*.

Hybrids

After reading the Canadian Automobile Association's findings that a 2010 Toyota Prius hybrid will cost slightly more to run than a $15,496 2010 Chevrolet Cobalt, it's hard to comprehend how the $27,800 hybrid can be called a money-saver.

As practical as the promise of ethanol fuel seemed at first, hybrids use a pie-in-the-sky alternative fuel system that requires expensive and complex electronic and mechanical components. A bare-bones Honda Civic can achieve the same fuel economy for about two-thirds the cost of the Prius without polluting the environment with exotic toxic metals leached from battery packs and powertrain components.

The Canadian Automobile Association's latest study of fuel savings of hybrids and conventional vehicles (*http://caa.ca/documents/CAA_Driving_Cost_English_2011_web.pdf*), released August 18, 2011, says conventional vehicles have much lower operating costs. The CAA study compared a Toyota Prius with a Chevrolet Cruze and a Dodge Grand Caravan. CAA researchers found the following:

> Based on 18,000 km, a Cruze costs $8,883.85 a year to operate, which is 49.4 cents per km. A Prius on the other hand is $9,496.20 or 52.8 cents per km to operate. The gap narrows at 32,000km/year where the Cruze's total cost is $11,333.85 (35.4 cents/km) compared to $11,484.20 (35.9 cents/km) for a Prius.

Overall, the Prius costs less to drive the more it is driven, as the fixed costs (purchase price, depreciation, etc.) can be amortized over greater kilometres. The downside? Cars are driven an average 20,000 km a year in Canada. To get within striking distance of the Cruze's lower operating costs, a Prius owner would have to put an extra 12,000 kilometres on the car.

How does this help the environment or your wallet?

Other disadvantages of hybrids are their mechanical and electronic complexities, dependence on specialized dealers for basic servicing, high depreciation rates and insurance costs, overblown fuel-efficiency numbers (owners report getting 40 percent less mileage than promised), and the $3,000 cost to replace their battery packs.

Finally, consider this: Hybrid vehicles like the Toyota Prius use rare earth minerals such as lanthanum, scandium, and yttrium mixed oxides and aluminas (which are used in almost all automotive emissions control systems). Neodymium is another rare element used in the lightweight permanent magnets that power hybrid motors. It's a radioactive substance mined almost exclusively in China, which has threatened to restrict its international sale in order to protect its domestic use and has slapped on heavy export duties. And there's a good reason why mining has been mostly restricted to China: The government there doesn't care if the mining and refining of these toxic minerals poisons the environment and sickens villagers—something North American "green" advocates overlook.

Western nations simply cannot afford to mine and refine neodymium within their borders due to the enormous environmental toxicity that mining it produces. In a sense, China has not cornered the neodymium market by virtue of their mineral reserves, but rather their willingness to sacrifice their environment and expose their populace to a higher cancer rate. In the end, North American motorists may trade a dependence on Middle Eastern oil for a troubling dependence on Chinese-sourced neodymium that's poisoning the Chinese people in the process.

Diesel and natural gas

These two fuels have the most promising potential of all the other alternative fuels so far considered, and that includes electric, ethanol, and hydrogen-power. Most importantly, both fuels have a distribution infrastructure and are widely available in Canada at a reasonable cost.

Diesel fuel is cleaner these days and far more fuel-efficient than ever before. Among the alternative fuels tested by independent researchers, diesel comes closest to the estimated fuel economy figures. It's also widely available and requires neither a steep learning curve in the service bay nor exotic replacement parts. Additionally, unlike hybrids, diesel-equipped vehicles are reasonably priced, hold their value quite well, and give an excellent return on investment.

As with the changeover to unleaded gasoline in the '80s, owners of diesel-equipped Detroit-made vehicles can expect some higher maintenance costs and repair downtime (mostly replacing injectors and integrating constantly changing emissions hardware and software. Ford's Power Stroke and GM's Duramax diesels have been the worst offenders. Additionally, beginning with the 2011 models, diesel engines now require that owners regularly fill up with urea—an unexpected extra expense and annoyance.

To pee or not to pee? Recent model diesels, like Mercedes' Bluetec, inject a urea solution—known as AdBlue—into the exhaust to reduce nitrous oxide (N_2O) emissions. Audi, BMW, VW, and the Detroit Three also use urea injection under different names.

A yearly urea refill can be expected since the urea tank contains roughly 8 gallons (U.S.), which is good for about 19,300 kilometres (12,000 miles) of standard operation. Generally, automakers will add the urea solution at every scheduled maintenance visit.

Mercedes-Benz Blutec diesels will not run if the urea tank doesn't contain a certain amount. If the tank reaches one gallon, the car notifies the driver. It does so again with only 20 starts remaining. To reset the system, at least two gallons of AdBlue—or four half-gallon bottles, at $7.75 each—must be added. Not a lot to help save the environment, you say? Read on.

Consumer Reports was charged an outrageous $317 to put 7.5 gallons of AdBlue in its Mercedes GL320 test car at $32/gallon for the fluid, even though 7.5 gallons would cost only $116.25 in half-gallon bottles elsewhere. So, what can you do if your car or truck is urea-immobilized, there is no dealership around, or you refuse to pay through the nose for a simple fill-up?

That brings us back to our original question: "To pee or not to pee?"

Don't pee, at least not into the urea tank. Yes, human urine contains 2–4 percent urea, but modern diesels won't use your pee because it's too diluted and full of other substances like salts, toxins, bile pigments, hormones, and up to 95 percent water. AdBlue, TDI, and other urea products have a concentration of 32.5 percent urea mixed with deionized water. If you put anything else in the urea tank, your car or truck won't start.

Natural gas

Compressed natural gas (CNG) is an excellent fuel source that's in abundant supply, particularly in Western Canada. Its advantages are many. It's a clean-burning fuel. Over the past few years natural gas prices have dropped by more than half. Better yet, car owners can equip their existing cars to run on natural gas at a minimal cost of $2,000 to $4,000 U.S.

The biggest obstacle to a major changeover to natural gas now is that CNG fuel outlets are few and far between and its extraction from the ground, through a process called "fracking," is a "dirty" process that pollutes the air and surrounding groundwater. At the present, natural gas industry pundits say adding more CNG fuel pumps at home and in shopping malls and eliminating environmental problems can be done through sustained investment and modern technology, giving Canada energy reserves for the next 300 years.

Sure, we have heard these "clean air" promises before. This time they might come true, at least that's what Wall Street energy analyst, Mike Kapsch says at *http:// seekingalpha.com/article/633881-investing-in-the-rise-of-natural-gas-vehicles*:

The Case for more natural gas vehicles

According to *Popular Mechanics*, "Nationwide, natural gas ranges from 79 cents to $1.50 for a gasoline gallon equivalent (GGE) of fuel." Let's say your car has a 15-gallon fuel tank. If you were to fill it up once a week at $1 per gallon with compressed natural gas (CNG), you would save over $2,000 per year with gas prices averaging $3.75 per gallon around the country. Savings like these are getting impossible to ignore. And car companies are increasingly taking action.

GM (NYSE: GM) announced the 2013 GMC Sierra and Chevy Silverado will have a bi-fuel option that can switch between running on compressed natural gas and gasoline.

Ford (NYSE: F) and Chrysler also said they'll be ramping up production on their bi-fuel trucks over the coming years.

Even car rental company Hertz (NYSE: HTZ) just stated it will begin renting CNG Honda Civics and CNG GMC Yukons at its Will Rogers World Airport location in Oklahoma City early next month.

In Europe, with gas prices close to $10 per gallon, the trend is catching on even faster. Just a few days ago, Fiat (Milan: F.MI), Italy's largest auto manufacturer, emphasized it's bypassing electric cars and will focus on CNG as its "go-to" alternative fuel for at least the rest of this decade. A little over a week ago, Volvo Trucks unveiled plans to launch a 13-liter natural gas engine schedule to hit the North American market in 2014.

Of course, the biggest problem around the world for natural gas-powered vehicles is the lack of infrastructure. In the United States, there are only 1,000 CNG refueling stations. And most of them aren't even available to the public. In Europe, that number is closer to the 2,000 mark. This is obviously where we'll need to see the most growth in order to make natural gas-powered vehicles a viable alternative to cars that strictly run on gasoline.

Canada has about 80 public CNG stations located in five provinces.

A Cheap, Reliable Vehicle

Overall vehicle safety and body fit and finish on both domestic and imported vehicles are better today than they were three decades ago. Premature rusting is less of a problem, and reliability is improving. Repairs to electronic systems and powertrains, however, are outrageously expensive and complicated. Owners of Chrysler, Ford, and GM cars and trucks still report serious engine and automatic transmission deficiencies, often during the vehicle's first year in service. Other common defects include electrical system failures caused by faulty computer modules; malfunctioning ABS; brake rotor warpage; early pad wearout; failure-prone air conditioning and automatic transmissions; and faulty engine head gaskets, intake manifolds, fuel systems, suspensions, and steering assemblies.

Nothing shows the poor quality control of the Detroit Three automakers as much as the poor fit and finish of body panels. Next time you're stuck in traffic, look at the trunk lid or rear hatch alignment of the vehicle in front of you. Chances are, if it's a Detroit-bred model, the trunk or hatch will be so misaligned that there will be a large gap on one side. Then look at most Asian products: Usually, you will see perfectly aligned trunks and hatches without any large gaps on either side.

Cutting Costs

Fuel economy misrepresentation

So if you can't make a gas-saving product that pours into your fuel tank or attaches to the fuel or air lines, you have to use that old standby: lie. Hell, if automakers and government fuel-efficiency advocates can do it, why not dealers?

Fuel economy misrepresentation is actionable, and Canadian jurisprudence allows for a contract's cancellation if the gas-mileage figures are false (see Part Two of this guide). Most people, however, simply keep the car they bought and live with the fact that they were fooled.

There are a few choices you can make that will lower fuel consumption. First off, choose a smaller version of the vehicle style you are interested in buying. Second, choose a manual transmission or an automatic with a fuel-saving Fifth or Sixth gear. Third, look for an engine with variable valve timing or a cylinder-deactivation feature, which will increase fuel economy by 3 and 8 percent, respectively.

Inflated maintenance fees

Inspections and replacement parts represent hidden costs that are usually exaggerated by dealers and automakers to increase their profits on vehicles that either rarely require fixing or are sold in insufficient numbers to support a service bay.

Alan Gelman, a well-known Toronto garage owner and co-host of *Dave's Corner Garage* on Toronto AM740, warns drivers:

> There are actually two maintenance schedules handed out by car companies and dealers. The dealer inspection sheets often call for far more extensive and expensive routine maintenance checks than what's listed in the owner's manual. Most of those checks are padding; smart owners will stick with the essential checks listed in the manual and have them done by cheaper, independent garages.

Getting routine work done at independent facilities will cost about one-third to one-half the price usually charged by dealers. Just be sure to follow the automaker's suggested schedule so no warranty claim can be tied to botched servicing. Additionally, an inexpensive ALLDATA service bulletin subscription (see page 61) will keep you current as to your vehicle's factory defects, required check-ups, and recalls; tell you what's covered by little-known "goodwill" warranties; and save you valuable time and money when troubleshooting common problems.

Use the legal and the stated warranty

There's a big difference between warranty promise and warranty performance. Most automakers offer bumper-to-bumper warranties that are good for at least the first 3 years/60,000 km, and most models get powertrain coverage up to 5 years/100,000 km, although Mitsubishi offers a 5-year/100,000 km base warranty and a 10-year/160,000 km powertrain warranty. It's also becoming an industry standard for car companies to pay for roadside assistance, a loaner car, or hotel accommodations if your vehicle breaks down while you're away from home and it's still under warranty. This assistance may be for as long as 5 years, without any kilometre restriction. *Lemon-Aid* readers report few problems with these ancillary warranty benefits.

Don't buy a car that's warranty-dependent

If you pick a vehicle rated Recommended by *Lemon-Aid,* the manufacturer's warranty won't be that important and you won't need to spend money on additional warranty protection. On those vehicles that have a history of engine and transmission breakdowns, but the selling price is too good to turn down, budget about $1,500 for an extended powertrain warranty backed by an insurance policy. If the vehicle has a sorry overall repair history, you will likely need a $2,000 comprehensive warranty. But first ask yourself this question: "Why am I buying a vehicle that's so poorly made that I need to spend several thousand dollars to protect myself until the warranty company grows tired of seeing my face?"

Just like the weight-loss product ads you see on TV, what you see isn't always what you get. For example, bumper-to-bumper coverage usually excludes stereo components, brake pads, clutch plates, and many other expensive parts. And automakers will pull every trick in the book to make you pay for their factory screw-ups. These tricks include blaming your driving or your vehicle's poor maintenance, penalizing you for using an independent garage or the wrong fuel, or simply stating that the problem is "normal" and it's really you who is out of whack.

Part Two has all the answers to the above lame excuses. There, you will find plenty of court decisions and sample claim letters that will make automakers and their dealers think twice about rejecting your claim.

Ferret out "secret" warranties

Automobile manufacturers are reluctant to publicize their secret warranty programs because they feel that such publicity would weaken consumer confidence in their products and increase their legal liability. The closest they come to an admission is to send out a "goodwill policy," "special policy," or "product update" service bulletin intended for dealers' eyes only. These bulletins admit liability and propose free repairs for defects that include rust damage, faulty paint, brake systems, emissions components, and engine and transmission failures. The seven sample secret warranties below show how much money can be saved by asking the right questions and not taking "No" for an answer when asking that a "goodwill policy" be applied to cover repair costs (many more secret warranties are listed in the 2012–13 *Lemon-Aid Used Cars and Trucks Guide*):

2001–02 **GM** Grand Prix, Impala, Monte Carlo, and Regal. **Problem:** Defective catalytic converters may cause vehicle to lose power or the dash warning light to come on. **Warranty coverage:** The converter warranty is extended to 10 years. Owners will also be reimbursed for previous converter/OBD system repairs or replacements.

2000–05 **GM** DeVille; 2002–06 Rendezvous; 2003–06 CTS; 2004–06 SRX; 2005–06 STS; and 2006 DTS. **Problem:** Roof rust perforation. **Warranty coverage:** GM will replace, repair, or repaint the roof for free up to 6 years/100,000 km.

2005–06 **GM** G6, Malibu, Maxx; 2008 G6, Malibu, Malibu Maxx, and Aura. **Problem:** Loss of power steering assist. **Warranty coverage:** Under Special Coverage Adjustment #10183, dated July 20, 2010, GM will replace the failed components free of charge up to 10 years/100,000 mi. (160,000 km).

2006–09 **Honda** Civic. **Problem:** Engine overheats or leaks coolant because the engine block is cracking at the coolant passages. **Warranty coverage:** Honda will install a new engine block assembly free of charge under a "goodwill policy," as stated in its TSB #10-048, issued August 17, 2010.

1995–2000 **Toyota** Tacoma and Tundra. **Problem:** Rust-damaged structural frames. The excessive rusting is caused by inadequate anti-corrosion undercoating applied at the factory. **Warranty coverage:** According to the April 14, 2008, edition of *Automotive News*, Toyota will repair or buy back the affected pickups. Dealers will inspect all affected Tacomas and Tundras free of charge and apply an extended 15-year frame-rust warranty. Trucks with minor frame pitting will be repaired for free; trucks with more serious damage will be bought back at 150 percent of the "excellent" value listed in the U.S.-published *Kelley Blue Book* guide, regardless of the truck's condition.

2004–07 **Toyota** Prius. **Problem:** Faulty electric water pump. **Warranty coverage:** According to Limited Service Campaign #A0N, Toyota will replace the water pump free of charge until November 30, 2013. There is no mileage limitation.

All automakers, years, and models. **Problem:** Premature wearout of brake pads, calipers, and rotors. Produces excessive vibration, noise, and pulling to one side when braking. **Warranty coverage:** *Calipers and pads:* "Goodwill" settlements confirm that brake calipers and pads that fail to last 2 years/40,000 km will be replaced for half the repair cost; components that last less than 1 year/20,000 km will be replaced for free. Rotors: If they last less than 3 years/60,000 km, they will be replaced at half price; replacement is free up to 2 years/40,000 km.

If you're refused full compensation, keep in mind that secret warranty extensions are, first and foremost, an admission of manufacturing negligence. You can usually find them in technical service bulletins (TSBs) that automakers send to dealers. Your bottom-line position should be to accept a pro rata adjustment from the manufacturer, whereby you, the dealer, and the automaker each accept a third of the repair costs. If polite negotiations fail, challenge the refusal in court on the grounds that you should not be penalized for failing to make a reimbursement claim under a secret warranty that you never knew existed!

Service bulletins are written by automakers in "mechanic speak" because service managers relate better to them that way. They're great guides for warranty inspections (especially the final one), and they're useful in helping you decide when it's best to trade in your car. Manufacturers can't weasel out of their obligations by claiming that they never wrote such a bulletin.

If your vehicle is out of warranty, show these bulletins to less-expensive, independent garage mechanics so they can quickly find the trouble and order the most recent upgraded part, ensuring that you don't replace one defective component with another.

Canadian service managers and automakers may deny at first that the bulletins even exist, or they may shrug their shoulders and say that they apply only in the States. However, when shown a copy, they usually find the appropriate Canadian part number or bulletin in their files. The problems and solutions don't change from one side of the border to another. Imagine American and Canadian tourists' cars being towed across the border because each country's technical service bulletins were different. Mechanical fixes do differ in cases where, for example, a bulletin is for California only, or it relates to a safety or emissions component used only in the States. But these instances are rare, indeed. What is quite gratifying is to see some automakers, like Honda, candidly admit in their bulletins that "goodwill" repair refunds are available. What a shame other automakers aren't as forthcoming!

The best way to get bulletin-related repairs carried out is to visit the dealer's service bay and to attach the specific ALLDATA-supplied service bulletin covering your vehicle's problems to a work order.

Getting your vehicle's service bulletins

Free summaries of automotive recalls and technical service bulletins listed by year, make, model, and engine can be found at the ALLDATA (*www.alldata.com/TSB*) and NHTSA (*www.safercar.gov*) websites. But, like the NHTSA summaries, ALLDATA's summaries are so short and cryptic that they're of limited use. You can download the complete contents of all the bulletins applicable to your vehicle from ALLDATA at *www.alldatadiy.com* if you pay the $26.95 (U.S.) annual subscription fee. Many bulletins offering "secret warranty" coverage are reproduced in Part Three.

Trim Insurance Costs

Insurance premiums can average between $900 and $2,000 per year, depending on the type of vehicle you own, your personal statistics and driving habits, and whether you can obtain coverage under your family policy.

There are some general rules to follow when looking for insurance savings. For example, vehicles older than five years do not necessarily need collision coverage, and you may not need loss-of-use coverage or a rental car. Other factors that should be considered are as follows:

- When you phone for quotes, make sure you have your serial number in hand. Many factors—such as the make of the car, the number of doors, if there's a sports package, and the insurer's experience with the car—can affect the quote. And be honest, or you'll find your claim denied, the policy cancelled, or your premium cost boosted.
- Where you live and work also determine how much you pay. In the past, auto insurance rates have been 25–40 percent lower in London, Ontario, than in downtown Toronto because there are fewer cars in London and fewer kilometres to drive to work. Similar disparities are found in B.C. and Alberta.
- Taking a driver-training course can save you hundreds of premium dollars.
- You may be able to include your home or apartment insurance as part of a premium package that's eligible for additional discounts.

InsuranceHotline.com, based in Ontario but with quotes for other provinces, says that it pays to shop around for cheap auto insurance rates. The group has found that the same insurance policy could vary in cost by a whopping 400 percent.

"Hidden" Costs

Depreciation

Depreciation is the biggest—and most often ignored—expense that you encounter when you trade in your vehicle or when an accident forces you to buy another vehicle before the depreciated loss can be amortized. Most new cars depreciate 30–45 percent during the first two years of ownership.

The best way to use depreciation rates to your advantage is to choose a vehicle listed as being both reliable and economical to own and then keep it for 10 years or more. Generally, by choosing a lower-depreciating vehicle—such as one that keeps at least half its value over four years—you are storing up equity that will give you a bigger down payment and fewer loan costs with your next purchase.

Gas Pains

With gas prices falling a dime toward the $1.20/L mark, motorists are scratching their heads trying to find easy ways to cut their fuel bill even more. Here are three simple suggestions:

1. Buy a used compact car for half its original price. Savings on taxes, freight fees, and depreciation: about $15,000.
2. Find low-cost fuel referrals on the Internet (*www.gasbuddy.com*). You can save about 15 cents a litre from between the highest- and the lowest-priced stations.
3. Convert your vehicle to use compressed natural gas if there is a supply source nearby. If not, consider installing a home gas-filling system ($5,000).

Diesel Details

The only reasons to buy a diesel-equipped vehicle are for their potential to deliver outstanding fuel economy and for their much lower maintenance and repair costs compared with similar-sized vehicles powered by gasoline engines. Unfortunately, independent data suggests that both claims by automakers may be false.

Let's examine the fuel-savings issue first. In theory, when compared with gasoline powerplants, diesel engines are up to 30 percent more efficient in a light vehicle and up to 70 percent cheaper to run in a heavy-duty towing and hauling truck or SUV. They become more efficient as the engine load increases, whereas gasoline engines become less so. This is the main reason diesels are best used where the driving cycle includes a lot of city driving—slow speeds, heavy loads, frequent stops, and long idling times. At full throttle, both engines are essentially equal from a fuel-efficiency standpoint. The gasoline engine, however, leaves the diesel in the dust when it comes to high-speed performance.

On the downside, fleet administrators and owners report that diesel fuel economy in real driving situations is much less than what's advertised—a complaint also voiced by owners of hybrids. Many owners say that their diesel-run rigs get about 30 percent less mileage than what the manufacturer promised.

Also undercutting fuel-savings claims is the fact that, in some regions, the increased cost of diesel fuel—because of high taxes and oil company greed, some say—makes it more expensive than regular fuel.

The diesel engine's reputation for superior reliability may have been true in the past, but no longer. This fact is easily confirmed if you cross-reference owner complaints with confidential automaker service bulletins and independent industry polling results put out by J.D. Power and others, a task done for you in Part Three's ratings section.

Many owners of diesel-equipped vehicles are frustrated by chronic breakdowns, excessive repair costs, and poor road performance. It's practically axiomatic that bad injectors have plagued Ford Power Stroke, GM Duramax engines, and (to a lesser extent) Dodge Cummins diesels.

In the past, defective injectors were often replaced at the owner's expense and at a cost of thousands of dollars. Now, GM and Ford are using "secret warranty" programs to cover replacement costs long after the base warranty has expired (11–13 years after the vehicle was originally purchased).

Hybrid cars

Automakers are offering hybrid vehicles like the Toyota Prius and Honda Civic and Accord Hybrids that use an engine/electric motor for maximum fuel economy and low emissions while providing the driving range of a comparable small car. Yet this latest iteration of the electric car still has serious drawbacks, which may drive away even the most green-minded buyers:

- Real-world fuel consumption may be 20 percent higher than advertised.
- Cold weather and hilly terrain can cut fuel economy by almost 10–30 percent.
- AC and other options can increase fuel consumption even more.
- Interior cabin heat may be insufficient.
- Electrical systems can deliver a life-threatening 275–500 volts if tampered with through incompetent servicing or during an emergency rescue.
- Battery packs can cost up to $3,000 (U.S.), and fuel savings almost equal the hybrid's extra costs only after about 32,000 km of use.
- Hybrids cost more to insure, and they depreciate just as quickly as non-hybrid vehicles that don't have expensive battery packs to replace.
- Hybrids make you a captive customer where travel is dependent on available service facilities.

If you find the limitations of an electric hybrid too daunting, why not simply buy a more fuel-efficient small car? Or, get a comfortable higher line of used car. Here are some environmentally friendly cars recommended by Toronto-based Environmental Defence Canada (*www.environmentaldefence.ca*):

- Ford Focus
- Honda Civic (2011) and Fit
- Hyundai Accent and Tucson
- Mazda3 and Mazda5
- Nissan Sentra and Versa (although the Versa received a two-star crash rating)

- Toyota Corolla and Yaris
- VW Golf/Jetta TDI

Rust Protection

Most vehicles built today are much less rust-prone than they were several decades ago, thanks to more-durable body panels and better designs. When rusting occurs now, it's usually caused by excessive environmental stress (road salt, etc.), a poor paint job, or the use of new metal panels that create galvanic corrosion or promote early paint peeling—the latter two causes are excluded from most rustproofing warranties.

Invest in undercoating, and remember that the best rustproofing protection is to park the vehicle in a dry, unheated garage or under an outside carport and then wash it every few weeks. Never bring it in and out of a heated garage during the winter months, since it is most prone to rust when temperatures are just a bit above freezing; keep it especially clean and dry during that time. If you live in an area where roads are heavily salted in winter, or in a coastal region, have your vehicle's undercoating sprayed annually.

Annual undercoating, which costs around $150, will usually do as good a job as rustproofing. It will protect vital suspension and chassis components, make the vehicle ride more quietly, and allow you to ask a higher price at trade-in time. The only downside, which can be checked by asking for references, is that the under-coating may give off an unpleasant odour for months, and it may drip, soiling your driveway.

Whether you are rustproofing the entire vehicle or just undercoating key areas, make sure to include the rocker panels (make a small mark inside the door panels on the plastic hole plugs to make sure that they were removed and that the inside was actually sprayed), the rear hatch's bottom edge, the tailgate, and the wheel-wells. It's also a smart idea to stay at the garage while some of the work is being done to see that the overspray is cleaned up and all areas have been covered.

Surviving the Options Jungle

The best options for your buck are a 5- or 6-speed automatic transmission, an anti-theft immobilizer, air conditioning, a premium sound system, and higher-quality tires—features that may bring back one-third to half their value come trade-in time. Rustproofing can also make cars easier to sell in some provinces where there's lots of salt on the roads in the winter, but paint protection and seat sealants are a waste of money. Most option packages can be cut by 20 percent, while extended warranties are overpriced by about 75 percent.

Dealers make more than three times as much profit selling options as they do selling most cars (50 percent profit versus 15 percent profit). No wonder their eyes light up when you start perusing their options list. If you must have some options, compare prices with independent retailers and buy where the price is lowest and the warranty is the most comprehensive. Buy as few options as possible from the dealer, since you'll get faster service, more comprehensive guarantees, and lower prices from independent suppliers. Remember, extravagantly equipped vehicles hurt your pocketbook in three ways: They cost more to begin with but return only a fraction of what they cost when the car is resold; they drive up maintenance costs; and they often consume extra fuel.

A heavy-duty battery and suspension, and perhaps an upgraded sound system, will generally suffice for American-made vehicles; most imports already come well equipped. An engine block heater with a timer isn't a bad idea, either. It's an inexpensive investment that ensures winter starting and reduces fuel consumption by allowing you to start out with a semi-warm engine.

When ordering parts, remember that purchases from American outlets can be slapped with a small customs duty if the part isn't made in the United States. And then you'll pay the inevitable GST or HST levied on the part's cost and customs duty. Finally, your freight carrier may charge a $15–$20 brokerage fee for representing you at the border.

Smart Options

The problem with options is that you often can't refuse them. Dealers sell very few bare-bones cars and minivans, and they option-pack each vehicle with features that can't be removed. You'll be forced to dicker over the total cost of what you are offered, whether you need the extras or not. So it isn't a case of "yes" or "no," but more a decision of "at what cost?"

Adjustable Pedals and Extensions

This device moves the brake and accelerator pedals forward or backward about 10 cm (4 in.) to accommodate short-statured drivers and protect them from airbag-induced injuries.

If the manufacturer of your vehicle doesn't offer optional power-adjustable pedals, there are several companies selling inexpensive pedal extensions by mail order through the Internet. If you live in Toronto or London, Ontario, check out Kino Mobility (*www.kinomobility.com*).

Adjustable Steering Wheel

This option allows easier access to the driver's seat and permits a more-comfortable driving position. It's particularly useful if more than one person will drive the vehicle.

Air Conditioning

AC systems are far more reliable than they were a decade ago, and they have a lifespan of five to seven years. Sure, replacement and repair costs can hit $1,000, but that's very little when amortized over an eight- to 10-year period. AC also makes your car easier to resell.

Does AC waste or conserve fuel when a vehicle is driven at highway speeds? Edmunds, a popular automotive information website, conducted fuel-efficiency tests and concluded that there isn't that much difference between open or closed windows, a finding confirmed by *Consumer Reports*. See *www.edmunds.com/advice/fueleconomy/articles/106842/article.html*:

> While the A/C compressor does pull power from the engine wasting some gas, the effect appears to be fairly minimal in modern cars. And putting the windows down tends to increase drag on most cars, canceling out any measurable gain from turning the A/C off. But this depends on the model you're driving. When we opened the sunroof in our SUV, the mileage did decrease even with the A/C off. Still, in our experience, it's not worth the argument because you won't save a lot of gas either way. So just do what's comfortable.

AC provides extra comfort, reduces wind noise (from not having to roll down the windows), and improves window defogging. Factory-installed units are best, however, because you'll get a longer warranty and improve your chances that everything was installed properly.

Anti-Theft Systems

You'd be a fool not to buy an anti-theft system, including a lockable fuel cap, for your Japanese compact or sports car, which are much coveted by thieves. Auto break-ins and thefts cost Canadians more than $400 million annually. There's a one-in-130 chance that your vehicle will be stolen, but only a 60 percent chance that you'll ever get it back.

Since amateurs are responsible for stealing most vehicles, the best theft deterrent is a visible device that complicates the job while immobilizing the vehicle and sounding an alarm. For less than $150, you can install both a steering-wheel lock and a hidden remote-controlled ignition disabler. Satellite tracking systems like GM's OnStar feature are also very effective.

Battery (Heavy-Duty)

The best battery for northern climates is the optional heavy-duty type offered by many manufacturers for about $100. It's a worthwhile purchase, especially for vehicles equipped with lots of electric options. Most standard batteries last only two winters; heavy-duty batteries give you an extra year or two for about 20 percent more than the price of a standard battery.

Make sure your new vehicle comes with a fresh battery—one manufactured less than six months earlier. Batteries are stamped with a date code, either on the battery's case or on an attached label. The vital information is usually in the first two characters—a letter and a numeral. Most codes start with a letter indicating the month: A for January, B for February, and so forth. The numeral denotes the year: Say, 0 for 2000. For example, "B3" stands for February 2003.

Don't order an optional battery with cold cranking amps (CCA) below the one specified for your vehicle, or one rated 200 amps or more above the specified rating. It's a waste of money to go too high. Also, buy a battery with the longest reserve capacity you can find; a longer capacity can make the difference between driving to safety and paying for an expensive tow.

Replacement batteries are very competitively priced and easy to find. DieHard batteries usually get top ratings from *Consumer Reports*. A useful link for finding the right battery with the most CCA for your car and year is *www.autobatteries. com/basics/selecting.asp.*

Central Locking Control

Costing around $200, this option is most useful for families with small children, car-poolers, or drivers of minivans who can't easily slide across the seat to lock the other doors.

Child Safety Seat (Integrated)

Integrated safety seats are designed to accommodate any child more than one year old or weighing over 9 kg (20 lb.). Since the safety seat is permanently integrated into the seatback, the fuss of installing and removing the safety seat and finding someplace to store it vanishes. When not in use, it quickly folds out of sight, becoming part of the seatback. Two other safety benefits: You know that the seat has been properly installed, and your child gets used to having his or her "special" seat in back, where it's usually safest to sit.

Electronic Stability Control (ESC)

The latest IIHS studies conclude that as many as 10,000 fatal crashes could be prevented if all vehicles were equipped with ESC. Its June 2006 report concluded that stability control is second only to seat belts in saving lives because it reduces the risk of fatal single-vehicle rollovers by 80 percent and the chance of having other kinds of fatal collisions by 43 percent.

Electronic stability control was first used by Mercedes-Benz and BMW on the S-Class and 7 Series models in 1995 and then was featured on GM's 1997 Cadillacs and Corvettes. It helps prevent the loss of control in turns, on slippery roads, or when you must make a sudden steering correction. The system applies the brakes to individual wheels or cuts back the engine power when sensors find the vehicle is beginning to spin or skid. It's particularly useful in maintaining stability with SUVs, but it's less useful with passenger coupes and sedans.

It's worrisome that in spite of 2012 federal standards governing the performance of these systems, car owners still say these stability control systems don't work as they should. In tests carried out by *Consumer Reports* on 2003 models, the stability control system used in the Mitsubishi Montero was rated "unacceptable," BMW's X5 3.0i system provided poor emergency handling, and Acura's MDX and Subaru's Outback VDC stability systems left much to be desired.

Engines (Cylinder Deactivation)

Choose the most powerful 6- or 8-cylinder engine available if you're going to do a lot of highway driving, if you plan on carrying a full passenger load and luggage on a regular basis, or if you intend to load up the vehicle with convenience features like air conditioning. Keep in mind that minivans, SUVs, and trucks with 6-cylinder or larger engines are easier to resell and retain their value the longest. For example, Honda's '96 Odyssey minivan was a sales dud in spite of its bulletproof reliability, mainly because buyers didn't want a minivan with an underpowered 4-cylinder powerplant. Some people buy underpowered vehicles in the mistaken belief that increased fuel economy is a good trade-off for decreased engine performance. It isn't. That's why there's so much interest in peppy 4-cylinders hooked to 5- or 6-speed transmissions and in larger engines with a "cylinder deactivation" feature.

In fact, cylinder deactivation is one feature that appears more promising than most other fuel-saving add-ons. For example, *AutoWeek* magazine found the overweight Jeep Commander equipped with a "Multiple Displacement System" still managed a respectable 13.8 L/100 km (17 mpg) on the highway in tests published in its March 2006 edition.

Honda employs a similar method, which cuts fuel consumption by 20 percent on the Odyssey. It runs on all six cylinders when accelerating, and on three cylinders when cruising. So far, there have been neither reliability nor performance complaints.

Engine and Transmission Cooling System (Heavy-Duty)

This relatively inexpensive option provides extra cooling for the transmission and engine. It can extend the life of these components by preventing overheating when heavy towing is required. It's a must-have feature for large cars made by Chrysler, Ford, or GM.

Extended Warranties

A smart buy if the dealer will discount the price by 50 percent and you're able to purchase the extra powertrain coverage only. However, you are throwing away

$1,500–$2,000 if you buy an extended warranty for cars, vans, or trucks rated Recommended in *Lemon-Aid* or for vehicles sold by automakers that have written "goodwill" warranties covering engine and transmission failures. If you can get a great price for a vehicle rated just Average or Above Average but want protection from costly repair bills, patronize garages that offer lifetime warranties on parts listed in this guide as being failure-prone, such as powertrains, exhaust systems, and brakes.

Buy an extended warranty only as a last resort, and make sure you know what it covers and for how long. Budget $1,000 after dealer discounting for the powertrain warranty. Incidentally, auto industry insiders say the average markup on these warranties varies from 50 to 65 percent, which seems almost reasonable when you consider that appliance warranties are marked up from 40 to 80 percent.

Keyless Entry (Remote)

This safety and convenience option saves you from fiddling with your key in a dark parking lot, or taking off a glove in cold weather to unlock or lock the vehicle. Try to get a keyless entry system combined with anti-theft measures such as an ignition kill switch or some other disabler. Incidentally, some automakers no longer make vehicles with an outside key lock on the passenger's side.

Paint Colour

Choosing a popular colour can make your vehicle easier to sell at a good price. DesRosiers Automotive Consultants say that blue is the preferred colour overall, but green and silver are also popular with Canadians. Manheim auctioneers say that green-coloured vehicles brought in 97.9 of the average auction price, while silver ones sold at a premium 105.5 percent. Remember that certain colours require particular care.

Black (and other dark colours): These paints are most susceptible to sun damage because of their heavy absorption of ultraviolet rays.

Pearl-toned colours: These paints are the most difficult to work with. If the paint needs to be retouched, it must be matched to look right from both the front- and side-angle views.

Red: This colour also shows sun damage, so keep your car in a garage or shady spot whenever possible.

White: Although grime looks terrible on a white car, white is the easiest colour to care for. But the colour is also very popular with car thieves, because white vehicles can be easily repainted another colour.

Power-Assisted Sliding Doors, Mirrors, Windows, and Seats

Merely a convenience feature with cars, power-assisted windows and doors are a necessity with minivans—crawling across the front seat a few times to roll up the passenger-side window or to lock the doors will quickly convince you of their value. Power mirrors are convenient on vehicles that have a number of drivers, or on minivans. Power seats with memory are particularly useful, too, if more than one person drives a vehicle. Automatic window and seat controls currently have few reliability problems, and they're fairly inexpensive to install, troubleshoot, and repair. As a safety precaution, make sure the window control has to be lifted. This will ensure no child is strangled from pressing against the switch. Power-sliding doors on minivans are even more of a danger. They are failure-prone on all makes and shouldn't be purchased by families with children.

Side Airbags

A worthwhile feature if you are the right size and properly seated, side airbags are presently overpriced and aren't very effective unless both the head and upper torso are protected. Side airbags are often featured as a $700 add-on to the sticker price; offer half as much.

Suspension (Heavy-Duty)

Always a good idea, this inexpensive option pays for itself by providing better handling, allowing additional ride comfort (though a bit on the firm side), and extending shock life by an extra year or two.

Tires

There are three rules to remember when purchasing tires. First, neither brand name nor price is a reliable gauge of performance, quality, or durability. Second, the cheapest prices are offered by tire discounters like Tire Rack (*www.tirerack. com*) and Discount Tire Direct (*www.discounttiredirect.com*), and their Canadian equivalents like Canadian Tire and TireTrends (*www.tiretrends.com/index.php3*). Third, choosing a tire recommended by the automaker may not be in your best interest, since traction and long tread life are often sacrificed for a softer ride and maximum EPA mileage ratings.

Two types of tires are generally available: all-season and performance. "Touring" is just a fancier name for all-season tires. All-season radial tires cost from $90 to $150 per tire. They're a compromise since, according to Transport Canada, they won't get you through winter with the same margin of safety as snow tires will and they don't provide the same durability on dry surfaces as do regular summer tires. In areas with low to moderate snowfall, however, these tires are adequate as long as they're not pushed beyond their limits.

Mud or snow tires provide the best traction on snowy surfaces, but actually decrease traction on wet roads. Treadwear is also accelerated by the use of softer rubber compounds. Beware of using wide tires for winter driving; 70-series or wider give poor traction and tend to float over snow.

Remember, too, that buying slightly larger wheels and tires may improve handling—but there's a limit. For example, many cars come with 16-inch original equipment tires supplied by the carmaker. Moving up to a slightly larger size, say a 17-inch wheel, could improve your dry and wet grip handling. Going any larger could have serious downsides, though, like making the vehicle harder to control or more subject to hydroplaning ("floating" over wet surfaces), providing less steering feedback, and causing SUVs and pickups to roll over more easily.

Don't over-inflate tires to lower their rolling resistance for better fuel economy. The trade-off is a harsher ride and increased risk of a blowout when passing over uneven terrain. Excessive tire pressure may also distort the tread, reducing contact with the road and increasing wear in the centre of the tread. Under-inflation is a far more common occurrence. Experts agree that tire life decreases by 10 percent for every 10 percent the tire is under-inflated, sometimes through lack of maintenance or due to the perception that an under-inflated tire improves traction. Actually, an under-inflated tire makes for worse traction. It breaks traction more easily than a tire that is properly inflated, causing skidding, pulling to the side when braking, excessive wheelspin when accelerating, and tire failure due to overheating.

Spare tires

Be wary of space-saver spare tires. They often can't match the promised mileage, and they seriously degrade steering control. Furthermore, they are usually stored in spaces inside the trunk that won't hold a normal-sized tire. The location of the stored spare can also have safety implications. Watch out for spares stowed under the chassis or mounted on the rear hatch. Frequently, the attaching cables and bolts rust out or freeze, so the spare falls off or becomes next to impossible to use when you need it.

Self-sealing and run-flat tires

Today, there are two technologies available to help maintain vehicle mobility when a tire is punctured: self-sealing and self-supporting/run-flat tires.

Self-sealing: Ideal if you drive long distances. Punctures from nails, bolts, or screws up to 3/16 of an inch in diameter are fixed instantly and permanently with a sealant. A low air-pressure warning system isn't required. Expert testers say a punctured self-sealing tire can maintain air pressure for up to 200 km—even in freezing conditions. The Uniroyal Tiger Paw NailGard ($85–$140, depending on the size) is the overall winner in a side-by-side test conducted by Tire Rack (*www. tirerack.com*).

Self-supporting/run-flat: Priced from $175 to $350 per tire, 25–50 percent more than the price of comparable premium tires, Goodyear's Extended Mobility

Tire (EMT) run-flat tires were first offered as an option on the 1994 Chevrolet Corvette and then became standard on the 1997 model. These tires reinforce the side wall so it can carry the weight of the car for 90 km, or about an hour's driving time, even after all air pressure has been lost. You won't feel the tire go flat; you must depend on a $250–$300 optional tire-pressure monitor to warn you before the side wall collapses and you begin riding on your rim. Also, not all vehicles can adapt to run-flat tires; you may need to upgrade your rims. Experts say run-flats will give your car a harder ride, and you'll likely notice more interior tire and road noise. The car might also track differently. The Sienna's standard Dunlop run-flat tires have a terrible reputation for premature wear. At 25,000 km, one owner complained that her Sienna needed a new set at $200 each. You can expect a backlog of over a month to get a replacement. Goodyear and Pirelli run-flat tires have been on the market for some time now, and they seem to perform adequately.

"Green" tires

No, these tires aren't coloured differently; they're simply tires with a lower rolling resistance that have been proven (through independent tests) to save fuel, which saves you money and contributes to lower greenhouse gas emissions. One fuel-efficient tire that provides good traction, reasonable tread life, and low rolling resistance is the Continental Pro-Contact with EcoPlus.

Michelin's Energy Saver A/S ranks highest for fuel savings; the Cooper GFE also gives good fuel economy, but its overall performance is only average. The Department of Transportation says fuel savings can be substantial, depending on the tire, knocking down fuel consumption by 4 percent in city driving and 7 percent on the highway. *Consumer Reports* magazine pegs the annual savings at $100 per set. Lower rolling resistance tires may also produce less road noise and have a longer tread life.

Nitrogen air refills

The National Highway Traffic Safety Administration (NHTSA) has seen reduced aging of tires filled with nitrogen. Claims have also been made that nitrogen maintains inflation pressure better than air. Though the data technically does support the claim that passenger car tires could benefit from being filled with nitrogen, tire manufacturers say that they already design tires to perform well with air inflation. And while nitrogen will do no harm, manufacturers say that they don't see the need to use nitrogen, which generally adds $5 or more per tire charge.

Consumer Reports says consumers can use nitrogen and might enjoy the slight improvement in air retention provided, but you can do just as well without paying an extra penny by performing regular inflation checks.

Which tires are best?

There is no independent Canadian agency that evaluates tire performance and durability. However, the U.S.-based NHTSA rates treadwear, traction, and resistance to sustained high temperatures; etches the ratings onto the side walls of all tires sold in the States and Canada; and regularly posts its findings on the Internet (*www.safercar.gov*). NHTSA also logs owner complaints relative to different brands. *Lemon-Aid* summarizes these complaints in the ratings of specific models in Part Three.

You can get more-recent complaint postings, service bulletins, and tire recall notices at the same government website. Also check out independent owner performance ratings as compiled by Tire Rack, a large tire retailer, at *www.tirerack. com/tires/surveyresults/index.jsp.*

Traction Control

This option limits wheelspin when accelerating. It is most useful with rear-drive vehicles and provides surer traction in wet or icy conditions.

Trailer-Towing Equipment

Just because you need a vehicle with towing capability doesn't mean that you have to spend big bucks. But you should first determine what kind of vehicle you want to do the job and whether your tires will handle the extra burden. For most towing needs (up to 900 kg/2,000 lb.), a passenger car, small pickup, or minivan equipped with a 6-cylinder engine will work just as well as a full-sized pickup or van (and will cost much less). If you're pulling a trailer that weighs more than 900 kg, most passenger cars won't handle the load unless they've been specially outfitted according to the automaker's specifications. Pulling a heavier trailer (up to 1,800 kg/4,000 lb.) will likely require a large vehicle equipped with a V8 powerplant.

Automakers reserve the right to change limits whenever they feel like it, so make any sales promise about towing an integral part of your contract. A good rule of thumb is to reduce the promised tow rating by 20 percent. In assessing towing weight, factor in the cargo, passengers, and equipment of both the trailer and the towing vehicle. Keep in mind that five people and luggage add 450 kg (almost 1,000 lb.) to the load, and that a full 227L (60 gal.) water tank adds another 225 kg (almost 500 lb.). The manufacturer's gross vehicle weight rating (GVWR) takes into account the anticipated average cargo and supplies that your vehicle is likely to carry.

Automatic transmissions are fine for trailering, although there's a slight fuel penalty. Manual transmissions tend to have greater clutch wear caused by towing than do automatic transmissions. Both transmission choices are equally acceptable. Remember, the best compromise is to shift the automatic manually for maximum performance going uphill and to maintain control while not overheating the brakes when descending mountains.

Unibody vehicles (those without a separate frame) can handle most towing chores as long as their limits aren't exceeded. Front-drives aren't the best choice for pulling heavy loads in excess of 900 kg, since they lose some steering control and traction with all the weight concentrated in the rear.

Whatever vehicle you choose, keep in mind that the trailer hitch is crucial. It must have a tongue capacity of at least 10 percent of the trailer's weight; otherwise, it may be unsafe to use. Hitches are chosen according to the type of tow vehicle and, to a lesser extent, the weight of the load.

Most hitches are factory-installed, even though independents can install them more cheaply. Expect to pay about $200 for a simple boat hitch and a minimum of $600 for a fifth-wheel version.

Equalizer bars and extra cooling systems for the radiator, transmission, engine oil, and steering are prerequisites for towing anything heavier than 900 kg. Heavy-duty springs and brakes are a big help, too. Separate brakes for the trailer may be necessary to increase your vehicle's maximum towing capacity.

Transmissions

Despite its many advantages, the manual transmission is an endangered species in North America, where manuals equip only 8–10 percent of all new vehicles (mostly econocars, sports cars, and budget trucks), and that figure is slated to fall to 6 percent this year as more vehicles adopt fuel-saving CVT transmissions, among other powertrain innovations. One theory on why the manual numbers keep falling: North American drivers are too busy with cell phones, text messaging, and cappuccinos to shift gears. Interestingly, European buyers opt for a manual transmission almost 90 percent of the time. (And they also drink cappuccinos, but usually not in 20 oz. paper takeout cups.)

Automakers are currently offering hybrid manumatic transmissions that provide the benefits of an automatic transmission while also giving the driver the NASCAR-styled fun of clutchless manual shifting. Or, if all you want is fuel savings, there are now 5- and 6-speed automatic models—and even 7- and 8-speed versions—that are fuel-sippers.

Some considerations: The brake pads on stick-shift vehicles tend to wear out less rapidly than those on automatics do; a transmission with five or more forward speeds is usually more fuel-efficient than one with three forward speeds (hardly seen anymore); and manual transmissions usually add a mile or two per gallon over automatics, although this isn't always the case, as *Consumer Reports* recently discovered. Their road tests found that the 2008 Toyota Yaris equipped with an automatic transmission got slightly better gas mileage than a Yaris powered by a manual tranny.

Unnecessary Options

All-Wheel Drive (AWD)

Mark Bilek, editorial director of *Consumer Guide*'s automotive website (*consumerguideauto.howstuffworks.com*), is a critic of AWD. He says AWD systems generally encourage drivers to go faster than they should in adverse conditions, which creates trouble for stopping in emergencies. Automakers like AWD as "a marketing ploy to make more money," Bilek contends. My personal mechanic adds, "Four-wheel drive will only get you stuck deeper, farther from home."

Anti-Lock Brakes (ABS)

Like adaptive cruise control and backup warning devices, ABS is another safety feature that's fine in theory but mostly impractical under actual driving conditions. (Though if you want the highly recommended electronic stability control (ESC), you must use anti-lock brakes.) The system maintains directional stability by preventing the wheels from locking up. This will not reduce the stopping distance, however. In practice, ABS is said to make drivers overconfident. Many still pump the brakes and render them ineffective; total brake failure is common; and repairs are frequent, complicated, and expensive to perform.

Cruise Control

Automakers provide this $250–$300 option, which is mainly a convenience feature, to motorists who use their vehicles for long periods of high-speed driving. The constant rate of speed saves some fuel and lessens driver fatigue during long trips. Still, the system is particularly failure-prone and expensive to repair, can lead to driver inattention, and can make the vehicle hard to control on icy roadways. Malfunctioning cruise-control units are also one of the major causes of sudden acceleration incidents. At other times, cruise control can be very distracting, especially to inexperienced drivers who are unaccustomed to sudden speed fluctuations.

Adaptive cruise control is the latest evolution of this feature. It senses a vehicle ahead of you and then automatically downshifts, brakes, or cuts your vehicle's speed. This commonly occurs when passing another car or when a car passes you, and it can make for a harrowing experience…especially when you are in the passing lane.

Electronic Instrument Readout

If you've ever had trouble reading a digital watch face or resetting your VCR, you'll feel right at home with this electronic gizmo. Gauges are presented in a series of moving digital patterns that are confusing, distracting, and unreadable in direct sunlight. This system is often accompanied by a trip computer and vehicle monitor that indicate average speed, signal component failures, and determine fuel use and how many kilometres you can drive until the tank is empty. Figures are frequently in error or slow to catch up.

Fog Lights

A pain in the eyes for some, a pain in the wallet for those who have to pay the high bulb replacement costs. Fog lights aren't necessary for most drivers who have well-aimed original-equipment headlights on their vehicles.

Gas-Saving Gadgets and Fuel Additives

Ah, the search for the Holy Grail. Magic software and miracle hardware that will turn your gas-hungry Hummer into a fuel-frugal Prius when the right additive is poured into your fuel tank.

The accessory market has been flooded with hundreds of atomizers, magnets, and additives that purport to make vehicles less fuel-thirsty. However, tests on over 100 gadgets and fuel or crankcase additives carried out by the U.S. Environmental Protection Agency have found that only a handful produce an increase in fuel economy, and the increase is tiny. These gadgets include warning devices that tell the driver to ease up on the throttle or shift to a more fuel-frugal gear, hardware that reduces the engine power needed for belt-driven accessories, cylinder deactivation systems, and spoilers that channel airflow under the car. The use of any of these products is a quick way to lose warranty coverage and fail provincial emissions tests.

GPS Navigation Systems

This navigation aid links a Global Positioning System satellite unit to the vehicle's cellular phone and electronics. Good GPS devices cost $99–$269 (U.S.) when bought from an independent retailer. Although GPS-enabled smartphones are gaining ground in the portable navigation market, the standalone portable navigation device (PND) bought from retail outlets is still very popular. PNDs have more features than ever, including audible driving directions with text-to-speech, spoken street names, real-time traffic updates, Internet connectivity for points-of-interest search, and easy-to-read screens that are no longer as obtrusive, distracting, washed out in sunlight, or hard to calibrate. Plus, when you trade in the car, the GPS can be put in another vehicle with all of your settings already calibrated.

On the downside: a PND is easily stolen in a "smash and grab" (unless you take it with you when leaving the car); the screen may not be as large as dealer-installed GPS units; and securing the device to the dash and hiding the power cord may take some do-it-yourself skill.

As a dealer option, you will pay $1,000–$4,000 (U.S.). For a monthly fee, the unit connects drivers to live operators who will provide driving directions, give repair or emergency assistance, or relay messages. If the airbag deploys or the car is stolen, satellite-transmitted signals are automatically sent from the vehicle to operators who will notify the proper authorities of the vehicle's location.

Besides the high cost, here are some other disadvantages associated with factory-supplied units: the GPS device can't be used on another vehicle; navigation maps are often out-of-date; the system won't enhance your trade-in's value since it will have been long out-of-date; and any of the dealer-installed systems' functions can be performed by a cheap cell phone. Here are the top five GPS models rated by CNET (*http://reviews.cnet.com/best-gps*):

The **Garmin Nuvi 3790T** is the best of the lot. It's an exceptional portable navigation device with just the right blend of form and function. Price: **$269.00**; 4 stars. Outstanding.

Garmin's Nuvi 50 carries a lower price this year, and its large 5-inch screen enhances value. More frugal buyers may opt for the smaller **Nuvi 30** or **Nuvi 40**, which offer the same functionality but with smaller, 4.7 and 3.5 inch, screens. Price: **$99.99–$149.99**; 4 stars. Very good.

The **Magellan RoadMate 5175T-LM Traveler** is a competent performer offering features to help plan vacations. Price: **$194.99–$279.95**; 4 stars. Very good.

The **TomTom GO Live 1535M**. The killer app here is TomTom's clever use of Twitter to automatically update friends and family on where you're going and when you'll be there. Price: **$165.00–$239.95**; 4 stars. Very good.

TomTom's VIA series of GPS navigators is a cheaper version of its top-tier brothers. There is an available lifetime map and traffic updates feature that ensures information will always be up-to-date. Price: **$149.99**; 4 stars. Very good.

High-Intensity Headlights

These headlights are much brighter than standard headlights, and they cast a blue hue. Granted, they provide additional illumination of the roadway, but they are also annoying to other drivers, who will flash their lights—or give you the middle finger—thinking that your high beams are on. These lights are easily stolen and expensive to replace. Interestingly, European versions have a device to maintain the light's spread closer to the road so that other drivers aren't blinded.

ID Etching

This $150–$200 option is a scam. The government doesn't require it, and thieves and joyriders aren't deterred by the etchings. If you want to etch your windows for your own peace of mind, several private companies will sell you a $15–$30 kit that does an excellent job (try *www.autoetch.net*), or you can wait for your municipality or local police agency to conduct one of their periodic free VIN ID etching sessions in your area.

Paint and Fabric Protectors

Selling for $200–$300, these "sealants" add nothing to a vehicle's resale value. Although paint lustre may be temporarily heightened, this treatment is less effective and more costly than regular waxing, and it may also invalidate the manufacturer's guarantee at a time when the automaker will look for any pretext to deny your paint claim.

Auto fabric protection products are nothing more than variations of Scotchgard, which can be bought in aerosol cans for a few dollars—a much better deal than the $50–$75 charged by dealers.

Power-Assisted Minivan Sliding Doors

Not a good idea if you have children. These doors have a high failure rate, opening or closing for no apparent reason and injuring children caught between the door and post.

Reverse-Warning System

Selling for about $500 as part of an option package, this safety feature warns the driver of any objects in the rear when backing up. Although a sound idea in theory, in practice the device often fails to go off or sounds an alarm for no reason. Drivers eventually either disconnect or ignore it.

Rollover-Detection System

This feature makes use of sensors to determine if the vehicle has leaned beyond a safe angle. If so, the side airbags are automatically deployed and remain inflated to make sure occupants aren't injured or ejected in a rollover accident. This is a totally new system that has not yet been proven effective. It could have disastrous consequences if the sensor malfunctions, as has been the case with front and side airbag sensors over the past decade.

Rooftop Carrier

Although this inexpensive option provides additional baggage space and may allow you to meet all your driving needs with a smaller vehicle, a loaded roof rack can increase fuel consumption by as much as 18 percent. An empty rack can increase your gas bill by about 10 percent.

Sunroof

Unless you live in a temperate region, the advantages of having a sunroof are far outweighed by the disadvantages. You aren't going to get better ventilation than a good AC system would provide, and a sunroof may grace your environment with painful booming wind noises, rattles, water leaks, and road dust accumulation. A sunroof increases gas consumption, reduces night vision because overhead highway lights shine through the roof opening, and can lose you several centimetres of headroom.

Tinted Glass

On the one hand, tinting jeopardizes safety by reducing your night vision. On the other hand, it does keep the interior cool in hot weather, reduces glare, and hides the car's contents from prying eyes. Factory applications are worth the extra cost, since cheaper aftermarket products (cost: about $150) distort visibility and peel away after a few years. Some tinting done in the United States can run afoul of provincial highway codes that require more transparency.

Cutting the Price

Bidding by Fax or Email

The process is quite easy: Simply fax or email an invitation for bids to area dealerships, asking them to give their bottom-line price for a specific make and model. Be clear that all final bids must be sent within a week. When all the bids are received, the lowest bid is sent to the other dealers to give them a chance to beat that price. After a week of bidding, the lowest price gets your business. When the Canadian loonie is near parity with the American dollar, try doing an Internet search for American prices and then using that lower figure to haggle with Canadian dealers.

Dozens of *Lemon-Aid* readers have told me how this bidding approach has cut thousands of dollars from the advertised price and saved them from the degrading song-and-dance routine between the buyer, sales agent, and sales manager ("he said, she said, the sales manager said").

A *Lemon-Aid* reader sent in the following suggestions for buying by fax or email:

> Based on my experience, I would suggest that in reference to the fax-tendering [or email-tendering] process, future *Lemon-Aid* editions emphasize:
>
> - Casting a wide geographical net, as long as you're willing to pick the car up there. I faxed up to 50 dealerships, which helped tremendously in increasing the number of serious bidders. One car was bought locally in Ottawa, the other in Mississauga.
> - Unless you don't care much about what car you end up with, be very specific about what you want. If you are looking at just one or two cars, which I recommend, specify trim level and all extended warranties and dealer-installed options in the fax letter. Otherwise, you'll end up with quotes comparing apples and oranges, and you won't get the best deal on options negotiated later. Also,

specify that quotes should be signed. This helps out with errors in quoting.

- Dealerships are sloppy: there is a 25–30 percent error rate in quotes. Search for errors and get corrections, and confirm any of the quotes in serious contention over the phone.
- Phone to personally thank anyone who submits a quote for their time. Salespeople can't help themselves, they'll ask how they ranked, and often want to then beat the best quote you've got. This is much more productive than faxing back the most competitive quote (I know, I've tried that too).

Getting a Fair Price

"We Sell Below Cost"

This is no longer a bait-and-switch scam. Many dealers who are going out of business are desperate to sell their inventory, sometimes for 40 percent below the MSRP. Assuming the vehicle's cost price was 20 percent under the MSRP, astute buyers are getting up to a 20 percent discount. In addition to the dealer's markup, some vehicles may also have a 3 percent carryover allowance paid out in a dealer incentive program. Finance contracts may also tack on a 2 percent dealer commission.

Holdback

Ever wonder how dealers who advertise vehicles for "a hundred dollars over invoice" can make a profit? They are counting mostly on the manufacturer's holdback.

In addition to the MSRP, the invoice price, dealer incentives, and customer rebates (available to Canadians at *www.apa.ca*), another key element in every dealer's profit margin is the manufacturer's holdback—the quarterly payouts dealers depend on when calculating gross profit.

The holdback was set up about 50 years ago by General Motors as a guaranteed profit for dealers tempted to bargain away their entire profit to make a sale. It usually represents 1–3 percent of the sticker price (MSRP) and is seldom given out by Asian or European automakers, which use dealer incentive programs instead. There are several free Internet sources for holdback information: The most recent and comprehensive are *www.edmunds.com* and *www.kbb.com*, two websites geared toward American buyers. Although there may be a difference in the holdback percentage between American automakers and their Canadian subsidiaries, it's usually not a significant difference.

Some GM dealers maintain that they no longer get a holdback allowance. They are being disingenuous—the holdback may have been added to special sales "incentive" programs, which won't show up on the dealer's invoice. Options are the icing on the cake, with their average 35–65 percent markup.

Can You Get a Fair Price?

Yes, but you'll have to keep your wits about you and time your purchase well into the model year—usually in late winter or spring.

New-car negotiations aren't wrestling matches where you have to pin the sales agent's shoulders to the mat to win. If you feel that the overall price is fair, don't jeopardize the deal by refusing to budge. For example, if you've brought the contract price 10 percent or more below the MSRP and the dealer sticks you with a $200 "administrative fee" at the last moment, let it pass. You've saved money and the sales agent has saved face.

Of course, someone will always be around to tell you how he or she could have bought the vehicle for much less. Let that pass, too.

To come up with a fair price, subtract two-thirds of the dealer's markup from the MSRP and then trade the carryover and holdback allowance for a reduced delivery and transportation fee. Compute the options separately, and sell your trade-in privately. Buyers can more easily knock $4,000 off a $20,000 base price if they shop early in the year, when Chrysler and GM hold their new year "fire" sales and ratchet up the competition. Remember, choose a vehicle that's in stock, and resist getting unnecessary options.

Beware of Financing and Insurance Traps

Once you and the dealer have settled on the vehicle's price, you aren't out of the woods yet. You'll be handed over to an F&I (financing and insurance) specialist, whose main goal is to convince you to buy additional financing, loan insurance, paint and seat cover protectors, rustproofing, and extended warranties. These items will be presented on a computer screen as costing only "a little bit more each month."

Compare the dealer's insurance and financing charges with those from an independent agency that may offer better rates and better service. Often, the dealer gets a kickback for selling insurance and financing. And guess who pays for it? Additionally, remember that if the financing rate looks too good to be true, you're probably paying too much for the vehicle. The F&I closer's hard-sell approach will take all your willpower and patience to resist, but when he or she gives up, your trials are over.

Add-on charges are the dealer's last chance to stick it to you before the contract is signed. Dealer pre-delivery inspection (PDI) and transportation charges, "documentation" fees, and extra handling costs are ways that the dealer gets extra profits for nothing. Dealer preparation is often a once-over-lightly affair, with a car seldom getting more than a wash job and a couple of dollars' worth of gas in the tank. It's paid for by the factory in most cases, but when it's not, it should cost no more than 2 percent of the car's selling price. Reasonable transportation charges are acceptable, although dealers who claim that the manufacturer requires the payment often inflate them.

"No Haggle" Pricing

All dealers bargain. They hang out the "No dickering; one price only" sign simply as a means to discourage customers from asking for a better deal. Like parking lots and restaurants that claim they won't be responsible for lost or stolen property, they're bluffing. Still, you'd be surprised by how many people believe that if it's posted, it's non-negotiable.

Price Guidelines

When negotiating the price of a new vehicle, remember that there are several price guidelines and dealers use the one that will make them the most profit on each transaction. Two of the more-common prices quoted are the MSRP (what the automaker advertises as a fair price) and the dealer's invoice cost (which is supposed to indicate how much the dealer paid for the vehicle). Both price indicators leave considerable room for the dealer's profit margin, along with some extra padding in the form of inflated transportation and preparation charges. If you are presented with both figures, go with the MSRP, since it can be verified by calling the manufacturer. Any dealer can print up an invoice and swear to its veracity. If you want an invoice price from an independent source, contact *www.apa.ca* or *www.carhelpcanada.com*.

Buyers who live in rural areas or in western Canada are often faced with grossly inflated auto prices compared to those charged in major metropolitan areas. A good way to get a more-competitive price without buying out of province is to check online to see what prices are being charged in different urban areas or in the States. Then compare the U.S. automakers' "Build Your Car" prices (for example, go to *Ford.com*, for suggested prices in the States and *Ford.ca* for Canada). Show the dealer printouts that list selling prices, preparation charges, and transportation fees, and then ask for his or her price to come closer to the advertised prices.

Another tactic is to take a copy of a local competitor's car ad to a competing dealer selling the same brand and ask for a better price. Chances are they've already lost a few sales due to the ad and will work a little harder to match the deal; if not, they're almost certain to reveal the tricks in the competitor's promotion to make the sale.

Dealer Incentives and Customer Rebates

Sales incentives haven't changed much in the past 30 years. When vehicles are first introduced in the fall, they're generally overpriced; early in the new year, they'll sell for about 20–30 percent less. After a year, they may sell for less through a combination of dealer sales incentives (manufacturer-to-dealer), cash rebates (manufacturer-to-customer), zero percent interest financing (manufacturer's-finance-company-to-customer), and discounted prices (dealer-to-customer).

In most cases, the manufacturer's rebate is straightforward and mailed directly to the buyer from the automaker. There are other rebate programs that require a financial investment on the dealer's part, however, and these shared programs tempt dealers to offset losses by inflating the selling price or pocketing the manufacturer's rebate. Therefore, when the dealer participates in the rebate program, demand that the rebate be deducted from the MSRP, not from some inflated invoice price concocted by the dealer.

Some rebate ads will include the phrase "from dealer inventory only." So if your dealer doesn't have the vehicle in stock, you won't get the rebate.

Sometimes automakers will suddenly decide that a rebate no longer applies to a specific model, even though their ads continue to include it. When this happens, take all brochures and advertisements showing your eligibility for the rebate plan to provincial consumer protection officials. They can use false advertising statutes to force automakers to give rebates to every purchaser who was unjustly denied one.

If you are buying a heavily discounted vehicle, be wary of "option packaging" by dealers who push unwanted protection packages (rustproofing, paint sealants, and upholstery finishes) or who levy excessive charges for preparation, "administration," loan guarantee insurance, and credit life insurance.

Leftovers

Last year's vehicles left over in stock can be good buys as long as they aren't actually used and you can amortize the first year's depreciation by keeping the vehicle for eight years or more. But if you're the kind of driver who trades every two or three years, you're likely to come out a loser by buying an end-of-the-season vehicle. The simple reason is that, as far as trade-ins are concerned, a leftover is a "used" vehicle that has depreciated at least 20 percent in its first year. The savings the dealer gives you may not equal that first year's depreciation (a cost you'll incur without getting any of the first year's driving benefits). If the dealer's discounted price matches or exceeds the 30 percent depreciation, you're getting a pretty good deal.

Ask the dealer for all work orders relating to the leftover vehicle, including the PDI checklist, and make sure that the odometer readings follow in sequential order. Remember as well that most demonstrators should have less than 5,000 km on the ticker and that the original warranty has been reduced from the day the vehicle was first put on the road. Also, make sure the vehicle is relatively "fresh" (about three months old) and check for warranty damage. With demos, have the dealer extend the warranty or lower the price about $100 for each month of warranty that has expired. If the vehicle's file shows that it was registered to a leasing agency or any other third party, you're definitely buying a used vehicle disguised as a demo. You should walk away from the sale—you're dealing with a crook.

Cash versus Financing

Up until recently, car dealers preferred financing car sales instead of getting cash, because of the 1–2 percent kickbacks lenders gave them. This is less the case now, because fewer companies are lending money, and those that do are giving back very little to dealers and don't want to give loans for more than two-thirds of the purchase price. Dealers are scrambling for equity and will sell their vehicles for less than what they cost if the buyer pays cash. Cash is, once again, king.

If you aren't offered much of a discount for cash, financial planners say it can be smarter to finance the purchase of a new vehicle if a portion of the interest is tax-deductible. The cash that you free up can then be used to repay debts that aren't tax-deductible (mortgages or credit card debts, for example).

Rebates versus Low or Zero Percent Financing

Low-financing programs have the following disadvantages:

- Buyers must have exceptionally good credit.
- Shorter financing periods mean higher payments.
- Cash rebates are excluded.
- Only fully equipped or slow-selling models are eligible.
- Buyers pay full retail price.

The above stipulations can add thousands of dollars to your costs. Remember, to get the best price, first negotiate the price of the vehicle without disclosing whether you are paying cash or financing the purchase (say you haven't yet decided). Once you have a fair price, you can then take advantage of the financing.

Getting a Loan

Borrowers must be at least 18 years old (the age of majority), have a steady income, prove that they have discretionary income sufficient to make the loan payments, and be willing to guarantee the loan with additional collateral or with a parent or spouse as a co-signer.

Before applying for a loan, you should have established a good credit rating via a paid-off credit card and have a small savings account with your local bank, credit union, or trust company. Prepare a budget listing your assets and obligations. This will quickly show whether or not you can afford a car. Next, prearrange your loan with a phone call. This will protect you from much of the smoke-and-mirrors showroom shenanigans.

Incidentally, if you do get in over your head and require credit counselling, contact Credit Counselling Service (CCS), a not-for-profit organization located in many of Canada's major cities (*www.creditcanada.com*).

Hidden Loan Costs

The APA's undercover shoppers have found that most deceptive deals involve major banking institutions rather than automaker-owned companies.

In your quest for an auto loan, remember that the Internet offers help for people who need an auto loan and want quick approval, but don't want to face a banker. The Bank of Montreal (*www.bmo.com*), RBC (*www.rbc.com*), and other banks allow vehicle buyers to post loan applications on their websites. Loans are available to those who aren't current BMO or RBC customers.

Be sure to call various financial institutions to find out the following:

- The annual percentage rate on the amount you want to borrow, and the duration of your repayment period
- The minimum down payment that the institution requires
- Whether taxes and licence fees are considered part of the overall cost and, thus, are covered by part of the loan
- Whether lower rates are available for different loan periods, or for a larger down payment
- Whether discounts are available to depositors, and if so, how long you must be a depositor before qualifying

When comparing loans, consider the annual rate and then calculate the total cost of the loan offer—that is, how much you'll pay above and beyond the total price of the vehicle.

Dealers may be able to finance your purchase at interest rates that are competitive with the banks' because of the rebates they get from the manufacturers and some lending institutions. Don't believe dealers that say they can borrow money at as much as five percentage points below the prime rate. Actually, they're jacking up the retail price to more than make up for the lower interest charges. Sometimes, instead of boosting the price, dealers reduce the amount they pay for the trade-in. In either case, the savings are illusory.

When dealing with banks, keep in mind that the traditional 36-month loan has now been stretched to 48 or 60 months. Longer payment terms make each month's payment more affordable, but over the long run, they increase the cost of the loan considerably. Therefore, take as short a term as possible.

Be wary of lending institutions that charge a "processing" or "document" fee ranging from $25 to $100. Sometimes consumers will be charged an extra 1–2 percent of the loan up front in order to cover servicing. This is similar to lending institutions adding "points" to mortgages, except that with auto loans, it's totally unjustified. In fact, dealers in the States are the object of several state lawsuits and class actions for inflating loan charges.

Some banks will cut the interest rate if you're a member of an automobile owners' association or if loan payments are automatically deducted from your chequing account. This latter proposal may be costly, however, if the chequing account charges exceed the interest-rate savings.

Loan Protection

Credit insurance guarantees that the vehicle loan will be paid if the borrower becomes disabled or dies. There are three basic types of insurance that can be written into an installment contract: credit life, accident and health, and comprehensive. Some car companies, like Hyundai, will make some of your loan payments if you become unemployed. Most bank and credit union loans are already covered by some kind of loan insurance, but dealers sell the protection separately at an extra cost to the borrower. For this service, the dealer gets a hefty 20 percent commission. The additional cost to the purchaser can be significant. The federal GST is applied to loan insurance, but retail sales tax may be exempted in some provinces.

Collecting on these types of policies isn't easy. There's no payment if your unemployment was due to your own conduct or if an illness is caused by some condition that existed prior to your taking out the insurance. Generally, credit insurance is unnecessary if you're in good health, you have no dependants, and your job is secure. Nevertheless, if you need to cancel your financial obligations, the same company that started up LeaseBusters now offers FinanceBusters (*www.finance-busters.com*). They provide a similar service to a lease takeover, but for customers who have vehicle loans.

Personal loans from financial institutions (particularly credit unions) now offer lots of flexibility, like fixed or variable interest rates, a choice of loan terms, and no penalties for prepayment. Precise conditions depend on your personal credit rating.

Leasing contracts are less flexible. There's a penalty for any prepayment, and rates aren't necessarily competitive.

Financing Scam: "Your Financing Was Turned Down"

This may be true, now that credit has become more difficult to get. But watch out for the scam that begins after you have purchased a vehicle and left your trade-in with the dealer. A few days later, you are told that your loan was rejected and that you now must put down a larger down payment and accept a higher monthly payment. Of course, your trade-in has already been sold.

Protect yourself from this rip-off by getting a signed agreement that stipulates that financing has been approved and that monthly payments can't be readjusted. Tell the dealer that your trade-in cannot be sold until the deal has closed.

The Contract

How likely are you to be cheated when buying a new car or truck? APA staffers posing as buyers visited 42 dealerships in four Canadian cities in early 2002. Almost half the dealers they visited (45 percent) flunked their test, and (hold onto your cowboy hats) auto buyers in western Canada were especially vulnerable to dishonest dealers. Either dealer ads left out important information or vehicles in the ads weren't available or were selling at higher prices. Fees for paperwork and vehicle preparation were frequently excessive.

Now, 10 years later, we know dealers are much more honest. Ahem…maybe.

The Devil's in the Details

Watch what you sign, since any document that requires your signature is a contract. Don't sign anything unless all the details are clear to you and all the blanks have been filled in. Don't accept any verbal promises that you're merely putting the vehicle on hold. And when you are presented with a contract, remember it doesn't have to include all the clauses found in the dealer's pre-printed form. You and the sales representative can agree to strike some clauses and add others.

When the sales agent asks for a deposit, make sure that it's listed on the contract as a deposit, try to keep it as small as possible (a couple hundred dollars at the most), and pay for it by credit card—in case the dealer goes belly up. If you decide to back out of the deal on a vehicle taken from stock, let the seller have the deposit as an incentive to cancel the contract (believe me, it's cheaper than hiring a lawyer and probably equal to the dealer's commission).

Scrutinize all references to the exact model (there's a heck of an upgrade from base to LX or Limited), prices, and delivery dates. Make sure you specify a delivery date in the contract that protects the price.

Contract Clauses You Need

You can put things on a more-equal footing by negotiating the inclusion of as many clauses as possible from the sample additional contract clauses found on the following page. To do this, write in a "Remarks" section on your contract and then add, "See attached clauses, which form part of this agreement." Then attach a photocopy of the "Additional Contract Clauses" and persuade the sales agent to initial as many of the clauses as possible. Although some clauses may be rejected, the inclusion of just a couple of them can have important legal ramifications later on if you want a full or partial refund.

ADDITIONAL CONTRACT CLAUSES

1. **Original contract:** This is the ONLY contract; i.e., it cannot be changed, retyped, or rewritten, without the specific agreement of both parties.

2. **Financing:** This agreement is subject to the purchaser obtaining financing at _____% or less within _____ days of the date below.

3. **"In-service" date and mileage:** To be based on the closing day, not the day the contract was executed, and will be submitted to the automaker for warranty and all other purposes. The dealership will have this date corrected by the automaker if it should become necessary.

4. **Delivery:** The vehicle is to be delivered by _____, failing which the contract is cancelled and the deposit will be refunded.

5. **Cancellation:**
   (a) The purchaser retains the right to cancel this agreement without penalty at any time before delivery of the vehicle by sending a notice in writing to the vendor.
   (b) Following delivery of the vehicle, the purchaser shall have two days to return the vehicle and cancel the agreement in writing, without penalty. After two days and before thirty-one days, the purchaser shall pay the dealer $25 a day as compensation for depreciation on the returned vehicle.
   (c) Cancellation of contract can be refused where the vehicle has been subjected to abuse, negligence or unauthorized modifications after delivery.
   (d) The purchaser is responsible for accident damage and traffic violations while in possession of the said vehicle.

6. **Protected price:** The vendor agrees not to alter the price of the new vehicle, the cost of preparation, or the cost of shipping.

7. **Trade-in:** The vendor agrees that the value attributed to the vehicle offered in trade shall not be reduced, unless it has been significantly modified or has suffered from unreasonable and accelerated deterioration since the signing of the agreement.

8. **Courtesy car:**
   (a) In the event the new vehicle is not delivered on the agreed-upon date, the vendor agrees to supply the purchaser with a courtesy car at no cost. If no courtesy vehicle is available, the vendor agrees to reimburse the purchaser the cost of renting a vehicle.
   (b) If the vehicle is off the road for more than two days for warranty repairs, the purchaser is entitled to a free courtesy vehicle for the duration of the repair period. If no courtesy vehicle is available, the vendor agrees to reimburse the purchaser the cost of renting a vehicle of equivalent or lesser value.

9. **Work orders:** The purchaser will receive duly completed copies of all work orders pertaining to the vehicle, including warranty repairs and the pre-delivery inspection (PDI).

10. **Dealer stickers:** The vendor will not affix any dealer advertising, in any form, on the vehicle.

11. **Fuel:** Vehicle will be delivered with a free full tank of gas.

12. **Excess mileage:** New vehicle will not be acceptable and the contract will be void if the odometer has more than 200 km at delivery/closing.

13. **Tires:** Original equipment Firestone or Bridgestone tires are not acceptable.

Date   Vendor's Signature   Buyer's Signature

"We Can't Do That"

Dealers and automakers facing bankruptcy can do almost anything to get your business. Don't take the dealer's word that "We're not allowed to do that"—heard most often in reference to reducing the PDI or transportation fee. Some dealers have been telling *Lemon-Aid* readers that they are "obligated" by the automaker to charge a set fee and could lose their franchise if they charge less. This is pure hogwash. No dealer has ever had their franchise licence revoked for cutting prices. Furthermore, the automakers clearly state that they don't set a bottom price, since doing so would violate Canada's *Competition Act*—that's why you always see them putting disclaimers in their ads saying the dealer can charge less.

The Pre-delivery Inspection

The best way to ensure that the PDI (written as "PDE" in some regions) will be done is to write in the sales contract that you'll be given a copy of the completed PDI sheet when the vehicle is delivered to you. Then, with the PDI sheet in hand, verify some of the items that were to be checked. If any items appear to have been missed, refuse delivery of the vehicle. If the items you check seem all in order and you accept delivery of the vehicle, once you get home, check out the vehicle more thoroughly, and send a registered letter to the dealer if you discover any incomplete items from the PDI.

Selling Your Trade-In

When to Sell

Used cars are worth more than ever because new cars are in short supply (especially Ford products), new prices are holding firm and aren't expected to drop before the new year, and used prices are rising. This makes it hard for most owners to figure out when is the best time to buy another vehicle, though it doesn't take a genius to figure out that the longer one keeps a vehicle, the less it costs to own.

If you're happy with your vehicle's styling and convenience features and it's safe and dependable, there's no reason to get rid of it. Shortly after your vehicle's fifth birthday (or whenever you start to think about trading it in), ask a mechanic to look at it to get some idea of what repairs, replacement parts, or maintenance work it will need in the coming year. Find out if dealer service bulletins show that it will need extensive repairs in the near future (see page 61 for how to order bulletins from ALLDATA). If it's going to require expensive repairs, you should trade the vehicle right away; if expensive work isn't predicted, you may want to keep it the 11 years that is the North American norm. Auto owners' associations provide a good yardstick. Industry experts say that the annual cost of repairs and preventive maintenance for the average vehicle is about $800–$1,100. If your vehicle is five years old and you haven't spent anywhere near $5,500 in maintenance, it would pay to invest in your old vehicle and continue using it for another few years.

Consider whether your vehicle can still be serviced easily. If it's no longer on the market, the parts supply is likely to dry up and independent mechanics will be reluctant to repair it.

Don't trade for fuel economy alone. Most fuel-efficient vehicles, such as front-drives, offset the savings through higher repair costs. Also, the more fuel-efficient vehicles may not be as comfortable to drive because of their excessive engine noise, lightweight construction, stiff suspension, and torque steer.

Reassess your needs. Has your family grown to the point that you need a new vehicle? Are you driving less? Are you taking fewer long trips? Let your car or minivan show its age, and pocket the savings if its deteriorating condition doesn't pose a safety hazard and isn't too embarrassing. If you're in sales and are constantly on the road, it makes sense to trade every few years—in that case, the vehicle's appearance and reliability become a prime consideration, particularly since the increased depreciation costs are mostly tax-deductible.

Getting the Most for Your Trade-In

Customers who are on guard against paying too much for a new vehicle often sell their trade-ins for too little. Before agreeing to any trade-in amount, read Part Three of *Lemon-Aid Used Cars and Trucks*. The guide will give your vehicle's dealer price and private selling price, and it offers a formula to figure out regional price fluctuations.

Now that you've nailed down your trade-in's approximate value, here are some tips on selling it with a minimum of stress:

- Never sign a new-vehicle sales contract unless your trade-in has been sold—you could end up with two vehicles.
- Negotiate the price from retail (dealer price) down to wholesale (private sales).

If you haven't sold your trade-in after two weekends, you might be trying to sell it at the wrong time of year or have it priced too high.

Make Money—Sell Privately

If you must sell your vehicle and want to make the most out of the deal, consider selling it yourself and putting the profits toward your next purchase. You'll likely come out hundreds of dollars ahead. Buyers will pay more for your vehicle because they know cars sold by owners are more reasonably priced: there's no dealer overhead or sales commissions to pay. The most important thing to remember is that there's a large market for used vehicles in good condition in the $5,000–$7,000 range. Although most people prefer buying from individuals rather than from used-car lots, they may still be afraid that the vehicle is a lemon. By using the following suggestions, you should be able to sell your vehicle quite easily:

1. Know its value. Study dealers' newspaper ads and compare them with the prices listed in *Lemon-Aid*. Undercut the dealer's price by $300–$800, and be ready to bargain down another 10 percent for a serious buyer. Remember, prices can fluctuate wildly depending on which models are trendy, so watch the want ads carefully.
2. Enlist the aid of the salesperson who's selling you your new car. Offer him or her a few hundred dollars to find you a buyer. The fact that one sale hinges on the other, along with the prospect of making two commissions, may work wonders.

3. Post notices on bulletin boards at your office or local supermarkets, and place a "For Sale" sign in the window of the vehicle itself. Place a newspaper ad only as a last resort.
4. Don't give your address right away to a potential buyer responding to your ad. Instead, ask for the telephone number where you may call that person back.
5. Be wary of selling to friends or family members. Anything short of perfection, and you'll be eating Christmas dinner alone.
6. Don't touch the odometer. If you do, you may get a few hundred dollars more—and a criminal record.
7. Paint the vehicle. Some specialty shops charge only $300 and give a guarantee that's transferable to subsequent owners.
8. Make minor repairs. This includes a minor tune-up and patching up the exhaust. Again, if any repair warranty is transferable, use it as a selling point.
9. Clean the vehicle. Go to a reconditioning firm, or spend the weekend scrubbing the interior and exterior. First impressions are important. Clean the chrome, polish the body, and peel off old bumper stickers. Remove butts from the ashtrays and clean out the glove compartment. Make sure all tools and spare parts have been taken out of the trunk. Don't remove the radio or speakers—the gaping holes will lower the vehicle's worth much more than the cost of the sound equipment. Replace missing or broken dash knobs and window cranks.
10. Change the tires. Recaps are good buys.
11. Let the buyer examine the vehicle. Insist that it be inspected at an independent garage, and then accompany the prospective buyer to the garage. This gives you protection if the buyer claims you misrepresented the vehicle.
12. Don't mislead the buyer. If the vehicle was in an accident or some financing is still to be paid, admit it. Any misleading statements may be used later against you in court. It's also advisable to have someone witness the actual transaction in case of a future dispute.
13. Keep important documents handy. Show prospective buyers the sales contract, repair orders, owner's manual, and all other documents that show how the vehicle has been maintained. Authenticate your claims about fuel consumption.
14. Write an effective ad, if you need to use one.

Selling to Dealers

Selling to a dealer means that you're likely to get 20 percent less than if you sold your vehicle privately, unless the dealer agrees to participate in an accommodation sale based on your buying a new vehicle from them. Most owners will gladly pay some penalty to the dealer, however, for the peace of mind that comes with knowing that their eventual buyer won't lay a claim against them. This assumes that the dealer hasn't been cheated by the owner—if the vehicle is stolen, isn't paid for, has had its odometer spun back (or forward to a lower setting), or is seriously defective, the buyer or dealer can sue the original owner for fraud. Sell to a dealer who sells the same make. He or she will give you more because it's easier to sell your trade-in to customers who are interested in only that make of vehicle.

Drawing Up the Contract

The province of Alberta has prepared a useful bill of sale applicable throughout Canada that can be accessed at *www.servicealberta.gov.ab.ca/pdf/mv/ BillOfSaleReg3126.pdf*. Your bill of sale should identify the vehicle (including the serial number) and include its price, whether a warranty applies, and the nature of the examination made by the buyer.

The buyer may ask you to put in a lower price than what was actually paid in order to reduce the sales tax. If you agree to this, don't be surprised when a Revenue Canada agent comes to your door. Although the purchaser is ultimately the responsible party, you're an accomplice in defrauding the government. Furthermore, if you turn to the courts for redress, your own conduct may be put on trial.

Summary

Purchasing a used vehicle and keeping it at least five years saves you the most money. It takes about eight years to realize similar depreciation savings when buying new. Giving the biggest down payment you can afford, using zero percent financing programs, and piling up as many kilometres and years as possible on your trade-in are the best ways to save money with new vehicles. Remember that safety is another consideration that depends largely on the type of vehicle you choose.

Buy Safe

Here are some safety features to look for:

1. High NHTSA and IIHS crashworthiness ratings for front, offset, and side collisions (pay particular attention to the side rating if you are a senior driver) and roof strength, plus a low rollover potential due to electronic stability control
2. Good-quality tires; be wary of "all-season" tires and Bridgestone/Firestone makes and follow *www.tirerack.com* consumer recommendations
3. Three-point seat belts with belt pretensioners and adjustable shoulder belt anchorages
4. Integrated child safety seats and seat anchors, safety door locks, and override window controls
5. Side airbags with head protection; unobtrusive, effective head restraints that don't push your chin into your chest; and pedal extenders
6. Front driver's seat with plenty of rearward travel and a height adjuster
7. Good all-around visibility; a dash that doesn't reflect onto the windshield
8. An ergonomic interior with an efficient heating and ventilation system

9. Headlights that are adequate for night driving and don't blind oncoming traffic
10. Dash gauges that don't wash out in sunlight or produce windshield glare
11. Adjustable head restraints for all seating positions
12. Delaminated side-window glass
13. Easily accessed sound system and climate controls
14. Navigation systems that don't require a degree from MIT to calibrate
15. Manual sliding doors in vans (if children are being transported)

Buy Smart

1. Buy the vehicle you need and can afford, not the one someone else wants you to buy, or one loaded with options that you'll probably never use. Take your time. Price comparisons and test drives may take a month, but you'll get a better vehicle and price in the long run.
2. Buy in winter or later in the new year to double-dip from dealer incentives and customer rebate or low-cost financing programs.
3. Sell your trade-in privately.
4. Arrange financing before buying your vehicle.
5. Test drive your choice by renting it overnight or for several days.
6. Buy through the Internet or by fax, or use an auto broker if you're not confident in your own bargaining skills, you lack the time to haggle, or you want to avoid the "showroom shakedown."
7. Ask for at least a 20 percent discount off the MSRP, and cut freight charges by at least 50 percent. Insist on a specific delivery date written in the contract, as well as a protected price in case there's a price increase between the time the contract is signed and when the vehicle is delivered. Also ask for a free tank of gas.
8. Order a minimum of options, and seek a 30 percent discount on the entire option list.
9. Put the vehicle's down payment on your credit card.
10. Avoid leasing. If you must lease, choose the shortest time possible, drive down the MSRP, and refuse to pay an "acquisition" or "disposal" fee.
11. Look at Japanese vehicles made in North America, co-ventures with American automakers, and rebadged imports. They often cost less than imports and are just as reliable. However, some European imports may not be as reliable as you might imagine—Mercedes' M-Class sport-utilities, for example. Get extra warranty protection from the automaker if you're buying a model that has a poorer-than-average repair history. Use auto club references to get honest, competent repairs at a reasonable price.

Now that the vehicle search is over and tough negotiations have produced a fair price, Part Two will show you how to get your money back if that "dream car" turns into a nightmare, or if the dealer goes bankrupt.

Part Two

THE ART OF COMPLAINING

"I Can't Get No Satisfaction"

San Francisco resident Henry Wolf is suing BMW, claiming the company's bike gave him an unexpected, unwanted and ongoing erection lasting more than two years. Wolf specifically blames an after-market ridge-like seat mounted on his 1993 Beemer bike for causing an acute case of priapism—a persistent, lasting erection—according to a complaint filed in San Francisco's state court. The 52-year-old Wolf says a four-hour ride in 2010 left him with the condition and that he "is now unable to engage in sexual activity, which is causing him substantial emotional and mental anguish."

WWW.NYDAILYNEWS.COM/AUTOS/MAN-SUES-BMW-MOTORCYCLES-GIVING-TWO-YEAR-ERECTION-ARTICLE-1.1071363#IXZZ1U24T1V3A

Honda Satisfies (Free Engine Blocks)

HONDA CIVIC ENGINE BLOCK EXTENDED WARRANTY	
BULLETIN NO.:10-048	DATE: JUNE 17, 2011

WARRANTY EXTENSION: ENGINE BLOCK

VEHICLES AFFECTED: On some 2006–08 and early production 2009 Civics, the engine (cylinder) block may experience engine coolant leaks, resulting in engine overheating. To increase customer confidence, American Honda is extending the warranty of the engine block to 8 years from the original date of purchase, with no mileage limit.

The warranty extension does not apply to any vehicle that has ever been declared a total loss or sold for salvage by a financial institution or insurer, or has a branded, or similar title under any states law.

That's right. Honda will replace defective engine blocks for free on 2006–09 Civics without any limitation as to mileage or number of previous owners. This represents an owner savings of over $4,000.

Refund Rights

Honda is doing the right thing. Too bad other automakers won't fess up to their own mistakes.

If you've bought an unsafe vehicle or one that was misrepresented, or you've had to pay for repairs to correct factory-related defects, this section's for you. It's intended is to help you get your money back—without going to court or getting frazzled by a dealer's broken promises or "benign neglect." But if going to court is your only recourse, this section also has the jurisprudence you'll need to cite in your complaint to get an out-of-court settlement or to win your case without spending a fortune on lawyers and research.

Remember the "money-back guarantee"? Well, that's long gone. Automakers are reluctant to offer any warranty that requires them to take back a defective car or minivan, because they know that there are a lot of lemons out there. Fortunately, our provincial consumer protection laws have filled the gap when the base warranty expires, so now any sales contract for a new or used vehicle can be cancelled—or free repairs can be ordered—in the following situations:

1. Vehicle is unfit for the purpose for which it was purchased
2. Vehicle was misrepresented verbally or in writing
3. Repairs are covered by a secret warranty or a "goodwill" warranty extension
4. Vehicle hasn't been reasonably durable, considering how well it was maintained, the mileage driven, and the type of driving that was done (this is particularly applicable to engine, transmission, and paint defects)

The four legal concepts enumerated above can lead to the sales contract being cancelled, the purchase price being partially refunded (*quanti minoris*), and/or damages being awarded. For example, if the seller says that a minivan can pull a 900 kg (2,000 lb.) trailer and you discover that it can barely tow half that weight or won't reach a reasonable speed while towing, you can cancel the contract for misrepresentation. In effect, what was bought was "unfit for the purpose intended"—a key provision of all provincial consumer protection and product liability laws.

The same principle applies to a seller's exaggerated claims concerning a vehicle's fuel economy or reliability, as well as to "demonstrators" that are, in fact, used cars with false (rolled-back) odometer readings. GM's and Chrysler's secret paint warranties and Ford's engine and transmission "goodwill" programs have all been successfully challenged in small claims court. And reasonable durability is an especially powerful legal argument that allows a judge to determine what the dealer and auto manufacturer will pay to correct a premature failure long after the original warranty has expired.

Abusive Contracts

Sales contracts aren't meant to be fair. Dealers' and automakers' lawyers spend countless hours making sure their clients are well protected with one-sided contracts that they hope will discourage the filing of buyer lawsuits, inhibit class actions, or limit the amount that can be claimed in damages, or will give them the right to choose the jurisdiction where the case will be heard. To this end, many businesses are using mandatory arbitration clauses that in theory are reasonable alternatives to court, but in practice are grossly unfair. Says the Quebec Union des Consommateurs:

> Consumer contracts commonly contain clauses forcing the consumer to submit to arbitration his [or her] claims against the company, while reserving to the company any recourse regarding its own claims against the consumer. Moreover, although Quebec and Ontario laws prohibit excluding exemplary damages, companies still insert such

Called "standard form contracts," or "contracts of adhesion," these agreements are looked upon by judges with a great deal of skepticism. They know the buyer had little or no bargaining power in drawing up these pre-printed, "take it or leave it" sales agreements, loan documents, insurance contracts, and automobile leases. Fortunately, when a dispute arises over terms or language used in this kind of document, judges have the latitude to interpret clauses in the way most favourable to the buyer.

Plaintiff Pitfalls

Except for lawyers, very few people complain for a living. Sure, we all know how to negotiate salaries, working conditions, etc., but sending off a claim letter or preparing a legal claim is much more difficult because we get so emotionally involved. In some cases our search for retribution can take over our lives.

When things go wrong, stay calm and try to avoid the following three pitfalls that can compromise your chance of getting compensation and closure.

1. **"I am not making any more payments. Come and get your lemon."** The dealer can seize the car, sell it for much less than it is worth, and sue you for the remaining amount, plus legal fees and seizure costs. The case will be tried in provincial court where more legal fees will be charged and there could be over a year's delay before your case is heard. All the while, you are carless. During the trial you will have to answer why the dealer wasn't given a reasonable chance to repair any problems you were having. That will be followed by the dealer service manager swearing that the car didn't have any defects, backed by the subsequent purchaser. Moral of this story: Have the vehicle checked by an independent mechanic and notify the dealer that the defects found must be repaired within five working days, failing which, you will tender the vehicle back to the dealership and sue.

2. **"You are a no good, lying, cheating *!*#*&*!"** Name-calling, threatening, or libeling the seller won't only make you look deranged, but could also weaken your case. These intemperate actions may burn any bridges to a settlement and result in you being charged with blackmail, trespass, libel, or slander.

3. **"Everyone says this car is a lemon; I have reports from NHTSA, *Consumer Reports*, and service bulletins about these cars."** This is inadmissible hearsay, unless a mechanic relates the service bulletin to your car's failures. It's essential that printed evidence and/or witnesses (relatives are not excluded) are available to confirm that a false representation actually occurred, that a part is failure-prone, or that its replacement is covered by a secret warranty. Stung by an increasing number of small claims court defeats, automakers are now asking small claims court judges to disallow evidence from *Lemon-Aid*,

service bulletins, or memos on the pretext that such evidence is hearsay (not proven) unless confirmed by an independent mechanic or unless the document is recognized by the automaker's or dealer's representative at trial ("Is this a common problem? Do you recognize this service bulletin? Is there a case-by-case 'goodwill' plan covering this repair?"). This is why you should bring in an independent garage mechanic or body expert to buttress your allegations, or authenticate a document. Sometimes, though, the service manager or company representative will make key admissions if questioned closely by you, a court mediator, or the trial judge. That questioning can be particularly effective if you call for the exclusion of witnesses until they're called (let them mill around outside the courtroom wondering what their colleagues have said).

Auto manufacturers often blame owners for having pushed their vehicle beyond its limits. Therefore, when you seek to set aside the contract or get a repair reimbursed, it's essential that you get the testimony of an independent mechanic and his or her co-workers in order to prove that the vehicle's poor performance isn't caused by negligent maintenance or abusive driving.

It Should Have Lasted Longer!

The reasonable durability claim is your ace in the hole. It's probably the easiest allegation to prove, since all automakers have benchmarks as to how long body components, trim and finish, and mechanical and electronic parts should last (see the "Reasonable Part Durability" chart on page 107). Vehicles are expected to be reasonably durable and merchantable. What "reasonably durable" means depends on the price paid, the kilometres driven, the purchaser's driving habits, and how well the vehicle was maintained by the owner. Judges carefully weigh all these factors in awarding compensation or cancelling a sale.

Whatever reason you use to get your money back, don't forget to conform to the "reasonable diligence" rule that requires you to file suit within a reasonable time after the vehicle's purchase or after you've discovered the defect. If there have been no negotiations with the dealer or automaker, this period shouldn't exceed a year. If either the dealer or the automaker has been promising to correct the defects for some time, or has carried out repeated unsuccessful repairs, the delay for filing the lawsuit can be extended from the time negotiations ended.

Refunds for Other Expenses

It's a lot easier to get the automaker to pay to replace a defective part than it is to obtain compensation for a missed day of work. Manufacturers seldom pay for consequential expenses like a ruined vacation, a vehicle not living up to its advertised hype, or an owner's mental distress, because they can't control the amount of the refund. Courts, however, are more generous, having ruled that all expenses (damages) flowing from a problem covered by a warranty or service bulletin are the manufacturer's or dealer's responsibility under both common law (which covers all provinces except Quebec) and Quebec civil law. Fortunately, when legal action is threatened—usually through small claims court—automakers quickly up their ante to include most of the owner's expenses because they know the courts will probably do the same.

One precedent-setting judgment (cited in *Sharman v. Ford*, found on pages 134–135) giving generous damages to a motorist fed up with his lemon Cadillac was rendered in 1999 by the British Columbia Supreme Court in *Wharton v. Tom Harris Chevrolet Oldsmobile Cadillac Ltd.* ([2002] B.C.J. No. 233, 2002 BCCA 78d). In that case, Justice Leggatt threw the book at GM and the dealer in awarding the following amounts:

(a) Hotel accommodations: $217.17
(b) Travel to effect repairs at 30 cents per kilometre: The plaintiff claims some 26 visits from his home in Ucluelet to Nanaimo. Some credit should be granted to the defendants since routine trips would have been required in any event. Therefore, the plaintiff is entitled to be compensated for mileage for 17 trips (approximately 400 km from Ucluelet to Nanaimo return) at 30 cents per kilometre.

     $2,040.00

TOTAL: $2,257.17

[20] The plaintiffs are entitled to non-pecuniary damages for loss of enjoyment of their luxury vehicle and for inconvenience in the sum of $5,000.

Warranties

It's really not that hard to get a refund if you take it one step at a time. Vehicle defects are covered by two warranties: the *expressed* warranty, which has a fixed time limit, and the *implied* (or legal) warranty, which is entirely up to a judge's discretion.

Expressed Warranties

The manufacturer's or dealer's warranty is a written or verbal "expressed" promise that a vehicle will perform as represented and be reasonably reliable, subject to certain conditions. Regardless of the number of subsequent owners, this promise remains in force as long as the warranty's original time/kilometre limits haven't expired. The expressed warranty given by most sellers is often full of empty promises, and it allows the dealer and manufacturer to act as judge and jury when deciding whether a vehicle was misrepresented or is afflicted with defects they'll pay to correct. Rarely does it provide a money-back guarantee.

Some of the more familiar lame excuses used in denying expressed warranty claims are "You abused the car," "It was poorly maintained," "It's normal wear and tear," "It's rusting from the outside, not the inside," and "It passed the safety inspection." Ironically, the expressed warranty sometimes says that there is no warranty at all, or that the vehicle is sold "as is." And, when the warranty's clauses (or lack thereof) don't deter claimants, some dealers simply say that a verbal warranty or representation as to the vehicle's attributes is unenforceable.

Fortunately, these attempts to weasel out of the warranty and limit the seller's liability seldom make it through judicial review. Justice Searle put it this way in the *Chams* decision (see pages 136–142):

> Ford's warranty attempts to limit its liability to what it grants in the warranty. It is ancient law that one who attempts to limit his liability by, for example, excluding common law remedies, must clearly bring that limitation to the attention of the person who might lose those remedies. The evidence in this case is clear: The buyer of even a new car does not get a warranty booklet until after purchasing the car although he "would be" told the highlights sooner.

Implied Warranties

Thankfully, car owners get another kick at the can with the implied warranty ("of fitness"). As clearly stated in the unreported Saskatchewan decision *Maureen Frank v. General Motors of Canada Limited* (found exclusively here in *Lemon-Aid* on pages 128–129)—in which the judge declared that paint discoloration and peeling shouldn't occur within 11 years of the purchase of a vehicle—the implied warranty is an important legal principle. It's solidly supported by a large body of federal and provincial laws, regulations, and jurisprudence, and it protects you primarily from hidden dealer- or factory-related defects. But the concept also includes misrepresentation and a host of other scams.

This warranty also holds dealers to a higher standard of conduct than private sellers because, unlike private sellers, dealers are presumed to be aware of the defects present in the vehicles they sell. That way, they can't just pass the ball to the automaker or to the previous owner and then walk away from the dispute. For instance, in British Columbia, a new-car dealer is required to disclose damage requiring repairs costing more than 20 percent of the price (under the *Motor Dealer Act* regulations).

Why the implied warranty is so effective

- It establishes the concept of "reasonable durability" (see "How Long Should a Part or Repair Last?" on page 105), meaning that parts are expected to last for a reasonable period of time (7–10 years/160,000 km for engines and transmissions, for example), as stated in jurisprudence, judged by independent mechanics, or expressed in extended warranties given by the automaker in the past.
- It covers the entire vehicle and can be applied for whatever period of time the judge decides.
- It can order that the vehicle be taken back, or that a major repair cost be refunded.
- It can help plaintiffs claim compensation for supplementary transportation,

inconvenience, mental distress, missed work, screwed-up vacations, insurance paid while the vehicle was in the repair shop, repairs done by other mechanics, and exemplary (or punitive) damages in cases where the seller was a real weasel.

• It is frequently used by small claims court judges to give refunds to plaintiffs "in equity" (out of fairness) rather than through a strict interpretation of contract law.

Faulty Tires

Consumers have gained additional rights following Bridgestone/Firestone's massive tire recall in 2001. Because of the confusion and chaos surrounding Firestone's handling of the recall, Ford's 575 Canadian dealers stepped into the breach and replaced the tires with any equivalent tires dealers had in stock, no questions asked.

This is an important precedent that tears down the traditional liability wall separating tire manufacturers from automakers in product liability claims. In essence, whoever sells the product can now be held liable for damages. In the future, Canadian consumers will have an easier time holding the dealer, automaker, and tiremaker liable, not just for recalled products but also for any defect that affects the safety or reasonable durability of that product. This includes tire valve stem failures as well as tire pressure monitoring systems (TPMS).

The Supreme Court of Canada (*Winnipeg Condominium v. Bird Construction* [1995] 1S.C.R.85) has ruled that defendants are liable in negligence for any designs that result in a risk to the public's safety or health. The Supreme Court reversed a long-standing policy and provided the public with a new cause of action that had not existed before in Canada. Prior to this Supreme Court ruling, companies dodged liability for falling bridges and crashing planes by warranty exclusion and "entire-agreement" contract clauses. In the *Winnipeg Condominium* case, the Supreme Court held that repairs made to prevent serious damage or accidents could be claimed from the designer or builder for the cost of repair in tort from any subsequent purchaser. Consumers with tire or other claims relating to the safety of their vehicles would be wise to insert the above court decision (with explanation) in their claim letter and then mail or fax it to the automaker's legal affairs or product liability department. A copy should also be deposited with the clerk of the small claims court, if you have to use that recourse.

Other Warrantable Items

Safety restraints, such as airbags and seat belts, have warranty coverage extended for the lifetime of the vehicle, following an agreement made between U.S. automakers and importers. In Canada, though, some automakers try to dodge this responsibility because they are incorporated as separate Canadian companies. That distinction didn't fly with B.C.'s Court of Appeal in the 2002 Robson decision (*www.courts.gov.bc.ca/jdb-txt/ca/02/03/2002bcca0354.htm*). In that class action petition, the court declared that both Canadian companies and their American counterparts can be held liable in Canada for deceptive acts that violate the provincial *Trade Practices Act* (in this case, Chrysler and GM paint delamination):

> At this stage, the plaintiffs are only required to demonstrate that they have a "good arguable case" against the American defendants. The threshold is low. A good arguable case requires only a serious question to be tried, one with some prospect of success: see *AG Armeno Mines*, supra, at para. 25 [*AG Armeno Mines and Minerals Inc. v. PT Pukuafu Indah* (2000), 77 B.C.L.R.(3d) 1 (C.A.)].

Aftermarket products and services—such as gas-saving gadgets, rustproofing, and paint protectors—can render the manufacturer's warranty invalid, so make sure you're in the clear before purchasing any optional equipment or services from an independent supplier.

How fairly a warranty is applied is more important than how long it remains in effect. Once you know the normal wear rate for a mechanical component or body part, you can demand proportional compensation when you get less than normal durability—no matter what the original warranty said.

Some dealers tell customers that they need to have original-equipment parts installed in order to maintain their warranty. A variation on this theme requires that routine servicing—including tune-ups and oil changes (with a certain brand of oil)—be done by the selling dealer, or the warranty is invalidated.

Nothing could be further from the truth. Canadian law stipulates that whoever issues a warranty cannot make that warranty conditional on the use of any specific brand of motor oil, oil filter, or any other component, unless it's provided to the customer free of charge.

Warranty Runaround

Sometimes dealers will do all sorts of minor repairs that don't correct the problem, and then, after the warranty runs out, they'll tell you that major repairs are needed. You can prevent this nasty surprise by repeatedly bringing your vehicle into the dealership before the warranty ends. During each visit, insist that a written work order include the specific nature of the problem as *you* see it and that the work order carry the notation that this is the second, third, or fourth time the same problem has been brought to the dealer's attention. Write it down yourself, if need be. This allows you to show a pattern of nonperformance by the dealer during the warranty period and establishes that it's a serious and chronic problem. When the warranty expires, you have the legal right to demand that it be extended on those items consistently reappearing on your handful of work orders. *Lowe v. Fairview Chrysler* (see page 143) is an excellent judgment that reinforces this important principle. In another lawsuit, *François Chong v. Marine Drive Imported Cars Ltd. and Honda Canada Inc.* (see page 150), a Honda owner forced Honda to fix his engine six times—until they got it right.

A retired GM service manager gave me another effective tactic to use when you're not sure that a dealer's warranty "repairs" will actually correct the problem for a reasonable period of time after the warranty expires. Here's what he says you should do:

> When you pick up the vehicle after the warranty repair has been done, hand the service manager a note to be put in your file that says you appreciate the warranty repair; however, you intend to return and ask for further warranty coverage if the problem reappears before a reasonable amount of time has elapsed even if the original warranty has expired. A copy of the same note should be sent to the automaker....Keep your copy of the note in the glove compartment as cheap insurance against paying for a repair that wasn't fixed correctly the first time.

Supplementary Warranties

Power Information Network data shows that 40 percent of car buyers purchase extended warranties, although only 10 percent of leased vehicles get the extra protection. Some extra warranties promise a refund of the warranty cost if no claim is made while the lease is in force. What buyers may not know, however, is that a call for roadside assistance made under the manufacturer's warranty may be counted as a claim under the extended warranty as well. Owners are also uncomfortable with the proviso that they must keep their vehicle for the life of the contract—sometimes up to 5 years.

The manufacturer, the dealer, or an independent third party may sell supplementary warranties that provide extended coverage, and this coverage is automatically transferred when a vehicle is sold. They cost between $1,500 and $2,000 and should be purchased only if the vehicle you're buying has a reputation for being unreliable or expensive to service (see the ratings in Part Three) or if you're reluctant to use the small claims courts when factory-related trouble arises. Don't let the dealer pressure you into deciding right away.

Dealers love to sell you extended warranties, whether you need them or not, because up to 60 percent of the warranty's cost represents dealer markup. Out of the remaining 40 percent comes the sponsor's administration costs and profit margin, calculated at another 15 percent. What's left to pay for repairs is a minuscule 25 percent of the original amount. The only reason that automakers and independent warranty companies haven't been busted for operating this Ponzi scheme is that only half of the vehicle buyers who purchase extended service contracts actually use them.

Those who do need help often find it difficult to collect a refund because independent companies frequently go out of business or limit the warranty's coverage through subsequent mailings. Provincial laws cover both situations. If the bankrupt warranty company's insurance policy won't cover your claim, take the dealer to small claims court and ask for the repair costs and a refund of the original warranty payment. Your argument for holding the dealer responsible is a simple one: By accepting a commission to act as an agent of the defunct company, the dealer also took on the obligations of that company. As for limiting the coverage after you have already bought the warranty policy, this practice is illegal and allows you to sue both the dealer and the warranty company for a refund of both the warranty and the repair costs.

Emissions-Control Warranties

These little-publicized warranties can save you big bucks if major engine or exhaust components fail prematurely. They come with all new vehicles and cover major components of the emissions-control system for up to 10 years/194,000 km, no matter how many times the vehicle is sold. Unfortunately, although owner's manuals vaguely mention the emissions warranty, most don't specify which parts are covered. The U.S. Environmental Protection Agency has intervened on several occasions, with hefty fines against Chrysler and Ford, and ruled that all major motor and fuel-system components are covered. These components include fuel metering, ignition spark advance, restart, evaporative emissions, positive crankcase ventilation (PCV), engine electronics (computer modules), and catalytic converter systems as well as parts like hoses, clamps, brackets, pipes, gaskets, belts, seals, and connectors. Canada, however, has no list defined by the government, so it's up to each manufacturer and the small claims courts to decide which emissions-control components are covered.

Some of the confidential technical service bulletins listed in Part Three show parts failures that are covered under the emissions warranty (stinky exhausts caused by defective catalytic converters, for example), even though motorists are routinely charged for their replacement. Faulty fuel gauges are also covered by the emissions warranty. Malfunctioning gauges are a common problem with all automakers, with repairs costing $300–$500.

Make sure to get your emissions system checked out thoroughly by a dealer or an independent garage before the emissions warranty expires or before having the vehicle inspected by provincial emissions inspectors. In addition to ensuring that you'll pass provincial tests, this precaution could save you up to $1,000 if your catalytic converter and other emissions components are covered by a "secret" warranty.

Pssst...More "Secret" Warranties

Few vehicle owners know that secret warranties exist. The closest automakers come to an admission is sending out a "goodwill policy," "product improvement program," or "special policy" technical service bulletin (TSB) to dealers or first owners of record. Consequently, the only motorists who find out about these policies are the original owners who haven't moved or haven't leased their vehicles. The other motorists who get compensated for repairs are the ones who read *Lemon-Aid* each year, wave TSBs, and yell the loudest.

Remember, second owners and repairs done by independent garages are included in these secret warranty programs. Large, costly repairs, such as blown engines, burned transmissions, and peeling paint, are often covered.

Here are a few examples of the most comprehensive secret warranties that have come across my desk during the last several years.

All Years, All Models

Automatic transmissions

Problem: Faulty automatic transmissions that self-destruct, shift erratically, gear down to "limp home mode," are slow to shift in or out of Reverse, or are noisy. **Warranty coverage:** If you have the assistance of your dealer's service manager, expect an offer of 50–75 percent (about $2,500). File the case in small claims court, and a full refund will be offered up to 7 years/160,000 km. Acura, Honda, Hyundai, Lexus, and Toyota coverage varies between seven and eight years.

Brakes

Problem: Premature wearout of brake pads, calipers, and rotors. Produces excessive vibration, noise, and pulling to one side when braking. **Warranty coverage:** *Calipers and pads:* "Goodwill" settlements confirm that brake calipers and pads that fail to last 2 years/40,000 km will be replaced for 50 percent of the repair cost; components not lasting 1 year/20,000 km will be replaced for free. *Rotors:* If they last less than 3 years/60,000 km, they'll be replaced at half the price; replacement is free up to 2 years/40,000 km. *ABS brake sensors and electrical connections:* Should last for at least 5 years/100,000 km.

Interestingly, premature brake wear, once mainly a Detroit failing, is now quite common with Asian makes as well. Apparently, brake suppliers for all automakers are using cheaper calipers, pads, and rotors that can't handle the heat generated by normal braking on heavier passenger cars, trucks, and vans. Consequently, drivers find routine braking causes rotor warpage that produces excessive vibrations, shuddering, noise, and pulling to one side when braking.

Engines

Problem: At around 60,000–100,000 km, the engine may overheat, lose power, and burn extra fuel, or possibly self-destruct. Under the best of circumstances, you may have to replace the engine's intake manifold gasket—a repair that will take a day and cost about $800–$1,000. **Warranty coverage:** If you have the assistance of your dealer's service manager, expect a full refund up to 7 years/160,000 km, although initial offers will hover at about 50 percent of the costs. If you must file a small claims court action, cite the *Chams* decision (see pages 136–142).

No matter which automaker you're dealing with, filing your claim in small claims court always sweetens the company's settlement offer. Furthermore, you likely won't have to step inside a courtroom to get your refund, since most small claims court filings are settled at the pretrial mediation stage.

Exhaust systems

Problem: A nauseating "rotten-egg" exhaust smell permeates the interior. **Warranty coverage:** At first, owners are told they need a tune-up. Then they are told to change fuels and to wait a few months for the problem to correct itself. When this fails, the catalytic converter will likely be replaced and the power control module recalibrated. The replacement and recalibration is free up to 8 years under the emissions warranty.

Chrysler, Ford, General Motors, Honda, Hyundai, and Mazda

Paint

Problem: Faulty paint jobs that cause paint to turn white, peel off of horizontal panels, or produce thin white scratches. **Warranty coverage:** Automakers will offer a free paint job or partial compensation up to six years with no mileage limitation. Thereafter, all these manufacturers offer 50–75 percent refunds on the small claims courthouse steps.

In *Frank v. GM*, the Saskatchewan small claims court set an 11-year benchmark for paint finishes. Three earlier Canadian small claims judgments extended the benchmark beyond the warranty and extended compensation to second owners and pickups.

> I wanted to let you and your readers know that the information you publish about Ford's paint failure problem is invaluable. Having read through your "how-to guide" on addressing this issue, I filed a suit against Ford for the "latent" paint defect. The day prior to our court date, I received a settlement offer by phone for 75 percent of what I was initially asking for.
>
> This settlement was for a 9-year-old car. I truly believe that Ford hedges a bet that most people won't go to the extent of filing a lawsuit because they are intimidated or simply stop progress after they receive a firm no from Ford.
>
> M.P.

How Long Should a Part or Repair Last?

Much longer than the manufacturer guarantees, or about as long as judges, industry service bulletins, and secret warranties indicate. How do you know when a part or service doesn't last as long as it should and whether you should seek a full or partial refund? Sure, you have a gut feeling based on your use of the vehicle, how you maintained it, and the extent of work that was carried out on it. But you'll need more than emotion to win compensation from garages and automakers.

You can definitely get a refund if a repair or part lasts longer than its guarantee but not as long as is generally expected. But you'll have to show what the auto industry considers to be "reasonable durability." Automakers, mechanics, and the courts all have their own benchmarks as to what they consider a reasonable period of time or mileage for a part or adjustment to last. Consequently, I've prepared a chart to show what most automakers consider to be reasonable durability, as expressed by their original and "goodwill" warranties.

Many of the guidelines on the following page were extrapolated from Chrysler and Ford payouts to thousands of dissatisfied customers over the past several decades, in addition to Chrysler's original seven-year powertrain warranty (applicable from 1991–95 and reapplied from 2001–04). Other sources for this chart were the Ford and GM transmission warranties outlined in their secret warranties; Ford, GM, and Toyota engine "goodwill" programs laid out in their internal service bulletins; and court judgments where judges have given their own guidelines as to what is meant by "reasonable durability."

Safety features—with the exception of anti-lock brake systems (ABS)—generally have a lifetime warranty.

Airbags are a different matter. Those that are deployed in an accident—and the personal injury and interior damage their deployment will likely have caused—are covered by your accident insurance policy. However, if there is a sudden deployment for no apparent reason, the automaker and dealer should be held jointly responsible for all injuries and damages caused by the airbag. You can prove their liability by downloading data from your vehicle's data recorder. This will likely lead to a more-generous settlement from the two parties and prevent your insurance premiums from being jacked up.

Use the manufacturer's emissions warranty as your primary guideline for the expected durability of high-tech electronic and mechanical pollution-control components, such as powertrain control modules (PCM) and catalytic converters. First look at your owner's manual for an indication of which parts on your vehicle are covered. If you come up with few specifics, ask the auto manufacturer for a list of all components covered by the emissions warranty.

Recall Repairs

Vehicles are recalled for one of two reasons: Either they are unsafe or they don't conform to federal pollution-control regulations. Whatever the reason, recalls are a great way to get free repairs and keep your car safe—if you know which ones apply to you and you have the patience of Job.

A recall doesn't mean your vehicle will become a long-term problem. Most vehicles will undergo two or three recalls during their life cycle. Indeed, recalls happen in even the best automotive neighbourhoods, with manufacturers from Acura to Rolls-Royce frequently subject to government-mandated recalls. Even

REASONABLE PART DURABILITY

ACCESSORIES

Air conditioner	7 years
GPS Navigation	7 years
Cruise control	5 years/100,000 km
Hybrid battery	10 years
Power doors, windows, Seats, locks	5 years
Radio	5 years
Headlights	5 years
Tire pressure sensor, Monitor	5 years

ENGINE AND DRIVETRAIN

CV joint	6 years/160,000 km
Differential	7 years/160,000 km
Engine (diesel)	15 years/350,000 km
Engine (gas)	7 years/160,000 km
Stability control	5 years/100,000 km
Turbocharger	5 years/100,000 km
Radiator	4 years/80,000 km
Transfer case	7 years/160,000 km
Transmission (auto.)	7 years/160,000 km
Transmission (man.)	10 years/250,000 km

BODY

Paint (peeling)	7–11 years
Rust (perforations)	7–11 years
Rust (surface)	5 years
Water/wind/air leaks	5 years

EXHAUST SYSTEM

Catalytic converter	8–11 years/100,000 km or more
Muffler	2 years/40,000 km
Tailpipe	3 years/60,000 km

BRAKE SYSTEM

ABS	100,000 km
Brake drum	120,000 km
Brake drum linings	35,000 km
Brake rotor	60,000 km
Brake calipers/pads	30,000 km
Master cylinder	100,000 km
Wheel cylinder	80,000 km

IGNITION SYSTEM

Cable set	60,000 km
Electronic module	5 years/80,000 km
Retiming	20,000 km
Spark plugs	20,000 km
Tune-up	20,000 km

quality-snob Toyota has sustained huge recalls on all of its models in the last couple of years, affecting some 15 million vehicles.

Millions of unsafe vehicles have been recalled by automakers for the free correction of safety-related defects since American recall legislation was passed in 1966 (a weaker Canadian law was enacted in 1971). During that time, NHTSA estimates that about 28 percent of the recalled vehicles never made it back to the dealership for repairs because owners were never informed, they just didn't consider the defect to be that hazardous, or they gave up waiting for corrective parts. This is unfortunate since one important study found that a 10 percent increase in the recall rate of a particular model will reduce the number of accidents involving that model by around 2 percent (*ms.cc.sunysb.edu/~hbenitezsilv/recall.pdf*).

The automaker has three options for correcting the defect: repair, replace, or refund. This probably means a trip to the dealer. However, in the case of a tire or child seat recall, you may mail in the defective item or go to the retailer that sold the product.

If you've moved, it's smart to pay a visit to your local dealer. Give the dealer your address to get a "report card" on which recalls, free service campaigns, and warranties apply to your vehicle. Simply give the service advisor the vehicle identification number (VIN)—found on your insurance card or on the dash, just below the windshield on the driver's side—and have the number run through the automaker's computer system. Ask for a computer printout of the vehicle's history (or have it emailed to you), and make sure you're listed in the automaker's computer as the owner. This process ensures that you'll receive notices of warranty extensions and emissions and safety recalls.

There are limitations on automotive recalls. Vehicle manufacturers are not required to perform free recalls on vehicles that are more than 10 years old. Getting repairs when the automaker says you're too late often takes a small claims court filing. But these cases are easy to win and are usually settled out of court. U.S. recalls may be voluntary or ordered by the U.S. Department of Transportation, and they can be nationwide or regional. In Canada, all recalls are considered voluntary. Transport Canada can only order automakers to notify owners that their vehicles may be unsafe; it can't force them to correct the problem. Fortunately, most U.S.-ordered recalls are carried out in Canada, and when Transport Canada makes a defect determination on its own, automakers generally comply with an owner notification letter and a recall campaign.

Voluntary recall campaigns—frequently called "Special Service" or "Safety Improvement" campaigns—are a real problem. The government does not monitor the notification of owners; dealers and automakers routinely deny there's a recall, thereby dissuading most claimants; and the company's so-called fix, not authorized by any governing body, may not correct the hazard at all. Also, the voluntary recall may leave out many of the affected models or unreasonably exclude certain owners.

Wherever you live or drive, don't expect to be welcomed with open arms when your vehicle develops a safety- or emissions-related problem that's not yet part of a recall campaign. Automakers and dealers generally take a restrictive view of what constitutes a safety or emissions defect, and they frequently charge for repairs that should be free under federal safety or emissions legislation. To counter this tendency, look at the following list of typical defects that are clearly safety-related. If you experience similar problems to these, insist that the automaker fix them at no expense to yourself, including paying for a car rental:

• Airbag malfunctions
• Corrosion affecting the safe operation of the vehicle
• Disconnected or stuck accelerators

- Electrical shorts
- Faulty windshield wipers
- Fuel leaks
- Problems with original axles, driveshafts, seats, seat recliners, or defrosters
- Seat belt problems
- Stalling, or sudden acceleration
- Sudden steering or brake loss
- Suspension failures
- Tire pressure monitor systems (TPMS)
- Tire valve airleaks
- Trailer coupling failures

Regional recalls

Don't let any dealer refuse you recall repairs because of where you live. In order to cut recall costs, many automakers try to limit a recall to vehicles in a certain designated region. This practice doesn't make sense, since cars are mobile and an unsafe, rust-cankered steering unit can be found anywhere—not just in certain rust-belt provinces or American states.

In 2001, Ford attempted to limit its recall of faulty Firestone tires to five American states. Public ridicule of the company's proposal led to an extension of the recall throughout North America.

Recall fatigue

Safety experts agree that the sheer number of auto recalls has resulted in "recall fatigue," where affected owners sometimes ignore urgent calls to get corrective repairs. The increasing number of recalls (for example, recalls for Toyota's sudden acceleration problem, brake failures, and rust-damaged suspension/steering systems) makes drivers immune to the message, leading them to believe that nothing bad will happen to them. However, if an item is relatively expensive or the perceived threat is immediate, consumers are more likely to seek recall assistance.

This finding is buttressed by one 2009 NHTSA study, which found that 73 percent of recalled autos were taken back to be fixed, while only 45 percent of child car seats were taken in for recall corrections. Evidently, the safety seat risk didn't seem as threatening.

Safety Defects Databases

If you wish to report a safety defect or want recall info, you may access Transport Canada's website at *www.tc.gc.ca/roadsafety/safevehicles/defectinvestigations/index. htm*. You can get recall information in French or English, as well as general information relating to road safety and importing a vehicle into Canada, and can access the recall database for vehicles with model years from 1970 to the present, but unlike NHTSA's website, owner complaints aren't listed, defect investigations aren't disclosed, voluntary warranty extensions (secret warranties) aren't shown, and service bulletin summaries aren't provided. You can also call Transport Canada at 1-800-333-0510 to get additional information.

For good measure, try NHTSA's website at *www.safercar.gov*. It's more complete than Transport Canada's—NHTSA's database is updated daily and covers vehicles built since the '50s. You'll get immediate access to four essential database categories applicable to your vehicle and model year: the latest recalls, current and closed safety investigations, defects reported by other owners, and a brief summary of service bulletins that apply.

Nailing Down a Refund

Step 1: Informal Negotiations

Most vehicle owners won't take the steps outlined in the previous sections; instead, they'll try to settle things informally with a phone call. This tactic rarely works, but it's worth trying. Customer service agents (who recite policies but don't make them) will tell you the vehicle's warranty doesn't apply. This brush-off usually convinces 90 percent of complainers to drop their claims after some angry venting.

Nevertheless, don't take no for an answer. Contact someone higher up who has the authority to bend policies to satisfy your request. Speak in a calm, polite manner, and try not to polarize the issue. Talk about cooperating to solve the problem. Let a compromise emerge—don't come in with a set of hardline demands.

At the start of this chapter we showed Honda's "engine block extended warranty" service bulletin #10-048 sent out June 17, 2011. Follow Brian's July narrative below and you will see how polite persistence pays off, although he still paid $800 that Honda owes him under its August bulletin guidelines (hope you read this, Brian):

Brian on July 7, 2010

My 07 Civic (99,600 miles) just had the same cracked engine block. All my maintenance and service was done on time and at correct intervals at the dealer, but it doesn't seem to matter. The service manager told me that Honda has seen this problem in the past. Service manager says Honda is willing to pay 50% of repair, but I am not satisfied. They should pay for the entire repair! I did call the customer service line and was told by the rep that Honda would not help me out. I told her I wanted to speak with someone with more authority, she put me on hold for 10 minutes, came back and said the case has been referred to a "local service rep" and they'll get back to me in a few days. In the meantime, I have no car and they will not provide loaner. I am totally dissatisfied w/ Honda right now.

July 9, 2010

7/9/10 – follow up. Dealership service manager originally said Honda would go 50 / 50 (approx. $2,500.00). Then he called me late Wednesday (7/7/10) and said Honda was stepping up more and my portion would be $1,700.00. Today (7/9/10) Honda customer service (1800-999-1009) has just informed me that I will be responsible for $1,500.00 (plus taxes) worth of the repair (and with her tone, I should consider myself lucky that Honda is chipping in at all). My car is supposed to be ready today so I will be paying the $1,500.00 plus tax…but my fight isn't over. By the way, according to the rep, the new motor is only coming with a 12,000 mile / 12 month warranty. I am going to continue to call Honda on the carpet over this situation.

•

July 10, 2010

7/9/10 – follow up 4:30pm. Honda dealer called and car is ready. Guess what the bill is!! $750.00 plus tax = $802.50 total!!! Maybe if I were to hold out a little longer, they'd be paying me! I think a lot of credit has to go to my dealership (Honda of Turnersville – NJ). They have been sympathetic, understanding, and more willing to work w/ me than corporate Honda. I just wish corporate Honda would get their heads out of their a**es.

An independent estimate of the vehicle's defects and the cost of repairing them is essential if you want to convince the dealer that you're serious in your claim and that you stand a good chance of winning your case in court. Prepare to use your estimate to challenge the dealer who agrees to pay half the repair costs and then tries to jack up the price 100 percent so that you wind up paying the whole shot.

Don't insist on getting the settlement offer in writing, but make sure that you're accompanied by a friend or relative who can confirm the offer in court if it isn't honoured. Be prepared to act upon the offer without delay so that if the dealer or automaker withdraws it, they won't be able to blame your hesitancy.

Dealer and service manager help

Service managers have more power than you may realize. They make the first determination of what work is covered under warranty or through post-warranty "goodwill" programs, and they're directly responsible to the dealer and manufacturer for their decisions. (Dealers hate manufacturer audits that force them to pay back questionable warranty decisions.) Service managers are paid to save the dealer and automaker money while mollifying irate clients—an almost impossible balancing act. Nevertheless, when a service manager agrees to extend warranty coverage, it's because you've raised solid issues that neither the dealer nor the automaker can ignore. All the more reason to present your argument in a confident, forthright manner with your vehicle's service history and *Lemon-Aid's* "Reasonable Part Durability" chart (see page 107) on hand.

Also bring as many technical service bulletins and owner complaint printouts as you can find from websites like NHTSA's. It's not important that they apply directly to your problem; they establish parameters for giving out after-warranty assistance, or "goodwill." Don't use your salesperson as a runner, because the sales staff are generally quite distant from the service staff and usually have less pull than you do.

If the service manager can't or won't set things right, your next step is to convene a mini-summit with the service manager, the dealer principal, and the automaker's rep. By getting the automaker involved, you run less risk of having the dealer fob you off on the manufacturer, and you can often get an agreement where the dealer and automaker pay two-thirds of the repair costs.

Step 2: Send a Registered Letter, Fax, or Email

Don't worry; no one feels comfortable writing a complaint. But if you haven't sent a written claim letter, fax, or email, you haven't really complained—or at least that's the auto industry's mindset. Send the dealer and manufacturer a polite registered letter or fax that asks for compensation for repairs that have been done or need to be done, insurance costs during the vehicle's repair, towing charges, supplementary transportation costs like taxis and rented cars, and damages for your inconvenience (see the following sample complaint letter).

Specify a reasonable time for either party to respond. If no satisfactory offer is made or your claim is ignored within five business days, file suit in small claims court. Make the manufacturer a party to the lawsuit, especially if an emissions warranty, a secret warranty extension, or a safety recall campaign is involved.

Step 3: Get the Government Involved

As a former Member of Parliament, let me assure you: a complaint letter copied to your local MP brings results. Manufacturer representatives want to lobby the government with a "clean slate" and to stay "on message." The last thing they want is an MP shoving unresolved owner complaints under their nose at some committee hearing. Another advantage in getting a government official involved is that MP offices have paid staff who know who to contact in the government and industry to apply extra pressure to get your problem resolved.

Step 4: Mediation and Arbitration

If the formality of a courtroom puts you off, or you're not sure that your claim is all that solid and don't want to pay the legal costs to find out, consider using mediation or arbitration offered by these groups: the Better Business Bureau (BBB), the Automobile Protection Association (APA), the Canadian Automobile Association (CAA), small claims court (mediation is often a prerequisite to going to trial), provincial and territorial government-run consumer mediation services, and the Canadian Motor Vehicle Arbitration Plan (CAMVAP):

NEW-VEHICLE COMPLAINT LETTER/FAX/EMAIL

WITHOUT PREJUDICE

Date: _____

Name: _____

Please be advised that I am dissatisfied with my new vehicle, a (state model), for the following reasons:

1.
2.
3.
4.
5.

In compliance with the provincial consumer protection laws and the "implied warranty" set down by the Supreme Court of Canada in *Donoghue v. Stevenson, Wharton v. GM*, and *Sharman v. Ford Canada*, I hereby request that these defects be repaired without charge. This vehicle has not been reasonably durable and is, therefore, not as represented to me.

Should you fail to repair these defects in a satisfactory manner and within a reasonable period of time, I shall get an estimate of the repairs from an independent source and claim them in court, without further delay. I also reserve my right to claim up to $1 million for punitive damages, pursuant to the Supreme Court of Canada's February 22, 2002, ruling in *Whiten v. Pilot*.

I have dealt with your company because of its honesty, competence, and sincere regard for its clients. I am sure that my case is the exception and not the rule.

A positive response within the next five (5) days would be appreciated.

(signed with telephone number, fax number, or email address)

I just won my case with Chrysler Canada over my 2003 Ram SLT 4×4 quad cab truck. I've been having PCV valves freezing up (5 PCVs in 9,000 km). After one month in the shop, I went to CAMVAP to put in my claim, went to arbitration, and won. They have agreed to buy back my truck.

CAMVAP (1-800-207-0685; *www.camvap.ca*) is the best-known organization offering free arbitration. Awards are no longer confidential (thanks to pressure exerted by the Quebec government), and the stipulation that no appeals are allowed doesn't seem enforceable, as CAMVAP says on its own website:

If you believe that the award or result of your hearing was improper because the arbitrator erred in law or erred in his or her assessment of the facts, then you may want to consider an appeal to the courts.

The agony of arbitration

Though CAMVAP presents its arbitration program as a free, fast, and fair process, some plaintiffs who have used CAMVAP's system say that the arbitration awards aren't enforced, multiple hearings may unduly delay a final judgment, and there is an undue reliance upon successive repair attempts before a final settlement is achieved.

In a June 2009 study done by Quebec's Union Des Consommateurs, *Consumer Arbitration and Effective Process*, the APA says this about the CAMVAP program:

> The published success rate for consumers is around 61%, but 54% of consent awards and 21% of arbitrated cases were ordered back to the dealer for yet another repair. For many consumers who have gone through the arbitration process, this is not a satisfactory resolution, but in CAMVAP's statistics they appear as a successful resolution.

According to the APA, CAMVAP falsely claims to be a program enabling a consumer who has purchased a "lemon" to obtain the vehicle's repurchase. The APA attributes the absence of guidelines regarding "lemons" to the program's control by industry, and to the low representation of consumers and governments within the program (*www.consommateur.qc.ca/union-des-consommateurs/docu/protec_conso/arbitrageE.pdf*).

Getting Outside Help

Don't let poor preparation scuttle your case. Ask government or independent consumer protection agencies to evaluate how well prepared you are before going to your first hearing. Also, use the Internet and media sources to ferret out additional facts and to gather support (*www.lemonaidcars.com* is a good place to start).

Auto Industry Groups

Ontario consumers may file an online complaint with the Ontario Motor Vehicle Industry Council (OMVIC) at *www.omvic.on.ca/services/consumers/file_complaint_info.htm*. Sure, OMVIC is the dealer's self-defence lobby—made up of around 9,000 registered dealers and 20,000 registered salespeople—but it has the following mandate:

> [T]o maintain a fair, safe and informed marketplace in Ontario by protecting the rights of consumers, enhancing industry professionalism and ensuring fair, honest and open competition for registered motor vehicle dealers.

The way your complaint is handled will test the veracity of the above-stated goals.

Alberta has a similar self-regulating auto industry group, the Alberta Motor Vehicle Industry Council (AMVIC; *www.amvic.org*). Since March 13, 2012, consumers with valid complaints can get compensation from a $1.5 million fund introduced by the Alberta government and AMVIC for financial losses where no other options for resolution with the business are available. While AMVIC can mediate, investigate, and lay charges, direct compensation when no other recourse is available should provide greater piece of mind, protection, and confidence for Albertans when dealing with the automotive industry.

AMVIC is responsible for regulating the automotive industry on behalf of the provincial government. The industry includes new, used, consignment, and lease automotive and RV dealerships as well as automotive repair and recycling businesses. The council investigates complaints against licensed automotive businesses and registered salespeople, and enforces Alberta's automotive industry regulations under the provincial *Fair Trading Act*. Since 1999 AMVIC has returned more than $20 million to Alberta consumers after investigating complaints against businesses and salespeople.

Complaints about a business practice can be filed online at *www.amvic.org/ consumers_complaintform_business.cfm;misleading*, auto advertising reports may be sent to *www.amvic.org/consumers_complaintform_advertising.cfm*, and queries about unlicensed businesses or tradespeople are taken at *www.amvic.org/consumers_ complaintform_report_an_unlicensed_business.cfm*.

Classified Ads and Media Exposés

Put an ad in the local paper describing your plight and ask for information from people who may have experienced a problem similar to your own. This approach alerts others to the potential problem, helps build a base for a class action or a group meeting with the automaker, and puts pressure on the local dealer and manufacturer to settle with you. Sometimes the paper's news desk will assign someone to cover your story after your ad is published. You may also gain attention by setting up a website.

Attract Media Attention

Television producers and their researchers need articulate consumers with issues that are easily filmed and understood. If you want media coverage, you must summarize your complaint and have visual aids that will hold the viewer's interest (viewers should be able to understand the issues with the sound turned off). Paint delamination? Show your peeling car. Bought a "lemon" vehicle? Show your repair bills. Holding a demonstration? Make it a "lemon" parade: Target one of the largest dealers, give your group a nifty name, and then drive past the dealership in vehicles decorated with "lemon" signs.

The Chrysler "death wobble" media campaign

Chrysler Canada wrote CBC TV Vancouver a letter that a Ram "death wobble" when passing over potholes "has no basis in fact." Yet a month earlier, U.S. Department of Transportation safety investigators had already determined there was a problem. The U.S. safety agency had told Chrysler on April 4, 2011:

> [We] are aware of 12 complaints of similar failures on 2008–2011 Ram 2500 & 3500 vehicles. A preliminary evaluation has been opened to assess ball joint related issues on the subject vehicles. This investigation will determine if the subject vehicles have a similar steering system design that might also present a risk of ball joint failure.

On May 17, a few days after Chrysler Canada's denial, CBC TV aired the story on *The National* evening news show, which featured excerpts from *Lemon-Aid* research and other experts. The newscast, researched by Associate Producer Enza Uda and reported by Kathy Tomlinson, interviewed a Canadian Ram truck owner who said his truck had a "death wobble" after passing over small potholes or uneven stretches of road.

Six weeks after the story was broadcast, Chrysler announced the recall of 242,780 Ram pickups manufactured between 2003 and 2011. This includes the 2008 Ram 1500 and 2003–11 Ram 2500 and 3500 Heavy Duty trucks. According to NHTSA, these trucks may have a defective left tie rod ball stud that can fracture during low-speed parking manoeuvres and could result in the potential loss of directional stability in the left-hand front wheel, increasing the risk of a crash.

In the end, it took a crusading CBC TV producer and determined reporter along with convincing independent research and visuals to force Chrysler to act after nine years of stonewalling governments and Ram pickup owners on both sides of the border.

This kind of failure isn't limited to Chrysler, and during the past 41 years *Lemon-Aid* has been published we've seen worse. From Volkswagen's self-starting "runaway Rabbits" to minivans with automatic sliding doors that open when they shouldn't or won't open when they should.

Other media tactics

Call a press conference in front of the agency with whom you are in disagreement. Show your vehicle and any documents that tell the story. Carry a small sign, decorate your vehicle appropriately, and be polite but firm. All you want is to meet with someone responsible to review the claim and perhaps reconsider their earlier decision.

This approach works with government functionaries just as well as it does with car dealers. It's the intensity of your story coupled with your reasonableness and some film or pictures showing your displeasure that will get the story on the afternoon radio news, the local TV news, and the next morning's newspaper—which will be picked up again by the open-line radio shows for another day.

An example of these tactics in action: Mario Girolami is a volunteer driver who parked his truck in downtown Calgary on May 19, 2011, to deliver aid for Slave Lake fire victims. His engine was running and he had the emergency lights lit for the few moments it took to unload bedding, etc. As he was pulling away, a Calgary Parking Authority (CPA) agent slapped him with s $315 parking ticket.

Girolami called the *Calgary Sun*, showed where he had been parked, and handed out copies of the ticket. Renato Gandia wrote the story, and the *Sun*'s "Page Five" picked it up. The upshot?

The next day the ticket was cancelled and the two Parking Authority bosses responsible were fired over their actions.

Yep, complaining works, anywhere in Canada, if it's done the right way.

Federal and Provincial Consumer Affairs

Although the beefed-up *Competition Act* has some bite in regard to misleading advertising and a number of other illegal business practices, the government has been more reactive than proactive in applying the law. The *Act* also had some teeth pulled by an amendment that forces the government to prove in civil court that not only did price fixing occur, but that it also was successful in influencing prices. There is now a more passive mindset among government staffers in investigating complaints of price fixing and misleading advertising.

Nevertheless, you never know what complaint will be taken seriously and lead to government action. So it pays to at least try. Use the online Enquiry/Complaint Form found at *www.competitionbureau.gc.ca*. Six years ago, an online complaint sent by *Lemon-Aid* made Toyota cease its Access price-fixing practices and pay out almost $2 million as a settlement fee.

On the provincial side, consumer affairs staffers can still help with investigation, mediation, and some litigation. Strong and effective consumer protection legislation has been left standing in most of the provinces, and resourceful consumers can use these laws in conjunction with media coverage to prod provincial consumer affairs offices into action. Furthermore, provincial elected officials and bureaucrats aren't as well shielded from criticism as their federal counterparts. A call to your MPP or MLA, or to their executive assistants, can often get things rolling and help you tap into a provincial compensation fund.

Protest Works

You can put additional pressure on a seller or garage by putting a "lemon" sign on your car and parking it in front of the dealer or garage, by creating a "lemon" website, or by forming a self-help group like the Chrysler Lemon Owners Group (CLOG) or the Ford Lemon Owners Group (FLOG). After forming your group, you can have the occasional parade of creatively decorated cars visit area dealerships as the local media are convened. Just remember to keep your remarks pithy and factual, don't interfere with traffic or customers, and remain peaceful.

One other piece of advice from this consumer advocate with more than 42 years of experience and hundreds of pickets and mass demonstrations under his belt: Keep a sense of humour, and never break off negotiations.

Finally, don't be scared off by threats that it's illegal to criticize a product or company. Unions, environmentalists, and consumer groups do it regularly (it's called "informational picketing"), and the Supreme Court of Canada reaffirmed this right in *R. v. Guinard* in February 2002. In that judgment, an insurance policyholder posted a sign on his barn claiming the Commerce Insurance Company was unfairly refusing his claim. The municipality of St-Hyacinthe, Quebec, told him to take the sign down. He refused, maintaining that he had the right to state his opinion. The Supreme Court agreed. This judgment means that consumer protests, signs, and websites that criticize the actions of corporations cannot be banned simply because they say unpleasant things.

Defamation and libel

Picketing a new car dealer or automobile manufacturer, having a "sit-in" at the local auto show, or placing an ad rounding up other "lemon" owners are all legitimate public-interest complaint tactics that get results—and lawsuits. However, the legal intimidation hanging over these actions is now a past threat thanks to a recent ruling of our Supreme Court.

In December 2009, the Canadian Supreme Court rendered two judgments that make it much harder for plaintiffs to win cases alleging defamation or libel. The first decision overturned a lower court award of $1.5 million to a forestry executive who sued the *Toronto Star*. The *Star* alleged that he had used political connections to get approval for a golf course expansion (see *Grant v. Torstar Corp.*).

The Supreme Court struck down the judgment against the newspaper because the earlier judgment had failed to give adequate weight to the value of freedom of expression. The court announced a new defense of "responsible communication on matters of public interest." In the court's opinion, anyone (journalists, bloggers, unions, picketers, etc.) can avoid liability if they can show that the information they communicated—whether true or false—was of public interest and they tried their best to verify it.

In another case, also involving a major Canadian newspaper, a former Ontario police officer sued the *Ottawa Citizen* after it reported that he had misrepresented his search-and-rescue work at Ground Zero in New York City after the attacks of September 11, 2001. The Supreme Court reversed the $100,000 jury award because the judges felt the article was in the public interest (see *Quan v. Cusson*).

Using the Courts

It is well known that disputes that go before the courts can last a very long time. The plaintiff may face interminable delays setting and postponing hearing dates; long, drawn-out hearings, procedural roadblocks, and appeals; and long-awaited judgments. For example, in the judicial district of Montreal, the period between filing a legal claim and the hearing date is 14 to 15 months. British Columbia's small claims division registered in 2006 a median period of 296 days from filing a legal claim to the hearing date.

Top 10 Legal Phrases You Should Know

When using Canadian courts it's a good idea to be trilingual, with a good knowledge of English, French, and Legalese. The following phrases are ones that you are mostly likely to encounter when filing or pleading a lawsuit:

Audi alteram partem: "Hear the other side." It is most often used to refer to the principle that no person should be judged without a fair hearing in which each party is given the opportunity to respond to the evidence against him or her.

Caveat emptor: "Let the buyer beware." Purchasers are responsible for checking whether goods suit their needs. This concept ruled the consumer protection movement until the publication of Ralph Nader's *Unsafe at Any Speed* in the '60s. That book, which exposed the Corvair's design deficiencies, argued that more effective legislation was needed to force a "seller beware" mindset. British Columbia, Saskatchewan, and Quebec were the first provinces to apply this doctrine in legislation relative to automobile warranties and the interpretation of what is reasonable durability.

Ex post facto law: "From after the action." A law that retroactively changes the legal consequences (or status) of actions committed or relationships that existed prior to the enactment of the law.

Ignorantia juris non excusat: "Ignorance of the law excuses no one." A legal principle holding that a person who is unaware of a law may not escape responsibility for violating that law.

Pro bono publico: "For the public good." The term is generally used to describe professional work undertaken voluntarily and without payment as a public service.

Mens rea: "A guilty mind." Considered one of the necessary elements of a crime. This goes to the defendant's intent.

Quanti minoris: "A reduced amount," or "diminished value." A partial refund may be claimed based upon the reduced value of a product due to the manufacturer's or seller's negligence or misrepresentation. This principle was used successfully against Nissan and Ford of Canada by the Automobile Protection

Association in hundreds of small claims court cases during the '70s. Refunds up to $300 were awarded as compensation to buyers who were sold "redated" new vehicles that were the previous year's model. Nissan appealed the awards to the Supreme Court of Canada, claiming small claims courts were unconstitutional because lawyers were barred from pleading. A second argument was that the small claims courts lacked jurisdiction because the proper remedy was a cancellation of the sale. This would have taken the cases out of the courts $300 maximum jurisdiction. The Supreme Court rejected both arguments (see *Nissan v. Pelletier*).

Ratio decidendi: "The point in a case which determines the judgment," or "the principle which the case establishes."

Res ipsa loquitur: "The thing speaks for itself." The elements of duty of care and breach can be sometimes inferred from the very nature of an accident or other outcome, even without direct evidence of how any defendant behaved.

Restitutio in integrum: "Restoration to the original condition." This is one of the primary guiding principles behind the awarding of damages in common law negligence claims. The general rule, as the principle implies, is that the amount of compensation awarded should put the successful plaintiff in the position he or she would have been in had the wrongful action not been committed. Thus, the plaintiff should clearly be awarded damages for direct expenses, such as medical bills and property repairs, and the loss of future earnings attributable to the injury (which often involves difficult speculation about future career and promotion prospects). This is also a term used to describe how far insurance companies must go in repairing accident damage.

When to Sue?

If the dealer you've been negotiating with agrees to make things right, give him or her a deadline for completing the repairs and then have an independent garage check them over. If no offer is made within 10 working days, file suit in court. Make the manufacturer a party to the lawsuit only if the original, unexpired warranty is still in place; if your claim falls under the emissions warranty, a TSB, a secret warranty extension, or a safety recall campaign; or if there is extensive chassis rusting caused by poor engineering.

Which Country?

Tepei v. Uniroyal: Canadians injured by an American-manufactured tire can file their claim in American courts where jury awards tend to be more generous (*www.crossborderlaw.com*). In this 2004 case, a Washington jury awarded $9.1 million (U.S.) in damages to the six Canadian plaintiffs (*www.crossborderlaw.com/PDF/CBL-Tepei-Verdict-040429.pdf*).

The jury found that a driver's negligence was the sole cause of the plaintiffs' injuries; nevertheless, the *Tepei v. Uniroyal* case shows that Canadian plaintiffs need a thorough knowledge of the laws on both sides of the border to maximize their recovery whenever United States law is implicated in litigation.

> The pre-trial legal maneuvering between the parties and Michelin over *forum non conveniens* and choice-of-law issues suggests that while U.S. corporate defendants will aggressively contest the efforts of Canadian plaintiffs to seek redress for injuries caused by defective American products, the American courts are generally open to such claims for relief.
>
> In Washington, as well as in the majority of states around the U.S. which have abandoned the *lex loci delecti* approach to choice-of-law issues, it is likely that a Canadian plaintiff who chooses to sue an American manufacturer in a state with some connection to the product in question would find the courts willing to entertain both jurisdiction over the case and the application of the American forum's products liability law—irrespective of where the injury to the plaintiff actually took place.

Indeed, many of the cases relied upon by Michelin in its attempt to suggest the place of the *Tepei* accident was "fortuitous" could be turned against a corporate defendant, supporting the argument that an injury occurring in Canada "could have occurred anywhere."

Which Court?

Most claims can be handled without a lawyer in small claims court, especially now that courts' jurisdictions vary from $5,000 to $25,000. Still, it's up to you to decide what remedy to pursue—that is, whether you want a partial refund or a cancellation of the sale. To determine the refund amount, add the estimated cost of repairing the existing mechanical defects to the cost of prior repairs. Don't exaggerate your losses or claim for repairs that are considered to be routine maintenance. A suit for the cancellation of a sale involves practical problems. The court requires that the vehicle be "tendered," or taken back, to the seller at the time the lawsuit is filed. This leaves you without transportation for as long as the case continues, unless you purchase another vehicle in the interim. If you lose the case, you must then take back the old vehicle and pay the accumulated storage fees. You could go from having no vehicle to having two—one of which is a clunker!

Generally, if the cost of repairs or the sales contract amount falls within the small claims court limit (discussed below), file the case there to keep your costs to a minimum and to get a speedy hearing. Small claims court judgments aren't easily appealed, lawyers aren't necessary, filing fees are minimal (about $125), and cases are usually heard within a few months. In fact, your suit is almost always best argued in the provincial small claims court to keep costs and frustrations down and to get a quick resolution within a few months.

Here's another reason not to be greedy: If you claim more than the small claims court limit, you'll have to go to a higher court—where costs quickly add up, lawyers routinely demand 30 percent of your winnings or settlement, and trial delays of a few years or more are commonplace, not counting more years to wait if the decision is appealed.

Small Claims Courts

Crooked automakers scurry away from small claims courts like cockroaches from bug spray, not because the courts can issue million-dollar judgments or force litigants to spend a fortune in legal fees (they can't), but because dealers and manufacturers don't want the bad publicity arising from the filings and eventual judgments. Other disincentives are that small claims courts can award sizeable sums to plaintiffs not represented by lawyers, and they make jurisprudence that other judges on the same bench are likely to follow.

For example, in *Dawe v. Courtesy Chrysler* (Dartmouth Nova Scotia Small Claims Court; SCCH #206825; July 30, 2004), Judge Patrick L Casey, Q.C., rendered an impressive 21-page decision citing key automobile product liability cases from the past 80 years, including *Donoghue*, *Kravitz*, and *Davis*. The court awarded $5,037 to the owner of a new 2001 Cummins engine–equipped Ram pickup with the following problems: It wandered all over the road; lost power, or jerked and bucked; shifted erratically; lost braking ability; bottomed out when passing over bumps; allowed water to leak into the cab; produced a burnt-wire and oil smell in the interior as the lights would dim; and produced a rear-end whine and wind noise around the doors and under the dash. Dawe had sold the vehicle and reduced his claim to meet the small claims threshold. Anyone with water leaking into the interior or problems with the engine, transmission, or suspension will find this judgment particularly useful.

Interestingly, "small claims" court is quickly becoming a misnomer, now that Alberta, Nova Scotia, British Columbia, Yukon, and Ontario allow claims of up to $25,000, and other provinces permit $5,000–$20,000 filings. The lowest fees in Canada for a claim before a small claims division are $15 in the Northwest Territories for any claim of $500 or less, and $39 for a claim exceeding $500. The highest fees for a claim filed by a consumer are in Alberta: $100 for any claim of $7,500 or less, and $200 for a claim of $7,501 to $25,000. Claims before small claims divisions don't generally incur other fees.

Check your provincial or territorial court's website for updated rules and increased claim limits.

There are small claims courts in most counties of every province, and you can make a claim in the county where the problem happened or where the defendant lives and conducts business. Simply go to the small claims court office and ask for a claim form. Remember, you must identify the defendant correctly, which may require some help from the court clerk (look for other recent lawsuits naming the same party). Crooks often change their company's name to escape liability; for example, it would be impossible to sue Joe's Garage (1999) if your contract is with Joe's Garage, Inc. (1984).

At this point, it wouldn't hurt to hire a lawyer or a paralegal for a brief walk-through of small claims procedures to ensure that you've prepared your case properly and that you know what objections will likely be raised by the other side. If, instead, you'd like a lawyer to do all the work for you, there are a number of law firms around the country that specialize in small claims litigation. "Small claims" doesn't mean "small legal fees," though. In Toronto, some law offices charge a flat fee of $1,000 for a basic small claims lawsuit and trial.

Remember that you're entitled to bring to court any evidence relevant to your case, including written documents, such as a contract, letter, or bill of sale or receipt. If your car has developed severe rust problems, bring a photograph (signed and dated by the photographer) to court. You may also have witnesses testify in court. It's important to discuss a witness's testimony prior to the court date. If a witness can't attend the court date, he or she can write a report and sign it for representation in court. This situation usually applies to an expert witness, such as an independent mechanic who has evaluated your car's problems.

If you lose your case in spite of all your preparation and research, some small claims court statutes allow cases to be retried in exceptional circumstances, at a nominal cost. If a new witness has come forward, additional evidence has been discovered, or key documents (that were previously not available) have become accessible, apply for a retrial.

Alan MacDonald, a *Lemon-Aid* reader who won his case in small claims court, gives the following tips on beating Ford over a faulty automatic transmission:

> I want to thank you for the advice you provided in my dealings with the Ford Motor Company of Canada Limited and Highbury Ford Sales Limited regarding my 1994 Ford Taurus wagon and the problems with the automatic transmission (Taurus and Windstar transmissions are identical). I also wish to apologize for not sending you a copy of this judgment earlier...(*MacDonald v. Highbury Ford Sales Limited*, Ontario Superior Court of Justice in the Small Claims Court London, June 6, 2000, Court File #0001/00, Judge J.D. Searle).
>
> In 1999, after only 105,000 km, the automatic transmission went. I took the car to Highbury Ford to have it repaired. We paid $2,070 to have the transmission fixed, but protested and felt the transmission failed prematurely. We contacted Ford, but to no avail: Their reply was we were out of warranty, period. The transmission was so poorly repaired (and we went back to Highbury Ford several times) that we had to go to Mr. Transmission to have the transmission fixed again nine months later at a further $1,906.02.
>
> It is at that point that I contacted you, and I was surprised, and somewhat speechless (which you noticed) when you personally called me to provide advice and encouragement. I am very grateful for your call. My observations with going through small claims court involved the following: I filed in January of 2000, the trial took place on June 1 and the judgment was issued June 6.

At pretrial, a representative of Ford (Ann Sroda) and a representative from Highbury Ford were present. I came with one binder for each of the defendants, the court and one for myself (each binder was about 3 inches thick, containing your reports on Ford Taurus automatic transmissions, ALLDATA Service Bulletins, Taurus Transmissions Victims (Bradley website), Center for Auto Safety (website), Read This Before Buying a Taurus (website), and the Ford Vent Page (website)).

The representative from Ford asked a lot of questions (I think she was trying to find out if I had read the contents of the information I was relying on). The Ford representative then offered a 50 percent settlement based on the initial transmission work done at Highbury Ford. The release allowed me to still sue Highbury Ford with regards to the necessity of going to Mr. Transmission because of the faulty repair done by the dealer. Highbury Ford displayed no interest in settling the case, and so I had to go to court.

For court, I prepared by issuing a summons to the manager at Mr. Transmission, who did the second transmission repair, as an expert witness. I was advised that unless you produce an expert witness you won't win in a car repair case in small claims court. Next, I went to the law school library in London and received a great deal of assistance in researching cases pertinent to car repairs. I was told that judgments in your home province (in my case Ontario) were binding on the court; that cases outside of the home province could be considered, but not binding, by the judge.

The cases I used for trial involved *Pelleray v. Heritage Ford Sales Ltd.*, Ontario Small Claims Court (Scarborough) SC7688/91 March 22, 1993; *Phillips et al. v. Ford Motor Co. of Canada Ltd. et al*, Ontario Reports 1970, 15th January 1970; *Gregorio v. Intrans-Corp.*, Ontario Court of Appeal, May 19, 1994; *Collier v. McMaster's Auto Sales*, New Brunswick Court of Queen's Bench, April 26, 1991; *Sigurdson v. Hillcrest Service & Acklands (1977)*, Saskatchewan Queen's Bench; *White v. Sweetland*, Newfoundland District Court, Judicial Centre of Gander, November 8, 1978; *Raiches Steel Works v. J. Clark & Son*, New Brunswick Supreme Court, March 7, 1977; *Mudge v. Corner Brook Garage Ltd.*, Newfoundland Supreme Court, July 17, 1975; *Sylvain v. Carroseries d'Automobiles Guy Inc. (1981)*, C.P. 333, Judge Page; [and] *Gagnon v. Ford Motor Company of Canada, Limited et Marineau Automobile Co. Ltée.* (1974), C.S. 422–423.

In court, I had prepared the case, as indicated above, [and] had my expert witness and two other witnesses who had driven the vehicle (my wife and my 18-year-old son). As you can see by the judgment, we won our case and I was awarded $1,756.52, including pre-judgment interest and costs.

Key Court Decisions

The following Canadian and U.S. lawsuits and judgments cover typical problems that are likely to arise. Use them as leverage when negotiating a settlement or as a reference should your claim go to trial. Legal principles applying to Canadian and American law are similar; however, Quebec court decisions may be based on legal principles that don't apply outside that province. You can find a comprehensive

In *Prebushewski v. Dodge City Auto (1985) Ltd. and Chrysler Canada Ltd.*, the Supreme Court ordered Chrysler to pay $25,000 in punitive damages for denying a Saskatoon Dodge Ram owner's refund request.

listing of Canadian decisions from small claims courts all the way to the Supreme Court of Canada at *www.canlii.org* (Canadian Legal Information Institute).

Additional court judgments can be found in the legal reference section of your city's main public library or at a nearby university law library. Ask the librarian for help in choosing the legal phrases that best describe your claim.

LexisNexis (*global.lexisnexis.com/ca*) and FindLaw (*www.findlaw.com*) are two useful Internet sites for legal research. Their main drawback, though, is that you may need to subscribe or use a lawyer's subscription to access jurisprudence and other areas of the sites. However, there is a free online summary of class actions filed in Canada at *http://classactionsincanada.blogspot.com*. It's run by Ward Branch, one of the legal counsels in the Canada-wide, $1.2 billion class action settled several years ago by General Motors for defective engine intake manifold gaskets.

An excellent reference book that will give you plenty of tips on filing, pleading, and collecting your judgment is Justice Marvin A. Zuker's *Ontario Small Claims Court Practice 2012* (Carswell, 2012). Judge Zuker's annual publication is easily understood by non-lawyers and uses court decisions from across Canada to help you plead your case successfully in almost any Canadian court.

Product Liability

Almost three decades ago, before *Robson*, the Supreme Court of Canada clearly affirmed in *Kravitz v. GM* that automakers and their dealers are jointly liable for the replacement or repair of a vehicle if independent testimony shows that it is afflicted with factory-related defects that compromise its safety or performance. The existence of secret warranty extensions or technical service bulletins also help prove that the vehicle's problems are the automaker's responsibility. For example, in *Lowe v. Fairview Chrysler* (see page 143), technical service bulletins were instrumental in showing in 1989 that Chrysler had a history of automatic transmission failures similar to what we see in Ford and GM vehicles today.

In addition to replacing or repairing the vehicle, an automaker can also be held responsible for any damages arising from the defect (refer to *Wharton*, page 98). This means that loss of wages, supplementary transportation costs, and damages for personal inconvenience can be awarded. However, in the States, product liability damage awards often exceed millions of dollars, while Canadian courts are far less generous.

When a warranty claim is rejected on the pretext that you "altered" the vehicle, failed to carry out preventive maintenance, or drove abusively, manufacturers *must* prove to the court that there's a link between their allegation and the failure (see *Julien v. General Motors of Canada Ltd. (1991)*, 116 N.B.R. (2d) 80).

Before settling any claim with GM or any other automaker, search the Internet to read the latest information from dissatisfied customers who've banded together and set up their own self-help websites.

Implied Warranty (Reasonable Durability)

This is that powerful "other" warranty that they never tell you about. It applies during and after the expiration of the manufacturer's or dealer's expressed or written warranty and requires that a part or repair will last a "reasonable" period of time. Look at the "Reasonable Part Durability" chart on page 107 for some guidelines on what you should expect.

Judges usually apply the implied or legal warranty when the manufacturer's expressed warranty has expired and the vehicle's manufacturing defects remain uncorrected. The landmark Canadian decisions upholding implied warranties in auto claims have been *Donoghue v. Stevenson*, [1932] A.C. 562 (H.L.), and *General Motors Products of Canada Ltd. v. Kravitz*, [1979] 1 S.C.R. 790.

In *Donoghue*, the court had to determine if the manufacturer of a bottle of ginger beer owed a duty to a consumer who suffered injury as a result of finding a decomposed snail in the bottle after consuming part of the bottle's contents. Lord Atkin, in finding liability against the manufacturer, established the principle of negligence. His reasons have been followed and adopted in all the common-law countries:

> The rule that you are to love your neighbour becomes in law, you must not injure your neighbour; and the lawyer's question, who is my neighbour? receives a restricted reply.

You must take reasonable care to avoid acts or omissions which you can reasonably foresee would be likely to injure your neighbour. Who, then, is my neighbour?

The answer seems to be persons who are so closely and directly affected by my act that I ought reasonably to have them in contemplation as being so affected when I am directing my mind to the acts or omissions which are called in question.

Over 45 years later, in Quebec, *Kravitz* said essentially the same thing. In that case, the court said the seller's warranty of quality was an accessory to the property and was transferred with it on successive sales. Accordingly, subsequent buyers could invoke the contractual warranty of quality against the manufacturer, even though they did not contract directly with it. This precedent is now codified in articles 1434, 1442, and 1730 of Quebec's Civil Code (see *Turdif v. Hyundai Motor America* at *www.canlii.org/fr/qc/qccs/doc/2004/2004canlii7992/2004canlii7992.html* for a full analysis of warranties, hidden defects, and misrepresentation relating to Hyundai's horsepower ratings).

Paint and Body Defects

The following settlement advice applies mainly to paint defects, but you can use these tips for any other vehicle defect that you believe is the automaker's or dealer's responsibility. If you aren't sure whether the problem is a factory-related deficiency or a maintenance fault, have it checked out by an independent garage or get a technical service bulletin summary for your vehicle. The summary may include specific bulletins relating to diagnosis and correction as well as information about ordering the upgraded parts needed to fix your problem.

Four good examples of favourable paint judgments are *Shields v. General Motors of Canada*; *Bentley v. Dave Wheaton Pontiac Buick GMC Ltd. and General Motors of Canada*; *Maureen Frank v. General Motors of Canada Limited*; and the most recent, *Dunlop v. Ford of Canada*.

In *Dunlop v. Ford of Canada* (No. 58475/04; Ontario Superior Court of Justice, Richmond Hill Small Claims Court; January 5, 2005; Deputy Judge M.J. Winer), the owner of a 1996 Lincoln Town Car that was purchased used in 1999 for $27,000 was awarded $4,091.64. Judge Winer cited the *Shields* decision (following) and gave these reasons for finding Ford of Canada liable:

Evidence was given by the Plaintiff's witness, Terry Bonar, an experienced paint auto technician. He gave evidence that the [paint] delamination may be both a manufacturing defect and can be caused or [sped] up by atmospheric conditions. He also says that [the paint on] a car like this should last ten to 15 years, [or even for] the life of the vehicle.

It is my view that the presence of ultraviolet light is an environmental condition to which the vehicle is subject. If it cannot withstand this environmental condition, it is defective.

In *Shields v. General Motors of Canada* (No. 1398/96; Ontario Court, General Division, Oshawa Small Claims Court; July 24, 1997; Robert Zochodne, Deputy Judge), the owner of a 1991 Pontiac Grand Prix had purchased the vehicle used with over 100,000 km on its odometer. Beginning in 1995, the paint began to bubble and flake, and it eventually peeled off. Deputy Judge Zochodne awarded the plaintiff $1,205.72 and struck down every one of GM's arguments that the peeling paint was caused by acid rain, UV rays, or some other environmental factor. Here are some other important aspects of this 12-page judgment, which GM didn't appeal:

1. The judge admitted many of the technical service bulletins referred to in *Lemon-Aid* as proof of GM's negligence.
2. Although the vehicle had 156,000 km on its odometer when the case went to court, GM still offered to pay 50 percent of the paint repairs if the plaintiff dropped his suit.
3. The judge ruled that the failure to protect the paint from the damaging effects of UV rays is akin to engineering a car that won't start in cold weather. In essence, vehicles must be built to withstand the rigours of the environment.
4. Here's an interesting twist: The original warranty covered defects that were present at the time it was in effect. The judge, taking statements found in the GM technical service bulletins, ruled that the UV problem was factory-related, existed during the warranty period, and, therefore, represented a latent defect that appeared once the warranty expired.
5. The subsequent purchaser was not prevented from making the warranty claim, even though the warranty had long since expired, both in time and mileage, and he was the second owner.

The small claims judgment in *Bentley v. Dave Wheaton Pontiac Buick GMC Ltd. and General Motors of Canada* (Victoria Registry No. 24779; British Columbia Small Claims Court; December 1, 1998; Judge Higinbotham) builds upon the *Shields* decision and cites other jurisprudence as to how long paint should last on a car. If you're wondering why Ford and Chrysler haven't been hit by similar judgments, remember that they usually settle out of court.

From *Maureen Frank v. General Motors of Canada Limited* (No. SC#12 (2001); Saskatchewan Provincial Court, Saskatoon, Saskatchewan; October 17, 2001; Provincial Court Judge H.G. Dirauf):

> On June 23, 1997, the Plaintiff bought a 1996 Chevrolet Corsica from a General Motors dealership. At the time, the odometer showed 33,172 km. The vehicle still had some factory warranty. The car had been a lease car and had no previous accidents.
>
> During June of 2000, the Plaintiff noticed that some of the paint was peeling off from the car and she took it to a General Motors dealership in Saskatoon and to the General Motors dealership in North Battleford where she purchased the car. While there were some discussions with the GM dealership about the peeling paint, nothing came of it and the Plaintiff now brings this action claiming the cost of a new paint job.

During 1999, the Plaintiff was involved in a minor collision causing damage to the left rear door. This damage was repaired. During this repair some scratches to the left front door previously done by vandals were also repaired.

The Plaintiff's witness, Frank Nemeth, is a qualified auto body repairman with some 26 years of experience. He testified that the peeling paint was a factory defect and that it was necessary to completely strip the car and repaint it. He diagnosed the cause of the peeling paint as a separation of the primer surface or colour coat from the electrocoat primer. In his opinion no primer surfacer was applied at all. He testified that once the peeling starts, it will continue. He has seen this problem on General Motors vehicles. The defect is called delamination.

Mr. Nemeth stated that a paint job should last at least 10 years. In my opinion, most people in Saskatchewan grow up with cars and are familiar with cars. I think it is common knowledge that the original paint on cars normally lasts in excess of 15 years and that rust becomes a problem before the paint fails. In any event, paint peeling off, as it did on the Plaintiff's vehicle, is not common. I find that the paint on a new car put on by the factory should last at least 15 years.

It is clear from the evidence of Frank Nemeth (independent body shop manager) that the delamination is a factory defect. His evidence was not seriously challenged. I find that the factory paint should not suffer a delamination defect for at least 15 years and that this factory defect breached the warranty that the paint was of acceptable quality and was durable for a reasonable period of time.

There will be judgment for the Plaintiff in the amount of $3,412.38 plus costs of $81.29.

Some of the important aspects of the *Frank* judgment are as follows:

1. The judge accepted that the automaker was responsible, even though the car had been bought used. The subsequent purchaser wasn't prevented from making the warranty claim, even though the warranty had long since expired, both in time and mileage, and she was the second owner.
2. The judge stressed that the provincial warranty can kick in when the automaker's warranty has expired or isn't applied.
3. By awarding full compensation to the plaintiff, the judge didn't feel that there was a significant "betterment" or improvement added to the car that would warrant reducing the amount of the award.
4. The judge decided that the paint delamination was a factory defect.
5. The judge also concluded that without this factory defect, a paint job should last up to 15 years.
6. GM offered to pay $700 of the paint repairs if the plaintiff dropped the suit; the judge awarded five times that amount.
7. Maureen Frank won this case despite having to confront GM lawyer Ken Ready, who had considerable experience arguing other paint cases for GM and Chrysler.

Other Paint and Rust Cases

Martin v. Honda Canada Inc. (March 17, 1986; Ontario Small Claims Court, Scarborough; Judge Sigurdson): The original owner of a 1981 Honda Civic sought compensation for the premature "bubbling, pitting, [and] cracking of the paint and rusting of the Civic after five years of ownership." Judge Sigurdson agreed with the owner and ordered Honda to pay the owner $1,163.95.

Thauberger v. Simon Fraser Sales and Mazda Motors (3 B.C.L.R., 193): This Mazda owner sued for damages caused by the premature rusting of his 1977 Mazda GLC. The court awarded him $1,000. Thauberger had also previously sued General Motors for a prematurely rusted Blazer truck and was awarded $1,000 in the same court. Both judges ruled that the defects couldn't be excluded from the automaker's expressed warranty or from the implied warranty granted by British Columbia's *Sale of Goods Act*.

Whittaker v. Ford Motor Company (1979) (24 O.R. (2d), 344): A new Ford developed serious corrosion problems despite having been rustproofed by the dealer. The court ruled that the dealer, not Ford, was liable for the damage for having sold the rustproofing product at the time of purchase. This is an important judgment to use when a rustproofer or paint protector goes out of business or refuses to pay a claim, because the decision holds the dealer jointly responsible.

See also:

- *Danson v. Chateau Ford (1976)* C.P. (Quebec Small Claims Court; No. 32-00001898-757; Judge Lande)
- *Doyle v. Vital Automotive Systems* (May 16, 1977; Ontario Small Claims Court, Toronto; Judge Turner)
- *Lacroix v. Ford* (April 1980; Ontario Small Claims Court, Toronto; Judge Tierney)
- *Marinovich v. Riverside Chrysler* (April 1, 1987; District Court of Ontario; No. 1030/85; Judge Stortini)

Safety-Related Failures

Sudden acceleration, chronic stalling, and ABS and airbag failures

These kinds of failures are not that difficult to win in Canada under the doctrine of *res ipsa loquitur* ("the thing speaks for itself"), meaning, in negligence cases, that liability is shown by the failure itself. In a nutshell, the exact cause doesn't have to be pinpointed, and judges are free to award damages by weighing the "balance of probabilities" as to fault.

This advantage found in Canadian law was laid out succinctly in the July 1, 1998, issue of the *Journal of Small Business Management* in its comparison of product liability laws on both sides of the border ("Effects of Product Liability Laws on Small Business" at *www.allbusiness.com/legal/laws-government-regulations/691847-1.html*):

> Although in theory the Canadian consumer must prove all of the elements of negligence (*Farro v. Nutone Electrical Ltd. 1990*; Ontario Law Reform Commission 1979; Thomas 1989), most Canadian courts allow injured consumers to use a procedural aid known as *res ipsa loquitur* to prove their cases (*Nicholson v. John Deere Ltd. 1986; McMorran v. Dom. Stores Ltd. 1977*). Under *res ipsa loquitur*, plaintiffs must only prove that they were injured in a way that would not ordinarily occur without the defendant's negligence. It is then the responsibility of the defendant to prove that he was not negligent. As proving the negative is extremely difficult, this Canadian reversal of the burden of proof usually results in an outcome functionally equivalent to strict product liability (*Phillips v. Ford Motor Co. of Canada Ltd. 1971; Murray 1988*). This concept is reinforced by the principal that a Canadian manufacturer does not have the right to manufacture an inherently dangerous product when a method exists to manufacture that product without risk of harm. To do so subjects the manufacturer to liability even if the safer method is more expensive (*Nicholson v. John Deere Ltd. 1986*).

In *Jarvis v. Ford* (United States Second Circuit Court of Appeal, February 7, 2002), a judgment was rendered in favour of a driver who was injured when her six-day-old Ford Aerostar minivan suddenly accelerated as it was started and put into gear. What makes this decision unique is that the jury had no specific proof of a defect. The Court of Appeal agreed with the jury award, and Justice Sotomayor (now a Supreme Court Justice) gave these reasons for the Court's verdict:

> [A] product may be found to be defective without proof of the specific malfunction:
>
> It may be inferred that the harm sustained by the plaintiff was caused by a product defect existing at the time of sale or distribution, without proof of a specific defect, when the incident that harmed the plaintiff:
>
> (a) was of a kind that ordinarily occurs as a result of product defect; and
>
> (b) was not, in the particular case, solely the result of causes other than product defect existing at the time of sale or distribution.
>
> Restatement (Third) of Torts: Product Liability § 3 (1998). In comment c to this section, the Restatement notes:
>
> > [There is] no requirement that plaintiff prove what aspect of the product was defective. The inference of defect may be drawn under this Section without proof of the specific defect. Furthermore, quite apart from the question of what type of defect was involved, the plaintiff need not explain specifically what constituent part of the product failed. For example, if an inference of defect can be appropriately drawn in connection with the catastrophic failure of an airplane, the plaintiff need not establish whether the failure is attributable to fuel-tank explosion or engine malfunction.

The jury awarded Ms. Jarvis $24,568 in past medical insurance premiums, $340,338 in lost earnings, and $200,000 in pain and suffering. For future damages, the jury awarded $22,955 in medical insurance premiums, $648,944 in lost earnings, and $300,000 for pain and suffering.

Incidents of sudden acceleration or chronic stalling are quite common. However, they are often very difficult to diagnose, and individual cases can be treated very differently by federal safety agencies. Nevertheless, getting corroborative proof may be far easier in the future, now that the U.S. Department of Transportation under NHTSA will require that automakers install "black box" accident data recorders in all vehicles and give out their access codes to accident investigators. In fact, a number of impaired drivers have already been sent to jail in Canada based on black-box-accessed data.

Sudden acceleration is considered to be a safety-related problem—stalling, only sometimes. Never mind that a vehicle's sudden loss of power on a busy highway puts everyone's lives at risk. The same problem exists with engine and transmission powertrain failures, which are only occasionally considered to be safety-related. ABS and airbag failures, however, are universally considered to be life-threatening defects. If your vehicle manifests any of these conditions, here's what you need to do:

1. Get independent witnesses to confirm that the problem exists. Your primary tools include an independent mechanic's verification, passenger accounts, downloaded data from your vehicle's data recorder, and lots of searching through Google. Search for the automaker name and the model and year along with a description of the problem. For example: "Toyota 2007 Camry sudden acceleration."
   Also, notify the dealer or manufacturer by email, fax, or registered letter that you consider the problem to be a factory-induced, safety-related defect. Make sure you address your correspondence to the manufacturer's product liability or legal affairs department. At the dealership's service bay, make sure that every work order clearly states the problem as well as the number of previous attempts to fix it. (You should end up with a few complaint letters and a handful of work orders confirming that this is an ongoing deficiency.) If the dealer won't give you a copy of the work order because the work is a warranty claim, ask for a copy of the order number "in case your estate wishes to file a claim, pursuant to an accident." (This wording will get the service manager's attention.) Leaving a paper trail is crucial for any claim you may have later on, because it shows your concern and persistence, and it clearly indicates that the dealer and manufacturer have had ample time to correct the defect.
2. Note on the work order that you expect the problem to be diagnosed and corrected under the emissions warranty or a "goodwill" program. It also wouldn't hurt to add the phrase on the work order or in your claim letters that "any deaths, injuries, or damage caused by the defect will be the dealer's and manufacturer's responsibility" because the work order (or email, fax, or letter) constitutes you putting them on "formal notice."

3. If the dealer does the necessary repairs at little or no cost to you, send a follow-up confirmation that you appreciate the "goodwill." Also, emphasize that you'll be back if the problem reappears—even if the warranty has expired—because the repair renews your warranty rights applicable to that defect. In other words, the warranty clock is set back to its original position. Understand that you won't likely get a copy of the repair bill, either, because dealers don't like to admit that there was a serious defect present and don't feel that they owe you a copy of the work order if the repair was done gratis. You can, however, subpoena the complete vehicle file from the dealer and manufacturer (this costs about $50) if the case goes to small claims or a higher court. This request has produced many out-of-court settlements when the internal documents show extensive work was carried out to correct the problem.

4. If the problem persists, send a email, fax, or letter to the dealer and manufacturer saying so, look for ALLDATA service bulletins to confirm that your vehicle's defects are possibly factory-related, and report the failure by contacting Transport Canada or NHTSA or by logging on to NHTSA's website. Also, you may want to involve the non-profit, Montreal-based Automobile Protection Association or the Nader-founded Center for Auto Safety in Washington, D.C. (*www.autosafety.org/auto-defects*) to get a lawyer referral and an information sheet covering the problem.

5. Now come two crucial questions: Repair the defect now or later? Use the dealer or an independent? Generally, it's smart to use an independent garage if you know the dealer isn't pushing for free corrective repairs from the manufacturer, if weeks or months have passed without any resolution of your claim, if the dealer keeps repeating that it's a maintenance item, and if you know an independent mechanic who will give you a detailed work order showing the defect is factory-related and not caused by poor maintenance. Don't mention that a court case may ensue, since this will scare the dickens out of your only independent witness. An added bonus is that the repair charges will be about half of what a dealer would demand. Incidentally, if the automaker later denies warranty "goodwill" because you used an independent repairer, use the argument that the defect's safety implications required emergency repairs, carried out by whoever could see you first.

6. Dashboard-mounted warning lights usually come on prior to airbags suddenly deploying, ABS brakes failing, or engine glitches causing the vehicle to stall out. (Sudden acceleration usually occurs without warning.) Automakers consider these lights to be critical safety warnings and generally advise drivers to immediately have their vehicle serviced to correct the problem when any of the warning lights come on (advice that can be found in the owner's manual). This fact bolsters the argument that your life was threatened, emergency repairs were required, and your request for another vehicle or a complete refund isn't out of line.

7. Sudden acceleration can have multiple causes, isn't easy to duplicate, and is often blamed on the driver mistaking the accelerator for the brakes or failing to perform proper maintenance. Yet NHTSA data shows that with the 1992–2000 Explorer, for example, a faulty cruise-control or PCV valve and

poorly mounted pedals are the most likely causes of the Explorer's sudden acceleration. So how do you satisfy the burden of proof showing that the problem exists and it's the automaker's responsibility? Use the legal doctrine called "the balance of probabilities" by eliminating all of the possible dodges the dealer or manufacturer may employ. Show that proper maintenance has been carried out, you're a safe driver, and the incident occurs frequently and without warning, and quote the *Jarvis* decision (p. 131).

8. If any of the above defects causes an accident, or if the airbag fails to deploy or you're injured by its deployment, ask your insurance company to have the vehicle towed to a neutral location and clearly state that neither the dealer nor the automaker should touch the vehicle until your insurance company and Transport Canada have completed their investigation. Also, get as many witnesses as possible and immediately go to the hospital for a check-up, even if you're feeling okay. You may be injured and not know it because the adrenalin coursing through your veins is masking your injuries. A hospital exam will easily confirm that your injuries are accident-related, which is essential evidence for court or for future settlement negotiations.

9. Peruse NHTSA's online accident and service bulletin database to find reports of other accidents caused by the same failure, bulletins that indicate part upgrades, current defect investigations, and reported failures that have resulted in recalls or closed investigations.

10. Don't let your insurance company bully you. Refuse to let them settle the case if you're sure the accident was caused by a mechanical failure. Even if an engineering analysis fails to directly implicate the manufacturer or dealer, you can always plead the aforementioned balance of probabilities. If the insurance company settles, your insurance premiums will soar and the manufacturer will get away with the perfect crime.

Toyota's "Lag and Lurch"

Toyota's sudden acceleration problems have been joined by another safety defect that delays acceleration from a stop and then suddenly shoots the car forward as the electronic sensors finally pick up the throttle command. This results in near rear-enders as the car appears to stall and then darts forward. Toyota has known about this "lag and lurch" safety hazard for well over a decade, and apparently it afflicts almost its entire fleet of vehicles.

Mental Distress (Minivan Doors)

In *Sharman v. Formula Ford Sales Limited, Ford Credit Limited, and Ford Motor Company of Canada Limited* (Ontario Superior Court of Justice; Oakville, Ontario; No. 17419/02SR; 2003/10/07), Justice Shepard awarded $7,500 to the owner of a 2000 Windstar for mental distress resulting from the breach of the implied warranty of fitness, plus $7,207 for breach of contract and breach of warranty. The problem with the Windstar was that its sliding door wasn't secure and leaked air and water after many attempts to repair it. The judge cited the *Wharton* decision as support for his award for mental distress:

The plaintiff and his family have had three years of aggravation, inconvenience, worry, and concern about their safety and that of their children. Generally speaking, our contract law did not allow for compensation for what may be mental distress, but that may be changing. I am indebted to counsel for providing me with the decision of the British Columbia Court of Appeal in *Wharton v. Tom Harris Chevrolet Oldsmobile Cadillac Ltd.*, [2002] B.C.J. No. 233, 2002 BCCA 78. This decision was recently followed in *Tiavra v. Victoria Ford Alliance Ltd.*, [2003] B.C.J. No. 1957.

In *Wharton*, the purchaser of a Cadillac Eldorado claimed damages against the dealer because the car's sound system emitted an annoying buzzing noise and the purchaser had to return the car to the dealer for repair numerous times over two-and-a-half years. The trial court awarded damages of $2,257.17 for breach of warranty with respect to the sound system, and $5,000 in non-pecuniary damages for loss of enjoyment of their luxury vehicle and for inconvenience, for a total award of $7,257.17....

In the *Wharton* case, the respondent contracted for a "luxury" vehicle for pleasure use. It included a sound system that the appellant's service manager described as "high end." The respondent's husband described the purchase of the car in this way: "[W]e bought a luxury car that was supposed to give us a luxury ride and be a quiet vehicle, and we had nothing but difficulty with it from the very day it was delivered with this problem that nobody seemed to be able to fix. So basically we had a luxury product that gave us no luxury for the whole time that we had it."

It is clear that an important object of the contract was to obtain a vehicle that was luxurious and a pleasure to operate. Furthermore, the buzzing noise was the cause of physical, in the sense of sensory, discomfort to the respondent and her husband. The trial judge found it inhibited listening to the sound system and was irritating in normal conversation. The respondent and her husband also bore the physical inconvenience of taking the vehicle to the appellant on numerous occasions for repairs.

In my view, a defect in manufacture that goes to the safety of the vehicle deserves a modest increase. I would assess the plaintiff's damage for mental distress resulting from the breach of the implied warranty of fitness at $7,500.

Free Engine Repairs

In the following judgments, Ford was forced to reimburse the cost of engine head gasket repairs carried out under the implied warranty—long after the expressed warranty had expired.

Dufour v. Ford Canada Ltd. (April 10, 2001; Quebec Small Claims Court, Hull; No. 550-32-008335-009; Justice P. Chevalier): Ford was forced to reimburse the cost of engine head gasket repairs carried out on a 1996 Windstar 3.8L engine.

Schaffler v. Ford Motor Company Limited and Embrun Ford Sales Ltd. (Ontario Superior Court of Justice, L'Orignal Small Claims Court; Court File No. 59-2003; July 22, 2003; Justice Gerald Langlois): The plaintiff bought a used 1995 Windstar in 1998. The engine head gasket was repaired for free three years later under Ford's seven-year extended warranty. In 2002, at 109,600 km, the head gasket failed again, seriously damaging the engine. Ford refused a second repair.

Justice Langlois ruled that Ford's warranty extension bulletin listed signs and symptoms of the covered defect that were identical to the problems written on the second work order ("persistent and/or chronic engine overheating; heavy white smoke evident from the exhaust tailpipe; flashing 'low coolant' instrument-panel light even after coolant refill; and constant loss of engine coolant"). The judge concluded that the dealer knew of the problem well within the warranty period and was therefore negligent. The plaintiff was awarded $4,941 plus 5 percent interest. This award included $1,070 for two months' car rental.

John R. Reid and Laurie M. McCall v. Ford Motor Company of Canada (Superior Court of Justice, Ottawa Small Claims Court; Claim No. 02-SC-077344; July 11, 2003; Justice Tiernay): A 1996 Windstar bought used in 1997 experienced engine head gasket failure in October 2001 at 159,000 km. Judge Tiernay awarded the plaintiffs $4,145 for the following reasons:

> A Technical Service Bulletin dated June 28, 1999, was circulated to Ford dealers. It dealt specifically with "undetermined loss of coolant" and "engine oil contaminated with coolant" in the 1996–98 Windstar and five other models of Ford vehicles. I conclude that Ford owed a duty of care to the Plaintiff to equip this vehicle with a cylinder head gasket of sufficient sturdiness and durability that would function trouble-free for at least seven years, given normal driving and proper maintenance conditions. I find that Ford is answerable in damages for the consequences of its negligence.

Chams v. Ford Motor Company of Canada, Limited, and Courtesy Ford Lincoln Sales, Limited (Ontario Superior Court of Justice, Small Claims Court; London, Ontario; Claim No. 5868, Court File No. 103/04; November 22, 2004; Deputy Justice J.D. Searle):

Reasons for Judgment

1. J.D. SEARLE DEPUTY J.: The defendant Ford Motor Company of Canada, Limited, hereinafter referred to as "Ford" is a corporation based in Oakville, Ontario and is a manufacturer of motor vehicles. The defendant Courtesy Ford Lincoln Sales Limited, hereinafter referred to as "Courtesy" is a corporation which carries on the business of a Ford dealer in the city of London in the county of Middlesex.
2. Samir Chams resides in the city of London. In 1997 he purchased from Courtesy a low kilometerage 1995 Ford Windstar van with a 3.8 liter engine. By 1998 at the latest Ford was aware the head gaskets of such engines had a defect which could destroy the engine. In 2000 it offered to the plaintiff and other owners an "additional warranty" for this defect but limited the warranty to seven years from the date the vehicle first went into service or 160,000 kilometers, whichever came first. Upon receiving notice of the additional warranty in 2000 the plaintiff took his van to Courtesy but no problems were manifest. For the plaintiff the

original warranty had expired by passage of time. The additional warranty expired on March 08, 2002 by passage of time.

3. On January 11, 2004, some 22 months after the additional warranty expired, the plaintiff's engine overheated and was destroyed within a matter of minutes. The van had only 80,000 kilometers on the odometer. In due course the engine was replaced at a cost of over $4,000.00 paid by the plaintiff. As the court understands the plaintiff's case he is suing outside the expired warranty. Against Ford he alleges manufacturing defect. Against Courtesy he alleges negligence in 2000 in not replacing the defective head gasket to avoid possible engine destruction or at least telling him that was an option at his own expense. He also invokes manufacturer's warranty.

4. Ford contends it has no responsibility beyond its warranty and the destruction of the engine was from a cause or causes other than the head gasket. The court finds the highly probable cause of destruction of the engine was failure of the head gasket. The allegation of alternate causes is speculation not supported by the evidence. Pure economic loss does not apply because there was damage to property. See also *Winnipeg Condominium Corporation No. 36 v. Bird Construction Co. Ltd.* [1995] 1 S.C.R. 85.

5. Courtesy contends it was not negligent: the additional warranty issued by Ford only applied to cases with manifest problems and to merely replace a head gasket at a cost to the customer of $1,200.00 to $1,400.00 in the absence of manifest problems did not make economic sense.

6. In the Nova Scotia case of *Ford v. Kenney* (2003, unreported) Boudreau J. of the Nova Scotia Supreme Court was hearing an appeal from a decision of the Small Claims Court Adjudicator. At page 5 of the oral reasons His Lordship said:

> Ford Motor Company has the right to decide which vehicles they are going to provide repairs to and which vehicles they are not. That doesn't mean that they couldn't be successfully challenged by that on negligent proper negligent manufacturing evidence, but there was not that evidence in this case.

7. *Campbell v. Ford* is a judgment of the Nova Scotia Small Claims Court rendered on January 31, 2002 and not reported. The plaintiff's 1995 Ford Windstar van was showing signs of head gasket problems and the head gasket was replaced at 168,000 [km] at the $1,600.00 expense of the plaintiff. At 207,000 kilometers the engine was destroyed. The engine was rebuilt or replaced at a much greater cost. In both instances the vehicle was beyond the kilometerage caps of both the original and additional warranties.

8. The Adjudicator dismissed the replacement of the head gasket as pure economic loss but said of the engine rebuilding or replacement:

> It is certainly arguable that if the head gasket failed and it was due to negligence of the designer/manufacturer and that failure in turn caused physical damage to the property of the Claimant, consequential damage to the engine itself, that may well be a recoverable head of damage and the basis for an action in negligence.

The Adjudicator found there was insufficient admissible and reliable evidence to establish a causal connection between the gasket failure sought to be corrected at 168,000 kilometers and the destruction of the engine at 207,000 kilometers. The important point is that the Adjudicator was discussing the potential liability of Ford quite apart from its original or additional warranties.

9. *Beshara v. Barry* is an Ontario Small Claims Court judgment of Tierney J. with reasons released a few days before trial in the case at bar and not yet reported. The unrepresented plaintiff sued the president of Ford for the estimated cost of replacing an engine similar to the one in the case at bar. The action was dismissed because the failure occurred after the expiry of Ford's original and additional warranties and the negligence alleged was that of the repairer and not Ford. The repairer was not a party.

10. The foregoing cases were furnished to the court by the agent for Ford. In each case involving Ford that company was successful. The court did additional research.

11. In *Kozoriz v. Chrysler Canada Ltd.* [1992] O.J. No. 3937 the problem was a transaxle seal which failed at 16,000 kilometers. Thereafter there was frequent leaking and repair work. As the van neared the 80,000 kilometer warranty expiry the 80,000 kilometer inspection was done at a Chrysler dealership and no problem was found with the trans-axle seal or the transmission. A few days later in Iowa there was an expensive failure of these apparently related parts. Tierney J. of the Ontario Small Claims Court found both parts failed due to a nearly continuous leak of the seal since 16,000 kilometers.

12. Chrysler pleaded the failure occurred after the expiry of the 80,000 kilometer warranty. In part the warranty described itself as "[a] guarantee of the quality and engineering excellence." Judge Tierney found that to be equivalent to a warranty that the product was free of defect. He found the axle seal was defective almost immediately and failed after only 16,000 kilometers and the defect led to the transmission damage after the expiry of the warranty. At page 3:

> Those damages occurred as a direct result of the manufacturer's breach of warranty. For that reason, it is my view that the amounts are recoverable as damages for breach of contract, even though the actual breakdown occurred after the warranty period had expired.

13. A similar case is *Shields v. General Motors of Canada Ltd.* [1997] O.J. No. 5434 (Ont. Sm. C.C.). A 1991 Pontiac with a three year warranty began losing an extensive amount of its paint in 1995. Zochodne, D.J. found the problem was a failure to ensure proper bonding when the vehicle was being painted originally. At page 6:

> The defect, which I have found, that is the lack of primer surfacer, occurred at the time the vehicle was manufactured. At that point, however, the defect was latent. The defect became patent when the paint began to bubble, flake and then peel off the vehicle.

That being the case His Honour found the warranty must respond to the loss. Judgment was in favour of the plaintiff.

14. *Schaffler v. Ford Motor Co. of Canada and Embrum Ford Sales Ltd.* [2003] O.J. No. 3165 (Ont. Sm. C.C.) is yet another Ford Windstar case involving an engine identical to the one involved in the case at bar. On March 02 of 2000, August 06 of 2001 and October 16 of 2001 the plaintiff took the van to Embrum with problems involving coolant levels, one of the indicia of head gasket failure. On those dates the respective kilometerages were 59,850, 84,000 and 89,000. The additional warranty expired by passage of time on August 07, 2002. Two months later there was serious damage to the engine as a result of head gasket failure.

15. Deputy Judge Langlois found the dealer liable for failure to diagnose the head gasket problem and Ford liable on its additional warranty which had been invoked by the plaintiff within the additional warranty period although the major damage occurred after expiry of the warranty.

16. It is distressing to note that although Barry Holmes was able in the case at bar to produce cases from both Ontario and Nova Scotia when Ford was successful he produced none where Ford was not successful. That includes the Schaffler case of one year ago and in which he was Ford's representative. In the case at bar he was Ford's agent and only witness.

17. In the case at bar the plaintiff received notice in 2000 from Ford of a potential problem with the head gasket in his van. His response was to take the van to Courtesy and enquire what should he done about it. Although they are only estimates the van was 5.5 years from the original warranty start date and had traveled 49,000 kilometers. Courtesy took in the van and gave the plaintiff and his family a ride home. About one half hour later Courtesy called and said the van was ready to be picked up. There was no paperwork introduced at trial evidencing this occurrence and it is probable none exists. William Taylor was the service manager and a helpful and credible witness at trial. He was not surprised at the absence of paperwork and said by way of summary that "[w]e do not charge for conversation."

18. It is probable that what happened is this: the plaintiff took his van to Courtesy, did not have the Ford notice with him, told Courtesy he had received a notice about head gaskets, asked what should [be] done and got a ride home. Courtesy was readily able to identify the van by its vehicle identification number and pull up its file on the vehicle, including at least references to technical service bulletins and notices affecting the plaintiff's vehicle and others in its class.

19. Having received no report from the plaintiff nor made any observations themselves the Courtesy service people would not be aware of any of the mostly gross symptoms Ford said could trigger warranty work on the head gasket. According to Mr. Taylor Courtesy had done "a lot" of gasket-related work under the warranty program in 1999 and 2000. In the absence of reports or observations of at least one of the gross symptoms Courtesy would inspect the head gasket only if the customer paid. The court finds the absence of paperwork on this visit by the plaintiff makes it a near certainty there was no gasket inspection.

20. One of the four symptoms listed in the Ford notice received by the plaintiff

in 2000 was "constant loss of coolant" and another was flashing of the "low coolant" sensor light. Neither the plaintiff nor his wife testified to the existence of either of these symptoms and Courtesy does not note, except perhaps informally on the back of a work order, whether coolant has been "topped up." The plaintiff's vehicle was well maintained and in otherwise good condition throughout with much of the servicing done at Courtesy and some oil changes at a large department store if Mrs. Chams was shopping there.

21. Based on what Courtesy knew at the time of this visit Mr. Taylor would not recommend changing the head gasket for two reasons: the cost would be $1,200.00 to $1,400.00 to head off a problem which was only potential and there is a risk of non-payment and alienation if the work is done and the customer starts contending it is warranty work. The mechanic who owns and operates the independent vehicle repair shop which eventually replaced the plaintiff's engine said that due to the problems which can arise from it he will not permit his shop to change a head gasket for the sole purpose of changing the head gasket.

22. Nothing more relevant to an engine problem happened until Sunday, January 11, 2004. The Chams family fueled the van and moved it a short distance to a car wash. While entering the wash the plaintiff noticed the engine temperature digital readout was climbing. It maximized after the wash when they were back on the street. Mr. Chams pulled into the next "Petro" or "petrol" station and looked under the hood but saw nothing awry. He drove about two blocks to his house where the engine would not restart.

23. He asked a friend knowledgeable about motor vehicles to come over. That person observed coolant coming from the exhaust and coolant mixed with oil under the hood. The van was towed to Courtesy that day or early the next.

24. The diagnosis was "coolant in cylinders, no start, no heat, intermittent hydraulic lock. No start due to coolant leak inside engine. Suspect head cracked." The recommendation was replacement of the engine with a rebuilt engine. The kilometerage was noted to be 80,671. The charge for the inspection was $79.00 plus tax, later voluntarily waived by Mr. Taylor in recognition of several members of the Chams family being good customers and, no doubt, because of the arising of a warranty issue. Further, according to Mr. Chams he had urged a friend with a similar vehicle to his to go to the dealer in 2000 and the result was the replacement of the head gasket.

25. Courtesy advised Mr. and Mrs. Chams the problem was not covered by warranty. The occurrence was 22 months after the expiry of the additional warranty. Mr. and Mrs. Chams spent time unsuccessfully trying to get Ford and Courtesy to take responsibility for the problem. Either directly or indirectly the Chams had the van towed to Automotive Solutions. That is a London vehicle repair shop owned and operated by Mohamed Omar who employs two class "A" automotive mechanics in the shop and who himself is in the final stage of his apprenticeship. Mr. Omar testified.

26. The van was stored at Automotive Solutions for about three months until a rebuilt engine and ancillary equipment was purchased by Mr. Chams and installed by Automotive Solutions on and about May 01.

27. When he studied the engine of the Chams van, seemingly in the company of

one of his licensed mechanics, Mr. Omar observed the engine appeared not to have been apart before. The head gasket was found to [be] "blown." Coolant was mixed with oil. The coolant had leaked into the inner part of the engine through the No. 1 cylinder where it could mix with the oil. Oil mixing with coolant can cause the head gasket to "blow." One purpose of the head gasket is to prevent coolant getting into the interior of the engine.

28. In the opinion of Mr. Omar if the head gasket failed in 2000 the vehicle could not be driven until 2004. Head gaskets in most cars do not fail by 80,000 kilometers. He was aware the 3.8 liter Ford engine had a head gasket problem and he has worked on "a few" with such a problem. He is not "100% sure" of the reason for the failure of the Chams engine.

29. William Taylor is the Courtesy service manager. Courtesy did "a lot" of head gasket related repairs to 3.8 liter engines in 1999 and 2000. He understands the problem is a head gasket wrongly configured or "too weak." He has not seen the Chams engine but testified that theoretically the damage could be caused by a defective head gasket, a cracked head or the timing cover.

30. Barry Holmes was Ford's agent and only witness. He is a licensed mechanic and is employed by Ford in its product liability department. His direct evidence was largely on the Ford warranty and there was little or no evidence by him on defect or otherwise the cause of the major engine damage. On cross examination he said he did not know the failure rate of the head gaskets in the affected 3.8 liter engines. On further examination he acknowledged it was possibly 85% but he was not sure and had not brought that information to court with him. The court does not accept that denial of knowledge. The court notes its comments above with respect to cherry picking of cases. Mr. Holmes is a Ford product liability employee. The figure of 85% figured in another case involving a Ford 3.8 liter engine. The case at bar is at least the third nearly identical case in which Mr. Holmes has been noted in the reasons for judgment as Ford's agent or witness or both. The court finds that Ford knows it has had a failure rate of at least 85% in this head gasket which is a component which can quickly destroy an engine if it fails. That makes it nearly a certainty that unless the offending gasket is replaced in time the engine will be destroyed by its failure.

31. As to warranty this court finds, as was found in the *Shields* case, (*supra*), the defect was in existence and known to the giver of the warranty not only during the period of the additional warranty but also during the period of the original warranty. Ford is therefore liable on its warranty.

32. As to negligence there can be no doubt the gasket has had a design or manufacturing defect which has existed since the time of design or manufacture. It is that defect which caused the destruction of the plaintiff's engine and made its replacement necessary.

33. Ford's warranty attempts to limit its liability to what it grants in the warranty. It is ancient law that one who attempts to limit his liability by, for example, excluding common law remedies, must clearly bring that limitation to the attention of the person who might lose those remedies. The evidence in this case is clear the buyer of even a new car does not get a warranty booklet until after purchasing the car although he "would be" told the highlights sooner.

34. Courtesy was not negligent nor in breach of any other obligation to the plaintiff.

Ford would not entertain repairs under either of its warranties unless certain "symptoms" had become manifest before the work was done. The court has no doubt Mr. Chams would have declined if Courtesy had asked if he would pay $1,200.00 to $1,400.00 to replace the head gasket in 2000 when his vehicle was manifesting no problem. The action is therefore dismissed against Courtesy with costs of $375.00 payable by Ford. This court will leave the fancy dancing of Bullock orders and the like to the higher courts.

35. At trial the focus was understandably on liability with damages consigned to the periphery. The rebuilt engine and ancillary parts were obtained from a NAPA dealer. The net NAPA bill is $2,375.67 but to that must be added a down payment of $250.00 and from it must be deducted a core deposit of $300.00. The old core is still available for credit. The radiator and water pump are valid expenses in that they are essential to obtaining a NAPA warranty on the rebuilt engine.

36. One legitimate Automotive Solutions bill is for $776.25 for towing and storage. The other is for $1,383.45 for labour, fluids, minor parts and an alternator. Storage is acceptable, particularly when one notes the absence of a substitute vehicle claim or loss of use. The alternator could not be proved as related to the engine failure and so $126.50 will be deducted.

37. Damages are assessed at $4,358.87 and there will be judgment in that amount against Ford. That sum will attract interest pursuant to the provisions of the *Courts of Justice Act* from January 12, 2004. The Clerk is requested to make that calculation.

38. As to costs a sealed document has now been opened and found to be an October 18, 2004 offer by Ford to settle by waiving allowable costs which stood at $25.00 or $75.00 at the time of the offer.

39. The trial was scheduled for two days but was completed in one. Mr. Ferguson was helpful to the court, particularly by creating document briefs for all parties, thus collecting dozens of potential exhibits into a handful. The court agrees with Mr. Ferguson's contention that many of the [I]nternet printouts collected by or on behalf of the plaintiff and included in one of the briefs were nevertheless inadmissible. Mr. Dupuis as agent for the plaintiff put in his client's case in a way that was economical in terms of trial time but nevertheless thorough and it underscores the need for reform of the law which does not currently permit the court to award a counsel fee with respect to agents even in substantial cases. The plaintiff shall have costs fixed at $200.00 against Ford.

General Motors Intake Manifold Gasket Class Action

A Canadian class action lawsuit was launched on April 24, 2006—with *Lemon-Aid*'s help—and sought $1.2 billion in damages to compensate owners of 1995–2004 GM vehicles with defective engine intake manifold gaskets. A year later, GM Canada settled out of court for an estimated $40 million.

Automatic Transmission Failures

Lowe v. Fairview Chrysler-Dodge Limited and Chrysler Canada Limited (May 14, 1996; Ontario Court (General Division), Burlington Small Claims Court; No. 1224/95): This judgment, in the plaintiff's favour, raises important legal principles relative to Chrysler:

- Internal dealer service bulletins are admissible in court to prove that a problem exists and certain parts should be checked out.
- If a problem is reported prior to a warranty's expiration, warranty coverage for the problematic component(s) is automatically carried over after the warranty ends.
- It's not up to the car owner to tell the dealer or automaker what the specific problem is.
- Repairs carried out by an independent garage can be refunded if the dealer or automaker unfairly refuses to apply the warranty.
- The dealer or automaker cannot dispute the cost of the independent repair if it fails to cross-examine the independent repairer.
- Auto owners can ask for and win compensation for their inconvenience, which in this judgment amounted to $150.
- Court awards add up: Although the plaintiff was given $1,985.94, with the addition of court costs and prejudgment interest, plus costs of inconvenience fixed at $150, the final award amounted to $2,266.04.

New-Vehicle Defects

Bagnell's Cleaners v. Eastern Automobile Ltd. (1991) (111 N.S.R. (2nd), No. 51, 303 A.P.R., No. 51 (T.D.)): This Nova Scotia company found that the new van it purchased had serious engine, transmission, and radiator defects. The dealer pleaded unsuccessfully that the sales contract excluded all other warranties except for those contained in the contract. The court held that there was a fundamental breach of the implied warranty and that the van's performance differed substantially from what the purchaser had been led to expect. An exclusionary clause could not protect the seller, who failed to live up to a fundamental term of the contract.

Burridge v. City Motor (10 Nfld. & P.E.I.R.; No. 451): This Newfoundland resident complained repeatedly of his new car's defects during the warranty period, and he stated that he hadn't used his car for 204 days after spending almost $1,500 for repairs. The judge awarded all repair costs and cancelled the sale.

Davis v. Chrysler Canada Ltd. (1977) (26 N.S.R. (2nd), No. 410 (T.D.)): The owner of a new $28,000 diesel truck found that a faulty steering assembly prevented him from carrying on his business. The court ordered that the sale be cancelled and that $10,000 in monthly payments be reimbursed. There was insufficient evidence to award compensation for business losses.

Fox v. Wilson Motors and GM (February 9, 1989; Court of Queen's Bench, New Brunswick; No. F/C/308/87): A trucker's new tractor-trailer had repeated engine malfunctions. He was awarded damages for loss of income, excessive fuel consumption, and telephone charges under the provincial *Sale of Goods Act.*

Gibbons v. Trapp Motors Ltd. (1970) (9 D.L.R. (3rd), No. 742 (B.C.S.C.)): The court ordered the dealer to take back a new car that had numerous defects and required 32 hours of repairs. The refund was reduced by mileage driven.

Johnson v. Northway Chevrolet Oldsmobile (1993) (108 Sask. R., No. 138 (Q.B.)): The court ordered the dealer to take back a new car that had been brought in for repairs on 14 different occasions. Two years after the car's purchase, the buyer initiated a lawsuit for the purchase price and general damages. General damages were awarded.

Julien v. GM of Canada (1991) (116 N.B.R. (2nd), No. 80): The plaintiff's new diesel truck produced excessive engine noise. The dealer claimed that the problem was caused by the owner's engine alterations. The plaintiff was awarded the $5,000 cost of repairing the engine through an independent dealer.

Magna Management Ltd. v. Volkswagen Canada Inc. (May 27, 1988; Vancouver (B.C.C.A.); No. CA006037): This precedent-setting case allowed the plaintiff to keep his new $48,325 VW while awarding him $37,101—three years after the car was purchased. The problems were centred on poor engine performance. The jury accepted the plaintiff's view that the car was practically worthless with its inherent defects.

Maughan v. Silver's Garage Ltd. (Nova Scotia Supreme Court; 6 B.L.R., No. 303, N.S.C. (2nd), No. 278): The plaintiff leased a defective backhoe. The manufacturer had to reimburse the plaintiff's losses because the warranty wasn't honoured. The court rejected the manufacturer's contention that the contract's exclusion clause protected the company from lawsuits for damages resulting from a latent defect.

Murphy v. Penney Motors Ltd. (1979) (23 Nfld. & P.E.I.R.; No. 152, 61 A.P.R., No. 152 (Nfld. T.D.)): This Newfoundland trucker found that his vehicle's engine problems took his new trailer off the road for 129 days during a seven-month period. The judge awarded all repair costs, as well as compensation for business losses, and cancelled the sale.

Murray v. Sperry Rand Corp. (Ontario Supreme Court; 5 B.L.R., No. 284): The seller, dealer, and manufacturer were all held liable for breach of warranty when a forage harvester did not perform as advertised in the sales brochure or as promised by the sales agent. The plaintiff was given his money back and reimbursed for his economic loss, based on the amount his harvesting usually earned. The court held that the advertising was a warranty.

Oliver v. Courtesy Chrysler (1983) Ltd. (1992) (11 B.C.A.C., No. 169): This new car had numerous defects over a three-year period, which the dealer attempted to fix to no avail. The plaintiff put the car in storage and sued the dealer for the purchase price. The court ruled that the car wasn't roadworthy and that the plaintiff couldn't be blamed for putting it in storage rather than selling it and purchasing another vehicle. The purchase price was refunded, minus $1,500 for each year the plaintiff used the car.

Olshaski Farms Ltd. v. Skene Farm Equipment Ltd. (January 9, 1987; Alberta Court of Queen's Bench; 49 Alta. L.R. (2nd), No. 249): The plaintiff's Massey-Ferguson combine caught fire after the manufacturer had sent two notices to dealers informing them of a defect that could cause a fire. The judge ruled under the *Sale of Goods Act* that the balance of probabilities indicated that the manufacturing defect caused the fire, even though there wasn't any direct evidence proving that the defect existed.

Western Pacific Tank Lines Ltd. v. Brentwood Dodge (June 2, 1975; B.C.S.C., No. 30945-74; Judge Meredith): The court awarded the plaintiff $8,600 and cancelled the sale of a new Chrysler New Yorker that suffered from badly adjusted doors, water leaks into the interior, and electrical short circuits.

Leasing

Ford Motor Credit v. Bothwell (December 3, 1979; Ontario County Court (Middlesex); No. 9226-T; Judge Macnab): The defendant leased a 1977 Ford truck that had frequent engine problems, characterized by stalling and hard starting. After complaining for one year and driving 35,000 km (21,750 mi.), the defendant cancelled the lease. Ford Credit sued for the money owing on the lease. Judge Macnab cancelled the lease and ordered Ford Credit to repay 70 percent of the amount paid during the leasing period. Ford Credit was also ordered to refund repair costs, even though the corporation claimed that it should not be held responsible for Ford's failure to honour its warranty.

Schryvers v. Richport Ford Sales (May 18, 1993; B.C.S.C., No. C917060; Justice Tysoe): The court awarded $17,578.47, plus damages, to a couple who paid thousands of dollars more in unfair and hidden leasing charges than if they had simply purchased their Ford Explorer and Escort. The court found that this price difference constituted a deceptive, unconscionable act or practice, in contravention of the *Trade Practices Act*, R.S.B.C. 1979, c. 406.

Judge Tysoe concluded that the total of the general damages awarded to the Schryvers for both vehicles would be $11,578.47. He then proceeded to give the following reasons for awarding an additional $6,000 in punitive damages:

> Little wonder Richport Ford had a contest for the salesperson who could persuade the most customers to acquire their vehicles by way of a lease transaction. I consider

the actions of Richport Ford to be sufficiently flagrant and high-handed to warrant an award of punitive damages.

There must be a disincentive to suppliers in respect of intentionally deceptive trade practices. If no punitive damages are awarded for intentional violations of the legislation, suppliers will continue to conduct their businesses in a manner that involves deceptive trade practices because they will have nothing to lose. In this case I believe that the appropriate amount of punitive damages is the extra profit Richport Ford endeavoured to make as a result of its deceptive acts. I therefore award punitive damages against Richport Ford in the amount of $6,000.

Salvador v. Setay Motors/Queenstown Chev-Olds (Hamilton Small Claims Court; Case No. 1621/95): Robert Salvador was awarded $2,000 plus costs from Queenstown Leasing. The court found that the company should have tried harder to sell the leased vehicle, and at a higher price, when the "open lease" expired.

Incidentally, about 3,700 dealers in 39 American states paid between $3,500 and $8,000 each in 2004 to settle an investigation of allegations that they and Ford Motor Credit Co. overcharged customers who terminated their leases early.

See also:

- *Barber v. Inland Truck Sales* (11 D.L.R. (3rd), No. 469)
- *Canadian-Dominion Leasing v. Suburban Super Drug Ltd. (1966)* (56 D.L.R. (2nd), No. 43)
- *Neilson v. Atlantic Rentals Ltd. (1974)* (8 N.B.R. (2nd), No. 594)
- *Volvo Canada v. Fox* (December 13, 1979; New Brunswick Court of Queen's Bench; No. 1698/77/C; Judge Stevenson)
- *Western Tractor v. Dyck* (7 D.L.R. (3rd), No. 535)

Return of security deposit

Dealers routinely keep much of their lease customers' security deposits when their leases expire. However, that action can always be challenged in court. In the following claim, settled out of court, Ontario lawyer Harvey Goldstein forced GMAC and a GM dealer to refund his $525 security deposit:

1. The Plaintiff Claims:
   (A) Return of his security deposit of $525.00; and a finding that no amount is owing to the Defendants;
   (B) Alternatively, damages in the above amount;
   (C) Prejudgment interest on $525.00 at the rate of 2% per month (24% per annum) from June 22, 2005, to the date of this Claim, and thereafter on the date of payment or Judgment at the rate of 4% per annum, pursuant to Section 128 of the *Courts of Justice Act*, R.S.O. (1990) as amended;
   (D) Post-judgment interest at the post-judgment rate of interest, pursuant to Section 129 of the *Courts of Justice Act*, R. S. O. (1990) as amended;

(E) His costs of this action;

(F) Punitive damages in an amount to be determined; and

(G) Such further and other relief as this Honorable Court deems just and proper.

•

4. On or about June 10, 2005, the Plaintiff advised the Defendant North York Chevrolet Oldsmobile Ltd. that he wanted it to inspect the said vehicle for chargeable damage prior to its return or that he be present when it was inspected after its return to the said Defendant.

5. The said Defendant advised that it had no control over the inspection process and that the Defendant GMAC Leaseco Limited would inspect the vehicle only after the lease expired, the vehicle was returned to the dealer and the Plaintiff was not present.

6. The Plaintiff sent an email on June 10, 2005 to the Defendant GMAC Leaseco Limited asking it for an inspection prior to the vehicle being returned.

7. The said Defendant did not respond to the request.

8. The Plaintiff called and spoke with a representative of the said Defendant on June 17, and wrote her a letter sent by fax the same day, again asking that an inspection be scheduled in his presence. The said Defendant did not respond to the letter.

9. On June 23, 2005, the Plaintiff again called the said Defendant. He was told that it had no record of the vehicle being returned to the dealership.

10. Shortly thereafter, the Plaintiff called the Defendant North York Chevrolet Oldsmobile Ltd. to enquire as to the status of his security deposit. The said Defendant advised that it had no record of the vehicle being returned to it.

11. Not having heard from either Defendant, the Plaintiff called the Defendant GMAC Leaseco Limited on July 15, 2005. He was advised that he owed the said Defendant $550.00, less the amount of the security deposit held by it. He was further advised that details of its claim to that amount could be found on the said Defendant's website. He was told that it did not inspect the said vehicle until July 7, 2005, 15 days after it was left in the dealership's service bay. He was told that the vehicle was at an auction and that he could not inspect the alleged damages for which the Defendants claimed compensation. He was advised that no adjustment would be made to their claim even though the vehicle was returned with 20,000.00 kilometers less than allowed by the lease agreement. Further, he was told that the alleged damages to the vehicle were not repaired prior to sending it to auction.

12. The Plaintiff denies that the vehicle required repairs claimed by the Defendants and puts them to the strict proof thereof.

13. The Plaintiff further claims that the process by which the Defendants seek to claim compensation from him is unfair, open to abuse and contrary to the principles of natural justice. The Defendants pay the fee of the alleged independent inspectors and deny the Plaintiff the opportunity to dispute the charges in any meaningful fashion. Further, its delay in inspecting the vehicle for 15 days, leaves open the question of when, if ever, the damages occurred.

Repairs: Faulty Diagnosis

Davies v. Alberta Motor Association (August 13, 1991; Alberta Provincial Court, Civil Division; No. P9090106097; Judge Moore): The plaintiff had a used 1985 Nissan Pulsar NX checked out by the AMA's Vehicle Inspection Service prior to buying it. The car passed with flying colours. A month later, the clutch was replaced, and then numerous electrical problems ensued. At that time, another garage discovered that the car had been involved in a major accident, had a bent frame and a leaking radiator, and was unsafe to drive. The court awarded the plaintiff $1,578.40 plus three years of interest. The judge held that the AMA set itself out as an expert and should have spotted the car's defects. The AMA's defence—that it was not responsible for errors—was thrown out. The court held that a disclaimer clause could not protect the association from a fundamental breach of contract.

False Advertising: Vehicle Not as Ordered

When you're buying a new vehicle, the seller can't misrepresent the vehicle through a lie or a failure to disclose important information. Anything that varies from what one would commonly expect or from the seller's representation must be disclosed prior to signing the contract. Typical scenarios are odometer turnbacks, accident damage, used or leased cars sold as new, new vehicles that are the wrong colour or the wrong model year, or vehicles that lack promised options or standard features.

Goldie v. Golden Ears Motors (1980) Ltd. (Port Coquitlam; June 27, 2000; British Columbia Small Claims Court; Case No. CO8287; Justice Warren): In a well-written eight-page judgment, the court awarded plaintiff Goldie $5,000 for engine repairs on a 1990 Ford F-150 pickup in addition to $236 court costs. The dealer was found to have misrepresented the mileage and sold a used vehicle that didn't meet Section 8.01 of the provincial motor vehicle regulations (unsafe tires, defective exhaust and headlights).

In rejecting the seller's defence that he disclosed all information "to the best of his knowledge and belief," as stipulated in the sales contract, Justice Warren stated the following:

> The words "to the best of your knowledge and belief" do not allow someone to be willfully blind to defects or to provide incorrect information. I find as a fact that the business made no effort to fulfill its duty to comply with the requirements of this form. The defendant has been reckless in its actions. More likely, it has actively deceived the claimant into entering into this contract. I find the conduct of the defendant has been reprehensible throughout the dealings with the claimant.

This judgment closes a loophole that sellers have used to justify their misrepresentation, and it allows for the cancellation of the sale and damages if the vehicle doesn't meet highway safety regulations.

Lister v. Scheilding (c.o.b. Kar-Lon Motors) [1983] (O.J. No. 907 (Co. Ct.)): Here, the plaintiff was entitled to rescind the contract because of the defendant's false representation. The defendant failed to state that the motor had been changed and was not the original motor.

MacDonald v. Equilease Co. Ltd. (January 18, 1979; Ontario Supreme Court; Judge O'Driscoll): The plaintiff leased a truck that was misrepresented as having an axle stronger than it really was. The court awarded the plaintiff damages for repairs and set aside the lease.

Seich v. Festival Ford Sales Ltd. (1978) (6 Alta. L.R. (2nd), No. 262): The plaintiff bought a used truck from the defendant after being assured that it had a new motor and transmission. It didn't, and the court awarded the plaintiff $6,400.

Bilodeau v. Sud Auto (Quebec Court of Appeal; No. 09-000751-73; Judge Tremblay): This appeals court cancelled the contract and held that a car can't be sold as new or as a demonstrator if it has ever been rented, leased, sold, or titled to anyone other than the dealer.

Chenel v. Bel Automobile (1981) Inc. (August 27, 1976; Quebec Superior Court (Quebec); Judge Desmeules): The plaintiff didn't receive Jacob brakes, essential to transporting sand in hilly regions, with his new Ford truck. The court awarded the plaintiff $27,000, representing the purchase price of the vehicle less the money he earned while using the truck.

Lasky v. Royal City Chrysler Plymouth (February 18, 1987; Ontario High Court of Justice; 59 O.R. (2nd), No. 323): The plaintiff bought a 4-cylinder 1983 Dodge 600 that had been represented by the salesman as being a 6-cylinder model. After putting 40,000 km on the vehicle over a 22-month period, the buyer was given her money back, without interest, under the provincial *Business Practices Act*.

Rourke v. Gilmore (January 16, 1928; Ontario Weekly Notes, Vol. XXXIII, p. 292): Before discovering that his new car was really used, the plaintiff drove it for over a year. For this reason, the contract couldn't be cancelled. However, the appeals court instead awarded damages for $500, which was quite a sum in 1928!

Fuel Economy Lies

Canadian courts are cracking down on lying dealers and deceptive sales practices, and the misrepresentation of fuel economy figures is squarely in the judiciary's sights. Ontario's *Consumer Protection Act, 2002* (*www.e-laws.gov.on.ca/html/statutes/english/elaws_statutes_02c30_e.htm*), for example, lets a vehicle buyer cancel a contract within one year of entering into an agreement if the dealer made a false, misleading, deceptive, or unconscionable representation. This includes using exaggeration, innuendo, or ambiguity as to a material fact or failing to state a material fact if such use or failure deceives or tends to deceive consumers.

This law means that new- or used-car dealers cannot make the excuse that they were fooled about the condition or performance of a vehicle, or that they were simply providing data supplied by the manufacturer. The law clearly states that both parties are jointly liable and that dealers are *presumed* to know the history, quality, and true performance of what they are selling.

Details like fuel economy can lead to a contract's cancellation if the dealer gives a higher-than-actual figure. In *Sidney v. 1011067 Ontario Inc. (c.o.b. Southside Motors)*, a precedent-setting case that was filed before Ontario's *Consumer Protection Act* was toughened in 2002, the buyer was awarded $11,424.51 plus prejudgment interest because of a false representation made by the defendant regarding fuel efficiency. The plaintiff claimed that the defendant advised him that the vehicle had a fuel efficiency of 800–900 km per tank of fuel when, in fact, the maximum efficiency was only 500 km per tank.

This consumer victory is particularly important as everyone from automakers to sellers of ineffective gas-saving gadgets make outlandishly false fuel economy claims. Not surprisingly, sellers try to use the expressed warranty to reject claims, while smart plaintiffs ignore the expressed warranty and argue for a refund under the implied warranty instead.

Secret Warranty Claims

It's common practice for manufacturers to secretly extend their warranties to cover components with a high failure rate. Customers who complain vigorously get extended warranty compensation in the form of "goodwill" adjustments.

François Chong v. Marine Drive Imported Cars Ltd. and Honda Canada Inc. (May 17, 1994; British Columbia Provincial Small Claims Court; No. 92-06760; Judge C.L. Bagnall): Mr. Chong was the first owner of a 1983 Honda Accord with 134,000 km on the odometer. He had six engine camshafts replaced—four under Honda "goodwill" programs, one where he paid part of the repairs, and one via a small claims court judgment.

In his ruling, Judge Bagnall agreed with Chong and ordered Honda and the dealer to each pay half of the $835.81 repair bill for the following reasons:

> The defendants assert that the warranty which was part of the contract for purchase of the car encompassed the entirety of their obligation to the claimant, and that it expired in February 1985. The replacements of the camshaft after that date were paid for wholly or in part by Honda as a "goodwill gesture." The time has come for these gestures to cease, according to the witness for Honda. As well, he pointed out to me that the most recent replacement of the camshaft was paid for by Honda and that, therefore, the work would not be covered by Honda's usual warranty of 12 months from date of repair. Mr. Wall, who testified for Honda, told me there was no question that this situation with Mr. Chong's engine was an unusual state of affairs. He said

that a camshaft properly maintained can last anywhere from 24,000 to 500,000 km. He could not offer any suggestion as to why the car keeps having this problem.

The claimant has convinced me that the problems he is having with rapid breakdown of camshafts in his car [are] due to a defect, which was present in the engine at the time that he purchased the car. The problem first arose during the warranty period and in my view has never been properly identified nor repaired.

I love the case highlighted above. Where most plaintiffs have to fight tooth and nail to get secret warranty refunds through the courts, Mr. Chong bit into Honda's rear end and hung on like a crazed Chihuahua until he was compensated each of the five times his Accord engine failed.

Honda's engine problems resurfaced with its 2006–09 Civic 1.8L cracked engine blocks, but this time Honda has the good sense to give free engine blocks to all owners without anyone having to resort to the courts (p. 94).

Thank you, Mr. Chong.

Punitive Damages

Punitive damages (also known as "exemplary damages") allow the plaintiff to get compensation that exceeds his or her losses as a deterrent to those who carry out dishonest or negligent practices. These kinds of judgments, common in the U.S., sometimes reach hundreds of millions of dollars. Canadian courts, however, seldom award substantial punitive damages.

"The insurance company from hell"

Nevertheless, there have been a few cases where the Supreme Court of Canada has shocked the business establishment by levying huge exemplary damage awards. One such case was the *Whiten v. Pilot Insurance Co.* decision rendered in 2002. In this case, the plaintiff's home caught fire and burned to the ground, destroying all of the home's contents and killing three pet cats. Pilot Insurance made a single $5,000 payment for living expenses and covered the family's rent for a couple of months, and then cut off the rent payments without forewarning the family. The insurance claim went to trial, based on the respondent's allegation that the family had torched their own home, even though the local fire chief, the respondent's own expert investigator, and its initial expert all said there was no evidence whatsoever of arson. The original trial jury awarded the plaintiff compensatory damages and $1 million in punitive damages. Pilot Insurance fought this decision at the Court of Appeal, where the punitive damages award was reduced to $100,000. The case was then taken all the way to the Supreme Court, where the trial jury's unprecedented award of $1 million was restored:

The jury's award of punitive damages, though high, was within rational limits. The respondent insurer's conduct towards the appellant was exceptionally reprehensible.

It forced her to put at risk her only remaining asset (the $345,000 insurance claim) plus $320,000 in costs that she did not have. The denial of the claim was designed to force her to make an unfair settlement for less than she was entitled to. The conduct was planned and deliberate and continued for over two years, while the financial situation of the appellant grew increasingly desperate. The jury evidently believed that the respondent knew from the outset that its arson defence was contrived and unsustainable. Insurance contracts are sold by the insurance industry and purchased by members of the public for peace of mind. The more devastating the loss, the more the insured may be at the financial mercy of the insurer, and the more difficult it may be to challenge a wrongful refusal to pay the claim.

Chrysler truck fire

Punitive damages are rarely awarded in Canadian courts against automakers. When they are given out, it's usually for sums less than $100,000. In *Prebushewski v. Dodge City Auto (1985) Ltd. and Chrysler Canada Ltd.*, the plaintiff got $25,000 in a judgment handed down in 2001 and confirmed by the Supreme Court in 2005. The plaintiff's 1996 Ram's running lights had shorted and caused her truck to burn to the ground, and Chrysler had refused her claim. The court basically said that aggrieved car owners may sue for much more than the depreciated value of what they bought under provincial consumer protection statutes. The Supreme Court reaffirmed the power of the lower courts to assess an additional financial penalty to punish automakers that treat their customers unfairly and ensure they don't repeat the offence.

Honda cycle

Vlchek v. Koshel (1988; 44 C.C.L.T. 314, B.C.S.C., No. B842974): The plaintiff was seriously injured when she was thrown from a Honda all-terrain cycle on which she had been riding as a passenger. The court allowed for punitive damages because the manufacturer was well aware of the injuries likely to be caused by the cycle. Specifically, the court ruled that there is no firm and inflexible principle of law stipulating that punitive or exemplary damages must be denied unless the defendant's acts are specifically directed against the plaintiff. The court may apply punitive damages "where the defendant's conduct has been indiscriminate of focus, but reckless or malicious in its character. Intent to injure the plaintiff need not be present, so long as intent to do the injurious act can be shown."

See also:

- *Granek v. Reiter* (Ontario Court, General Division; No. 35/741)
- *Morrison v. Sharp* (Ontario Court, General Division; No. 43/548)
- *Schryvers v. Richport Ford Sales* (May 18, 1993; B.C.S.C., No. C917060; Judge Tysoe)
- *Varleg v. Angeloni* (B.C.S.C., No. 41/301)

Provincial business practices acts cover false, misleading, or deceptive representations and allow for punitive damages should the unfair practice toward the consumer amount to an unconscionable representation (see *Canadian Encyclopedic Digest* (C.E.D.), Third Edition, s. 76, pages 140–145). Here are some specific cases to keep in mind:

- Exemplary damages are justified where compensatory damages are insufficient to deter and punish. See *Walker et al. v. CFTO Ltd. et al.* (1978; 59 O.R. (2nd), No. 104; Ontario C.A.).
- Exemplary damages can be awarded in cases where the defendant's conduct was "cavalier." See *Ronald Elwyn Lister Ltd. et al. v. Dayton Tire Canada Ltd.* (1985; 52 O.R. (2nd), No. 89; Ontario C.A.).
- The primary purpose of exemplary damages is to prevent the defendant and all others from doing similar wrongs. See *Fleming v. Spracklin* (1921).
- Disregard of the public's interest, lack of preventive measures, and a callous attitude all merit exemplary damages. See *Coughlin v. Kuntz* (1989; 2 C.C.L.T. (2nd); B.C.C.A.).
- Punitive damages can be awarded for mental distress. See *Ribeiro v. Canadian Imperial Bank of Commerce* (1992; Ontario Reports 13 (3rd)) and *Brown v. Waterloo Regional Board of Commissioners of Police* (1992; 37 O.R. (2nd)).

Now that you know how to get the best deal for less money and what to do to get your money back, let's take a look in Part Three to see which cars and trucks to pick and which ones to run from.

REVIEWS AND RATINGS

When we compared their gas mileage with that of the standard versions, we found that the Cruz Eco saves you only $20 a year; the Focus SFE and Civic HF save you $145 and $135, respectively. So you'd need to own them between three and 38 years, depending on the model, for the fuel savings to offset the higher price.

CONSUMER REPORTS
JULY 2012

All automakers build bad cars and trucks—some more often than others. The trick is to know which models and years have the most problems. Like wine, vintage is important.

For example, four decades ago most Japanese small cars were underpowered rustbuckets; British cars were electrical system nightmares (joke: "Lucas is the Prince of Darkness and inadvertently invented the intermittent windshield washer"); the Italians used fuel systems that seldom held their "tune" and came packaged in biodegradable bodies; and the Germans made bizarre-behaving, hard-to-diagnose, parts-challenged models that included VW's self-starting, fire-prone Rabbits (garage owner and Toronto 740AM radio broadcaster Alan Gelman knows the stories—he had to jury-rig VW "fix-it" kits so rainwater wouldn't run down the antenna mount and into the wiring, closing the circuit and starting the car).

Since then, some automakers, like Acura, Honda, Hyundai, Mazda, Nissan, Subaru, Suzuki, and Toyota, have gotten much better at building reliable, fuel-efficient vehicles. Others, like Audi, BMW, Cadillac, Chrysler, Jaguar, Jeep, Mini, and Saab (now bankrupt), have gotten worse. Ford, Kia, Mercedes, Mitsubishi, Nissan, Toyota, Volkswagon, and Volvo quality control has improved or declined, depending upon the model.

Most surprising of all, during the 2009 model year when the U.S. recession began to pummel auto sales, Detroit automakers' quality improved. In February 2012, J.D. Power and Associates released the following statement:

> Strong initial quality of 2009 model-year vehicles—which were produced during one of the toughest years for the automotive industry—has translated into historically high levels of vehicle dependability in 2012, according to the J.D. Power and Associates 2012 U.S. Vehicle Dependability Study....

> The study measures problems experienced during the past 12 months by original owners of three-year-old (2009 model-year) vehicles. Overall dependability is determined by the level of problems experienced per 100 vehicles (PP100), with a lower score reflecting higher quality.

> In 2012, overall vehicle dependability averages 132 PP100—an improvement of 13 percent from the 2011 average of 151—which is the lowest problem rate since the inception of the study in 1990. The strong dependability of these models reflects their high levels of initial quality when measured three years ago. According to the J.D. Power and Associates 2009 Initial Quality Study, overall initial quality of 2009 model-year vehicles was, at the time, the highest level of initial quality since the inaugural IQS in 1987.

> Fully 25 of 32 brands have improved in dependability from 2011, while only six have declined and one has remained stable. Domestic nameplates have improved in 2012 at a slightly faster rate than imports, narrowing the dependability gap to 13 PP100 from 18 PP100 in 2011....

> However, there are several brands that have performed very well in dependability during the past several years but still face challenges with customer perceptions of their reliability. In particular, during the past four years models from Buick, Cadillac, Ford, Hyundai, and Lincoln have achieved consistently strong levels of dependability but still have relatively high proportions of new-vehicle buyers expressing reliability concerns. Lexus ranks highest in vehicle dependability among all nameplates in 2012. In addition, the Lexus LS has the fewest problems in the industry, with just 72 PP100. Rounding out the five highest-ranking nameplates are Porsche, Cadillac, Toyota, and Scion, respectively. Mini and Scion posted the greatest year-over-year improvements from 2011—by 60 PP100 and 55 PP100, respectively.

> Toyota continues to perform well in long-term dependability and garners eight segment awards—more than any other automaker in 2012—for the Lexus ES 350 (in a tie with the Lincoln MKZ); Lexus RX 350; Scion tC; Scion xB; Toyota Prius; Toyota Sienna; Toyota Tundra; and Toyota Yaris.

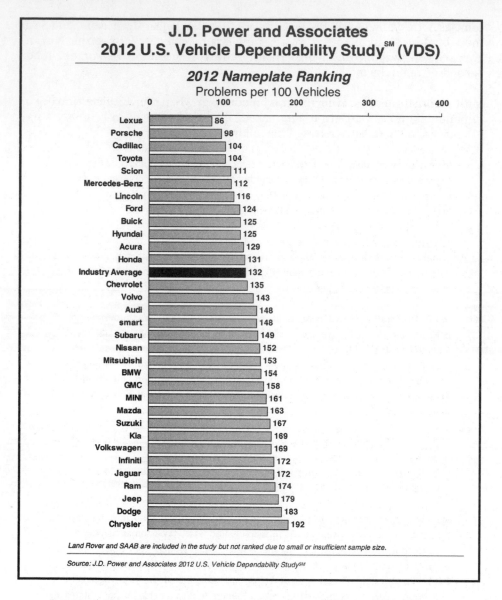

J.D. Power and Associates
2012 U.S. Vehicle Dependability Study[SM] (VDS)

2012 Nameplate Ranking
Problems per 100 Vehicles

Lexus	86
Porsche	98
Cadillac	104
Toyota	104
Scion	111
Mercedes-Benz	112
Lincoln	116
Ford	124
Buick	125
Hyundai	125
Acura	129
Honda	131
Industry Average	132
Chevrolet	135
Volvo	143
Audi	148
smart	148
Subaru	149
Nissan	152
Mitsubishi	153
BMW	154
GMC	158
MINI	161
Mazda	163
Suzuki	167
Kia	169
Volkswagen	169
Infiniti	172
Jaguar	172
Ram	174
Jeep	179
Dodge	183
Chrysler	192

Land Rover and SAAB are included in the study but not ranked due to small or insufficient sample size.

Source: J.D. Power and Associates 2012 U.S. Vehicle Dependability Study[SM]

Ford Motor Company receives three model awards for the Ford Explorer (in a tie with the Nissan Murano); Ford Fusion; and Lincoln MKZ (in a tie). General Motors (Buick Lucerne and Chevrolet Equinox) and Nissan Motor Co., Ltd. (Nissan Frontier and Nissan Murano, in a tie with the Ford Explorer) each receive two awards. In addition, the Hyundai Genesis also receives an award. Although there are no awards in their respective segments due to an insufficient number of award-eligible models, or insufficient market share of award-eligible models in the segment, these models also perform particularly well: Ford Mustang, GMC Yukon, and Porsche 911.

Neither *Lemon-Aid* nor *Consumer Reports* agree with all of J.D. Power's choices, particularly because *CR*'s database comprises 1.3 million subscriber/respondents and *Lemon-Aid*'s data is reinforced by the automakers' own confidential service bulletins.

J.D. Power and Associates offers the following tips for consumers regarding vehicle dependability:

- Consumer perceptions of vehicle quality and dependability are often based on historical experiences or anecdotes and may be out of line with the current reality. Consumers should gather as much information as they can on the latest models from a variety of sources to make an informed decision.
- Historically, initial quality has been a good indicator of likely long-term dependability. If a model has high levels of quality when new, it is more likely to be dependable over the long term.
- Vehicle dependability is at an all-time high, and resale values are also very high by historical standards. If your vehicle has been properly maintained and is in good working condition, it may be worth more than you think if you are considering trading it in.

"Hot" Cars: One Chance in 100

Car buyers have a new menace to consider: Radiation.

In the three months following the March 11, 2011, meltdown of four nuclear power plants at the Fukushima-Daiichi facility situated on Japan's east coast, four shipping ports (one in Chile; three in Russia) have quarantined or sent back 84 radiation-contaminated new and used vehicles. The Japan Automobile Manufacturers Association says it has begun radiation testing on all vehicle shipments for the domestic and export markets.

Radiation-contaminated cars are still getting through. In fact, The Associated Press estimates that about 1 percent of new Japanese cars shipped into South America are radioactive. Radiation levels outside the Japanese reactors are eight times the normal level. This is the minimal amount of radiation some cars could be trailing back to the States. Although this is not considered a public health danger, if some cars were exposed to iodine-131, this could trigger thyroid cancer.

No one wants to buy a car, truck, or SUV that has a 1 percent chance of emitting residual radiation. Yet, there's little that can be done, except for scanning every vehicle imported into our country. Even that isn't enough, though. There are many auto suppliers on Fukushima's doorstep that distribute parts for automakers around the world, including the Detroit Three.

Those parts will probably be radioactive.

"YESSIR, THE CAR IS HOT AND IT GLOWS IN THE DARK."

What Makes a Good Car Good?

It would help if it doesn't glow in the dark. But seriously, any new vehicle should live up to the promises made by the manufacturer and dealer. It must be reasonably priced, provide safe highway performance, protect occupants in a crash, be fuel-efficient, and be capable of lasting 15 years without a series of major repairs; it should cost no more than about $800 a year to maintain; and it should provide you with a fair resale value a few years down the road. Parts should be affordable and easily available, and competent servicing shouldn't be hard to find.

And don't believe for one moment that the more you spend, the better the vehicle. For example, most Hondas are as good as more-expensive Acuras. The same is true of Toyota and Lexus. Even more surprising is that some luxury makes offer you merely a dressed-up entry model with a luxury-car price. The extra money buys you more features of dubious value and newer, unproven technology, like rear-mounted video cameras, failure-prone electronic gadgetry, and tire pressure monitors that frequently fail, or cost you an arm and a leg to reset each year.

J. D. Power and Associates has noted in both its 2011 and 2012 dependability studies that high-tech improvements increase the chance something will go wrong. Said David Sargent, vice president of global vehicle research at J.D. Power and Associates, after he singled out Ford's poorly designed computer/driver interaction deficiencies as one reason for owner discontent:

> Automakers, as a whole, have made significant improvements in reducing traditional problems, particularly with vehicle interiors; engines and transmissions; and steering

and braking during the past several years. However, as manufacturers add new features and technologies to satisfy customer demand and new legislation, they face the potential for introducing new problems.

In terms of road performance, at the very minimum, every vehicle must be able to merge safely onto a highway and have adequate passing power for two-lane roads. Steering feel and handling should inspire confidence. The suspension ought to provide a reasonably well-controlled ride on most road surfaces. Ideally, the passenger compartment will be roomy enough to accommodate passengers comfortably on extended trips. The noise level should not become tiresome or annoying. As a rule, handling and ride comfort are inversely proportional—good handling requires a stiff suspension, which pounds the kidneys, while a softer suspension that cushions those kidneys leaves you lacking in the handling department.

Five Steps to Honest, Accurate Ratings

Lemon-Aid follows these five simple rules when rating new vehicles:

1. We believe the best rating approach is to combine a driving test with an owners' survey of past models (only *Consumer Reports* and *Lemon-Aid* do this).
2. Owner responses must come from a large owner pool (over a million responses from *CR* subscribers, for example). Anecdotal responses should then be cross-referenced, updated, and given depth and specificity through NHTSA's safety complaint prism. Responses must again be cross-referenced through automaker internal service bulletins to determine the extent of a defect over a specific model and model-year range and to alert owners to problems that are likely to occur.
3. Rankings should be predicated upon important characteristics measured over a significant period of time, unlike "Car of the Year" contests or polls of owners who have just bought their car.
4. Data must come from unimpeachable sources like *Consumer Reports*, *Which?*, Alldata, and NHTSA (crash and safety reports). There should be no conflicts of interest, such as advertising, consultant ties, or self serving tests done under ideal conditions for an extra fee.
5. Tested cars must be bought or rented, and serviced—not borrowed from the car company and pampered as part of a journalists' fleet lent out for ranking purposes.

Responsible auto critics shouldn't hit up dealers or manufacturers for free test vehicles under any circumstances, but most auto columnists and some consumer groups compromise their integrity by doing so. Test vehicles should be rented or borrowed from an owner.

I've adopted this practice from my early experience as a consumer reporter. Nissan asked me to test drive its new 1974 240Z—no strings attached. I took the car for a week, had it examined by an independent garage, spoke with satisfied and dissatisfied owners, and accessed internal service bulletins and government-logged owner safety complaints. The car's poor brake design apparently made it unsafe to drive, and I said so in my report. Nissan sued me for $2 million, fixed the brakes through a "product improvement campaign," and then dropped the lawsuit two years later. I was never offered another car.

Definitions of Terms

ALERT! This caution is used to indicate important facts related to cost, safety, or performance to consider while in the showroom or the service bay.

Key Facts

This year, we rate many more cars, trucks, and SUVs than ever before, and include previews of some 2013 and 2014 models for readers planning to buy a new vehicle in mid-2013. We also include "miles per gallon" (mpg) in addition to our usual "litres per 100 kilometres" (L/km) in deference to our metric-challenged readers. American prices are given as benchmarks for haggling successfully with Canadian dealers or when negotiating cross-border deals.

Prices: We list the manufacturer's suggested retail price (MSRP) range, in effect at press time and applicable to standard models. That price will likely fluctuate considerably during the year as customer rebates and manufacturer-to-dealer sales incentives kick in, particularly in the new year. Check the latest MSRP figure periodically on both sides of the border by accessing each manufacturer's Canadian and American websites (like *www.honda.com* and *www.honda.ca*). Vehicles that aren't selling well usually carry the heftiest discounts and/or rebates; check the "Cost Analysis" section for a vehicle's predicted price negotiability.

Destination charges and the pre-delivery inspection (PDI) fee, which may reach $2,000, are quasi-fraudulent "back doors" into your wallet. Offer half of the indicated figure. Also, don't fall for the $99–$1,100 "administration fee" scam, unless the bottom-line price is so tempting that it won't make much difference. Sticking to your principles is one thing; losing an attractive deal is another.

Tow limit: Note that towing capacities differ depending on the kind of powertrain/suspension package or towing package you buy. And remember that there's a difference between how a vehicle is rated for cargo capacity or payload and how heavy a boat or trailer it can pull. Do not purchase any new vehicle without receiving very clear information from the dealer about a vehicle's towing capacity and the kind of special equipment you'll need to meet your requirements. Better yet, go across town and ask the manufacturer/retailer or local garage which model and year vehicle would best meet your requirements. (Say, "What are most people buying to pull this thing?") Confirm that information on the Internet. Whichever model is chosen, make sure to have the towing capacity and included equipment written into the dealer sales contract.

Load capacity: This is defined as the safe combined weight of occupants and cargo (such as luggage). It is taken from the manufacturer's rating or from *Consumer Reports*' calculated safe load. Exceeding this maximum weight can adversely affect a vehicle's handling.

Ratings

We rate vehicles on a scale of one to five stars, with five stars as our top ranking. We use owner complaints, confidential technical service bulletins (TSBs), and test drives to ferret out serious factory-related defects, design deficiencies, and servicing glitches.

This guide emphasizes important new features that add to a vehicle's safety, reliability, road performance, and comfort, and points out those changes that are merely gadgets and styling revisions. Also noted are important improvements to be made in the future, or the dropping of a model line. In addition to its overall rating, each vehicle's strong and weak points are summarized.

Interestingly, some vehicles that are identical but marketed and serviced by different automakers may have different ratings. This variation occurs because servicing and after-warranty assistance may be better within one dealer network than another.

It takes about six months to acquire enough information for a fair-minded evaluation of a car's or truck's first year on the market, unless the vehicle has been available elsewhere under another name. Most new cars and trucks hit the market before all of the bugs have been worked out, so it would be irresponsible to recommend them before owner reports and internal service bulletins give them an "okay." Sadly, as we have seen with Toyota's sudden, unintended acceleration problems and Chrysler's poorly shifting transmissions, it may take several years to correct some factory powertrain glitches.

Recommended: This rating indicates a "Best Buy," and it applies to many Asian models. Recommended vehicles usually combine a high level of crashworthiness with good road performance, few safety-related complaints, decent reliability, and a better-than-average resale value. Servicing is readily available, and parts are inexpensive and easy to find.

Above Average: Vehicles in this class are pretty good choices. They aren't perfect, but they're often more reasonably priced than their competition. Most vehicles in this category have quality construction, good durability, and plenty of safety features as standard equipment. On the downside, they may have expensive parts and servicing, too many safety-related complaints, or only satisfactory warranty performance—one or all of which may have disqualified them from the Recommended category.

Average: Some deficiencies or flaws make these good second choices. In many cases, certain components are prone to premature wear or breakdown or don't perform as well as the competition. An Average rating can also be attributed to such factors as substandard assembly quality, lack of a solid long-term reliability record, a substantial number of safety-related complaints, or a deficient parts and service network.

Below Average: This rating category denotes an unreliable or poorly performing vehicle that may also have a poor safety record. Getting an extended warranty is advised.

Not Recommended: Chances of having major breakdowns or safety-related failures are omnipresent. Inadequate road performance and poor dealer service, among other factors, can make owning one of these vehicles a traumatic and expensive experience, no matter how cheaply it's sold.

Vehicles that have not been on the road long enough to assess, or that are sold in such small numbers that owner feedback is insufficient, are either given a Not Recommended rating or left unrated.

Road performance

This is principally about power to merge and handling that's sufficient to avoid accidents.

Quality and reliability

Lemon-Aid bases its quality and reliability evaluations in the "Rating" and "Overview" sections on owner comments, confidential manufacturer service bulletins, and government reports from NHTSA safety complaint files. We also draw on the knowledge and expertise of professionals working in the automotive marketplace, including mechanics and fleet owners. The aim is to have a wide range of unbiased (and irrefutable) data on quality, reliability, durability, and ownership costs. Allowances are made for the number of vehicles sold versus the number of complaints, as well as for the seriousness of problems reported and the average number of problems reported by each owner.

Technical Service Bulletins (TSBs) give the most probable cause of factory-related defects on previous model years that will likely be carried over to the 2013 versions. TSBs are reliable sources of information because manufacturers depend on the dealer corrections outlined in their bulletins until a permanent, cost-effective engineering solution is found at the factory, which often takes several model years and lots of experimentation.

As you read through the ratings and manufacturers' confidential service bulletins, you'll quickly discover that most Japanese and South Korean manufacturers are far ahead of Chrysler and GM in terms of maintaining a high level of quality control in their vehicles. European makes are even worse performers, especially with VW/Audi's failure-prone DGS 6-speed transmissions.

Safety

Some of the main features weighed are a model's crashworthiness score, the availability of front and side airbags, assisted stability and traction control, rollover resistance, head-restraint effectiveness, and front and rearward visibility.

Frontal and side crash protection figures are taken from the National Highway Traffic Safety Administration's (NHTSA) New Car Assessment Program. For the front crash test, vehicles are crashed into a fixed barrier, head-on, at 57 km/h (35 mph). NHTSA uses star rankings to show the likelihood, expressed as a percentage, of belted occupants being seriously injured. The more stars, the greater the protection.

NHTSA's side crash test represents an intersection-type collision with a 1,368 kg (3,015 lb.) barrier moving at 62 km/h (38.5 mph) into a standing vehicle. The moving barrier is covered with material that has "give" to replicate the front of a car.

A vehicle's rollover resistance rating is an estimate of its risk of rolling over in a single-vehicle crash, not a prediction of the likelihood of a crash. The lowest-rated vehicles (one star) are at least four times more likely to roll over than the highest-rated vehicles (five stars) when involved in a single-vehicle crash.

In 2009, NHTSA upgraded the government safety standard governing roof crush resistance, a major factor in rollover accidents. The new rule requires that vehicles weighing 6,000 lb. or less must be able to withstand a force equal to three times their weight applied alternately to the left and right sides of the roof. However, vehicles weighing between 6,000 lb. and 10,000 lb. need only withstand 1.5 times their own weight on the roof.

The Insurance Institute for Highway Safety (IIHS) rates head-restraint and frontal, offset, roof, and side crash protection as "Good," "Acceptable," "Marginal," or "Poor." In the Institute's 64 km/h (40 mph) offset test, 40 percent of the total width of each vehicle strikes a barrier on the driver's side. The barrier's deformable face is made of an aluminum honeycomb, which makes the forces in the test similar to those involved in a frontal offset crash between two vehicles of the same weight, each going just less than 64 km/h.

Though IIHS's 50 km/h (31 mph) side-impact test is carried out at a slower speed than NHTSA's side test, the barrier uses a front end shaped to simulate the typical front end of a pickup or SUV. The Institute also includes the degree of head injury in its ratings.

"KILLER" LUXURY CARS: IIHS has retooled its front-end collision safety tests to demonstrate the need for more safety features even on some luxury cars that have excelled at meeting existing crashworthiness standards. The institute modified its tests to address what they say is happening in about a quarter of these head-on collisions involving the front corner. When only a corner of the car slammed into a structure, researchers found there was greater risk of serious injury to occupants because that part of the car offers the least crash protection.

Small overlap crashes primarily affect a car's outer edges, which aren't well protected by crush-zone structures. Crash forces go directly into the front wheel, suspension system and firewall. Sometimes, the wheel is forced rearward into the footwell, contributing to even more intrusion in the occupant compartment and resulting in serious leg and foot injuries.

In recent crash-tests of 11 luxury cars, IIHS found only the Acura TL, Volvo S60, and Infiniti G series earned a "Good" or "Acceptable" rating. The eight that failed the test include the Acura TSX, BMW 3 Series, Lincoln MKZ, and the Volkswagen CC, which were rated "Marginal." The Audi A4, Lexus ES 350, Lexus IS 250/350, and Mercedes C-Class earned "Poor" ratings. In one test, a Volkswagen CC door sheared off during the accident.

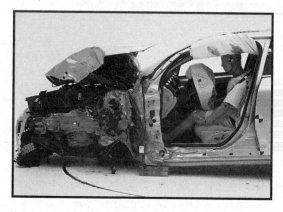

Volkswagen 2012 CC: A four-door becomes a three-door.

IIHS found that airbags don't always provide adequate protection during these accidents, allowing drivers to hit their heads against part of the windshield frame, known as the A pillar. Side curtain airbags, in particular, may not extend far enough forward to protect someone from the A pillar.

Often, there is no airbag protection: the side airbags don't deploy at all and the steering wheel-mounted airbag shifts to the middle of the car during impact. In the Lincoln MKZ crash-test, for example, the driver's head missed all of the airbags during the collision.

IIHS plans to test other models and will post the new test results in future safety ratings.

Owner Costs and Best Alternatives

Winter prices for the 2013 models will start out much higher than last year's prices on some vehicles, such as full-sized trucks, SUVs, and vans. As long as fuel costs stay high, this trend is likely to continue. As the cost of oil dips below $85 (U.S.) a barrel, large vehicles become more in demand and carry higher prices. Small cars and hybrids, in this case, would be less popular and discounted accordingly.

Leasing deals are also expected to pick up now that the American automakers have renewed their links with major lending agencies.

In our selection of alternative buys, we consider whether a vehicle's 2012 or scheduled 2013 redesign measurably improves that vehicle's performance over the previous model. If it doesn't, we suggest you choose the earlier model or consider a different vehicle.

MSRP and PDI fees scam

If you buy a new Acura ZDX in Canada, you will pay $9,000 more than what it sells for less than an hour's drive away in the States. That's the startling conclusion reached by CBC investigators in a new report aired June 13, 2012 (*www.cbc.ca/news/canada/ottawa/story/2012/06/12/ottawa-car-price-disparity-border-shopping.html*).

CBC News looked at the relative prices of 24 models made in Ontario by Ford, GM, Chrysler, Honda, and Toyota. In 18 cases, the models cost thousands of dollars more to buy in Ontario than in the United States, including Hawaii.

Honda Canada said Canada's price was determined by a number of factors, including exchange rates, market conditions, Canadian-specific content, and the cost of doing business in two official languages.

Balderdash! Bullcrap!

There is no justification for this rip-off that has been going on for decades. Three things leap to mind:

1. We are being hosed by automakers who were recently on their knees getting millions of dollars in federal and provincial handouts after going bankrupt.
2. The freight and pre-delivery inspection (PDI) fee buyers pay in Canada (for vehicles *made in Canada*) is almost double what consumers are charged in the States.
3. Senator Pierrette Ringuette said she invited representatives from the Big Three automakers in the U.S. to appear before the Senate finance committee to explain the price disparities, but they declined.

In other words, GM, Ford, Chrysler, Honda, and Toyota are telling Canadians and Parliament (to borrow a phrase from our late prime minister Pierre Trudeau) to go "fuddle-duddle."

The only way to combat this dishonesty is for Parliament to haul these automakers before the appropriate committees for answers and for Canadians to do their shopping across the border for big-ticket vehicles.

NEW-VEHICLE PRICE DISPARITY

VEHICLE	CANADA MSRP (CDN)	U.S. MSRP (U.S.)	MANUFACTURED IN
Acura ZDX	$54,990	$46,120	Alliston, ON
Acura MDX	$52,690	$43,030	Alliston, ON
Chrysler Town & Country	$31,645	$29,995	Windsor, ON
Dodge Grand Caravan	$19,995	$20,995	Windsor, ON
Chrysler 300	$32,995	$28,670	Brampton, ON
Dodge Charger	$29,995	$24,495	Brampton, ON
Dodge Challenger	$26,995	$24,995	Brampton, ON
Ford Edge	$27,999	$27,525	Oakville, ON
Lincoln MKX (AWD)	$47,650	$41,395	Oakville, ON
Ford Flex	$30,499	$30,885	Oakville, ON
Chevy Camaro	$27,965	$23,280	Oshawa, ON
Chevy Impala	$28,125	$25,760	Oshawa, ON
Buick Lacrosse	$34,935	$30,170	Oshawa, ON
Chevy Equinox	$26,445	$23,530	Ingersoll, ON
GMC Terrain	$28,395	$25,560	Ingersoll, ON
Cadillac XTS 2013	$48,995	$44,075	Oshawa, ON
Honda Civic sedan	$14,990	$15,995	Alliston, ON
Civic Si	$25,990	$22,555	Alliston, ON
Civic coupe	$18,240	$15,755	Alliston, ON
Toyota Corolla	$15,540	$16,130	Cambridge, ON
Lexus RX350 (AWD)	$44,950	$40,710	Cambridge, ON
Toyota Matrix	$16,795	$18,845	Cambridge, ON
Toyota Rav4	$24,865	$22,650	Woodstock, ON
Volkswagen Routan	$28,575	$27,020	Windsor, ON

1 $2,280 credit available some places
2 $2,000 credit available some places
3 Add $1,595 destination fee
4 Freight and PDI of $1,465 in Canada, $760 in U.S.
5 Freight and PDI of $1,565 in Canada, $810 in U.S.

(Sources: Manufacturers online listings and CBC Ottawa)

Owner satisfaction

We measure owners' satisfaction through their responses to almost 1.4 million questionnaires sent by *Consumer Reports* and J.D. Power and Associates, automaker internal service bulletins, and the thousands of owner safety-related complaints posted by NHTSA at *safercar.org*. We then cross-reference the data to see which complaints constantly reappear.

Dealer servicing

A large number of complaints come from drivers who find dealer servicing is far costlier than expected, less competent than it should be, and takes longer than promised. *Consumer Reports* targeted this problem in its 2012 edition and concluded that owners who prefer independent repairers drove Chrysler, Dodge,

Jaguar, Jeep, Nissan, Mercedes-Benz, and Volvo makes. Bringing up the rear was Land Rover, whose owners were least satisfied with dealer repairs among the 32 brands surveyed.

2012–13 HIGHLIGHTS

NEW MODELS	REDESIGNED	DISCONTINUED
Acura ILX	Acura RDX	Dodge Caliber
BMW X1	BMW 3 Series	Dodge Nitro
Buick Encore	Chevrolet Malibu	Ford Escape Hybrid
Cadillac ATS	Dodge Ram	Hyundai Veracruz
Cadillac XTS	Ford Escape	Jeep Compass
Chevrolet Spark	Ford Fusion	Jeep Liberty Lotus Elise
Dodge Dart	Honda Accord	Mercedes-Benz R-Class
Ford C-Max	Hyundai Azera	Mercedes-Benz SL
Infiniti JX	Lexus ES 350/Hybrid	Saab, all models
Mazda CX-5	Lexus GS	Tesla Roadster
Mitsubishi i	Lincoln MKZ	
Scion FR-S	Mercedes-Benz GL	
Subaru BRZ	Nissan Altima	
Subaru XV Crosstrek	Nissan Pathfinder	
Tesla Model S	Porsche 911	
Toyota Prius C	Viper SRT	

AMERICAN VEHICLES

Volt and Leaf Are "Unappealing"

A few recent driving impressions, including one in the well-read magazine *Consumer Reports,* have pointed to the limited range, high cost and potentially annoying traits that are likely to make the Volt and its main competitor, the Nissan Leaf, unappealing to the majority of drivers. After months of buildup and often gushing reviews, it seems now as if the automotive consumer sector is exhaling and rediscovering skepticism.

JONATHAN WELSH
THE WALL STREET JOURNAL
MARCH 6, 2011

Chevrolet Volt: Victim of the Loony Right?

The loony right has its jaws sunk into the Volt with all the stupid determination of a terrier who has locked his teeth into the mailman's butt. And with the same result: painful, but without any useful purpose. So, if this continues, will we see the Republican presidential campaign centered on the Volt, with catchy slogans like "Vote Republican! Kill the Volt before it kills you!"? The current insanity is of such magnitude that it wouldn't surprise me.

FORMER GM VICE CHAIRMAN BOB LUTZ
WWW.FORBES.COM
MARCH 12, 2012

Touchy, touchy, Bob.

Do you honestly believe *The Wall Street Journal* is loony? Take a whiff of the marketplace and you will see that the Volt—yes, your baby from conception to showroom—is a resounding flop. And the Nissan Leaf isn't far behind.

Fortunately, GM and the rest of the foreign and domestic automakers have done quite well after the 2009 shakeout of the American auto industry, which left Ford as the only clear winner—without government handouts (okay, there was former president Bush's $50 billion handout to Detroit as an incentive to build more fuel-efficient cars). All this contributed to huge Ford profits with smaller, option-laden, fuel-efficient cars generating much of the revenue.

But now the picture is much more sombre. Ford sales are falling again, simply because its million-dollar "brain trust" didn't see the resurgence of consumer demand for 2011 and 2012. Ford misjudged the market, so now its dealers are crying for product. Ironically, Honda and Toyota have a similar problem, caused by natural disasters flattening their factories and supply lines. This means Japanese models will be in scarce supply until the end of 2012. For 2013, Ford brings back a redesigned Focus, with an all-electric plug-in, and a revamped Escape and Fusion.

Chrysler/Fiat/Jeep

Chrysler Plays Catch-Up

Chrysler invented the minivan and still does very well there, and the company should do better as both Toyota and Honda, its main competitors, struggle to overcome the effects of the earthquake disaster. Other segments look, well, rougher. The sedans are stylish, but they're going up against superior cars from Chevy, Ford, and even the upstart Koreans. There's always hope in pickups, but the Ram brand is a perennial number three to Ford's F-150 and Chevy's Silverado.

MATTHEW DEBORD
BNET
MAY 2, 2011

Chrysler is out of crisis mode for the time being, thanks to its recent bankruptcy, bailouts by Ottawa and Washington, and the purchase of the company by Fiat. The Fiat "rescue" is all the more ironic now that the Italian automaker needs cash from Chrysler to support its lagging European sales. Chrysler's predicted $1.5 billion net profit by the end of 2012 will go a long way to meet Fiat's cash flow problems.

The Chrysler/Fiat plan is to give Chrysler responsibility for large cars, trucks, SUVs, and vans and leave the smaller vehicles to Fiat. Chrysler will handle engines larger than 2 litres, hybrids, and electrics, while Fiat will handle smaller engines and small- to mid-sized diesels. For 2013, Chrysler is focused on tweaking its powertrains, boosting the horsepower of its V6 engines, slightly restyling some models, and offering a wider range of optional equipment.

Chrysler's Dart has been a huge success during its first year on the market. 2013 discounts will be rare.

This year's Viper gets 640 horsepower, 600 foot-pounds of torque, and a 100-pound weight reduction, while Chrysler will concentrate on its just-launched compact four-door Dodge Dart (now where have we heard that name before?). Dodge's Dart fills the gap left by the compact Neon. Although it has stiff competition from the Chevrolet Cruze, Honda Civic, Mazda3, Toyota Corolla, and VW Golf, sales have been quite good. Derived from the C-Evo platform, along with the Fiat Bravo,

The 2012 Dodge Avenger: Gone and easily forgotten for 2013. May return as a Barracuda...ouch!

Alfa Milano, and others, the Dart is built at Chrysler's Belvidere, Illinois, plant, where the Neon and Patriot SUV were once assembled.

The Caliber was discontinued for 2012, and the small-car gap it created will be filled by Fiat for 2013. Though there were announcements that Dodge's Avenger (a Sebring twin) and the Chrysler 200 would also be axed for 2013, this may not be the case. Industry insiders now say these mid-size sedans could return as rear-drives, sharing the Alfa Romeo Giulia, Dart, and SRT Barracuda platform.

SUV, truck, and van changes for 2013: The Liberty will be replaced in mid-2013 by a similar-sized Jeep/Fiat design based on a stretched and widened Alfa Romeo Giulietta platform, also used by the Dodge Dart. It will be powered by a 3.2L version of the Pentastar V6 coupled to a 9-speed automatic transmission. The Nitro SUVs will be dropped, and the 2013 Dodge Journey will be heavily discounted and have some trim and option changes before it is cut from the lineup next year. There will also be a new version of the Jeep Compass.

One mid-sized SUV that will sell for full price is the recently redesigned Grand Cherokee; dealers can't keep this vehicle in stock. A diesel-powered Jeep Grand Cherokee is set to arrive later in the year to supplement the current 3.6L V6, 5.7L V8, and 6.4L V8. The diesel is expected to be the same 237 hp 3.0L turbocharged V6 that's sold in Europe. It will be much more fuel-efficient than the Grand Cherokee's gasoline engines, which (combined) post an estimated 8.4 L/100 km (28 mpg) in Europe.

Chrysler knows that its Ram pickup has lagged behind the competition in overall refinement and quality control. That's why it's good to see a redesigned base Ram 1500 truck that replaces the 3.7L V6 and 6-speed transmission with a 3.6L V6 Pentastar hooked to an 8-speed transmission, boosting horsepower by 42 percent. Quality? Time will tell; hold off buying until mid-summer 2013 while we see how the new powertrain setups work out.

Quality Control

Type in "automatic transmission failures," and Google throws up a picture of a Chrysler minivan (well, almost). All kidding aside, Chrysler has gone from a company noted for engineering innovation and strong, high-performance muscle cars to being known for ABS, AC, electrical system, and minivan automatic sliding door failures and automatic transmissions that need replacing after only a few years. Poor fuel economy and subpar fit and finish, with the associate clunks, squeaks, rattles, and exhaust drone, combined with a mediocre ride and handling, are other Chrysler traits you won't see mentioned in the company's brochures.

Pentastar V6 under fire

Chrysler came out a few years ago with a new Pentastar V6 engine that is already showing serious reliability problems, although the company has minimized the extent of the engine failures and has tried to put some of the blame on owners.

Nevertheless, Chrysler is replacing defective cylinder heads on its Pentastar V6 engines with "more robust" parts. In August 2012, there were around 1,300 vehicles waiting several weeks for replacement parts. To its credit, Chrysler says it will pay for rentals until the engines are fixed under warranty. The automaker estimates it is getting almost 500 requests per week for new engines built with more reliable cylinder heads.

The company insists the defect affects *only* 7,500 engines built since 2010, but independent repairers say the failures are more widespread. Early signs of the problem are an engine ticking noise, increased gas consumption, loss of power, and stalling-out. Also, the Check Engine light illuminates on all affected engines. Chrysler says the engine failures are caused by a combination of factors, that include the type of fuel used, owner driving habits, and how well the vehicle was maintained. Owners call this corporate nonsense. They believe the cylinder head failure is caused by faulty design and poor-quality engine parts. Although Chrysler hasn't yet issued any technical service bulletins on the issue, its decision to install more durable engine components in the Pentastar V6 certainly gives credibility that the engine problem is factory-related.

The engine techs at *Flatratetech.com*, a website run by independent auto repairers, have complained about the valve guides on Pentastars for some time:

> The new Pentastar 3.6L engine has been having problems with cylinder heads. The exhaust valve guide is too sloppy, and allows the valve to wobble. Usually it's the number three or five cylinder, but it's not isolated to those two.

The stakes are high for Chrysler because the 3.6L Pentastar V6 powers most of its vehicle lineup. It's the standard powerplant in some minivans, the Grand Cherokee and Wrangler, Chrysler 300, and Dodge Charger sedans and Journeys, and this fall will be available on the 2013 Ram 1500 pickup. And Chryslers are not the only affected vehicles. Volkswagen's Routan minivan, a Chrysler Town & Country clone, uses the same Pentastar, and VW owners are asking for similar warranty coverage for the problem.

Finally, despite Chrysler's assurances that the dealer-repaired engines are just as good as the factory-installed versions, owners are skeptical and add that the present engine woes are driving down resale values.

Chrysler and Cross-Border Shopping

Chrysler Canada kicks Canadians in the teeth after pocketing their bankruptcy bailout money and dumping the North American Free Trade Agreement (NAFTA) in their Windsor, Ontario, outhouse. UCanImport Publications (*www.ucanimport. com/Warranty_Policies.aspx*) says:

> Chrysler calls itself "Canada's Choice." And to make sure it stays that way, the company has elected to void your OEM warranty if you import one of their vehicles from the United States into Canada. If you still wish to purchase a product from this company, UCanImport suggests you request a discount from the U.S. dealership equal to the manufacturer's warranty allocation (which the manufacturer builds into the price of each vehicle) and purchase a third-party warranty.

Just to rub salt into our wounds, the Ford Canada OEM warranty is valid in Canada and offers complete coverage. Hmm…and Ford didn't ask for a government bailout, either.

The Dodge Avenger.

RATING: Not Recommended. As Scott Burgess, auto critic for the *Detroit Free Press* puts it: "The 200 shows how Band-Aids on sheet metal never really stick." The next step down from the Chrysler 300, the 200 is a reworked Sebring in disguise. Now that the 200 and Avenger are scheduled to be dumped next year, there is no incentive for Chrysler or its dealers to invest in parts or mechanic training for two cars that are essentially "dead men, walking." **Road performance:** Considerably improved with stiffened body mounts, a smoother suspension, a raised roll centre, an upgraded rear sway bar and tires, improved noise reduction, and a softened ride. The base 4-cylinder engine coupled to the Jurassic 4-speed tranny is a puny performer and lacks reserve power for passing and merging. **Strong points:** A more stylish appearance; a gentler, more comfortable ride; better handling; and a classier, quieter interior. V6 engine gives plenty of power. Easy access to the interior. Standard side curtain airbags and electronic stability control. **Weak points:** The optional 6-speed transmission helps the acceleration, but shifts are harsh and too frequent. Only average fuel economy. Uncomfortable front seats have insufficient thigh room. Interior feels small, closed in. Smallish trunk. Because the 200 was rushed into production and is based on the mediocre Sebring and Avenger twins, there is a high likelihood the car will be dropped by Fiat before the 200's first-year defects are corrected. **Safety:** Three-quarter rear visibility is seriously compromised by the C-pillars. NHTSA awarded four stars for frontal crash and rollover protection and three stars for side crashworthiness. IIHS rates the 200 sedan "Good" in front, side, rollover, roof strength, and rear crashworthiness tests. The convertible version scored similarly, except there was no roof rating. **New for 2013:** Nothing.

ALERT! Test the car for a high-pitched screeching noise when the rear window is opened; be wary of under-rated tires; and be on the lookout for a suspension "death wobble," a well-known Chrysler trait that usually affects its trucks. One Chrysler 200 owner describes it this way:

> When driving the vehicle at speeds 30–70 mph [48–113 km/h] in a straight line and encountering slight dips or bumps in the road surface, a dramatic loss of directional control was experienced at the left rear of the vehicle. The condition is best described as a sudden, violent swerving from the left to the right. The vehicle was very difficult to keep within the lane. This was a rental car from a commercial agency.

•

> The tires on the V6 200 with the upgraded wheels have a performance rating of "T," however after talking to several tire shops and looking at similarly equipped cars, this seems to be an unreasonably low rating for this particular car. It results in severe understeer, harsh cornering, poor braking distance, and could result in a blow out. The 4-cylinder version of this same car comes with tires that have a much higher rating.

KEY FACTS

Canadian Price (SOFT): *LX:* $19,995, *Touring:* $22,995, *Limited:* $26,995, *Convertible LX:* $29,995, *Convertible Touring:* $36,495, *Convertible Limited:* $38,495; *Avenger SE:* $19,995, *Avenger SXT:* $23,995, *Avenger SXT V6:* $25,200, *RT:* $28,995 **U.S. Price:** *LX:* $19,245, *Touring:* $21,540, *Limited:* $23,945, *S:* $26,240, *Convertible Touring:* $26,445, *Convertible Limited:* $31,440, *Convertible S:* $31,940, *Avenger Express:* $19,245, *Avenger Mainstreet:* $21,340, *Avenger LUX:* $23,745, *Avenger Heat:* $23,840, *Avenger R/T:* $23,545, *Avenger R/T AWD:* $25,545 **Canadian freight:** $1,400 **U.S. freight:** $750

POWERTRAIN (FRONT-DRIVE)
Engines: 2.4L 4-cyl. (173 hp) • 3.6L V6 (283 hp), Transmissions: 4-speed auto. • 6-speed manumatic.

DIMENSIONS/CAPACITY (SEDAN)
Passengers: 2/3; Wheelbase: 108.9 in.; H: 58.4/L: 191.7/W: 72.5 in.; Legroom F/R: 42.4/36.2 in.; Cargo volume: 13.6 cu. ft.; Fuel tank: 62L/regular; Tow limit: 1,000 lb.; Load capacity: 865 lb.; Turning circle: 36.5 ft.; Ground clearance: 6.1 in.; Weight: 3,389 lb.

OVERVIEW: Like its Dodge Avenger twin, the 200 carries a base 2.4L 4-cylinder or an optional 3.6L Pentastar V6 engine. Entry-level models use a 4-speed automatic transmission, while the 6-speed automatic is optional. A 6-speed dual-clutch automatic (an automatically shifted manual transmission) will be optional on the much-awaited 4-cylinder Limited model.

The Chrysler Sebring *cum* 200 and the Dodge Avenger are two sides of the same coin. What you save from a low selling price you will lose through frequent repairs, excessive depreciation, and time spent waiting for a tow, a taxi, or a mechanic. *Consumer Reports* put out this warning to readers on March 18, 2011:

> Reliability out of the box was lousy, and both cars have hovered at the bottom of our family sedan Ratings. Further dampening our impressions, we had a *Consumer Reports*–owned Sebring that almost stranded our staff members on several occasions.

COST ANALYSIS: Wait for the reworked, Fiat-inspired model. It will offer a 9-speed automatic transmission and several engine variants. **Best alternatives:** The Ford Fusion, Mazda3, Honda Accord, and Hyundai Elantra. **Options:** As the 4-banger is a sad joke, hobbled by its 4-speed gearbox, get the better-performing—make that the *only* performing—V6 powerplant. **Rebates:** $1,500–$2,500 rebates and discounts plus low-cost financing. **Depreciation:** Very fast, and likely to get faster. For example, a 2012 200 LX that originally sold for $19,995 (plus $1,400 freight) is now worth about $12,500. **Insurance cost:** Average. **Parts supply/cost:** Parts are mostly taken from the Sebring and Avenger bin, so they are reasonably priced and easily found, for now. **Annual maintenance cost:** Average. **Warranty:** Bumper-to-bumper 3 years/60,000 km; powertrain 5 years/100,000 km; rust perforation 5 years/160,000 km. **Supplementary warranty:** Getting an extended powertrain warranty is a smart idea; choosing a different car is an even better idea. **Highway/city fuel economy:** *2.4L 4-speed auto.: 6.7/9.9 L/100 km, 42/29 mpg. 2.4L 6-speed auto.: 6.4/10.5 L/100 km, 44/27 mpg. 3.6L 6-speed auto.: 6.8/11.0 L/100 km, 42/26 mpg. Convertibles: 2.4L 4-speed auto.: 6.9/10.3 L/100 km, 41/27 mpg. 2.4L 6-speed auto.: 6.8/11.5 L/100 km, 42/25 mpg. 3.6L 6-speed auto.: 6.8/11.0 L/100 km, 42/26 mpg.*

OWNER-REPORTED PROBLEMS: Brake, transmission, suspension, fuel, electrical, and audio system failures; electrical malfunctions; unprotected battery terminals; paint peeling; and poorly assembled body panels:

> Just bought a 2011 200 S series a week ago and already having paint peeling problems. Took it back to the dealer and they are looking at repainting back bumper and trunk...the paint color is Blackberry. My 200 has a lot of little defects in the paint. Dust particles and such. Not a good finish. Not to mention that it had some type of overspray on it when I picked it up.... I did get Chrysler to repaint my back bumper... looks great...now having electrical problems...MIL (Check Engine) Light turns on... ESP Lights turns on for no apparent reason...loud noise in engine compartment...car stops after 3 minutes using remote start.... "WHAT A PIECE OF ****."

SERVICE BULLETIN-REPORTED PROBLEMS: Long crank time and RPM fluctuations; rear-door wind noise; and paint defects:

LIGHT TO MODERATE PAINT IMPERFECTIONS

BULLETIN NO.: 23-003-12   DATE: JANUARY 10, 2012

2012 Models
LIGHT TO MODERATE PAINT SURFACE IMPERFECTIONS ON FACTORY APPLIED PAINT FINISH
OVERVIEW: This bulletin involves removing light to moderate paint surface imperfections on factory applied paint finishes revealing a swirl-free, durable, protected finish. SYMPTOM/CONDITION: Isolated light to moderate paint surface imperfections (scratches, bird dropping stains, chemical etching, etc.) on factory applied paint.

CHALLENGER, CHARGER ★ ★ ★ / ★ ★

Both the Challenger (above) and Charger are afflicted with sudden, unintended deceleration.

RATING: *Charger:* Below Average, because it costs more, depreciates faster; and elicits more safety-related complaints than its cheaper, high-performance brother. *Challenger:* Average. In a nutshell, the Challenger remains the premiere muscle car with a retro look and a small horsepower edge over its Dodge rival, while the Charger continues as Dodge's slightly higher-priced muscle car, now sporting an 8-speed automatic transmission. Both cars offer a choice of the Hemi or the Pentastar V6. **Road performance:** In past model years, the Challenger's lack of agility made it more of a Clydesdale than a "pony car," but last year's suspension and steering tweaks have made the car more responsive. The Charger's performance is also better than average, particularly with the 8-speed automatic transmission. **Strong points:** These are comfortable, spacious, and affordable sports cars with a healthy dose of muscle car flair (especially the 2012 Challenger). Challenger's bigger back seat and larger trunk give it an edge when compared with

KEY FACTS

Canadian Price (Soft): *Challenger SXT:* $26,995, *Challenger SXT Plus:* $28,995, *Challenger R/T:* $36,695, *Challenger R/T Classic:* $38,690, *Challenger SRT8:* $47,995, *Charger SE:* $29,995, *Charger SXT:* $32,745, *Charger SXT Plus:* $34,745, *R/T:* $37,995, *R/T AWD:* $39,996, *SRT8:* $47,995 **U.S. Price:** *Challenger SE:* $24,895, *Challenger Rallye:* $26,895, *Challenger R/T:* $29,895, *Challenger R/T Plus:* $31,895, *Challenger R/T Classic:* $33,195, *Challenger SRT8:* $43,780, *Charger SE:* $25,395, *Charger Rallye:* $27,645, *Charger Rallye Plus:* $29,395, *Charger R/T:* $30,395, *Charger R/T Plus:* $32,395, *Charger R/T Road and Track Package:* $33,395, *Charger R/T Max:* $32,495 **Canadian Freight:** $1,400 **U.S. Freight:** $995

POWERTRAIN (REAR-DRIVE/AWD)

Engines: 3.6L V6 (292 hp) • 3.6L V6 (305 hp) • 5.7L V8 (370 hp) • 5.7L V8 (375 hp) • 6.4L V8 (470 hp); Transmissions: 5-speed auto. • 8-speed auto.; Challenger: 6-speed man. • 6-speed auto.

DIMENSIONS/CAPACITY

Passengers: 2/3; Wheelbase: 116 / 120 in.; *Challenger:* H: 57/L: 198/W: 76 in., *Charger:* H: 58/L: 200/W: 75 in.; Headroom F/R: *Charger:* 2.5/2.0 in.; Legroom F/R: *Charger:* 41.5/28.0 in.; Cargo volume: 16 cu. ft.; Fuel tank: 68–72L/regular; Tow limit: *Challenger:* Not recommended, *Charger:* 1,000–2,000 lb.; Load capacity: 865 lb. est.; Turning circle: 41 ft.; Ground clearance: 4.5 in.; Weight: *Challenger:* 3,720–4,140 lb., *Charger:* 3,728–4,268 lb.

the Chevrolet Camaro and Ford Mustang. It's undeniable that both Dodge muscle cars have exceptional styling, horsepower to burn (as in, "What do you mean, the fuel tank is on empty again?"), and cachet. The 305 hp 3.6L V6 has proven to be much more reliable than any of the three V8s, and it burns less fuel, but, as with the last few years of Mustang production, powertrain dependability has come under fire from owners of 2009–11 models. Various interior improvements; tighter suspension and steering; and an all-new adaptive suspension system for the SRT8. This system automatically tunes the suspension system and also has manual controls that the driver can set to "Auto" or "Sport" mode to tune the suspension to his or her preference. Outward visibility has also been improved by an enlarged windshield area. **Weak points:** Despite recent upgrades to improve performance and comfort, you will still find a stiff, jarring ride, handling that's not particularly agile, overly assisted steering that requires constant correction, and marginal rear headroom. The Challenger is in dire need of an interior facelift similar to the Charger's. There are many quality issues that mostly concern the airbags, suspension, steering, brakes, suspension, climate system, and fit and finish. **Safety:** *Challenger:* NHTSA gave the Challenger five stars for front and side crashworthiness and four stars for rollover resistance. *Charger:* Four stars for frontal collision and rollover protection and three stars for side crashworthiness. The IIHS rates the Charger "Good" for frontal, side, and head-restraint protection and roof strength. **New for 2013:** Not much. The Challenger will get rear parking assist. Most other features will be carried over unchanged from the 2012 model year. An 8-speed automatic will be offered on V6 Chargers. Challengers aren't expected to get 8-speeds until 2014.

ALERT! Check out the SRT8 dash illumination system during daytime driving. Many owners say the instruments may come on only with the headlights, they are partially hidden, the sun washes out the readings, and illumination is minimal even when set to the maximum brightness level.

Also, stay away from the "skip shift" feature, as this 2012 Challenger owner wishes he had done:

> This feature is already the cause of several near misses of me being rear-ended because from a stop, I am unexpectedly prevented from shifting from first into 2nd gear to maintain expected acceleration in traffic. I realize what the skip shift is intended for but in the real world of traffic, the skip shift feature is inherently dangerous and is a safety issue. Whenever anyone is behind me at a stop or a left or right turn, when it's time to go, the skip shift feature puts me at risk of being rear ended every time it engages. There is a display on the instrument panel when skip shift is engaged but to take your eyes off the road to refocus and look for this display while at the same time driving in traffic is as dangerous as the skip shift feature itself.
>
> Additionally, being forced to shift from first to fourth is damaging to the clutch, transmission and engine. The engine knocks and pings terribly if I try to [accelerate] in fourth gear at such a low speed. Oftentimes I am frantically double clutching trying to override the feature by trying to yank and jam the transmission into second gear all the while decelerating with following traffic honking or yelling verbal abuse. There needs to be a way to disable the skip shift feature on these 6-speed manual transmissions.

A Challenger costs $3,000 less than a Charger, yet performance and comfort don't differ much. For once, the cheaper buy is the better buy. The Challenger's front passenger-side airbag electrical harness may short out and disable the airbag, activating the Airbag dash warning light. During your test drive, carry a passenger to check out the electrical connection.

OVERVIEW: Using the same platform and engines as the Chrysler 300, the Charger and Challenger combine a potent mixture of Hemi V8 power, rear-drive, and an independent suspension supplied by Mercedes. Combined with the company's Multi-Displacement System (MDS), which shuts down half the cylinders under light load, the 5.7L Hemi engine produces more horsepower and slightly better fuel economy than previous engines. The downside is finding suitable Hemi engine repairs from a trimmed dealership network with limited parts inventories.

Although these cars are fun to drive and buy you entry into the high-performance "winner's circle," in the end the cost may not be worth the prize. High fuel, insurance, and depreciation costs will quickly thin out your wallet. Plus, the absence of a comprehensive seven-year or lifetime powertrain warranty is like performing a high-wire act without a net. Chrysler revived the Hemi name in 2002 with a 5.7L Hemi V8 engine used in its pickups and then extended it to the 300 Ram Wagon sedan—a winning combination that has revived lagging pickup, sedan, and wagon sales.

COST ANALYSIS: Look for discounts and rebates to cut the Charger's transaction price by about 10 percent. Challenger prices will remain firm as long as oil prices stay under $90 (U.S.) a barrel. The Challenger will continue with its 305 hp V6 and Hemi V8 engines to better compete with the Chevrolet Camaro and horsepower-boosted Ford Mustang V6. It's also the largest, roomiest, and heaviest entrant among these classic American sport coupes. **Best alternatives:** Chevrolet Camaro and Hyundai Genesis. Why not the Mustang? Way too many safety-related defects and internal service bulletins decrying the 'Stang's poor highway performance and abysmal reliability. **Options:** You'll want the 305 hp 3.6L V6 engine for better all-around performance with less of a fuel penalty. Servicing will be easier and less expensive than with any of the Hemi powerplants. **Rebates:** $3,000–$5,000 rebates and discounts, plus zero percent financing by the spring of next year. **Depreciation:** Talk about fast depreciation! A 2011 Challenger SE that originally sold for $27,000 is now worth about $18,000. Depreciation is even faster with the Charger: A 2011 Charger SE that once sold for $30,000 is now worth $11,000 less, and the SXT takes a $9,000 hit. **Insurance cost:** What the market can bear. You want high performance, you get high insurance rates. **Parts supply/cost:** Parts are not a problem due to the many different models using the same Chrysler 300 parts. Engine and body components are expensive and complex to troubleshoot, especially now that Chrysler has fewer dealers, parts suppliers, and skilled mechanics. **Annual maintenance cost:** Average; higher than average once the warranty expires. **Warranty:** Bumper-to-bumper 3 years/60,000 km; powertrain 5 years/100,000 km; rust perforation 5 years/160,000 km. **Supplementary warranty:** An extended powertrain warranty is a wise choice, since Chrysler is too cheap to provide Canadians with a lifetime powertrain warranty like the one offered in the States. **Highway/city fuel economy:** *Challenger 3.6L:* 7.3/11.7 L/100 km, 39/24 mpg. *Challenger 5.7L, man.:* 8.2/13.8 L/100 km, 34/20 mpg. *Challenger 6.4L, SRT8:* 8.8/15.1 L/100 km, 32/19 mpg. *Challenger 6.4L, SRT8 auto. with fuel saver:* 9.2/15.6 L/100 km, 31/18 mpg. *Charger 3.6L:* 7.3/11.7 L/100 km, 39/24 mpg. *Charger 5.7L with fuel saver:* 8.0/13.5 L/100 km, 35/21 mpg. *Charger 5.7L AWD with fuel saver:* 8.5/14.4 L/100 km, 33/20 mpg.

OWNER-REPORTED PROBLEMS: *Challenger:* Not an inordinate number of problems reported, but some are quite serious: A fractured tie rod caused the front passenger-side wheel to fall off; a fire may ignite in the rear; and airbags don't deploy when they should or are deactivated by a shorted-out wiring harness:

> I was rear ended, (at 4,200 miles [6,760 km] on my new vehicle), while at a dead stop for a traffic light by a Ford F250 pickup truck traveling at 45 mph [72 km/h] pulling a utility trailer hauling approximately 6,000–7,000 pounds which hit my 2012 Dodge Challenger in the right rear end, pushing me into the back end of a Nissan Altima, and not one of the air bags deployed in my Challenger. I had a prior problem with the Challenger at approximately 2,300 miles [3,700 km] on the vehicle where the Air Bag warning light came on and had the vehicle serviced at the dealer to fix the problem they said was a faulty wiring harness from the factory in the drivers seat for the air bag system, and after the dealer replaced said faulty wiring harness it turned the warning light off prior to this accident. The accident occurred...causing extensive damage to the rear and major damage to the front of the vehicle from the impact. Again not one of the air bags deployed. The dealer service department also stated to me when I had the vehicle in for repair of the warning light prior to the accident that

they were having this problem with all of these new Challengers of a faulty wiring harness from the factory causing the Air Bag light to come on. I can only be led to believe at this time that the problem is not only the wiring harness but that there is a much bigger problem in the air bag system.

Other owner complaints concern engine, transmission, brake, fuel system, and suspension/steering failures:

The components causing the most problems are the suspension and steering components, such as the struts, strut plates, control arm, bushings and tie rod ends, the axles, rear suspension arms, and the U-joint connectors for the driveshaft.

There has been one report of a fire igniting at the rear driver's side of the car, and another incident where the SRT8 suddenly shut down on the highway. *Charger:* Owners report many more problems with the airbags, transmission, brakes, suspension, body construction, and electrical malfunctions. Chronic stalling or a sustained loss of power are constant worries plaguing Charger drivers:

While turning left to cross multiple lanes on the highway, I accelerated to go and the car began coasting. I pressed on the gas and nothing! The car would not accelerate. With oncoming traffic and cars swerving to keep from plowing into me.

Not to mention the numerous electrical glitches:

They found a wire from the front driver seat air bag that needed to be repaired. Based on the technician, one of the pins of the wire was out of position. The technician repaired it and corrected the code. After one day working good without the Air Bag light on, a chime sound and the Air Bag symbol appeared, again.

·

Trunk opens by itself, you can hear the relay click and release the trunk. Door handles do not unlock the car, airbag light comes on and goes off after restarting, UConnect control touch screen not functioning, dash lights stay on even when the car is locked, and all other lights off.

One 2012 Charger owner describes his car's computer as acting out a role in *2001: A Space Odyssey:*

Car has stalled and shut off when driving. Car locks you out and will not open unless you use the key. Electrical module that controls car is like 'HAL' from *2001: A Space Odyssey*: It does what it wants and the dealer has to reprogram it twice a month. The computer turns the AC on by itself in freezing weather.

SERVICE BULLETIN-REPORTED PROBLEMS: Long crank time and RPM fluctuations; rear-door wind noise; light to moderate paint defects; and free replacement of the coolant hose. *Challenger:* Intermittent no-start; automatic transmission malfunctions; booming noise at idle; door glass self-cycling/battery drain; passive door handles inoperative; and deck lid and trunk can be opened without the key fob nearby. *Charger:* Automatic transmission controls cause a shudder, shift concern; deck lid spoiler rattle, chatter; front-door wind noise; battery drain; radio powers itself on with the ignition off; cluster chime locks up; fix for the rear chime; false chime from the blind spot system; trunk won't open with passive switch; and coolant leaks.

300, 300C, 300S ★★★

The Chrysler 300S.

RATING: Average. These cars were modestly refined and restyled for the 2011 model year. They carry the new Pentastar 3.6L V6 coupled to a 6-speed automatic transmission. Popular 8-speed automatic transmissions are back ordered at least three months. **Road performance:** The new 3.6L V6 gives the car the power it needs; the V8 gives much more, but it guzzles fuel. Either engine gives you better-than-average power and handling. **Strong points:** There's plenty of power with the latest V6 hooked to the 6-speed automatic gearbox. You will also enjoy acceptable handling, a remarkably quiet and spacious interior, and a large trunk. The touring model gives a smoother, more-comfortable ride than does the 300C, which is the performance-oriented variant. Chrysler has also enlarged the window area for better visibility and reworked the interior so that it feels less claustrophobic, is more user-friendly, and looks classier. **Weak points:** Hemi-equipped models are way overpriced, and the 300's resale values have fallen considerably. Standard towing capability is less than one would expect from a rear-drive. Some of the electronics derived from Mercedes' luxury models have had serious reliability problems. **Safety:** Impressive crashworthiness, says NHTSA, which gives the 300 five stars for frontal and side crash protection and four stars for rear protection. The IIHS is even more enthusiastic, giving five stars for front, side, roof, and rear crashworthiness. **New for 2013:** The Chrysler 300 and 300C are expected to get a V6 power boost and a leaner lineup. There will be four basic Chrysler 300 models: 300, 300S, 300C, and 300C Luxury Series (plus SRT8). The

Hemi V8 will be available as part of a package on 300S, 300C, and 300C Luxury Series. All models will have standard leather, UConnect Voice, and Bluetooth. AWD is promised for base models, while the V6-equipped Chrysler 300C will feature an 8-speed automatic that will be phased in for the V8 models. The relatively new 292 hp 3.6L V6 will be standard; a 363 hp 5.7L V8 is optional. SRT8s will use a production version of the 6.4L Hemi with 465 hp and MDS for better gas mileage (expected in late 2012).

ALERT! Some of the optional features can be haggled down by 50 percent. Airbag warnings are constant and not always meaningful.

OVERVIEW: Front-drives are out, and rear-drives are in, again, along with all-wheel drive and complicated Hemi V8 engines—all the ingredients for endless repair waits and extra expenses as these elegantly styled, complicated-to-service sedans start putting on the miles and coming closer to their warranty expiry dates. The V8 is rather exceptional in that it features Chrysler's Multi-Displacement System, which uses eight cylinders under load and then switches to 4-cylinder mode when cruising. So far, this feature has worked reliably well.

KEY FACTS

Canadian Price (Very Negotiable): *Touring:* $32,745, *Limited:* $35,745, *C:* $39,995, *AWD:* $41,995, *S:* $35,995, *AWD:* $37,995, *V8:* $39,995, *V8 AWD:* $41,995, *SRT8:* $48,995 **U.S. Price:** *300:* $27,170, *Limited:* $31,170, *C:* $38,170 **Canadian Freight:** $1,400 **U.S. Freight:** $935

POWERTRAIN (REAR-DRIVE/AWD)

Engines: 3.6L V6 (292 hp) • 5.7L V8 (363 hp); 6.4L V8 (465 hp) Transmissions: 5-speed auto. • 8-speed auto.

DIMENSIONS/CAPACITY (BASE)

Passengers: 2/3; Wheelbase: 120 in.; H: 58.4/L: 199/W: 75 in.; Headroom F/R: 4.5/2.5 in.; Legroom F/R: 41.8/40.1 in.; Cargo volume: 16.3 cu. ft.; Fuel tank: 68L/regular; Tow limit: 2,000 lb.; Load capacity: 865 lb.; Turning circle: 41 ft.; Ground clearance: 4.7–5.0 in.; Weight: *300:* 3,961–4,513 lb.

COST ANALYSIS: Excess weight and large engines drive up fuel costs; consequently, resale values are dropping because buyers are shifting to smaller, more-economical sedans. **Best alternatives:** Ford Fusion, Honda Accord Crosstour, Subaru Forester or Legacy, Suzuki SX4 Hatchback, and Toyota Sienna. **Options:** You may want to order the $2,000 SafetyTec Package. True, these options add complexity to the car's innards and increase the risk of electronic failures, but some of the safety features are worthwhile. They include blind-spot alert, cross-path detection, forward collision warning, a front- and rear-obstacle-detection system, adaptive cruise control, driver-side automatic day/night mirror, mirror-mounted turn signals, universal garage door opener, rain-sensing wipers, rear fog lights, and steering-linked adaptive and self-dimming bi-xenon headlights. The $3,300 Limited Luxury Package is not so useful; it gives the dealer a $4,000 profit and adds little to your driving experience or safety, except for the power-adjustable pedals. A "premium" paint job is not worth its $1,000 premium, either; even the $300 "special" paint application is of doubtful value. **Rebates:** Expect $2,000–$3,000 discounts or rebates and low-interest financing programs by late winter. **Depreciation:** Higher than average. For example, a 2009 Chrysler 300C SRT8 equipped with a Hemi V8 sold new for $53,695; today its resale value is barely $20,000. No, that's not a misprint: $20,000. A 2011 base 300 version that sold new for $33,000 is now worth about $19,000. **Parts supply/cost:** Expect long delays and high costs. **Annual maintenance cost:** Higher than average. **Warranty:** Bumper-to-bumper 3 years/60,000 km; powertrain 5 years/100,000 km; rust perforation 5 years/160,000 km. **Supplementary warranty:** Get an extended powertrain warranty thrown in the deal. **Highway/city fuel economy:** *3.6L:* 7.3/11.7 L/100 km, 39/14 mpg. *5.7L 300C (cylinder deactivation):* 8.0/13.5 L/100 km, 35/30 mpg. *5.7L AWD:* 8.7/13.4 L/100 km, 32/21 mpg. Owners report, however, that real-world fuel consumption for both engines is far more than these estimates.

OWNER-REPORTED PROBLEMS: Forward-Collision warning system light comes on when no threat is imminent; Airbag light comes on for no reason; hard starts and no-starts; car wouldn't shift from Neutral to Drive in a car wash; warning chime that there is another vehicle in close proximity doesn't work; poor headlight and side light illumination; rear-view and side-view mirrors give too dark an image; fuel spills out after refuelling, causing a foul smell in the cabin; computer malfunction causes excessive amounts of fuel to be dumped into the engine cylinders; and headlight fogging.

SERVICE BULLETIN-REPORTED PROBLEMS: Not a lot of problems reported. Some radio malfunctions and a fix for water infiltrating into the mirror turn-signal housing.

GRAND CARAVAN, TOWN & COUNTRY ★★★

The Chrysler Grand Caravan.

RATING: Average. 2011 refinements corrected many of these minivans' past deficiencies, giving both minivans an upgraded rating from Below Average to Average. It will take several years to find out if the use of the new Pentastar V6 and an upgraded automatic transmission (introduced on the 2011s) cures Chrysler's decades-old powertrain maladies, but owner feedback is quite positive—so far. As for long-term servicing, it seems repairs and parts shouldn't be a problem. **Road performance:** The tight chassis and responsive steering provide a comfortable, no-surprise ride. Stiffer springs have greatly improved handling and comfort. Manoeuvring around town is easy, though high-speed merging with a full load requires some forethought and patience. The new powertrain introduced in 2011 has been very problematic. The engine tends to run roughly and suddenly lose power, and the transmission shifts erratically and loses fluid. Dealers believe the cause of these failures is both electrical shorts and malfunctioning electronic control modules, but so far most fixes haven't worked. Power steering is vague and over-assisted as speed increases. Downshifting from the electronic gearbox provides practically no braking effect. The brake pedal feels mushy, and the brakes tend to heat up after repeated applications, causing considerable loss of effectiveness (fade) and warping of the front discs. The ABS has proved to be unreliable on older vans, and repair costs are astronomical. **Strong points:** Very reasonably priced and subject to deep discounting. Lots of innovative convenience features; user-friendly instruments and controls; two side-sliding doors; easy entry and exit; and plenty of interior room. Dual airbags include knee bolsters to prevent front occupants from sliding under the seat belts. Remote-controlled power door locks can be programmed to lock when the vehicle is put in gear. Chrysler has developed a mechanism that releases the power door locks and turns on the interior lights when the airbag is deployed. **Weak points:** A sad history of chronic powertrain, AC, ABS, and body defects that are exacerbated by the automaker's hard-nosed attitude in interpreting its after-warranty assistance obligations. Get used to a cacophony of rattles, squeals, moans, and groans caused by the vehicle's poor construction and subpar components. Fuel consumption is worse than advertised. **Safety:** Both vehicles were given NHTSA's top, five-star rating for frontal and side crashworthiness; rollover resistance earned four stars. IIHS ranks frontal offset, side impact, roof strength, and head-restraint protection as "Good." The chrome ring around the passenger-side heater deck may cause a distracting reflection in the side-view mirror in the Town & Country; the backup camera image is too dim in daytime to be useful; and the third-row seat belt is a hostage-taker:

KEY FACTS

Canadian Price (Very Negotiable): *Grand Caravan Cargo:* $29,495, *SE:* $27,995, *SXT:* $30,995, *Crew:* $33,995, *R/T:* $38,795, *Town & Country Touring:* $39,995, *with leather:* $41,995, *Limited:* $45,995 **U.S. Price:** *Grand Caravan Cargo:* $21,800, *Express:* $23,995, *Mainstreet:* $25,845, *Crew:* $28,795, *R/T:* $30,695, *Town & Country Touring:* $30,260, *Touring L:* $32,660, *Limited:* $39,825 **Canadian Freight:** $1,400 **U.S. Freight:** $835

POWERTRAIN (FRONT-DRIVE)

Engine: 3.6L V6 (283 hp); Transmission: 6-speed auto.

DIMENSIONS/CAPACITY

Passengers: 2/2/3; Wheelbase: 121 in.; H: 69/W: 77/L: 203 in.; Headroom F/R1/R2: *Grand Caravan:* 6/5/0 in., *Town & Country:* 3.5/4.5/0.0 in.; Legroom F/R1/R2: *Grand Caravan:* 41.0/30.5/27.0 in., *Town & Country:* 41/31/25 in.; Cargo volume: 61.5 cu. ft.; Fuel tank: 76L/regular; Tow limit: 3,800 lb.; Load capacity: 1,150 lb.; Turning circle: 41 ft.; Ground clearance: 5.0 in.; Weight: *Grand Caravan:* 4,600 lb., *Town & Country:* 4,755 lb.

The driver side rear third row seat belt suddenly locked with a passenger in the seat. While trying to loosen the seat belt, it only continued to tighten around the passenger. The seat belt was eventually cut and the passenger received minor bruises to the abdomen as a result.

New for 2013: An upgraded suspension. Fed up with jokes about its minivans being only for soccer moms, Chrysler now sells a lower-sitting R/T high-performance model described as a "man van." Town & Country will be put out to pasture in 2014; a redesigned Grand Caravan will appear in 2015.

ALERT! GM offered an optional $5,000 Sit-N-Lift power seat on its last production run of minivans (2005–08). It's the only automotive manufacturer in the U.S. to offer a fully motorized, rotating lift-and-lower passenger seat to assist physically challenged passengers. The seat meets all safety regulations and hasn't shown any reliability problems. These seats are now installed by independent mechanics and some dealers. Contact GM Canada and your local association for the physically challenged, and scout Internet want ads. • Sliding side doors make it easy to load and unload children and carry seniors, but they are failure-prone and have a sorry history of seriously injuring passengers. • In your test drive, also look for sudden, unintended deceleration—a common occurrence. • A night drive is a prerequisite to check out headlight illumination, which many have called inadequate.

OVERVIEW: These versatile minivans return with a wide array of standard and optional features that include anti-lock brakes, child safety seats integrated into the seatbacks, flush-design door handles, and front windshield wiper and washer controls located on the steering-column lever for easier use. Childproof locks are standard. Chrysler mated the Pentastar V6 to a 6-speed automatic transmission, which is just as fuel-thrifty as the much less powerful outgoing model. Beginning with the 2011 models, there was an important improvement in emergency handling and stopping power, and a new fuel economizer switch that changes the transmission shift schedule for better mileage. There's a new spoiler, LED tail lights, a lower ride height, lower rolling resistance tires, reduced brake and rear bearing drag (this increases gas mileage), and a retuned suspension with different spring rates. No more Swivel 'n Go seats, but the new seats are more comfortable, and captain's chairs in the middle row have returned. Except for the following, there is not much new that's specific to the 2013s: 17" standard wheels, trailer sway dampening, and second-row floor mat retainers. Power fold-in exterior mirrors will be standard on the Limited and optional on the Touring L.

COST ANALYSIS: Go for a practically identical, though cheaper 2012 model. **Best alternatives:** First, think small and consider the six-passenger Mazda5. Honda's Odyssey should be your next choice, with the Toyota Sienna placing third. Full-sized GM rear-drive vans are also worth looking at. They are more affordable and practical buys if you intend to haul a full passenger load or do regular heavy hauling, are physically challenged, use lots of accessories, or take frequent motoring excursions. Sure, they're less fuel-efficient, but they are discounted over 30 percent and fuel costs have dipped 25 percent during the last year. Don't splurge on a new luxury Chrysler minivan: Chrysler's upscale Town & Country may cost up to $10,000 more than a Grand Caravan yet be worth only a few thousand dollars more after five years on the market. **Options:** Town & Country's $2,000 leather interior isn't worth the extra cost. You may wish to also pass on the tinted windshields—they seriously reduce visibility. Ditch the failure-prone Goodyear original-equipment tires. **Rebates:** The 2012 models will likely get $3,000–$6,000 discounts on the Grand Caravan and Town & Country or zero percent financing throughout the year. **Depreciation:** Faster than average. Check this out: A $39,995 2011 Town & Country is now worth $23,500; a 2011 Grand Caravan SE that sold for $27,995 now has a $18,000 resale value. **Insurance cost:** About average for a minivan. **Parts supply/cost:** Higher than average, especially for AC, transmission, and ABS components, which are covered under a number of "goodwill" warranty programs. **Annual maintenance cost:** Repair costs are average during the warranty period. **Warranty:** The base warranty is inadequate if you plan to keep your minivan for more than five years. Bumper-to-bumper 3 years/60,000 km; powertrain 5 years/100,000 km; rust perforation 5 years/160,000 km. **Supplementary warranty:** An extended powertrain warranty is a must-have. If buying the warranty separately, bargain it down to about one-third of the $2,000 asking price. Chrysler minivans can be expected to have some brake, suspension, AC, body, and electrical system deficiencies similar to previous versions. Quality control has been below average since these vehicles were first launched more than 20 years ago and, surprisingly, got much worse after the 1990 model year introduced limp-prone transmissions. **Highway/city fuel economy:** 3.6L: 7.9/12.2 L/100 km, 36/23 mpg.

OWNER-REPORTED PROBLEMS: Very few complaints recorded by NHSTA; those failures that are listed and confirmed by confidential Chrysler service bulletins concern primarily—you guessed it—the engine and automatic transmission:

> I noticed a fluid leak in my driveway and based on the red color I eliminated the possibility that it was from the power steering because the reservoir was at the max level. I was later informed that the transmission side cover was leaking. I sent the vehicle to the dealer where dye was added and was informed that fluid was leaking in the area of the bell housing and the transmission would require disassembly to ascertain what the cause is.

> •

> I have a transmission manufacturing defect that should be afforded the same consumer protection as the 2012 Grand Caravans with engine sludge. My pump and axle seals began leaking while I was driving at 45 mph [72 km/h]. I didn't notice until 20 miles [32 km] were on the odometer. The dealership refused to examine it before I had to release it to AMS Vans for wheelchair conversion. It was returned to me with 36 miles [58 km] on the odometer and it was leaking during the additional 16 miles [26 km]. Unless Chrysler is willing to provide documentation that this transmission cannot be damaged by running it without fluid it should have been replaced under the 5 year 50,000 mile drive train warranty. But Chrysler and the dealership have

refused to do so, replacing only the fluid and seals and leaving me with a damaged transmission on my new vehicle.

 When dealers do only a partial repair under warranty, they and the manufacturer are liable for any subsequent repairs related to the same issue. The warranty clock is set back for that one problem.

Owners say rpms surge up and down at idle, causing the Caravan to launch forward when put into Drive and shake violently at highway speeds and then slow to 1300 rpms. This makes merging a roll of the dice. When parked on a slope with the nose pointing down and the tranny in Reverse, the vehicle will roll forward. Sliding-door failures make owners afraid to drive these minivans, lest the doors crush passengers as they enter or exit, or start an electrical fire:

> The contact rented a 2011 Dodge Grand Caravan. The contact stated while the vehicle was parked, it burst into flames. No one was injured during the fire and the vehicle was destroyed. The fire department was notified and extinguished the fire. The Fire Marshall stated during the fire the passenger side sliding door was open. The contact stated the Saturday before the fire, as his daughter was exiting the vehicle, the door began to close on her. The rest of the day the door handle would not work, but the key remote and the driver's side button would operate the door. The manufacturer was notified of the failure and the vehicle was inspected; however, the inspector did not find a defect with the vehicle. The failure mileage was 23,000. The fire dept. observed the greatest amount of heat damage was in the area of the passenger rear door.

Owners also say the sliding doors rub the rear body panels and leave black marks on the rear wheelwells. Complaints also focus on other electrical glitches, erratic AC performance, and early brake wear (see *forum.chryslerminivan.net*). In one NHTSA-logged complaint, the minivan, used as a hearse, was deemed unsafe to transport...dead bodies?

> All electrical equipment stopped working on the way home from the dealership. No gauges, no power windows or doors, no turn signals, no brake lights, no A/C, no radio. The only thing[s] working were the windshield wipers, which came on by themselves and I could not shut them off. All the warning lights on the dash lit up. Made it home and called the dealership. Van has less than 100 miles [160 km] on it and already in for service. Called dealership Monday afternoon, they can't find any problems, must be the TIPM (Totally Integrated Power Module). They have ordered the part, but it is on backorder until who knows when. Van has been deemed unsafe to drive until repaired. Dealership provided me with a small sedan to drive until fixed, but this van was purchased by my funeral home to use for body transportation, stretchers, caskets, etc. Sedan is totally useless for my business.

The speed control feature automatically shifts transmission into low gear with a thud, and high engine revs whenever the vehicle goes down an incline. At other times, the vehicle will lose all power until the ignition key is reinserted. Also, vehicle may shut down whenever both wheels pass over a pothole or speed bump. Other owners note the premature wearout of the cooling system, clutch, front suspension components, wheel bearings, air conditioning, and body parts (trim, weather stripping becomes loose and falls off; plastic pieces rattle and break easily). The front brakes need constant attention, if not to replace the pads or warped rotors after two years or 30,000 km, then to silence the excessive squeaks when braking. Tire valve stems frequently fail, resulting in the tire going flat.

SERVICE BULLETIN-REPORTED PROBLEMS: Light to moderate paint imperfections. AC condenser road debris damage can be avoided by installing a condenser guard supplied by Chrysler (under warranty, of course). TSB #23-047-06 is very useful for determining when a cracked windshield should be replaced under warranty. Power liftgate failures can be easily corrected by recalibrating the power control module, says TSB #08-045-06. NHTSA has recorded numerous complaints of airbags deploying unexpectedly—when passing over a bump in the road or simply when turning the vehicle on—or failing to deploy in an accident. Owners who find the sliding door obstruction detection feature too sensitive need to reflash the electronic module.

2009 CHRYSLER TOWN & COUNTRY 3.8L V6

All Technical Service Bulletins

NUMBER	DATE	TITLE
08-012-12	02/14/2012	Instruments—VIC Software Enhancements
L41	02/09/2012	Campaign—PCM Software Error in O2 Heater Sense Circuit
23-003-12	01/10/2012	Body—Light to Moderate Paint Imperfections
17-003-11	11/22/2011	Suspension—Low Speed Noise from Rear on Uneven Surface
05-007-11	10/11/2011	Brakes—Front End Vibration When Braking
18-043-11	09/14/2011	Engine Controls—MIL ON/Multiple O2 Sensor DTCs Set
08-053-11	08/27/2011	Antitheft—Alarm Sounds without Reason/Vehicle No Start
18-037-11	08/02/2011	Engine Controls—MIL ON/DTCs P06DE/P054A/P0298/P054C
13-002-11	07/27/2011	Engine, A/T—Front End Pop When Shifting from Park
08-024-11A	07/01/2011	Keyless Systems—No Start/Intermittent RKE Function
02-001-11	06/24/2011	Steering/Suspension—Steering Wheel out of Alignment
08-027-11	06/17/2011	Interior, A/C—Heated Front Seat Inoperative
23-023-11	06/17/2011	Body—Quarter Glass Weatherstrip Not Seated Properly
23-014-11	04/20/2011	Interior—Power 3rd Row Seat Won't Fully Stow
08-015-11	04/06/2011	Cell Phone—Loss Of HFM Communication
24-005-11	04/02/2011	A/C—Whistle Noise from Dash with A/C in Floor Mode
18-018-11	03/29/2011	Engine Controls—MIL ON/DTCs P06DD/P0522/P0108/P1239
18-006-11A	02/26/2011	Engine Controls—MIL ON/DTC P0128 Stored In Memory
21-001-11	02/15/2011	Engine, A/T—Knocking/Rattling Noise from A/T Area
18-033-10	12/18/2010	Engine Controls—MIL ON/Camshaft Position Sensor DTCs

Source: www.alldata.com

RAM 1500, 2500, 3500 PICKUP ★ ★ ★

The RAM 1500.

KEY FACTS

Canadian Price (Very Negotiable): *1500 ST Short Cab V6 4×2:* $26,570 **U.S. Price:** *1500 ST:* $20,810 **Canadian Freight:** $1,400 **U.S. Freight:** $975
POWERTRAIN (REAR-DRIVE/PART-TIME/FULL-TIME AWD)
Engines: 3.6L V6 (305 hp) • 4.7L V8 (310 hp) • 5.7L V8 (395 hp) • 6.7L Diesel (Cummins); Transmissions: 6-speed auto. • 8-speed auto.
DIMENSIONS/CAPACITY (BASE)
Passengers: 3/2; Wheelbase: 141 in.; H: *1500:* 77, *2500:* 79/W: 80/L: 228 in.; Headroom F/R: 6/4 in.; Legroom F/R: *1500:* 40.5/25.0 in., *2500:* 40/26 in.; Fuel tank: 132L/regular; Tow limit: 5,655 lb.; Load capacity: *1500:* 1,120 lb., *2500:* 1,945 lb.; Turning circle: *1500:* 50 ft., *2500:* 51 ft.; Ground clearance: *1500:* 10.5 in., *2500:* 8.0 in.; Weight: *1500:* 5,655 lb., *2500:* 7,130 lb.

RATING: Average. **Road performance:** Compare the stability and ride with Toyota trucks, and you will be impressed by the newest Ram's better handling and more-comfortable ride. Mercifully, this may mean the end of the Chrysler/Ram "death wobble," where the truck loses steering control after passing over potholes or uneven terrain. **Strong points:** The crew cab model comes with a cargo bed that's longer than that of most of the competition but not as huge as the Mega Cab; the Crew Cab has a roomy rear seat and the interior is relatively quiet and well-appointed. The lockable "Ram box" storage compartment keeps items secure and out of the weather. **Weak points:** The Pentastar and 8-speed tranny have yet to prove they are dependable performers. So far, Pentastar hookups with 6-speeds aren't that impressive. The fuel-thirsty Hemi V8 isn't a wise choice, either. Its cylinder-deactivation feature is helpful, but not very. The Hemis are also complicated to service, and parts are often back ordered. Full-time AWD and electronic stability control (ESC) are optional. The "Ram box" takes up some of the bed width. **Safety:** The 2013 Ram 1500s return with standard safety features like head-protecting side curtain airbags for both front and rear seating and an anti-skid system that includes trailer-sway control. *2010 1500 four-door Regular Cab, 1500 four-door Crew Cab, and 1500 four-door Quad Cab:* NHTSA awarded five stars for frontal crashworthiness and four stars for rollover resistance.

2010 2500 Extended Cab 42 and 44: These models earned four and three stars, respectively, for rollover resistance. *All 2010 1500 models:* IIHS gave frontal crash protection and head restraints a "Good" rating. IIHS gave side crash protection a "Marginal" rating. Mediocre braking. If you are a short driver, you may not be able to see over the raised hood. **New for 2013:** This year's 1500 gets an 8-speed automatic transmission coupled to a more powerful (305 hp), fuel-frugal 3.6L Pentastar V6. Obviously, Chrysler has been spooked by Ford's new EcoBoost engines that have given that company's trucks and small cars much more power and better fuel economy. Chrysler knows its venerable Hemi V8 has become yesterday's news and can't bring in the crowds attracted by Ford's EcoBoost-equipped models, hence Chrysler's launch of a new powertrain setup and other new fuel-saving features. There's a stop/start feature that stops the engine at lights and restarts it as soon as the foot is lifted off the brake. More fuel is saved through the use of a new electric-powered steering system, a revised alternator, and low-rolling-resistance tires. The Ram 2500 gets a compressed natural gas (CNG) option for fleets.

ALERT! The new Rams won't arrive until year's end, which is a blessing because new-car hoopla and prices usually subside going into the new year. Smart buyers will wait for a better-built second-series Ram that will reach dealer lots in early spring. • Be wary of "pain in the neck" front head restraints. They could be a deal-breaker. Check them out during the test drive, or rent the truck for a weekend. • Look for paint flaws, particularly on the hood.

OVERVIEW: These trucks are considerably improved, and so many have been sold over the years that their maintenance can be carried out by most independent garages—with the exception of the Hemi engine, which requires more specialized dealership support. The only reason these trucks have not been given a higher rating is their infamous powertrain failures.

Ram 2500 and 3500 models feature either the Hemi gas engine or the highly desirable Cummins diesel. As for power, Ford's new diesel has higher peak torque, but the Cummins is still the best choice for providing low-end torque. *2011 Ram 2500/3500/4500/5500 Chassis cab:* The Ram 2500's tow rating increased on 2011 models from 20,000 to 22,000 lb. with the diesel and 4.1 axle ratio, thanks to a beefier rear suspension and axle. Both the 2500 and 3500 have a standard EVIC (Electronic Vehicle Information Center), standard tire pressure monitoring, and standard trailer brake control on all but ST models.

COST ANALYSIS: Go for the much-improved 2013 second-series 1500. If you're inclined to stick with the V8s—including the problematic Hemi—go for a 2013, as well. The ideal combination is the diesel engine coupled to a manual transmission to dodge (pun intended) Chrysler's automatic transmission breakdowns. **Best alternatives:** Honda Ridgeline and the Nissan Frontier. Ford's F-Series is the best Detroit alternative to the Ram. It was also redesigned at the same time as the Ram with a more-solid-feeling structure and larger cabs and cargo beds, as well as additional compartments and dividers. Ford F-Series trucks took a big step forward on the powertrain front last year with its introduction of the twin-turbocharged EcoBoost V6 and a strong new base V8 engine. Base Silverado and Sierra models aren't a smart buy, despite what may be a bargain price. On the other hand, the redesigned 2011 and later Heavy Duty (HD) versions are much more refined than previous model years, though they have a less accommodating, less comfortable crew cab. **Options:** The air suspension option hasn't proven itself. **Rebates:** These trucks will likely get $3,000–$5,000 rebates or discounting plus zero percent financing throughout the year as higher fuel prices cut into the sales of the bigger rigs. **Depreciation:** Average, but much faster than average for the V8-equipped models. Diesels with manual transmissions hold their value best. **Insurance cost:** Average. **Parts supply/cost:** Parts prices are higher than average, especially for Hemi engine, AC, transmission, and ABS components; parts are often back ordered. **Annual maintenance cost:** Repair costs are average during the warranty period; however, this doesn't include lost wages or lost use of the truck due to long waits for back-ordered parts, which is a frequent complaint. **Warranty:** The base warranty is inadequate if you plan to keep your pickup for more than five years. Bumper-to-bumper 3 years/60,000 km; powertrain 5 years/100,000 km; rust perforation 5 years/160,000 km. **Supplementary warranty:** Consider buying an extended powertrain warranty. If buying the warranty separately, bargain it down to about one-third of the $2,000 asking price. **Highway/city fuel economy:** *3.7L V6:* 10.0/14.8 L/100 km, 28/19 mpg. *4.7L V8:* 10.0/15.6 L/100 km, 26/18 mpg. *5.7L V8 MDS:* 10.2/15.4 L/100 km, 28/18 mpg. *5.7L V8 44 MDS:* 10.8/16.2 L/100 km, 26/17 mpg.

OWNER-REPORTED PROBLEMS: Recall repairs to the rear axle spindle delayed until September 2012:

> The problem is...the rear axle pinion bearing on my truck may not receive adequate lubrication under certain driving conditions. This lack of lubrication condition could cause the pinion bearing to seize and cause a loss of vehicle control and/or a crash without warning. I have contacted three different servicing dealers, and have been told three different stories. The one common factor they have is that parts are not available, and backorders weren't being processed. I feel like I'm getting the run-around.

Owners report Chrysler is also delaying the carrying out of a steering and door latch recall. Sudden, unintended acceleration; gas pedal stuck to the floor; vehicle suddenly downshifts:

> The problem is when traveling, uphill-downhill or on level, if you are above 45 mph [72 km/h] and you stop applying gas pedal to coast. The vehicle will coast until you reach approximately 40 mph [64 km/h] at which time the transmission will downshift into 3rd gear. This causes an abrupt slowing without alerting vehicle behind you. This could in effect cause a rear collision because the brake lights are not activated, and the gearing is low in rear axle which causes the vehicle to slow at a faster rate than normal.

If you open the rear passenger-side window when driving, the vehicle shakes violently. Gas spews out of filler tube when filling up; wheel lug nuts sheared and wheel flew off truck; defective suspension front struts; sudden steering lockup; windshield wipers fall off because they no longer have a retention bolt; recurrent horn failures:

> Told that the horn did not have a sufficient ground. The vehicle was repaired a second time but the horn continued to fail intermittently. The horn would also sound independently any time the contact was attempting a turn in either direction, or when a slight road bump was driven over.

SERVICE BULLETIN-REPORTED PROBLEMS: N/A.

JEEP

WRANGLER ★★

RATING: Below Average. In spite of its dated design, the Wrangler is one of the most off-road-capable Jeeps ever made, but it falls far short when driven on-road. Nevertheless, the Jeep cachet attracts many first-time buyers who want the off-road thrills and know this little SUV's limits. **Road performance:** This entry-level Jeep's impressive "bush" performance is taken away by its overall poor reliability and dangerous on-road performance, highlighted by the powertrain suddenly jumping out of gear when the outside temperature drops, or the steering and suspension going into a "death wobble" after passing over potholes or speed bumps. Plus, its short wheelbase, loud and porous cabin, and mediocre highway performance makes the Wrangler annoying at best as a daily commuter and

KEY FACTS

Canadian Price (Firm): *two-door Sport:* $19,345, *four-door Unlimited:* $24,445, *two-door Sahara:* $26,245, *two-door Rubicon:* $29,245, *four-door Unlimited Rubicon:* $34,495 **U.S. Price:** *two-door Sport:* $22,045, *Sport S:* $24,245, *Sahara:* $27,745, *Sahara 70th:* $29,055, *Mojave:* $29,975, *Rubicon:* $29,820 **Canadian Freight:** $1,400 **U.S. Freight:** $800

POWERTRAIN (REAR-DRIVE/PART-TIME/FULL-TIME AWD)

Engine: 3.6L V6 (285 hp); Transmissions: 6-speed man. • 5-speed auto.

DIMENSIONS/CAPACITY (BASE)

Passengers: 2/3; Wheelbase: 116 in.; H: 71/W: 74/L: 173 in.; Headroom F/R: 5.5/5.0 in.; Legroom F/R: 41/28 in.; Cargo volume: 34.5 cu. ft.; Fuel tank: 70L/regular; Tow limit: 3,500 lb.; Load capacity: 850 lb.; Turning circle: 43 ft.; Ground clearance: 8 in.; Weight: *Sport:* 3,849 lb., *Rubicon:* 4,165 lb.

outright uncomfortable as a road trip vehicle. The V6 engine is powerful enough for most chores, but fuel economy suffers with the automatic 5-speed. Handling is compromised by vague steering and low cornering limits (standard stability control is a plus). Violent shaking makes the vehicle practically uncontrollable when passing over small bumps at cruising speeds. A rigid frame makes for a stiff, jiggly ride and clumsy handling. All Wranglers are four-wheel drive and feature a low-range gear for off-road use that shouldn't be left engaged on dry pavement. **Strong points:** The Wrangler comes with a roomy, plush cabin with plenty of headroom. Unlimited models with four doors have 1.6 inches more legroom in the back and lots of cargo space. **Weak points:** These little SUVs are selling at their full list price and are not likely to be discounted by much as the year progresses. Getting in and out takes some acrobatics and patience; the two-door interior isn't very uncomfortable; and there is only a small amount of cargo room in the back. Fuel economy? Much less than advertised (don't believe government-posted figures). **Safety:** Safety features include stability control with rollover sensing, hill-start assist, and anti-lock brakes. **New for 2013:** Trailer sway dampening; Quadra Coil suspension; upgraded seats; an auto-dimming rear-view mirror; a better tire-pressure monitoring system; revised LED courtesy lights; dual windshield wiper nozzles; and a premium softtop. 2014s get a heavy-duty 8-speed transmission.

ALERT! Owners report that the Wrangler's off-road prowess is compromised by poor original equipment tires and thin body panels. Although there's not much you can do about the body panels, *www.tirerack.com* can give you invaluable, unbiased tips on the best and cheapest tires for the kind of driving you intend to do.

OVERVIEW: The Wrangler is the smallest and least expensive (we're talking bare bones here) Jeep you can find. It's an iconic SUV that can easily handle open-air off-road driving anywhere you choose and still be presentable for Saturday night cruising downtown. How's this for versatility? The standard softtop can be folded down, or the available hard top can be taken off. Then, if you want more adventure, the doors can be removed and the windshield folded down—in effect, creating many different vehicles out of one.

The two-door Wrangler is offered in Sport, Sahara, and Rubicon trim with standard four-wheel drive powered by a 285 hp 3.6L V6 engine, hooked to a standard 6-speed manual with Overdrive or an optional 5-speed automatic with Overdrive. Also standard is electronic stability control with roll control, traction control, brake assist, and hill hold control. The Rubicon offers equipment that off-road enthusiasts usually pick up for less money from independent suppliers, like heavy-duty axles, front and rear electronic locking differentials, 32-inch BF Goodrich mud tires, a sway bar disconnect system, rock rails, and a heavy-duty transfer case with a 4:1 low-gear ratio. The Unlimited is a four-door Wrangler that carries five people and their luggage.

COST ANALYSIS: The 2013 model has enough new equipment to make it a better buy than a 2012 leftover. **Best alternatives:** Honda CR-V or Element, Hyundai Tucson, Nissan Xterra, Subaru Forester, and Toyota RAV4. Remember, none of these other models do as well as the Wrangler off-road. **Options:** Softtop models are nice touches, but beware of water and wind leaks. Keep an eye out for the optional suspension system, which includes larger shock absorbers and heavy-duty springs. An aftermarket anti-theft system is also a plus. Ditch the Firestone tires. **Rebates:** The 2012 models are practically sold out, and they are expected to stay in short supply. Therefore, expect to buy a 2013 with a small discount of no more than 5 percent on the higher-end models, if you are lucky. Four-door models are even harder to find, and they are selling at a premium with little haggling allowed. **Depreciation:** Average, despite their overall popularity. A 2009 two-door X model that sold for $19,995 is worth barely $11,000 today. Even the much-in-demand 2009 four-door, entry-level Unlimited Sport version that originally retailed for $25,695 is now fetching only about $14,500. This is why you should hold onto your Wrangler until the depreciation losses have levelled off after five to eight years. **Insurance cost:** Higher than average. **Parts supply/cost:** Parts are frequently back ordered, and they can be costly. This is especially true for AC, transmission, and ABS components. Repair costs are average during the warranty period. **Warranty:** Bumper-to-bumper 3 years/60,000 km; powertrain 5 years/100,000 km; rust perforation 5 years/160,000 km. **Supplementary warranty:** Get an extended powertrain warranty because early reports on the Pentastar V6 aren't encouraging. Also, brake, powertrain, and exhaust system repairs should be carried out by franchised independents that provide extensive warranties on their work (lifetime). **Highway/city fuel economy:** *3.6L V6 man.:* 9.3/12.7 L/100 km, 30/22 mpg. *3.6L V6 auto.:* 9.5/12.6 L/100 km, 30/22 mpg.

OWNER-REPORTED PROBLEMS: Owners report frequent engine, transmission, fuel system, steering clock spring, and brake failures, in addition to subpar fit and finish. Other complaints include a fire igniting in the front end while vehicle was parked; engine exhaust valves leaking; misfiring/low compression at #2 engine cylinder (faulty exhaust camshaft phasers); and #2 engine cylinder ticking with intermittent loss of power:

> Engine developed a ticking sound on driver's side engine bay. Sounds like engine is missing or tapping on driver's side. Loss of power/stalls more common now. Took vehicle to Chrysler and they say that my engine is just "loud" compared to all other 2012's and that it's normal. They told me to just drive it until it fails and then bring it back in

because Chrysler corporate will not allow a dealership to work on the engine and fix it until a failure occurs.

The automatic transmission Tiptronic shift is much too sensitive, and the manual transmission is hard to shift and often pops out of gear:

Automatic transmission with "electronic range select" allows a downshift with a move of the shift lever to the left when in "D" drive. A move to the right up-shifts. Accidental downshifts occur frequently because of "hair-trigger" nature of shift lever controls. The slightest, barely perceptible movement left causes a downshift, often unintended and unexpected. Up-shifting requires a definite movement to the right. Discussion of the issue with 2012 automatic Wranglers drivers on Jeep Internet forums suggests a number of people experience and have a problem with this, while a number of drivers state their shifter requires a definite move left to downshift. I experience frequent, accidental downshifts on every trip due to this defect.

•

The transmission became difficult to engage 1st gear. Shifting into all others was very notchy. Finally, in traffic, it became impossible to engage 1st gear at all. The vehicle had to be started in 2nd gear. The vehicle had limped in to the dealer. Upon inspection it was found that the 1st gear synchro had cracked and failed. This can create a hazardous situation in busy traffic. This transmission has been reported by various user forums as faulty and prone to failure, including popping out of gear and difficult shifting. Popping out of gear in a busy intersection could be dangerous, especially if you are unable to engage another gear.

•

My 2012 Wrangler Sport (6sp) has a faulty transmission. It makes a horrible rattle at high rpms in 3rd and 4th gear, the gears whine and 1st is really h[a]rd to engage when the vehicle is slowly rolling. Sometimes I have to double clutch it just to get 1st gear to work when rolling. Reverse grinds. The gear shifter shakes excessively when vehicle is in 4th and 5th gear. Shifting from 1st to 2nd is notchy as is 5th to 6th and when putting it into Reverse. The clutch often has a crunchy feel when I press the pedal to the floor.

Loose horn pads; steering pulls to the right; brake squealing; fuel spills out during fill-ups; and when it rains, water leaks through the firewall and collects on the inside front floorboards.

SERVICE BULLETIN-REPORTED PROBLEMS: Countermeasures to eliminate engine misfiring. *2011–12 models:* Manual transmission pops out of gear (January 12, 2012, TSB #21-002-12). Light to moderate paint imperfections. Water leak onto front floor.

RATING: Below Average, for two important reasons: First, during the past decade the Grand Cherokee has been beset with chronic automatic transmission, brake system, and electrical system defects in addition to abysmally bad fit and finish. Take, for example, the fact that Jeep placed 27th out of 33 brands in J.D. Power and Associates' ranking of initial quality released in June 2010. Second, this year's 2013 model is mostly a carryover of the 2012, which is noted for some of the same powertrain and body deficiencies decried in the past. *Lemon-Aid* has learned from 42 years of rating Chrysler cars and trucks that revamped Chrysler models can be much more problematic than previous models. **Road performance:** The Grand Cherokee is built on a proven rear-drive unibody platform that the Mercedes-Benz ML has used for years; when combined with front and rear independent suspension systems, the result is enhanced on-road handling and comfort. Also, the stiffer body reduces noise, vibration, and harshness. The 3.6L V6 is adequate, but it has to be pushed to move this heavy SUV; the V8 makes a better match. Low-range gearing for off-road driving is lacking on most models, though it's available with the Quadra-Drive II option. **Strong points:** The 290 hp Pentastar V6

KEY FACTS

Canadian Price (Firm): *Laredo:* $37,995, *Laredo X:* $43,185, *Limited:* $47,195, *Overland:* $50,195 **U.S. Price:** *Laredo:* $30,215, *Laredo X:* $34,215, *Limited:* $36,715, *Overland:* $39,260, *SRT8:* $49,000 **Canadian Freight:** $1,400 **U.S. Freight:** $750

POWERTRAIN (REAR-DRIVE/PART-TIME/FULL-TIME AWD)

Engines: 3.6L V6 (290 hp) • 5.7L V8 (360 hp) • 6.4L V8 (470 hp) Transmissions: 5-speed auto. • 6-speed auto. • 8-speed auto.

DIMENSIONS/CAPACITY (BASE)

Passengers: 2/3; Wheelbase: 114.8 in.; H: 69.4/W: 84.8/L: 189.8 in.; Cargo volume: 36.3 cu. ft.; Fuel tank: 80L/ regular; Tow limit: 3,500–7,200 lb. (the higher towing capacity applies to the 4×2 model); Load capacity: 850 lb.; Turning circle: 37.1 ft.; Ground clearance: 11.1 in.; Weight: *Sport:* 3,849 lb., *Rubicon:* 4,165 lb.

boosts power with 80 horses more than the previous 3.8L V6 engine. It features Variable Valve Timing, showing an increase of 33 percent in horsepower and 11 percent in torque over its predecessor, while also supposedly improving fuel economy up to 11 percent. The cabin is quiet and well-appointed. **Weak points:** Grand Cherokees sell at a premium, and prices will remain high until production is ramped up in early 2013. A good reason to wait until mid-2013 to buy the new Grand Cherokee: The engine, automatic transmission, and electrical system have shown some quality glitches in the first-series production. Fit and finish is quite poor (especially the doors), and the touch screen radio isn't user-friendly. **Safety:** NHTSA gives the 2011–13 4×2 four stars for frontal crash protection, five stars for side-impact crashworthiness, and only three stars for rollover resistance. The 4×4 model has a similar rating, except that rollover resistance was a bit better, at four stars. The IIHS awarded a "Good" ranking for frontal offset, side, and rear collision protection (head restraints). Roof strength was also judged "Good." Other important safety features: An electronic feature on all models offers automatic crash notification, emergency calls, roadside assistance calls, remote door unlock, and stolen vehicle location assistance. There's also electronic stability control; electronic roll mitigation; trailer-sway control; hill-start assist and hill-descent control; full-length side curtain airbags to protect front and rear outboard passengers; seat-mounted side thorax airbags; active head restraints that deploy in the event of a rear collision; an optional park assist system that detects stationary objects; a blind spot/rear cross-path detection system; adaptive cruise control that decreases a vehicle's preset cruise-control speed when closing in on another vehicle or when another vehicle pulls into the same lane (this has been a failure-prone feature in the past); a forward collision warning system that detects when the vehicle may be approaching another vehicle too rapidly; and a remote starting feature. **New for 2013:** The Grand Cherokee returns unchanged until the debut of the 2014 model year in January 2013, when it picks up an 8-speed automatic and an optional 241 hp 3.0L diesel coupled to a 5-speed automatic transmission.

ALERT! Make sure the headlights provide sufficient illumination during a night road test; many dissatisfied drivers wish they had tested this before buying their Grand Cherokee:

> The headlight system is tilted down so visibility distance is very low. There is about 20 to 30 feet [6–9 m] of visibility then there is a black wall of darkness in front of the car. You can't drive the car safely at night on unlit roads. Jeep refuses to admit they know of any problem despite the countless people on the Internet that claim they have this problem.

OVERVIEW: Almost 20 years ago, Jeep created its premium SUV segment with the introduction of its upscale Grand Cherokee, which was an immediate hit. However, it soon lost sales momentum by falling behind in highway performance and quality control. Jeep sold about 300,000 Grand Cherokees in 1999 and roughly 50,300 in 2009. The 2014 model's powertrain upgrades seek to recapture the lost ground in a competitive field that Asian automakers, GM, and Ford dominate.

COST ANALYSIS: Don't waste your money on the short-lived 2013 version; a second-series 2014 diesel would be a better investment. This will give the factory more time to get the 2014 redesign bugs fixed. **Best alternatives:** Honda CR-V or Element, Hyundai Tucson, Subaru Forester, and Toyota RAV4. Remember, none of these other models can follow the Grand Cherokee off-road, but on the other hand, they won't be following it to the repair bay, either. **Options:** The $1,250 sunroof option will only add more rattles and noise while giving you less headroom. Ditch the Firestone and Bridgestone tires. **Rebates:** Brisk sales have caused the 2012 models to be seriously back ordered, and the shortened 2013 model year won't help matters much. Wait until production picks up and rebates are sweetened during early spring or summer. Also, it's axiomatic that redesigned models produced during the second half of the model year have fewer factory-related glitches. **Depreciation:** About average. A 2010 entry-level North V6 that sold for $41,645 is now worth about $25,000. **Insurance cost:** Higher than average. **Parts supply/cost:** Parts are slow to arrive and may cost more than expected, especially for AC, transmission, and ABS components. **Annual maintenance cost:** Repair costs are average during the warranty period. **Warranty:** Bumper-to-bumper 3 years/60,000 km; powertrain 5 years/100,000 km; rust perforation 5 years/160,000 km. **Supplementary warranty:** Get an extended powertrain warranty. Also, brake, powertrain, and exhaust system repairs should be carried out by independent agencies that provide extensive warranties on their work (lifetime). **Highway/city fuel economy:** 3.6L: 8.9/13.0 L/100 km, 32/22 mpg. 5.7L: 10.6/15.7 L/100 km, 27/18 mpg (thanks to the Multi-Displacement System (MDS) feature on the V8).

OWNER-REPORTED PROBLEMS: Most complaints centre on the automatic transmission, electrical system (especially vehicle stalling, or not starting), and fit and finish problems. Two under-hood fires reported while vehicle was underway; sudden engine power loss and violent shaking; engine surges when brakes are applied:

> I was going approximately 20–25 [32–40 km/h] approaching a signal light. I let off the gas and applied the brake as the light was red. As I let off the gas, the engine began to rev higher and as I applied the brake I had to apply it harder and harder as the engine continued to rev even higher. I began to smell the brakes burning as they tried to hold the car back. Fortunately, I had the foresight to put the car in Neutral. It continued to rev for about 5 seconds and then went down to normal. It has happened once. No warning lights went on. The dealer said that they contacted the Detroit technical bureau and they suggested that maybe it was the floor mat, or my foot, etc, etc but claimed they had no other reports of this occurring. I don't have carpets as I opted for rubber mats and they sit tight to the floor. And my foot was not stuck on the gas.

The 6-speed manual transmission sometimes pops out of gear; the automatic transmission slips erratically in and out of Second gear, suddenly downshifts, and leaks fluid:

> Transmission shifted into 4 wheel drive (4WD) low, suddenly, accompanied by a clunk and change in vehicle speed from downshifting. Lights came on in the dash indicating

loss of traction control and 4WD service needed. This event continued to happen sporadically while driving until we made it back to the dealership. Since downshifting into 4WD occurred while driving at normal roadway operating speeds (approximately 20–40 mph [32–64 km/h]) it certainly felt like a safety issue, compounded by the fact that traction control was lost as a result. Once back at the dealership, the service department found that the transfer case had an internal failure. The vehicle was in the shop for about 3 weeks while the transfer case was replaced under warranty.

Yes, there are reports of sudden, unintended acceleration, too:

The contact owns a 2011 Jeep Grand Cherokee 4×4. While stopped at the light, the Check Engine light illuminated and the vehicle suddenly accelerated while the brake was depressed. There was an abnormal increase in RPMs to 3,000. The contact placed the gear in park, turned the vehicle off and the engine returned to normal for a moment before continuing to accelerate abnormally. The vehicle was taken to the dealer who performed a diagnostic and located the failure at the throttle body. The dealer replaced the accelerator pedal and the throttle body but to no avail as the failure continued to recur. The manufacturer was contacted and they advised the contact to take the vehicle back to the dealer. The vehicle was not repaired. The failure mileage was 4,000 [6,440 km] and the current mileage was 4,300 miles [6,920 km].

•

On March 24th, 2011 it was beginning to snow, I was stopped at the corner stop sign waiting to make a right turn and the car surged forward into the intersection, skidding onto the sidewalk, just missing a pedestrian and a utility pole. If it was my daughter driving, who is a new driver, I don't think she would have been so lucky as to miss the pedestrian or the pole. This time I called the dealer and told them I almost died in the car, due to the same problem, sudden acceleration, Engine and Throttle light on. They actually had the nerve to tell me to drive the car to the dealer for service.... There were 3 electrical failures leading up to the complete electrical and engine system shutting down while driving.

Frequent airbag failures, fuel-tank leaks, fuel-pump failures, malfunctioning fuel gauges, front end torsion bar failures and fluid leaks, and clutch failures. The power steering locks up, and there's excessive and premature brake wear, leading to brake failures. Other brake complaints concern the vehicle pulling to the left when braking, the rear brakes suddenly locking up while driving in the rain and approaching a stop sign, and the vehicle going into open throttle position when the brakes are applied. There have also been many instances where drivers mistook the accelerator for the brake because the pedals are so close together. The tire-pressure monitoring system is malfunction-prone. Body welds and seams are susceptible to premature rusting; there have been frequent complaints about peeling paint and water leaks. Doors fail to latch due to faulty hinges; tailgate back glass exploded when the tailgate was opened, and Chrysler denied the warranty claim.

SERVICE BULLETIN-REPORTED PROBLEMS: *2012 Grand Cherokees:* Troubleshooting engine misfiring and power loss. Engine power sag, hesitation may be fixed by replacing the power control module. On the other hand, a shudder felt when accelerating, decelerating, or when coasting may require only the reflashing or changing of the drivetrain control module. Power liftgate won't open or close. A rear shock absorber buzz, squeak, or rattle may signal the need to replace both rear upper shock mounts. Excessive exhaust noise can be corrected by replacing the exhaust pipe/catalytic converter assembly. Steering fluid leak, noise. Light to moderate paint imperfections.

Ford

Ford Is Out of Sync

Ford Sync module stopped working and when you prompt the system to go into mobile apps, Sync responds "no mobile apps found." Took to Ford dealer and after days of troubleshooting got the module replaced. 2 days later it failed again. It's not my phone. Phone works just fine in exact same vehicle on lot.

2012 FOCUS OWNER

SAFERCAR.GOV COMPLAINTS

Ford Safety Not Automatic

I was told this car had "automatic transmission". After a few hundred miles on it, I noticed the transmission shifted sporadically and with no prediction. Engine shuddered, car lost power and was not safe to drive. The key here is no prediction as to how the car will react when under acceleration. Took to dealer and was told "this isn't an automatic transmission—it's a computer-controlled manual that has to learn how you drive". Dealer uploaded a computer update from Ford. The next hundred miles of driving almost caused numerous accidents due to lack of acceleration and uneven performance. 6/4/2012 I tried to merge into traffic and car refused to speed up. I almost caused a major accident, but numerous drivers slammed on their brakes and/or swerved and averted multiple collisions. Took the car to the dealer. 6/5/2012 Was told by head tech "It just has to get used to how you drive". I told him there were three different people driving this Focus. He said we can't because that would just end up totally "confusing" the computer.

2012 FOCUS OWNER

SAFERCAR.GOV COMPLAINTS

Ford Quality Plummets

J.D. Power and Associates' 2012 Initial Quality Study (IQS) results released last June hammered Ford over its poor quality and complicated MyFord Touch and MyLincoln Touch electronic systems and other controls. The company's dual-clutch automatic transmission was also singled out as being balky and unpredictable. Owners said Ford's Power Shift automatic transmission, found in the Ford Fiesta and Ford Focus, was particularly troublesome. This is quite a blow to Ford, which has trumpeted other poll results that show its overall vehicle quality control has improved over the past few years.

Although ranked fifth last year, Ford fell to 23rd this year, with an estimated 116 problems per 100 vehicles. This is up from 93 last year and worse than the industry average of 107 owner-reported problems. The Lincoln division didn't do much better; it dropped from number 8 to 17 this year, with 111 problems.

Quality and Performance

Some of Ford's latest model offerings fall far short of the company's carefully orchestrated hype. Highway performance is much less than promised, head restraints are poorly designed, interior instruments and controls are far from user-friendly, high-tech communication and navigation gizmos are needlessly complicated, and quality control is woefully inadequate (see the reports on "lag and lurch" self-destructing manual transmissions in the Mustang section and failure-prone automatics in the Fusion section). Yet, Ford's products represent the best of what was formerly called the Detroit Big Three—shows how far the benchmark has been lowered.

In the past decade, powertrain defects, faulty suspensions and steering components, and premature brake wear and brake failures were the primary concerns of Ford owners. The company's engine and automatic transmission deficiencies affected most of its products, and these deficiencies have existed since the early '80s, judging by *Lemon-Aid* reader reports, NHTSA complaints, confidential Ford internal documents, and technical service bulletins. And we aren't talking about mechanical and electronic components only; Ford's fit and finish has traditionally also remained far below Japanese and South Korean standards.

In fact, four 2012 models, the Fiesta, Focus, Mustang, and Explorer, have already proven to be major disappointments, say owners, *Motor Trend*, *Consumer Reports*, and Ford's own confidential service bulletins.

While it's "debugging" these cars, Ford must extend its base warranty to cover powertrain defects for at least seven years. Additionally, the automaker should be generous in giving out free "goodwill" repairs to correct other factory-related problems. With pressure from *Lemon-Aid* and the Canadian Automobile Protection Association, Ford did just this with its rust-cankered lineup in the '70s, and a decade later, the automaker extended its engine and transmission warranties to compensate thousands of Canadian car owners whose original warranty had expired. Both actions created a sales surge that gave back to Ford Canada the market share it had lost due to the bad publicity surrounding its powertrain failures and rust-prone body panels.

Ford's much ballyhooed, redesigned 2011 Explorer handles less like a truck and provides better fuel economy now that Ford has replaced its body-on-frame platform with a car-like unibody chassis. Unfortunately, the reworked Explorer also brings with it serious performance and quality control deficiencies decried by both *Consumer Reports* and *Motor Trend*. Surprisingly, *Consumer Reports* gave the Explorer an easier time than *Motor Trend* did in this May 2011 article:

> We didn't like driving the Explorer very much.... Massive, freaky, comical torque steer (the vehicle pulls to one side when accelerating). The big Ford also rode worse than much of the competition.... We also had issues with the seating position...the chassis needs some refinement.... Car feels wobbly at speed—not confidence inspiring.... The My Ford Touch system shut down for about 60 seconds, taking away all climate, stereo, phone, and navigation controls.

Consumer Reports' June 2011 edition confirms many of *MT*'s findings: *CR* points out that the 6-speed automatic transmission shifts slowly at times, the engine is noisy, handling is mediocre with excessive body roll when cornering, and the slow steering transmits little road feedback. Interior ergonomics and comfort apparently wasn't Ford's "Job 1" with the reworked Explorer, either: The driving position is described as "flawed," with limited footroom, a poorly placed footrest, and pedals that are mounted too close together. Front seat cushions felt narrow and too short; rear cushions too hard, too low, or too short. *CR* rated fit and finish as average, and the MyFord Touch system was judged to be overly complicated, with the Sync-voice-command system often misunderstanding simple commands.

Ford is shifting its product mix to smaller vehicles that use more-reliable Japanese components and are assembled more cheaply in Mexico or offshore. Like most major automakers, the company is copying European designs, importing some models directly from Europe, then transferring their production to North America. By selling and building worldwide models that are virtually identical, Ford can keep production costs down and quickly get to market more agile, fuel-efficient, and highway-proven vehicles that follow the marketplace's shifting trends.

Improved Safety Features

Ford has been a leader in developing more crashworthy cars and trucks and is now offering innovative inflatable rear seat belts. In fact, we can balance out some of our negative 2012 Explorer comments by stressing that the 2011 Explorer was the first vehicle to offer the industry-first rear inflatable seat belts, and is a IIHS Top Safety Pick. In total, Ford has 12 vehicles named as 2011 Top Safety Picks.

EcoBoost

Get used to the term "EcoBoost." It is used by Ford to describe its new family of turbocharged and direct-injected 4-cylinder and 6-cylinder gasoline engines that deliver power and torque consistent with larger displacement powerplants. Engines using the EcoBoost design are touted to be 20 percent more fuel-efficient than naturally aspirated engines. Ford says the EcoBoost's power output and fuel efficiency rival hybrid and diesel engine technology, and the company intends on using it extensively in future vehicle applications. The F-150 trucks' 3.5L EcoBoost engine, utilizing turbo and direct injection, is giving other competitors a run for their money. Already Chrysler and GM have redesigned their small pickups to be more fuel-efficient.

FIESTA ★★

KEY FACTS

Canadian Price (Firm): *Sedan S:* $14,000, *Sedan SE:* $15,999, *Hatchback SE:* $16,001, *Titanium:* $19,001 **U.S. Price:** *S:* $14,200, *SE:* $16,200, *Titanium:* $18,200, *Hatchback:* $14,200 **Canadian Freight:** $1,500 **U.S. Freight:** $795 **POWERTRAIN (FRONT-DRIVE)** Engine: 1.6L DOHC 4 (120 hp); Transmissions: 5-speed man. • 6-speed manumatic.

DIMENSIONS/CAPACITY

Passengers: 2/3; Wheelbase: 98 in.; H: 58 /L: 173.6/W: 66.8 in.; Legroom F/R: 42.2/31.2 in.; Cargo volume: 12.8 cu. ft.; Fuel tank: 45L/regular; Tow limit: Not recommended; Turning circle: 34.4 ft.; Ground clearance: 6.7 in.; Weight: 2,578 lb.

RATING: Below Average. Powertrain problems are worrisome. **Road performance:** Responsive steering, easily-modulated brakes and nimble, better-than-average handling. A choppy ride on some highways. The PowerShift automatic transmission shifts erratically and unexpectedly. **Strong points:** Stylish. The car accelerates well with the manual gearbox. There is also just adequate space in the front of this five-seater for the driver and passenger (the Honda Fit provides more room for passengers and cargo). Little noise intrudes into the well-appointed cabin. Most gauges and instruments are easy to see and access. A tilt and telescopic steering wheel, height-adjustable driver's seat, and capless fuel filler also come with the car. A relatively high ground clearance reduces "belly drag" in the snow (an inch higher than the Toyota Yaris and VW Jetta); the cabin is welcoming; and luxury features are available. **Weak points:** Owners report that the automatic transmission cuts gas mileage by almost 15 percent. Rear passenger space is cramped; even Honda's Fit has more storage space than the Fiesta five-door hatchback. Drivers find the head restraints force a chin-to-chest driving position that's so uncomfortable they're removing the head restraints altogether. Seats could use a bit more lumbar and thigh bolstering. Armrest is too far forward on the Fiesta's door. Rear seatbacks may not lock into position, allowing any cargo to fly forward as a deadly projectile in a sudden stop. Limited cargo and rear seat space. The dash houses angled keys that look good but lack functionality. **Safety:** Available safety features include ABS, traction control, an anti-skid system, side curtain airbags, front side airbags, and a driver knee airbag. Fiesta earned four stars for frontal crash protection and rollover resistance and garnered five stars for side crashworthiness from NHTSA. IIHS gave it top marks in frontal offset, side, and rear impact occupant protection, as well as protection from excessive roof intrusion into the cabin. **New for 2013:** Nothing significant.

ALERT! Don't get sucked in by frivolous options: A power moonroof adds $745 to the bottom line, a Fiesta stripe graphic adds $195, and an interior style package adds $925. Check out the added versatility of the hatchback models. Also be wary of the front head restraints:

> The headrest is causing me to have headaches due to the forward leaning position of the headrest. I have tried all the situations of the seat and it is the same for all of them. I am 5'2" and in my research have found most other short people have the same issue.

OVERVIEW: Available as a five-door hatchback or sedan, this 120 hp 1.6L 4-cylinder minicar is a front-drive subcompact manufactured and marketed throughout the world since 1976. Its return to Canada and the U.S. in the fall of 2010 makes it the first Fiesta model to be sold in North America since 1980. Essentially, Ford plans to import the little car from Europe until it can transfer production to Canada and the United States. Without a doubt, the Fiesta has what it takes to be a fine small car, in theory. The only caveat is that Ford has never imported a European-derived vehicle that went on to become a success in North America. Poor quality, performance, and servicing have afflicted most of these imports and sent them packing back to Europe. Will the Fiesta repeat history? Don't be the first to find out.

COST ANALYSIS: The 2012 and 2013 Fiesta models aren't very different from each other; go for the 2013, since prices aren't expected to increase by much and the extra year will give Ford time to fix the car's first-year factory-related bugs, like those affecting the automatic transmission:

> This vehicle, bought new in September, 2010, had loud sounds coming from the engine area. Ford has put 2 new transmissions in it. The 3rd repair attempt was diagnosed as a problem that "engineering has to come up with a solution". Ford, on two of the 3 repair attempts, sent out a field engineer to inspect the vehicle. The first engineer (on the 2nd repair attempt) said to put another new transmission in the vehicle, (the 2nd new transmission to be put on the vehicle). This still did not solve the problem. The problem, according to the service manager (on the 3rd repair attempt—2 at the dealer, and this 1st attempt at another dealer, third overall) said "It's the clutch. We took other cars out, and with the laptop we were able to duplicate it on every one of them." The duplication he was

speaking of involves the transmission and its clutch system, just introduced this model year of 2011 by Ford. It is the 6 speed automatic transmission, with a dual clutch. The situation is that when you come to a sudden stop, the transmission does not downshift to a lower gear fast enough. When you try to accelerate, after a sudden stop, the vehicle seems stuck in a higher gear. The car momentarily stalls before taking off. This is very dangerous when trying to cross lanes of a highway at busy times. We do not feel safe in it. We were told, in an email, by a Ford customer service manager, "As I explained to you on the phone the Ford engineers are aware and are researching a solution for your vehicle's concern. Your vehicle is safe to drive so you may continue to enjoy it while waiting to be contacted by [name withheld] service manager at the dealer and myself".

Another sudden, unintended acceleration experience may be related to the cruise control feature:

While driving with the cruise control set at 40 mph [64 km/h], the vehicle suddenly accelerated up to 60 mph [97 km/h] and the rpms increased to over 500 rpms. The contact shut the cruise control off and the speed resumed its normal state. The vehicle was taken to an authorized dealer where the computer was reprogrammed. The failure occurred again and the vehicle was taken back to the dealer. The manufacturer had not been notified. The failure mileage was 8,000 miles [12,870 km].

And if the cruise control is okay, watch out for the ventilation duct falling:

Ventilation duct falls onto driver's right foot during vehicle operation, inhibiting the driver's ability to control the accelerator.

Interestingly, Fiesta models take a huge price jump with the bundled optional AC included. **Best alternatives:** Honda Civic (2011) or Fit, Hyundai Accent or Elantra, Kia Rio, Mazda2 or Mazda3, and Nissan Versa. The Ford Focus is the better buy, if you must buy a Ford. Its fuel economy is similar, and you get a more comfortable ride with more room. **Options:** Be wary of original equipment Firestone or Bridgestone tires. **Rebates:** $500 to $1,000 in early 2013; probably more once word gets out about the poor quality. **Depreciation:** Below average. **Insurance cost:** Below average. **Parts supply/cost:** Average. **Annual maintenance cost:** Estimated to be average. **Warranty:** Bumper-to-bumper 3 years/60,000 km; powertrain 5 years/100,000 km; rust perforation 5 years/ unlimited km. **Supplementary warranty:** A good idea for the powertrain, judging by owner complaints and internal service bulletins covering the first-year 2011 models. **Highway/city fuel economy:** *Man.:* 5.3/7.1 L/100 km, 53/40 mpg. *SFE auto:* 4.9/6.8 L/100 km, 58/42 mpg. *Auto.:* 5.1/6.9 L/100 km, 55/41 mpg.

OWNER-REPORTED PROBLEMS: Airbags failed to deploy; fuel leaked under the car; oil pan, water pump, and front crank seal leaks; engine stalling and surging along with poor transmission performance; electrical shorts; excessive steering-wheel vibration; noisy brakes; and various fit and finish deficiencies (for example, door panel fell apart).

Brake and accelerator pedals are placed too close together. When the brake is released while in Drive, the car rolls backward:

> Ford Service explained that it is due to the double clutch transmission. The driver has 3 seconds to press the accelerator before the brake releases.

One car had so many electrical problems, it was bought back by Ford; another Fiesta caught fire:

> Attorney writes on behalf of clients in regards to vehicle catching fire while driving: The driver of the vehicle stated he was driving with the cruise control activated, when suddenly the vehicle began to lose power and the heater stopped working. The driver stopped the vehicle, after seeing a glare at the driver's side window. He turned the vehicle off and removed the key. The fire started in the front of the vehicle under the dashboard. According to the fire report, the fire was due to an electrical problem.

Sudden power-steering failure. Driver's seat belt latch may not "catch." A rust-prone muffler is a common issue. One owner says passing other cars is a death-defying experience, with the car suddenly speeding up and then losing power. Fuel economy rating and odometer readings are not believable.

SERVICE BULLETIN-REPORTED PROBLEMS: *2011–12:* AC lack of heat; blower motor frozen in cold weather. Steering column pop, clunk, knock during slow-speed turns. *2011:* Customer Satisfaction Program 11B31 (secret warranty) calls for a free upgraded clutch replacement on the DPS6 automatic transmission. Engine stalling and surging along with poor transmission performance may be due to a malfunctioning transmission control module. Automatic transmission fluid leak from the clutch housing will require a major repair covered by the base warranty (TSB #11-6-8). Poor or no engine start, or transmission engagement. Engine block heater coolant leakage and spillover into the spark plug well.

FOCUS ★★

RATING: Below Average. **Road performance:** This small car is fun to drive and a fairly good highway performer when the transmission is working properly—which isn't often. Like with the Fiesta's similar transmission, overall performance both on the highway and in town is hampered by a failure-prone, poorly designed, and badly calibrated PowerShift automatic that stumbles and surges. Its deficiencies compromise safety and fuel economy and lead to white-knuckle driving when merging or when slowing down. Nevertheless, the car usually gives a smooth, supple ride, shows excellent handling and road holding, and provides a commanding view of the highway. **Strong points:** Stylish, with a well-appointed interior and plenty of high-tech options. Impressive fuel economy. Very reliable from 2005–10, which is all the more surprising because the 2000–04 models were quintessential lemons. **Weak points:** Infotainment controls can be finicky, and backseat legroom is minimal. **Safety:** Standard ABS, stability and traction

KEY FACTS

Canadian Price (Negotiable): *Sedan S:* $14,869, *Sedan SE:* $16,219, *Hatchback:* $17,020, *SEL:* $18,444, *Hatchback:* $19,245, *Titanium:* $21,114, *Hatchback:* $21,648, *Electric:* $ 41,199 **U.S. Price:** *Sedan S: $16,500, Sedan SE: $17,400, Five-door: $18,200, SEL:* $20,300, *Titanium:* $23,200 **Canadian Freight:** $1,500 **U.S. Freight:** $795

POWERTRAIN (FRONT-DRIVE)

Engine: 2.0L DOHC 4 (160 hp) • Electric motor (143 hp); Transmissions: 5-speed man. • 6-speed auto.

DIMENSIONS/CAPACITY

Passengers: 2/3; Wheelbase: 104.3 in.; H: 57.8/L: 178.5/W: 71.8 in.; Headroom N/A; Legroom F/R: 43.7/33.2 in.; Cargo volume: 13.2 cu. ft.; Fuel tank: 47L/ regular; Tow limit: Not recommended; Turning circle: 36 ft.; Weight: 2,970 lb.

control, and side curtain airbags. Another plus is the Focus's standard torque vectoring control—a first for a car in this class. This feature increases vehicle stability by adding brake force to wheels on one side during turns, which helps keep the vehicle under control. NHTSA gave the four- and five-door 2012 Focus four stars for frontal crashworthiness and rollover resistance and five stars for side protection. IIHS gave its top rating ("Good") for frontal offset, rear, and side crash protection and roof strength. However, head restraints receive criticism for being angled downward too sharply, forcing the head to bend forward. **New for 2013:** A slight restyling. A 1.0L EcoBoost 3-cylinder engine, incorporating direct injection and turbocharging will likely arrive in 2013 and be used by the Fiesta, Focus, and its B-Max and C-Max derivatives. Debut of ST and Electric models.

ALERT! Once again, watch out for the driver head restraints pushing your chin to your chest, especially with the Recaro-equipped ST.

The Focus Electric

A limited number of electric-powered models arrived in the States in late 2011 and sell for almost $40,000, minus government and Ford rebates that could reach $8,000. Ford says the Focus EV will beat the Chevrolet Volt and Nissan Leaf fuel-economy numbers. Charge time on the Focus Electric is predicted to be three to four hours using a 240-volt system—half the time needed by the Leaf, thanks to an onboard charger that is twice as powerful as the Nissan's. A charge on regular 120-volt household current, though, will take almost 20 hours, or about the same time as a Leaf. Ford includes a

120-volt cord with the EV. Best Buy Canada sells a Ford-made 240-volt home charger for approximately $1,500, including installation.

Best Buy supplies the charging station and includes consultation and installation services through its own Geek Squad and third-party licensed electrical contractors. Focus Electric owners can work with their Ford dealer or contact Best Buy directly to set up an in-home consultation and installation.

During the appointment, a Geek Squad agent will conduct a quick electrical survey to ensure the residence can support the charging station. Then, the Geek Squad agent will schedule a master electrician for a charging station installation. The charging unit can be plugged into a 240-volt outlet, instead of being hard-wired into the electrical breaker box. This makes removal and replacement as simple as unplugging and plugging back in, meaning the device can be replaced or upgraded without the use of tools in the event the owner moves. Warranty and repair claims for the charging station will be fielded by Best Buy.

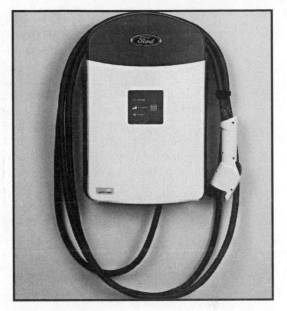

The 240-volt home charging station will allow Focus Electric owners to fully charge their cars in as little as three to four hours. COURTESY FORD

The Electric employs a 143 hp electric motor that has less horsepower but more torque than the 160 hp, 2.0L 4-cylinder engine in the conventional 2012 Focus. A single-speed transmission will get you to a top speed of 135 km/h (84 mph). Aside from the quieter operation and smooth, shiftless power distribution, owners have to contend with the Electric's 700 extra pounds when compared with a gas-powered five-door. Obviously, that much weight degrades both the ride and handling, but what the heck, the energy is *free* (not).

OVERVIEW: The Focus provides better fuel economy, gives a supple ride, and competes with the Chevrolet Cruze, Honda Fit, Hyundai Elantra, and Mazda3. The sedan comes with basics like an audio system with an AM/FM radio, single-disc CD player and MP3 capability, an auxiliary input jack, and a tilt and telescopic steering wheel. Hatchbacks include a few more standard features, like MyKey. All models use a 2.0L 4-cylinder engine, torque vectoring control, and airbags with adaptive venting technology that reduce pressure for smaller occupants.

COST ANALYSIS: Your best bet is to steer clear of the Focus due to its serious quality problems seen with last year's models. If you still want one, pay a bit more for the latest 2013 and cross your fingers that Ford has solved its quality glitches. **Best alternatives:** Take a good look at the Honda Fit—one of the roomiest and most practical hatchbacks around. The Fit is thousands of dollars cheaper than the Focus hatch and sedan. Don't overlook the Hyundai Accent or Elantra and Mazda3 trio, either. They also will appeal to budget-minded shoppers who value performance, cabin space to comfortably seat five, high fuel economy, and a reasonable sales price. **Options:** Ditch the original equipment Firestones. **Rebates:** $1,500–$2,500. **Depreciation:** Average. **Insurance cost:** Average. **Parts supply/cost:** Average. **Annual maintenance cost:** Average. **Warranty:** Bumper-to-bumper 3 years/60,000 km; powertrain 5 years/100,000 km; rust perforation 5 years/unlimited km. **Supplementary warranty:** A good idea for the powertrain. **Highway/city fuel economy:** *Man.:* 5.6/8.0 L/100 km, 50/35 mpg. *Auto.:* 5.8/8.2 L/100 km, 49/34 mpg.

OWNER-REPORTED PROBLEMS: What a difference a year makes; good thing *Lemon-Aid* is an annual guide, because the redesigned 2012–13 Focus has been transformed back into its lemony former state. Last year, 2011 Focus owners posted only seven incidents and *Lemon-Aid* recommended the car. Not this year. So far, NHTSA has recorded 95 complaints (25 would be average) on the 2012 model. The car's deficiencies are legion—mostly related to the powertrain (engine and transmission), brakes, electrical system, steering, and fit and finish:

> Automatic transmission does not shift smoothly. Intermittent vibrates, bucks, hesitates, slips & jerks. Can't rely on take-off acceleration whether it will engage properly, pulling into traffic is very dangerous. Stop and go traffic is very dangerous. It's like someone driving a stick shift and not having the clutch & gas in sync, only it's an automatic so you can't do anything about it. I have had the car in to the service department on 3 occasions. The first time the tech laughed at me and told me it was just the "new" 6-speed transmission. 2nd time, they replaced some parts in the transmission. 3rd time, they had the car 4 days & said there was nothing out of the ordinary happening.

> •

> I bought the 2012 Ford Focus SEL on May 5th 2012. The car has had both front struts replaced, at 69 miles!! The car jerks and refuses to go when you give it gas after being completely stopped, I was almost hit pulling out onto a busy road because the car would not go!!!! The transmission needs to be replaced in this car, however, they will not do that.

SERVICE BULLETIN-REPORTED PROBLEMS: *2012:* Engine controls/drivability issues; automatic transmission controls—various drivability concerns; free transmission clutch replacement; steering wander; front-end crunching, creaking when passing over bumps; MyFord Touch glitches (see next page). Other issues include the loss of steering power assist; erratic fuel gauge readings; and a visible depression in the hood's surface. *2011:* Ford says excessive road wander, steering drift, or uneven rear tire wear may require the installation of a new right rear lower control arm (January 25, 2011, TSB #11-1-1). *2008–11:* An underbody squeak or creaking noise may be silenced by replacing the parking brake cables and routing eyelets (December 16, 2011, TSB #10-24-06). Paint damage? Here is Ford's "secret warranty" that will pay for a new paint job. Shh!

MYFORD TOUCH—VARIOUS FUNCTIONAL ISSUES

BULLETIN NO.: 11-7-29   DATE: JULY 28, 2011

VARIOUS FUNCTIONALITY CONCERNS WITH MYFORD TOUCH

FORD: 2012 Focus

ISSUE: Some 2012 Focus vehicles equipped with MyFord may experience various concerns in the following areas: Blank/black display screen, Radio switches from off to on or changes state after ending a phone call or voice command, phone pairing, incorrect Sirius channel selection using voice command, unable to download photo resolution 800x378, Sirius travel link download time, Sirius channel art logo mismatch, phone book downloads.

LOWER BODY PAINT ABRASION/DAMAGE

BULLETIN NO.: 10-15-6   DATE: AUGUST 16, 2010

PAINT DEGRADATION/ROAD ABRASION

2008–11 Focus

ISSUE: Some 2008–11 Focus vehicles may experience paint damage or road abrasion on the rocker panel and on the side of the vehicle located slightly ahead of the rear tires on both 2 door and 4 door models. Rocker Panel, 1/4 panel, dog leg and/or rear door, dependent on model. This has been reported in geographical areas that commonly experience snow and ice conditions and use various forms of traction enhancers.

ACTION: Follow the Service Procedure steps to correct the condition.

NOTE: Per the warranty and policy manual paint damage caused by conditions such as chips, scratches, dents, dings, road salt, stone chips or other acts of nature are not covered under the new vehicle limited warranty. However, paint abrasion at the dog leg area due to the above circumstances is a unique condition on the focus and, as a result, repairs are eligible for basic warranty coverage.

FUSION, MKZ   ★★/★★★

The Ford Fusion.

KEY FACTS

Canadian Price (Very Soft): *Fusion S 2.5:* $18,784, *SE:* $19,499, *SEL:* $22,169, *SEL V6 AWD:* $26,619, *Sport AWD:* $30,268, *Hybrid:* $29,884, *MKZ Front-drive:* $34,022, *AWD:* $36,260, *Hybrid:* $37,518 **U.S. Price:** *Fusion S:* $19,850, *ST:* $24,495, *Hybrid:* $28,600, *MKZ Front-drive:* $34,645, *Hybrid:* $34,645 **Canadian Freight:** $1,600 **U.S. Freight:** $850

POWERTRAIN (FRONT-DRIVE/AWD)

Engines: *Fusion:* 1.6L EcoBoost 4-cyl. (179 hp) • 2.0L EcoBoost 4-cyl. (240 hp) • 2.5L 4-cyl. (170 hp) • 2.0L 4-cyl. hybrid (185 hp) and plug-in electric; *Fusion ST:* 2.0L EcoBoost 4-cyl. (252 hp); *Lincoln:* 3.7L V6 (300 hp) • 2.0L 4-cyl. hybrid (188 hp); Transmissions: 6-speed man. • 6-speed auto. • CVT

DIMENSIONS/CAPACITY (FUSION)

Passengers: 2/3; Wheelbase: 107 in.; H: 56.9/L: 190.6/W: 72.0 in.; Headroom F/R: 2.5/2.5 in.; Legroom F/R: 40.5/ 28.0 in.; Cargo volume: 16 cu. ft.; Fuel tank: 45L/regular; Tow limit: No towing; Load capacity: 850 lb.; Turning circle: 39 ft.; Ground clearance: 5.0 in.; Weight: 3,285 lb.

RATING: *Fusion:* Below Average. *MKZ:* Average. **Road performance:** *Fusion:* Good acceleration and fair handling; steering is tight, precise, and vibration-free; and the 4-cylinder and V6 engines borrowed from Mazda are competent, thrifty, and dependable. Added rigidity and additional chassis tweaking have resulted in a car that will seat five passengers (four in comfort) and corner reasonably well. Some negatives: Fusion carries a dangerously flawed automatic transmission; brake performance is unreliable; and the car tends to wander all over the road. *MKZ:* The Lincoln accelerates and handles without a hitch. Ride comfort and interior amenities are average. **Strong points:** Stylish. Overall reliability (except for the automatic transmission) is average with the Lincoln MKZ. The Fusion/MKZ Hybrid fuel economy estimates are better than most of the competition's. It can run on one or both of its power sources (to balance acceleration and fuel economy) and requires no plug-in charging. **Weak points:** Cramped rear seating and head restraints can be pure torture. Super-fast depreciation with both the Fusion and Lincoln: A 2007 Fusion SE V6 that sold for $26,899 is now worth only $7,500. A base 2007 Lincoln MKZ that first sold for $37,499? Its resale value is about $10,500. **Safety:** Standard eight airbags and electronic stability control (ESC). NHTSA gives the 2012 Fusion/MKZ four stars for front and side crashworthiness and four stars for rollover resistance and side crash protection; frontal crashworthiness merited three stars. The AWD model earned five stars for rollover resistance. IIHS ranked the 2012 Fusion/MKZ "Good" for roof strength, frontal offset, side, and rear crash safety. The Fusion has a cross-traffic sensor that alerts the driver to vehicles approaching from the side when the car is in Reverse. Owners note poor visibility through the rear windshield. **New for 2013:** The Fusion's V6 option has been dropped; the car has been slightly restyled with new headlights and tail lights; and a shielded underbody helps improve vehicle aerodynamics and reduce noise inside the cabin. All-wheel drive is again available, but only on the 2.0L model. A fuel-saving engine stop-start system is standard on 1.6L models, and hybrid buyers get a new 2.0L. An Atkinson-cycle 4-cylinder will replace the outgoing 2.5L. The high-performance Fusion ST will use a more refined version of the EcoBoost 2.0L powerplant. On the Lincoln side, a new dramatic design incorporates a large, panoramic glass roof panel, an Audi A7–like sloping C-pillar, and a high deck lid with an integrated spoiler. There's also a new standard turbocharged 240 hp 2.0L 4-cylinder engine, and a 300 hp 3.7L V6 that's more potent than what the previous MKZ offered. Another standard feature is Lincoln

Drive Control, which tailors the driving experience for different modes, including Sport, Normal, and Comfort. Inside, the gear lever has been replaced by push-button controls, there is a new four-spoke steering wheel, and the dash has been upgraded.

ALERT! Lincoln is under heavy fire to increase sales this year, or face having the brand merge with another Ford division or be sold to another automaker as Ford has done with money-losing Jaguar. This means you can haggle aggressively, because dealers will get basketfuls of rebates and other sales incentives to move these luxe cars. Costco members get a $1,000 discount.

OVERVIEW: These practically identical mid-sized sedans are set on a lengthened Mazda6 platform. The Fusion offers three gasoline engines and two hybrids. The smaller engines can be coupled to either a 6-speed manual or a 6-speed automatic transmission; there's no choice with the V6, which comes with a 6-speed automatic. The 4-cylinder comes solely in front-drive; the 2.0L is available in front-drive or all-wheel drive. The hybrid variant is a spinoff of the Mazda6 and the Ford Escape Hybrid—two vehicles that have been recommended for years by *Lemon-Aid* for both their quality and performance.

So why are these cars so bad if they come from such good stock? The answer is that Ford has failed to correct factory-related defects during the Fusion's first year of production, and the defects continue to accumulate. For example, NHTSA recorded 80 safety-related complaints on the 2011 Fusion, but the 2012 model is already up to the 95 complaints mark, indicating the car is getting less reliable each year. The 2010 model has generated almost 200 complaints, or almost four times the benchmark of 50 complaints per model year used by *Lemon-Aid*. Only four complaints have been posted relative to the 2010 Lincoln.

Why does *Consumer Reports* rate the Fusion and MKZ as Recommended while *Lemon-Aid* rates them as Below Average and Average? Mostly because we count the many transmission and brake complaints reported by owners. *Lemon-Aid* gets tipped off early to the presence of safety- and performance-related defects by studying thousands of consumer complaints logged by NHTSA and then comparing these complaints to factory-generated confidential service bulletins sent weekly to auto dealerships. *Consumer Reports* drives the vehicle and publishes its member comments. No service bulletins or NHTSA-logged complaints are studied, nor are non-members polled.

COST ANALYSIS: Be careful. The reworked 2013 powertrains are likely to come with lots of factory-related defects, and the 2012s have their own engine and transmission deficiencies. **Best alternatives:** *Fusion:* Honda Accord, Hyundai Elantra or Tucson, Mazda6, Nissan Altima, and Toyota Camry. *MKZ:* Toyota Avalon, BMW 5-Series, and Mercedes-Benz E-Class. **Options:** Pass on the original equipment Firestone/Bridgestone tires. **Rebates:** Don't expect much discounting on the 2012s until the spring of next year. Expect to see a $5,000 rebate on the 2012 model. **Depreciation:** Much faster than average. **Insurance**

cost: Average; the hybrid premium costs more than average. **Parts supply/cost:** Average availability and cost, except for hybrid components, which may be hard to get. Hybrid part costs are moderately expensive, although most parts are taken from the Mazda or Escape Hybrid bins. **Annual maintenance cost:** Repair costs have been average during the three-year warranty period. **Warranty:** Bumper-to-bumper 3 years/60,000 km; powertrain 5 years/100,000 km; rust perforation 5 years/160,000 km. **Supplementary warranty:** A good idea. Their first three years on the market have shown the Fusion to be prone to serious automatic transmission failures, making an extended powertrain warranty worthwhile. **Highway/city fuel economy:** (2012 models) *2.5L:* 6.9/9.4 L/100 km, 41/30 mpg. *Auto.:* 6.9/9.4 L/100 km, 44/30 mpg. *3.0L:* 7.3/11.1 L/100 km, 29/35 mpg. *3.0L AWD:* 7.8/11.8 L/100 km, 36/24 mpg. *3.5L AWD:* 8.3/12.7 L/100 km, 34/22 mpg. *Hybrid:* 5.4/4.6 L/100 km, 52/61 mpg.

OWNER-REPORTED PROBLEMS: Vehicle tends to drift to the left, and owners say the front seats are painful to sit in:

MKZ front seats have a hard block I think is the box for the seat controls that if you sit in it for more than a few minutes starts hurting the back of your legs. It actually takes your attention away because it is so uncomfortable you are always adjusting the way you are sitting. I took it in for service and the service tech felt it and told me he thought something was wrong too. He called me the next day and told me that the seat was the standard and that is the way they were made, there wasn't anything they could do. When I went back to the dealer to pick up my MKZ I went into the show room to feel the seats in the new MKZs and there are all the same.

Lincoln airbags failed to deploy in an accident, and both front seatbacks collapsed in a rear-ender. Fusion owners say the knee airbag restricts brake pedal access and the brakes are too weak. Chronic automatic transmission failures and erratic shifting with the Fusion:

The transmission seized while travelling at 100 kilometers per hour, causing rapid deceleration while on highway. Shortly after coming to a stop on the side of the road, the transmission failed to engage, despite engine running.

•

Automatic transmission shifting is unpredictable. 1–2 and 2–3 gear shift will rev at high rpm and slam into gear. Merging into traffic or at any intersection where cross traffic does not stop is very dangerous as acceleration is non-existent until it slams hard into gear. The car has done this from 1st week of ownership. Besides safety issue, the transmission at this rate will not last long. This issue is mainly present when 1) cold or 2) after the car has sat for a couple days making it difficult for the dealer to act on anything. This is a very well known problem with 2010 Ford Fusions and now many people are complaining of this issue with the 2011 Fusion (not the Sport model as it uses different transmission).

•

I bought a 2011 Ford Fusion on Nov. 26, 2010. The day I brought it home, the problems started. It bangs so hard into reverse that it feels like someone ran into the car with a bulldozer. It has dead spots in the acceleration, and often goes above 5000 rpm when shifting just going down a normal flat highway. The problems have gotten worse and more frequent and are completely random. It happens with a warm engine, cold engine, in rain, snow, sun, and even after being driven for 4 hours straight. I now have over 6000 miles [9,660 km] on the car and the dealership has done nothing because Ford won't authorize anything because the car is not "putting out any codes." They say they have never heard of such problems, but online forums have hundreds of the same complaints with 2010 Fusions. My fear is that the acceleration will fail when I am on the expressway or in heavy traffic or that my transmission will just fall out completely. This is my first new car, and I can't afford to get another one or a long court battle. Help! It's not just an inconvenience, it's unsafe.

Sudden stalling when the car is underway; Hybrid brake pedal is mounted too close to the accelerator pedal; head restraints force driver's head forward and downward (chin to chest).

MUSTANG ★★/★

RATING: *Automatic transmission–equipped models:* Below Average. *Manual transmission–equipped versions:* Not Recommended. The Mustang has been downgraded this year due a flood of 2011 and 2012 owner complaints relating to chronic "unfixable" electrical shorts, electronic module malfunctions, and transmission failures. **Road performance:** Fast acceleration and impressive handling and braking. The V8 is a pocket rocket. The automatic transmission robs the engine of some of its performance; the manual tranny is more responsive with crisp short-throws. **Strong points:** Base models come equipped with a host of safety, luxury, and convenience features. There's easy access into the interior and comfortable, upright front seating gives an excellent view of the road. Resale value is better than average. **Weak points:** A poorly performing manual transmission that can get you killed; all bets are off on the GT500 powertrain's long-term durability. Rear seatroom is limited, and fit and finish is unimpressive. **Safety:** Better-than-average past crashworthiness. NHSTA gives the 2013 Mustang four stars for frontal and side protection; rollover resistance got the top, five star-star

KEY FACTS

Canadian Price (Firm): *Coupe V6:*
*$23,999, V6 Premium: $26,999, V6
Premium Convertible: $31,999, Coupe
GT: $39,299, Convertible GT: $44,299,
Boss Coupe: $48,799, Shelby GT500:
$61,549, Shelby GT500 Convertible:
$66,249* **U.S. Price:** *Coupe V6: $22,495,
V6 Premium: $26,495, GT: $30,595,
GT Premium: $34,595, Premium
Convertible: $31,495, GT Convertible:
$35,595, GT Premium Convertible:
$39,595, Boss 302: $42,995, Shelby
GT500: $54,995, Shelby GT500
Convertible: $59,995* **Canadian Freight:**
$1,500 **U.S. Freight:** $825

POWERTRAIN (REAR-DRIVE)

Engines: 3.7L V6 (305 hp) • 5.0L
V8 (402 hp) • 5.0L V8 (444 hp) •
Supercharged 5.8L V8 (650 hp);
Transmissions: 6-speed man. • 6-speed
auto.

DIMENSIONS/CAPACITY

Passengers: 2/2; Wheelbase: 107.1 in.;
H: 55.8/L: 188.5/W: 73.9 in.; Headroom
F/R: 5.0/1.0 in.; Legroom F/R: 40.5/
23.5 in.; Cargo volume: 13.4 cu. ft.; Fuel
tank: 60.1L/regular; Tow limit: 1,001 lb.;
Load capacity: 720 lb.; Turning circle:
33.4 ft.; Ground clearance: 5.7 in.;
Weight: 3,585 lb.

designation. The IIHS's rating is not as positive: Although frontal offset collision protection and head restraints were rated "Good," side crashworthiness was ranked only "Acceptable." Ironically, the convertible version, a car style that usually doesn't do well in crash tests, outperformed the two-door model with a "Good" rating in all three categories. **New for 2013:** Eight more horses for the Shelby GT V8's 5.0L engine, and a 650 hp 5.8L V8, new front-end styling, and some interior tweaks.

ALERT! Mustangs equipped with a Chinese-built manual transmission can commit the "perfect crime" when failing to shift or popping out of gear. Accident investigators will blame driver error or reckless driving (after all, it is a sports car), and the accident will wipe out any proof that the transmission was at fault:

My 2012 Mustang GT was most likely totaled tonight when the transmission did not allow a shift into 5th gear. It slid into 3rd [gear] and caused the wheels to spin resulting in the car fishtailing and hitting a tree in the median.

•

2012 Mustang V6 Manual 6-speed transmission. Hard to shift into 1st gear. Stopped at a red light with my 3-year-old and baby daughter in the baby seat in the back behind me. I saw a driver behind me coming in too fast. I started prepping if I had to move forward into the intersection that had no traffic just in case. Car could not shift into 1st gear no matter what I tried. Quickly I shifted into 2nd and saw the driver smash the brakes while his tires were smoking as he was approaching my rear end in a slide. My car found enough power to move me forward 10 feet and avoid a collision.

There is a huge markup on higher-end Mustangs in Canada versus the States; it's well worth a trip south. Xenon high-intensity headlights are standard; they will likely be stolen.

OVERVIEW: Mustang has gone back to its muscle car roots while keeping prices in check. The perfect "back to the future" retro sports car, the Mustang's body panel creases reign supreme. And more than four decades after its debut, the original pony car still stands strong, both stylistically and in its highway performance. The Mustang offers a V6 or a V8 in the GT engines.

There was a huge horsepower boost on the base 2011 Mustang that turned a wimpish 210 hp V6 into a sizzling 305 hp. Incidentally, the 2011–12 GT500 ratcheted up performance by a few notches, too, with an aluminum-block engine that produced 550 hp. Other goodies on the 2011–12 Mustangs: a new limited-clip differential, larger brakes (taken from the 2010 GT), electronic power steering, a retuned suspension, stiffer rear anti-roll bars, and convertibles get less body flexing through the use of shock-tower braces. Another big change was fold-down rear head restraints to improve rear visibility. For parents, there's still the MyKey system, which allows owners to limit the car's maximum speed and audio volume. The 2013 Mustang will hopefully have its transmission and electrical problems fixed. *Shelby:* The Shelby GT500 has had successive power boosts and other refinements during the past couple of years to improve engine cooling and performance. Ford says its revamped transmission and final-drive gearing give better acceleration off the starting line with improved highway fuel economy. The GT500 comes in both coupe and convertible versions.

COST ANALYSIS: Get a 2013 model that will have hopefully corrected the serious redesign glitches carried over from the 2011 version. Anyhow, there are few unsold 2012s available, and those that are on dealer lots aren't discounted by much. Finally, this may be the ideal car to buy in the States if you live close to a large American city; the price difference may be at least $3,000–$12,000, and availability shouldn't be a problem. **Best alternatives:** The resurrected Camaro is looking better and better when compared to the failure-prone Mustang. Although the Mustang still has a competitive price and performs well, the racing thrills quickly fade when you pay exorbitant garage repair bills. Furthermore, confidential internal reports and owner complaints now show that Mustangs have more factory-related problems than the Camaro. Forget about the Dodge Challenger. Its 250 hp engine and heavy body take it out of the running. Plus, rumour has it that the model is likely to be dropped next year. In summary, four fun and reliable competitors are the Chevrolet Camaro, Hyundai Genesis, 2012 Infiniti G25 or G27, and Mazda Miata. **Options:** An anti-theft system (one that includes an engine immobilizer) and good tires recommended by *www.tirerack. com.* Stay away from the notchy, erratic-shifting 6-speed Getrag manual transmission. It has performed poorly on 2011–12 models and the jury's still out on the 2013s (see *http://mustangsdaily.com/blog/2011/11/09/ford-responds-to-nhtsas-investigation-of-the-mustangs-mt82-6-speed-transmission*). You may wish to invest in a full-sized spare tire:

> The contact owns a 2012 Ford Mustang. While driving approximately 45 mph [72 km/h], the contact noticed that the rear passenger side tire had blown. The contact attempted to replace the tire with the spare and noticed there was no spare tire. The contact stated there was only a spare tire repair kit and felt that the repair kit was unsafe and would not work properly.

Rebates: $500–$1,500 rebates, plus low-interest financing. **Depreciation:** Fairly slow. For example, a new $27,000 2011 base Mustang now costs almost

$19,000 used. The convertibles fare even better: An entry-level 2011 that sold for $31,399 has a resale value of $26,000. Expect the boosted horsepower on the entry-level V6 engine (which rivals that of the 2010 GT V8) to send the older GT's resale value plummeting. **Insurance cost:** Way higher than average. **Parts supply/cost:** Inexpensive and easily found among independent suppliers; some delays getting engine, transmission, and body components. **Annual maintenance cost:** Lower than average. **Warranty:** Bumper-to-bumper 3 years/60,000 km; powertrain 5 years/100,000 km; rust perforation 5 years/ unlimited km. **Supplementary warranty:** Not necessary. Put your money into handling options and theft protection. **Highway/city fuel economy:** Fuel consumption is cut in the new 3.7L V6 (manual) to a frugal 6.9/11.2 L/100 km, 41/25 mpg. *3.7L V6 auto.:* 6.4/10.7 L/100 km, 44/26 mpg. *3.7L V6 convertible auto:* 7.8/11.9 L/100 km, 36/24 mpg. *5.0L V8 man.:* 7.7/12.2 L/100 km, 37/23 mpg. *5.0L V8 auto.:* 7.9/11.8 L/100 km, 36/24 mpg. *5.4L V8 man.:* 8.8/14.5 L/100 km, 32/19 mpg.

OWNER-REPORTED PROBLEMS: When the redesigned 2011 Mustang came out, factory-related safety defect reports posted at NHTSA started pouring in. At first, they concerned mostly the manual transmission, but they have since included the automatic, as well. The MT82 manual transmission is designed by and built in China. It represents the majority of NHTSA-logged safety complaints. Here is how the Japlonik Forum (*http://jalopnik.com/5792482/faulty-chinese+built-transmissions-plague-new-ford-mustang*) describes the problem, followed by some typical NHTSA-registered owner complaints:

The MT82 transmission in question is built by Ford and supplier Getrag at a joint venture in Nanchang, China—a point that has only added to the ire of some customers. And it's not the first time owners of that transmission have reported trouble shifting; the same problems were reported by owners of Land Rover Defenders.

Since the first complaints surfaced [two years ago], Ford has attempted to soothe angry owners and quietly offered several possible fixes, from replacing bolts in the flywheel to new clutches to even swapping out the transmission fluid. While some of those repairs have satisfied customers, several report that the problems returned—especially the balky 1st–2nd shift.

•

I am having frequent issues with shifting on my 2012 Mustang GT 6-spd. It has been difficult to shift Into 5th gear at times. Shifting from 1st to 2nd is now producing a brief grinding sound with every shift. At times, the transmission will not allow shifting into 4th on the first try, and this also occurs from 4th to 5th at times. A second shift attempt usually works but there is the loss of [getting] up to speed in each case. In addition, the skip-shift feature often engages at too low an rpm range causing the engine to "lug" with very little power. This has nearly caused an accident twice as I accelerate from a stop, shift (being forced to 4th gear from 1st by the skip shift) and lose power. Once, the engine died following the skip-shift from 1st to 4th, causing a serious risk. After having these Issues with the manual transmission, I found many, many complaints on Internet forums and this NHTSA site and do not understand why there is no action to encourage Ford to address this well-known and extremely well-documented issue. This situation is [getting] close to justifying class-action activity.

•

The 2012 Mustang has a shifter that will not retain its position and I believe it is related to the skip shift feature implemented for fuel economy. Commonly it tries to force the shifter from 1st to 4th. As a result the driver ends up fighting the stick shift to get to 2nd. This often results in reduction in speed and a loss of real control of the vehicle and increases the risk of being struck from behind. In virtually every gear at some point I have lost the ability to down shift or up shift creating a driving scenario of real danger and potential of being struck by other motorists.

Some head restraints force drivers to adopt a chin-to-chest posture (Ford corrected this oversight in early 2012—make sure the improved version is on your car); airbags deploy for no reason; sudden, unintended acceleration; car loses power when accelerating; transmission leaks; AC comes on by itself; Brembo brakes wear out prematurely and constantly squeak; original equipment tires wear out within the first six months; more reasons why Ford's lack of a spare tire is such a dangerous, stupid idea (I wonder if women were consulted?):

I am senior citizen and love my 2012 Mustang, except that the V-6 model does not have a spare tire wheel. I am greatly concerned that if a large piece of metal ruins my tire or causes my tire to blow out, I will be stranded on a bridge, rural road or the interstate, without a spare tire to get me to safety. I would have to be stranded until help arrived, and what if at night, and I can't get a new tire until the next day. This, I feel is a safety matter for the motorist. A mini spare should be standard on all cars. You never know who might stop while you are stranded and attack or rob you. Even the police can't help you with no spare tire, and you have to sit in a dangerous place until a tow truck arrived. I complained to Ford and their reply was buy a GT V-8 model, which does come with a spare tire and wheel. I feel this is a safety complaint and that Ford should supply a mini spare tire and jack at little or no cost.

Control arm failures; suspension clunking; windshield water leaks; poor windshield wiper design impairs the view of the road in rainy conditions (the degree of travel by the passenger-side wiper needs to be modified); inaccurate exterior temperature gauge; and the emergency flashers turn on when the AC is adjusted.

SERVICE BULLETIN-REPORTED PROBLEMS: *2005–12:* May have a major fluid leak from the rear axle vent. *2011–12:* Manual transmission may be difficult to shift in cold weather. Front-end suspension may produce a grunt, creak, chirp, or squeak. *2012:* Engine cold start-up ticking noises with 3.5L and 3.7L engines; the repairs require installing a camshaft kit that takes two hours of labour. Automatic transmission fluid leak from the bell housing. Squealing, squeaking rear brakes. Sync voice recognition system may ignore your voice…"Hello, Hal, do you hear me?"

ESCAPE ★★★★

KEY FACTS

Canadian Price (Negotiable): *S FWD auto.:* $22,204, *SE FWD auto.:* $26,080, *SE 4×4 auto.:* $28,038, *SEL FWD man.:* $30,263, *4×4:* $32,221, *Titanium 4×4:* $35,514, *(2012) Hybrid 4×2:* $38,599, *(2012) Hybrid 4×4:* $40,999 **U.S. Price:** *S 4×2 man.:* $22,470, *SE:* $25,070, *SEL FWD:* $27,870, *Titanium:* $30,370 *(2012) Hybrid 4×2:* $30,570, *4×4:* $32,320, *Limited:* $33,080, *4×4:* $34,830 **Canadian Freight:** $1,500 **U.S. Freight:** $825

POWERTRAIN (FRONT-DRIVE)

Engines: 1.6L 4-cyl. (178 hp) • 2.0L 4-cyl. (240 hp) • 2.5L 4-cyl. (168 hp); Transmission: 6-speed manumatic

DIMENSIONS/CAPACITY

Passengers: 2/3; Wheelbase: 105.9 in.; H: 66.3/L: 178.1/W: 72.4 in.; Headroom F/R: 3.0/4.0 in.; Legroom F/R: 43.1/36.8 in.; Cargo volume: 34.3 cu. ft.; Fuel tank: 62L/ regular; Tow limit: 1,500 lb.; Load capacity: 1,000 lb.; Turning circle: 37 ft.; Ground clearance: 7.9 in.; Weight: 3,598 lb.

RATING: Above Average. Totally redesigned by Ford. The Escape Hybrid has been dropped in favour of two direct-injected and turbocharged 1.6L and 2.0L EcoBoost 4-cylinder engines that use less fuel than the 2012 model. The 2013 model also features improved interior space and technology, and accessibility that tops the previous model and the competition. **Road performance:** Improved considerably. The new Escape is much more agile and comfortable now that it shares its underpinnings and the majority of its suspension components with the new Focus. **Strong points:** Peppy performance and a roomy, well-finished interior that provides lots of high-tech content and plenty of cargo space. **Weak points:** There is an unacceptably large price difference between the Canadian and American high-end models. First-year Fords have always been less reliable than later versions, and the 2013 Escape will likely be no different. High-tech means a high probability of things going wrong. For example, the new EcoBoost engines will likely be the main troublemaker. Already owners are complaining EcoBoost engines don't always deliver the promised fuel savings and work poorly with automatic transmissions. **Safety:** NHTSA gave the 2011 and 2012 Escape only Average crashworthiness scores (three stars) for front, side, and crash protection. The

IIHS gave its top rating ("Good") to the Escape for frontal offset, side, and rear crash protection (head-restraint effectiveness); roof strength was ranked "Marginal." **New for 2013:** Everything (see "Overview").

ALERT! With an attractive base price for the S trim near $23,000, the Escape starts off competitively. Once customers step up to the SE, SEL, and Titanium models, however, the price jumps quickly and—after adding options—could easily surpass $30,000 and top out around $42,000. Unfortunately, the similar Mazda Tribute is no longer around as a cheaper alternative; it's been replaced by the Mazda CX-5.

OVERVIEW: The decade-old Escape is a good buy, with many standard features and reasonably good overall reliability, but it was in dire need of the 2012 redesign to save fuel, provide a roomier interior, and improve ride and handling.

First, the most evident change this year is the new styling features, which give it a sleek, less boxy appearance and are said to make the vehicle 10 percent more aerodynamic than the previous model. Of course, the newest Escape also has more room than the previous model, with 68.1 cubic feet of space behind the first row of seats and 34.3 cubic feet behind the second row.

Ford has done away with its popular hybrid version of the Escape for 2013 because it wants to cut fuel consumption using old ideas married to new technology. In place of the Hybrid, customers will be able to choose between two EcoBoost engines: a 1.6L and a 2.0L featuring direct injection and turbochargers. The standard Escape engine will be the normally aspirated 2.5L inline 4-cylinder engine. The non-turbocharged 2.5L is only available in front-drive, and Ford has offered only one transmission choice for the 2013 Escape: a 6-speed "SelectShift" automatic.

The drivetrain has been upgraded to make the new Escape more off-road capable than ever before by using a "drive-by-wire" intelligent four-wheel-drive system that monitors 25 external data points, including wheel speed, accelerator position, and steering-wheel angle.

How's this for an answer to a problem no one has asked? This year's Escape has an automatically opening rear hatch activated by waving your foot under the rear bumper: "You put your right foot in; you put your right foot out...." I can't wait to see this little jig being performed at the West Edmonton Mall as Escape owners find their remote fob and right foot are out of step.

And speaking of being out of step, after a ton of complaints over the past several years from owners of models equipped with faulty voice command and electronic device failures in the cockpit, Ford has finally installed an upgraded MyFord Touch system in the 2013 Escape, hopefully making for easier communication between car and driver. "You put your right foot in...."

COST ANALYSIS: The 2013s are radically different from last year's model and will likely enjoy no-haggle pricing until more Asian competition hits the marketplace in early 2013. The new powertrain is bound to cause headaches for first-year buyers hit by factory-related snafus and mechanics who aren't used to troubleshooting the EcoBoost engines, transmissions, and electronic modules. Actually, if you can afford to wait, don't buy a 2013 until next summer; if you can't wait, get a discounted 2012 version. **Best alternatives:** Chevrolet Equinox, GMC Terrain, Honda CR-V, Hyundai Tucson, Kia Sportage, Mazda CX-5, Nissan Rogue, and Toyota RAV4. **Options:** Nothing that is essential. **Depreciation:** Average. **Insurance cost:** Average. **Parts supply/cost:** Reasonably priced parts for gasoline-powered models, but parts are frequently back ordered. If you are buying a leftover 2012 Hybrid, parts will be expensive and harder to find due to fewer suppliers and the dropping of that model this year. Same holds true for the Mazda Tribute. **Annual maintenance cost:** Average. **Warranty:** Bumper-to-bumper 3 years/60,000 km; powertrain 5 years/100,000 km; rust perforation 5 years/unlimited km. **Supplementary warranty:** Getting an extended powertrain warranty is a good idea. **Highway/city fuel economy:** *FWD, 2.5L: 6.3/9.5 L/100 km. FWD, 2.0L: 6.7/9.5 L/100 km. AWD, 2.0L: 6.9/9.8 L/100 km. 2012 Hybrid: 6.5/5.8 L/100 km, 43/49 mpg. Hybrid AWD: 7.4/7.0 L/100 km, 39/43 mpg.*

OWNER-REPORTED PROBLEMS: Airbags fail to deploy, driver's seat collapses, or seat belt latch pops open; spontaneous windshield cracks and sunroof/side window shattering; distorted windshields; liftgate glass exploded, and Ford denied warranty claim despite putting out the service bulletin on the following page that confirms it is a Ford manufacturing defect:

> I was closing the back hatch on my 5 week old 2011 Ford Escape when the back glass shattered everywhere. I contacted Ford Motor Company and they related to me that the back glass was not covered. So, of course I had to replace my back glass for approx $400. Exactly 2 days after the new glass was installed, it happened again. When closing the liftgate the back glass shattered. This time the glass company replaced it for free, but when contacting the Ford company and dealership they were very rude and disrespectful.

Transmission fluid leakage (possible causes: a faulty AC condenser hose or condenser; cost to replace: $750–$1,025 U.S.). Oil filler tube is located directly above the exhaust manifold, creating a fire risk; cable lines fail, causing pedal to become inoperable; vehicle will not hold when stopped on an incline; sudden loss of braking ability or power steering; excessive steering noise may require the replacement of the entire steering assembly; one vehicle's parking brake failed, and the vehicle rolled backwards down a hill; excessive glare from the instrument panel blinds driver; LED readout is washed out by sunlight; tire jack won't raise the vehicle high enough to change the tire. *Hybrid:* Surprisingly for a vehicle that has such a complicated electrical system, there aren't any complaints concerning the hybrid components. One would normally expect to see, on average, 50 or so reports per model year. Owners do report some brake failures.

SERVICE BULLETIN-REPORTED PROBLEMS: 2.5L engine drone or rattle; 2.0L and 2.5L engines may constantly cause the MIL light to come on; harsh or delayed shifts; broken liftgate window, and water leaks from the liftgate area:

INTERMITTENT LIFTGATE GLASS WATER LEAKS

BULLETIN NUMBER: 12-2-2   DATE: MARCH 2, 2012

FORD: 2009–12 Escape

ISSUE: Some Escape, and Mariner vehicles may exhibit an intermittent water leak originating from the liftgate glass/seal.

EXPLORER ★★

RATING: Below Average. Problematic quality control and poor highway performance hobble what should have been Ford's best SUV. **Road performance:** The Explorer's unibody construction cuts weight and gives car-like road manners to the SUV. It offers front-drive, all-wheel drive, or four-wheel drive that can be left engaged on dry pavement, and has a low-range gear for off-roading. Downshifts can be slow and abrupt, and braking may be hard to modulate on hills. **Strong points:** Average performance and reliability with the V6; an optional fuel-efficient turbocharged 4-cylinder is also available. Abundant high-tech features, and an upscale cabin. **Weak points:** Transaction prices are too high, but they will start to decline in the new year. The longer you delay your purchase, the better quality you'll likely find as Ford tackles quality and design deficiencies that usually hang around for a few years on new designs. The most likely areas of concern for the next several years: Costly powertrain failures in addition to faulty brake, electrical system, steering and suspension components, and subpar body construction. We are also seeing electronic devices that are distracting and failure-prone; a dash offering a confusing array of small buttons, crowded displays, and redundant controls; and head restraints that are literally a pain in the neck. The cabin is an adequate size, but it's not quite as roomy as what is offered by the Dodge Durango, Ford Flex, or Chevy Traverse. Cargo space is the smallest of the group, and the third row is somewhat cramped. **Safety:** NHTSA gave the 2012–13

222

KEY FACTS

Canadian Price (Very Negotiable):
Base FWD: $29,539, *EcoBoost FWD:* $30,399, *Base V6 4WD:* $32,769, *XLT V6 FWD:* $33,690, *XLT EcoBoost FWD:* $34,550, *XLT V6 4WD:* $37,360, *Limited V6 FWD:* $38,407, *Limited EcoBoost FWD:* $39,267, *Limited V6 4WD:* $42,077, *Sport:* $41,545 **U.S. Price:** *Base:* $28,695, *XLT:* $32,170, *Limited:* $37,680, *Sport:* $40,545 **Canadian Freight:** $1,500 **U.S. Freight:** $825

POWERTRAIN (FRONT-DRIVE/4×4/AWD)

Engines: 2.0L 4-cyl. (240 hp) • 3.5L V6 (290 hp); *Sport:* 3.5L twin-turbo V6 (350 hp); Transmission: 6-speed auto.

DIMENSIONS/CAPACITY

Passengers: 2/3/2; Wheelbase: 112.6 in.; H: 70.4/L: 197.1/W: 74 in.; Headroom F/R1/R2: 2.5/4.0/0.5 in.; Legroom F/R1/R2: 40.6/39.8/33.2 in.; Cargo volume: 80.7 cu. ft.; Fuel tank: 70.4L/regular; Tow limit: 5,000 lb.; Load capacity: 1,275 lb.; Turning circle: 39.2 ft.; Ground clearance: 7.6 ft.; Weight: 4,557 lb.

Explorer five stars for frontal and side crashworthiness and four stars for rollover resistance, while IIHS scored frontal offset protection as "Good" and side protection and head-restraint effectiveness as "Acceptable." Standard safety features on every Explorer include AdvanceTrac with Roll Stability Control and Curve Control function, traction control, anti-lock disc brakes, and a tire-pressure monitor, as well as Ford's MyKey owner control feature and six airbags. Industry-first second-row inflatable seat belts are available on XLT and Limited models, packaged with a Blind Spot Information System (BLIS) with cross-traffic alert. Other options include Active Park Assist and adaptive cruise control with collision warning. **New for 2013:** A front-passenger knee airbag is now standard, while the XLT model gets a six-way power front passenger seat. Other improvements: A crisper steering response; a stiffened suspension for better driving dynamics; Lane Departure Warning and Lane Keep Assist are standard features with the Limited trim; and optional high-intensity discharge (HID) headlights with automatic high-beam control. *Sport:* The biggest change for 2013 is the arrival of the high-performance Sport with a 350 hp twin-turbo V6, a sport suspension, 20-inch wheels, a brake upgrade, a reworked Terrain Management System to manage the 3.5L EcoBoost engine's extra torque in all conditions, larger shock tower braces, and a new cross tunnel brace for added rigidity.

ALERT! Some things to check out at the dealership: Drivers say there's insufficient footroom; the brake and accelerator pedals are mounted too close to each other; narrow, poorly cushioned seats lack sufficient thigh support; and the small rear window cuts visibility. Be wary of the headlights option: HID headlights are thief magnets.

OVERVIEW: The seven-passenger Explorer is available in both front-drive and four-wheel-drive configurations, with a choice of four trim levels: Base, XLT, Limited, and Sport. A 290 hp 3.5L Ti-VCT V6 engine and 6-speed automatic transmission with SelectShift manual mode are standard on all trims. The 4×4 models get a user-friendly terrain management system, while an efficient 240 hp 2.0L turbocharged Ecoboost 4-cylinder engine with direct fuel injection is available for front-drive models. Explorer Base trims are well-equipped with 17-inch wheels, air conditioning, cruise control, MP3 capability, and MyFord driver connect technology; XLT trims add 18-inch aluminum wheels, fog lights, and a reverse sensing system, along with a USB port, satellite radio, and the Sync communications and entertainment system. Limited trims are further outfitted with 20-inch aluminum wheels, dual-zone automatic climate control, heated front seats, leather upholstery, HD radio, Intelligent Access with push-button start, and a rear-view camera. Third-row seating increases carrying capacity to seven passengers. Explorer's capless fuelling system allows owners to fill their fuel tanks without having to remove a gas cap, and the optional Sync voice-activated cell phone and MP3 player control system is particularly useful.

COST ANALYSIS: Many competitive car-based crossover SUVs that are more refined and better performing can beat Ford's prices; most of them are just as family-friendly, too, while offering a wide array of safety features, better fuel economy, and a less troublesome powertrain setup. Remember, Ford's past redesigns have always been afflicted with numerous factory-related powertrain defects and inflated prices for the first couple of years. **Best alternatives:** Honda CR-V or Ridgeline, Hyundai Tucson or Santa Fe, and Toyota RAV4. **Options:** Watch out for costly options bundled into different packages. They can easily send a Sport model over to the far side of $50,000. **Rebates:** On the 2012s, look for $4,000 rebates, $3,000 discounts, and zero percent financing. The 2013 Explorers will likely get 10 percent discounts and zero-interest financing by the summer of 2013. **Depreciation:** Much faster than average. A 2009 base Explorer 4×4 that sold for $36,000 is now worth about $18,000. **Insurance cost:** Above average. **Parts supply/cost:** Parts are easy to find and are reasonably priced. **Annual maintenance cost:** Average while under warranty; higher than average thereafter, primarily because of powertrain breakdowns. **Warranty:** Bumper-to-bumper 3 years/60,000 km; powertrain 5 years/100,000 km; rust perforation 5 years/unlimited km. **Supplementary warranty:** Getting an extended powertrain warranty would be wise. **Highway/city fuel economy:** 3.5L V6: 8.0/11.9 L/100 km, 35/24 mpg; 4×4: 8.8/12.5 L/100 km, 32/23 mpg.

OWNER-REPORTED PROBLEMS: Owners continue to complain that the head restraints are literally a pain in the neck and can be dangerous if the airbags deploy:

> The head rest pushes the driver's head towards the windshield due to its perpendicular design.... If the air bag were to deploy, the driver could become seriously injured. The contact called the manufacturer and was informed that the vehicle was designed in that manner and no compensation would be provided.

Mediocre automatic transmission performance and fit and finish deficiencies; sun visors are poorly designed; driver's foot presses on the foot rest bar when attempting to apply the brakes:

> The contact stated that when he tried to apply the brakes, his foot pressed on a bar that's next to the brake pedal, instead of the pedal. The vehicle was taken to the dealer who stated that was the way the vehicle was designed and they could not alter it.

Sudden power-steering failure:

I stopped at a stop sign and took a left hand turn as I proceeded down a hill. My steering wheel wouldn't turn, like the wheel locked up, and the brakes were hard to push, not slowing me down. The Explorer went off the road, striking a concrete pole. It destroyed the entire right front end, and destroyed the pole. The dealer said that they could fix the problem with the steering, and the brakes, but they are not responsible for the damage. They said that it's not Ford's fault for the damage.

Under hard acceleration, sudden, unintended acceleration accompanied by loss of brakes; exhaust fumes enter the cabin; gas leaks out when fuelling; rear seat belts don't retract; and Sync and MyTouch work erratically:

The My Sync function that was installed in the vehicle caused the computer system to fail, including the air conditioner, heating system, radio and defroster system. All systems remained at a constant rate if activated and he was unable to change the function. The failure recurred intermittently. The dealer stated that the computer system was faulty but he did not currently have a remedy for the failure. The manufacturer was made aware of the failure but failed to offer any assistance. No repairs were performed. The current mileage was 5,200 miles [8,370 km] and the failure mileage was 2,000 miles [3,220 km].

•

I bought a new 2012 Ford Explorer. In the words of one of the several Ford Motor Co. Customer Care case mangers I've spoken to since I purchased this vehicle about 6 weeks ago, Ford's MyTouch system is "totally dysfunctional". The software upon which this system is based was apparently co-authored by Microsoft and Ford is currently telling customers they have to wait for the next release, supposedly due to be released in "the first quarter of next year". Has anyone ever heard this kind of message before…think MS Vista! My Explorer has an approx 8"×5" touchscreen in the middle of the dash. It is supposed to come on when I start the vehicle and many functions of the vehicle are controlled by touching icons on the screen. Unfortunately, when the screen fails to come on, usually for about the initial 20 minutes after starting the vehicle, the driver controls are unavailable. This includes features like being able to view the rear-view camera, turning on the heated seats, climate control features, dealing with phone calls and selecting music sources and radio channels, etc. MyTouch also includes a feature where it's supposed to sync the driver's mobile phone, but this only works intermittently at best. The worst problem with this system, which I believe makes the vehicle unsafe for nighttime driving, is when the touchscreen, which cannot be turned off or dimmed, starts flickering (Ford's term is "strobing") very rapidly while driving after dark. This can continue for up to 30 minutes at a time, and is incredibly distracting while trying to drive. I've posted a video on YouTube under the heading "Ford MyTouch Strobing". This problem has been known to Ford since the 2011 model year and they continue to sell these problematic vehicles without telling customers until after they take possession.

SERVICE BULLETIN-REPORTED PROBLEMS: Power liftgate malfunctions. *2011–12:* Intermittent front brake squeal; forward centre console storage bin door hard to open; interior rattle or buzz; and front bumper creaking.

The Ford F-150.

RATING: Below Average. The F-150 has seen the best of times and the worst of times, and it's now coming out of a multi-year sales slump that almost forced Ford into bankruptcy. Ford's stock is nudging $10 a share (down from $40), and serious engine and electronic deficiencies are showing up on the Internet and in internal service bulletins. Has Ford simply replaced one set of defects for another? **Road performance:** Handling is a breeze, although the ride is a bit stiff; best in its class for towing. On the downside: The powertrain is a bit rough and loud, and braking is just acceptable. **Strong points:** Easily negotiated prices as fuel prices rise and truck prices fall. Offers lots of upgrade options, a roomy cab with lots of convenient storage bins, a power-opening centre rear window, and a spring-assisted tailgate. **Weak points:** High sticker price; less comfortable than comparable models; and long-term reliability has yet to be determined. This is especially important because these trucks have disappointed owners after each redesign since the mid-'80s. **Safety:** NHTSA gave the 2013 F-150 five stars for side crashworthiness and four stars for frontal collision protection and rollover resistance. The F-250 wasn't tested. IIHS also gave the F-150 top marks ("Good") for frontal offset, side, and rear crashworthiness. **New for 2013:** *Limited:* Powered by Ford's 365 hp 3.5L Ti-VCT EcoBoost V6 engine and mated to a 6-speed automatic transmission. Look for a lavishly appointed cockpit, heated and cooled memory seats, ambient lighting, a moonroof, a rear-view camera, a multimedia hub, a Sony audio system, Sync with MyFord Touch, and voice-activated navigation connected to Sirius Travel Link. Additional hardware includes high-intensity discharge headlights, a Reverse-Sensing system, power-folding side mirrors, and power running boards. *Raptor SVT:* A minor facelift; upgraded with new beadlock-capable forged alloy wheels; HID headlights; and Sync with MyFord Touch.

KEY FACTS

Canadian Price (2012): *F-150 Regular:* $21,549, *F-150 Super Cab:* $23,947, *Super Crew Cab:* $31,129, *F-250 XL 4x2 Super Duty Regular Cab:* $35,499, *Super Cab:* $38,599, *4×4:* $38,899 *Crew Cab long bed:* $40,599, *XLT 4x2 Crew Cab long bed:* $46,849, *Lariat 4×2 Crew Cab long bed:* $55,049, *Crew Cab:* $28,781, *F-350 Regular:* $26,230, *Super Cab:* $28,466, *Crew Cab:* $29,928, *F-450 4×2:* $41,968, *F-450 4×4:* $45,064 **U.S. Price (2012):** *F-150 XL:* $22,790; *STX:* $25,880; *XLT:* $26,500, *FX2:* $33,460, *Lariat:* $34,495, *FX4:* $37,010, *SVT Raptor:* $41,935, *King Ranch:* $42,175, *Platinum:* $44,635 *Lariat LTD:* $47,580, *Harley Davidson:* $48,380; *F-250:* $28,505, *F-350:* $29,225, *F-450:* $48,835 **Canadian Freight:** $1,500 **U.S. Freight:** $975

POWERTRAIN (REAR-DRIVE/PART-TIME 4×4/AWD)

Engines: 3.6L V8 (248 hp) • 4.6L V8 (292 hp) • 5.4L V8 (310 hp) • 6.2L V8 (411 hp) • 6.4L V8 diesel (350 hp) • 6.7L V8 diesel (385 hp) • 6.8L V10 (362 hp) • 3.5L V6 (365 hp) EcoBoost • 3.7L V6 (302 hp) • 5.0L V8 (360 hp) • 6.2L V8 (411 hp); Transmissions: 4-speed auto. • 5-speed auto. • 6-speed auto. • 6-speed man.

DIMENSIONS/CAPACITY

Passengers: 2/1 up to 3/3; Wheelbase: 121 in.; H: 69/L: 201/W: 77 in.; Headroom F/R: 4.5/3.5 in.; Legroom F/R: 40.0/29.5 in.; Cargo volume: 55.4 cu.ft.; Fuel tank: 98.4L/regular, *Raptor:* 94L/regular, *Harley-Davidson:* 136L/regular; Tow limit: *F-150:* 5,400 lb.; *F-250:* 12,500 lb.; Load capacity: 1,480–5,100 lb.; Turning circle: 48 ft.; Ground clearance: 8.5 in.; Weight: 5,620 lb.

ALERT! In your test drive, pay particular attention to the position of the front head restraints. Owners confirm that these poorly designed head restraints force your chin to your chest. Ford's new EcoBoost engines have been heralded as providing plenty of turbo power and using less fuel than previous powerplants. This is true, but these redesigned engines have a nasty habit of losing power when most needed, thereby exposing passengers and pedestrians to serious injury or death:

> Major safety issue with F150 EcoBoost trucks. Hundreds of owners with this issue: [*www.blueovalforums.com/forums/index.php?/topic/49606-f-150-ecoboost-shutter*] while taking off from T-intersection and turning left crossing oncoming traffic the truck started to take off then lost all power for approximately 3–5 seconds. This left my family and I sitting in the oncoming traffic lane on a blind corner. The truck did not die (I thought it did), I mashed the accelerator to the floor and the truck did not respond whatsoever. My wife was screaming frantically at me asking what I was doing while I attempted to get the truck to move out of the oncoming lane. After approximately 5 seconds the truck regained power and accelerated normally. This has occurred 3X now and I am afraid to drive the truck but do and my wife will not drive it at all…. Ford has done nothing to address the problem and has promised a fix for the last 3 months. While the truck has other major issues, this specific problem is going to result in deaths. It's not a matter of if, but when.

OVERVIEW: The Ford F-Series ruled the roost for three decades as the bestselling pickup in North America. Then Ford's house of cards came tumbling down. Abetted by lousy diesel engines, failure-prone powertrains, suspensions, and steering assemblies, and body construction that would make the Marquis de Sade cry, Ford began to lose market share a decade ago and has only recently bounced back. Its 2009–12 models give hope that some of the worst design deficiencies have been corrected and that Ford is finally on the road to better truck quality. So far, NHTSA-logged complaints and *Consumer Reports* member survey feedback gives the impression these are better-made pickups. I am not convinced.

COST ANALYSIS: Unless you're looking for a high-performance Raptor or are in dire need of an engine boost, look for a cheaper, leftover 2012 version (discount should be in the 10–15 percent realm). Check lower American prices on the Internet by searching "Ford USA," and compare the prices to "Ford Canada." With high-end pickups, $10,000 or more can be saved. **Best alternatives:** GM's Silverado or Sierra base models or HD series, Honda's Ridgeline, Nissan's Titan, and dead-last Chrysler's "Jurassic" Ram equipped with a Cummins diesel and a more-reliable manual transmission. Nissan's Frontier or King Cab are also worth considering. **Options:** Take a pass on the Firestone/Bridgestone tires, heated seats, and Lariat Chrome package. **Rebates:** $3,000–$5,000 rebates and low-cost financing on the larger trucks. **Depreciation:** Faster than average during the first three years of ownership. For example, a 2009 entry-level F-150 that sold new for $24,199 is now worth about $10,000 less. **Insurance cost:** Above average. **Parts supply/cost:** Reasonably priced parts are easy to find, mainly because many independent suppliers specialize in new and used F-Series parts. EcoBoost engine components may be in short supply. **Annual maintenance cost:** Average. **Warranty:** Bumper-to-bumper 3 years/60,000 km; powertrain 5 years/100,000 km; rust perforation 5 years/unlimited km. **Supplementary warranty:** Getting an extended bumper-to-bumper warranty is a good idea. **Highway/city fuel economy:** 3.5L V6: 9.0/12.9 L/100 km, 31/22 mpg; 6.2L V8: 11.4/16.9 L/100 km, 25/17 mpg; 3.5L V6 4×4: 9.0/12.9 L/100 km, 30/20 mpg; 6.2L V8 4×4: 12.7/18.3 L/100 km, 22/15 mpg; 3.7L V6: 8.9/12.9 L/100 km, 32/22 mpg; 3.7L 4×4: 9.8/13.4 L/100 km, 21/15 mpg; 5.0L V8: 9.7/13.9 L/100 km, 29/20 mpg; 5.0L V8 4×4: 10.5/15.0 L/100 km, 27/19 mpg; *Raptor* 6.2L V8 4×4: 14.2/19.1 L/100 km, 20/15 mpg.

OWNER-REPORTED PROBLEMS: One fire started under the driver's door, another ignited via the exhaust system, a third broke out near the brake master cylinder on an F-250; another F-250 suddenly accelerated; a familiar litany of engine, transmission and steering failures. Head restraints are uncomfortable and dangerous:

> Headrest forces driver's chin into the chest. Dealer stated that this is the new safety design. Headrests are non-adjustable. Also, they are very wide and, in conjunction with the frame post at the rear of the doors, create a blind spot on both sides of the pickup.

•

> The truck owner stated that the driver's and passenger side headrests were not adjustable and constantly struck him in the back of the neck. The manufacturer stated that this was a new design for safety. He was concerned that his neck could be seriously injured due to the air bags in the event of a crash.

SERVICE BULLETIN-REPORTED PROBLEMS: Troubleshooting a variety of engine malfunctions:

ENGINE CONTROLS—MIL ON/VARIOUS DTCS SET

BULLETIN NO.: TSB 12-2-10   DATE: FEBRUARY 17, 2012

FORD: 2011–12 F-150.

ISSUE: Some 2011–12 F-150 vehicles built on or before 2/7/2012 and equipped with a 3.5L gasoline turbocharged direct injection (GTDI) engine may exhibit a malfunction indicator lamp (MIL) with various diagnostic trouble codes (DTC) and driveability concerns.

SERVICE PROCEDURE: The calibration update contains improvement actions and enhancements to address the following conditions:

- Intermittent engine surge during moderate to light loads at cruise.
- Enhancements to misfire monitor detection.
- Powertrain control module (PCM) DTC P0430 and/or P0096.

1. If the vehicle exhibits DTC P0430 replace the left bank catalytic converter. Refer to WSM section 309-00. Proceed to Step 2.
2. Reprogram the PCM to the latest calibration using IDS release 77A.03A or higher. This new calibration is not included in the 2012.1A DVD. Calibration files may also be obtained at the website.

NOTE: Please advise the customer that this vehicle is equipped with an adaptive transmission shift strategy which allows the vehicle's computer to learn the transmission's unique parameters and improve shift quality. When the adaptive strategy is reset, the computer will begin a re-learning process. This re-learning process may result in firmer than normal upshifts and downshifts for several days.

WARRANTY STATUS: eligible under provisions of new vehicle limited warranty coverage and emissions warranty coverage

---

This is typical of the driving dangers Ford's lineup of EcoBoost engines present. Fortunately, the emissions warranty gives you an extended warranty to fix the troublesome turbo-powered engines.

General Motors

The Mailman's Butt

The Chevrolet Volt is again cast in its familiar role as the poster child of President Obama's socialist meddling in the free automotive market.... [The latest attacks come] from the rabid, sadly misinformed right... U.S. jobs are in jeopardy because major portions of the American public believe, as [*Fox News*] Lou Dobbs and Bill O'Reilly claimed, that they "catch fire."... [T]he imperious, self-glorifying O'Reilly, unquestioned ruler of the "No Spin Zone," once again kicked the Volt around and proclaimed "several have caught fire."... So, the loony right has its jaws sunk into the Volt with all the stupid determination of a terrier who has locked his teeth into the mailman's butt. And with the same result: painful, but without any useful purpose.

BOB LUTZ
WWW.FORBES.COM/SITES/BOBLUTZ/2012/03/12/
THE-CHEVY-VOLT-BILL-OREILLY-AND-THE-POSTMANS-BUTT

Lutz is right about the safety of GM's Volt electric car. The car isn't fire-prone. But 475,000 2011–12 Chevrolet Cruz sedans are. Last June, GM recalled the popular compact to modify the engine shield design that could cause fires in the engine compartment. Fire can ignite when oil or other flammable fluids drip onto a hot plastic shield below the engine.

New Models

Goodbye, Aveo; hello, Spark. GM's newest small compact hit the showrooms this summer, and sales have been brisk. The Buick Encore, Cadillac ATS and XTS, Buick Verano, and a redesigned Malibu round out the revamped lineup of GM's 2013 models. Most of the equipment changes have to do with new engines, a wider availability of 6-speed transmissions, more powerful V6 engines, better fuel economy, and "decontenting" through option package deletions.

The Chevrolet Malibu.

This year, GM's model lineup will have lots of overlap as GM sells thinly disguised Chevrolets and Daewoos (Aveo/Sonic) through Chevrolet-Buick-GMC dealers. This shoring up of Buick dealers has hurt Cadillac, whose products look more and more like upscale Buicks with little Cadillac cachet. In China, where Buicks were once the car driven by top government officials, the brand is losing steam as the Chinese economy cools off.

Nevertheless, car sales were on the upswing for GM throughout 2011–12, and it looks like they will stay positive well into 2013. Fleet sales have rebounded, and residual values remain strong. Historically, low resale values have long plagued the industry, driving down the value of both new and used products. But that has turned around this year, with used-car sales particularly strong.

New and redesigned models, less Japanese product, a souring European economy, and pent-up buyer demand in North America have given GM, Chrysler, and Ford a year's sales advantage, which is apparently coming to an end in the last quarter of 2012 as Japanese automakers recapture market share (especially Honda and Toyota).

General Motors has already seen a first-quarter reduction in North American market share from 19.6 to 17.5 percent. Nevertheless, it is making more money than ever, while selling fewer cars. It has done this through reducing incentives last year and loading up its products with optional features that increase the profit on each sale. This said, incentives returned in the first quarter of 2012, where they were 9 percent higher than the industry average.

"Sticker Shock" Returns

Greed has returned to the truck and SUV market as automakers take advantage of consumer demand and a lessening of Japanese competition to announce huge price increases for 2013 models and tack on a slew of unjustified extra charges in the process. Fortunately, prices will fall after the December holidays, as they always do. In effect, prices will likely fall by at least 15 percent, depending on how much Asian automakers want to spend on discounts and sales incentives to recapture lost sales during the past disaster-ridden year.

Smart buyers will wait out the Auto Show hoopla and pick up discounted bargains. Just remember to carefully scrutinize ads and offers for bogus delivery and dealers' fees.

Increased Fuel Economy

Earlier this year, GM introduced its eAssist, or "light electrification," fuel-saving technology. This feature uses a small lithium-ion battery and a 15 kw motor-generator that gives electric boost during sustained acceleration, cuts off fuel during deceleration, regenerates during braking, and switches to electric power when stopped.

This technology is expected to cut fuel consumption by 25 percent, which rivals the mileage claims of Ford's new EcoBoost turbocharged engines and hybrids, without the extra hybrid cost. Look for eAssist as a standard feature in the 2012–13 Buick LaCrosse and as an optional item in the 2012–13 Buick Regal and the 2013 Chevy Malibu.

Other fuel-saving measures will come from a shift to 4-cylinder engines. Last year, 46 percent of GM's sales were 4-cylinder vehicles, up from only 25 percent five years ago. The engines are changing, too: Turbocharging, variable-valve timing, active fuel management, direct injection, and new liquid petroleum gas (LPG) alternative-fuel vehicles will soon be seen everywhere.

Trucks and SUVs

General Motors' truck and SUV division is halfway through its own restructuring as GM confronts stricter fuel-economy standards, lower diesel-fuel NO_x emissions rules that require regular urea fill-ups, gas price spikes that drive product planners batty, and a buying public that wants both car-like handling and performance in their truck or SUV while the engine barely sips fuel. Although the Tahoe, Yukon, Suburban, and Yukon XL will likely soldier on until at least 2014, the smaller, last-in-class Colorado and Canyon pickups will be discontinued for 2012.

GM dealers are stockpiling pickups in expectation of GM's 29-week idling of its plants to retool for the 2014 models, scheduled to arrive in the spring of 2013. Industry insiders say that General Motors turned on the incentive spigot in the first quarter of 2012 and will sweeten incentives early in the new year, offering heftier discounts, rebates, and low-interest financing to sell the aging full-sized trucks before the revamped versions hit dealer showrooms.

As buyers downsize from Detroit SUVs to CR-Vs, RAV4s, Foresters, and Tucsons, GM comes to the party a bit late; nevertheless, its SUVs and pickups are credible competitors that are gaining market share from the downsized boom and limited Asian production.

Quality Control

Not good, when measured against Asian products, but a bit better than what is offered by Ford and Chrysler. Ford's pickup lineup has shown some quality improvements in the past two years; however, its changeover to new fuel-frugal powertrains and the adoption of innovative, glitz-prone electronic gadgetry has created a customer backlash that threatens sales. Chrysler has similar problems. Except for the Dart and Ram pickup makeover, Chrysler's lineup and low quality scores haven't changed much. The company's future is riding on a new V6 powertrain that has so far not delivered the quality promised. Back to GM, the company has a strong truck and SUV lineup, plus the Malibu and Impala redesigns will help the company's bottom line. Even the little Aveo/Sonic has performed well during its first year on the market.

Like Chrysler and Ford, where GM has fallen down is in providing quality servicing and prompt parts delivery. Buyers are finding dealers unable to fix annoying, sometimes dangerous, defects because of inadequate manufacturing support. The company lets problems carry over year after year (a quick glance at the service bulletins in this section will confirm this) making small problems into big ones, and driving customers to the competition.

GM's quality control needs serious improvement. Buyers are suspicious, and its engines and automatic transmissions still aren't as reliable or as durable as those of the Asian competition. Furthermore, GM brake and electronic components often fail prematurely and cost owners big bucks to diagnose and repair. The quality and assembly of body components remains far below Asian standards.

SONIC	★★★★

RATING: Above Average. The Sonic proves that cheap subcompact cars don't mean you have to endure an uncomfortable ride and white-knuckle highway performance. **Road performance:** Fast and smooth acceleration; the optional turbocharged 1.4L (1.4T) engine has more torque and a nicely refined power curve. Its 0–60 mph acceleration time is only a bit over 8 seconds. RS models offer either a 6-speed manual or a 6-speed automatic transmission. Manual trannies have closer ratios, and the automatic gets a shorter final drive. Steering is

KEY FACTS

Canadian Price (Firm): *LS Sedan:* $14,495; *LT:* $16,495; *LTZ:* $20,495; *LS Hatch:* $15,495; *LT Hatch:* $17,495; *LTZ Hatch:* $20,995 **U.S. Price:** *LS Sedan:* $14,495, *LS Hatch:* $15,395; *LT:* $15,695, *LT Hatch:* $16,495, *LTZ Sedan:* $17,295; *LTZ Hatch:* $17,995 **Canadian Freight, Dealer Fees, and AC Tax:** $1,745 (Pay half of the freight charge, nothing for "dealer fees," and $100 AC tax) **U.S. Freight:** $975

POWERTRAIN (FRONT-DRIVE)

Engines: 1.8L 4-cyl. (138 hp) • 1.4L 4-cyl. turbo (138 hp); Transmissions: 5-speed man. • 6-speed man. • 6-speed auto.

DIMENSIONS/CAPACITY

Passengers: 2/3; Wheelbase: 99.4 in.; H: 59.7/L: 173.1/W: 68.3 in.; Legroom F/R: 41.8/34.6 in.; Cargo volume: 14.9 cu. ft.; Fuel tank: 45L/regular; Tow limit: Not recommended; Turning circle: 17.3 ft.; Ground clearance: 4.9 in.; Weight: 2,727 lb.

precise and responsive, with no torque steer pulling the car to the side when accelerating. **Strong points:** Reasonably priced, refined, and well-appointed. The interior is comfortable and practical, with little noise intrusion into the cabin. Sedans are about a foot longer than hatchbacks. Production has moved from South Korea to the States. **Weak points:** Firm pricing. A high probability of first-year factory-related defects. The hatchback's load floor is quite high—the Honda Fit is more useful and versatile. Mushy brakes. **Safety:** Earned five stars from NHTSA for front, side, and rollover crash protection. IIHS also gave its "Good" top score for frontal offset, side, rear, and roof crashworthiness. **New for 2013:** Chevrolet has a sporty RS variant that keeps the same 138 hp 1.4L engine but adds a stiffer suspension and rear disc brakes, different front and rear fascias, rocker-panel extensions, special fog lamps, 17-inch wheels, and a retuned exhaust. Inside: standard sport seats, a thicker steering wheel, aluminum pedals, a distinctive instrument-cluster design, special trim, and Chevrolet's MyLink infotainment system, which features a 7-inch touch screen and Bluetooth connectivity.

ALERT! The 2012 Chevrolet Sonic, Hyundai Accent, and Kia Rio excelled in road tests from *Consumer Reports* due to their "improvements in performance, equipment levels, and comfort." Owners note that the Sonic wanders with original equipment tires and wheels; consider getting alternatives.

OVERVIEW: Basically a second-generation Aveo, the Sonic offers more refinement, enhanced crashworthiness, better performance, and impressive fuel economy. It fits into GM's small car lineup between the Spark and Cruze.

COST ANALYSIS: Get the improved 2013 version; it will have fewer factory-related glitches. **Best alternatives:** Honda Fit, Hyundai Accent, Mazda2, Nissan Versa, and Toyota Yaris. **Rebates:** A $500 discount later in the new year. **Options:** The torquier 1.4L turbocharged 4-cylinder engine, because the 1.8L quickly runs out of steam when loaded. **Depreciation:** Predicted to be average. **Insurance cost:** Should be average. **Parts supply/cost:** Because the car is built on an all-new global small-car platform (the only one in its class assembled in the U.S.) and borrows powertrain components (including both engines) from the larger Cruze sedan, parts should be easy to find and be competitively priced. **Annual maintenance cost:** Expected to be average. **Warranty:** Bumper-to-bumper 3 years/60,000 km; powertrain 5 years/160,000 km; rust perforation 6 years/160,000 km. **Supplementary warranty:** A good idea. **Highway/city fuel economy:** *RS 6-speed man.:* 5.9/8.1 L/100 km, 40/29 mpg. *RS 6-speed auto.:* 7.6/8.7 L/100 km, 31/27 mpg.

OWNER-REPORTED PROBLEMS: Front passenger-side airbag sensor doesn't recognize that the seat is occupied; car rolls backwards when stopped on a hill, even though Hill Holder is engaged; engine dies when the windshield wipers are engaged; transmission hesitates up to 30 seconds before shifting; driver window button sticks; chronic rear brake squeal (corrosion); burning plastic smell in the cabin; front end of the vehicle is too low and drags on the ground when passing over uneven terrain; steering shake and excessive steering effort required:

> The steering wheel started "hunting" (shaking left and right) and resisted attempts to steer the vehicle. Although the car was still controllable, it was difficult to handle. This happens both while stopped and while driving. The problem is intermittent and is not thermal (will happen both at cold start-up and when vehicle is up to operating temperature). The dealer reprogrammed the electronic brake control module with SPS 155 WT40, stating the current programming was incorrect. The invoice reported a code: "C0710 symptom 4B sensor not learned relearn steering sensor". The problem returned after approx 100 miles [160 km] of use.

SERVICE BULLETIN-REPORTED PROBLEMS: Tires leak air or suddenly go flat (clean and resurface the wheel bead seat); a drivetrain clunk noise heard when shifting is an acceptable characteristic of GM transmissions, says TSB #01-07-30-042G, issued September 22, 2011:

2–3 UPSHIFT OR 3–2 DOWNSHIFT CLUNK

BULLETIN NO.: 01-07-30-042G   DATE: SEPTEMBER 22, 2011

INFORMATION ON 2–3 UPSHIFT OR 3–2 DOWNSHIFT CLUNK NOISE

2012 and Prior GM Passenger Cars and Light Duty Trucks Equipped with 4L60-E, 4L65-E or 4L70-E Automatic Transmission (RPOs M30, M32, M70).

IMPORTANT: For 2005 model year full-size utilities and pickups, refer to Corporate Bulletin Number 05-07-30-012. Some vehicles may exhibit a clunk noise that can be heard on a 2–3 upshift or a 3–2 downshift. During a 2–3 upshift, the 2–4 band is released and the 3–4 clutch is applied. The timing of this shift can cause a momentary torque reversal of the output shaft that results in a clunk noise. This same torque reversal can also occur on a 3–2 downshift when the 3–4 clutch is released and the 2–4 band applied. This condition may be worse on a 4-wheel drive vehicle due to the additional tolerances in the transfer case. This is a normal condition. No repairs should be attempted.

Can you believe it? General Motors is the only automaker that claims a clunking automatic transmission on its entire lineup of vehicles for the past several decades is a "normal condition."

Some airbags may not have a felt patch; power-steering fluid leaks; shock absorber/strut fluid leaks; tire slowly goes flat/warning light on; carpeted floor mats missing; automatic transmission clunk noise; engine hesitation at start-up requires reprogramming the engine control module.

CRUZE ★★★★

RATING: An Above Average compact sedan that's still relatively untested. Remember, the Daewoo-engineered Cruze is brought to you by the same quality-challenged company that made the unimpressive Aveo (with Chevrolet), the Reno and Forenza (with Suzuki), and the gone-but-not-lamented Pontiac LeMans (all on its own). **Road performance:** A peppy, smooth, and efficient turbocharged engine, plus good steering and handling. The firm suspension makes you feel every bump in the road. **Strong points:** An upscale interior, large trunk, quiet cabin, and comfortable front seats. The Eco gives impressive fuel economy. **Weak points:** Fuel economy is not extraordinary with base models. The Bluetooth feature often disconnects during phone calls; cramped rear seating with seat cushions set too low; rear-view mirror blocks the view through the front windshield; limited storage area; a boring exterior; and unproven long-term reliability. **Safety:** Five stars for frontal and side protection; rollover resistance scored four stars. IIHS rates frontal, side, head-restraint, and roof crash protection as "Good." **New for 2013:** More infotainment features; a long-awaited diesel engine will make the 2014 a Recommended buy.

ALERT! The latest fire recall solves one problem but may create others, says this owner:

> The recall fix for the Chevrolet Cruze was performed on my car. The fix was to cut the engine, or under the engine area, skid plate exposing this area. I believe this to be a safety issue that could result in further damage to the car, engine, exhaust, oil pan and other components that are now exposed. This is a safety concern because during the act of driving this vehicle, it may be exposed to road conditions, foreign objects, or other miscellaneous environmental factors that will affect the performance and overall safe handling of this vehicle.

KEY FACTS

Canadian Price (Firm): *LS:* $17,400, *LS:* $19,260, *LT TURBO:* $20,600, *LT TURBO+:* $21,580, *ECO:* $22,065, *LTZ TURBO:* $27,835 **U.S. Price:** *LS:* $16,525, *ECO:* $18,425, *1LT:* $18,425, *2LT:* $20,925, *LTZ:* $22,225 **Canadian freight, dealer fees, and AC tax:** $1,750 (This is padded profit. Pay half of the freight charge, nothing for "dealer fees," and $100 for AC tax.) **U.S. Freight:** $795

POWERTRAIN (FRONT-DRIVE)

Engines: 1.8L 4-cyl. (136 hp) • 1.4L turbocharged 4-cyl. (138 hp); Transmissions: 6-speed man. • 6-speed auto.

DIMENSIONS/CAPACITY

Passengers: 2/3; Wheelbase: 105.7 in.; H: 58.1/L: 181/W: 70.7 in.; Legroom F/R: 42.3/35.4 in.; Cargo volume: 15.0 cu. ft.; Fuel tank: 59L/regular; Tow limit: 1,000 lb. (No towing for Eco model.); Turning circle: 35.7 ft.; Ground clearance: 6.5 in.; Weight: 3,056 lb.

OVERVIEW: The Chevrolet Cruze is built in Lordstown, Ohio, and last year replaced the poor-selling Chevrolet Cobalt and its Pontiac G5 twin as the leading homegrown compact car from GM. This wasn't hard to do, since the Cobalt ranked a disappointing 24th out of 30 "affordable small cars" rated by *U.S. News & World Report.*

Cruze comes as a four-door sedan equipped with a fuel-frugal 136 hp 1.8L 4-cylinder engine. The Eco version uses a 138 hp turbocharged 1.4L 4-cylinder engine. Diesel power is also on its way; a turbocharged 2.0L 4-cylinder will join the lineup in late 2013 or 2014.

A 6-speed manual transmission is standard on the LS and Eco; a 6-speed automatic is optional on those models, but comes standard on the LT and LTZ. Buyers get a wide choice of standard safety features that include ABS, traction control, an anti-skid system, side curtain airbags, front and rear side airbags, and front knee airbags. The Eco models come with tires that have ultra-low rolling resistance (meaning they are better at gripping the road) and other aerodynamic improvements designed to enhance fuel economy.

European and Australian car columnists who have tested earlier, local versions of the Cruze have mixed opinions. They praise the Cruze for its interior quality/space and modern styling, while criticizing the car's weight, wimpy engines, and mediocre handling. Drivers don't want just style or fuel economy; they want performance, too, which may stop the Cruze dead in its tracks if fuel costs stay reasonable enough for drivers to stick with less-fuel-efficient but better-performing vehicles.

COST ANALYSIS: Buy a 2013 model. It will have fewer factory-related problems and cost only about $500 more. You may wish to wait for a diesel-equipped Cruze next year. It will likely be patterned after the Australian 2.0L 4-cylinder version and could boost gas mileage to around 4.7 L/100 km (50 mpg). This almost ties with Toyota's Prius gas/electric hybrid ($27,800), which gets 4.6L/100 km (51 mpg) in the city and 4.9L/100 km (48 mpg) on the highway, according to tests run by the Washington-based Environmental Protection Agency. Cars with diesel engines generally cost more than those with gasoline engines. **Best alternatives:** Some good alternative models are the Honda Fit, Hyundai Accent, Mazda2 (after it has been on the market a while), and VW Jetta (with a more-reliable manual transmission). **Options:** The turbocharged 4-banger and premium tires. **Rebates:** $500 rebates at year's end. **Depreciation:** Average. **Insurance cost:** Average. **Parts supply/cost:** Average supply and cost. **Annual maintenance cost:** Average. **Warranty:** 60-day money-back guarantee as long as you don't drive more than 4,000 km. Bumper-to-bumper 3 years/60,000 km; powertrain 5 years/160,000 km; rust perforation 6 years/160,000 km. **Supplementary warranty:** An extended powertrain warranty would be a wise investment. **Highway/city fuel economy:** *Eco 1.4L man.:* 4.6/7.2 L/100 km, 55/36 mpg. *Eco 1.4L auto.:* 5.1/7.8 L/100 km, 51/33 mpg. *1.8L man.:* 5.4/7.8L/100 km, 52/36 mpg. *1.8L auto.:* 5.6/9.2 L/100 km, 50/31 mpg. Despite the preceding figures put out by the federal government (*http://oee.nrcan.gc.ca/transportation/tools/fuelratings/ratings-search.cfm*), Cruze owners say real gas mileage is much less than what is advertised.

OWNER-REPORTED PROBLEMS: Sudden, unintended acceleration, "lag and lurch" when accelerating; loss of braking when backing up (vacuum pump suspected); loss of braking when underway:

> While driving approximately 10 mph [16 km/h], the contact depressed the brake pedal but the vehicle would not respond and the brake pedal fell to the floorboard abnormally. The contact used the emergency brake in order to stop the vehicle. The vehicle was taken to the dealer for diagnostics where the technician advised that the booster kit, retainer, cylinder kit and the valve kit would have to be replaced. The vehicle was repaired, however, the failure recurred. The vehicle was taken back to the dealer for diagnostic testing where the technicians were unable to diagnose the failure.

Faulty struts "pop" when braking; coolant smell in the cabin even though coolant hose and thermostat housing had been changed:

> I think we have an anti-freeze smell inside the car whenever the heater is used. I can no longer drive the car if I am going to need heat. Dealer worked on the car 4 times and has not fixed the problem. The only smell GM will admit to is a hot plastic smell. Even if it is hot plastic, what is it doing to people's health? I feel sick and [nauseated] when using the heater.

Axle seal leaks; chronic automatic transmission failures and malfunctions (often caused by a faulty transmission control module):

> At 65 miles an hour [105 km/h] my 2011 Chevy Cruze (14,500 miles [23,340 km]) suddenly began slowing and the engine was revving high. I pulled over and a light on the dash appeared indicating "emissions problems" according to the manual. It is an automatic transmission but the car wouldn't seem to shift any higher than 3rd gear and would go no faster than 30–35 miles an hour [48–58 km/h] without revving in the danger zone. Car was towed to dealer. The transmission control module failed. $1300 for the part plus labor costs and not covered by warranty.

Airbags fail to deploy when they're needed; "spongy" brakes accompanied by a delayed response; floor mats slide up under the pedals; original equipment Firestone tires cause the car to shake excessively, and tires deflate when driven over winding roads; excessive headlight glare from the rear-view mirror; the rear-view mirror vibrates constantly; windshield wipers are too slow to be effective; power steering failures; and in one incident, the steering wheel came off in the driver's hand:

> While driving my new 2011 Chevy Cruze on Highway 10 in Minnesota, without any warning or any other indications the steering wheel fell off in the hands of the driver. We crossed several lanes of traffic and finally got the car stopped just inches from hitting the guardrail.

SERVICE BULLETIN-REPORTED PROBLEMS: Some airbags may not have a felt patch; power-steering fluid leaks; shock absorber/strut fluid leaks; tire slowly goes flat/ warning light on; carpeted floor mats are missing; automatic transmission clunk noise; and engine hesitation at start-up requires reprogramming the engine control module.

MALIBU ★★

KEY FACTS

Canadian Price (Very Negotiable):
LS: $26,040, *LT:* $28,390, *Platinum:*
$30,040, *LTZ:* $35,040 **U.S. Price:** *LS:*
$23,150, *LTZ:* $28,590, *LTZ Turbo:*
$30,925 *Eco:* $25,235, *Hybrid:* $26,095
**Canadian Freight, Dealer Fees, and AC
Tax:** $2,045 (This is price gouging. Pay
half of the freight charge, nothing for
"dealer fees," and $100 for the AC Tax.)
U.S. Freight: $760
POWERTRAIN (FRONT-DRIVE)
Engines: 2.4L 4-cyl. (182 hp) • 2.5L
4-cyl. (197 hp); Transmission: 6-speed
auto.
DIMENSIONS/CAPACITY
Passengers: 2/3; Wheelbase: 107.8 in.;
H: 57.6/L: 191.5/W: 73 in.; Headroom
F/R: N/A; Legroom F/R: 42.1/36.8;
Cargo volume: 13.2 cu. ft.; Fuel tank:
61L/regular; Tow limit: 1,000 lb.; Load
capacity: 915 lb.; Turning circle: 18.7
ft.; Ground clearance: 5.0 ft.; Weight:
3,500 lb.

RATING: Below Average. The Malibu has never been a spectacular performer, and its redesign this year will likely saddle the car with more reliability problems. **Road performance:** The Malibu's performance has been strengthened by this year's redesign; hopefully, a decline in quality won't ensue. Nevertheless, the base 4-cylinder engine with an automatic transmission is barely adequate for highway driving with a full load. The car does give a comfortable though firm ride and better-than-average handling, thanks to its independent suspension. **Strong points:** Well-appointed, with many advanced high-tech features; adequate passenger and luggage space; few squeaks and rattles; higher-grade materials used in the interior; and the Eco's high fuel economy. **Weak points:** As with earlier redesigns, expect lots of powertrain and brake problems during the first year of use. Less rear legroom than in other cars in this class; transmission makes the Eco model feel sluggish; and overpriced bundled option packages. The car, despite its restyling, still seems to be more plastic than metal. Controls appear to be a bit more complicated than those used in previous years. **Safety:** NHTSA awarded the Malibu its five-star crashworthiness score for frontal and side protection and four stars for frontal rollover resistance. IIHS says frontal offset, side, rear, and roof crash protection is "Good." **New for 2013:** Revamped and set on GM's new Epsilon II platform, shared with the Buick Regal and LaCrosse. The platform change makes the Malibu slightly wider and a little taller, thereby creating a roomier interior that gives better access to instruments and controls.

ALERT! Consider the standard 2.5L-equipped models, instead of snapping up the more expensive, feeble, and untested mild-hybrid Eco version.

OVERVIEW: The Malibu is a popular front-drive, mid-sized sedan distinguished by its nice array of standard features. A new 2.5L 4-cylinder arrived this summer as standard equipment, and an optional turbocharged 2.0L 4-cylinder engine will show up later in the year.

COST ANALYSIS: The 2013 2.5L-equipped Malibu has a better frontal crashworthiness rating, its powertrain will be more suitable for hard driving, and factory-related snafus will likely be fewer. The Eco's high fuel economy is only 1 mpg better than what the 4-cylinder-powered Hyundai Sonata and Toyota Camry achieve. **Best alternatives:** The Honda Accord has more usable interior space, is super reliable, and has quicker and more-accurate steering; Hyundai's Elantra is cheaper and just as well put together, and Toyota's Camry is plusher, though not as driver-oriented. Other cars worth considering are the Mazda3 or Mazda6 and Nissan Sentra. **Options:** Careful, careful. The few options that might be worthwhile come with other features that aren't worth the extra money. **Rebates:** $500 rebates should kick in sometime during the new year. **Depreciation:** Average. **Insurance cost:** Higher than average. **Parts supply/cost:** Malibu uses generic GM parts that are easy to find and reasonably priced. **Annual maintenance cost:** Average. **Warranty:** 3 years/60,000 km; powertrain 5 years/160,000 km; rust perforation 6 years/160,000 km. **Supplementary warranty:** An extended powertrain warranty would be a wise investment. **Highway/city fuel economy:** *2.4L:* 6.5/9.5 L/100 km, 43/30 mpg. *2.4L 6-speed:* 5.9/9.4 L/100 km, 48/30 mpg. *V6:* 7.8/12.2 L/100 km, 36/23 mpg.

OWNER-REPORTED PROBLEMS: Power-steering failure; the electronic stability control light comes on and the car loses all power, and at other times no warning light comes on:

> This car suddenly lost power as it began to slow down on a busy street, and then would not drive. The car continued to run, but would not go forward, even after gas pedal was pushed to the floor. It, in fact, started coasting backwards when it was on a slight incline. No indicator light came on. It happened suddenly, and without warning. Service dpt. at dealership can find nothing wrong. We feel that this brand new car has a faulty computer system and is very dangerous to drive.

SERVICE BULLETIN-REPORTED PROBLEMS: Power-steering fluid leaks; Airbag warning light comes on intermittently (likely caused by a loose, missing, or damaged connector position assurance retainer); shock absorber fluid leaks; tires slowly go flat; wet front or rear passenger-side carpet (this condition may be caused by a plugged HVAC evaporator drain—in some cases, water from the HVAC system

PART THREE • AMERICAN VEHICLES

will drain back though the front of the dash); clunking automatic transmission shifts are called "normal" by GM; and there's a gap at the rear edge of the shifter trim plate.

IMPALA, LACROSSE   ★ ★ ★

The Chevrolet Impala.

RATING: Average. **Road performance:** The V6 provides smooth acceleration and works well with the 6-speed automatic transmission, though it could use more high-speed torque. Handling and ride are better than average, owing to recent suspension and steering refinements. Three years ago, the mid-sized LaCrosse was completely restyled and its four-wheel independent suspension was retuned to improve the ride and handling. The available all-wheel-drive system employs a limited-slip differential to send torque to whichever wheel has more traction for better control on slippery roads. **Strong points:** *Impala:* Comes with an array of standard features, provides a comfortable ride, and has an easily accessed interior, highlighted by a convenient flip-down centre console in the middle of the bench seats and rear seatbacks that fold flat, opening up cargo storage space. *LaCrosse:* Adequate rear legroom, and a front bench seat. LaCrosse also has a much better reliability record than the Impala. **Weak points:** *Impala:* Rear seating is uncomfortable for three and obstructs rear visibility due to the tall, wide rear-seat head restraints:

> I cannot see when using the rear view mirror due to the reduced visibility caused by the head rests on the rear seats. The view when using the rear view mirror is obstructed significantly with only 4 inches of visibility between the ceiling of the car and the top of the head rests. Also, the side mirrors are small increasing the poor visibility in this vehicle. The head rests problem would have been noticed if the car salesman had not sat in backseat in the middle. The car dealership suggested that the car be

taken to a local seat cover company to have the headrests rebuilt. This is a new car and should not have problems such as this.

Safety: NHTSA gave the 2013 Impala and LaCrosse a five-star crashworthiness rating for front and side protection and four stars for rollover resistance. IIHS judged front, side, and rear crashworthiness as "Good" on the 2012 Impala, while roof strength and rear crash protection (head restraints) were judged to be only "Acceptable." The 2012 LaCrosse was rated as "Good" by IIHS for front, side, roof, and rear crashworthiness. **New for 2013:** The V8 is no longer on the option list for the 2013 remake. Instead, GM uses a 302 hp 3.6L V6 and two 4-cylinder alternatives. This year shall see additional safety features, like a lane departure warning system and blind-spot detection. There is also a new state-of-the-art infotainment system with a pop-up LCD screen at the top of the centre console that conceals a hidden cubbyhole used to store—and recharge—a mobile phone or MP3 player. The infotainment system includes the new MyLink system, which not only allows hands-free Bluetooth communication but also can be used to control smartphone apps such as Pandora radio.

ALERT! *Impala:* During the test-drive listen for engine knocking/ticking and fuel pump noise/vibration while accelerating. *LaCrosse:* Can you adjust to the front pillar partially obstructing your view?

OVERVIEW: Impala has become one of GM's least competitive products and should have been culled from the herd years ago. Keeping the Impala without major upgrades weakens the Chevrolet brand and gives Ford's Fusion and Chrysler's 200 a boost. With the V8 option gone, the car is overwhelmed by its unimpressive highway performance and overall lack of quality. It will soldier on until 2014 without any significant changes. Everyone agrees that GM has given up on large front-drive sedans as a competitive volume product and is relying instead on crossovers and downsized SUVs to take up the slack. Last year's better-performing powertrain with cylinder deactivation is an important upgrade, but it should have been offered a decade ago; it may have arrived too late to save the nameplate.

KEY FACTS

Canadian Price (Very Negotiable): *Base Impala LS:* $29,970, *LT:* $30,960, *LTZ:* $36,115, *Base LaCrosse:* $34,400, *AWD:* $39,270 **U.S. Price:** *Impala LS:* $25,860, *Base Lacrosse:* $31,660, *Premium 1:* $35,285, *Premium 2:* $36,705 **Canadian Freight, Dealer Fees, and AC Tax:** $1,745 (pay half of the freight charge, nothing for "dealer fees," and $100 for the AC tax.) **U.S. Freight:** $825

POWERTRAIN (FRONT-DRIVE/AWD)
Engines: *Impala:* 3.6L V6 (300 Hp) • 3.9L V6 (230 Hp) • 5.3L V8 (303 Hp), *Lacrosse:* 2.4L 4-Cyl. (182 Hp) • 3.0L V6 (255 Hp) • 3.6L V6 (280 Hp); Transmissions: *Impala:* 4-Speed Auto., *Lacrosse:* 6-Speed Auto.

DIMENSIONS/CAPACITY
Passengers: 2/3; Wheelbase: *Impala:* 110.5 in., *LaCrosse:* 111.7 in.; *Impala:* H: 58.7/L: 200.4/W: 72.9 in.; *LaCrosse:* H: 58.9/L: 197.0/W: 73.1 in.; Headroom: F/R: 4.0/1.5 in.; Legroom F/R: 42.3/37.6 in.; Fuel tank: 64L/regular/premium; Cargo volume: 16 cu. ft.; Tow limit: 1,000 lb.; Load capacity: *Impala:* 945 lb., *LaCrosse:* 915 lb.; Turning circle: 38.8 ft.; Ground clearance: 6.0 in.; Weight: *Impala LS, LT:* 3,555 lb., *LTZ:* 3,649 lb., *LaCrosse CX:* 3,948 lb..

COST ANALYSIS: 2012 Impala and LaCrosse models are discounted about 10 percent and are practically identical to the 2013s. **Best alternatives:** The more-reliable, better-performing Honda Accord, Mazda6, Hyundai Elantra, and Toyota Camry or Avalon. Those wanting a bit more performance should consider the BMW 3 Series. More room and better performance can be had by purchasing a Hyundai Tucson or a Honda CR-V. **Options:** Pass on the Impala's rear spoiler, which obstructs rear visibility and is of doubtful utility. **Rebates:** *Impala:* The Impala is in a marketing segment that's steadily losing ground to Japanese entries. The longer you wait, the cheaper these cars will become. Look for the return of $2,500 rebates on Impalas throughout 2013. *LaCrosse:* Its recent redesign has created some buying buzz, and this has kept the price higher than it should be; GM will reinstate $2,000 rebates throughout the year. **Depreciation:** *Impala:* Incredibly fast; a 2007 Impala LS that sold new for $25,230 is now worth only $9,500. *LaCrosse:* Again, depreciation is a big minus. A 2007 LaCrosse (which was called the Allure from 2005–09) CX that sold for $26,395 is now worth $8,500. **Insurance cost:** Higher than average. **Parts supply/cost:** Moderately priced parts that aren't hard to find. **Annual maintenance cost:** Higher than average. Independent garages can perform most non-emissions servicing; however, cylinder deactivation makes you a prisoner of GM dealer servicing. **Warranty:** A 60-day money-back guarantee, as long as you don't drive more than 4,000 km. Bumper-to-bumper 4 years/80,000 km; powertrain 5 years/160,000 km; rust perforation 6 years/160,000 km. **Supplementary warranty:** Essential, especially after the third year of ownership. Get an extended powertrain warranty to protect you from the usual GM engine and transmission problems. **Highway/city fuel economy:** *Impala 3.5L:* 6.7/10.8 L/100 km, 42/26 mpg. *3.9L:* 7.4/12.0 L/100 km, 38/24 mpg. *LaCrosse 2.4L:* 6.5/10.8 L/100 km, 43/26 mpg. *3.6L:* 7.3/12.2 L/100 km, 39/23 mpg. *AWD 3.6L:* 7.7/12.7 L/100 km, 37/22 mpg.

OWNER-REPORTED PROBLEMS: Engine rear main seal leak; loud engine knocking, ticking noise; chronic stalling; car was parked with transmission in "Park," and it rolled away; wheel lug nut studs snap off; and a noisy, vibrating high-pressure fuel pump.

SERVICE BULLETIN-REPORTED PROBLEMS: Automatic transmission clunks when shifted; power-steering leakage; Airbag warning light comes on intermittently; shock absorber fluid leaks; tires slowly go flat; and carpeted floor mats may be missing.

CAMARO ★★★★

RATING: Above Average going into its third year on the market. **Road performance:** Impressive V6 and V8 acceleration with reasonable fuel economy and nice steering/handling. **Strong points:** Interior trim looks and feels to be of better quality, and the seats provide good lateral support and are easy to adjust. Very few serious reliability complaints. **Weak points:** No headroom; if you are 6'2" or taller, your head will be constantly brushing up against the headliner; rear seating is a "knees-to-chin" affair; not much cargo room; small trunk and trunk

opening. Owners report that fit and finish glitches are everywhere; exterior styling seems to have been slapped together by a committee; the rear, especially, is ugly and obstructs rear visibility; plus, the car is set too high to look "sporty." **Safety:** NHTSA awarded the Camaro its top five-star rating for frontal, side, and rollover crashworthiness. IIHS hasn't yet crash-tested the Camaro. **New for 2013:** Nothing much new except for more infotainment gadgetry and the rollout of a 1LE performance model for Camaro SS Coupes. The 2016 model will be redesigned.

ALERT! Listen for front strut shock noise when passing over uneven terrain or small bumps. Some drivers also report that the steering gives way to any imperfections in the road.

OVERVIEW: The 2012–13 Chevrolet Camaro continues to breathe life into General Motors' iconic high-performance two-door coupe and convertible pony car. This year, we see the return of the LS, 1LT, 2LT, 1SS, and 2SS models offered with either a base 323 hp 3.6L V6 or the choice of two V8s. The 1SS and 2SS come with a manual transmission hooked to a 426 hp 6.2L V8; automatic-equipped versions get the same V8, but harness "only" 400 hp and GM's Active Fuel

KEY FACTS

Canadian Price (Very Negotiable): *1LS man.:* $28,200, *2LS auto.:* $29,400, *1LT man.:* $30,110, *2LT man.:* $34,390, *1SS:* $39,580, *2SS:* $39,580, *1LT Conv.:* $36,300, *2LT Conv.:* $40,250, *1SS man.:* $38,350, *2SS auto.:* $43,220, *1SS Conv.:* $44,820, *2SS Conv.:* $49,100 **U.S. Price:** *LS man.:* $23,345, *2LS auto.:* $24,545, *1LT man.:* $25,760, *2LT man.:* $28,685, *1SS man.:* $31,330, *2SS man.:* $36,135, *ZL1 man.:* $54,350, *1LT Conv.:* $30,660, *2LT Conv.:* $34,435, *1SS Conv.:* $38,685, *2SS Conv.:* $41,285 *ZL1:* $59,545

Canadian Freight, dealer fees, and AC Tax: $1,500 (Cut the freight charge in half, pay nothing for "dealer fees," and hand over $100 for the AC tax.) **U.S. Freight:** $900

POWERTRAIN (REAR-DRIVE)
Engines: 3.6L V6 (323 hp) • 6.2L V8 (400–426 hp) • 6.2L supercharged V8 (580 hp); Transmissions: 6-speed man. • 6-speed auto.

DIMENSIONS/CAPACITY
Passengers: 2/2; Wheelbase: 112.3 in.; H: 54.2/L: 190.4/W: 75.5 in.; Cargo volume: 11.3 cu. ft.; Fuel tank: 71.9L/regular; Tow limit: No towing; Turning circle: 37.7 ft.; Weight: 3,769–3,849 lb.

Management cylinder deactivation. Available safety features include ABS, traction control, an anti-skid system, front side airbags, and side curtain airbags.

COST ANALYSIS: Camaros are "hot," and this year's sales have beaten the equally popular Ford Mustang by a small margin. This means there will be no bargains; dealers can ask for (and get) the full suggested retail price. Smart buyers will wait on the more reasonably priced, leftover models available in the spring of 2013. **Best alternatives:** The Hyundai Genesis Coupe, not the Mustang. Ford gave its new 'Stang everything but quality. **Options:** Buying the GPS navigation aids, special wheels, and xenon headlights from independent retailers can save you thousands, but don't waste your money on the power sunroof, leather upholstery, or heated seats. And don't let the dealer sell you poorly performing original-equipment summer tires. **Rebates:** Rebates and discounts of only $1,000–$2,000 because the Camaro is still seen as a "hot" American-built sports car. **Depreciation:** Very slow. A 2010 base model that sold for $26,995 is now worth $18,000. Not much lost for almost three year's use. **Insurance cost:** Much higher than average. **Parts supply/cost:** Not easily found and quite costly. At present, dealers have a monopoly on parts and service. **Annual maintenance cost:** Higher than average; there's no competition. **Warranty:** A 60-day money-back guarantee, as long as you don't drive more than 4,000 km. Bumper-to-bumper 4 years/80,000 km; powertrain 5 years/160,000 km; rust perforation 6 years/unlimited km. **Supplementary warranty:** An extended powertrain warranty is a good idea, considering that the Camaro is going into only its fourth year on the market. **Highway/city fuel economy:** *3.6L V6:* 7.1/12.4 L/100 km, 40/23 mpg. *Auto.:* 6.8/11.4 L/100 km, 42/25 mpg. *SS man. and 6.2L V8:* 8.2/13.2 L/100 km, 34/21 mpg. *Auto.:* 8.0/13.3 L/100 km, 35/21 mpg.

OWNER-REPORTED PROBLEMS: Passenger-side airbag doesn't recognize the seat is occupied; the vehicle shudders in all shift modes; and noisy suspension struts:

> I constantly get a very annoying clunking sound from both driver and passenger side front strut or shock area when driving [over] uneven pavement or hitting bumps when driving at any speeds, the sound has begun to get louder, the steering gives way to any imperfections on roads or highways regardless of speed which has now given me the concern of safety. General Motors for some reason has denied that this is a problem, stating that this is a characteristic of this vehicle.

SERVICE BULLETIN-REPORTED PROBLEMS: Sound change in 3- or 4-cylinder mode; automatic transmission makes a clunk sound when shifted; recalibration of the electronic brake control module to improve cold-weather braking performance; power-steering fluid leaks; moisture from vent when AC is on/car may be wet; lower rear window seal loose or missing; side window glass won't clear moulding; tips on removing scratches and scuffs on the radio display screen; door light bar inoperative or loses intensity; noisy six-way power front seats; rear bumper fascia contacting body/paint peeling; door and quarter panel paint appearance; and convertible top spots, indentation/damage.

RATING: Average; a brawny, bulky sport coupe that's slowly evolving into a more-refined machine. But quality control continues to be subpar, and safety-related transmission and body deficiencies are common. The Corvette does deliver high-performance thrills—along with suspension kickback, numb steering, and seats that need extra bolstering. Overall, get the quieter and less temperamental base Corvette; it delivers the same cachet for a lot less money. **Road performance:** A powerful and smooth powertrain that responds quickly to the throttle; the 6-speed gearbox performs well in all gear ranges and makes shifting smooth, with short throws and easy entry into all gears. Easy handling; enhanced side-slip angle control helps to prevent skidding and provides better traction control. No oversteer (in fact, steering is a little vague), wheel spinning, breakaway rear ends, or nasty surprises, thanks partly to standard electronic stability control. Better-than-average braking; the ABS-vented disc brakes are easy to modulate, and they're fade-free. **Strong points:** The car has a relatively roomy interior, user-friendly instruments and controls, and lots of convenience features. There's a key-controlled lockout feature that discourages joy riding by cutting engine power in half. All Corvettes are also equipped with an impressively effective

KEY FACTS

Canadian Price (Very Negotiable): *1LT:* $50,575, *2LT:* $52,720, *3LT:* $56,570, *4LT:* $60,070, *Grand Sport:* $56,975, *Convertible:* $77,040, *Grand Sport Convertible:* $83,740, *Z06:* $95,705, *ZR1:* $128,600 **U.S. Price:** *1LT:* $50,575, *2LT:* $52,720, *3LT:* $56,570, *4LT:* $60,070, *Grand Sport 1LT:* $56,975, *2LT:* $59,120, *3LT:* $62,970, *4LT:* $66,470, *Z06 1LZ:* $76,575, *2LZ:* $81,235, *3LZ:* $85,435, *ZR1 1ZR:* $113,575, *3ZR:* $123,575 **Canadian Freight, dealer fees, and AC Tax:** $1,745 (Pay half of the freight charge, nothing for "dealer fees," and $100 for the AC tax) **U.S. Freight:** Included.

POWERTRAIN (REAR-DRIVE)

Engines: 6.2L V8 (430 hp) • 7.0L V8 (505 hp) • 6.2L V8 Supercharged (638 hp); Transmissions: 6-speed man. • 6-speed auto.

DIMENSIONS/CAPACITY

Passengers: 2; Wheelbase: 106 in.; H: 49/L: 175/W: 73 in.; Headroom: 4 in.; Legroom: 41 in.; Cargo volume: 11 cu. ft.; Fuel tank: 68.1L/ premium; Tow limit: Not recommended; Load capacity: 390 lb.; Turning circle: 42 ft.; Ground clearance: 4.5 in.; Weight: 3,280 lb.

PassKey theft-deterrent system that uses a resistor pellet in the ignition to disable the starter and fuel system when the key code doesn't match the ignition lock. All models come with standard side airbags and revised interiors. Convertibles get a trunk spoiler, and cars equipped with manual transmissions get a Performance Traction Management system that modulates the engine's torque output for fast starts. This feature also manages engine power when the driver floors the accelerator when coming out of a corner. The car is so low that its front air dam scrapes over the smallest rise in the road. Expect lots of visits to the body shop. **Weak points:** Limited rear visibility; inadequate storage space; poor-quality powertrain; mediocre fit and finish; cabin amenities and materials aren't up to the competition's standards. The Corvette's sophisticated electronic and powertrain components have low tolerance for real-world conditions. **Safety:** No crashworthiness or rollover data available from NHTSA or IIHS. **New for 2013:** GM fetes the last year of the C6 model with the 427 convertible, equipped with a 505 hp 7.0L V8. 2014 models will see a longer wheelbase and more-refined engines.

ALERT! Save your money for the radically improved 2014 model.

OVERVIEW: Standard models come with a 430 hp 6.0L V8 mated to a 6-speed manual or optional automatic transmission, keyless access with push-button start, large tires and wheels (18-inch front, 19-inch rear), HID xenon lighting, power hatch pull-down, heated seats, and an AM/FM/CD/MP3 player with seven speakers and in-dash six-CD changer.

Z06

Although not quite as fast as the Dodge Viper, this is the fastest model found in the Corvette lineup (0–100 km/h in 3.6–4.2 seconds). It's also the lightest Z06 yet, thanks to the magic of Detroit reengineering. Instead of just adding iron and components to carry extra weight, GM has reinforced the rear axle and 6-speed clutch, installed coolers everywhere, adopted a dry-sump oil system to keep the engine well oiled when cornering, and added wider wheels and larger, heat-dissipating brakes. These improvements added about 50 kg of weight, which was trimmed by using cast-magnesium in the chassis structure and installing lighter carbon-fibre floorboards and front fenders. Net result: a monster Vette that is rated for 300+ km/h and weighs less than the base model.

To be honest, the Z06 chassis isn't very communicative to the driver, so the car doesn't inspire as much driving confidence as does the European competition, although it does feature standard stability control for when you get too frisky.

COST ANALYSIS: Keep in mind that premium fuel and astronomical insurance rates will further drive up your operating costs. A word about the ZR1: It's like investing in Cisco or Dell—don't! A 2010 ZR1 that sold new for $128,515 is now worth $83,000. **Best alternatives:** Other sporty models worth considering are the Ford GT or Shelby GT500 Mustang and the Porsche 911 or Boxster. The Nissan 370Z looks good on paper, but its quality problems carried over year after year make it a risky buy, much like Nissan's attractively styled Quest. **Options:** Remember, performance options rarely increase performance to the degree promised by the seller; the more performance options you buy, the less comfort you'll have, the more things can go wrong, and the more simple repairs can increase in complexity. Run-flat tires are not a good investment, either. They are hard to find and expensive. Forget about the head-up instrument display that projects speed and other data onto the windshield; it's annoyingly distracting, and you'll end up turning it off. **Rebates:** The Corvette is so popular that GM normally doesn't have to offer rebates to boost sales, but there will be some discounting starting late in 2012. If gasoline prices spike, Corvette sales will fall and rebates will be substantially higher. **Depreciation:** Much faster than you would imagine, and nowhere near the resale prices promised by salespeople. For example, an entry-level 2007 Corvette coupe that sold for $68,565 new is now worth about $24,000. **Insurance cost:** Astronomical. **Parts supply/cost:** Parts are pricey and often back ordered. **Annual maintenance cost:** Higher than average. **Warranty:** A 60-day money-back guarantee, as long as you don't drive more than 4,000 km. Bumper-to-bumper 3 years/60,000 km; powertrain 5 years/160,000 km; rust perforation 6 years/160,000 km. **Supplementary warranty:** A smart idea to protect you from frequent drivetrain failures. **Highway/city fuel economy:** 6.2L man.: 7.7/12.9 L/100 km, 37/22 mpg. Auto.: 8.1/14.3 L/100 km, 35/20 mpg. 7.0L man.: 8.2/14.2 L/100 km, 34/20 mpg. Auto.: 8.2/14.2 L/100 km, 34/20 mpg. ZR1 man.: 10.2/15.5 L/100 km, 28/18 mpg.

OWNER-REPORTED PROBLEMS: Poor-performing original equipment Goodyear tires:

> My model is equipped with Goodyear "Eagle F1 Supercar Gen2 Tires" featuring an [asymmetrical] tread pattern. They are very hard and treacherous in cold rainy weather and have a tendency to "float" on any kind of ponding water on the road (particularly expressways) causing the vehicle to act as if it is going to move laterally from one lane to the next. It is disconcerting at best and potentially dangerous at worst.

SERVICE BULLETIN-REPORTED PROBLEMS: Wheel hop, differential chatter; under-hood rattle, tapping noise; automatic transmission clunks; power-steering and shock absorber fluid leakage; Airbag warning light comes on intermittently; cracks in transparent removable roof panel; convertible headliner frayed at outer edges; and troubleshooting tips for eliminating various noises from lift-off roof while driving.

CTS ★★★

RATING: Average. As Cadillac reinvents itself in a futile attempt to lure younger buyers, its cars are becoming more complex and less distinctive. **Road performance:** Competent and secure handling; a pleasant ride; three manually tuned suspension settings for all tastes; and available all-wheel drive. The 3.6L V6 is smooth and powerful. **Strong points:** Roomier cabin than with other cars in

this class (the Sport Wagon's generous cargo space is especially noteworthy); a tasteful, well-appointed interior loaded with high-tech gadgetry. **Weak points:** Not as agile as its rivals; poor rear visibility; and an awkward driving position caused by uneven pedal depth and limited knee room due to the intrusion of the centre stack. Rear occupants have tight seating. Owners also complain of embarrassingly evident fit and finish defects and frequent electronic module malfunctions. Rear-seat access requires some acrobatics due to the low rear roofline, and the rear seatback could use additional bolstering. Also, the trunk's narrow opening adds to the difficulty of loading bulky items. **Safety:** NHTSA has given five stars for side crashworthiness and four stars for front crash protection and rollover resistance. IIHS awarded its top rating of "Good" for frontal offset, side, roof, and rear (head-restraint) crashworthiness. **New for 2013:** Nothing important. By year's end, the 2014 model will arrive with a longer, sleeker Alpha platform used by the smaller ATS.

ALERT! The only changes on the 2013 CTS will be the addition of two-piece front brake rotors and red Brembo brake calipers. Save your money and buy a 2012 version instead.

OVERVIEW: *CTS sedan and coupe:* A 270 hp 3.0L V6 is the standard engine; the 304 hp 3.6L is optional. *CTS Sport Wagon:* Slightly shorter than the CTS sedan, the CTS Sport Wagon provides 7.6 metres (25 feet) of cargo space accessible via a power-assisted liftgate. The Sport Wagon also carries a base 3.0L and optional 3.6L V6 and employs either a rear-drive or all-wheel-drive system, plus a suspension that can be adjusted from cushy to sporty (firm). *CTS-V sedan and coupe:* This 556 hp "muscle" Cadillac returns with no significant changes. The coupe version uses a smaller 3.6L V6. Standard safety features include anti-lock disc brakes, traction control, stability control, front-seat side airbags, full-length side curtain airbags, and GM's OnStar emergency communications system.

COST ANALYSIS: Buy the cheaper, 2012 model this fall when Asian competition heats up, forcing prices down and leading to more-generous customer rebates and dealer sales incentives. Think carefully about whether you want all-wheel drive: That option will cost you about $4,500 more with the base 3.0L engine or $2,600 when coupled to the 3.6L engine. **Best alternative:** Acura TL SH-AWD, BMW 3 Series, Hyundai Genesis, Infiniti G37, and Lincoln MKS or Town Car. **Options:** Neither the adaptive cruise control nor the advanced DVD navigation system is worth the extra money. **Rebates:** $4,000–$6,000 in sales incentives. **Depreciation:** Unbelievably fast. A 2007 base CTS that sold new for $35,800 is now worth $12,000; a 2007 CTS-V that went for $70,670 new now sells for no more than $16,000. **Insurance cost:** Higher than average. **Parts supply/cost:** Parts are often back ordered, and electronic components are quite pricey. **Annual maintenance cost:** Higher than average. **Warranty:** A 60-day money-back guarantee, as long as you don't drive more than 4,000 km. Bumper-to-bumper 4 years/80,000 km; powertrain 5 years/160,000 km; rust perforation 6 years/160,000 km. **Supplementary warranty:** A good thing to have. **Highway/city fuel economy:** 3.0L: 7.2/11.23 L/100 km, 39/25 mpg. 3.6L: 6.9/11.4 L/100 km, 41/25 mpg. 3.6L AWD: 7.9/13 L/100 km, 36/22 mpg. CTS-V man.: 10.5/14.9 L/100 km, 27/19 mpg. CTS-V auto.: 11/17.5 L/100 km, 28/16 mpg.

OWNER-REPORTED PROBLEMS: Car wash power loss danger:

> I took my car through a car wash and afterwards, the traction control system indicated a failure on the dash warning light. At the same time the engine lost significant power, and I'm told by the dealer that this is due to inhibiting half of the injectors if the TC system fails. The TC system "healed itself" after the car dried out for a day.... Anyone can drive a car safely without a traction control system in operation, however, a non-responsive engine due to the programmed shutdown of half the injectors is extremely dangerous. The car was barely able to accelerate in street traffic, and if the TC failure had happened on the freeway, I would have been in a very bad situation, unable to maintain safe speed just to get off of the freeway.

SERVICE BULLETIN-REPORTED PROBLEMS: Tire slowly goes flat; missing carpeted floor mats; slow, noisy operation of the front door glass; power steering/shock absorber

KEY FACTS

Canadian Price (Very Negotiable):
Coupe RWD: $42,860, *Coupe AWD:* $44,675, *3.0L Sedan:* $37,095, *AWD:* $41,420, *3.0L Wagon:* $44,130, *AWD:* $46,755, *3.6L Performance Wagon:* $50,760, *Performance AWD Wagon:* $53,795, *CTS-V Coupe:* $71,250, *Sedan:* $72,565 **U.S. Price:** *3.0 V6 Sedan Luxury:* $39,990, *3.6 V6 Sedan AWD Luxury:* $44,815, *3.6 V6 Sedan Performance:* $44,235, *3.6 V6 Sedan AWD Performance:* $46,135, *3.6 V6 Sedan Premium:* $49,185, *3.6 V6 Sedan AWD Premium:* $51,085, **Canadian Freight, dealer fees, and AC tax:** $1,745 (Pay half of the freight charge, no "dealer fees," and $100 for the AC tax.) **U.S. Freight:** Included.

POWERTRAIN (REAR-DRIVE/AWD)
Engines: 3.0L V6 (270 hp) • 3.6L V6 (304 hp) • 6.2L V8 (556 hp); Transmissions: 6-speed man. • 6-speed auto.

DIMENSIONS/CAPACITY (BASE CTS)
Passengers: 2/3; Wheelbase: 113 in.; H: 58/L: 192/W: 73 in.; Headroom F/R: 3.0/1.5 in.; Legroom F/R: 44.0/28.5 in.; Cargo volume: 14 cu. ft.; Fuel tank: 70L/premium; Tow limit: 1,000 lb.; Load capacity: 890 lb.; Turning circle: 38 ft.; Ground clearance: 5.0 in.; Weight: 3,940 lb.

leaks; the Airbag warning light comes on intermittently. Here's an easy, inexpensive way to eliminate a chatter-type noise or rear axle clunk:

EQUINOX, TERRAIN ★★★★

The Chevrolet Equinox.

RATING: Above Average. **Road performance:** These tall wagons handle very well, provide a comfortable ride, and are easily controlled with precise steering. Thrilling acceleration with the V6 and manual transmission; the 4-cylinder engine and automatic gearbox are acceptable and fairly quiet, but the V6 is the better performer with little fuel penalty. **Strong points:** Other handy features include remote engine start, a navigation system, a wireless mobile phone link, DVD entertainment, a hard drive for storing digital audio files, a rear-view camera, and a power liftgate. GMC's MultiFlex rear seat can be moved 20 cm (8 in.) fore and aft to better accommodate people and cargo. The Terrain shares its basic design and powertrain with the Chevrolet Equinox. Besides a plethora of airbags, the Terrain also comes with ABS, traction control, and an anti-skid system. A rear-view camera is standard on all Terrain models. Acceptable handling and braking combined with a comfortable ride. Plenty of passenger room; a quiet interior; most controls are well laid out; very comfortable seating. **Weak points:** The 4-cylinder engine comes up short when passing other vehicles or merging into traffic; handling is better with the Honda competition; tall head restraints cut rear visibility; the dash buttons all look the same; cheap-looking, easily scratched, and hard-to-keep-clean door panels and dash materials. Overall reliability has been only average: The transmission, suspension, electrical, and fuel systems have been problematic, and fit and finish continues to get low marks. Not quite as much cargo space as seen in some rival makes; and some dash controls are difficult to reach. **Safety:** NHTSA gives the 2013 Equinox and its Terrain twin four stars for rollover resistance and frontal occupant protection; side crash protection was given a five-star rating. After testing both vehicles, IIHS gave a "Good" designation for frontal, side, roof, and rear (head-restraint) crash protection. Most of the important safety devices are standard (traction control, an anti-skid system, front side airbags, and side curtain airbags). **New for 2013:** The most important change is the potent 301 hp 3.6L V6; which has 14 percent more horsepower and 22 percent more torque than last year's 3.0L V6. Interestingly, fuel-economy figures for the 3.6L are the same as with the 3.0L. There's a standard MyLink infotainment system tied into the optional navigation system; new forward-collision alert and lane-departure warning systems; a power passenger seat; and a new FE2 suspension set-up.

ALERT! These cars are hobbled by the turbocharged 4-cylinder engine.

OVERVIEW: With seating for five, this four-door crossover SUV offers a choice of two engines: a base 182 hp 2.4L 4-cylinder and an optional 301 hp 3.6L V6. Both variants are teamed with a smooth-performing 6-speed automatic transmission, and front-drive and all-wheel drive are available with all models.

KEY FACTS

Canadian Price (Firm): *LS:* $26,315, *AWD:* $28,885, *2LT:* $30,955, *LT w/1LT:* $29,920, *LT w/2LT:* $31,720, *AWD:* $37,425, *LTZ:* $35,900, *AWD:* $37,850, *Terrain: SLE-1:* $28,695, *AWD:* $30,645, *SLE-2:* $31,040, *AWD:* $32,990, *SLT-1:* $32,665, *AWD:* $34,615, *SLT-2:* $37,145, *AWD:* $39,000, *Denali:* $39,830, *AWD:* $41,780 **U.S. Price:** *LS:* $23,530, *2LT:* $26,220, *LTZ AWD:* $31,795 *Terrain: SLE-1:* $25,835, *Denali:* $35,350 **Canadian Freight, dealer fees, and AC tax:** $1,500 (Cut the freight charge in half, pay nothing for "dealer fees," and give $100 for the AC tax.) **U.S. Freight:** $950
POWERTRAIN (FRONT-DRIVE/AWD)
Engines: 2.4L 4-cyl. (182 hp) • 3.6L V6 (301 hp); Transmission: 6-speed auto.
DIMENSIONS/CAPACITY
Passengers: 2/3; Wheelbase: 112.5 in.; H: 66.3/L: 187.8/W: 72.5 in.; Headroom: N/A; Load capacity: 1,183 lb.; Legroom F/R: 41.2/39.9 in.; Cargo volume: 63.7 cu. ft.; Fuel tank: 59L/regular; Tow limit: 1,500 lb. (*LS*), 1,500–3,000 lb. (all others); Turning circle: 40 ft.; Ground clearance: 7.8 in.; Weight: 3,786 lb.

COST ANALYSIS: This is one of the few times you should choose a 2013 model over a 2012. Engine power and other refinements make next year's cars an even better choice. **Best alternatives:** Honda CR-V, Hyundai Tucson, Mazda CX5, Nissan Rogue, Subaru Forester, and Toyota RAV4. **Options:** Get the 3.6L V6; however, the $1,000 moonroof is a frivolous expense. **Rebates:** $500 rebates at year's end. **Depreciation:** Average. **Insurance cost:** Average. **Parts supply/cost:** Average supply and cost. **Annual maintenance cost:** Average. **Warranty:** A 60-day money-back guarantee, as long as you don't drive more than 4,000 km. Bumper-to-bumper 3 years/60,000 km; powertrain 5 years/160,000 km; rust perforation 6 years/160,000 km. **Supplementary warranty:** Not needed. **Highway/city fuel economy:** *2.4L auto.:* 6.1/9.2 L/100 km, 46/31 mpg. *AWD:* 6.9/10.1 L/100 km, 41/28 mpg. *3.0L auto.:* 8.1/12.4 L/100 km, 35/23 mpg. *AWD:* 8.6/12.9 L/100 km, 33/22 mpg. Despite these figures put out by the federal government (*http://oee. nrcan.gc.ca/transportation/tools/fuelratings/ratings-search.cfm*), Equinox owners say real gas mileage is much less than what is advertised:

> Sales agent assured my wife the 2011 Equinox would get better than 30 mpg [7.8 L/100 km]. And if it didn't get the mileage it could be fixed. Well, after multiple trips to three dealerships it is very obvious that we were lied to. After 5000 miles [8,000 km] we still only get around 22 mpg [10.7 L/100 km] highway. I called the Chevrolet complaint line just to be told that that mpg was under best driving conditions. In other words they were going to do nothing to fix the problem even though the sales person lied to my wife right in front of my sister. I will tell you this: I have bought my last Chevrolet.

OWNER-REPORTED PROBLEMS: Sudden power loss while cruising; power-steering loss while in Reverse; tire side wall damage; steering groan; placement of the cruise-control button makes it easy to accidently activate the feature; vehicle blind spot makes it impossible to see pedestrians walking in front of the vehicle; some phones are useless in many new Chevys:

> Chevy has known for almost 2 years that Android and BlackBerry phones do not work with many new Chevys. They have a software glitch that they cannot repair. This means that owners are not able to safely use their phones while in their cars. I believe that there should be a recall to fix this problem. I personally purchased this vehicle with the knowledge that I had a Bluetooth in it. I make and receive a lot of calls while in my car and I cannot do this safely with the Equinox.

And the rear hatch falls down and "beans" people in its way:

> Four different times the rear hatch was open and has unexpectedly come down and hit people in the back. No buttons have been pushed to start this action. One time the hatch raised unexpectedly. The Chevy dealer has studied the problem and replaced two parts which did not solve the problem. The dealer says they cannot get more information from GM Central on solving the problem. A person with a GM Terrain had the same problem...I found seven instances of unexpected hatch actions on the Net that are from various GM SUVs. The GM dealers have found nothing in their GM sites.

SERVICE BULLETIN-REPORTED PROBLEMS: Automatic transmission clunks when shifting; troubleshooting tips to plug transfer case fluid leaks:

TRANSFER CASE LEAKING FLUID

BULLETIN NO.: 09-04-21-004B   DATE: JANUARY 23, 2012

TRANSFER CASE FLUID LEAKAGE AT THE LEFT HAND WEEP HOLE OR BETWEEN TRANSFER CASE TO TRANSMISSION INTERFACE (REPLACE TRANSFER CASE INPUT SHAFT SEAL-LEFT OR TRANSFER CASE O-RING SEAL).

2008–12 Buick Enclave; 2008–09 Chevrolet Equinox Sport; 2009–12 Chevrolet Traverse; 2010–12 Chevrolet Equinox; 2007–12 GMC Acadia; 2010–12 GMC Terrain; 2008–09; Pontiac Torrent GXP; 2007–10 Saturn Outlook; 2008–10 Saturn; VUE; and 2007–09 Suzuki XL-7 models equipped with 6T45/70/75 Automatic Transmission RPOs MHC/MH4/MH6 for GM or AF33-5 AWD/PTU Automatic Transmission (RPO M45) for 2007–08 Suzuki and Getrag 760 or 790 Power transfer case.

CONDITION: Some customers may comment on a fluid leak from the automatic transmission or transfer case area. Upon further diagnosis, the technician may find fluid leaking between the transmission to transfer case interface or from the transfer case left hand weep hole.

Power steering, shock absorber leaks; roof panel flutters/rattle noise when doors close; tires slowly go flat; tire-pressure monitor system update for Canadians only; and carpeted floor mats may be missing.

ENCLAVE, TRAVERSE, ACADIA ★★★★

The Chevrolet Traverse.

RATING: Above Average. These are practically identical seven- and eight-passenger crossover SUVs, with the Traverse being the most recent addition. **Road performance:** The smooth-running 3.6L V6 has plenty of power for most chores

KEY FACTS

Canadian Price (Very Negotiable):
Enclave 2×4 CX: $43,750, *AWD:*
$46,750, *Traverse 1LS 2×4:* $35,910,
AWD: 38,910; *LT:* $38,570, *AWD:*
$41,570, *AWD:* $41,570, *LTZ:* $47,835,
AWD: $50,835, *Acadia: SLE-1:* $38,440,
AWD: $41,440, *SLE-2:* $41,010, *SLT-
1:* $46,450, *AWD:* $49,450, *SLT-2:*
$50,005, *Denali:* $58,090 **U.S. Price:**
Enclave Base: $38,120, *AWD:* $40,120;
Traverse: LS: $29,660, *LT:* $31,660, *2LT:*
$35,905, *AWD:* $37,905, *LTZ:* $39,035,
AWD: $41,035 *Acadia: SLE-1:* $38,440,
AWD: $41,440, *SLE-2:* $41,010,
AWD: $41,010, *SLT-1:* $46,450, *AWD:*
$49,450, *SLT-2:* $50,005, *Denali:*
$58,090, **Canadian Freight, dealer fees,
and AC tax:** $1,500 (Pay half of the freight
charge, ignore the "dealer fees," and give
$100 for the AC tax.) **U.S. Freight:** $825
POWERTRAIN (FRONT-DRIVE/AWD)
Engine: 3.6L V6 (288 hp); Transmission:
6-speed auto.
DIMENSIONS/CAPACITY (ENCLAVE)
Passengers: 7/8; Wheelbase: 119 in.;
H: 72.5/L: 201.5/W: 79 in.; Headroom:
N/A; Load capacity: 1,470 lb.; Cargo
volume: 115.3 in. (behind 1st row);
67.5 in. (behind 2nd row); 23.2 in.
(behind 3rd row); Fuel tank: 83L/regular;
Tow limit: 5,000–5,200 lb.; Turning
circle: 40.4 ft.; Ground clearance: 8.4 in.;
Weight: 4,780–4,985 lb.

and isn't as fuel-thirsty as other SUVs in the same class; a taught and comfortable ride; and standard stability control. On the negative side: The automatic transmission sometimes hesitates when shifting. **Strengths:** Strong acceleration; many powertrain configurations; a quiet interior; good towing capability; parts aren't hard to find and are reasonably priced; mechanical/body failures aren't excessive; and repairs can be done by independent garages. **Weak points:** Side airbags sometimes fail to deploy; head restraints force your chin into your chest; transmission oil leaks and malfunctions; fuel-pump flow module fails, making the engine run rough or stall; inaccurate fuel gauges; a noisy suspension; and headlight failures. **Safety:** NHTSA gave these vehicles four stars for front and rollover protection; side protection earned five stars. IIHS awarded these models a "Good" rating for front, side, roof, and rear collision crash protection. An airbag has been placed between the two front passengers. Limited rear visibility. **New for 2013:** A restyled front end; a revised suspension to better control body roll and improve the ride; minor interior improvements; and the addition of GM's MyLink system.

ALERT! Again, those pesky head restraints can make your driving a living hell if you are not the ideal size. Check this out with a test drive.

OVERVIEW: These large SUVs are an endangered species, and GM is likely to pull the plug at any time. Still, they are tough and versatile; prices are easily bargained down.

COST ANALYSIS: Buy an almost identical, discounted 2012 for the best price/quality advantage now that higher fuel prices and new products are pushing leftover SUV and truck base prices way down; $10,000 discounts are commonplace. **Best alternatives:** The Ford Flex, Honda Pilot, Hyundai Veracruz, and Mazda CX-9. If you don't mind downsizing a notch, consider the Ford Edge, Hyundai Santa Fe, and Nissan Xterra. **Options:** Stay away from Firestone and Bridgestone original-equipment tires; *www.tirerack.com* is your best contact for dependable and well-performing tires. **Rebates:** $1,000 rebates throughout 2012. **Depreciation:** Faster than average. **Insurance cost:** Much higher than average. **Parts supply/cost:** Parts aren't hard to find and are competitively priced. **Annual maintenance cost:** Average. **Warranty:** Bumper-to-bumper 4 years/80,000 km; powertrain 5 years/160,000 km; rust perforation 6 years/160,000 km. **Supplementary warranty:** Not needed. **Highway/city fuel economy:** *Front-drive:* 8.4/12.7 L/100 km, 34/22 mpg. *AWD:* 9.0/13.4 L/100 km, 31/21 mpg.

OWNER-REPORTED PROBLEMS: Middle-row passenger windows vibrate and make a loud noise when partially rolled down; side panels create a huge blind spot; and excessive seat creaking and squeaking.

SERVICE BULLETIN-REPORTED PROBLEMS: Engine won't shut off, and electrical/water issues:

ELECTRICAL—ENGINE WON'T SHUT OFF/ELECTRICAL ISSUES

BULLETIN NO.: 08-08-57-003C   DATE: JULY 15, 2011

FLOOR WET UNDER CARPET/ENGINE CONTINUES TO RUN WITH KEY OFF/POSSIBLE NO CRANK/NO START/COMMUNICATION LOSS/VARIOUS ELECTRICAL CONCERNS (SEAL SEAM)

2008–12 Buick Enclave; 2007–12 GMC Acadia; and the 2007–10 Saturn Outlook.

CONDITION: Some customers may comment on any, or a combination of, the following conditions:
- Evidence of a water leak at the right side A-pillar and/or the right front floor is wet under the carpet.
- Various electrical concerns such as: Engine Continues to Run with Key Off/Possible No Crank/No Start/ Communication Loss/Various Electrical Concerns, which may be a result of a water leak on the IP BEC.
- Other electrical related conditions that may be communication issues between certain electrical modules due to water dripping on the IP BEC.

CAUSE: Water from the right front sunroof drain hose exits the vehicle through the plenum (upper arrow) and may re-enter through the un-sealed seam at the front of the dash. In more current models and years, sunroof drain hose and windshield related issues have sometimes been found to be a source of a water leak in the A-pillar area. This water can also sometimes leak on the IP BEC and/or onto the floor area.

Troubleshooting tips to plug transfer case fluid leaks; power-steering, automatic transmission clunks; steering-column squeak or rattle; shock absorber leaks; tires slowly go flat; carpeted floor mats may be missing; and second-row "Easy Entry" seats may not work.

ESCALADE, TAHOE, YUKON   ★★★★

RATING: Above Average; these large SUVs are for those who need rugged, truck-like capabilities, a nine-passenger capacity, and lots of cargo space. All three vehicles are practically identical, though the Escalade comes with a 6.2L V8 and a plusher interior and is also more gadget-laden. **Road performance:** Surprisingly good handling for an SUV this large. Comfortable for highway cruising, and pretty agile around town as well. **Strengths:** Strong acceleration; many powertrain configurations; standard stability control; a quiet interior and comfortable ride; good towing capability; parts aren't hard to find and are reasonably priced; and repairs can be done by independent garages. A hybrid version is available. **Weaknesses:** Extremely poor fuel economy; rapid depreciation; small third-row

The Cadillac Escalade.

seat sits too low and doesn't fold into the floor; long braking distances; and terrible fit and finish. Specific problem areas include loss of brakes; faulty powertrain, suspension, and climate controls; and various body glitches. **Safety:** NHTSA gave these three SUVs plus the 2013 hybrid five stars for frontal and side passenger protection and three stars for rollover resistance. IIHS hasn't yet tested these vehicles for crashworthiness. **New for 2013:** Nothing; 2014 models get a small-block V8 and Escalade EXT is axed.

ALERT! Keep a wary eye on the rear hatch when loading or unloading cargo. It can suddenly fall down and seriously injure anyone in its way.

OVERVIEW: These three trucks are only masquerading as car-like SUVs and will likely not last another two years if fuel prices continue their upward ride.

COST ANALYSIS: In the new year, prices will fall and you will get these large SUVs for almost a third off their original price. **Best alternatives:** Many SUV buyers purchase more than they need. If you don't have the need to tow more than 6,500 lb., you can get eight-passenger seating and better fuel economy and manoeuvrability in the cheaper Chevy Traverse. Other choices are the Buick Enclave, Chevrolet Equinox or Terrain, Ford Flex, GMC Acadia or Traverse, Honda Pilot, Hyundai Santa Fe, Mazda CX-5 or CX-9, and Toyota Highlander. The Ford Flex and the Mazda CX-9 get good fuel economy and are easier to drive, and their third-row seating outclasses what GM offers. Plus, crossover SUVs are available with all-wheel drive, which can provide a good amount of all-weather capability. **Options:** Don't accept factory Bridgestone or Firestone tires. Independent suppliers will sell you better tires for less money. Also, stay away from the $2,065 glitch-prone power-sliding sunroof. **Rebates:** Escalade buyers get $2,500 throughout the year. **Depreciation:** Incredibly fast. Good for used-car buyers, but a kick in the pants for owners selling after two to five years. Let's look at how much we lose with the top-of-the-line model of each brand: A 2007 Escalade ESV that sold new for $79,030 is now worth $25,000; the same model year $61,075 Tahoe LTZ AWD sells for $17,500; and a 2007 GMC Yukon XL that sold new for $66,170 won't fetch more than $19,000. **Insurance cost:** Much higher than average. **Parts supply/cost:** Parts are easy to find and competitively priced. **Annual maintenance cost:** Average. **Warranty:** Bumper-to-bumper 4 years/80,000 km; powertrain 5 years/ 160,000 km; rust perforation 6 years/160,000 km. **Supplementary warranty:** Not needed. **Highway/city fuel economy:** Escalade AWD: 10.8/17.7 L/100 km, 26/16 mpg. Other models should produce similar figures. Hybrid figures are not available.

OWNER-REPORTED PROBLEMS: Barely half a dozen owner complaints when 150 would be the norm. Consumer Reports subscribers confirm the vehicles' powertrain and electrical system shortcomings in addition to major complaints relative to subpar body construction and low-quality materials. Chrome-plated door handles peel and cut fingers; as the rear window was closing, one passenger's finger was trapped in the weather stripping and was amputated. Escalade power rear cargo door may be hazardous, says one father, who is thankful his son wasn't killed when the door failed:

> 2011 Cadillac Escalade ESV 26771 power rear cargo door is a serious safety hazard. Son was seriously hurt at airport luggage claims when a power rear cargo door was closing, came down on his head and face without warning of any kind that this door was closing. The door is so large and heavy as it comes down, it's fast and does not retract back up when it hits something. The driver had no warning that a person was behind him as he closed the door. This is a very serious problem that could kill someone and should be corrected. This door should be changed so that it cannot open from overhead. This door is too large and heavy to have something coming down from that distance

KEY FACTS

Canadian Price (Very Negotiable): *Escalade EXT Base:* $84,955, *Escalade Luxury:* $91,855, *Platinum:* $108,205, *ESV:* $88,685, *EXT:* $79,945, *Escalade Hybrid:* $95,110, *Tahoe LS 2×4:* $49,555, *LT:* $54,960; *Tahoe Hybrid 2×4:* $68,815, *4×4:* $761,800, *Yukon SLE 2×4:* $49,555, *4×4:* $54,015, *Denali AWD:* $73,355, *Hybrid 2×4:* $68,815, *4×4:* $71,800, *4×4 Denali:* $80,557 **U.S. Price:** *Escalade:* $63,170, *Platinum:* $79,395, *Luxury:* $67,395, *Tahoe LS 2×4:* $40,075, *4×4:* $44,135, *LT 2×4:* $45,225, *4×4:* $48,075, *LTZ 2×4:* $54,290, *4×4:* $57,395, *Hybrid 2×4:* $53,290, *4×4:* $56,095, *Yukon SLE 4×2:* $41,430, *SLE 4×4:* $45,440, *SLT:* $46,915, *4×4:* $49,770, *Denali:* $56,355, *4×4:* $59,350

Canadian Freight, dealer fees, and AC tax: $1,500 (Pay half of the freight charge, refuse to pay anything for "dealer fees," and give $100 for the AC tax.) **U.S. Freight:** $975

POWERTRAIN (FRONT-DRIVE/AWD)
Engines: 5.3L V8 (320 hp) • 6.2L V8 (403 hp) • 6.0L V8 (332 hp); Transmissions: 6-speed auto. • CVT

DIMENSIONS/CAPACITY
Passengers: *Escalade:* 3/3/2; *Tahoe:* 3/3/3; Wheelbase: *Escalade:* 116 in.; *Hybrid:* 202.5 in.; H: 74.3/L: 202.5/W: 79 in., Cargo volume: 16.9 cu. ft. (behind 3rd row); Fuel tank: 98L/regular; Tow limit: *Escalade:* 8,100 lb.; *Hybrid:* 5,600 lb.; Payload: *Escalade:* 1,609 lb.; *Hybrid:* 1,484 lb.; Turning circle: 40.4 ft.; Ground clearance: 9.0 in.; Weight: *Escalade:* 5,691–5,943 lb.; *Hybrid:* 6,116 lb.

that's above the top of the Escalade. This is a very serious safety problem someone will be killed or lose body parts if this design is not changed.

Owners also report serious electrical shorts and drive system malfunctions. Hard automatic transmission shifts also noted. For over a decade, owners have decried the slapdash fit and finish of these top-of-the-line vehicles.

SERVICE BULLETIN-REPORTED PROBLEMS: Engine knocking on a cold start (GM says, "Don't worry, be happy"); power-steering, shock absorber leaks; tires slowly go flat; Airbag warning light comes on intermittently; airbag isn't flush with the dash; exhaust leak, rattle, rumble noise; tapping, clicking, and ticking noise at windshield area; sun visor fails to stay in the up position; sticking, binding door-mounted seat switches; front-door window regulator squeaks; third-row seat hard to remove and install; front seat cushion cover becomes detached; and warped, wavy front or rear fender liners.

SILVERADO 1500, 2500, 2500 HD / SIERRA ★★★★

The Chevrolet Silverado 1500.

RATING: Above Average. GM's 1500 pickups are slowly improving, but they are still held back by a platform dating to model year 2007. All the more reason why GM should eliminate the duplication of its divisions and merge GMC with Chevrolet. Money saved should go into a major redesign of the 1500 series to match the improvements now seen with GM's Heavy Duty (HD) series. **Road performance:** Since its 2008 redesign, the Silverado handles fairly well, offers plenty of power, and provides a more-controllable ride (no more "Shakerado"). Nevertheless, Ford's F-150 and the Ram 1500 have both had more-recent redesigns and, as a result, have better interiors and more capable powertrains that give a more-comfortable ride. **Strong points:** *1500:* Comfortable seating; a quiet interior; lots of storage capability; generally good crashworthiness scores; and acceptable fuel economy with the 6-speed automatic transmission coupled to the 5.3L V8. *2500:* These heavy-duty work trucks are built primarily to be load-carrying vehicles capable of working off-road; the independent front end improves handling and smoothes out the ride. The standard engine is a powerful 360 hp 6.0L V8 backed up by a 397 hp 6.6L turbodiesel. On the other hand, the GM Allison transmission dates to the late '40s, yet it hasn't performed as well as Ford's TorqShift 6-speed found in the Super Duty models. **Weak points:** *1500:* Powertrain smoothness and reliability doesn't measure up to what the Honda Ridgeline and Nissan Titan can provide, especially when comparing the performance of the V8 4×4 model. GM Duramax-equipped pickups need diesel exhaust fluid (urea) refills every 8,000 km (5,000 mi.). This is more frequent than the oil change one usually does every 12,000 km (7,500 mi.). Furthermore, the urea-filling process can be costly and complicated, as this diesel owner found out and posted to NHTSA:

> The contact owns a 2011 Chevrolet Silverado 3500HD(NA). The contact stated that the computer was programmed to limit the speed of the vehicle when the diesel exhaust fluid was too low. He noticed that when he filled the fuel tank, the computer did not recognize that the tank was full and the diesel warning light continued to illuminate on the instrumental panel. The vehicle had not been inspected by a dealer but was contacted; they informed him that the only remedy was for them to drop the diesel tank and empty the fluid for the computer to reprogram itself. The vehicle had not been repaired. The failure mileage was approximately 6,500 miles [10,400 km].

Safety: NHTSA gave the 2013 Silverado 1500 and 1500 Hybrid five stars for side crash protection and four stars for frontal crashworthiness and rollover resistance; the 2500 has scored between three and four stars for rollover resistance, three stars for frontal crash protection, and four stars for side crashworthiness. The 3500 series hasn't yet been rated. IIHS has given the Silverado 1500 a "Good" rating for frontal offset protection and an "Acceptable" score for side-impact crashworthiness and head-restraint

KEY FACTS

Canadian Price (Very Negotiable): *1500 WT Standard Cab 4×2:* $28,600, *LT Standard Long Cab 4×2:* $32,430, *Standard Cab 4×4:* $36,580, *Hybrid:* $47,715 **U.S. Price:** *1500 WT 4×2:* $23,590 *4×4:* $27,630, *Hybrid 1HY 2×4:* $40,885, *4×4:* $51,040 **Canadian Freight, dealer fees, and AC tax:** $1,500 (Pay half of the freight charge, nothing for "dealer fees," and $100 for the AC tax.) **U.S. Freight:** $950

POWERTRAIN (REAR-DRIVE/4×4)

Engines: 4.3L V6 (195 hp) • 4.8L V8 (302 hp) • 5.3L V8 (315 hp) • 6.0L V8 (360 hp) • 6.2L V8 (403 hp) • 6.6L V8 TD (397 hp) • *Compressed Natural Gas (CNG):* 6.0L V8 (279 hp) • *Hybrid:* 6.0L V8 (332 hp) • 6.6L Diesel (397 hp); Transmissions: 4-speed auto • 6-speed auto , *Hybrid:* CVT

DIMENSIONS/CAPACITY

Passengers: *1500:* 2/1, *2500:* 3/3; Wheelbase: *1500:* 144 in., *2500:* 133.6–167 in.; *1500:* H: 74/L: 230/W: 80 in., *2500:* H: 77/L: 240/W: 80 in.; Headroom F/R: *1500:* 6.5/6.0 in., *2500:* 6.0/5.0 in.; Legroom F/R: 41.5/29 in., *2500:* 40.5/27 in.; Load capacity: 1,695–1,794 lb.; Fuel tank: 129L/regular; Tow limit: *Hybrid:* 6,100 lb., *1500:* 7,500 lb., *2500:* 13,600 lb., *HD Turbo Diesel:* 15,600 lb.; Load capacity: *1500:* 1,570 lb., *2500:* 2,260 lb.; Turning circle: *1500:* 50 ft., *2500:* 55 ft.; Ground clearance: 9.5 in.; Weight: *1500:* 5,435 lb., *2500:* 6,920 lb.

effectiveness. IIHS says the 1500's roof crashworthiness merits a "Marginal" rating. Seat pelvic-thorax and side curtain airbags are available but aren't standard on the 2500HD; Ford Super Duty trucks have them as a standard safety feature. **New for 2013:** Only some new colours and improved downhill braking, which reduces brake rotor temperatures by more than 200 degrees by downshifting transmission gears, thereby reducing brake applications during long downhill sections. 2014 1500 models will be lighter and use a small-block V8 with cylinder deactivation, perhaps coupled to an 8-speed tranny.

ALERT! Diesel owners can save money buying urea at independent retailers.

OVERVIEW: All V8s are flex-fuel capable, and the 4.8L and 5.3L engines have variable valve timing. Trucks with the 5.3L engine were also given a 6-speed automatic transmission and a revised rear axle ratio. All 1500 models have standard electronic stability control, seat-mounted side airbags, and side curtain airbags. All stereos also get a USB port. The Chevrolet Silverado 1500 didn't get a new turbodiesel V8 engine because GM is putting most of its money on changes to the HD lineup. Basically, this large pickup is a twin of the GMC Sierra and is offered in regular-, extended-, and crew-cab body styles. Regular cabs seat up to three passengers; extended cabs and crews can carry six. There are three bed lengths: 5.8, 6.6, and 8.0 feet. Silverados offer two interiors: "pure pickup" and "luxury inspired." The 5.3L V8 saves fuel through Active Fuel Management cylinder deactivation. V6 and 4.8L V8 Silverados are coupled to a 4-speed automatic transmission. A 6-speed automatic is used with the 5.3L and 6.2L V8s. Rear-drive is standard and two four-wheel-drive systems are optional: a part-time setup that shouldn't be left engaged on dry pavement, and GM's AutoTrac, which can go anywhere. Both have a low-range gear for off-roading.

The Silverado 1500 Hybrid has a 6.0L V8 that pairs with an electric motor, producing 332 hp. It can run on one or both of its power sources depending on driving demands, and doesn't need to be plugged in. The hybrid has a continuously variable automatic transmission and a maximum towing capacity of 6,100 lb.

COST ANALYSIS: Save your money; buy the almost identical, but cheaper, 2012 base 1500 series, or HD if you need the additional power. The 2014 models get all the improvements. Remember, safety and performance ratings and owner complaints will probably apply to the Sierra and Hybrid models as well, with just a few exceptions. **Best alternatives:** The Honda Ridgeline and Nissan Titan. Chrysler and Ford trucks still have some problems to work out. But Chrysler's new suspension gives it one of the smoothest rides of any full-size pickup, and its Laramie Longhorn trim is well worth the extra cost. Ford's F-150 trucks have these advantages: They have the highest tow rating of any full-size pickup truck; they're comfortable to drive; and the EcoBoost engine gets good fuel economy (but not good reliability reports). **Options:** Consider the $600 Exterior Plus package, which includes a remote starter, fog lights, a garage door opener, and a locking tailgate with the EZ Lift feature. Also, consider getting adjustable gas and brake pedals if you need to put extra space between you and the steering-wheel-mounted airbag. **Rebates:** $4,000 in sales incentives on the 2012 and 2013 HD models; about half as much on the 1500 series. As summer approaches, the rebates may almost double. **Depreciation:** Faster than average. **Insurance cost:** Much higher than average. **Parts supply/cost:** Parts aren't hard to find and are competitively priced by independent suppliers. **Annual maintenance cost:** Higher than average. **Warranty:** A 60-day money-back guarantee, as long as you don't drive more than 4,000 km. Bumper-to-bumper 4 years/80,000 km; powertrain 5 years/160,000 km; rust perforation 6 years/160,000 km. **Supplementary warranty:** Recommended. **Highway/city fuel economy:** *4.3L 2WD:* 10.0/14.1 L/100 km, 28/20 mpg. *4.3L 4WD:* 11.3/14.9 L/100 km, 24/19 mpg. *4.8L 2WD:* 10.6/14.7 L/100 km, 27/19 mpg. *4.8L 4WD:* 11.1/15.4 L/100 km, 25/18 mpg. *5.3L 2WD:* 10.1/14.5 L/100 km, 28/19 mpg. *5.3L 4WD:* 10.3/14.7 L/100 km, 27/19 mpg. *6.2L AWD:* 10.8/17.7 L/100 km, 26/16 mpg. *Hybrid 2WD:* 9.2/9.8 L/100 km, 31/29 mpg. *Hybrid 4WD:* 9.8/10.5 L/100 km, 29/27 mpg.

OWNER-REPORTED PROBLEMS: Fuel and drive system failures are a major complaint, in addition to sloppy fit and finish. Owners also target the powertrain's "Reduced Power Mode" feature and automatic transmission malfunctions:

I have had a recurring problem with my new 2012 Chevrolet Silverado 1500 LT (5.3 liter engine) going into "Reduced Engine Power Mode" which also results in the disabling of stability control and traction control. This is a dangerous condition in that it results in a loss of power while operating the vehicle upon the roadway. An authorized repair facility has replaced the number one and two throttle sensors, the accelerator pedal assembly, the throttle body, the alternator, the computer, and a large ground wire behind the dash. A GM engineer has flown in and now the repair center is replacing the engine wiring harness. The vehicle (which was purchased less than three months ago) has been out of service for approximately 30 days. In researching this matter I have found that Chevy has had an ongoing problem with this in various vehicles in its product line since 2003. Although several service bulletins have been produced there does not seem to be a consensus regarding the cause of this problem. All of the parts associated with trouble codes C0242, P2127, and P2138 have been replaced without result. This condition could result in the affected vehicles being rear-ended, or, because of the loss of stability and traction control, result in a rollover. This needs to be addressed immediately.

•

Transmission shifts hard from a complete stop as 1st gear was being engaged. Drove it until break-in period was over and took it back to the dealer where the transmission body and valves were replaced. Now getting more problems with the transmission shifting between gears at a speed of 35–45 mph [56–72 km/h]. Transmission disengages and I have no power going to the wheels, like it shifts to Neutral for 5–10 seconds. This will cause an accident if transmission does not reengage while driving in traffic you will get rear ended.

A distracting high-pitched noise comes from behind the dash; original equipment tires (Goodyear Eagle LS-2) provoke sliding when accelerating or cornering; and the trailer lights' electrical connection may be unsafe:

> Chevrolet/GM has changed the wiring in their vehicles so that electric trailer brake controllers no longer illuminate the trailer brake lights when the electric brake controller is operated independently from the vehicle brakes. All brake lights work fine when the foot brake is applied but no brake lights illuminate when the controller override is applied to operate the trailer brakes independently. There are times when trailering that one only wishes to use the trailer brakes to settle down swaying on long downhill grades. 2012 vehicles are not wired so that brake lights also work off the controller override switch. I have been towing for over 26 years and brake lights have always worked both on the foot brake and controller override brake switch. This is a potential accident waiting to happen.

EXCESSIVE WIND NOISE FROM REAR INTERIOR

BULLETIN NO.: 10-08-58-001F   DATE: DECEMBER 14, 2011

2007–12 Chevrolet Silverado and 2007–12 GMC Sierra.

CONDITION: Some customers may comment on hearing excessive wind noise coming from the rear interior of the vehicle.

CAUSE #1 (2007–10 MODEL YEARS ONLY): This condition may be caused by a void in the body filler within the C-pillar.

CAUSE #2: This condition may be a result of the design of the body rear panel acoustic insulator that is mounted behind the rear seat. The insulator could be one of several early designs (1 or 2 in the above graphic), which demonstrated a lesser success of minimizing wind noise.

GM has allowed this problem to continue for the past six model years—from before to after bankruptcy. Can you blame motorists who say Detroit automakers still consider quality to be "job last"? This service bulletin is proof the company is negligent and, under the implied warranty (refer to Part Two), must foot the bill for any repair—long after the normal warranty has expired.

SERVICE BULLETIN-REPORTED PROBLEMS: Excessive wind noise coming from rear interior of vehicle:

Airbag light comes on intermittently; side roof-rail airbags may not deploy as designed, says GM Customer Satisfaction Campaign bulletin #11288 (shh…it's a "secret warranty"—the fix is free); automatic transmission clunks when shifted; rear suspension clunk and squeaks; rattle noise from wheel or hubcap; underbody pop, clunk when turning; rear leaf-spring slap or clunk noise; exhaust leak, rattle, or rumble; front-door regulator squeak; tapping, clicking, or ticking at the windshield area; shock absorber and power-steering leaks; sun visor won't stay up; water leaks through the headliner near the sunroof; warped or wavy fender liners; excessive rear-view mirror shake; musty odours emitted from the AC; tires may slowly go flat; and excessive front brake vibration:

BRAKE INDUCED PULSATION/VIBRATION FELT IN STEERING WHEEL, RUMBLE NOISE FROM UNDERBODY DURING DOWNHILL DESCENT (VERIFY CONDITION AND REPLACE FRONT BRAKE PADS WITH A BRAKE PAD KIT.)

2008–12 Chevrolet Silverado Light Duty (LD) and 2008–12 GMC Sierra Light Duty (LD).

CONDITION: Some customers may comment on a pulsation or vibration mostly concentrated in the steering wheel during downhill descent as specifically described. This condition will most often begin as an increasing rumbling noise coming from the underbody or the front of the vehicle. This condition is exhibited mostly in mountainous regions.

This condition occurs ONLY under the following conditions:

- On a downhill descent on a fairly steep grade (approximately 5% or greater).
- On taller hills (roughly 1.5 km [1 mi.] road length or greater), without sharp turns.
- At speeds above 64 km/h (40 mph).
- Using the brakes just enough to maintain the speed limit when moving downhill.

A rumbling noise will be heard first, building in intensity, followed by increasing pulsation, or vibration, felt in the steering wheel, then typically felt in the floor panel. The condition will be eliminated once the vehicle is driven on relatively flat ground, typically for 1.5–3.0 km (1–2 mi).

CAUSE: This condition may be caused by interaction between the front brake lining material and the front brake rotors.

This is a warranty repair. Instead of using a brake pad kit to fix this defect since 2008, why weren't problem-free brakes installed at the factory four years ago?

ASIAN VEHICLES

Toyota's *Dawn of the Dead*: Sudden Acceleration

Throughout 2009–2010, Toyota found itself squirming in the harsh light of the press—and the federal government's crosshairs—as it struggled to answer questions of so-called "sudden acceleration" issues involving vehicles like the 2010 Toyota Sequoia full-sized SUV, the popular Toyota Camry sedan, and the Lexus ES. [Floormats], not electronics, were ultimately determined to be the cause of the issue. Toyota either removed or replaced the floormats promptly, and reshaped the nearby gas pedal. The automaker would ultimately recall over nine million vehicles worldwide and paid nearly $50 million in fines.... Toyota just announced it is recalling two more of its vehicles due to the sudden acceleration recall. The automaker will be issuing a safety recall notification in August to owners of its 2010 Lexus RX 350 and RX 450h hybrid mid-sized crossovers.

JOEL ARELLANO
JUNE 29, 2012
BLOGS.AUTOMOTIVE.COM

Asian Comeback

2011 was the year Asian automakers suffered one blow after another, including a North American recession, two earthquakes, a tsunami, four nuclear reactor meltdowns, and allegations that their cars were deathtraps.

CANADIAN AUTO SALES, JUNE 2012

RANK	AUTOMAKER	JUNE 2012	% CHANGE	YEAR TO DATE (YTD)	YTD % CHANGE
1	Toyota	16,957	+70.1%	88,318	+25.7%
2	Hyundai	13,761	+2.4%	71,642	+4.3%
3	Honda	12,047	+42.6%	64,544	+23.5%
4	Nissan	9,116	−14.7%	43,100	+6.9%
5	Kia	7,782	+10.0%	39,298	+18.7%
6	Mazda	7,250	+3.4%	37,607	+8.0%
7	Subaru	2,576	+3.7%	14,700	+3.7%
8	Mitsubishi	2,089	+9.3%	10,310	−0.2%
9	Acura	1,510	+33.3%	7,290	+12.9%
10	Lexus	1,340	+48.4%	7,036	+8.4%
11	Infiniti	756	+24.5%	4,005	+23.4%
12	Scion	807	+34.9%	2,678	+17.3%
13	Suzuki	507	+ 10.9%	2,560	−10.1%

Source: Polk and *Automotive News*

All that was missing was an invasion of frogs and locusts.

Nevertheless, this year, following one of the worst worldwide recessions in living memory and a series of cataclysmic natural disasters, the Asian auto industry is back on its feet and posting healthy sales numbers in Canada.

South Korean vehicles—once the laughing stock of car columnists and consumer advocates—have caught up to within a hair's breadth of the Japanese competition in terms of quality and sales. This is partly due to Hyundai finally putting better-quality parts in its Kia subsidiary's cars, SUVs, and minivans.

Everybody knows the Japanese and South Koreans know how to build reliable, fuel-sipping vehicles. Whether they're cars, minivans, sport-utilities, or pickups, and whether they're built in Japan, Canada, Mexico, or the United States, Asian cars give you much more performance and fuel economy for your money than if you were to buy the equivalent vehicle made by Chrysler, Ford, or General Motors—or by most European automakers, for that matter. Most of all, you can count on most Asian vehicles to be easy to repair and relatively slow to depreciate—both admirable qualities in a volatile auto market where models quickly disappear and hapless owners may be left with irreparable, worthless pieces of junk in their driveways (hello, Jaguar, Land Rover, Saab, and Volvo). Undoubtedly, Asian automakers have a more-realistic mix of models that can withstand the vagaries of the marketplace as fuel prices rise and fall. They also know how to squeeze the most profit out of the cars they sell.

It's simple, really. Sell vehicles with less quality content at a higher price. No matter if this practice makes the cars unsafe and unreliable. This is the crisis we are facing today, thanks to the penny-pinching bean-counters who have emigrated from Detroit to Honda, Hyundai, Kia, and Toyota.

No, automakers don't always learn from their past mistakes.

Acura

Acura, Honda's luxury division, sells seven different models in Canada. They are the entry-level ILX compact (rated in the Appendix), a TSX sport sedan, the TL performance luxury sedan, a ZDX four-door sport coupe, an RL luxury performance sedan, soon to be replaced by the RLX (both models are profiled in the Appendix), a turbocharged RDX luxury crossover SUV, and the MDX luxury SUV.

Acuras are good buys, but let's not kid ourselves—most Acura products are basically fully loaded Hondas with a few additional features and unjustifiably higher prices.

Automobile magazine on its June edition cover calls Acura "a lost brand"—a harsh judgment of the first Japanese nameplate (four years before Lexus) to take on the U.S. luxury market with the popular 1986 Legend and Integra. The brand is now less distinctive than it once was when Acura was a showcase for advanced technology. It has lost its leadership edge and now offers what everybody else provides, at a discount. The case could easily be made that Acura has moved away from affordable, nimble, sporty cars to be a builder of high-end SUVs like the MDX—its bestseller that accounts for one-third of all Acura sales.

Despite the fact that Acura and Honda dealers have abhorred real price competition for years, declining sales during the past few years have forced them to give sizeable rebates and other sales incentives to customers to keep market share. In their own right, maintenance costs are low, depreciation is generally slower than average, though there are some exceptions, and reliability and quality are much better than average. What few defects Acuras have are usually related to squeaks, rattles, minor trim glitches, and accessories such as the navigation, climate control, and sound systems.

Here's a tip for penny-pinchers: Despite being the bestselling vehicle in Acura Canada's lineup, Honda axed the Acura CSX after the 2011 model year and replaced it with the Civic-based ILX (see Appendix "Reviews and Previews"). Smart shoppers should consider buying a fully loaded 2011 CSX Sedan Tech for $20,000; a reasonable price for a car that originally sold for $26,000.

The 2013 Acura TSX.

RATING: Average. Essentially a modified Accord with less interior room. **Road performance:** Good handling with very little body lean, though there's a slight tendency to understeer (the car turns wider than the driver wants it to). Sporty driving is compromised by vague steering. Smooth and responsive 6-speed manual and 5-speed automatic transmissions. The 4-cylinder is loud and underpowered until it gets into the higher rpms; the V6 sounds great but is overpriced and shows some torque-steer wander. **Strong points:** Powerful V6; slick-shifting automatic transmission; generously appointed; instruments and controls are well laid out; good navigation system controls; brakes are easy to modulate, producing short, controlled stops; impressive fit and finish; and reasonable fuel economy. **Weak points:** Premium fuel negates the small engine's fuel-sipping savings; cabin centre console houses too many buttons; the interior is a bit snug, especially in the rear; rear seats have insufficient thigh support; trunk hinges limit utility; and the low roofline hampers rear access. **Safety:** NHTSA crash tests awarded the 2013 TSX five stars for rollover resistance. Occupant protection in offset, side, and rear crashes is "Good," according to IIHS. Roof strength was also rated "Good." **New for 2013:** No important changes or additions; 2014 model may be dropped.

KEY FACTS

Canadian Price (Negotiable): *Base:* $31,890, *Sport Wagon:* est. $30,000, *Premium:* $33,690, *TECH package:* $37,990, *V6 TECH package:* $41,890
U.S. Price: *Base:* $29,610, *Sport Wagon:* $30,960 **Canadian Freight:** $1,895
U.S. Freight: $895

POWERTRAIN (FRONT-DRIVE/AWD)

Engines: 2.4L 4-cyl. (201 hp) • 3.5L V6 (280 hp); Transmissions: 5-speed auto. • 6-speed man.

DIMENSIONS/CAPACITY

Passengers: 2/3; Wheelbase: 107 in.; H: 57/L: 186/W: 73 in.; Headroom F/R: 3.0/2.5 in.; Legroom F/R: 41/27.0 in.; Cargo volume: 13 cu. ft.; Fuel tank: 70L/premium; Tow limit: 1,000 lb.; Load capacity: 850 lb.; Turning circle: 36.7 ft.; Ground clearance: 5.9 in.; Weight: 3,440 lb.

ALERT! When you consider the TSX's price is about $7,000 more than a base Honda Accord, you have to wonder whether the vehicle has that much cachet—or if its manufacturer has just a lot of nerve. Overly sensitive seat sensors may disable the airbag, even when an average-sized adult is seated.

OVERVIEW: The TSX is an entry-level sports car/wagon equipped with a base 201 hp 2.4L 4-cylinder engine and an optional 280 hp 3.5L V6 that competes in a luxury-sedan niche where V6 power is commonplace. The car is sportier than the TL, yet it isn't as harsh as the discontinued high-performance RSX. The V6 option doesn't give you sportier handling than the 4-banger.

COST ANALYSIS: Get a cheaper, almost-identical 2012 model. Acura has thrown in a cornucopia of standard safety, performance, and convenience features—like standard stability and traction control, and head-protecting side airbags—to make the luxury sedan and sport wagon attractive to shoppers who feel size and V6 power aren't everything. **Best alternatives:** Other cars worth considering, although they aren't as well made as the TSX, are the Audi A4, BMW 328i, Infiniti G37, Lexus IS 250 or 350, and Lincoln MKZ. The BMW 3 Series and Mercedes C-Class look good but aren't as reliable as the TSX and will likely cost a bundle to maintain. The TSX's size and good looks outclass the TL by far, and the V6 puts it about where the former TL was in size and power. **Options:** Ditch the Bridgestone and Firestone original equipment tires for better-performing Michelin, Yokohama, or Pirelli tires. **Rebates:** $3,000 rebates, some discounting, and low finance rates. **Depreciation:** Faster than average; a 2009 TSX that sold new for $33,000 is now worth about $18,500. **Insurance cost:** Higher than average. **Parts supply/cost:** Easily found and moderately priced, especially most mechanical and electronic components. **Annual maintenance cost:** Less than average. **Warranty:** Bumper-to-bumper 5 years/100,000 km; rust perforation 5 years/unlimited km. **Supplementary warranty:** Not needed. **Highway/city fuel economy:** *4-cyl. man.:* 6.8/9.9 L/100 km, 42/29 mpg. *4-cyl. auto.:* 6.2/9.3 L/100 km, 46/30 mpg. *V6 auto.:* 7.0/10.7 L/100 km, 40/26 mpg.

OWNER-REPORTED PROBLEMS: "Lag and lurch" when letting off the accelerator:

> When accelerating from stop light and the car in front slows down, I let off of accelerator, then press down on accelerator again when appropriate, the car stalls and then leaps forward. This causes an immediate problem and the brakes have to be applied or the car in front gets rear ended. The Acura dealer tells me that they have had numerous complaints about this, but, they can't fix the problem because Acura won't fix it.

Excessive steering vibration with the wagon; noisy brake pads, and premature brake caliper and rotor wear; paint peeling and spotting; and malfunctioning power accessories and entertainment systems.

SERVICE BULLETIN-REPORTED PROBLEMS: The retractable master key does not lock in its extended position.

TL ★★★

RATING: Average. **Road performance:** Comes in front-drive and all-wheel drive; a limited-slip differential provides impressive acceleration in a smooth and quiet manner. Handling is acceptable, with a firm suspension that provides a comfortable ride. The car isn't as agile as some of the competition; steering is a bit numb; and the suspension may be too firm for some. **Strong points:** Good fuel economy. Well-constructed, with quality mechanical and body components. **Weak points:** Tight rear seating and some acrobatics required for tall passengers entering the rear-seat area; excessive road noise for a luxury car of this calibre and expense; and buttons, buttons, everywhere. **Safety:** NHTSA ranked frontal and side crash safety four stars; rollover protection earned five stars. Given a "Good" rating by IIHS for frontal offset, side, and rear crashworthiness and roof strength. The side mirrors are a bit narrow, reducing rear visibility. **New for 2013:** No significant changes; wait for the 2014 model redesign.

ALERT! Everything about the TL screams, "Accord! Accord!" So why not simply buy a cheaper Accord? Both the TL and Accord depreciate at the same rate.

OVERVIEW: The TL combines luxury and performance in a nicely styled, front-drive, five-passenger sedan that uses the same chassis as the Accord. Two engines are offered and are mated to either a 6-speed manual or a 6-speed automatic Sequential SportShift automatic transmission. Interior accommodations are better than average all around; the cockpit layout is very user-friendly, although learning which buttons perform which tasks takes some practice. Visibility fore and aft is

KEY FACTS

Canadian Price (Negotiable): *Base:* $39,490, *TECH:* $42,990, *SH-AWD:* $43,490, *TECH:* $46,990, *Elite:* $48,990 **U.S. Price:** *SH-AWD:* $39,255, *TECH:* $39,435 **Canadian Freight:** $1,895 **U.S. Freight:** $895

POWERTRAIN (FRONT-DRIVE/AWD)

Engines: 3.5L V6 (280 hp) • 3.7L V6 (305 hp); Transmissions: 6-speed man. • 6-speed auto.

DIMENSIONS/CAPACITY

Passengers: 2/3; Wheelbase: 109.3 in.; H: 57.2/L: 194/W: 74 in.; Headroom F/R: 3.5/3.5 in.; Legroom F/R: 42.5/36.2 in.; Cargo volume: 13.1 cu. ft.; Fuel tank: 70L/premium; Tow limit: 1,000 lb.; Load capacity: 850 lb.; Turning circle: 38.4 ft.; Ground clearance: 5.9 in.; Weight: 3,726–3,948 lb.

unobstructed. Standard safety features include ABS, stability and traction control, front seat belt pretensioners, and head-protecting airbags.

COST ANALYSIS: Get the cheaper, practically identical 2012 model. **Best alternatives:** Consider the Hyundai Genesis, Lexus ES, Nissan Maxima, and Toyota Avalon. **Options:** Ditch the Bridgestone and Firestone tires. **Rebates:** $2,500 rebates; some discounting. **Depreciation:** Slower than average. **Insurance cost:** Higher than average. **Parts supply/cost:** Easily found and moderately priced, especially most mechanical and electronic components, with the exception of some body parts. **Annual maintenance cost:** Less than average. **Warranty:** Bumper-to-bumper 5 years/100,000 km; rust perforation 5 years/unlimited km. **Supplementary warranty:** Not needed. **Highway/city fuel economy:** *3.5L:* 6.8/10.4 L/100 km, 42/27 mpg. *3.7L AWD man.:* 8.0/11.9 L/100 km, 35/24 mpg. *3.7L AWD auto.:* 7.6/11.4 L/100 km, 37/25 mpg.

OWNER-REPORTED PROBLEMS: Very few complaints, except for electrical shorts, minor body fit and finish deficiencies, and premature brake wear.

SERVICE BULLETIN-REPORTED PROBLEMS: Ticking, tapping noise from the rear wheelwell area (2009–12 models); rear shelf area clicks, taps, or ticks; and the master key won't lock in the extended position.

ZDX ★★

RATING: Below Average for a luxury car that could have been made by Tonka toys. **Road performance:** The V6 and 6-speed automatic combine to provide smooth and sufficient power for all driving situations; a firm ride; and handles reasonably well. **Strong points:** Plenty of safety, performance, and convenience features that are luxurious and high-tech; a well-appointed interior; and outstanding reliability. **Weak points:** Location, location, location. Where to put your passengers? Where to put your cargo? Where do you put your head to see out the side and back windows? This is a claustrophobia-inducing small SUV that is a poster child for poor design. It has a cramped back seat, Cirque du Soleil rear-seat access, limited cargo space, a low roof, and a tall beltline. **Safety:** NHTSA gives five stars for side crash protection and four stars for frontal protection and rollover resistance. **New for 2013:** Returns slightly restyled and equipped with some new technology. Slow sales cloud its future.

ALERT! The small side windows and narrow rear window seriously impair outward visibility.

OVERVIEW: An MDX-based coupe-like luxury SUV, the ZDX carries a hefty 300 hp 3.7L V6 that is coupled to a 6-speed automatic transmission. If you're looking for a utilitarian family-hauler with towing capability and comfortable back seats, the ZDX is the wrong car for you.

KEY FACTS

Canadian Price (Negotiable): *Base:* $54,990 **U.S. Price:** *Base:* $46,020
Canadian Freight: $1,895 **U.S. Freight:** $895
POWERTRAIN (AWD)
Engine: 3.7L V6 (300 hp); Transmission: 6-speed auto.
DIMENSIONS/CAPACITY
Passengers: 2/3; Wheelbase: 108.3 in.; H: 62.8/l.; 192.4/W: 78.5 in.; Headroom: N/A; Legroom F/R: 42.2/35.7 in.; Cargo volume: 26.2 cu. ft.; Fuel tank: 79.5L/ premium; Tow limit: 1,500 lb.; Load capacity: 870 lb.; Turning circle: 38.5 ft.; Ground clearance: 7.9 in.; Weight: 4,410 lb.

COST ANALYSIS: Get the practically identical 2012 model, and seriously consider saving $10,000 by getting your ZDX in the States, where both the base price and freight charges are much less. You could drive the car a year and still sell it for almost what you paid in the States. Be prepared for a big depreciation hit: A 2010 Tech Package version that first sold for $59,590 is now worth only $32,000. **Best alternatives:** The Acura MDX has more rear passenger and cargo space, with the same interior quality and technology, all for about $4,000 less than the ZDX and with only slightly worse fuel economy. The BMW X6 is also worth considering. **Rebates:** Look for $4,000 rebates on the 2012s, and a similar amount in the summer of 2013, applicable to the early 2013 models. **Options:** Nothing more is needed. **Depreciation:** Fairly rapid. **Insurance cost:** Higher than average. **Parts supply/cost:** Most mechanical and electronic components are used on other Acura models, so they are easily found and moderately priced. Body parts are unique and not easily found due to low-volume ZDX sales; this can add to collision repair time and cost. **Annual maintenance cost:** Average. **Warranty:** Bumper-to-bumper 5 years/100,000 km; rust perforation 5 years/unlimited km. **Supplementary warranty:** Not needed. **Highway/city fuel economy:** 8.8/12.7 L/100 km, 32/22 mpg.

OWNER-REPORTED PROBLEMS: None.

SERVICE BULLETIN-REPORTED PROBLEMS: None.

KEY FACTS

Canadian Price (Negotiable): *Base:* $40,990, *TECH package:* $42,990
U.S. Price: *Base:* $32,620, *TECH package:* $35,720 **Canadian Freight:** $1,895 **U.S. Freight:** $895
POWERTRAIN (AWD)
Engines: 3.5L V6 (273 hp); Transmission: 6-speed auto.
DIMENSIONS/CAPACITY
Passengers: 2/3; Wheelbase: 104.3 in.; H: 65.1/L: 182.4/W: 73.6 in.; Headroom F/R: 4.0/3.5 in.; Legroom F/R: 40.5/27.5 in.; Cargo volume: 27.8 cu. ft.; Fuel tank: 72.7L/premium; Tow limit: 1,500 lb.; Load capacity: 870 lb.; GVWR: 5,732 lb.; Turning circle: 41 ft.; Ground clearance: 6.2 in.; Weight: 3,941 lb.

RATING: Average. **Road performance:** Adequate power, with some turbo lag (a delay between throttle application and acceleration). The buzzy, fuel-thirsty 4-cylinder engine competes in a class where 6- and 8-cylinders are the norm; stiff-riding, with some jostling when passing over uneven terrain; more pavement noise than one would expect in a luxury car. Handles like a tall sports car: tight and responsive, with excellent braking. **Strong points:** Seating and driving positions work for occupants of all sizes. The nicely appointed interior is well laid out, with plenty of small storage areas; the seats have good thigh and back support; above-average reliability; and top-quality mechanical components. **Weak points:** Difficult to learn computerized audio, climate, and navigation systems; the turbo boost gauge is superfluous; the small space-saver spare tire has no place in a car this expensive. **Safety:** NHTSA has tested the 2012 version for rollover protection only, and has awarded the RDX four stars. On the other hand, the 2013 RDX has received the highest possible safety rating of Top Safety Pick from IIHS, earning a score of "Good" in all categories. **New for 2013:** This crossover SUV returns with increased ride and interior comfort, utility, and power, along with class-leading fuel economy. The new 3.5L V6 has 33 more horsepower (273 horsepower) than the previous model, a better 6-speed automatic transmission, and an upgraded all-wheel-drive system. Other standard features include leather seating, heated power front seats, a power moonroof, and a 360-watt audio system. New technologies such as the Pandora Internet radio interface, an SMS text messaging function, a Keyless Access System with push-button start, an Active

Noise Control system, and a rear-view camera system with three unique viewing angles are also provided.

ALERT! This year's V6 is a better-performing, more-durable engine than the turbocharged 4-banger used in the 2012 model and is worth the 2013's extra cost.

OVERVIEW: A Honda CR-V spin-off, the RDX takes over from the MDX as Acura's entry-level crossover SUV. Although its dimensions are similar to that of the CR-V, the RDX uses a unique platform developed to handle the vehicle's advanced all-wheel-drive system and peppy turbocharged engine.

COST ANALYSIS: Get the upgraded 2013 model for the horsepower and equipment boost, and compare prices in the States—there are sizeable reductions south of the border. The premium for the RDX can be whittled down to about half as much through smart haggling. The extra dough gets you a more-powerful drivetrain, a more-refined interior, more tech gadgets, and different front-end styling. If these attributes don't turn you on, then save yourself the $4,000–$8,000 and get a CR-V. **Best alternatives:** Subaru Forester, Toyota RAV4, BMW X3, Honda CR-V, Infiniti EX, and Mazda CX-5. **Rebates:** Look for $3,000 rebates on the 2012s, and a similar amount applicable to the early 2013 models in the summer of 2013. **Options:** The Bluetooth satellite navigation system should be compared with the less-expensive Garmin devices. The $4,000+ technology package—the 10-speaker audio system with satellite radio and the full computerized navigation package with backup camera—is a money-waster. **Rebates:** With a base price of $40,990, there are at least $5,000 worth of rebates and discounts that you can use to bring the suggested list price down to an acceptable level. **Depreciation:** Much faster than average: A first-year 2010 base model that sold for $42,000 now fetches $27,000. **Insurance cost:** Higher than average. **Parts supply/cost:** Except for turbo components, most mechanical and electronic components are easily found and moderately priced. Body parts may be hard to come by, and they can be expensive. **Annual maintenance cost:** Average. **Warranty:** Bumper-to-bumper 5 years/100,000 km; rust perforation 5 years/unlimited km. **Supplementary warranty:** Not needed. **Highway/city fuel economy:** 8.7/11.7 L/100 km, 32/24 mpg.

OWNER-REPORTED PROBLEMS: Moonroof suddenly shattered; engine oil leaks at the front of the engine block; malfunctioning gauges, instruments, AC, and entertainment devices; electrical short circuits; and noisy brakes that wear out prematurely.

SERVICE BULLETIN-REPORTED PROBLEMS: The master key won't lock in the extended position.

MDX ★★★

KEY FACTS

Canadian Price (negotiable): *Base: $51,190, TECH package: $57,290, Elite package: $61,990* **U.S. Price:** *Base: $42,230, TECH package: $45,905* **Canadian Freight:** $1,895 **U.S. Freight:** $895

POWERTRAIN (AWD)

Engine: 3.7L V6 (300 hp); Transmission: 6-speed auto.

DIMENSIONS/CAPACITY

Passengers: 2/3/2; Wheelbase: 108.3 in.; H: 68.2/L: 191.6/W: 78.5 in.; Headroom F/R: 4.0/4.0 in.; Legroom F/R: 41.2/38.7 in.; Cargo volume: 42 cu. ft.; Fuel tank: 72.7L/premium; Tow limit: 5,000 lb.; Load capacity: 1,160 lb.; GVWR: 5,732 lb.; Turning circle: 37.6 ft.; Ground clearance: 8.2 in.; Weight: 4,550 lb.

RATING: Average. **Road performance:** The MDX has it all—sporty performance, good value, and interior comfort—if you have the money. Power is supplied smoothly via the slick and quiet 6-speed automatic transmission, and steering and handling are superb. **Strong points:** Loaded with goodies; above-average reliability; and top-quality body and mechanical components. **Weak points:** Overpriced and overweight; the rear third seat is a tight fit; the dash console isn't user-friendly; audio and navigation systems are needlessly complicated; and fuel consumption is on the high side. **Safety:** NHTSA gives the MDX a five-star crashworthiness rating for side occupant protection and a four-star rating for frontal protection and rollover resistance. IIHS says rear, offset, side, and roof protection are "Good." **New for 2013:** Nothing; wait for the redesigned 2014 model.

ALERT! This mid-size SUV's sporty performance may not sit well with passengers who expect a smoother ride. The Lexus RX is much smoother, even over the roughest roads. Another advantage of the RX is its lower starting price and reasonable fuel economy for an all-wheel-drive.

OVERVIEW: The MDX is one of the best-handling SUVs available in this price range. Its price is competitive with many other vehicles that don't offer the same package of safety, performance, and convenience features.

COST ANALYSIS: Get a discounted, practically identical 2012 version. **Best alternatives:** The BMW X5, Buick Enclave, Chevrolet Traverse or Terrain, Infiniti FX35, and Lexus RX series. Would you like comparable Asian performance and reliability for about $11,000 less? Try a Honda Pilot (the MDX's cheaper cousin) for its additional passenger- and cargo-hauling capability, a Nissan Xterra, or a Toyota Highlander. The Volvo XC90 and Mercedes ML320, ML350, or ML550 have adequate cargo room with all the rows down, but they have neither comparable cargo room behind the second row nor comparable quality control and dealer servicing. Furthermore, now that Volvo has been sold to Chinese interests, Volvo sales and servicing in North America may become problematic. **Options:** Forget the satellite navigation system. **Rebates:** Look for $3,000 rebates on leftover 2012s, and a similar amount in the late winter applicable to the early 2013 models. **Depreciation:** Much faster than average; a 2010 base MDX is barely worth $36,000 (quite a comedown for a vehicle that sold originally for $52,000). **Insurance cost:** Higher than average. **Parts supply/cost:** Most mechanical and electronic components are easily found and moderately priced. Body parts may be hard to come by, and they can be expensive. **Annual maintenance cost:** Average. **Warranty:** Bumper-to-bumper 5 years/100,000 km; rust perforation 5 years/unlimited km. **Supplementary warranty:** Not needed; the base warranty is fairly applied. **Highway/city fuel economy:** 9.6/13.2 L/100 km, 29/21 mpg.

OWNER-REPORTED PROBLEMS: Noisy brake pads and premature brake wear; malfunctioning power accessories and entertainment systems. No complaints on the 2012s have been reported to NHTSA.

SERVICE BULLETIN-REPORTED PROBLEMS: Running board step plate pad doesn't lay flat, and the master key won't lock in the extended position.

Honda

Picking Up the Pieces

Honda, Nissan, and Toyota were the auto manufacturers hit hardest by natural disasters in Japan early last year, yet all three companies are rebounding with increased auto sales and production. Honda and Toyota are both expected to break their 2007 records for North American output this year, thanks to strong pent-up demand for cars in spite of a lagging North American economy. And, in an effort to shorten its supply chain, More than 87 percent of the Honda and Acura models sold in the U.S. are now made in North America, up from 84 percent a year earlier.

Nevertheless, it has been a particularly hard 18 months for Honda, whose sales have fallen by double digits, posting its worst June results since 1997, says *Edmunds*:

Honda's plants have taken longer to resume full production both in Japan and the U.S. than those of Toyota Motor Corp. and Nissan Motor Corp. Honda said its net profit for the 2012 fiscal year will decline by 63%, mainly because of the impact of the quake. Honda expects lingering issues to slow production of its popular Civic due to parts shortages.

Additionally, many parts suppliers will need much more time to rebuild their factories and reestablish new working relationships with other factories to ensure they can provide quality parts at reasonable prices. Yes, Humpty Dumpty can be fixed, but it will take more time than the automakers are letting on, and the pieces might not fit together very well at first, causing quality to suffer.

Honda is still smarting from *Consumer Reports*' 2012 Civic downgrade, and Toyota's sudden, unintended acceleration problems are growing. Just this July, the company's Lexus division recalled runaway 2010 models after reassuring the public that its cars were safe.

In a bid to keep up sales momentum, Honda will offer buyers more-generous rebates, low-cost financing, and cheap leases to make room for the 2013s and to poach buyers from competitors. Smart consumers should take advantage of these sweetened deals and add a clause to the sales contract specifying a firm delivery date and a penalty that the dealer must pay if that date is missed.

Most of Honda's 2013 lineup will have standard backup cameras in preparation for expected 2014 federal government regulations requiring their use.

Another plus for the 2013 models is the addition of a standard backup camera on the redesigned Honda Accord, along with the Crosstour, Odyssey, Pilot, Ridgeline, CR-Z, and 2012 Honda Fit EV. With this change, Honda's 12-model lineup goes from having just two models with a standard backup camera to nine models. The 2012 Honda CR-V and FCX Clarity hydrogen vehicle got the camera last year. The Honda Insight has a backup camera available as part of a costly navigation package. The Honda Fit and Civic have no backup camera options, though that could change next year.

FIT ★★★★★

RATING: Recommended. Fit ranks first out of 41 affordable small cars rated by *U.S. News & World Report* based on the analysis of 37 published reviews and test drives and other reliability and safety data. This four-door, five-passenger mini hatchback is surprisingly roomy and reasonably fuel-efficient, thanks to its small, 1.5L 4-cylinder engine mated to a 5-speed manual or automatic transmission.

Slotted below the Civic, the Fit is one of the better choices among the 2013 small cars. **Road performance:** Plenty of smooth, quiet power with either the manual or automatic transmission; handles and brakes like a sports car. Handling is easy and predictable, but the ride is somewhat choppy due to the car's small size. **Strong points:** Honda offers lots of standard features; outstanding resale value; good interior ergonomics; ample and flexible interior space; quality craftsmanship; and good resale value. Almost no reliability complaints, which is amazing for a car that was redesigned last year. **Weak points:** Engine struggles going uphill with a full load; a busy ride; front seats aren't height-adjustable; and more legroom is needed for taller passengers. **Safety:** NHTSA gives the Fit its top rating of five stars for occupant protection in a frontal collision, five stars for driver protection in a side impact, and four stars for side passenger protection and rollover prevention. IIHS ratings are "Good" for offset frontal, side, rear, and roof crashworthiness. Traction control and an anti-skid system are available, but only on the more-expensive models. **New for 2013:** Riding on last year's redesign; 2014 EV has limited range. Look for it and Hybrid suspension refinements.

ALERT! Welcome to head-restraint hell:

KEY FACTS

Canadian Price (Firm): *DX:* $14,580, *DX-A:* $15,880, *LX:* $16,980, *Sport:* $18,880 **U.S. Price:** *LX:* $16,115 *Sport:* $16,860, *Sport with Navi* $19,240
Canadian Freight: $1,495 **U.S. Freight:** $790

POWERTRAIN (FRONT-DRIVE)
Engine: 1.5L 4-cyl. (117 hp);
Transmissions: 5-speed man. • 5-speed auto.

DIMENSIONS/CAPACITY
Passengers: 2/3; Wheelbase: 97 in.;
H: 60/L: 157/W: 66 in.; Headroom F/R: 5.5/3.5 in.; Legroom F/R: 40/26 in.; Cargo volume: 21 cu. ft.; Fuel tank: 41L/regular; Tow limit: No towing; Load capacity: 850 lb.; Turning circle: 34.3 ft.; Ground clearance: N/A; Weight: 2,535 lb.

The head rest pushes my head forward and strains my neck to the point that I either have to sit upright away from the seat or stretch my neck far out in pain. Either way it is not safe, whether in case of accident or generally for my health. With no cool-off period on new cars in California, I cannot return the car, which at this point has 12 miles [19 km] on it, so I am forced to drive unsafely. I ran Google search for Honda head rest complaints and found out that customers have been complaining about Honda's new head rests for the same very reason since 2007 for most of their models—from Accord and Odyssey to Fit.

What makes the matter worse is that you cannot reverse the headrest as there are grooves only on one of the two support poles. By making head restraint extremely uncomfortable to use, Honda is forcing its customers to drive unsafely, specifically without head restraint. I spoke to [the] service manager at my dealer and he told me that Honda does not have adjustable or reversible head restraints.

He is also aware of the complaints from the customers. Solution should be easy to implement by making the head rest reversible for those like me with neck or back problems. I drove Hondas for 18 years and cannot believe that Honda has not responded to 3 years of continuous complaints.

OVERVIEW: The 2013 Honda Fit is small on the outside but big on the inside. It sips fuel and still performs well. Sure, its 1.5L engine isn't in the big leagues, but you will seldom realize you're driving a mini-compact. Hey, nine seconds to 100 km/h using a manual gearbox? That's outstanding, considering the competition. Innovative seats allow you to lift the rear seat's base up against the backrest to make room for bulky items, or the seat can be folded flat, which doubles the cargo space. You can even configure the seats to make a small bed.

COST ANALYSIS: Buy the practically identical 2013 version, since Honda says it won't increase the car's price. And the latest model will have corrected most of last year's design glitches. Also, the cheaper, base model has everything you will need. **Best alternatives:** Other good econocars are the Honda Civic (2011), Hyundai Accent or Elantra, Mazda2 or Mazda3, and Nissan Versa. Mercedes' Smart Car and Toyota's Yaris aren't as refined as the Fit. The Smart is especially weak, with Canadian sales tumbling from 4,080 units in 2008 to 1,851 in 2011 and 957 through June of 2012. **Options:** Nothing worth the extra money. The Fit is really a small wagon that outshines some compact SUVs for room and utility while giving much better fuel economy. **Rebates:** Look for $1,000 rebates on the leftover 2012 models and half as much for the 2013s. Remember, prices are firm. **Depreciation:** A little slower than average. For example, a 2010 Fit that sold for $14,480 is still worth about $9,500. **Insurance cost:** Average. **Parts supply/cost:** No trouble finding parts at a fair price. **Annual maintenance cost:** Less than average. **Warranty:** Bumper-to-bumper 5 years/100,000 km; rust perforation 5 years/unlimited km. **Supplementary warranty:** Basic warranty is sufficient. **Highway/city fuel economy:** *Man.:* 5.7/7.2 L/100 km, 50/39 mpg. *Auto.:* 5.5/7.1 L/100 km, 51/40 mpg. Interestingly, tests prove the automatic gearbox is more fuel-efficient than the manual transmission. Whichever transmission you choose, owners say fuel economy claims are overstated by about 30 percent.

OWNER-REPORTED PROBLEMS: Best-in-class reliability and durability, judging by *Consumer Reports* member surveys and NHTSA posted reports, as well as European owner reviews of the Jazz/Fit. The redesigned 2012 has only three owner complaints posted on NHTSA's website (*www.safercar.gov*): The right rear seat belt would not unlatch and kept tightening around a child passenger's neck; vehicle wouldn't accelerate from a standstill if the wheels were turned to the right or left; and the fuel tank understated the amount of remaining fuel. Only seven complaints were logged by NHTSA for the 2011 models when 100 would be the norm. On older models, owners report sudden acceleration and airbag failures; windshield stress fractures; seat belts break, and the tire jack may bend sideways when lifting the car; periodic brake failures; paint chipping and premature cosmetic rusting; insufficient legroom causes drivers to apply the brakes and accelerator at the same time; and the dashboard's elevated design obstructs forward visibility.

Other complaints include airbags that fail to deploy; a narrow view out the rear window; some transmission seal leaks; a weak AC; a small gas tank; a fuel sloshing noise heard under the front seats; touchy, squeaky brakes; the vehicle tends to sway and wander when buffeted by moderate side winds; jerky acceleration when driving in traffic; excess gear shifting over hilly terrain; some interior engine and road noise; bland exterior and interior styling; and some paint peeling and delamination. Road debris easily destroys the AC condenser—an expensive repair not covered under warranty—but repair discounts are given under a "goodwill" warranty.

SERVICE BULLETIN-REPORTED PROBLEMS: None.

CIVIC ★★★/★★

RATING: *2013:* Average; *2012:* Below Average. The Civic's redesign last year is no big deal, and it certainly is no reason to go out and buy a 2013 thinking all of the 2012 flaws have been corrected. They haven't. There are better buys available, like the Chevrolet Cruze and Hyundai Elantra, that are cheaper, more stylish, and better equipped. The Civic was once one of the best-performing small cars around. However, that was then, and this is now. Honda's 2012 redesign brings with it lots of factory- and supplier-related mistakes that will take several years to correct, as was painfully true with the Accord's 2008 redesign, as well. **Road performance:** These cars are noted for good acceleration; and a smooth-shifting automatic transmission. Some minuses are mediocre handling, a choppy ride, and vague steering:

> My 2012 Honda Civic LX Coupe has extremely vague steering feel at speeds greater than 55 mph [89 km/h], causing excessive and repeated correction to maintain

KEY FACTS

Canadian Price (negotiable): *DX:* $14,990, *LX Coupe:* $17,990, *EX-L Sedan:* $24,390, *Si Sedan:* $25,990, *Hybrid Sedan:* $27,350 **U.S. Price:** *DX 2d. manual Sedan:* $15,955, *LX 2d manual Sedan:* $18,005, *EX:* $20,655; *EX-L:* $22,105 *Si 2d manual:* $22,205, *Base Hybrid:* $24,200 **Canadian Freight:** $1,495 **U.S. Freight:** $790 **POWERTRAIN (FRONT-DRIVE)**
Engines: (Hybrid)1.5L 4-cyl. (110 hp) plus electric motor (23 hp) • 1.8L 4-cyl. (140 hp) • 2.4L 4-cyl. (201 hp); Transmissions: 5-speed man. • 5-speed auto. • 6-speed man. • CVT auto.

DIMENSIONS/CAPACITY (SEDAN)
Passengers: 2/3; Wheelbase: 105.1 in.; H: 56.5/L: 177.3/W: 69 in.; Headroom F/R: 3.0/2.0 in.; Legroom F/R: 42.0/36.2 in.; Cargo volume: 12.5 cu. ft.; Fuel tank: 50L/regular; Load capacity: 850 lb.; Turning circle: 35.4 ft.; Weight: 2,672 lb.

DIMENSIONS/CAPACITY (Hybrid)
Passengers: 2/3; Wheelbase: 105.1 in.; H: 56.5/L: 177.3/W: 69 in.; Headroom F/R: 3.0/2.0 in.; Legroom F/R: 42.0/36.2 in.; Cargo volume: 10.7 cu. ft.; Fuel tank: 47L/regular; Tow limit: N/A; Load capacity: 850 lb.; Turning circle: 35.4 ft.; Ground clearance: 5.4 in.; Weight: 2,853 lb.

the steering wheel towards the left to continue driving straight. The dealer has performed a 4-wheel alignment twice without resolution. They have also inspected the steering and suspension components.

Strong points: Instruments and controls are easily accessed; a tilt/telescoping steering wheel is standard; and interior space is more than adequate for most adults. Thankfully, considering all of the potential problems, Civics have a strong resale value (because not everyone reads *Lemon-Aid*). **Weak points:** The 2012s aren't as reliable, or perform as well, as previous models, and the 2013s are question marks. Brakes require a long stopping distance, and interior materials look and feel cheap. Head restraints must have been designed by the Marquis de Sade working under the tutelage of Toyota CEO Akio—"I didn't know our cars would suddenly accelerate, with no brakes… sniff, sniff"—Toyoda. An expansive dash shelf and sloping nose make it tough to judge distance when parking, and rear visibility isn't impressive, either; the suspension may be too firm for some; the coupe's interior noise is less isolated than in the sedan; the coupe's rear access takes some effort, and trunk hinges intrude into the cargo area; and there are some fit and finish problems. **Safety:** NHTSA awarded the 2012 four-door Civic five stars for front and side crash protection and four stars for rollover resistance. The two-door version got a four-star rating across the board. The 2011s didn't do as well: four stars for front protection and rollover resistance, and only two stars for side crashworthiness. The 2013 models have yet to be tested. IIHS results for the 2012 SI's rear crash protection were "Good." The 2012 four-door Civic received a "Good" rating in all categories. The 2011 two-door was "Good" in frontal offset crash tests and "Acceptable" for side protection. The coupe's steeply raked front windshield cuts forward visibility. **New for 2013:** Honda promises the major design changes will correct many of the 2012's faults.

ALERT! Honda's policy of no-haggle pricing has been dropped. Although sales haven't done that poorly, the company is now offering sizeable rebates and sales incentives to counter the panning of the Civic by *Consumer Reports*, *Lemon-Aid*, and other critics earlier this year. This means you should politely tell your Honda dealer that the list price isn't acceptable and that you want at least a 5 percent discount. As competition in the new year heats up with Chevrolet, Ford, and Toyota, Honda dealers will cut prices and offer other sales incentives.

The head restraint pushes the driver's head too far forward:

> I have tilted the seat back as far as I safely can and still be able to drive. I am [a] 53 year old female, 5'3" tall, and wear bifocals. I am having difficulty focusing from tachometer to speedometer to road because I cannot [move] my head to use the right part of my glasses to see. I cannot tilt my head back at all because of the headrest. I also experienced a headache that evening as well due to eye strain. The NHSTA changed their headrest regulations in 2008. Test dummies for large males were used and then standards were put in place. After spending thousands of dollars on a new car, I am unable to safely drive it. I have to either remove, turn around, or jerry-rig a remedy for the headrest in order to drive and not suffer neck, back, shoulder, and visual pain. The cost is my safety in an accident. Or, I can leave the headrest and drive with my posture in a horrid position. I cannot sit up straight, my head is forced downward so I cannot use my bifocals properly, and I cannot tilt the seat back any further and still see over the dashboard.

Dunlop and Firestone tires have a history of sudden tread separation; demand upgraded tires before signing the contract. During the test drive, listen for a loud sloshing noise caused by fuel banging against the gas tank walls:

> The dealer let me know that the noise I was hearing was the fuel moving around in the fuel tank, due to a design change in the 2012 model which removed the fuel tank baffles.

Also look for excessive windshield glare:

> I am just documenting that this vehicle has a real glare problem due to size and slant of windshield. The entire image of the dash appears on the windshield and

the glare is very distracting while driving. I'm sure Honda has tried to deal with this issue due to the matte finish on the dash, but it isn't working. I feel like I've made one of the biggest mistakes by buying this vehicle. I hope I don't run someone over, lost in the glare.

OVERVIEW: Honda's 2012 revision targeted greater fuel economy on its entry-level Civic and added a paltry four more horses to the Si model's output. Engines are hooked to either a 5-speed manual or automatic transmission (competitors use 6-speeds), while the costlier Si makes do with a 6-speed manual. There's also a cheap-looking plastic two-tier instrument panel, and the car is about 40 pounds lighter. The wheelbase is shorter by an inch and a half, and the Si gets stiffer suspension settings and a limited-slip differential. 2012 Civic hybrids now carry a 1.5L engine, instead of the previous model's 1.3L; the electric motor has slightly more horsepower and uses a stop-start fuel-saving mode; and a new lithium ion battery has been added. HF hybrids are styled more aerodynamically and roll on low-resistance tires.

COST ANALYSIS: Reputation degrades slowly, but when it does, prices and sales usually tumble. So far, Honda has kept sales relatively stable by cutting prices and stressing the Civic's overall reliability, borne out by *Consumer Reports* yet contradicted by posted NHTSA owner complaints (see "Owner-Reported Problems"). This has been seen before: The domestic automakers managed to make mediocre cars for years before their customers started to abandon them. Honda knows it can sell mediocre Civics for a while, too, but eventually people will start to catch on and buy American or switch to the South Korean or German automakers. On the bright side, Civics still retain higher resale values than most cars. Even the much-maligned 2012 loses only about 15 percent of its value after one year's use. **Best alternatives:** Chevrolet's popular fuel-efficient Cruze, the fuel-efficient and more aggressively styled Hyundai Elantra, a peppy and stylish Mazda3, the "pocket rocket" Kia Forte, and a larger and less expensive VW Jetta. **Options:** Try to get a free extra set of ignition keys written into the contract; Honda's anti-start, theft-protection keys may cost as much as $150 per set. Steer clear of the standard-issue radio and problematic Firestone or Bridgestone tires. **Rebates:** Mostly related to leasing and low-cost financing. **Depreciation:** Slower than average. A 2011 Civic Coupe that once sold for $19,000 is still worth almost $13,500. **Insurance cost:** Average. **Parts supply/cost:** Reasonably priced and easily found at dealers and independent suppliers. Hybrid parts may be back ordered due to production cutbacks in Japan. **Annual maintenance cost:** Much less than average. **Warranty:** Bumper-to-bumper 3 years/60,000 km; powertrain 5 years/100,000 km; rust perforation 6 years/unlimited km. **Supplementary warranty:** Not needed. **Highway/city fuel economy:** *1.8L (140 hp) man.:* 5.4/7.4 L/100 km, 52/38 mpg. *Auto.:* 5.7/8.2 L/100 km, 50/34 mpg. *Hybrid:* 5.3 L/100 km (combined highway/city), 44 mpg.

OWNER-REPORTED PROBLEMS: Let's start with faulty seat belts and airbags: A fire ignited in the seat belt wiring under the passenger seat; seat belts tighten progressively when connected; a child was injured when he became entangled in an unfastened rear centre shoulder belt, which retracted, cutting off his air; seat belts don't always retract into the harness; Airbag warning light stays lit even though an adult passenger occupies the seat; seat belts fail to lock up in a sudden panic stop; and there have been a multitude of complaints of inadvertent side airbag deployment, or airbags failing to deploy in collisions:

> I was trying to back into a parking space with my 8-month-old 2012 Honda Civic. As I took my foot off the gas pedal to put the car into reverse and before I could step on the brake, the car surged forward at a tremendous rate of speed, jumped a curb and went straight into a brick building. The car bounced backwards onto the parking lot and I was able to step on the brake and regain control. This happened in a matter of a split second with no time to jam the brake on as the car lurched forward. Even though the car jolted tremendously, the airbag did not go off, but a service light came on the dash board indicating "Check Airbag System."

Mechanical and body failures are legion. Most common failings are fractured front tie rods, causing complete steering loss; sudden acceleration or surging when AC or heater is engaged, or when the steering wheel is turned sharply; car veers sharply to the right when braking; and the brake and accelerator pedal are mounted too close together. Vehicle hesitates when accelerating from a stop and there's engine surging when exiting on an off-ramp or when the brakes are applied:

> Car suddenly stops dead while accelerating to make left-hand turn. It will resume acceleration only after a four-second pause. Turning into oncoming traffic with a dead vehicle is going to cause an accident involving injuries or death. This is the third time that this incident has occurred to my vehicle. The Honda dealer cannot find the cause.

•

> The contact owns a 2012 Honda Civic. The contact was reversing into a residential garage when the vehicle abnormally accelerated forward as the brake was disengaged. On a different occasion, while driving uphill and releasing the brakes, the vehicle accelerated in reverse instead. In order to prevent the vehicle from rolling backward, the contact would continuously depress the accelerator pedal. The Civic was taken to the dealer who stated that the failure was normal.

Cruise control doesn't stay at its set speed, and chronic stalling accompanied by steering-wheel lock-up; engine momentarily maintains high rpm when decelerating; fuel leakage into the engine compartment while vehicle is underway; car has to warm up a few minutes before brakes will work properly; vehicle rolls back when stopped on an incline with automatic transmission engaged; transmission surges forward when put in Reverse (blamed on transmission solenoid); automatic transmission will suddenly downshift in traffic; when accelerator pedal is tapped at less than 5 km/h, vehicle suddenly passes from Drive to Neutral to Reverse; transmission won't easily go into First gear; steering wheel wouldn't lock when parked; steering wheel shakes when turned sharply to the left or right; sunlight reflection from the dashboard to the windshield reduces visibility; taller drivers' vision blocked by nonadjustable, windshield-mounted rear-view mirror; driver's sun visor keeps falling down, obstructing vision; loose driver's seat; windshield cracked suddenly; difficult to see through bottom of windshield; with AC engaged at night, a film covers rear windshield (said to be caused by either an engine head gasket failure or "outgassing" from the interior's plastic trim); the AC has been blamed for emitting toxic fumes; and water leaks into the engine compartment through the front hood lip and grill.

Other factory-related annoyances that may mostly injure your wallet, or fry your nerves: Hard starts, engine won't crank, or suddenly stalls; engine oil leaks; car won't move in Drive; early automatic transmission replacement, transmission fluid leaks, and noisy engagement; stalling in Reverse or Drive; manual transmission grinds when shifting into Third gear; heater blower motor overheats or blows a fuse; malfunctioning alternator; noise from the wheel bearing, brake pedal booster, clutch pedal, or master cylinder; oil leaks from the lower engine block crack; motor mounts failure; faulty main rear crankshaft seal; sluggish performance when it rains or when passing through a large puddle; transmission periodically won't shift into Third or Fourth gear (torque converter replaced); premature wheel bearing replacement; excessive steering shimmy; front strut leakage causes noise and difficult handling; tire rims easily collect snow, ice, and dirt; and the premature wearout of brake pads and discs:

> My Honda Civic has only 13,000 miles [21,000 km] on it and my brake pads have already worn down to nothing and had to be replaced yesterday. The repair guy told me there is absolutely no way that at such low miles that this should have happened. There must have been a problem with the original breaks on my car and $378 later, I already had to replace them.

Body fit and finish and accessories are also problematic: A-pillar, dash, or sunroof rattles; windows bind or come out of run channels; doors and trunk lid are hard to close; inoperable fuel-door handle; body and bumper paint peeling and cracking; poorly mounted driver's seat; inoperable door locks and power windows; trunk cannot be opened from the cabin area; a driver-side window that won't roll back up; sun visors that fall apart; an erratic fuel gauge, speedometer, and tachometer; an interior light that hums as it dims; lousy radio speakers; water leaks through the door bottoms, from the tail light into the trunk, and onto the driver-side footwell carpet; windows that often come off their tracks; trunk springs fail; exterior and interior lights dim to an unsafe level; rear running lights fail due to a faulty fuse box; heated side mirrors gradually lose their reflective ability; an AC condenser that is easily destroyed by road debris and doesn't cool properly, and condensate that drips from under the glove compartment (heating core needs to be replaced to fix the problem); dashboard buzzing; front and rear windshield creaking; and loose, rattling seat belt adjusters, door panels, and door latches.

SERVICE BULLETIN-REPORTED PROBLEMS: Modules and control units updated, and the correction of the rear spring upper mounting cushion. *Hybrid:* Steering-wheel controls software update.

INSIGHT ★

bad buy

RATING: Not Recommended. As much as Canadian sales reps say they have a long-term commitment, Honda insiders say the Insight's days are numbered. **Road performance:** Lethargic acceleration; a jumpy, jerky ride; and mediocre handling. **Strong points:** The Insight will save you a bit on fuel, and it costs less than the more-refined Toyota Prius. It also has a versatile hatchback design. Long-term reliability has been exceptional; only four NHTSA-posted complaints on the 2011, and none for the 2012. **Weak points:** For the small savings over a Prius, you'll have to accept crawling up hills, occasional brake failures (just like with the Prius), a hard-to-access, cheap-looking interior, and poorly supported, knees-to-your-chin rear seats that are real head-bangers every time the car passes over uneven terrain. Get used to a howling engine when accelerating. **Safety:** NHTSA gave the 2013 Insight four stars for rollover resistance. IIHS awarded the 2012 model its top rating of "Good" for frontal offset, side, and rear impact protection and roof strength—an improvement over 2010–11 models, which were rated only "Acceptable." **New for 2013:** Nothing noteworthy.

KEY FACTS

Canadian Price (negotiable): *(2012) LX:* $21,990 **U.S. Price:** *Base:* $18,500, *LX:* $20,275, *EX:* $21,965 **Canadian Freight:** $1,495 **U.S. Freight:** $790
POWERTRAIN (FRONT-DRIVE)
Engine: 1.3L 4-cyl. (98 hp);
Transmission: CVT
DIMENSIONS/CAPACITY
Passengers: 2/3; Wheelbase: 100.3 in.; H: 56.1/L: 172.2/W: 66.6 in.; Headroom F/R: 5.0/1.5 in.; Legroom F/R: 40.5/26.5 in.; Cargo volume: 15.8 cu. ft.; Fuel tank: 50L/regular; Tow limit: Not recommended; Load capacity: 850 lb.; Turning circle: 36 ft.; Ground clearance: N/A; Weight: 2,755 lb.

ALERT! Check out the front head restraints; many drivers find them a real pain. Also, make sure to test drive the Insight over hilly terrain to better judge its limitations:

This car should not charge the battery on climbs. As a result of this, extra load is added on the engine. This could be very dangerous as you don't have enough power to climb at a certain rate other cars are capable of. If you visit *insightcentral.net* there are a lot of complaints about this. Honda needs to re-program the cars not to force charge during climbs. I understand that if the battery was very low or drained that force charging on climbs are a necessary evil. But my battery was 75% full!

OVERVIEW: The Insight sells for less than the Accord, and the car comes with multiple airbags, automatic climate control, power windows and locks, heated mirrors, CD audio with auxiliary jack, and anti-lock brakes. The EX gives you Bluetooth connectivity, a USB interface, paddle shifters, stability control, and a navigation system of doubtful utility.

COST ANALYSIS: This car has very little to offer, except for some fuel savings and the cachet of buying a "green" car. Be especially wary of the "environmentally friendly" hype: Your "green machine" uses toxic rare earth elements that kill workers in developing countries, and its electrical energy comes from coal-burning utilities. And the cost for a new battery pack is best left unsaid. **Best alternatives:** The Hyundai Accent, Mazda3, Nissan Sentra, Suzuki SX4, and Volkswagen Jetta TDI. **Options:** Steer clear of the standard-issue radio and problematic Firestone or Bridgestone tires. **Rebates:** A $2,500 rebate early in the new year. **Depreciation:** Faster than average—a 2010 LX that sold originally for $24,000 is now worth about $15,500. **Insurance cost:** Higher than average. **Parts supply/cost:** Electronic parts are expensive and hard to find. **Annual maintenance cost:** Lower than average. **Warranty:** Bumper-to-bumper 3 years/60,000 km; powertrain 5 years/100,000 km; rust perforation 6 years/unlimited km. **Supplementary warranty:** Not needed. **Highway/city fuel economy:** *LX:* 4.5/4.8 L/100 km, 63/59 mpg. *EX:* 4.6/ 5.0L/100 km, 61/56 mpg.

OWNER-REPORTED PROBLEMS: Airbags failed to deploy in a frontal collision. Sudden brake failures in Drive and Reverse (hybrids from all automakers have a history of sudden brake failures). When coasting to a stop, the car will suddenly accelerate; low beams don't adequately light up the road; there is no way to restrict access to the fuel-filler nozzle; and the tire-pressure monitor will indicate a low tire pressure when the pressure is within normal limits.

CR-V ★★★★★

best buy

RATING: Recommended. **Road performance:** A smooth-running 4-banger handles most chores well, but owners could use a bit more grunt for merging and tackling steep grades with a full load. Also, owners say a persistent hesitation-before-acceleration problem crops up from time to time. The 5-speed automatic transmission performs flawlessly, and braking is first-class. The ride is firm but comfortable, though the steering is a bit stiff and vague. High-speed cornering is not recommended, due to excessive body lean. Also, annoying highway noises are omnipresent when at cruising speeds. **Strong points:** The CR-V has more

legroom than ever before, thanks to the roomy rear seats that recline and slide independently and fold down to create a flat cargo floor. A low loading floor also helps to get cargo in and out of the car. Amenities abound in the ultra-functional, well-laid out interior. The lift-up tailgate is much more convenient than the swing-out version used in previous years. **Weak points:** Styling is confused, with rear-quarter styling trumping a decent outward view (think Pontiac Aztek). No V6, and ABS is a standard feature only as part of a more-expensive trim package. **Safety:** NHTSA gave the 2013 CR-V five stars for frontal and side crash protection and four stars for rollover resistance. IIHS awarded the 2012 model its top rating of "Good" in frontal offset, side, and rear impacts, and also for roof strength. **New for 2013:** Nothing significant added.

ALERT! Again, painful head restraints:

> 2012 Honda CR-V headrest—when sitting with my back completely against the car seat, the top part of the headrest is pitched forward at such an angle that it forces my head forward regardless of the height of placement. In order to correctly align my head with my spine while driving, I have to sit forward. This is not a feasible position. I am 5'10" tall and already suffer from cervical spine problems without this headrest creating more!!! I did not realize the situation with the headrest until I'd had the vehicle for about a week... The only solution I could find was to turn

KEY FACTS

Canadian Price (negotiable): *LX:* $27,300, *LX 4WD:* $29,300, *EX:* $31,500, *EX 4WD:* $33,000, *EX-L 4WD:* $34,500, *EX-L Navi. 4WD:* $35,500
U.S. Price: *LX:* $22,545, *LX 4WD:* $23,795, *EX:* $24,845, *EX 4WD:* $25,595, *EX-L:* $27,795, *EX-L 4WD:* $29,745 **Canadian Freight:** $1,395
U.S. Freight: $810
POWERTRAIN (FRONT-DRIVE/AWD)
Engine: 2.4L 4-cyl. (180 hp); Transmission: 5-speed auto.
DIMENSIONS/CAPACITY
Passengers: 2/3; Wheelbase: 103.1 in.; H: 66.1/L: 177.8/W: 71.6 in.; Headroom F/R: 4.0/4.0 in.; Legroom F/R: 40.1/ 29.0 in.; Cargo volume: 25.5 cu. ft.; Fuel tank: 50L/regular; Tow limit: 1,500 lb.; Load capacity: 850 lb.; Turning circle: 39 ft.; Ground clearance: 7.2 in.; Weight: 3,404 lb.

the headrest around and attach a cushion to it in case of an accident. These headrests may have been designed to fit current safety measures, but one size does not fit all!!

Snakes on a Plane? No—spiders in a Honda!

While driving a few weeks ago I noticed a very yellow large spider crawling across my dashboard. I almost ran off the road finding a napkin to kill it so it didn't get on me as it was making its way to me very quickly from the dash towards the steering wheel!!! Then a couple days later, another spider.... Then a couple days later another spider and this morning while at the Dunkin Donuts drive-thru, another spider!!!!! All of these I have managed to kill which only tells me that there are a bunch of spiders in my dashboard or something!!! The one today came out of the vent just over the A/C vent driver's side!??!?! Each time I see one, it's on the dashboard initially and then quickly moves around. This is the last thing I need and I want the car torn apart to find out where they are coming from and have them removed immediately! I'm freaking out! I am waiting on call backs from both Hollman Honda (the dealership which has never heard about any spider issues) as well as the customer service department of Honda itself to open a case about this matter. Being that they are poisonous (Mazda had a recall about this very issue evidently although Honda isn't issuing a recall at the moment). The car is brand new and I paid cash for it, otherwise I would trade it in if it were a lease. I am terrified of spiders and these are poisonous!!!! Help!! I can't keep driving this car! Scared out of my mind and needing a remedy fast!

OVERVIEW: A Honda bestseller, the CR-V has distanced itself from the Toyota Sienna and enhanced the driving experience by making a driver-communicative SUV that is as reliable as it is cheap to service. This is a driver's car, with a peppy, fuel-saving 4-cylinder engine that has sufficient power for most occasions (okay, going uphill fully loaded isn't the 4-banger's forte) and sips gas. You always feel in control, contrary to the experience in many of the larger SUVs where the vehicle cocoons the driver into a quasi-somnolent state.

CR-Vs are equally manoeuvrable in tight quarters as they are on winding roads, and they don't get blown about as much when cruising in stiff crosswinds. The Real Time 4WD system works well on slippery roads, where the feature automatically engages the wheels for maximum traction. Another interesting high-tech improvement is the Grade Logic Control, which automatically downshifts or upshifts when driving up or down a hill. Also, Honda has reduced engine idle vibration and noise.

COST ANALYSIS: Buying a cheaper 2012 model is not very realistic; likely they will have all been sold, and you will miss out on the 2013's improvements. Delay your purchase until mid-2013, when quality will be better and prices more negotiable. **Best alternatives:** The CR-V's biggest competitor is the Toyota RAV4. If you don't mind going downscale a bit, consider a Hyundai Tucson. **Options:** Steer clear of the standard-issue radio and the Continental, Firestone, or Bridgestone tires. **Rebates:** Not likely. **Depreciation:** Much slower than average. **Insurance cost:** Average. **Parts supply/cost:** Reasonably priced and easily found at dealers and independent suppliers. **Annual maintenance cost:** Much less than average. **Warranty:** Bumper-to-bumper 3 years/60,000 km; powertrain 5 years/100,000 km; rust perforation 6 years/unlimited km. **Supplementary warranty:** Not needed. **Highway/city fuel economy:** *Front-drive:* 7.1/9.8 L/ 100 km, 40/29 mpg. *AWD:* 7.5/10.1 L/100 km, 38/28 mpg. Expect a tad more fuel economy with the 6-speed automatic.

OWNER-REPORTED PROBLEMS: Sudden, unintended acceleration:

> I bought a new 2011 Honda CR-V and have a serious safety issue. The engine maintained its speed or accelerated on four separate occasions when I applied the brake and tried to stop. The worst incident occurred when I tried to come to a stop at a red light with cars in front of me. I applied brake and car stopped but engine raced. I had to apply very strong pressure to brake to hold car in place. Engine was racing and car was pulling forward. I shifted to neutral, engine continued to race and then I heard a loud knocking sound come from engine like a washing machine makes when it is out of balance. I was very scared. I turned engine off and then at green light turned engine on and it was OK. This happened four separate times when the car had just over 200 miles [320 km] on it, just over 400 miles [640 km], 723 miles [1,160 km], and 819 miles [1,320 km].

> I did not have a foot on both gas and brake, the mats are the Honda mats that come with car and are fastened to the floor and were not on the gas.... Reported to Honda and took car in twice. Honda said there were no codes and the brakes looked OK. They said to call American Honda which I did.... Honda said someone would get in touch with me the next day. It's been a week and no one has contacted me. I have owned the car for 40 days and driven it less than 850 miles [1,370 km] and this has happened four times and been in the shop twice.

Some owners would like a little "intended" acceleration: There are reports that when the accelerator is pressed hard, there is a loss of power and downshifting is delayed, just when extra power is needed (see "Service Bulletin-Reported Problems"):

> In stop and go traffic, with and without the Econ button on, the car hesitates to accelerate to the point that it has nearly caused accidents. Took it to Honda and asked them to drive to witness the problem. I don't think they drove it. The problem is somewhat intermittent, so you never know when it will happen. You have to adjust your driving just in case it might happen. The dealer told me not to drive with Econ button in city driving conditions. That doesn't make a difference. It will cause accident eventually.

Traction control has also been a problem with earlier models. Key frequently gets stuck in the ignition; driver's side window suddenly shattered; electrical system shorts; premature brake wear; airbags fail to deploy; AC condenser is destroyed by road debris (a chronic failure on most of Honda's lineup); bent wheel studs can easily snap; brake rotors wear out prematurely; the engine oil pan leaks; the driver's and passenger's sun visors fall out of their mounting; windshield washer nozzles freeze up in cold weather; omnipresent vibrations, rattles and clunking, knocking sounds; and poor stability and rapid tread wear experienced with Continental original equipment tires.

SERVICE BULLETIN-REPORTED PROBLEMS: An engine oil leak at the rear of the cylinder head cover may be caused by a defective No. 5 rocker shaft holder. The left rear wheelwell doesn't have enough seam sealer, which may allow water to leak into the interior under the rear seat on the 2011s—Honda has set up a free repair campaign to apply sealer. A loss of power when accelerating may be caused by faulty PGM-FI software.

ACCORD, CROSSTOUR ★★★★

The Honda Accord.

RATING: *Accord and Crosstour:* Above Average buy because these cars have much more content and are better performers than last year's model. Why not five stars? Simply because past Honda redesigns always took a couple of years to get the factory kinks corrected and we need more time to see if this is still the case. Interestingly, the Accord Crosstour has registered much fewer safety complaints over the past three years. **Road performance:** Excellent acceleration with all engines. Going against the "smaller is better" trend, Honda gives owners the option of a V6 engine, while Chevrolet (Malibu), Ford (Fusion), and Hyundai (Sonata) offer only four cylinders in their new midsize cars. The Accord also handles and rides well, thanks to large tires, a sturdy chassis, and standard stability control. Like most Hondas, this is a driver's car, while its primary competitor, the Toyota Camry, is more of a mobile cocoon. *Crosstour:* Responsive handling, a comfortable ride, and a car-like driving position. **Strong points:** Roomy and well-equipped with user-friendly instruments and controls as well as a telescoping steering column. **Weak points:** Mediocre fuel economy with the V6, and some

KEY FACTS

Canadian Price (negotiable): *Accord Coupe DX:* $26,290, *EX-L Navi:* $29,990, *EX-L V6 Navi:* $35,390, *Accord Sedan LX:* $23,990, *Sport:* $25,490, *EX-L:* $29,090, *V6:* $32,790, *V6 Touring:* $35,290; *Accord Crosstour EX-L:* $34,990, *EX-L 4WD:* $36,990, *EX-L 4WD Navi.:* $38,990 **U.S. Price:** *Accord Coupe DX:* $15,755, *LX:* $17,805, *EX:* $19,855, *EX-L:* $22,105, *EX-L Navi.:* $22,155, *Sedan LX:* $21,680, *Sport:* $23,930, *EX:* $24,605, *EX-L:* $27,995, *EX-L V6:* $30,070, *EX-L V6 Navi.:* $32,070, *Touring:* $33,430; *Accord Crosstour EX:* $27,755, *FX V6:* $30,440 *FX-I · $30,805, *EX-L V6 4WD Navi.:* $34,540 **Canadian Freight:** $1,640 **U.S. Freight:** $830

POWERTRAIN (ACCORD FRONT-DRIVE)
Engines: 2.4L 4-cyl. (185 hp) • 2.4L 4-cyl. (189 hp) • 3.5L V6 (278 hp); Transmissions: 6-speed man. • 6-speed auto. • CVT

DIMENSIONS/CAPACITY (ACCORD SEDAN)
Passengers: 2/3; Wheelbase: 110.2 in.; H: 58.1/L: 194.0/W: 72.6 in.; Headroom F/R: 6.5/3.5 in.; Legroom F/R: 41.5/30 in.; Cargo volume: 14 cu. ft.; Fuel tank: 65L/regular; Tow limit: 1,500 lb.; Load capacity: 850 lb.; Turning circle: 37.7 ft.; Ground clearance: 6.2 in.; Weight: 3,236–3,298 lb.

POWERTRAIN (CROSSTOUR FRONT-DRIVE/4WD)
Engines: 2.4L 4-cylinder (192 hp) • 3.5L V6 (271 hp); Transmission: 6-speed auto.

DIMENSIONS/CAPACITY (CROSSTOUR SEDAN)
Passengers: 2/3; Wheelbase: 110.1 in.; H: 58.1/L: 196.8/W: 74.7 in.; Headroom F/R: 6.5/3.5 in.; Legroom F/R: 41.5/30 in.; Cargo volume: 25.7 cu. ft.; Fuel tank: 65L/regular; Tow limit: 1,500 lb.; Load capacity: 850 lb.; Turning circle: 40.2 ft.; Ground clearance: 8.1 in.; Weight: 3,852–4,070 lb.

road noise intrusion into the cabin area. An astoundingly high number of performance and reliability defects on the 2008–09 models, with apparently biodegradable brakes topping the list. Annoying windshield dash reflection; distorted windshields; and creaks and rattles. Many owner reports of airbags that explode for no reason or fail to deploy, brake failures, and sudden, unintended acceleration. *Crosstour:* Strut towers intrude into storage space, and the sloping rear-end styling compromises the Crosstour's utility. **Safety:** Accord has earned five-star crashworthiness scores from NHTSA for front, side, and rollover protection. The car was also given a "Good" rating by IIHS for head-restraint effectiveness, frontal offset, side, rear, and roof crashworthiness. *Crosstour:* NHTSA scores: five stars for frontal and side occupant crash protection and four-star rollover resistance. IIHS rated frontal offset, side, and rear crashworthiness as "Good"; roof crash protection was "Mediocre." Limited rear visibility. **New for 2013:** An increase of 4 percent in hp with the base four-banger and 5–7 percent better fuel economy, thanks to the V6's cylinder deactivation system that puts the engine into 3-cylinder mode to improve fuel economy. A shorter wheelbase and length, a lower height, and increased width make the new Accord less boxy-looking and add passenger and trunk space. Soundproofing material has been added and the dash revised to reduce cabin noise—a common complaint. The once-lumpy seats are more supportive and LED headlights are standard. More goodies? Sure. Each new Accord is equipped with alloy wheels, and a rearview camera, an Expanded View Driver's Mirror, Bluetooth HandsFreeLink, USB/iPod integration, Pandora Internet radio compatibility, SMS text message function, dual-zone automatic climate control, and a 160-watt AM/FM/CD audio system.

A Sport and Touring model have been added. The Sport offers 18-inch alloy wheels, fog lights, 10-way power driver's seats, a spoiler, dual chrome exhausts, paddle shifters (CVT models only), a stiffer tower strut bar, and retuned suspension and steering. Landing between the Accord LX and Accord EX, the Sport model comes with a 2.4L VTEC engine coupled to either a 6-speed manual or Continuously Variable Transmission (CVT). The Sport model is value priced with a manufacturer's suggested retail price of $23,390 plus a destination and handling charge. The V6 Coupe is also available with a 6-speed manual. (Honda will start selling an Accord Plug-in Hybrid next year with a new electric-coupled CVT.)

ALERT! During the test drive, make sure the seat and head restraint design don't cause neck or back pain and that your right leg doesn't go numb. Make sure the front head restraints don't force your head into a chin-to-chest driving position and make driving a pain:

> The new style of headrest is forcing my head too far forward, and is causing me neck and shoulder pain. There is no adjustment between the seat back and the headrest, so I cannot adjust this angle. If I lean too far back, causing a natural forward lean to my head, I cannot drive comfortably, as I must move the seat too far forward, and my arms are overextended. I cannot adjust to make long distance driving comfortable—and I commute 60 miles, and over 1.5 hours, daily. My 1999 Honda Accord had no such problems. I am extremely disappointed with this situation, and the dealership is no help. My husband has back and neck problems (service-related), and he was ready to throw the passenger headrest out the window on our first freeway trip to our daughter's house—only 12 miles down the freeway.

•

> After driving off the lot with the 2012 Accord my wife and I noticed a "lump" in both the driver's and passenger seat. We had not noticed these lumps during our 15–20 minute test drive. By the time we got home, approximately 30 minutes, the lumps had become uncomfortable. The longer the drive the more uncomfortable the seats are. We have had the car just over a week and the lumps are still there (no settling in) and we have not acclimated to the seats. The lumps are above the adjustable lumbar support on the drivers side. Pulling forward on the headrest makes the "lump" disappear. This leads me to believe the lump is associated with the active head restraint system.

OVERVIEW: A well-designed family car, the Accord was last redesigned for the 2008 model year and jumped leagues ahead of the competition by giving owners superior road performance and a roomy interior with loads of safety and convenience features thrown in. Too bad build quality and reliability deteriorated so much following that last redesign. This hasn't been the case with the Crosstour, which has had few owner complaints despite its new design.

If you want good fuel economy and performance with a conventional powertrain, choose one of the two 4-cylinder engines. The V6 is a bit of a gas hog and is necessary only for highway travel with a full load. Ride comfort and responsive handling are assured by a suspension and steering set-up that enhances driver control. And what about space? Accord sedans are roomier than ever before, with interior dimensions and capacity that provide more interior space than you'll likely need.

Fast and nimble without a V6, this is the mid-sized sedan of choice for drivers who want maximum fuel economy and comfort along with lots of space for grocery hauling and occasional highway cruising. With the optional V6, the Accord is one of the most versatile mid-sized cars you can find. It offers something for everyone, and its reasonable resale value after five years means there's no way you can lose money buying one.

Accord Crosstour

The three-year-old Crosstour is billed as a "crossover utility vehicle," which is Honda-speak for a high-riding hatchback family station wagon equipped with four-wheel drive capability. This five-seater Accord spin-off offers a disappointing 25.7 cubic feet of cargo space and 51.3 cubic feet with the rear seatbacks folded. It is 300–500 pounds heavier than the Accord, depending on whether you choose the base or AWD model.

COST ANALYSIS: Buy the 2013 and hope the seats have been improved and the car's other 2012 deficiencies have been rectified. Accord prices are firm, but the Crosstour prices have plummeted due to poor sales, its controversial rear-end styling, and limited cargo space. **Best alternatives:** BMW 3 Series, Hyundai Elantra or Sonata, Mazda6, and Toyota Camry. *Crosstour:* Nissan Murano, Subaru Outback, and Toyota Venza. **Options:** The V6 gives a smoother ride and has lots of reserve power for passing and merging, though the 4-banger will do for most driving needs. The DVD navigation with voice control found on the EX and V6 coupe is a bit gimmicky, but it's easier to use and more understandable than most of the competition's systems (especially the system Ford has adopted). **Rebates:** Not likely until early 2013, except for some attractive leasing and financing deals. *Crosstour:* Look for $3,000–$5,000 sales incentives as Honda tries to boost sales. **Depreciation:** About average. For example, a 2010 Accord EX-L that sold for $30,790 is now worth no more than $21,000; a 2010 Crosstour EX-L that once went for $34,900 is now worth about $24,000. **Insurance cost:** Higher than average. **Parts supply/cost:** Good availability, and moderately priced. **Annual maintenance cost:** Less than average. **Warranty:** Bumper-to-bumper 3 years/60,000 km; powertrain 5 years/100,000 km; rust perforation 5 years/ unlimited km. **Supplementary warranty:** Not needed. **Highway/city fuel economy:** *2.4L 4-cylinder auto.:* 5.8/8.8 L/100 km, 42/39 mpg (with fuel-saving feature). *3.5L V6 6-speed man.:* 7.8/12.6 L/100 km, 22/36 mpg (with fuel-saving feature). *Auto.:* 6.7/11 L/100 km, 26/42 mpg (with fuel-saving feature). *Crosstour auto. 2WD:* 7.2/11.5 L/100 km, 39/25 mpg (with fuel-saving feature). *Auto. 4WD:* 8.0/12.3 L/100 km, 35/23 mpg (with fuel-saving feature).

OWNER-REPORTED PROBLEMS: *(2012 models)* Until the 2008 revamping, each Accord model year would usually have a few dozen reliability problems reported by owners to various government agencies and to *Lemon-Aid*; however, Honda's don't tolerate redesigns very well. For example, following the 2008 Accord's changes, an incredible 938 consumer complaints were logged by NHTSA, which is almost four times the average for most vehicles. This complaint ratio falls to about average with the 2011 and 2012 models, which registered 71 and 46 complaints, respectively. Interestingly, from 2008 to 2012 the areas of concern remain mostly the same: the powertrain, suspension, and brakes, painful front seats and head restraints, and assorted body defects.

As the reworked 2013 Accords arrive in the showrooms this fall, one wonders if history will repeat itself. It likely will, considering that these cars were rushed into production when Honda was reeling from a series of natural disasters, sales losses, and disrupted production and supply lines. As always, you can mitigate the number of factory-related defects by picking an Accord made during the second-half of the 2013 model year (March or later).

Here are some of the most-frequent problems reported on this year's 2012 models: Airbag failed to deploy; sudden, unintended acceleration:

> Vehicle suffers from an un-commanded acceleration/throttle problem which is completely reproducible. It affects the low-speed behavior of the vehicle particularly during turns where there is potential for loss of control.

Engine lags and lurches when accelerating; severe shimmy at 80 km/h; frequent windshield cracks; passenger side mirror suddenly shatters; rats eat the wiring:

> ABS lights on purchase after 5 months. I purchase my car on 30/12/11. On 30/5/12 I saw the lights on, I dropped my car for 1 day at Boardwalk Honda service. Next day, when I went to take my car, the manager told me that rodents had eaten the wiring. The place where I park my car, there were three other cars also parked every day. They never have such kind of problem. I think because their car is old and my car is new so rodents like to eat new wires not old wires. The manager told me that you have to pay for this and it will be more than $1,000. I completely disagree. Why should I pay. Still it's past 5 months. I am looking forward to fix this problem by Honda free of charge.

Newer Hondas have biodegradable wire coverings that attract rodents. It is hard to imagine a small claims court judge ruling against you since this "rodent hazard" is well-known by automakers who take more precautions to keep their vehicles rodent-free.

Dunlop SP Sport tires shred, blow out, or slide on metal surfaces in rainy weather; chronic premature wearout of the front and rear brake pads (especially the rear pads); loud and constant brake squealing or clicking (not a brake rotor/pad failure):

Dealer has checked to be sure there has not been a re-design of pads—and there has not been. A check on *Consumer Reports* web site under the forum for Honda shows this is a widespread problem. Although most got at least 12 to 15 thousand miles [19,000–24,000 km], I live in hills, which may explain part of the difference. Having to replace rear brake pads every 9,000 or 10,000 miles [14,500 or 16,000 km] is a safety problem.

Hole in AC condenser likely caused by road debris; metal creaking sound around the rear shelf deck likely due to broken spot welds in the rear shelf of the car; when the AC is activated, the headlights and interior lighting dim or flicker; remote door locking and unlocking failures; spontaneous shattering of the sunroof; and steering wheel locking up when making a left-hand turn. *Crosstour*: rear visibility obstructed:

Honda Accord Crosstour design defect impedes proper rear-view vision. The rear window of the vehicle has a heavy bar running horizontally in the middle of the window. The bar may have been required for the structure of the rear door, but it substantially blocked the rear vision for the driver.

SERVICE BULLETIN-REPORTED PROBLEMS: N/A.

ODYSSEY ★★★★

RATING: Above Average. The Odyssey outclasses Toyota's Sienna in driving pleasure and is just a bit more reliable. In a Sienna, the driver is "driven"; in an Odyssey, the driver does the driving by being more actively involved in the overall performance of the vehicle. There have, however, been frequent reports of safety- and performance-related failures, notably involving the electrical system, and this is likely to occur more frequently with future redesigns. Of particular concern are airbag malfunctions, brake defects leading to sudden brake loss, and the frequent replacement of the brake calipers and rotors. **Road performance:** Plenty of

KEY FACTS

Canadian Price (negotiable): *LX:* $29,990, *EX:* $33,990, *EX RES:* $35,490, *EX-L RES:* $40,990, *Touring:* $46,990 **U.S. Price:** *LX:* $28,075, *EX:* $31,225, *EX-L:* $34,725, *EX-L Navi.:* $36,725, *Touring:* $41,030, *Touring Elite:* $43,525 **Canadian Freight:** $1,495 **U.S. Freight:** $810

POWERTRAIN (FRONT-DRIVE)

Engine: 3.5L V6 (244 hp); Transmission: 5-speed auto.

DIMENSIONS/CAPACITY

Passengers: 2/3/3; Wheelbase: 118.1 in.; H: 68.8/L: 202.1/W: 77.1 in.; Headroom F/R1/R2: 4.5/5.5/2.0 in.; Legroom F/R1/R2: 41.5/31/28 in.; Cargo volume: 38.4 cu. ft.; Fuel tank: 80L/regular; Tow limit: 3,500 lb.; Load capacity: 1,320 lb.; Turning circle: 36.7 ft.; Ground clearance: 5 in.; Weight: 4,387 lb.

power for high-speed merging and lots of mid-range torque means less shifting when the engine is under load. Car-like ride and handling. Unlike with the Sienna, all-wheel drive isn't available and there is some tire rumble, rattling, and body drumming at highway speeds. **Strong points:** The Odyssey comes with an extensive list of standard equipment, and most controls and displays are easy to reach and read. There's a spacious, versatile, and quiet interior; comfortable seats; and numerous safety and convenience features. The second-row middle seat can be folded down as an armrest or removed completely, much like the middle-row captain's chairs, which can slide fore or aft, in unison or separately; second-row power windows; floor-stowable, 60/40-split third-row seats; easy back seat entry and exit; and a convenient second driver-side door and a power tailgate. **Weak points:** Fuel consumption isn't as low as Honda promises, despite its innovative cylinder deactivation system. Second-row head restraints block visibility; front-passenger legroom is marginal, owing to the restricted seat travel; and it's difficult to calibrate the radio without taking your eyes off the road. The storage well won't take any tire larger than a "space saver," meaning you'll carry your flat in the back. **Safety**: Impressive crash safety scores: NHTSA gives the 2013 Odyssey five stars for front and side crashworthiness and four stars for rollover protection. IIHS rates as "Good" the frontal, side, rear, and roof crash protection. Safety is enhanced with standard vehicle stability assist and traction control to prevent rollovers and improve handling; side curtain airbags with rollover sensors for all rows; and adjustable brake and accelerator pedals. On a not so positive note, owners say the van's headlights may be projected into oncoming drivers' eyes:

> Majority flash me that my high beams are on. They are not. Honda says all perfect. I cannot look into light—it is sun-like. My headlights come up into oncoming eyes constantly—Honda says aimed perfectly. I assert that this is simply highly dangerous; Honda will do nothing for me. All is perfect, they say. Even if I don't cause someone else's accident, the quantity of people flashing me appears to be evidence of spreading anger, because I can do nothing. My sun-like lights 'flash' them again and again. Pity the poor driver in front of me, in my lane. My bulbs are halogen, not the 'high intensity discharge' type.

New for 2013: A standard backup camera.

ALERT! During your test-drive see if the van has a tendency to lag and lurch when accelerating, or has the emissions warning light coming on intermittently. Some owners say the headlights don't project far enough—check that out, too.

OVERVIEW: The Odyssey has a lean look, but the interior is wide and long enough to accommodate most large objects. Sliding doors are standard equipment, and if you buy the EX version, they will both be power-assisted. Sufficient power is supplied by a competent V6, which includes variable cylinder deactivation to increase fuel economy. The engine's ability to automatically switch between 6-cylinder and 3-cylinder activation, depending on engine load, may cut gas consumption by up to 10 percent.

The Odyssey has remained relatively unchanged since the 2011s got a restyled interior and wider/lower exterior; a reworked front end; and user-friendly instruments and controls. The wider interior houses a multi-configurable second-row bench seat that spreads the seats out and uses a total of five latch positions for child seats, as well as more-ample third-row seats. If you need extra cargo space, you can easily fold the third-row seats, add the cargo, and bring the kids up into the second row. Additional comfort and infotainment features include an HDMI port; a wide screen to play one movie for all or play two separate video feeds simultaneously (copying Toyota's Sienna); a removable console with a hidden bin; and a small cooler in the central stack of the dash. Honda also boasts that not only has its 4-cylinder engine fuel economy improved, but its 3.5L V6 is more fuel-frugal than the Sienna's 4-banger. The brakes were made larger, and independent rear suspension was added.

COST ANALYSIS. The addition of a standard backup camera doesn't justify the higher cost of a 2013 version; get the cheaper 2012 model. Slow sales over the past year have forced Honda dealers to discount their upgraded 2012s by as much as 10 percent through lower transaction prices and attractive lease/loan programs. That's the better buy if you can find some leftovers on dealers' lots. **Best alternatives:** For better handling and reliability, the closest competitor to the Odyssey is Toyota's Sienna minivan. One major difference between the two models is the seating. Toyota's are like La-Z-Boy armchairs and are a chore to remove. Honda seats are more basic and are easier to install or remove. The Mazda5 and Chrysler's Caravan are acceptable choices for different reasons: The Mazda5 has less room but burns less fuel (without a high-tech engine add-on), and Chrysler's minivans aren't as reliable as the Odyssey or Mazda but offer better prices, lots of room for people and things, and plenty of convenience and safety features. The Kia Sedona minivan is also a decent choice. If you're looking for lots of towing "grunt" and plenty of usable space, rear-drive GM full-sized vans are fairly reliable vehicles that often carry sizeable discounts that will get larger as Toyota and Nissan ramp up production in the last quarter of 2012. Try to resist the gimmicky video entertainment, DVD navigation system, and expensive leather seats. See if you can trade the original-equipment Firestone or Bridgestone tires for something better (check with *www.tirerack.com*). **Rebates:** Any patient haggler will get a few thousand dollars cut from the base price; your goal should be to get at least 10 percent taken off of the MSRP. Low-cost financing and leasing programs will also help bring down the transaction price. **Depreciation:** Average. Expect half the resale value to be lost after four years. For example, a 2009 DX that originally sold for $31,490 is now worth about $15,500; a 2008 LX can be picked up for $12,500. **Insurance cost:** Higher than average. **Annual maintenance cost:** Average. **Parts supply/cost:** Moderately priced parts; availability is better than average because the Odyssey uses many generic Accord parts. CVT transmission and cylinder deactivation parts may be costly and could be hard to find outside the Honda dealer network. **Warranty:** Bumper-to-bumper 3 years/60,000 km; powertrain 5 years/100,000 km; rust perforation 5 years/unlimited km. **Supplementary warranty:** Not needed. **Highway/city fuel economy:** 8.5/13.3 L/100 km, 33/21 mpg. *EX-L & Touring:* 7.8/2.3 L/100 km, 36/23 mpg.

OWNER-REPORTED PROBLEMS: Odysseys are very reliable and durable, in fact, the 17 owner safety-related complaints registered by NHTSA for the 2012 model is only one-third the average most vehicles elicit. Some of the incidences described in the NHTSA-registered reports: airbags didn't deploy after a severe rear-ender and after hitting a deer; airbag cover warps; early engine failure; severe drivetrain judder and bucking as vehicle accelerates uphill; electrical malfunction causes a partial or complete shutdown requiring a tow to the dealership (see *www.odyclub. com/forums/54-2011-Odyssey/137322-battery-charge-low.html*):

I am getting the "Battery Charge Low" warning. Have taken the car to the dealership and spoke to them. They state it's not a problem and I need to drive the car more. It is concerning that the car shuts the dome lights, even the dash lights, off automatically. This is a supposed safety item of the car that I am to ignore? I am deeply concerned regarding this issue. First, Honda is not acknowledging the seriousness of this—"Ignore it. It's not a problem." Second, this issue, I feel, is potentially placing my family in danger if the battery cannot stay charged. Finally, this is not an infrequent issue as evidenced by the number of posts/complaints on the NHTSA website and other forums on the web (*www.odyclub.com*) yet Honda continues not to put out a TSB regarding this problem.

•

The wife is worried that if it is real and ignored she may be left stranded, which could be a danger to her in these times. Honda has sent a "service news article" to their dealers about this problem but again, their comment to fix the problem is to charge the battery and momentarily disconnect the battery sensor for 10 sec, and again this was done to our vehicle and was only a short-term fix.

Engine surges to 6000 rpms in Neutral with both feet on the brakes; automatic transmission breakdowns; transmission slams into gear or suddenly locks in low gear while the vehicle is underway; erratic downshifts; steering pulls continually to the right; premature replacement of the front strut assemblies; poor handling in snow, despite traction control; many complaints of road debris destroying the AC condenser; tire pressure monitoring system is disabled by a cell phone:

I purchased a brand new 2011 Honda Odyssey Touring Elite 4 weeks ago. As I drove home from the lot my TPMS (tire pressure monitoring system) light came on and stayed on. I immediately drove back to the dealer service center. Initially they thought it was just tire pressure but quickly realized it was an actual error of the TPMS system. One of the techs said he has seen this on one other 2011 Odyssey and that it is triggered by smart cellular phone interference. He told me it would probably happen again if I used my cell phone in the van. So they reset the TPMS error and I turned off my cell and drove for 30 minutes with no issues. So then I turned my cell phone on, and still no issues for another 5 minutes. Then my wife called and at the exact moment my cell phone rang the TPMS went into error again. So the service center tells me this is something they can't fix.

Windshield shattered on its own; excessive wind noise from the passenger and driver pillar area; ambient footwell lighting is too dim; third-row folding seat collapsed and broke a child's fingers; side sliding door frequently malfunctions by closing unexpectedly, opening when the vehicle is underway, and failing to retract when closing on an object. The EXL's running board is dangerously slippery when wet; some near-falls, many bruised shins. Brakes are another major problem area highlighted by sudden brake loss after the VSA light comes on (some dealers suggest unplugging the VSA); brake loss when backing out of a parking lot; brake pedal sometimes sinks to the floor; premature front brake wear and excessive noise; and a history of mushy braking:

We noticed the brakes appeared to be soft and spongy. When I finally took it in for service, I was told it needed a new master cylinder (at 2,800 miles [4,500 km]), which they replaced. After I picked it up, I drove it a few miles and the brakes still felt soft and spongy, so I drove back to the dealership. The service manager then drove the car and told me, "That's the way the Odyssey brakes are."

SERVICE BULLETIN-REPORTED PROBLEMS: *2008–12 models*—Engine ticking or knocking at idle:

ENGINE TICKING OR KNOCKING AT IDLE	
BULLETIN NO.: 08-017	DATE: NOVEMBER 23, 2011

PROBABLE CAUSE: The rocker shaft bridge has excessive clearance which causes the rocker shaft to rotate and make noise.
CORRECTIVE ACTION: Loosen and retorque the rocker shaft bridge bolts.

PILOT ★★★★

RATING: Above Average; if it weren't for some drivetrain, starting, and fit and finish issues, the Pilot would have earned a five-star Recommended rating. **Road performance:** The second-generation Pilot has grown into a large-sized people-carrier that offers adequate power for highway cruising, superb handling, and a fairly comfortable ride. Some minuses: mediocre acceleration when fully loaded

KEY FACTS

Canadian Price (negotiable): *LX:* $34,820, *LX 4WD:* $37,820, *EX 4WD:* $40,720, *EX-L 4WD:* $43,020, *EX-L res 4WD:* $44,620, *Touring 4WD:* $48,420 **U.S. Price:** *LX:* $29,450, *LX 4WD:* $29,920, *EX:* $31,170, *EX 4WD:* $32,770, *EX-L:* $34,270, *EX-L 4WD:* $35,870, *Touring 2WD:* $39,070, *Touring 4WD:* $40,670 **Canadian Freight:** $1,495 **U.S. Freight:** $830

POWERTRAIN (FRONT-DRIVE/AWD)

Engine: 3.5L V6 (250 hp); Transmission: 5-speed auto.

DIMENSIONS/CAPACITY

Passengers: 2/3/3; Wheelbase: 109.2 in.; H: 71.0/L: 190.9/W: 78.5 in.; Headroom: F/R1/R2: 40/39.8/38.2 in.; Legroom: F/R1/R2: 41.4/38.5/32.1 in.; Cargo volume: 18 cu. ft.; Fuel tank: 79.5L/ regular; Tow limit: 3,500–4,500 lb.; Load capacity: 1,320 lb.; Turning circle: 36.7 ft.; Ground clearance: 8.0 in.; Weight: 4,319 lb.

and so-so braking. **Strong points:** A versatile interior that could be more refined; plenty of passenger space; seating for up to eight; the third-row seat folds flat into sections to free up storage space; and there's a small storage area in the floor. Chock full of safety and convenience features and the GPS and voice operation feature are easy to use—with a little practice. Overall reliability has been better than average. **Weak points:** Unimpressive fuel economy—the much-heralded cylinder deactivation system doesn't save as much fuel as Honda fantasizes. Interior plastic materials and overall fit and finish aren't up to Honda's reputation for quality, and some road noise is omnipresent. The centre console and other controls' many buttons can be confusing to operate until you've mastered the layout. **Safety:** Very positive ratings. NHTSA: four stars for frontal and rollover protection, and five stars for side protection. IIHS: "Good" offset frontal, side, rear, and roof crash protection. The Pilot also has standard vehicle stability assist and traction control to prevent rollovers and enhance handling, side curtain airbags with rollover sensors for all rows, and adjustable brake and accelerator pedals. **New for 2013:** A standard backup camera.

ALERT! Pilot sales have rebounded this year, but dealers are willing to dicker a bit over prices, as Honda sweetens its leasing and financing deals.

OVERVIEW: It's the mouse that sometimes roars and at other times squeaks. The Pilot is truck-like on the outside, but it's a much tamer vehicle when you look closely. It combines car-like comfort and handling in a crossover package where ride comfort, utility, and passenger accommodations are foremost.

COST ANALYSIS: Unsold 2012 Pilots are rare, but the 2013s will be eligible for all kinds of automaker incentives that will drive down their prices during the first quarter of 2013. Be prepared to delay your purchase until then. **Best alternatives:** GM's heavily discounted Tahoe and Yukon SUVs are selling at bargain prices. A GM Terrain or Traverse would also be worth considering. **Options:** Nothing essential. **Rebates:** Early in 2013, $2,000–$4,000 discounts, attractive low financing rates, and special leasing prices will be commonplace. **Depreciation:** Slower than average. **Insurance cost:** Higher than average. **Annual maintenance cost:** Below average. **Parts supply/cost:** Average availability. Most parts are moderately priced, except for cylinder deactivation components, which may be costly because only Honda dealers sell them. **Warranty:** Bumper-to-bumper 3 years/60,000 km; powertrain 5 years/100,000 km; rust perforation 5 years/unlimited km. **Supplementary warranty:** A waste of money. **Highway/city fuel economy:** *Front-drive:* 8.7/12.7 L/100 km, 32/22 mpg. *AWD:* 9.1/13.1 L/100 km, 31/22 mpg.

OWNER-REPORTED PROBLEMS: Owners reported only 16 complaints to NHTSA for the 2012 Pilot when 50 would have been normal. Some of the reported incidents: airbags failed to deploy; fuel leak under the vehicle; sudden, unintended acceleration and brake failure; transmission lurches back and forth between Fourth and Fifth gear:

> Mechanic says this is a known problem, but there is no fix. He said it's due to the torque converter. He said it is the same on the Odyssey models but Honda released some software updates but they weren't successful. He said if it happens just speed up or slow down (he really said this). He said if Honda releases any software updates they'll contact me. Wow.

Mushy brakes that lose pressure:

> Traveling at low or at highway speeds the brake pedal has excessive travel and causes an excessively long delayed stop. Also, when coming to a stop and waiting with the brake pressed for several minutes, i.e., 3–5 minutes at a red light or longer time at a railroad stop, the brake paddle will slowly start traveling to the floor. Have to pump the brake to bring it back up, then, the problem keeps repeating.

Electrical failures may cause car to shut down; stalling and hard starting:

> 2012 Honda Pilot—does not start consistently and often stalls. The dealer's service department reported to me that Honda of America is aware of the problem an trying to fix it. They promised to keep me posted on the status of the Honda of America engineers' progress on the issue. Six weeks went by, and the problem persisted with intermittent

calls to my local service manager. I was told not to bother to bring it in for service each time it stalled because they were waiting for a recall/fix from corporate. After six weeks, multiple stalls, which were all reported to my dealer as requested, dealer agreed to trade my vehicle in for a different pilot. Within less than 24 hours of owning this second 2012 Honda Pilot, my new car stalled. I have recently been on YouTube and discovered that this is a common problem with the 2012 Honda Pilots, and has also been reported with some 2011 Honda Pilots.

Front wheel fell off; several owners warn that unprotected wiring in the undercarriage area could be life-threatening if damaged:

Wheel sensor wires on 2011 Honda Pilot are exposed and unprotected under the vehicle which when damaged, disable anti-lock braking system (ABS), vehicle stability assist (VSA), and the variable torque management (VTM-4) systems. Exposed wires are prone to be cut or damaged by road debris and hazards. Due to the wire being exposed, it was damaged and caused an out-of-pocket expense of approx. $266.00 to repair.

Automatic transmission fluid leaks; secondary hood latch failed when passing over rough roads; rear tailgate window exploded while vehicle was parked in a garage (window was replaced under warranty, which shows Honda realizes this is a quality issue and not a routine insurance claim for damage caused from an outside source). Original-equipment Goodyear tire sidewall failures; the rear AC system will not shut off from the front control panel; and the driver's seat height adjustment lowers on its own while the Pilot is underway.

Pilot dealer servicing has also been found wanting:

Spontaneous star crack in lower center windshield, spontaneous rear hatch and passenger door opening while driving with my young child in the rear passenger seat (with "locked" doors), transmission rattle upon slow acceleration or coast at second and third gears…Honda dealer said call insurance about windshield, something must have "hit" windshield without me knowing it, said "found no abnormal noises" and "cannot duplicate" rattle noise because different people have different driving patterns, said "cannot duplicate" doors opening while driving, dealer did not "fix" any of these safety issues, just told us to pick up the car.… After research on Internet, I believe these to be manufacturer defects.

SERVICE BULLETIN-REPORTED PROBLEMS: *2011–12 models:* Engine ticking or knocking at idle (see Odyssey).

 RIDGELINE

RATING: Recommended; not only a top-performer, but well-appointed, and more reliable, as well. **Road performance:** Sustained and quiet acceleration; a smooth-shifting automatic transmission; and secure handling and good cornering control, thanks to communicative, direct steering and well-tuned shocks that also

give a comfortable, supple ride. **Strong points:** A friendly cabin environment where everything is easily accessed and storage spaces abound; an all-weather, lockable trunk beneath the cargo bed; the tailgate opens either vertically or horizontally; and there's no intrusive wheel arch in the five-foot-long bed. Reliability and overall dependability are legendary, and crashworthiness is exemplary. **Weak points:** High sales price; excessive road noise; bed is too small for some needs; not well-suited for off-roading. **Safety:** Exceptionally high marks for passenger crash protection. NHTSA: 2013 model earned four stars for rollover resistance; other categories not tested; IIHS: "Good" offset frontal, side, rear, and roof crash protection. Standard vehicle stability assist and traction control to prevent rollovers and enhance handling, side curtain airbags with rollover sensors for all rows, and adjustable brake and accelerator pedals. **New for 2013:** A standard backup camera.

ALERT! Remember, small and mid-sized pickups retain a higher resale value than most cars. So, even if you pay more than expected, you will probably recoup the difference come trade-in time.

OVERVIEW: The Ridgeline mixes performance with convenience. It's an ideal truck for most jobs, as long as you keep it on the highway. Off-road, this unibody pickup

KEY FACTS

Canadian Price (negotiable): *DX:* $34,990, *VP:* $36,690, *EX-L:* $41,490, *EX-L Navi.:* $43,690 **U.S. Price:** *RT:* $29,150, *RTS:* $31,855, *RTL:* $34,730, *RTL Navi.:* $37,080 **Canadian Freight:** $1,395 **U.S. Freight:** $810

POWERTRAIN (FRONT-DRIVE/4WD)

Engine: 3.5L V6 (250 hp); Transmission: 5-speed auto.

DIMENSIONS/CAPACITY

Passengers: 2/3; Wheelbase: 122 in.; H: 70.3/L: 207/W: 69 in.; Headroom F/R: 6.5/4.5 in.; Legroom F/R: 42/28 in.; Cargo volume: N/A; Fuel tank: 83.3L/regular; Tow limit: 5,000 lb.; Load capacity: 1,554 lb.; Turning circle: 42.6 ft.; Ground clearance: 7.5 in.; Weight: 4,504 lb.; GVWR: 6,051 lb.

offers only medium performance relative to its nearest body-on-frame competitors, the Toyota Tacoma and the Nissan Frontier. Its long wheelbase and independent rear suspension give the Ridgeline an impressive in-bed trunk and excellent road manners, but make it difficult for the truck to traverse anything that's rougher than a stone road or has a breakover angle greater than 21 degrees. NHTSA and IIHS crashworthiness ratings are outstanding.

COST ANALYSIS: Some room for price haggling, mostly on financing and leasing deals. Go for the identical 2012 models and bypass the costlier 2013s. Weak sales have built up dealer inventories, and the general car-buying population hasn't discovered these trucks yet. **Best alternatives:** Other pickups worth considering are the GM Silverado and Sierra duo, and Nissan Frontier. **Options:** Firestone and Bridgestone original-equipment tires will not give you the best performance or durability; try to trade them for something better. **Rebates:** Look for $2,000– $4,000 rebates in the winter of 2012. **Depreciation:** Slower than average; a 2008 model that sold new for $35,000 now costs about $20,000. **Insurance cost:** Higher than average. **Parts supply/cost:** Mostly reasonably priced and easily found at dealers and independent suppliers. Body parts are a bit costly and harder to find. **Annual maintenance cost:** Laughably low. **Warranty:** Bumper-to-bumper 3 years/60,000 km; powertrain 5 years/100,000 km; rust perforation 6 years/unlimited km. **Supplementary warranty:** A waste of money. Very few safety-related incidents have been reported to NHTSA federal investigators or by *Consumer Reports* members within the last four model years. Also, internal manufacturer service bulletins show no major failure trends. **Highway/city fuel economy:** 9.8/14.1 L/100 km, 29/20 mpg.

OWNER-REPORTED PROBLEMS: None that are significant; mostly minor fit and finish flaws.

SERVICE BULLETIN-REPORTED PROBLEMS: N/A.

Hyundai

Hyundai and its Kia lineup are racking up impressive sales across Canada for three reasons: Their vehicles are relatively cheap when compared with the competition, their quality is almost equal to the best that comes from Japan, and owners can count on getting a comprehensive base warranty that other companies don't offer. The company is on a much surer footing than it was in the late '70s, when Hyundai Canada made money by dumping cheap, poor-quality Pony, Stellar, and Excel compacts into the market to compete against equally poor-quality American small cars. At that time, Hyundai got an important toehold in the North American market because Detroit iron was too expensive and not very fuel-efficient and fuel prices were going through the roof. However, when fuel became relatively cheap again, you couldn't give a Hyundai away.

Korean Quality?

No kidding. Hyundai car quality over the past several decades has gone from risible to reliable, except for some redesigned models like the glitch-ridden 2011 Sonata. This general quality turnaround has been accomplished through the use of better-made components and corporate espionage. Hyundai hired away a bevy of Toyota's top quality-control engineers in 2003—and got a satchel-full of Toyota's secret documents in the bargain. Following a cease-and-desist letter from Toyota in 2006, Hyundai returned the pilfered papers and assured Toyota that they never looked at the secret reports stolen from the company (wink, wink; nudge, nudge). Industry insiders say the privileged information was a major factor in Hyundai's leapfrogging the competition with better quality-control systems.

It's ironic, too, that Hyundai and Kia have copied the marketing strategy employed by Japanese automakers since the early '70s: Secure a solid beachhead in one car segment, like the Accent econocar, and then branch out from there with new models like the Elantra compact and the Genesis sports coupe and sedan.

Hyundai Pony

Hyundai Genesis

"The $4,750 entry-level Pony was undoubtedly cheap and generally 'craptastic', but it was a beginning. I knew a guy who drove one—and to say it was less than reliable would be an understatement." (See "Hyundai Pony, 1984-87" at *www.autos.ca/forum/index.php?topic=73546.0*.) On the other hand, *Consumer Reports* loves the Hyundai Genesis, which today costs seven times the original price of a Pony. Says *CR*: "This upscale sedan delivers virtually everything a $50,000 sedan does, but for $10,000 less."

Hyundai redesigns its lineup every three years. Models that don't sell, like the Entourage minivanand Elantra, get dumped. Hyundai is also sharing components with its Kia subsidiary to keep production costs down while raising Kia quality (yes, *Consumer Reports* now recommends the Kia Forte, Soul, and Sorento).

Has the quality bubble burst?

Unfortunately, all is not rosy for Hyundai from a quality perspective. Its redesigned 2011 Sonata (the Kia Optima is the same car with different badging) is a mess—a potentially lethal mess—with 611 safety-related complaints reported to NHTSA (a hundred complaints would be the norm after two years on the market).

So far the 2012 Sonata has only 67 safety-related incidents reported to NHTSA, indicating that Hyundai is quietly correcting most of its first-year redesign screw-ups. Owners of 2011–12s decry sudden, unintended acceleration, malfunctioning powertrains, headlights that give inadequate lighting, and steering malfunctions that drive the Sonata to one side of the road or the other:

The reworked 2011 Sonata has been a quality nightmare, yet Hyundai's Kia Optima, a Sonata clone, has escaped the Sonata's curse. Will Hyundai learn from Kia and correct its mistakes? Wait and see.

2012 Sonata will not drive straight, it pulls to the left mostly but also to the right. Basically the car swerves all over the road, especially at higher speeds. I took it back to the dealership and they told me all foreign cars drive like this. They adjusted the tire pressure but that did not solve the problem. I do not feel safe driving the car. Hyundai issued a service campaign to fix the 2011 Sonatas for this exact problem, why can't they just do the same for the 2012s?

•

After purchasing the car new in Sept of 2011, we received notice from Hyundai advising of recall due to pulling while driving. We contacted the local dealer multiple times and were advised they were waiting on the technical specification on how to fix the problem. This has continued since November of 2011 (letter written June 12, 2012). The driving condition of the car has continued to decline and has even caused the front two tires excessive wear. The front tires already need replacement. The car drifts off to the right severely when you release the steering wheel, causing fatiguing of the arms due to continued correction of the steering.

To a lesser degree, similar safety problems (notably, steering malfunctions) have affected the Elantra. Could it be that Hyundai is following Toyota and Honda production practices a little too closely and is giving owners less content for more money?

During 2012, the South Koreans continued to invest heavily in North America as they trolled for dealers recently dumped by the bankrupt Chrysler and General Motors. They have brought out an extensive lineup of fuel-efficient new cars, minivans, and SUVs, and are targeting increasingly upscale customers without forgetting their entry-level base. For example, Hyundai has enhanced its luxury lineup with the Genesis luxury sedan and the Genesis Coupe, a Camaro/Mustang stalker. The 2012 Equus is a $64,499 (now worth $10,000 less, used) V8-powered rear-drive luxury sedan aimed squarely at the BMW 5 Series and the Mercedes-Benz E-Class. Equus was developed on the rear-drive Genesis sedan platform, but the wheelbase was stretched by 10.9 cm (4.3 in.). It's 29 cm (11.4 in.) longer than the 2010 Mercedes E-Class.

At the other end of the fuel economy spectrum, both Hyundai and Kia are focusing on fuel-frugal small cars and plan to offer drivers fuel-saving options that include smaller engines, direct-injection gasoline engines, plug-in hybrids, and fuel cell technology. Hyundai calls the fuel economy initiative "Blue Drive"—a fancy name for cheaper models with less content, less weight, and more miles per gallon. For example, Blue Edition models have a lower gear ratio and tires with less rolling resistance. Power windows and door locks, as well as other formerly standard amenities, will become optional, thereby trading convenience for cash savings.

Hyundai is also giving each Sonata a Blue Link communications system that provides a direct connection to emergency services in the event of an accident. The feature also gives traffic and weather updates and allows owners easy access to roadside assistance. Smartphones can be connected with Blue Link to help owners locate their vehicle in large shopping malls or to follow "Junior" when he takes the car out on the weekend. The system can keep track of where the vehicle is being driven and how fast it's going.

Unless it's a 2011 Sonata, which likely hadn't gone anywhere, having taken up permanent residence in the dealer's repair bay.

ACCENT ★★★★

RATING: This year's Accent has been upgraded to an Above Average buy. **Road performance:** Good engine and automatic transmission performance in most situations; easy handling; a reasonably comfortable and quiet ride; a relaxed driving position with good visibility. Some drivers feel the engine could use a bit more torque and noise-vibration dampening and that the ride is a bit on the firm, jittery side. **Strong points:** Well-appointed, with nicely laid-out controls; a fair amount of interior room in the front; comfortable and height-adjustable, form-fitting bucket seats that provide plenty of support; an incredibly good reliability

KEY FACTS

Canadian Price (negotiable): *Hatchback L:* $13,699, *Auto:* $14,899, *Sedan L:* $13,299, *Auto:* $14,499, *GL:* $15,199, *Auto:* $16,399, *GLS:* $18,249 **U.S. Price:** *GLS:* $14,545 (plus $1,200 for an automatic transmission), *GS:* $14,795 ($1,000 more for an automatic tranny), *SE:* $16,095 (again, $1,000 more for an automatic gearbox) **Canadian Freight:** $1,495 **U.S. Freight:** $775
POWERTRAIN (FRONT-DRIVE)
Engine: 1.6L 4-cyl. (138 hp); Transmissions: 6-speed man. • 6-speed auto.
DIMENSIONS/CAPACITY (SEDAN)
Passengers: 2/3; Wheelbase: 101.2 in.; H: 57.1/L: 172/W: 66.9 in.; Headroom F/R: 4.5/2.0 in.; Legroom F/R: 41.8/33.3 34.3 in.; Cargo volume: 13.7 cu. ft.; Fuel tank: 43L/regular; Tow limit: N/A; Load capacity: 850 lb.; Turning circle: 34.1 ft.; Ground clearance: 5.5 in.; Weight: *L:* 2,396; *auto.:* 2,462 lb.

record, with few complaints relative to safety or quality control; and it's cheap on gas. **Weak points:** Acrobatic rear-seat entry/exit with the hatchback; cramped rear seating; and some noise intrusion into the cabin. **Safety:** NHTSA crash tests give the 2013 Accent four stars for frontal, side, and rollover crash protection. IIHS rated the 2012 Accent as "Good" in all crash scenarios. **New for 2013:** Nothing important.

ALERT! Insist upon a spare tire instead of a tire repair kit, and keep the car in the garage if you live in a woodsy area: Rodents see your yummy wiring insulation as Tim Hortons take out.

OVERVIEW: Hyundai has transformed its entry-level Accent into a larger, upscale compact the same way the Civic was incrementally improved and enlarged to join the Accord in the family car class. All of these improvements have added to the Accent's base price over the years, however, it is still one of the cheapest and most reliable feature-laden small cars sold in North America. Carrying a homegrown direct-injection 1.6L 4-cylinder engine coupled to a standard 6-speed manual transmission (the 6-speed automatic is optional), the Accent offers bare-bones motoring, but includes standard features such as a height-adjustable driver's seat, four-wheel disc brakes, active front head restraints, a tilt steering wheel, power locks, CD/MP3 stereo with USB and iPod interface, and floor mats.

COST ANALYSIS: Go for a 2013 model; some of the higher-end versions are less expensive than last year's Accent. **Best alternatives:** Chevrolet Cruze, Honda Fit or Civic (2011), Mazda3, Nissan Versa or Sentra, Suzuki SX4, and Toyota Yaris. **Options:** Not needed. **Rebates:** $1,000–$2,000 through low-cost financing, leasing deals, and discounting. **Depreciation:** Slower than average. **Insurance cost:** Average. **Parts supply/cost:** Parts aren't hard to find, and they're reasonably priced. **Annual maintenance cost:** Average. **Warranty:** Bumper-to-bumper 5 years/100,000 km; rust perforation 5 years/unlimited km. **Supplementary warranty:** No longer needed, such is the improvement in quality control. **Highway/city fuel economy:** *Man.:* 4.9/6.7 L/100 km, 58/42 mpg. *Auto.:* 4.8/7.8 L/100 km, 59/36 mpg.

OWNER-REPORTED PROBLEMS: Airbags failed to deploy; sudden loss of power; owners get a tire repair kit rather than a spare tire (a spare costs extra):

I purchased a 2012 Hyundai Accent 5 door 03/02/2012 and discovered after the purchase there was no spare tire just a repair kit. I was not told before the purchase. Who would even think that a spare was not included? This is a safety issue, especially if you are on the side of the road in the dark and it's inclement weather. The tire kit instructions are also hard to understand…Hyundai's explanation was it was for better mileage and the dealer told me that Hyundai now makes a spare for the 2012 Elantra for a price and the spare for the Accent is in process, once again for a price. Better mileage is great but so is safety.

Tire sidewall failures; steering-wheel lock-up:

While driving my car in a 25 mph [40 km/h] speed limit school zone, my steering wheel locked making it impossible to control my car on what coincidentally was a curvy road after having just made a right turn. Therefore as I had just begun to pick up speed, having to follow a curve about 500 yards thereafter, my steering wheel remained in the position I had placed it in order to follow the curve, locking immediately after. In losing control of my car, my initial reaction was to try to shift the steering wheel but as it didn't budge, I hit about 2 or 3 concrete median blocks, at about 15 mph [24 km/h].

One owner reports that groundhogs love to snack on the car's undercarriage cables thereby disabling the tranny and important dash gauges:

I put down moth balls and fox scent to ward the hogs off, but they love Accent wires; losing the transmission and speedometer can make driving a little dangerous.

SERVICE BULLETIN-REPORTED PROBLEMS: Harsh delayed shift diagnosis on the 6-speed automatic transmission. Reducing wind noise from the front door mirror area.

ELANTRA, TOURING ★★★★/★★★

RATING: *Elantra:* Downgraded to Above Average due to the car's severe steering "pull"; *Touring:* Average; also has strong steering pull to one side. **Road performance:** 4-cylinder engine has plenty of pep for daily chores and comes with a smooth-shifting 6-speed automatic transmission; however, the engine feels sluggish when in Active Eco mode, there's excessive engine noise when accelerating, and the steering pulls strongly to one or the other side. Good handling and a comfortable ride; electronic stability control comes with the SE trim. *Touring:* This compact wagon handles well and has excellent braking. Not as good a performer as the Elantra, though. First and second gear are too far apart, the ride is quite firm, there's little steering feedback, and engine noise invades the cabin. **Strong points:** The 2011 revamping gave the car a more fluid, stylish exterior and a well-appointed and spacious interior; comfortable seats; the seatback slides far back enough to easily accommodate drivers over six feet tall; and a classy, quiet interior. *Touring:* A compact wagon with a spacious, versatile interior. **Weak points:** Noisy brakes are sometimes a bit grabby and take some

The Hyundai Elantra.

KEY FACTS

Canadian Price (negotiable): *L:* $15,949, *L auto.:* $17,149, *GL:* $18,249, *GL auto.:* $19,449, *GLS man.:* $19,949, *GLS auto.:* $21,149, *Limited:* $23,199, *GLS Limited/Navigation:* $25,199, *GT GL man.:* $19,149, *GT GL auto.:* $20,349, *GT GLS man.:* $21,349, *GT GLS auto.:* $22,549, *GT SE auto.:* $24,349, *GT SE TECH:* $26,349, *Touring GL man.:* $18,199, *Touring GL auto.:* $19,399, *Touring GLS man.:* $20,649, *Touring GL auto.:* $21,849 **U.S. Price:** *GLS auto.:* $17,995, *Limited:* $20,945, *GS Coupe:* $17,445, *SE Coupe:* $19,745, *GT man.:* $18,395, *GT auto.:* $19,395 **Canadian Freight:** $1,495 **U.S. Freight:** $775

POWERTRAIN (FRONT-DRIVE)
Engine: 1.8L 4-cyl. (148 hp); Transmissions: 6-speed man. • 6-speed auto.
DIMENSIONS/CAPACITY (TOURING)
Passengers: 2/3; Wheelbase: 106.3 in.; H: 56.5/L: 178.3/W: 69.9 in.; Headroom F/R: 2.5/2.0 in.; Legroom F/R: 43.6/33.1 in.; Cargo volume: 14.8 cu. ft.; Fuel tank: 48L/regular; Tow limit: 2,000 lb.; Load capacity: 850 lb.; Turning circle: 34.8 ft.; Ground clearance: 5.5 in., Weight: 2,701 lb.

skill to modulate; a bit too much wind and road noise; and the dash vents would be more effective if they were mounted higher. *Touring:* Fuel economy isn't as good as the Elantra. **Safety:** NHTSA gives the 2013 model five stars for side crash protection and four stars for frontal and rollover occupant protection. NHTSA rated the 2011 Touring version four stars for rollover resistance. IIHS ranks the 2012 "Good" for occupant protection in all types of collisions. Large blind spots caused by the left and right front pillars:

> This car has large blind spots caused by both the left and right front pillars. The positioning of the rear view mirror only makes the right blind spot larger as there is only the space from the bottom of the mirror to the right pillar to view outside of the car. As a result, I almost hit someone crossing the street from my right to my left. Thankfully, I saw them in time to apply my brakes. This happens frequently with the car. And, at

intersections where there is a four-way stop or, when I am entering the lane, I can often not see a car coming from either direction.

New for 2013: A 2013 Elantra GT hatchback will replace the Touring wagon and the Limited gets a standard power driver seat, a feature that wasn't available last year. An upgraded steering system lets drivers choose between normal, sport, and comfort settings.

ALERT! No need for optional equipment; Elantra comes with all the right standard features, including air conditioning, cruise control, telescoping steering wheel, UV windshield glass, and 16-inch wheels. One feature that may be missing is a spare tire. Check it out:

> Spare tire not included with new vehicle—side wall puncture on freeways or rural/ mountain roads will create a personal safety hazard.

OVERVIEW: Elantra's sharp new styling is hard to miss and its roomy interior pushes the car into the mid-size category. A wagon version, called the Touring, arrived in early 2009. A 148 hp 1.8L 4-cylinder engine is coupled to a 6-speed manual or automatic transmission.

COST ANALYSIS: The 2013 is the better buy, considering that its additional standard features balance out most of this year's price increase. **Best alternatives:** The Chevrolet Cruze, Honda Accord or Civic (2011), Mazda3, Suzuki SX4, and Toyota Corolla. **Options:** Go for the automatic transmission: It's quieter and has smoother shifting than the manual, and fuel economy isn't much affected. **Rebates:** $2,000 rebates and low-cost financing. **Depreciation:** Slower than average, which is surprising because it's not often that you see a 2009 South Korean vehicle (Elantra L) worth more than half its $15,845 original price. **Insurance cost:** Average. **Parts supply/cost:** Parts are easy to find and reasonably priced, with heavy discounting by independents. **Annual maintenance cost:** Average. **Warranty:** Bumper-to-bumper 5 years/100,000 km; rust perforation 5 years/unlimited km. **Supplementary warranty:** Not needed. **Highway/city fuel economy:** *1.8L man.:* 4.9/6.8 L/100 km, 58/42 mpg. *Auto.:* 4.9/69 L/100 km, 58/41 mpg. *Touring 2.0L man.:* 6.4/8.9 L/100 km, 44/32 mpg. *Touring auto.:* 6.5/8.7 L/100 km, 43/32 mpg.

OWNER-REPORTED PROBLEMS: Sudden engine shutdown on the highway; hood suddenly flew up while vehicle was underway; dangerous airbag deployment:

> Drivers side air bag deployed and metal bracket deployed with air bag from headliner area, also. It sliced my ear in half…Could have been my neck…

Airbags failed to deploy:

> My wife and I were involved in an accident. Another car ran the red light and hit us. My wife and I were injured and our car was totaled. None of the airbags went off on

our brand new Hyundai Elantra. We were later told by Hyundai that passenger airbags don't always go off because of weight variations in some adults. My wife is 5'4" and her weight is normal for her height.

In another incident, both airbags deployed for no reason; airbag warning light and tire-pressure monitoring system alert come on for no reason; sudden, unintended acceleration accompanied by loss of braking capability; cruise control suddenly resets itself to a higher speed; throttle sensor sticks when cruising; automatic transmission jumps out of gear. Complete electrical shutdown:

Traveling on interstate, vehicle suddenly jerked (as if I hit something on the road), complete electrical failure. Dash, radio, navigation, power steering went dead. A few seconds later power came back while vehicle was still rolling and was able to restart by depressing brake and "start/stop" button. A few minutes later while traveling at lower speed, the event repeated. This time power would not return.

Defective solenoids blamed for early transmission failures; car may roll away even with emergency brake applied; faulty electronic stability control:

Dry day, normal acceleration, traction control killed power upon entering highway traffic, leaving us sitting in 50–55 mph [80–89 km/h] traffic, then cleared up, twice within 3 hours. Also on same day, 60 mph [97 km/h] on a two-lane road, the skid control light came on and applied the left front brake pulling me into oncoming traffic, The Skid Control light came on then went back out both times. One failure seemed to be the traction control, the other was the skid control. I suspect a bad wheel speed sending unit.

Transmission malfunctions:

Transmission would not shift properly out of 1st gear. RPMs and engine continued to operate, but transmission was continuing to grind, bang, jump and not shift. Drove car to dealership at roughly 15 mph. Car continued to balk and jump. A new transmission was ordered and replaced. Interesting to know if other 2011 and 2012 owners have had same problem. May lead to a total recall of the automatic transmissions.

Sudden steering lock-up; the car continually pulls to the right or left when cruising or when coming to a stop:

My car began pulling strongly to the left at various speeds. I contacted the dealership and arranged to have them look at it. Our dealership first suggested a roadforce balance and wheel alignment and wanted to charge us $250. Since the car had recently been to them for service including tire balancing and rotation, I pushed back and refused this suggested remedy. I had read online how people were experiencing this "pulling" problem. It does make your arms tired fighting to stay on the road. I called the dealership management and informed them of the identical complaints I was finding online. To the manager and our salesman's credit, they made the service dept look harder. A thorough inspection found that the steering "toe" was not calibrated properly. It should have been at zero (0), but instead was at +1. The service department reset the toe back to zero. Everything has been fine so far (2 weeks).

•

Purchased Elantra 3 days ago and noticed car pulling to left. On highway especially nearly went off road, veered into other lanes. Must keep constant pressure on wheel, wants to pull away if hand pressure releases. Car at 200 miles went to dealer after 2 days, they acted surprised as if they never heard of it happening. Dealership looked at car (2 hours) stated they centered the steering wheel? and did an alignment. During test drive later with mechanic, car veered to left constantly and nearly went off the road several times when I let go of steering wheel. Mechanic reported that car performed within standards.

•

While driving on straight roads the vehicle veers hard towards the right. We have to fight to keep it on the road. It feels like we are driving on a slippery icy road, always steering the car back and forth in order to keep it on the road. It is physically exhausting driving this car, hanging on hard to the steering wheel to keep it out of the ditch. Dealership claims nothing is wrong with electronic steering.

Brakes freeze up when vehicle is driven through snow; a history of front windshield cracks; Continental, Kumho Solus, and Hankook original equipment tires are noted for sidewall failures ("bubbling"). Elantra owners consider the lack of a spare tire and canned air in the trunk to be unsafe practices:

Car dealers are allowed to sell new cars with no spare tire or jack. Their policy is to only include a can of air which may or may not work when needed. They are also not keeping replacement tires in stock. This can of air is a hazard to keep in a car in Arizona when the temperatures in the summer reach 115 degrees [46°C]. And with the dealership not stocking the tires, my car was not drivable and strands the motorist.

SERVICE BULLETIN-REPORTED PROBLEMS: Free rear door harness and centre muffler rattle noise repair; excessive driveshaft noise (creaking or popping); troubleshooting an automatic transmission that stays in Third gear, goes into "failsafe mode," or has an illuminated MIL alert; and touch screen recalibration.

SONATA ★★

RATING: Below Average. Like Honda, Hyundai cars don't tolerate redesigns very well (see "Owner-Reported Problems"). Nevertheless, it looks like Hyundai has been diligent in correcting most 2011 factory-induced deficiencies. If the company continues to clean up its redesigned rubbish and compensates owners 100 percent for their repairs and inconvenience, *Lemon-Aid* will upgrade Sonata's rating—next year. **Road performance:** Sizzling, smooth V6 performance; acceptable handling; and a comfortable ride. The suspension is somewhat bouncy and noisy;

KEY FACTS

Canadian Price (negotiable): *GL:* $22,699, *GL auto.:* $24,299, *GLS auto.:* $26,499, *Limited:* $29,899, *2.0T Limited:* $31,799 *Hybrid:* $28,999 **U.S. Price:** *GLS auto.:* $20,895, *SE:* $23,34, *SE 2.0T:* $24,895, *Limited:* $25,845, *2.0T Limited:* $28,095, *Hybrid:* $25,795 **Canadian Freight:** $1,565 **U.S. Freight:** $760

POWERTRAIN (FRONT-DRIVE)

Engines: 2.4L 4-cyl. (198 hp) • 2.0L 4-cyl. turbo (274 hp); Transmissions: 6-speed man. • 6-speed auto.

DIMENSIONS/CAPACITY

Passengers: 2/3; Wheelbase: 110 in.; H: 57.9/L: 189: 8/W: 72.2 in.; Headroom F/R: 3.0/3.0 in.; Legroom F/R: 45.5/34.6 in.; Cargo volume: 16.4 cu. ft.; Fuel tank: 70L/regular; Tow limit: N/A; Load capacity: 860 lb.; Turning circle: 35.8 ft.; Ground clearance: 5.5 in.; Weight: 3,161–3,316 lb.

there's too much body lean under hard cornering; and the steering lacks sufficient feedback. **Strong points:** A credible alternative to most Detroit-bred family cars. V6 engine burns only a bit more gas than the 4-banger does. Well-equipped and stylish; user-friendly controls and gauges; spacious trunk, a conveniently low lift-in height; and the fairly quiet cabin comfortably seats three in the back. The standard Blue Link communications feature is part "Big Brother" and part emergency caller. **Weak points:** Quality, judging from the 2012's upward swing, is improving. Still, the problems reported are worrisome because many have been carried over from the 2011 model redesign; prices have been boosted thousands of dollars during the past few years without any real justification; and fuel economy could be better. **Safety:** NHTSA awarded the 2013 Sonata five stars for side and rollover crashworthiness and four stars for frontal occupant safety. IIHS says the Sonata deserves a "Good" rating for front offset protection, head-restraint effectiveness, roof crush-resistance, and side-impact protection. Poor left-side visibility out of the front windshield due to the position of the rear-view mirror. Excessive steering wander and severe pulling to the left or right continue to plague these cars. **New for 2013:** The manual transmission has been dropped.

ALERT! Dealer will likely try to pawn off on you original equipment Hankook tires. Don't take them. They are prone to sidewall bubbling that is often blamed on driver error in hitting road debris, potholes, etc. Also, check out front left side visibility and the headlight intensity:

The consumer stated the low beams did not project adequately when driving up and down hills and driving around curves. The low beam headlight projection decreased up to 50% and sometimes more than 50% depending on the size of the hill or curve.

OVERVIEW: This mid-sized sedan is a *Consumer Reports* top-rated pick and its sales, particularly since the 2011 redesign, have been spectacular. Unfortunately, the car is not reliable, nor is it safe to drive, judging from owner experiences with the 2011 version.

How could *CR* miss this? Probably because they did not compare their annual member survey comments with government NHTSA safety failure reports, nor with Hyundai's own confidential service bulletins.

Until the 2011 model was redesigned, only a few dozen owner complaints would appear on NHTSA's safety database each year. For example, the 2010 model has 39 incidents reported where the two-year norm would be a hundred reports. Contrast that with the redesigned 2011 model's profile: up through July 2012, that model year alone elicited 601 safety-related reports posted on NHTSA's website at *www-odi.nhtsa.dot.gov/complaints/results.cfm*. In the past, incremental powertrain, performance, safety, convenience, and styling changes were quickly corrected by Hyundai without provoking such large-scale owner dissatisfaction.

Is Hyundai fixing the above mentioned safety deficiencies? Apparently, yes, partly. The 2012 Sonata has been the object of only 68 safety reports, almost average for one year of use. Does that mean we go out and risk buying a 2012 or 2013?

No. Be patient. It is too early to judge how thorough Hyundai has been in "debugging" its 2011 changes.

In fact, a large number of the 68 safety complaint on the 2012 Sonata concern—you guessed it—excessive steering wander and severe pulling to the right or left. This is in spite of a recall to fix the defect. For five years, Honda and Toyota swept these problems under the rug (or, with Toyota runaway acceleration, under the floor mat). But most of the time, these redesign-related screwups were corrected in the next three-year redesign. In the interim, failures are usually fixed through secret warranties, as was the policy of Honda and Toyota. This is what Hyundai will likely do.

Styled similarly to the Honda Accord, the redesigned Sonata meets or exceeds the engine performance standards of its competitors, although its fuel economy isn't as good. The Sonata rides on a double-wishbone front suspension and a multi-link rear suspension that is more softly sprung than usual, making the car a bit "bouncier" than its competitors.

Hyundai has added standard safety features that have proven their worth. For example, this year's model includes four-wheel ABS; stability and traction control; front and side curtain airbags; front and rear seat belt pretensioners; an integrated rear child safety seat; and a "smart" passenger-side airbag that won't deploy if the passenger weighs less than 30 kg (66 lb.). Well, at least that's the theory—in practice, owners report the airbag in previous year models often switched itself off, no matter what the passenger's weight.

COST ANALYSIS: Stay away from the 2011–13 models, no matter how cheap a leftover may be. You are likely to spend your savings in the service bay, or in an emergency room. Instead, wait a year or so for the 2013's problems to be fixed. Remember, it took Honda two model years to get the Accord back on track and we are still keeping our fingers crossed. **Best alternatives:** The Chevrolet Cruze, Honda Accord, Hyundai Elantra, Nissan Sentra, Mazda5 or Mazda6, and Toyota Camry. **Options:** Choose the V6 engine for better performance and handling; you will lose only a bit of fuel economy. If you get the 4-banger, keep in mind that good fuel economy means putting up with more engine noise. Be wary of the sunroof; it eats up a lot of headroom and has a history of leaking. Hankook tires? I think not. **Rebates:** As you get into the new year, expect $3,000 rebates and zero percent financing or attractive leasing deals on all models. **Depreciation:** Average; a $26,000 2010 GLS Sonata is now worth about $12,500. **Insurance cost:** Average. **Parts supply cost:** Easy to find and relatively inexpensive. **Annual maintenance cost:** Average. **Warranty:** Bumper-to-bumper 5 years/100,000 km; rust perforation 5 years/unlimited km. **Supplementary warranty:** Not needed. **Highway/city fuel economy:** *Auto. 2.0L:* 6.0/9.3 L/100 km, 47/30 mpg. *Man. 2.4L:* 5.7/8.7 L/100 km, 50/32 mpg. *Auto. 2.4L:* 5.7/9.4 L/100 km, 50/30 mpg. *Hybrid:* 4.6/5.5 L/100 km, 61/51 mpg.

OWNER-REPORTED PROBLEMS: Sudden, unintended acceleration when passing other cars; same thing happens when shifting to Reverse; cruise control resets itself to a higher speed; sudden hybrid engine failure due to water intrusion in rainy weather:

> Engine can easily become hydro-locked in heavy rain and road splash-back from other vehicles due to the design of the direct air intake of the Sonata Hybrid. With its design, it does not have any water baffles to prevent water from entering the air filter and once it enters the air filter box, there are no drain holes for it to drain out. This forces the water through the engine as that is the only way for it to get out of the filter box.

> When the engine stalled, no electronic control warning lights were illuminated and the car remained in the "ready" state. This could lead to damage of the HEV system and battery pack. Per the technician servicing the car, they stated that the HEV warning light only illuminated when the HEV battery reaches 15% charge (the point at which they have to replace it).

> This contradicts with the owner's manual as well as counteracts the purpose of a warning lamp. Due to the nature of the design where the computer controls when the engine starts/stops, the engine can damage itself before preventative action can be taken. For example, when the engine stalls due to water ingestion through the air filter and the oxygen sensor determines it cannot compensate, the engine will stall, but before the

situation can be rectified, the computer attempted to restart the engine causing it to become hydro-locked.

Sudden electrical shutdown; passenger side airbag disabled when normal-sized adult occupies the seat; airbags fail to deploy in a high-speed collision; parked vehicle rolled downhill, even though transmission was left in Drive; manual transmission lunges forward when shifting from First to Second gear; poorly-located cruise control Resume button inadvertently activates the feature:

> While using the cruise control the car leaped ahead several times after I had applied the brake (because I was getting too close to the car in front of me) and was temporarily handling speed without the cruise control. Nearly had an accident on two such occasions. Then I figured out what was happening. The "resume" button is so close to the rim of the wheel, and so exposed that the heel of my right hand was touching it inadvertently and the cruise control reengaged when I didn't want it to and didn't know it was happening. [In my opinion,] your button needs to be relocated or protected by a ridge.

Vehicle pulls sharply to the left or right when accelerating, requiring constant correction.

The relative of a driver who died when her 2011 Sonata inexplicably ran into the left-side guardrail believes the car may have been at fault; a recent 2012 model incident shows the safety hazard has been carried over to the latest models:

> There are numerous complaints about the power steering of 2011 Sonatas on various websites. One of them is the website of auto recalls for consumers (*www.argc.org/complaints/2011/Hyundai/Sonata/steering/problem.aspx*). 117 out of 266 complaints (67%) on 6/12/2011 are related to the steering column. This is a safety concern, because it pulls the vehicle to the left stronger and stronger as the speed accelerates above 25 mph [40 km/h].

·

> I purchased a 2012 Sonata in late June. Technically this is the second one I purchased. I can explain it this way. The first one I bought had a horrible pulling issue. It pulled right aggressively. Before I took delivery I test drove it and had the salesman drive with me. Even he said this is dangerous and not right. The dealership put it in the shop and they said they fixed it with an alignment. I test drove it again and it was even worse. I refused to buy that car. They found me another one. At first it seemed to drive fine on the test drive. I should have driven it more than a couple blocks. Same issue as the first one after I took delivery. The car pulled and still pulls right, especially at highway speeds. Borderline dangerous on the highway. So, the dealership took it in again and worked the camber. Unpredictable....There are people all over the country having the same problem with the 2012 Sonata steering. Some Sonata techs say it's the same problem they had in 2011 when the recall was announced.

Premature wearout of the rear brakes; noisy shocks/struts; low-beam headlights give inadequate illumination:

There is a sharp boundary between headlight illumination on the lower area and darkness above. On all but level roadway, this hazardous defect is apparent. Many roads where I live in Pennsylvania are twisting and hilly. Traversing those roads with this Sonata using the low-beam headlights [is] unnerving and dangerous. When the front of the car dips into even a slight downgrade, the road ahead is illuminated to about 40 feet [12 m] in front of car. Line of sight through windshield has at least half the view unlit.

Left tail light fell out of its mounting inside the trunk due to the plastic mount crumbling; rear windshield exploded after door was closed; Hankook original equipment tires continue to fail due to sidewall bubbling; sun visors are not long enough (vertically) to keep sun from blinding the driver; the horn is weak, makes a short sound, and sometimes won't sound at all:

Wife activated the horn to get my attention. It sounded one short beep and went dead. Has not worked since. Horn can hardly be heard standing next to the car let alone trying to get someone's attention inside a vehicle with the windows rolled up and the radio on....There are hundreds of complaints about the sound or failure of these horns on the Internet forums.

Hard starts, no-starts:

The only reliable solution for starting the car is to depress the brake pedal and depress the Engine Start button for a minimum of 10 seconds. I've placed the key fob in several locations in the car (dashboard, cup holder, smart key holder) with no repeatable success. After a visit to the dealership, they cannot find a problem. However, a search on the Internet shows other owners experiencing the same problem.

SERVICE BULLETIN-REPORTED PROBLEMS: Automatic transmission malfunctions caused by faulty solenoids and other electronic failures. The transmission may shift harshly, drop into a "safe" default mode, or hesitate between shifts.

GENESIS COUPE, SEDAN ★★★★★

RATING: Upgraded to Recommended. The Genesis coupe and sedan are impressive upscale rear drive vehicles with different performance characteristics and widely varying retail prices. **Road performance:** The 3.8L engine gives breathtaking power to the coupe and quick acceleration when used with the sedan, although the sedan's 5.0L V8 is a real tire burner. The coupe's 4-cylinder turbo is both noisy and hooked to an imprecise 6-speed manual transmission; the optional 4.6L V8 is like having a sixth finger: It's there, but not all that useful. Expect the coupe to have a choppy, stiff ride, while the sedan has some body roll in hard cornering due to its more supple, "floaty" suspension (Infiniti and BMW models have stiffer suspensions that produce a more-secure feeling.) **Strong points:** Well-appointed, first-class interior fit and finish; a quiet, vibration-free, and spacious cabin; and clear and easy-to-read gauges. The sedan has plenty of room fore and aft and has posted impressive crashworthiness rankings. **Weak points:** Cramped rear seating

The Hyundai Genesis Coupe.

with the coupe; navigation and audio system controls are cumbersome. Hyundai recommends premium fuel for extra horsepower from the 4.6L V8, but it's not worth the higher fuel cost for just a few more horses. V6 reliability is above average; V8s are average. Actual fuel consumption is much higher than advertised. **Safety:** NHTSA gave the 2011–13 models five stars for rollover resistance. The 2010 coupe and sedan were given the top, five-star rating for front, side, and rollover occupant protection; IIHS frontal offset, side-impact, roof, and head-restraint protection were rated "Good" on the 2012 models. Strategically placed crumple zones, six airbags, and side-impact door beams enhance crashworthiness. Plus, there's a full complement of active safety features including electronic stability control and traction control. Rear seatbelts may be poorly-designed:

The rear center seat belt anchor and the left seat belt anchor are reversed. When one passenger fastens their seatbelt it covers the anchor point for the other passenger. The only way to connect both is to twist the seat belts across each other. In the event of an accident, the applied forces would not be in line with the seat belt anchor points and would most likely not conform to the intended designs parameters.

The Hyundai dealer has looked at the problem and agrees that the anchor points are backwards. Thus far Hyundai has refused to acknowledge that there is any problem.

KEY FACTS

Canadian Price (negotiable): *Coupe 2.0T:* $26,499, *auto.:* $28,299, *2.0T GT man.:* $31,149, *2.0T R-SPEC man.:* $28,799, *3.8 man.:* $32,999, *3.8 GT man.:* $36,999, *auto.:* $38,799, *Sedan:* $39,999 **U.S. Price:** *Coupe 2.0T:* $24,250, *R-SPEC:* $26,500, *2.0T Premium:* $28,750, *3.8 R-SPEC:* $28,750, *3.8 Grand Touring:* $32,000, *3.8 Track:* $33,000, *Sedan:* $34,200 **Canadian Freight:** *Coupe:* $1,565, *Sedan:* $1,760 **U.S. Freight:** $875

POWERTRAIN (REAR-DRIVE)
Engines: 2.0L Turbo 4-cyl. (274 hp) • 3.8L V6 (348 hp) • 4.6L V8 (378 hp) • 5.0L V8 (429 hp); Transmissions: 6-speed man. • 6-speed manumatic • 8-speed manumatic

DIMENSIONS/CAPACITY (COUPE)
Passengers: 2/3; Wheelbase: 115.6 in.; H: 58.3/L: 195.6/W: 73.4 in.; Headroom: N/A; Legroom F/R: 44.3/38.6 in.; Cargo volume: 15.9 cu. ft.; Fuel tank: 65L–73L/regular/premium; Tow limit: 5,000 lb.; Ground clearance: 5.2 in.; Load capacity: N/A; Turning circle: 36 ft.; Weight: 3,748 lb.

New for 2013: Restyled to look more aggressive, and the new powertrains pack more punch and a few more gears as well. For example, the Coupe's 3.8L V6 now generates 348 hp and the 2.0T is rated at 274 hp, a 30 percent increase over the previous engine. Cabin amenities have also been improved with easier-to-read gauges and extra seat bolstering.

ALERT! Fuel consumption figures are straight out of Harry Potter; expect to get 20 percent less than what Hyundai promises:

> This vehicle is rated at 20 mpg city, 30 mpg highway. The mileage has consistently been poor. It now has 4,200 miles on it and highway mileage with the cruise control on, in warm weather, with no load other than the driver is around 24 mpg. I had it checked by Hyundai and they replaced the O2 sensor. This improved the highway mileage slightly from 23 to 24 mpg. It has never approached 25 mpg let alone 30 mpg. I have read about others complaining about the poor mileage on 4-cylinder Genesis Coupes. If the mileage ratings had been more accurate I would not have even considered buying this car.

OVERVIEW: Hyundai's Genesis targets BMW and Mercedes-Benz big spenders with its own luxury rear-drive until the Equus gets its footing. The smaller Genesis Coupe was launched in 2010, a year after the sedan, and targets the Chevrolet Camaro, Dodge Challenger, Ford Mustang, and Nissan 370Z.

These luxury cars are loaded with high-tech safety gear that includes ABS, traction control, an anti-skid system, side curtain airbags, front side airbags, and rear side airbags. There's also a heated and cooled driver's seat, wireless cell phone link, a navigation system with a hard drive for storing digital music files, a rear-view camera, and front and rear obstacle detection. A knob in the centre console governs audio, navigation, and other functions.

COST ANALYSIS: Coupe or sedan? Both are excellent buys. Any cheaper 2012 leftovers are not worth the 2013 upgrades you will miss. **Best alternatives:** *Sedan:* The BMW 3 Series, Ford Taurus, Lincoln MKS, Mercedes-Benz E-Class, and Toyota Avalon. *Coupe:* The Chevrolet Camaro and—for sheer sportster thrills without the bills—the Mazda MX-5. **Options:** Rubber floor mats ($90 and $65) and a trunk cargo net ($70) are worth buying from an independent retailer for about half the Hyundai price. **Rebates:** These cars are hot and are likely to stay that way. A $1,000–$1,500 rebate may be offered if Ford and GM cut their pony-car prices, which is doubtful. **Depreciation:** Varies from average to slower than average, depending on whether you buy the coupe or the sedan. For example, a 2010 base Genesis sedan that originally sold for $39,000 is now worth $23,000. The coupe from the same year does better: original selling price was $24,500, value today is $19,500.

Insurance cost: Higher than average. **Parts supply/cost:** Parts are likely to be expensive and in short supply; due to the low volume and warranty, independent suppliers generally don't carry Genesis parts. **Annual maintenance cost:** Should be average. **Warranty:** Bumper-to-bumper 5 years/100,000 km; rust perforation 5 years/unlimited km. **Supplementary warranty:** Not needed. **Highway/city fuel economy:** *Coupe 2.0L man.:* 6.6/10 L/100 km, 43/28 mpg. *Coupe 2.0L auto.:* 6.7/10.5 L/100 km, 42/27 mpg. *Coupe 3.8L man.:* 7.6/12 L/100 km, 37/24 mpg. *3.8L auto.:* 7.3/12.2 L/100 km, 39/26 mpg. *3.8L 8-spd. auto.:* 6.9/11.1 L/100 km, 41/25 mpg. *Sedan 3.8L:* 7.2/11.4 L/100 km, 39/25 mpg. *Sedan 4.6L:* 8.1/12.6 L/100 km, 35/22 mpg. *5.0L 8-spd. auto.:* 8.1/13.1 L/100 km, 41/25 mpg.

OWNER-REPORTED PROBLEMS: Only eight safety-related complaints reported to NHTSA: Cruise control malfunctions; loud manual transmission knocking while the clutch is disengaged and the transmission is in Neutral; three-blink turn signal continues blinking after it is no longer needed; electronic stability control (ESC) locked driver's brakes when he was turning the vehicle; more ESC and Bluetooth malfunctions; early replacement of the automatic transmission; small pebble damaged the AC condenser ($800). *Coupe:* Stalling upon acceleration:

> While trying to normally accelerate, the car virtually died. Acceleration flat spot. Somewhat similar to the old carbureted cars. Very infrequent, however, the other day losing acceleration almost caused a major accident.

Sedan: Sudden, unintended acceleration:

> While attempting to park, the vehicle suddenly accelerated causing the Genesis to crash twice into a parked vehicle and then into a pole.

SERVICE BULLETIN-REPORTED PROBLEMS: A faulty transmission solenoid may activate the Check Engine alert and send the transaxle into "Fail-Safe" limp mode. Harsh, delayed shift diagnosis. Touch screen recalibration. *Coupe:* Sunroof switch replacement campaign. *Sedan:* Troubleshooting speed sensor malfunctions (replace valve body assembly).

TUCSON ★★★★

RATING: Above Average. **Road performance:** V6 engine provides smooth, sustained acceleration; sure-footed (thanks to the standard stability control); and effective, easy-to-modulate braking. Owners report the 4-cylinder engine struggles with a full load, the vehicle isn't as agile as others in its class, and the electric steering feels vague and lacks feedback at highway speeds:

> The electronic power steering feels stuck, vague, and hard. Lacks maneuverability and feedback while driving the vehicle. Feeling the sensation that you will lose control of the vehicle. Vehicle pulls to either the left or right side, giving the impression that you are going to crash. Also it is very difficult to maintain the vehicle aligned on the road; it has to be corrected constantly, requiring more physical effort than normal driving.

Strong points: Reasonably priced and well equipped; has a roomy and easily accessed cabin; and above average reliability. **Weak points:** Stiff-riding; poor

KEY FACTS

Canadian Price (negotiable): *L man.:* $19,999, *auto.:* $22,899, *GL auto.:* $24,599, *GL AWD:* $26,599, *GLS:* $26,899, *GLS AWD:* $28,899, *Limited AWD:* $32,349, *Limited AWD Navi.:* $34,349 **U.S. Price:** *GL:* $20,070, *GLS:* $23,420, *Limited AWD:* $26,270
Canadian Freight: $1,595
U.S. Freight: $825
POWERTRAIN (FRONT-DRIVE/AWD)
Engines: 2.0L 4-cyl. (165 hp) • 2.4L 4-cyl. (176 hp); Transmissions: 5-speed man. • 6-speed manumatic
DIMENSIONS/CAPACITY
Passengers: 2/3; Wheelbase: 103.9 in.; H: 65.2/L: 173.2/W: 71.7 in.; Headroom F/R: 5.0/4.0 in.; Legroom F/R: 41.2/38.7 in.; Cargo volume: 25.7 cu. ft.; Fuel tank: 58L/regular; Tow limit: 1,000–2,000 lb.; Load capacity: 860 lb.; Turning circle: 34.7 ft.; Ground clearance: 6.7 in.; Weight: 3,139–3,488 lb.

styling limits cargo space; rear seat needs more bolstering for thigh support; some road noise; and expected fuel economy doesn't materialize. **Safety:** NHTSA gave the 2013 Tucson a five-star crashworthiness rating for side-impact occupant protection and a four-star rating for frontal and rollover protection. The 2012 Tucson was a top-scorer with the IIHS after earning a "Good" designation for frontal offset, side, rear, and roof crashworthiness. **New for 2013:** Carried over relatively unchanged; 2014 model to be restyled.

ALERT! Does the car's rear styling cut your rearward visibility too much? Test the 4-cylinder engine for merging and steep grade performance. Also, check the steering performance and look for excessive road wander.

OVERVIEW: The Tucson is Hyundai's compact crossover that was first introduced for the 2005 model year. It is smaller than the Santa Fe and built on the same Elantra-based platform as the Kia Sportage. The optional all-wheel-drive system can send 99 percent of the power to the front wheels or split the traction between the front and rear wheels.

COST ANALYSIS: Buy a 10 percent cheaper second series 2012; it's practically identical to this year's version and there are plenty of leftovers. **Best alternatives:** The Honda CR-V and Toyota RAV4. **Options:** Nothing important. **Rebates:** Expect $2,000 discounts, zero percent financing, and attractive leasing deals on all models in early 2013. **Depreciation:** Less than average. A 2009 base Tucson originally sold for $21,195; today, it is worth $15,000. **Insurance cost:** Average. **Parts supply/cost:** Easy to find and relatively inexpensive. **Annual maintenance cost:** Less than average. **Warranty:** Bumper-to-bumper 5 years/100,000 km; rust perforation 5 years/unlimited km. **Supplementary warranty:** Not needed. **Highway/city fuel economy:** 2.0L man.: 7.4/10.1 L/100 km, 38/28 mpg. *Auto.:* 6.5/9.1 L/100 km, 43/31 mpg. 2.4L man.: 6.9/10 L/100 km, 41/28 mpg. *Auto:* 6.3/9.5 L/100 km, 45/30 mpg. 4WD auto.: 7.1/10 L/100 km, 40/28 mpg.

OWNER-REPORTED PROBLEMS: Firewall insulation caught fire; rear window shattered spontaneously; automatic transmission jerks and slams into gear:

> Sudden downshifting with loud clunk and lurching of vehicle at 35 mph [55 km/h]. Felt as if I had been hit from behind by another vehicle. Instinctively hit the brakes and pulled over to check for exterior damage, and found none. Continued down the road and experienced unusual increases in rpms. When I arrived at my destination, the vehicle would not go in Reverse. Owned vehicle only 11 days. Incident occurred at 500 miles [800 km].

Key can be taken out of the ignition and transmission placed in Park and the Tucson will still roll downhill; loss of brakes for a couple of seconds after passing over speed bumps or small potholes; when accelerating to merge with traffic, the vehicle hesitates and then decelerates while the gas pedal is fully depressed; power steering seized; vehicle sways left and right while cruising; rear of the vehicle slides as if it were on ice; rear-tire lock-up; and speed sensor wires are vulnerable to road debris:

> Wires are located behind the tires and are fully exposed to road debris. They can be easily severed, thereby affecting ABS and traction control. The wire sticks out 3 inches in open air of the undercarriage and are located close enough to the tires that if they kick up any debris, it is in the direct path of the wire.

SERVICE BULLETIN-REPORTED PROBLEMS: N/A.

SANTA FE ★★★★★

KEY FACTS

Canadian Price (negotiable): *2.4 GL:* $23,999, *2.4 GL Premium front-drive.:* $27,699, *3.5 GL auto.:* $28,999, *3.5 GL AWD:* $29,699, *3.5 GL FWD Sport:* $31,299, *3.5 GL AWD Sport:* $33,299, *Limited:* $35,799, *Limited Navi.:* $37,599 **U.S. Price:** *GLS:* $21,845, *SE:* $26,145, *Limited:* $27,195 **Canadian Freight:** $1,595 **U.S. Freight:** $810 **Powertrain (front-drive/awd)** Engines: 2.4L 4-cyl. (190 hp) • 2.0L 4-cyl turbo. (264 hp) • 3.3L V6 (290 hp); Transmission: 6-speed auto.

DIMENSIONS/CAPACITY

Passengers: 2/3; Wheelbase: 106.3 in.; H: 67.9/L: 184.1; W: 74.4 in.; Headroom N/A; Legroom F/R: 42.6/36.8 in.; Cargo volume: 41 cu. ft. and 35.4 cu. ft (Sport); Fuel tank: 75L/regular; Tow limit: 3,500 lb.; Load capacity: 1,120 lb.; Turning circle: 35.4 ft.; Ground clearance: 8.1 in.; Weight: 3,725–3,875 lb.

RATING: Recommended. This SUV does almost everything right, although side-impact crash protection is Below Average. **Road performance:** Acceptable acceleration with the base 2.4L 4-cylinder, but the 2.0L turbo four 3.3L V6 gives you more power and acceptable fuel economy as well. You will also enjoy the smooth-shifting automatic transmission; fairly agile comportment; and a comfortable, controlled ride. Less enjoyable: The 2.4L four could use more low-end power; vague steering; and the ride quality may be too stiff for some. **Strong points:** A long list of standard equipment; standard stability/traction control and full-body side curtain airbags; a roomy interior that easily accommodates both passengers and cargo; enhanced by comfortable seats; simple, user-friendly controls; improved fuel economy, and better than average quality control. **Weak points:** You will have to get used to some annoying suspension and road noise. **Safety:** NHTSA gave the 2012 Santa Fe a four-star rating for frontal offset crashworthiness and rollover resistance; side-impact protection earned only two stars. IIHS rated frontal, side, rear, and roof crashworthiness as "Good." **New for 2013:** Once production of the long-wheelbase Santa Fe seven-passenger starts in early 2013, the top-of-the-line Veracruz will be phased out. Hyundai promises that prices will be lower for the larger Santa Fe compared to the Veracruz. A two-row 2013 Sport model equipped with a 2.4L and optional 2.0L turbocharged four is now available. A new all-wheel-drive system can reduce unwanted understeer or oversteer and an upgraded steering system allows for three steering settings (Comfort, Normal, and Sport).

ALERT! Take a night test-drive; headlight illumination may be insufficient:

> Low beam headlights illuminated, the contact experienced extremely poor visibility. When the contact drove down a hill, she stated that the headlights provided limited view. The high beam headlights had to be illuminated in order to see the road clearly.

OVERVIEW: The Santa Fe is a competitively priced family SUV that is at the small end of the mid-size sport-utility lineup. It offers impressive room, good build quality, and many standard safety and performance features that cost a lot more when bought with competing models. Revamped last year, the Santa Fe now has better-performing, fuel-thrifty powertrains and additional cabin space.

COST ANALYSIS: Don't waste your money on a 2012. Instead, buy the more powerful and fuel-efficient 2013 model. **Best alternatives:** GM Terrain, Traverse, Acadia, or Enclave; Nissan Xterra; and Toyota RAV4 or Highlander. Although the Santa Fe is 2.1 inches shorter than the Lexus RX330, its seats have more head, leg, and shoulder room than the RX, with additional room for an optional third-row seat, missing in the Lexus. The Hyundai also has a 2.9-inch wider track width than Toyota's Highlander, providing improved handling. **Rebates:** Expect $3,000 rebates on the long-wheelbase, 7-passenger version, and zero percent financing and cheap leases on all models, starting in the spring. Sport models are expected to sell at full price. **Depreciation:** Average. **Insurance cost:** Average. **Parts supply/cost:** Easy to find, and relatively inexpensive. **Annual maintenance cost:** Average. **Warranty:** Bumper-to-bumper 5 years/100,000 km; rust perforation 5 years/unlimited km. **Supplementary warranty:** Not needed. **Highway/city fuel economy:** 2.4L man.: 7.7/11 L/100 km, 37/26 mpg. Auto: 7.2/10.4 L/100 km, 39/27 mpg. 2.4L 4WD: 8.0/10.6 L/100 km, 35/27 mpg. 3.5L: 7.6/10.2 L/100 km, 37/28 mpg. 3.5L 4WD: 7.7/10.6 L/100 km, 37/27 mpg.

OWNER-REPORTED PROBLEMS: Sudden acceleration accompanied by loss of braking:

> Driver was pulling into a parking space when Santa Fe suddenly surged or lunged forward and to the right causing car to jump over a concrete bumper and into another car parked at a 90-degree angle. After the accident investigation was cleared driver proceeded to the local dealership. Enroute the Santa Fe would not shift out of low gear.

When accelerating, vehicle pulls sharply to the side; hesitation when accelerating; raw gas smell both inside and outside the vehicle; Santa Fe frequently shuts down when underway; a loud knock and transmission jerk occurs whenever the vehicle is first started; when shifting, the jerkiness of the transmission feels like someone is hitting the rear end; and loss of brakes, as the pedal descended to the floor.

SERVICE BULLETIN-REPORTED PROBLEMS: Tips on reducing excessive driveshaft noise (creaking or popping).

VERACRUZ (2012) ★ ★ ★

KEY FACTS

Canadian Price (negotiable): *GL:* $33,499, *AWD:* $35,499, *GLS:* $39,999, *Limited:* $41,999 **U.S. Price:** *GLS:* $28,345, *Limited:* $34,495 (AWD on all models costs $1,750–$1,900 more) **Canadian Freight:** $1,595 **U.S. Freight:** $825

POWERTRAIN (FRONT-DRIVE/AWD)
Engine: 3.8L V6 (260 hp); Transmission: 6-speed auto.

DIMENSIONS/CAPACITY
Passengers: 2/3/2; Wheelbase: 110.4 in.; H: 68.9/L: 190.6/W: 76.6 in.; Headroom F/R1/R2: 3.0/4.0/1.0 in.; Legroom F/R1/R2: 42.6/38.4/31.5 in.; Cargo volume: 40 cu. ft.; Fuel tank: 78L/regular; Tow limit: 3,500 lb.; Load capacity: 1,160 lb.; Turning circle: 36.7 ft.; Ground clearance: 8.1 in.; Weight: 4,266–4,431 lb.

RATING: Average. **Road performance:** The V6 is smooth and quiet, and gives acceptable acceleration, though it could use a few more horses. The automatic transmission hesitates when shifting. Expect a comfortable ride, however, the car isn't as agile as the competition. **Strong points:** Very competitively priced; lots of standard features and gadgets galore; a quiet interior; and backed by a comprehensive base warranty. **Weak points:** There is some suspension noise; not much cargo space with the third seat in use; and cramped third-row seating. Fuel economy is disappointing. **Safety:** NHTSA gave the 2012 four stars for rollover crash protection, while IIHS scored offset and front- and side-impact protection as "Good." Head-restraint effectiveness was rated "Acceptable." **New for 2013:** Carried over unchanged.

ALERT! The 2012's transaction price should undercut the manufacturer's suggested retail price (MSRP) by at least 20 percent. Parts and servicing shouldn't be a problem, either, since Veracruz parts can be easily found in the Santa Fe parts bin.

OVERVIEW: The seven-passenger Veracruz uses a stretched Santa Fe platform and offers all the safety, performance, and convenience features you'll find on SUVs that cost $10,000 more. Problem is the car is a bit underpowered and burns too much fuel.

COST ANALYSIS: Buy the more powerful and cheaper to run 2013 Santa Fe. **Best alternatives:** The Honda Pilot, Hyundai's long-wheelbase Santa Fe, Kia Sorento, Lexus RX series, Mazda CX-9, and Nissan Murano. **Options:** Stay away from original-equipment Bridgestone or Dunlop tires; Michelins are much better performers and are more durable. **Rebates:** Expect $3,000–$5,000 rebates, low-interest financing, and sweet leasing deals. **Depreciation:** Faster than average. A 2010 AWD Limited GLS that originally sold for $41,000 is now worth barely $19,500. **Insurance cost:** Above average. **Parts supply/cost:** Acceptable. **Annual maintenance cost:** Higher than average. **Warranty:** Bumper-to-bumper 5 years/100,000 km; rust perforation 5 years/unlimited km. **Supplementary warranty:** Not needed. **Highway/city fuel economy:** *4WD:* 8.5/12.7 L/100 km, 33/22 mpg. *AWD:* 8.9/13.2 L/100 km, 32/21 mpg.

OWNER-REPORTED PROBLEMS: Airbag warning light comes on for no reason; sudden, unintended acceleration accompanied by loss of braking capability; premature wearout of brake calipers and out-of-round rotors:

> Hyundai has brake and rotor issues and won't do anything about it....The vehicle off the lot had rotor problems. Had them shaved, then replaced and they were worn out within a year... If you search Internet you will find brake issue with all vehicles from Hyundai!

Rear hatch opens on its own; opened rear hatch may suddenly fall down; rear doors sometimes won't open; tire pressure warning light comes on intermittently for no reason.

SERVICE BULLETIN-REPORTED PROBLEMS: Tips on reducing excessive driveshaft noise (creaking or popping).

Infiniti

Unlike Toyota's Lexus division, which started out with softly sprung vehicles akin to your dad's fully loaded Oldsmobile, Nissan's luxury brand has historically stressed performance over comfort and opulence, and offered buyers lots of high-performance, cutting-edge features at what were initially very reasonable prices. But the company got greedy during the mid-'90s, and its vehicles became more mainstream as they lost their price and performance advantage.

But Infiniti is fighting to get that performance edge back and is seriously considering launching a plug-in hybrid

Goodbye, G25 (shown above); hello, Infiniti LE EV. The LE electric vehicle is innovative and unique: It uses many of the Leaf EV components and comes with a wireless charging system that makes a plug-in charger unnecessary. Owners can install a charging pad in their garage, driveway or other parking space. They'll simply park over the pad and the charging system will take care of the rest. In the morning, the car can be driven away, fully-charged.

mid-engine sports car and adding more high-performance models to its product mix. Jumping into a new product niche, this summer Infiniti introduced the JX, a new entry aimed at Acura and Audi customers who want a three-row luxury import crossover. This year shoppers will also see greater stylistic differences between Nissan and Infiniti vehicles, even though most models share the same platform. Infinitis usually add more-powerful engines, more gears, more-luxurious interior appointments, and steering and suspensions tweaked for sportier driving.

Infiniti has trimmed its 2013 lineup by dropping the low-end G25 in favour of the G37 and has slated the G series for a redesign in 2014. Last year's 3.5L V6 engine, which powered the EX and FX crossovers, has been replaced by a more powerful and fuel-thrifty 3.7L V6.

Although Infinitis are sold and serviced by a small dealer network across Canada, this limited support base compromises neither availability nor quality of servicing. Furthermore, these cars are reasonably dependable, so there is less need for service. The only two drawbacks are that powertrain and body parts are sometimes in short supply and that adding on complicated high-tech features drives up servicing costs and practically guarantees a higher failure rate for electronic components.

G25, G37 ★★★/★★★

The Infiniti G25.

RATING: *G25:* Average. *G37:* Above Average. **Road performance:** *G25:* This entry-level sedan is fitted with a 218 hp 2.5L V6 that skimps on acceleration but burns about 15 percent less fuel. Generally, the car is fairly agile, quiet, and comfortable, but the engine is noisy when pushed. There is no manual transmission or sports package option. *G37:* A powerful, smooth, and responsive powertrain; predictable, sporty handling; and a firm but comfortable ride. The convertible (325 hp) has five horses less than the coupe (330 hp) but lots more than you'll find with the competition. **Strong points:** *G25:* Only a handful of owner complaints posted on the NHTSA (*safercar. gov*) website. **Weak points:** The $1,950 freight and pre-delivery inspection fee is highway robbery. *G25:* You get less power and less equipment than with the G37, and the resale value will plummet when the car is dropped in December 2012. *G37:* There's a small rear seat and cargo area; towing is not advised; and the convertible model has even less room and has yet to be crash tested. **Safety:** The 2012 G25 and G37 models earned five stars for rollover resistance; IIHS found front and side protection to be "Good," though roof strength and head restraints were judged to be only "Acceptable" and "Marginal," respectively. **New for 2013:** An IPL (Infiniti Performance Line) G Convertible joins the IPL G lineup with an array of special performance and luxury upgrades like 18 extra horsepower (343 hp), 19-inch IPL split seven-spoke aluminum-alloy wheels with graphite finish, sport brakes, an IPL-tuned exhaust and suspension, a unique front fascia and side sills, and climate-controlled front seats. The G37 sedan returns unchanged, with three available models: the Sedan Journey, Sedan 6MT Sport, and G37x AWD Sedan. G37 convertibles are carried over practically unchanged. Infiniti has axed the G25 and G37 Coupe, Sport Appearance Edition, and Limited Edition.

ALERT! As the G25 is phased out in the last quarter of 2012, Infiniti will ratchet up the rebates and sales incentives for these leftover models.

OVERVIEW: The G37 is a premium mid-sized car with SUV pretensions. It is sold as a two-door coupe, a four-door sedan, and a two-door convertible with a power-retractable hardtop. The G37 targets shoppers who would normally buy the Acura RDX or the BMW 328i or X3. The convertible model is priced right within striking range of BMW's 328i/335i Cabriolet and the Lexus IS 250 or IS 350 C convertible. The Mercedes-Benz CLK350 AMG Edition Cabriolet has priced itself out of that market.

COST ANALYSIS: The 2012 G25's greatest advantage compared with the competition is its price—the base model starts at $36,390—thousands of dollars less than most

KEY FACTS

Canadian Price (negotiable): *G25 Sedan:* $36,390, *G25x AWD Sedan:* $40,450, *G25x AWD Sedan Sport:* $45,540, *G37x AWD Sedan:* $43,450, *G37x AWD Sedan Sport:* $48,640, *G37x AWD Sedan M6 Sport:* $47,540, *G37 Coupe:* $46,800, *G37x AWD Coupe:* $49,200, *G37x AWD Sport Coupe:* $51,700, *G37x AWD M6 Sport Coupe:* $49,200, *G37 IPL G Coupe:* $57,200, *G37 Convertible Sport:* $58,300, *G37 Convertible Sport M6:* $58,400, *G37 Convertible Premier Edition:* $61,700 **U.S. Price:** *G25 Sedan:* $33,100, *G25 Journey:* $34,500, *G25x AWD:* $36,100, *G37 Journey:* $36,900, *G37x AWD:* $38,500, *G37 Sport 6MT:* $41,500, *G37 Coupe Journey:* $39,800, *G37x Coupe AWD:* $41,450, *G37x Coupe Sport MT:* $44,900, *G37 IPL G Coupe:* $52,400, *G37 Convertible:* $47,200, *G37 Convertible Sport 6MT:* $52,000 **Canadian Freight:** $1,950 **U.S. Freight:** $895

POWERTRAIN (REAR-DRIVE/AWD)
Engines: 2.5L V6 (218 hp) • 3.7L V6 (325 hp sedan, 330 hp coupe, 325 hp convertible); Transmissions: 6 speed man. • 7-speed auto.

DIMENSIONS/CAPACITY
Passengers: 2/2, 2/3; Wheelbase: 112.2 in.; H: 54.7–55.3/L: 183.1/W: 71.8 in.; Headroom F/R: 2.5/1.5 in.; Legroom F/R: 41/27.5 in.; Cargo volume: 7.4–13.5 cu. ft.; Fuel tank: 76L/premium; Tow limit: 1,000 lb.; Load capacity: 900 lb.; Turning circle: 35.4 ft.; Ground clearance: 5.1 in.; Weight: 3,642–3,847 lb.

competitors, like the BMW 328i. This advantage may be purely illusory when the exorbitant $1,950 freight costs and some trim upgrades are taken into account. Look for a discounted 2012 version. You can also save big bucks by shopping in the States for some of the pricier G37 models (just look at the preceding price differences). **Best alternatives:** The BMW 328i Series or X3. **Options:** The limited-slip differential in the Sport package. **Rebates:** $3,000+ discounts, low-cost financing, and attractive leases; discounts will be sweetened in early 2013. **Depreciation:** Average. **Insurance cost:** Higher than average. **Parts supply/cost:** Expensive parts that can be easily found in the Maxima parts bin. **Annual maintenance cost:** Lower than average. **Warranty:** Bumper-to-bumper 4 years/100,000 km; powertrain 6 years/110,000 km; rust perforation 7 years/unlimited km. **Supplementary warranty:** Not needed. **Highway/city fuel economy:** *G25*: 6.8/10.3 L/100 km, 42/27 mpg. *G25x*: 7.3/10.6 L/100 km, 39/27 mpg. *G37 3.7L 6-speed man.*: 7.9/12.3 L/100 km, 36/23 mpg. *G37 3.7L 6-speed man. convertible*: 8.4/12.9 L/100 km, 34/22 mpg. *G37 3.7L 7-speed auto. convertible*: 7.8/11.9 L/100 km, 36/24 mpg. *G37 3.7L 6-speed man. coupe*: 7.9/12.3 L/100 km, 36/23 mpg. *G37 3.7L 7-speed auto. coupe*: 7.4/11.0 L/100 km, 38/26 mpg. *G37x 3.7L 7-speed auto.*: 7.8/11.7 L/100 km, 36/24 mpg. (See the fuel savings with the new engine/tranny combo?)

OWNER-REPORTED PROBLEMS: Only 22 owner complaints posted by NHTSA on the 2011 and 2012 models. Gas station automatic fuelling nozzles shut off after a few seconds; vehicle suddenly accelerated while in Park with the engine running; engine surges when braking (confirmed by TSB #ITB07-048), or is slow to brake:

> While pulling into a parking place in a shopping center, with my right foot on the brake and the car stopped, the motor raced and the back tires spun at high speed, I turned the car off and had it towed to the dealer where it is now. This is the second time this has happened. I believe this is very dangerous. I find online this has happened to other [Infiniti] owners.

•

> Made a fairly hard brake for a red light—car slid a little to a stop, but continued accelerating at 2500 to 3500 rpms while I held both feet on the brake to keep it in place. It was like holding back a revved up jet—rpms would not come down even when I shifted car to Neutral.

The convertible has some body shake; engine tapping, clicking sound at start-up requires the use of a costlier "factory" oil; transmission suddenly downshifted to 15 km/h from 100 km/h:

> A chip was changed. However, the failure occurred three more times. The dealer then stated that the fluid in the vehicle was too full and was the cause of the failure.

The manual transmission gears grind when shifting, causing a delayed shift, especially in Sixth gear; transmission was replaced under warranty. The anti-traction feature activated on its own and caused the wheels to lock on a rainy day; defective Bridgestone Pole Position tires; Tire Pressure light did not come on when tire went flat; premature brake replacement; the area between the gas pedal and centre console gets quite hot; audio system malfunctions; and poor fit and finish. Incidentally, this car is not as much a "chick magnet" as it is a rodent attractant:

> Infiniti G37 has electrical wiring insulation made of soy-based polymer. Soy-based polymer is apparently biodegradable. The problem is that it is also attractive to rodents, who eat the wiring, creating electrical safety hazards. It also creates an economic stress on consumers and insurers who have to pay for repairs done to these automobiles, which Infiniti claims are not covered under any existing warranty.

SERVICE BULLETIN-REPORTED PROBLEMS: Troubleshooting multiple transmission problems; steering pull/drift, or steering wheel is off-centre; automatic transmission shifter boot may come loose; drivebelt noise; and the warranty is extended under Campaign PO308 in relation to the radio seek function and Campaign PO385 relative to reprogramming the G25's engine control module (ECM). *G37:* Bluetooth voice recognition issues; convertible top water leak at windshield header; AC blows warm air at idle; and door accent garnish replacements.

EX37 ★★★

RATING: Average. The EX and G series are entry-level Infinitis with the most to offer from a price and quality perspective—as long as you have short legs or never ride in the rear seat. **Road performance:** Not as sporty as Infiniti's sport sedans or some of BMW's crossovers; the EX performs like a car with power to spare; and the smooth, responsive manumatic transmission works flawlessly with the new V6 and 7-speed tranny. Overall, the car is much more agile, quiet, and comfortable than the G series. **Strong points:** Larger V6 engine means there will be 28 more

KEY FACTS

Canadian Price (negotiable): *EX37 AWD:* $42,200 ($2,200 more than the 2012 EX35) **U.S. Price:** *Base:* $35,200, *AWD:* $36,600, *Journey:* $37,400, *Journey AWD:* $38,800 **Canadian Freight:** $1,950 **U.S. Freight:** $895

POWERTRAIN (REAR-DRIVE/AWD)

Engine: 3.7L V6 (325 hp); Transmission: 7-speed manumatic

DIMENSIONS/CAPACITY

Passengers: 2/3; Wheelbase: 110.2 in.; H: 61.9/L: 182.3/W: 71 in.; Headroom F/R: 3.0/3.0 in.; Legroom F/R: 42/26 in.; Cargo volume: 18.6 cu. ft.; Fuel tank: 76L/premium; Tow limit: N/A; Load capacity: 860 lb.; Turning circle: 36 ft.; Ground clearance: 5.5 in.; Weight: 3,757–3,979 lb.

horsepower on tap in the EX. Not a car for serious off-road use, but definitely a comfortable, well-equipped, and versatile vehicle for most driving needs. **Weak points:** A smallish interior makes the EX a four-seater; limited cargo space; back seat occupants must keep a knee-to-chin posture when the front seats are pushed all the way back; taller drivers will want more headroom (especially with the sunroof-equipped Journey model); right-rear visibility is compromised by right-rear head restraint and side pillar; and fuel economy is unimpressive. **Safety:** NHTSA gives the 2013 EX37 four stars for rollover protection; no other tests have been done. **New for 2013:** A 3.7L V6.

ALERT! Both the Infiniti EX and FX crossovers are now powered by the automaker's 325 hp 3.7L V6, replacing last year's 3.5L V6. Naturally, the cars have been rebadged the EX37 and FX37 for 2013. Don't be confused and buy a lesser-performing leftover 2012 model. At $42,200, this year's model costs only $2,200 more than the 2012 EX35.

OVERVIEW: Offering the room of a compact station wagon, the EX37 is a small, upscale SUV wannabe that targets shoppers who would normally buy the Acura RDX or the BMW X3. Smaller than the Infiniti FX, it is priced in the same range as the Infiniti G series and is essentially a G wagon.

COST ANALYSIS: The 2013 model is a better buy, due to its more-powerful engine and increased fuel economy. Wait until the winter or spring for lower prices when extra rebates and other sales incentives kick in. The new 7-speed manumatic may give a slight boost to fuel economy, but keep in mind that any new powertrain is a risky buy during its first year on the market. Also, the larger, 18-inch wheels may make for a bumpier ride and cut your gas mileage. **Best alternatives:** Acura RDX, BMW 3 Series or X3, and Lincoln MKX. **Options:** The Navigation Package is overpriced and mostly fluff. **Rebates:** $4,000+ discounts, low-cost financing, and cheaper leases. **Depreciation:** Average. **Insurance cost:** Higher than average. **Parts supply/cost:** Expensive parts that can be easily found in the Maxima parts bin. **Annual maintenance cost:** Lower than average. **Warranty:** Bumper-to-bumper 4 years/100,000 km; powertrain 6 years/110,000 km; rust perforation 7 years/unlimited km. **Supplementary warranty:** Not needed. **Highway/city fuel economy:** *2012 3.5L 6-speed man.:* 7.9/12.3 L/100 km, 33/23 mpg. (No federal-sourced fuel economy figures yet on the 2013 3.7L 7-speed automatic transmission combo.)

OWNER-REPORTED PROBLEMS: The only safety problem reported concerns the accelerator and brake pedals being mounted too close together.

SERVICE BULLETIN-REPORTED PROBLEMS: Steering pull/drift, or steering wheel is off-centre; Bluetooth voice recognition issues; and door accent garnish replacements.

FX37, FX50 ★★★★

The Infiniti FX37.

RATING: Above Average. **Road performance:** Both engines have power to spare (22 more ponies are available in the new V6), delivered by a smooth and quiet drivetrain, though the ride is a bit stiff. Handling is precise and secure. Decent towing capacity and torque. **Strong points:** The roomy interior uses high-quality materials and simple controls. Body hardware and fit and finish get top marks. **Weak points:** Not much cargo room, and engine noise invades the cabin. **Safety:** NHTSA hasn't yet crash tested the 2013 FX or EX models. The 2012 EX35 got a "Good" score in all crash tests carried out by the IIHS, and the 2012 FX was rated "Good" only for frontal and rear crash protection. Limited rear visibility. **New for 2013:** A new 325 hp 3.7L V6 engine. Other enhancements for the new model year include the addition of the advanced Moving Objection Detection (MOD) to the Around View system (standard on the FX50, but optional on the FX37).

KEY FACTS

Canadian Price (negotiable): FX37: $53,350, FX50: $65,100 **U.S. Price:** FX35: $42,600, AWD: $44,050, FX50: $57,600 **Canadian Freight:** $1,950 **U.S. Freight:** $895
POWERTRAIN (REAR-DRIVE/AWD)
Engines: 3.7L V6 (325 hp) • 5.0L V8 (390 hp); Transmission: 7-speed auto.
DIMENSIONS/CAPACITY
Passengers: 2/3; Wheelbase: 113.5 in.; H: 66.1/L: 191.2/W: 75.9 in.; Headroom: N/A; Legroom: F/R: 44.7/34.6 in.; Cargo volume: 24.7 cu. ft.; Fuel tank: 90L/premium; Tow limit: 3,500 lb.; Load capacity: N/A; Turning circle: 36.7 ft.; Ground clearance: 7.3 in.; Weight: 4,299 lb., 4,575 lb.

ALERT! These are well-appointed, luxury crossover SUVs that drive and ride like heavy sports sedans—not agile, but acceptably responsive. The primary difference between the two vehicles is their engines, plus a few additional features.

OVERVIEW: The Infiniti FX received a number of exterior and refinements just last year. For 2013, the biggest change is under the hood—a 325 hp 3.7L V6 replaces the 3.5L V6 used by the 2012 models. Now named the FX37, it is available in three models: FX37 RWD, FX37 AWD, and FX37 AWD Limited Edition. Also offered is the top-of-the-line FX50 AWD, with its standard 390 hp 5.0L V8 and Infiniti Intelligent All-Wheel Drive. Both engines are paired with a standard 7-speed automatic transmission, featuring Adaptive Shift Control (ASC) and available solid magnesium paddle shifters.

Carried over from last year are a double-wishbone front/multi-link rear suspension and large four-wheel disc brakes, along with available Continuous Damping Control (CDC), Rear Active Steer, Intelligent Brake Assist and six-spoke 21-inch super lightweight aluminum-alloy wheels (FX50 Sport Technology Package).

The FX's driver-oriented cockpit has intuitive controls. Sport seating is available, and advanced audio, navigation, and technology ranges from an 11-speaker Bose-developed audio system to Infiniti Intelligent Key and Intelligent Cruise Control.

COST ANALYSIS: It will be hard to haggle before the new year, due to the popularity of the FX series and their short supply. The huge difference in price between Canada and the States make these vehicles prime candidates for cross-border shopping. South of the border, the price may be cut by $10,000 and the freight fee reduced by $1,000. **Best alternatives:** BMW X6 xDrive. **Options:** Nothing is needed. The lane-departure warning system may sound false alerts. **Rebates:** Look for discounts of about 10 percent as well as some very attractive leasing deals in the first quarter of 2013. **Depreciation:** Average. **Insurance cost:** Higher than average. **Parts supply/cost:** Expensive powertrain and body parts that aren't easily available. **Annual maintenance cost:** Higher than average. **Warranty:** Bumper-to-bumper 4 years/100,000 km; powertrain 6 years/110,000 km; rust perforation 7 years/unlimited km. **Supplementary warranty:** Not needed. **Highway/city fuel economy:** *FX37:* 9.3/13.3 L/100 km, 30/21 mpg. *FX50 AWD 7-speed auto:* 10.1/14.6 L/100 km, 28/19 mpg.

OWNER-REPORTED PROBLEMS: Early replacement of brake calipers and rotors.

SERVICE BULLETIN-REPORTED PROBLEMS: *FX37/50:* Steering pull/drift, or steering wheel is off-centre; Bluetooth voice recognition issues; improper seat climate control operation; and door accent garnish replacements.

The Infiniti M37.

RATING: *M37, M56:* Above Average buys, but Canadian buyers are victimized by price-gouging. Nevertheless, performance, luxury, and user-friendly tech features highlight the Infiniti M series as a strong player among luxury large cars. The major difference between the M37 and M56 is engine size, plus additional performance and convenience gadgets. *Hybrid:* An Average buy that's even more overpriced in Canada. **Road performance:** Both vehicles have superior acceleration and handle extremely well. While both V6- and V8-powered cars are competent on twisty roads, the V6 powered M37 is much more agile due to its lighter weight. *Hybrid:* A competent performer that quickly loses power with the Eco drive engaged. It also lacks all-wheel drive and the Sports Package's more responsive suspension. **Strong points:** Well-appointed with high-quality materials and electronics, and the cabin electronics are easy to understand and far more user-friendly than what's offered by BMW and Mercedes; easy entry and exit; head restraints lower into the seatback; comfortable and supportive front seats; and respectable fuel economy with the V6 coupled to the 7-speed automatic transmission. **Weak points:** High prices, some road noise, taller rear-seat passengers will want more headroom; small rear seats could use more thigh support; and the V8 is a gas hog. Hybrid

KEY FACTS

Canadian Price (negotiable): *M37:* $52,400, *M37x AWD:* $54,900, *M37 Sport:* $63,400, *M56:* $66.200, *M56x AWD:* $68,700, *M56 Sport:* $73,400, *M Hybrid:* $67,300 **U.S. Price:** *M37:* $47,700, *M37x AWD:* $49,850, *M56:* $59,100, *M56x AWD:* $61,600, *M Hybrid:* $54,200 **Canadian Freight:** $1,950 **U.S. Freight:** $895

POWERTRAIN (REAR-DRIVE/AWD)

Engines: 3.7L V6 (330 hp) • 5.6L V8 (420 hp) • *Hybrid:* 3.5L V6 (360 net hp); Transmission: 7-speed auto.

DIMENSIONS/CAPACITY

Passengers: 2/3; Wheelbase: 114.2 in.; H: 59.1/L: 194.7/W: 72.6 in.; Headroom F/R: 4.0/3.0 in.; Legroom F/R: 41/30 in.; Cargo volume: 14.9 cu. ft.; Fuel tank: 90L/premium; Load capacity: 860 lb.; Ground clearance: 7.4 in.; Turning circle: 36.7 ft.; Weight: 3,858 lb., 4,012 lb.

batteries cut trunk space. **Safety:** NHTSA gives the M37 five stars for side protection and a four-star frontal protection and rollover resistance rating. Innovative safety features are standard: Blind Spot Warning (BSW) helps alert the driver if another vehicle is detected in the blind spot area; Blind Spot Intervention (BSI) helps the driver return the vehicle back toward the centre of the lane of travel; Lane Departure Warning (LDW) and Lane Departure Prevention (LDP) systems; Intelligent Brake Assist (IBA) with Forward Collision Warning (FCW); and Front Pre-crash Seat Belts. **New for 2013:** Not much new, except for auto-dimming side-view mirrors and an auto-trunk cincher.

ALERT! The Sport Package makes for a stiffer, harsher ride; not a good idea for rough road travel.

OVERVIEW: The M37 and M56 rear-drive/AWD luxury sedans ride on a four-wheel independent suspension and carry either a V6 or V8 engine. They share the QX's drivetrain but are set on a shorter wheelbase. Because of their lighter curb weight and their potent engines, these cars can do 0–100 km/h in less than six seconds. For the 2013 model year, the Infiniti M Sedan returns with five well-equipped performance luxury models—the M37 RWD, M37x AWD, M56 RWD, M56x AWD, and M35h RWD with the 3.5L Direct Response Hybrid System. The M37 is powered by a 330 hp 3.7L V6 engine, while the M56 offers a 420 hp 5.6L V8. Both the M37 and M56 are available with rear-wheel drive or Infiniti's Intelligent All-Wheel Drive system. A special Sport Package, available for the first time on AWD and RWD models, includes 4-Wheel Active Steer (4WAS) on the RWD only, a sport-tuned suspension, sport brakes, and 20-inch wheels and tires (refer to the preceding "Alert!" section).

The Infiniti M Hybrid delivers V8 performance with 4-cylinder fuel efficiency. It is the first V6 true luxury performance "driver's" hybrid—and the only such vehicle to offer more than 350 horsepower (360 net horsepower) and exceptional fuel economy.

COST ANALYSIS: The cheaper 2012 M37 is the better buy. **Best alternatives:** The Acura RL V6, BMW 5 Series, and Mercedes E-Class. **Options:** All-wheel drive can cost up to $2,500 on the M37x and M56x and cut into the cars' performance on windy roads. **Rebates:** $4,000+ discounts, low-cost financing, and attractive leases; discounts will be sweetened in early 2013. **Depreciation:** Average. **Insurance cost:** Higher than average. **Parts supply/cost:** Expensive parts that aren't that hard to find. **Annual maintenance cost:** Lower than average. **Warranty:** Bumper-to-bumper 4 years/100,000 km; powertrain 6 years/110,000 km; rust perforation 7 years/unlimited km. **Supplementary warranty:** Not needed. **Highway/city fuel economy:** *M37 rear-drive:* 7.6/11.4 L/100 km, 37/25 mpg. *M37 AWD:* 8.3/12 L/100 km, 34/24 mpg. *M37 Sport:* 7.6/11.4 L/100 km, 37/25 mpg. *M56:* 8.0/12.9 L/100 km, 35/22 mpg. *M56 AWD:* 8.5/13.4 L/100 km, 33/21 mpg. *M56 Sport:* 7.6/11.4/L/100 km, 35/22 mpg.

OWNER-REPORTED PROBLEMS: No problems reported with the 2012s.

SERVICE BULLETIN-REPORTED PROBLEMS: *M37:* Harsh shifts, multiple diagnostic trouble codes set, and vibration; steering pull/drift, or steering wheel is off-centre; low battery voltage, or no-starts; driver's power seat won't adjust; and Bluetooth voice recognition issues. The warranty is extended under Campaign PO336 and PO328 relative to navigation and four-wheel steering software updates. *M56:* All of the above, plus a rough cold idle, steering-wheel finish peeling, and Campaign PO353 (ECM update).

QX (QX56) ★★★

RATING: Average. Now called the QX, this is a large SUV that trades fuel economy and handling for power and comfort. **Road performance:** The QX uses a smooth-shifting automatic transmission that delivers more than enough power in all gear ranges and provides more towing capacity and torque than your average brontosaurus. Predictable, responsive handling (thanks to the independent rear suspension); a stiff, jarring ride; and road handling is mediocre. **Strong points:** Comfortable and powerful, the car has a plush interior and standard navigation system plus more gadgets and convenience features than you will ever need. You'll also find plenty of interior room. **Weak points:** Way overpriced—a poster child for cross-border shopping. Fuel economy is brutal, although not as bad as with previous models because of the 7-speed transmission. The high step into the interior isn't for shy ladies. Steering-wheel-mounted controls are needlessly

KEY FACTS

Canadian Price (negotiable): *Base:* $73,000 **U.S. Price:** *Base:* $58,700, *4WD:* $61,800 **Canadian Freight:** $1,950 **U.S. Freight:** $895

POWERTRAIN (AWD)

Engine: 5.6L V8 (400 hp); Transmission: 7-speed auto.

DIMENSIONS/CAPACITY

Passengers: 2/3/2; 2/3/3; Wheelbase: 121.1 in.; H: 62.6/L: 208.3/W: 79.9 in.; Cargo volume: 16.6 cu. ft.; Fuel tank: 98L/premium; Tow limit: 8,500 lb.; Load capacity: N/A; Turning circle: 41.6 ft.; Ground clearance: 9.2 in.; Weight: 5,850 lb.

complex. The jury's still out over the car's long-term reliability. **Safety:** NHTSA gives the 2010 QX56 a five-star ranking for front-impact occupant protection and three stars for rollover resistance. **New for 2013:** Moving Object Detection (MOD) has been added to the standard Around View Monitor.

ALERT! This eight-seat, truck-based SUV is more than most people need. If you can get by with a bit less off-roading and towing muscle, choose a reliable luxury crossover like the Acura MDX, RDX, or ZDX, BMW X3, Infiniti EX35 or FX, and Lexus RX 350 instead.

OVERVIEW: This is Infiniti's SUV luxury flagship, loaded with every conceivable safety, performance, and convenience feature one could ever imagine. Yet, someone forgot to design a decent-sized third-row rear seat that's large enough for most people.

COST ANALYSIS: It will be hard to haggle, due to the popularity of the QX series. Thus, you have two recourses: Wait until spring of 2013 for prices to moderate by about $5,000 or buy the car in the States and save up to $14,000 U.S. (if you include the reduced freight fees). **Best alternatives:** Nissan's Armada and GM's Tahoe, Yukon, Denali, or Escalade. The GM vehicles are deeply discounted, ride better, have greater curb appeal, and are quieter. **Options:** Nothing is needed. **Rebates:** Look for discounts of about 10 percent as well as some very attractive leasing deals in the first quarter of 2013. **Depreciation:** Faster than average. A new 2009 that sold for $70,000 now sells for $37,500. **Insurance cost:** Higher than average. **Parts supply/cost:** Expensive parts that aren't easily found with independent suppliers. **Annual maintenance cost:** Higher than average. **Warranty:** Bumper-to-bumper 4 years/100,000 km; powertrain 6 years/110,000 km; rust perforation 7 years/ unlimited km. **Supplementary warranty:** A good idea for the powertrain. **Highway/city fuel economy:** 10.3/15.7 L/100 km, 27/18 mpg.

OWNER-REPORTED PROBLEMS: Hazardous suspension/steering wobble when passing over uneven terrain; models equipped with the Technology Package may cause the driver's foot to be caught under the mechanical/electrical device that comes with it:

> The tip of my shoe keeps getting caught under this mechanical device and on multiple occasions in the first week of ownership it has caused a momentary delay in quickly moving from the accelerator to the brake pedal. The hang up of the tip of my shoe is exaggerated greatly by dress shoes with a firmer tip of the sole of the shoe. Again, this device is only present on QX models with the technology package. This tech package device also gets in the way as you go to push on the gas pedal. The only way to avoid this problem is to always remember to place your right heel at least 2" away from the base of the gas pedal and push it only with your toes. Moving your heel away from the bottom of the pedal results in the tip of your shoe touching the pedal lower and just brushing the underside of the tech package device. I have contacted consumer support at Infinity USA and they have told me that they have had complaints but "that's just the way it is for people with bigger feet". I guess they don't have size 12 in Japan. This is a hazard when the tip of my right shoe gets caught and prevents me from moving quickly to the brake.

Windshield crack appeared under the wiper while the vehicle was parked in a garage overnight; some brake failures, and frequent brake repairs; malfunctioning rear air-levelling suspension makes the rear bottom out without any alert sent to the driver and makes trailer towing a white-knuckle experience; power accessories often malfunction; and the sound system is glitch-prone.

SERVICE BULLETIN-REPORTED PROBLEMS: Harsh shifts, multiple diagnostic trouble codes set, hesitation, vibration, and other automatic transmission issues; steering pull/drift, or steering wheel is off-centre.

Kia

The Good, the Bad, and the Dangerous

With its nimble handling and well-equipped cabin, the Kia Rio EX outpointed the Hyundai Accent and Chevrolet Sonic as the top-rated subcompact sedan in *Consumer Reports*' latest tests. The Rio's hatchback version scored lower, but it sits firmly in third place behind the previously tested and higher-rated Honda Fit and Nissan Versa SL among the subcompact hatchbacks tested with automatic transmissions.

CONSUMER REPORTS
PRESS RELEASE; MARCH 22, 2012

Kia has gone from buffoon to bestseller. Especially now that it doesn't make every model a failure-prone jack-in-the-box full of costly repair surprises, as it did five years ago.

Buyers now have more confidence in Kia cars, SUVs, and minivans that have become more functional, fuel-efficient, and stylish than ever before. Hyundai and its Kia subsidiary are breaking sales records with a much improved lineup crafted during an economic recession and covering practically all the market niches, with the exception of trucks.

While Hyundai goes upscale with high-tech and fuel-frugal models placed throughout its model lineup, Kia is putting its money into an expanded lineup of less-expensive fuel-efficient vehicles that carry more standard features, are freshly styled, and have fewer reliability problems. For example, the Sedona minivan has been dropped for 2013 and will be replaced in mid-2013 with a more-refined 2014 version.

On the other hand, Kia's quality ratings are not uniformly good. Sudden, unintended acceleration, steering/suspension wander, and atrocious fit and finish haunt the entire Kia lineup, along with automatic transmission and brake failures. Nevertheless, *Consumer Reports* has been recently won over by Kia's improved quality control after decades of listing most of the Kia lineup as "Not

Recommended." *CR* has consistently criticized the automaker for making unreliable, unsafe vehicles. Now, in a surprising turnaround, it has many Kia models on its "Recommended" list published in April.

Not so, *Lemon-Aid*. We will maintain the Sorento's and Optima's Not Recommended designations in view of the large number of life-threatening transmission and steering failures we have discovered. We are also hopeful Kia and its dealers will stop saying these failures are "normal" and will correct these and other safety hazards before lives are lost.

RIO, RIO5 ★ ★ ★ ★

The Kia Rio.

RATING: Above Average. The Rio sedan and Rio5 hatchback combine good fuel economy and interior room with useful standard features. **Road performance:** The 1.6L engine with the manual transmission is usually adequate for most chores; handling is exceptionally good, with plenty of steering feedback; good brakes; and a comfortable, though sometimes busy, ride. Slow acceleration with the automatic transmission; insufficient highway passing power; excessive engine noise at higher speeds; harsh ride when passing over small bumps. **Strong points:** Lots of standard features that cost extra on other cars; a well-equipped, roomy cabin housing good quality materials, user-friendly controls, and high-end electronics; strong brakes; and impressive fuel economy. **Weak points:** Trunk lid hinges intrude into the trunk area. **Safety:** Crash protection is a mixed bag. NHTSA awarded the 2013 Rio five stars for side crash protection and four stars for frontal and rollover crashworthiness; IIHS rates the 2011 Rio's frontal offset, rear, and roof crash protection as "Acceptable" and gives a "Poor" crashworthiness score for side collisions. Limited rear-corner visibility with the Rio5. **New for 2013:** Carried over relatively unchanged, except for standard steering-wheel paddle shifters (SX and EX models) and a cargo-floor tray and net (SX five-door models).

ALERT! Taller drivers will appreciate the front headroom and legroom.

OVERVIEW: The base Rio sedan won't spoil you with electronic gadgets and la-di-da comfort and convenience features, but it's an adequately equipped, solid econocar. Available as a four-door sedan or as the five-door hatchback Rio5, it comes with a manual transmission or an optional 6-speed automatic, wind-up windows, and manual door locks. On the other hand, safety features that are extra-cost items on more-expensive cars—like front seat belt pretensioners, disc brakes on all four wheels, and six airbags (dual frontal, front-seat side-impact, and full-coverage side curtain)—are standard features.

COST ANALYSIS: The discounted 2012s are cheaper buys than the almost identical 2013 versions, but the price difference isn't that much. **Best alternatives:** The Chevrolet Sonic has a small performance edge and upfront occupant knee airbags. Honda's Fit is roomier, with versatile seating that accommodates five people. Other contenders: The Hyundai Accent, Mazda3, and Nissan Versa are more-refined small cars that offer better performance while also conserving fuel. **Options:** Rio's optional Idle Stop and Go, which helps to cut fuel consumption, is a worthwhile $400 option. Kia's voice-activated infotainment system is an optional feature that stands out among competing small cars. **Rebates:** Look for $1,500 rebates or discounts and low financing rates in late 2012. **Depreciation:** Slower than average. **Insurance cost:** Average. **Parts supply/cost:** Average costs; parts aren't hard to find. **Annual maintenance cost:** Less than average. **Warranty:** Bumper-to-bumper 5 years/100,000 km; powertrain 5 years/100,000 km; rust perforation 5 years/unlimited km. **Supplementary warranty:** A wise buy for the engine/tranny, considering Kia's previous powertrain troubles. **Highway/city fuel economy:** *Man.:* 5.8/7.1 L/100 km, 49/40 mpg. *Auto.:* 5.6/7.7 L/100 km, 50/38 mpg.

OWNER-REPORTED PROBLEMS: Sharing the Accent platform and using more Hyundai components has undoubtedly improved Kia's quality, judging by J.D. Power survey results and the small number of owner complaints registered with NHTSA. In fact, the Rio and Rio5 have registered fewer owner complaints than the newer Kia Soul. Nevertheless, these serious problems have been reported: fuel hose vent line may leak fuel into the back seat area; automatic transmission malfunctions; tie rod and ball joints broke away from the chassis while vehicle was turning; poor fit and finish; premature brake repairs; electrical shorts; airbags failed to deploy in a frontal collision; passenger-side airbag was disabled, even though an average-sized

KEY FACTS

Canadian Price (Firm): *Rio LX:* $13,895, *Rio LX+:* $15,395, *EX:* $17,395, *Rio SX UVO:* $20,695, *Rio5 LX:* $14,395, *Rio5 LX+:* $16,984, *Rio5 EX:* $17,695, *Rio5 SX:* $20,984 **U.S. Price:** *LX sedan:* $13,600, *LX hatch.:* $13,800, *EX:* $16,500, *SX:* $17,700, *Rio5 LX auto.:* $15,095, *SX auto.:* $16,395 **Canadian Freight:** $1,455 **U.S. Freight:** $750

POWERTRAIN (FRONT-DRIVE)
Engine: 1.6L 4-cyl. (138 hp); Transmissions: 6-speed man. • 6-speed auto.

DIMENSIONS/CAPACITY (Rio)
Passengers: 2/3; Wheelbase: 101.2 in.; H: 57.3/L: 171.9/W: 67.7 in.; Headroom F/R: 4.5/2.0 in., Legroom F/R: 43.8/31.1 in.; Cargo volume: 13.7 cu. ft.; Fuel tank: 45L/regular; Tow limit: Not recommended; Load capacity: 850 lb.; Ground clearance: 5.5 in.; Turning circle: 34.5 ft.; Weight: 2,410–2,480 lb.

occupant was seated; sudden acceleration in Reverse, with loss of brakes; brakes locked up when applied; and the rear window shattered when the driver's door was closed.

SERVICE BULLETIN-REPORTED PROBLEMS: Troubleshooting instrument panel noise, and fixing an outside mirror cover gap; steering-wheel noise and vibration repair.

SOUL ★★★★

RATING: Above Average; poor-quality materials and craftsmanship bring down the car's rating. **Road performance:** Some powerful engines and fuel-sipping powertrains (the 2.0L is a better choice for reserve power), although the base engine could use more grunt at low engine rpm; a compliant suspension, without undue body roll or front-end plow; and fairly agile cornering, with good steering feedback. A busy highway ride. **Strong points:** Inexpensive and well equipped with safety devices like ABS, stability control, six airbags, and active head restraints—features that are rare on entry-level small cars. User-friendly, simple controls; plenty of interior room, especially when it comes to headroom; excellent front and side visibility; and comfortable seats. **Weak points:** Omnipresent rattles; excessive wind and road noise; and many body and fit and finish glitches. Poor-quality, easily broken, or prematurely worn interior items. Fuel economy is seriously overstated. **Safety:** Soul does well in crashworthiness tests: NHTSA gives the 2013 model four stars for front and rollover crash protection and five stars for side crashworthiness. IIHS rates the 2012 Soul as "Good" in frontal offset, side, and roof crash protection. Poor rearward visibility through the small rear windshield and thick rear pillars. **New for 2013:** Nothing significant.

ALERT! What? No spare tire? Tell the dealer this is a deal-breaker:

The 2012 Kia Soul does not come with a spare tire, instead it comes with a can of Fix-A-Flat and an air pump. There is no jack either. The flat may be fixed if the damage is on the tread and the hole is under ¼ inch in diameter. If the damage is on the sidewall or greater than ¼ inch, the vehicle has to be towed. For those people that have no cell phone or are in an area that gets no reception they will be stranded until another motorist comes along and these days most motorists don't stop for other drivers. Kia offers roadside assistance with the vehicle, but if you are traveling in a remote area, in the southwest (like Death Valley for example) what do you do without a spare? If your cell phone quits, you're done. Even if you have AAA, their driver will have to tow the vehicle as he won't have a spare either.

OVERVIEW: Fairly well equipped, the Soul is a cheap little four-door hatchback/wagon that combines safety with acceptable urban performance while keeping your fuel bills low. The best combination is the 2.0L engine hooked to a 6-speed manual transmission. Invest in the ABS and stability control by moving upscale.

COST ANALYSIS: Forget the cheaper, leftover 2012s; the extra cost for a 2013 model is insignificant. **Best Alternatives:** Other contenders are the Hyundai Elantra, Nissan Cube or Versa, and Toyota Corolla. **Options:** Larger, 18-inch wheels and the driver's seat height adjuster. **Rebates:** Look for $1,000 rebates and low financing rates in late 2012. **Depreciation:** Slightly faster than average. A base 2010 Soul that retailed for $15,495 is now worth $9,000. **Insurance cost:** Average. **Parts supply/cost:** Average costs; some parts delayed. **Annual maintenance cost:** Average. **Warranty:** Bumper-to-bumper 5 years/100,000 km; powertrain 5 years/100,000 km; rust perforation 5 years/unlimited km. **Supplementary warranty:** A wise buy for the engine/tranny, considering Kia's previous powertrain troubles. **Highway/city fuel economy:** *1.6L man.:* 4.9/6.6 L/100 km, 58/43 mpg. *1.6L auto.:* 4.9/6.8 L/100 km, 58/42 mpg.

OWNER-REPORTED PROBLEMS: Only 21 safety-related complaints reported to NHTSA, when 50 would have been normal for the 2012 model year. Airbags failed to deploy; brake pedal is too small; rear brake failure caused a rear-ender; automatic transmission slips and often sticks in gear or grinds when going into Second gear; sometimes the transmission suddenly downshifts for no reason; when the vehicle is shifted into Park, the doors are automatically unlocked; fuel spews out when refuelling; driver's door fails to latch; the steering column came off while the car was cruising on the highway; the electronic stability control may engage for no reason and lock up the steering:

KEY FACTS

Canadian Price (negotiable): *1.6:* $16,795, *2.0 2U:* $19,195, *2.0 4U:* $22,895, *2.0 4U Luxury:* $25,595 **U.S. Price:** *1.6L:* $14,400, *Plus Hatch.:* $17,700, *Exclaim Hatch.:* $19,900

Canadian Freight: $1,650 **U.S. Freight:** $750

POWERTRAIN (FRONT-DRIVE)

Engines: 1.6L 4-cyl. (138 hp) • 2.0L 4-cyl. (164 hp); Transmissions: 6-speed man. • 6-speed auto.

DIMENSIONS/CAPACITY

Passengers: 2/3; Wheelbase: 100.4 in.; H: 63.4 in./L: 162.2 in./W: 70.3 in.; Headroom F/R: 5.0/5.5 in.; Legroom F/R: 42.1/39 in.; Cargo volume: 19.3 cu. ft.; Fuel tank: 48L/regular; Load capacity: 850 lb.; Tow limit: 2,000 lb.; Ground clearance: 6.5 in.; Turning circle: 34.4 ft.; Weight: 2,689–2,764 lb.

The steering wheel was locked up and could only be turned if considerable force was applied to it. I carefully pulled over to the side of the road. The Kia dealer service shop ultimately had to replace the entire steering column to "fix" the problem. About two months later I was driving down the interstate and attempted to do a lane change. Again the electronic stability control falsely activated and caused me to collide with the vehicle directly in front of me. When the ESC activated, the steering wheel locked up and caused a sudden loss of control, resulting in the accident.

The AC defroster may not clear the windshield. Owners decry a plethora of fit and finish deficiencies, including excessive condensation in the headlights, chips in the glass and paint, and door panels that scratch with the slightest touch.

SERVICE BULLETIN-REPORTED PROBLEMS: Rio and Rio5 have registered fewer owner complaints than the newer Kia Soul. Steering-wheel noise and vibration repair.

FORTE, FORTE KOUP ★★★

The Kia Forte.

RATING: Average. Good value for your money. Kia slew the poor-quality dragon a few years back; now, Kia's roomy compact sedan, coupe, and hatchback have the engine, suspension, and equipment refinements the lineup lacked in the past. Among the various models, the hatchback is the most versatile for access and storage. **Road performance:** Base engine doesn't pack much of a punch; a smooth-shifting automatic transmission; sure-footed and precise, confidence-inspiring handling and a comfortable, though jittery, ride; and engine and road noise is pervasive and gets louder as speed increases. **Strong points:** Lots of standard features, like four-wheel disc brakes and easily accessed and intuitive controls, plus Bluetooth and steering-wheel controls with voice activation. Nicely bolstered, comfortable front seats; lots of interior room; heated side-view windows; fewer rattles and body glitches (but still too many); a large dealer network, with both Kia and Hyundai providing servicing; and a comprehensive base warranty. Prices will become more negotiable by the end of the year. Overall quality is much improved, with few complaints posted on the NHTSA website. **Weak points:** Five passengers is a squeeze; steering wheel tilts but doesn't telescope (EX trim excepted). **Safety:** NHTSA gives the 2013 Forte four stars for front, side, and rollover crash protection. IIHS awarded the 2012 Forte top marks for front, side, rear, and roof crashworthiness. **New for 2013:** Nothing important.

ALERT! The Honda Fit might be a better choice. It's the roomiest hatchback in this class and is also the most versatile, thanks to seats that accommodate long and tall items. The Fit is also less expensive than the Forte hatchback, and is a better performer.

OVERVIEW: All these body styles have what it takes to satisfy the needs of the daily commuter as well as excite the most ardent high-performance fan. Two different 4-cylinder engines deliver power without wasting fuel. The upgraded 2.4L inline 4-banger that delivers 173 hp is the better engine by far. Handling is a breeze, thanks to the Forte's front-drive unibody frame and four-wheel independent suspension, which provide a firm and sporty ride with a minimum of noise, vibration, and harshness.

KEY FACTS

Canadian Price (Firm): *LX man.:* $15,995, *auto.:* $17,195, *EX:* $18,595, *SX:* $23,095, *EX Koup:* $19,095, *auto.:* $20,295, *SX Koup:* $22,395, *auto.:* $23,595, *SX:* $22,395, *SX Luxury:* $24,695 **U.S. Price:** *LX:* $15,400, *EX:* $17,800, *EX hatch.:* $18,300, *SX:* $19,300, *EX Koup hatch.:* $16,995, *auto.:* $17,995, *SX man.:* $18,395, *auto.:* $19,395 **Canadian Freight:** $1,455 **U.S. Freight:** $750
POWERTRAIN (FRONT-DRIVE)
Engines: 2.0L 4-cyl. (156 hp) • 2.4L 4-cyl. (173 hp); Transmissions: 6-speed man. • 6-speed auto.
DIMENSIONS/CAPACITY
Passengers: 2/3; Wheelbase: 104.3 in.; H: 57.5/L: 178.3/W: 69.9 in.; Headroom F/R: 4.0/2.5 in.; Legroom F/R: 43.3/35 in.; Cargo volume: 14.7 cu. ft.; Fuel tank: 51.9L/regular; Load capacity: 850 lb.; Turning circle: 33.9 ft.; Ground clearance: 5.9 in.; Weight: 2,729–2,849 lb.

COST ANALYSIS: Price increases on the 2013 entry-level models have been minimal, so get the latest model year. **Best Alternatives:** The Honda Fit, Kia Forte EX, Kia Soul Plus, Mazda3 Touring, Suzuki SX4 Technology, and Toyota Matrix (base model). **Options:** The $395 rear spoiler is a crock; save your money. **Rebates:** Look for $2,500 rebates or discounts and low financing rates early in 2013. **Depreciation:** Average. **Insurance cost:** Average. **Parts supply/cost:** Average. **Annual maintenance cost:** Average. **Warranty:** Bumper-to-bumper 5 years/100,000 km; powertrain 5 years/100,000 km; rust perforation 5 years/unlimited km. **Supplementary warranty:** Not needed. **Highway/city fuel economy:** *2.0L man.:* 5.7/8.1 L/100 km, 50/31 mpg. *Auto.:* 5.5/8.0 L/100 km, 51/27 mpg. *2.4L:* 6.2/9.2 L/100 km, 46/31 mpg.

OWNER-REPORTED PROBLEMS: Minor audio and fit and finish complaints; major paint defects; and the windshield may not be installed securely at the factory:

> Our technician was able to push most of the windshield out without having to cut the urethane bead. The urethane bead pulled right off the windshield, and was only adhered

to about 1/3 of the windshield perimeter. This vehicle was not involved in an accident, but had it been, the windshield would not have remained intact. The safety of the vehicle occupants due to this factory-installed improper installation was compromised.

SERVICE BULLETIN-REPORTED PROBLEMS: An ECM software upgrade to address the MIL warning light.

OPTIMA

bad buy

RATING: Not Recommended. Optima's rating has been downgraded due to persistent steering failures with past models (as with the Hyundai Sonata), other serious safety-related defects, poor powertrain performance, and slow parts delivery. **Road performance:** The base engine performs well, the ride is comfortable, and handling is secure. The optional 4-cylinder turbocharged engine is powerful and fuel-efficient, but V6-equipped rivals give a smoother and quieter performance. Considerable body lean when turning. *Hybrid:* Minimal body roll when cornering, and an excellent ride. On the other hand, the electrically assisted steering is a bit numb, the powertrain's jerky when going from gas to electric power (see "Service Bulletin-Reported Problems"), and the regenerative brakes could be more responsive. **Strong points:** Nicely appointed; has good overall visibility; provides plenty of front headroom; uses firm, supportive front bucket seats with plenty of fore and aft travel; a spacious trunk; and posts better-than-average fuel economy figures with regular fuel. Another plus: Servicing can be done by both Hyundai and Kia dealers. *Hybrid:* Nicely styled and well-appointed; intuitive, easily accessed controls; and plenty of room in front and back. **Weak points:** Mediocre braking; average rear headroom; excessive wind and tire noise; low rear seats; difficult rear access; trunk has a small opening; and fit and finish isn't up to Asian or European automakers' standards. *Hybrid:* Repair parts have been hard to find and can be costly. **Safety:** NHTSA gave the 2013 Optima and

Optima Hybrid five stars for front, side, and rollover crashworthiness. IIHS wasn't so generous. Tests of the 2011 model resulted in an "Acceptable" score for frontal offset and roof crash protection and a "Poor" rating for side crashworthiness. The 2012 Optima's head-restraint performance was rated "Good." The front passenger seat is too low for some. Limited rear visibility:

> I purchased this new car in January and have had a difficult time adapting to the blind spots out of the rear window. The rear headrests of this car were designed too large. Even in the down position, these headrests block nearly 2 thirds of the rear window visibility.

New for 2013: Minimal changes: The Optima LX receives a standard automatic transmission, cruise control, and aluminum wheels; the EX Turbo has been dropped.

ALERT! Despite the hype, real-world fuel economy is not all that impressive.

OVERVIEW: Kia's mid-sized sedan is essentially a rebadged Hyundai Sonata. All models include front side airbags, side curtain airbags, seat belt pretensioners, ABS, four-wheel disc brakes, and anti-whiplash head restraints that have received IIHS's top safety rating. The car is available in three trim levels: LX, EX, and SX. The LX and EX are equipped with a naturally aspirated 200 hp 2.4L 4-cylinder, while the SX uses a turbocharged 274 hp 2.0L 4-cylinder. A Sportmatic 6-speed automatic is standard.

Optima Hybrid

Kia's Optima Hybrid can be driven on battery power alone, or in blended gas-electric mode. When the car is stopped, the engine shuts off to save fuel. It uses a lithium polymer battery that will hold its charge up to 25 percent longer than hybrids with nickel metal hydride batteries.

The Hybrid also is one of the first full hybrid systems to use a typical automatic transmission—a compact 6-speed automatic that debuted on the 2011 Kia Sorento SUV. An external electrically driven oil pump provides the pressure needed to keep the clutches engaged when the vehicle is in idle stop mode.

COST ANALYSIS: Save money with an almost identical 2012 model. Hold out for major discounting and generous rebates to cut the retail price by at least 15

KEY FACTS

Canadian Price (negotiable): *LX:* $21,995, *LX+:* $25,795, *EX:* $26,795, *EX Turo:* $29,095, *EX Luxury:* $30,895, *SX:* $33,995; *Hybrid:* $30,595 (2012) **U.S. Price:** *LX:* $21,200, *EX:* $23,500, *SX:* $26,800, *Hybrid:* $25,700 **Canadian Freight:** $1,455 **U.S. Freight:** $750

POWERTRAIN (FRONT-DRIVE)

Engines: 2.4L 4-cyl. (200 hp) • 2.0L Turbo 4 (274 hp) • *Hybrid:* 2.0L 4-cyl (206 net hp); Transmissions: 6-speed man. • 6-speed auto.

DIMENSIONS/CAPACITY

Passengers: 2/3; Wheelbase: 107 in.; H: 57.3/L: 190.7/W: 72.1 in.; Headroom F/R: 4.5/3.0 in.; Legroom F/R: 45.5/34.7 in.; Cargo volume: 15.4 cu. ft.; Fuel tank: 62L/regular; Tow limit: *2.4L:* No towing, *2.7L:* 1,000–2,000 lb.; Load capacity: 905 lb.; Turning circle: 35.8 ft.; Ground clearance: 5.3 in.; Weight: 3,206–3,385 lb.

DIMENSIONS/CAPACITY (Hybrid)

Passengers: 2/3; Wheelbase: 110.1 in.; H: 57.3/L: 190.7/W: 72.1 in.; Headroom: N. A.; Legroom F/R: 45.5/34.7 in.; Cargo volume: 9.9 cu. ft.; Fuel tank: 62L/regular; Tow limit: *2.4L:* No towing, *2.7L:* 1,000–2,000 lb.; Ground clearance: 5.1 in.; Turning circle: 35.8 ft.; Weight: 3,490 lb.

percent. **Best alternatives:** Consider the Chevrolet Cruze, Honda Accord, Kia Rondo, Mazda3, Suzuki Kizashi, and Toyota Camry. **Options:** Save your money. **Rebates:** Look for $2,000 rebates or discounts and low financing rates early in 2013. **Depreciation:** Average. **Insurance cost:** Average. **Parts supply/cost:** Average, but Hybrid parts can be costly and are sometimes hard to find. **Annual maintenance cost:** Average. **Warranty:** Bumper-to-bumper 5 years/100,000 km; powertrain 5 years/100,000 km; rust perforation 5 years/unlimited km. **Supplementary warranty:** A wise buy for the engine and transmission. **Highway/city fuel economy:** *2.0L auto.:* 5.8/9.2 L/100 km, 49/31 mpg. *2.4L man.:* 5.7/8.7 L/100 km, 50/32 mpg. *2.4L auto.:* 6.5/8.6 L/100 km, 50/33 mpg. *Hybrid:* 4.9/5.6 L/100 km, 58/50 mpg.

OWNER-REPORTED PROBLEMS: As with its Sonata cousin, the Optima pulls sharply to one side when accelerating:

> Vehicle hard to control and steer straight, especially at highway speeds. Severe pull to the left, though occasionally it drifts to the right. At city speeds, the steering problem is not as noticeable. I took the car to the dealer, and they checked the alignment. Minor adjustments, and tire inflation change, resulted in no significant change in the problem… It remains severe. If you let go of the steering wheel, then the car swiftly moves across to the left lanes.

Other scary failures: Airbags failed to deploy; sudden, unintended acceleration:

> The contact owns a 2012 Kia Optima. While driving approximately 5 mph [8 km/h], the vehicle suddenly accelerated independently and crashed into the median. The vehicle was towed to the dealer for diagnostic testing where the technician advised that the front passenger side tire and axle would have to be replaced. The failure recurred four times. The fourth time the failure recurred, the contact crashed into another vehicle. The manufacturer refused to repair the vehicle because they stated there were no defects within the vehicle. Approximate failure mileage was 11,000 [17,700 km].

•

> For 3 to 5 seconds, no response from engine at idle when accelerator depressed and the car is stopped (e.g., for traffic signal). Then, without warning, the engine went from idle (about 800 rpm) to rapid (surging) acceleration, often with screeching tires. This occurred each time I started from a stopped position.

Catastrophic transmission failure; a parked car will roll down an incline, despite being put in First gear or having the emergency brake engaged; driver-side floor mat bunches up around the brake pedal; Brake warning light comes on for no reason; side view mirror fell off while driving along the freeway; no spare tire.

SERVICE BULLETIN-REPORTED PROBLEMS: The tire monitor system can be affected by radio signals. Remote Start system module software upgrade. Remedy for vehicles that stick in Park. *Hybrid:* Jarring gear shifting:

CHARACTERISTIC ACCELERATION FEEL (OPTIMA HYBRID)

This bulletin provides information relating to the Optima Hybrid which features an advanced hybrid powertrain of the parallel variety. This means that the vehicle can operate under either electric power only ("EV Mode") gasoline engine power only or a combination of the two ("HEV Mode"). The two power sources are selected automatically by an engine clutch which may provide a new and different driving feel to customers who are accustomed to conventional vehicles or other hybrid vehicles.

Part of this new driving feel is a slight oscillation in forward acceleration which may be described as a slight shudder judder or jerking motion. This happens after the powertrain transitions out of EV Mode and into HEV Mode by engaging the engine clutch. This oscillation may occur in multiple situations but it is particularly noticeable when the following combination of events occur:

- After cold-start; and
- At low speed (less than 20 mph [32 km/h]); and
- Under light accelerator pedal input (less than 20%).

Oscillations under these conditions can be mitigated by temporarily turning off ActiveEco mode with the steering wheel-mounted eco button or by adjusting driving style (using different accelerator pedal inputs) when circumstances allow. Because the oscillation is reduced after vehicle warm-up the customer may elect to re-enable ActiveEco after the vehicle is warmed up typically after 5–10 minutes of driving time.

Based upon the technology used in the Optima Hybrid this oscillation is a normal characteristic is not an indication of a [defect] and is integral to the Optima Hybrid powertrain design that maximizes fuel economy and durability.

SPORTAGE ★★

RATING: Below Average. This downgrade reflects the Sportage's serious steering problems. The Sportage has become a 4-cylinder "crossover" similar to the Tucson. Question: Why not simply buy a Tucson in light of the Sportage's dangerous road wander? **Road performance:** Kia's Sportage SX comes with a 256 hp 2.0L turbocharged engine and lots of performance enhancements. The boost in power

KEY FACTS

Canadian Price (negotiable): *LX:* $21,995, *EX:* $27,595, *EX Luxury:* $34,095, *SX:* $37,395 **U.S. Price:** *Base man.:* $19,000, *LX auto.:* $21,200, *EX auto.:* $24,200, *SX auto.:* $26,900 **Canadian Freight:** $1,650 **U.S. Freight:** $800

POWERTRAIN (FRONT-DRIVE/AWD)

Engines: 2.4L 4-cyl. (176 hp) • 2.0L 4-cyl. Turbo (256 hp); Transmissions: 6-speed man. • 6-speed auto.

DIMENSIONS/CAPACITY

Passengers: 2/3; Wheelbase: 103.5 in.; H: 66.7/L: 171.3/W: 70.9 in.; Headroom F/R: 5.5/4.0 in.; Legroom F/R: 42/29 in.; Cargo volume: 28 cu. ft.; Fuel tank: 58L– 65L/regular; Tow limit: 2,000 lb.; Load capacity: 925 lb.; Turning circle: 38 ft.; Ground clearance: 6.0 in.; Weight: 3,230–3,527 lb.

is accompanied by a sport-tuned suspension with tauter shock and strut valving. The base engine on other models is a lively, competent 4-banger. Sportage provides a comfortable, quiet ride, interspersed with moments of terror as the car wanders into oncoming traffic. On paper, the powertrain setup and suspension system scream performance, but on the road, the Sportage takes it down to a whisper. Roadway feedback is barely noticeable, and the car exhibits excess body roll and, like the Optima, wanders all over the road in addition to pulling sharply to one side or the other. **Strong points:** Standard stability control and curtain airbags. **Weak points:** Styled like a Pontiac Vibe with upscale Audi headlights and LED lighting; interior hard plastic garnishments cheapen the look; the firm leather seats look good but are hard on the butt. **Safety:** NHTSA gives the 2013 Sportage five stars for frontal and side occupant crash protection; rollover protection was given four stars. "Good" IIHS scores across the board. **New for 2013:** Updated suspension for a smoother ride; a restyled 2014 model.

ALERT! During your test drive, check the car for excessive wander or pulling:

While travelling at highway speeds, or any speed above 50 km/h on a straight road, vehicle requires constant correction to track in a straight line. Without constant correction, the vehicle would leave the road surface. The resistance to steering pressure in correlation to speed does not seem properly programmed. The best way to describe this is to drive a car that would otherwise track down the road correctly, now throw control arms with worn out bushing and ball joints. It acts exactly like that, except a car with worn out control arm bushings and ball joints would in no way shape or form pass a safety inspection in any state. This problem, on trips over 45 minutes excessively fatigues the driver. (I thought I was going crazy on a 4.5 hour trip mostly expressway speeds). Over 110 km/h this problem seems to be eliminated...but not worth the endangerment to others using the roadway.

OVERVIEW: The Sportage has been around forever. Now—in its downsized configuration, resting on the Hyundai Tucson's frame, and using Kia's ubiquitous 2.4L 4-cylinder engine—Sportage offers power, car-like handling, and better dependability. Standard equipment for the base LX version, which has a 4-cylinder engine hooked to a manual 6-speed transmission, includes power windows and door locks, cruise control, tilt steering, power side mirrors, and four-wheel disc brakes with ABS.

COST ANALYSIS: Go for the 2013 version; prices haven't been boosted by much. **Best alternatives:** The Honda CR-V, Hyundai Tucson, Kia Rondo, Mazda Tribute, and Toyota RAV4. **Options:** The LX V6; the EX version is padded with nonessentials. **Depreciation:** Average. **Insurance cost:** Average. **Parts supply/cost:** Average cost; some delays for parts. **Annual maintenance cost:** Average. **Warranty:** Bumper-to-bumper 5 years/100,000 km; powertrain 5 years/100,000 km; rust perforation 5 years/unlimited km. **Supplementary warranty:** Worth considering. **Highway/city fuel economy:** *2.4L man.:* 6.9/10 L/100 km, 41/28 mpg. *2.4L auto.:* 6.2/9.4 L/100 km, 46/30 mpg. *2.4L 4WD:* 7.0/9.9 L/100 km, 40/29 mpg. *2.0L 4WD:* 7.7/10 L/100 km, 37/28 mpg.

OWNER-REPORTED PROBLEMS: Excessive steering wander/pull; vehicle moves forward when transmission lever is put in Park:

> The contact attempted to stop the vehicle by utilizing the emergency brake. He also opened the driver side door in the event that he would have to jump from the vehicle. The vehicle crashed into two parked vehicles, trapping the contact between the vehicles. The contact received injuries to the arms, shoulders and ribs. The current mileage is 3,500 miles [5,600 km].

Noisy, ineffective brakes; brake pedal grip padding falls off; windshield cracking; and minor problems with the audio system and fit and finish.

SERVICE BULLETIN-REPORTED PROBLEMS: Outside radio signals may cause the tire-pressure monitoring system to malfunction; steering-wheel noise and vibration repair.

SORENTO ★

bad buy

KEY FACTS

Canadian Price (negotiable): *LX: $26,895, LX V6: $29,495, EX: $32,295, EX V6: $34,295, EX V6 Luxury: $38,795, SX: $41,295* **U.S. Price:** *2.4L LX auto.: $23,150, 3.5L LX V6: $25,700, 2.4L EX: $26,950, 3.5L EX V6: $27,950* **Canadian Freight:** $1,650 **U.S. Freight:** $800
POWERTRAIN (REAR-DRIVE/4WD)
Engines: 2.4L 4-cyl. (175 and 191 hp) • 3.5L V6 (276 hp); Transmission: 6-speed auto.
DIMENSIONS/CAPACITY
Passengers: 2/3; 2/3/2; Wheelbase: 106.3 in.; H: 68.7/L: 183.9/W: 74.2 in.; Headroom F/R/R1: 5.5/5.5/0.1 in.; Legroom F/R: 41/27/26 in.; Cargo volume: 37.5 cu. ft.; Fuel tank: 80L/regular; Tow limit: 3,500 lb.; Load capacity: 1,120 lb.; Turning circle: 38 ft.; Ground clearance: 7.5 in.; Weight: 3,571–3,682 lb.

RATING: Not Recommended. Poor reliability and future orphanhood make the Sorento's 2013 carryover model a very poor buy. **Road performance:** At first glance, this is an off-roader's delight, with low-range gearing and good ground clearance, but there's always that pesky reliability thing. The base engine will do what is required. **Strong points:** Okay, it is well-appointed and you get more SUV for fewer bucks, but what you do get may be all show and no go—and not very reliable, either. (Not really "strong points," eh?) You also have a fairly roomy interior with good fit and finish. **Weak points:** Your off-roading fun will end as soon as the tranny, steering, or brakes give out. (Did we mention reliability?) Fuel consumption is much higher than represented. **Safety:** NHTSA gives five stars for side crash protection and four stars for frontal and rollover crashworthiness. IIHS scores the 2013 Sorento "Good" in all categories. **New for 2013:** Nothing significant.

ALERT! 250 safety-related complaints have been registered by the NHTSA on the redesigned 2011 model.

OVERVIEW: The Sorento represents good value in theory, with its strong towing capacity and excellent safety ratings. However, it falls far short on reliability, safety, quality control, fuel economy, and ride quality. The 2011 redesign adopted a new unibody platform and an additional third-row seat, making the Sorento longer and wider than previous models.

COST ANALYSIS: If you feel lucky, opt for a 2013, but steer clear of the poor-quality 2012 models. **Best alternatives:** The Honda CR-V and Hyundai Tucson. **Options:** The Sport package isn't worth its cost. **Rebates:** Look for $5,000 rebates and low financing and leasing rates in late 2012. **Depreciation:** Faster than average for an Asian make. For example, a 2009 4WD Sorento that originally sold for $30,000 is now worth only $12,500. **Insurance cost:** Average. **Annual maintenance cost:** Higher than average. **Warranty:** Bumper-to-bumper 5 years/100,000 km; powertrain 5 years/100,000 km; rust perforation 5 years/unlimited km. **Supplementary warranty:** A wise buy, considering Kia's previous transmission troubles. **Highway/city fuel economy:** *2.4L man.:* 7.4/10.6 L/100 km, 38/27 mpg. *2.4L auto.:* 6.2/9.5 L/100 km, 46/30 mpg. *2.4L 4WD:* 7.1/10.1 L/100 km, 40/28 mpg. *V6 4WD:* 8.2/11.5 L/100 km, 34/25 mpg.

OWNER-REPORTED PROBLEMS: This is a bad car. Normally one would expect to see an average of 50 complaints posted on the NHTSA website for a one-year-old vehicle. The 2011 Sorento has five times as many. Here's a summary of the most serious and life-threatening defects reported on the 2012 models: Sudden, unintended acceleration, as brakes wouldn't work and airbags failed to deploy; car stalls out when cruising; transmission hesitates or fails to upshift:

Transmission broken for the 4th time. Vehicle towed for 4th time.

•

The contact stated that the transmission failed to switch gears while driving 55 mph [88 km/h]. The contact had to shut off the engine to allow the vehicle to cool in order to proceed with driving. The vehicle was taken to the dealer for diagnosis where they were unable to diagnose or duplicate the failure. The vehicle was not repaired. The VIN is unavailable. The failure mileage was 3,000 [4,800 km].

•

On three occasions during the first month I owned the vehicle, I have experienced uncommanded downshift from 6th gear to 4th gear at speed. Transmission then locks in 4th gear until shut down and restarted. Very violent event when it occurs, with an instantaneous bang and corresponding immediate loss of speed.

Vehicle jerks, stutters, and stalls when accelerating:

Almost immediately started experiencing the occasional hesitation problem when pulling into traffic from a stop. On a couple occasions it put us in a very dangerous situation as we were crossing 2 lanes of traffic. Took the vehicle to dealer 4 times, they could not duplicate the problem. Finally they got us a 2012 near identical Sorento V6, and on the 3rd day had the same experience w/ 50 miles [80 km] on the vehicle. We now have 500+ [800 km] on it and have had a total of 7 similar situations.

Early brake wearout; chrome bezel instrument panel creates a painful and annoying reflection; rear sunroof exploded for no reason; headlight illumination is too short; sudden tire blowouts; and poor outward visibility:

New SUVs are adding huge pillars to the rear of vehicles, shrinking rear third windows, shrinking rear trunk door windows, pushing driver seats tightly up against the driver door—to shrink the car and boost gas mileage. On top of that, they are pursuing "quietness" & part of that is shrinking the exterior mirrors. Add this all up & you can hide a semi in the blind spot of this car. It was like driving a windowless cargo van w/o the big cargo van mirrors. The mirrors are small like what belongs on an economy car. Yes, my driver side mirror was well adjusted to only show a sliver of the vehicle. I just couldn't see. As I continued SUV shopping, I found this new design in many new SUVs. Gigantic blind spots are now the new design. I couldn't see to change into the left lane. When I looked over my shoulder my face was so close to the window, all I could see behind me were the separating pillars. Changing lanes was a guess.

SERVICE BULLETIN-REPORTED PROBLEMS: Steering-wheel noise and vibration repair. Transmission shift improvement. Steering wander or pull troubleshooting:

SUB-FRAME AND SUSPENSION ADJUSTMENT FOR DRIFT CONCERN

This bulletin provides information related to a drift condition and adjusting/settling the suspension components under load as assembly variation can remain on the suspension. Camber and Caster may need slight adjustment depending on actual road conditions. To improve this condition the dealer is requested to first follow the TSB CHA 032 (Drift/Pull Diagnosis and Best Practices Tips) for specifications and if they are outside the parameters then perform the instructions as directed in this TSB.

Lexus

Accelerating Lies

No one had heard of Lexus vehicles suffering from sudden, unintended acceleration with attendant brake loss—until a few years ago. At that time, Toyota, the owner of the Lexus luxury brand, insisted the accidents and deaths were due to driver error. However, after some delay the automaker did a turnabout and in late 2009 recalled almost its entire Toyota lineup (4.4 million vehicles), to better secure floormats and fix a sticky throttle, while insisting that most of its higher-end Lexus models weren't involved.

This denial lasted until June 20, 2010, when the National Highway Traffic Safety Administration (NHTSA) asked Toyota to recall 2010 Lexus RX 350 and RX 450 H vehicles "for a serious safety issue involving potential pedal entrapment by the floor mat"—the same defect affecting vehicles involved in the 2009 recall campaign.

Safety regulators have warned Toyota that it might face another investigation as to whether the company "met its obligation to notify the agency and conduct a recall in a timely manner." Previously, after the brake failures and sticky throttles were investigated by NHTSA, Toyota paid record federal fines for failing to promptly inform regulators of defects in its vehicles and for delaying recalls.

Toyota has received complaints from consumers about floormat entrapment since 2004.

Lexus's impeccable reputation for quality and safety has taken a beating by the past several years' news barrage of owner complaints, recalls, and serial *mea culpas* issued by Toyota's president that "Ahem, well, you know—the company lost its way."

Former executives who have testified against the automaker say Toyota simply believes it is above the law—showing the same arrogant attitude it manifested earlier in Canada when it tried to fix new-car prices under an "Access" price scheme. Caught with its pants down by Ottawa anti-competition investigators who were acting on a *Lemon-Aid* complaint, Toyota paid a $2 million settlement to charity and beat the rap. In the States, the automaker paid almost $50 million for dragging its feet on recalls.

The combination of bad press, an economic recession, and Japan's Fukushima earthquake hasn't seriously hurt sales for either Toyota or Lexus. Luxury car sales took a hit during the first year, but the Lexus brand has since bounced back sharply. Luxury car buyers, though, are no longer saying "I'm gonna buy a Lexus." Instead, they are looking at vehicles offered in the luxury class and then making their choice.

To make sure that choice is a Lexus, luxury car shoppers will be tempted by substantial rebates and other sales incentives throughout the 2013 model year.

Lexus is a luxury automaker on its own merits, even though many models are mostly dressed-up Camrys. Unlike Acura and Infiniti, Lexus is seen by some as the epitome of luxury and comfort, with a small dab of performance thrown in. Lexus executives know that no matter how often car enthusiast magazines say that drivers want "road feel," "responsive handling," and "high-performance" thrills, the truth of the matter is that most drivers simply want cars that look good and that give them bragging rights for safety, performance, convenience, and comfort; they want to travel from point A to point B, without interruption, in cars that are more than fully equipped Civics or warmed-over Maximas. Lexus executives figure that hardcore high-performance aficionados can move up to its sportier models and the rest will stick with the Camry-based ES series.

Although these imports do, in most cases, set advanced benchmarks for quality control, they don't demonstrate engineering perfection, as proven by a recent spate of engine failures, including sludge buildup and automatic transmissions that hesitate and then surge when shifting. And yes, cheaper luxury cars from Acura, Hyundai, Kia, Nissan, and Toyota give you almost as much comfort and reliability, but without as much cachet and resale value.

Speaking of resale values, don't believe that buying a Lexus is akin to investing in an RRSP. Some models are money-losers. Take, for example, a 2008 entry-level ES 350: New, it sold for $42,900; today you can get one for about $19,000. What? A four-year-old Lexus selling for less than half its original value? Welcome to the real world.

Technical service bulletins show that Lexus models have been affected mostly by powertrain and electrical malfunctions, faulty emissions-control components, computer module miscalibrations, and minor body fit and trim glitches. To Lexus' credit, many owners haven't heard of these problems because Lexus dealers have been particularly adept at fixing defects early.

Most of the 2013 Lexus models are carryovers from last year, so don't look for sweeping changes apart from cosmetic updates and refinements to existing technologies.

ES 350, ES 300H (HYBRID) ★★★

The Lexus ES 350.

KEY FACTS

Canadian Price (negotiable): *Base:* $39,500, *Premium:* $41,500, *Navi.:* $44,250, *Touring:* $48,550, *Technology:* $51,750 **U.S. Price:** *Base:* $36,100, *ES 300h Hybrid:* $38,850 **Canadian Freight:** $1,950 **U.S. Freight:** $875

POWERTRAIN (FRONT-DRIVE)

Engines: 3.5L V6 (268 hp) • *Hybrid:* 2.5L 4-cyl. (200 hp); Transmissions: 6-speed auto. • *Hybrid:* CVT

DIMENSIONS/CAPACITY

Passengers: 2/3; Wheelbase: 111 in.; H: 57.1/L: 192.7/W: 71.7 in.; Headroom F/R: 2.5/1.5 in.; Legroom F/R: 41.9/40 in.; Cargo volume: 15.2 cu. ft.; Fuel tank: 65L/regular; Load capacity: 900 lb.; Turning circle: 37.4 ft.; Ground clearance: 6.1 in.; Weight: 3,549 lb. *Hybrid:* 3,541 lb.

RATING: Average. Shh—this is a pricey near-luxury sedan that's really a gussied-up Camry. **Road performance:** Good acceleration; a pleasantly quiet ride; steering feel is muted; and overall handling (excessive body roll) isn't as nimble as with its BMW or Mercedes rivals. Dangerous erratically performing automatic transmission that hesitates and surges when shifting; **Strong points:** Aggressive styling and a well-appointed interior; lower curb weight and some engine tinkering nudges up fuel economy a bit; and better-than-average quality control. **Weak points:** Brakes are disappointing, in that the small discs are the same size as those found on the much lighter Camry and brake fade after successive stops is evident. Numb steering is another annoyance. The car is primarily a four-seater, as three adults can't sit comfortably in the rear; headroom is inadequate for tall occupants; trunk space is limited (low liftover, though); and some of the dash instruments and controls look a bit outdated. **Safety:** The 2013 models were given a four-star NHTSA rating for frontal and rollover crashworthiness, but side crash protection merited only two stars—unusually low for a higher-end car. IIHS gave "Good" ratings for front, side, and roof protection, but subsequent IIHS tests downgraded this ranking (see the "Alert!" section). Head restraints were rated "Marginal." Rear-corner visibility is hampered by the high rear end. **New for 2013:** There are two ES models: the naturally aspirated ES 350 and the ES 300h hybrid. They are practically identical at first glance—the hybrid model is distinguished by unique 17-inch alloy wheels, a rear decklid spoiler, and a fuel-frugal 2.5L Atkinson-cycle inline-four. This sixth-generation ES now uses the Toyota Avalon platform and gains 1.7 inches of additional wheelbase (111.0 total), 1 inch of additional length (192.7), and 0.8 inches of height. Lexus has managed to add 4 inches of additional rear legroom.

ALERT! In recent front-corner crash tests, IIHS gave the 2012 ES 350 a "Poor" rating. There's a drive-select knob on the centre console that can be dialed to Normal, Eco, and Sport modes, and the steering and throttle response is altered to match your choice. Only problem: The differences between the Normal and Eco settings are more mental than mechanical.

OVERVIEW: This entry-level Lexus front-drive carries a 268 hp V6 mated to an electronically controlled 6-speed automatic transmission that handles the 3.5L engine's horses effortlessly, without sacrificing fuel economy. All ES 350s feature dual front and side airbags, anti-lock brakes, double-piston front brake calipers, an optional Adaptive Variable Suspension, power-adjustable pedals with memory setting, 60/40 split-folding rear seats, a DVD navigation system, a 10-way power-adjustable driver's seat with memory, rain-sensing wipers, and one of the rarest features of all: a conventional spare tire.

COST ANALYSIS: A discounted leftover 2012 model will be cheaper and practically identical to the 2013. Consider getting the usurious freight/PDI fee cut in half. **Best alternatives:** An all-dressed Camry, the Acura TL, the BMW 3 Series, and the Toyota Avalon. **Options:** Don't fall for the frivolous $7,000 Ultra Luxury Package. **Rebates:** Mostly low-cost financing. **Depreciation:** Much lower than average. **Insurance cost:** Much higher than average. **Parts supply/cost:** Good availability, and parts are moderately priced. **Annual maintenance cost:** Below average. **Warranty:** Bumper-to-bumper 4 years/80,000 km; powertrain 6 years/120,000 km; rust perforation 6 years/unlimited km. **Supplementary warranty:** May be needed to cover automatic transmission malfunctions. **Highway/city fuel economy:** 7.2/10.9 L/100 km, 39/26 mpg.

OWNER-REPORTED PROBLEMS: Sudden, unintended acceleration; stuck accelerator; automatic transmission shifts erratically, suddenly accelerates, or slips and hesitates before going into gear; some minor transmission malfunctions; car lurches forward when the cruise control is reengaged; brake failure and premature brake wearout; radio system glitches; fit and finish imperfections; tire monitor system malfunctions; Bluetooth cell phone voice distortion; and an inoperative moonroof.

SERVICE BULLETIN-REPORTED PROBLEMS: Nothing serious reported.

IS 250, IS 350, IS F ★★★★

The Lexus IS 250.

KEY FACTS

Canadian Price (negotiable): *IS 250:* $32,900, *Auto.:* $34,500, *AWD:* $38,000, *250C:* $49,100, *350C:* $57,000, *IS C:* $49,000, *IS F:* $69,850 **U.S. Price:** *IS 250:* $34,465, *AWD:* $36,925, *RWD MT:* $33,295, *250C RWD:* $42,360, *250C RWD MT:* $41,190, *IS 350:* $39,720, *AWD:* $42,180, *350C:* $46,640, *IS F:* $60,660 **Canadian Freight:** $1,895 **U.S. Freight:** $875

POWERTRAIN (REAR-DRIVE/AWD)

Engines: 2.5L V6 (204 hp) • 3.5L V6 (306 hp) • 5.0L V8 (416 hp); Transmissions: 6-speed man. • 6-speed auto.

DIMENSIONS/CAPACITY

Passengers: 2/3; Wheelbase: 107.5 in.; H: 55.7/L: 182.5/W: 70.9 in.; Headroom F/R: 2.0/2.0 in.; Legroom F/R: 41.5/25.5 in.; Cargo volume: 10.8 cu. ft.; Fuel tank: 65L/premium; Tow limit: 1,500 lb.; Load capacity: 825 lb.; Turning circle: 33.5 ft.; Ground clearance: 4.7–5.3 in.; Weight: 3,814 lb.

RATING: Above Average. **Road performance:** The IS 350 has a competent standard 3.5L engine, but the IS 250's 2.5L feels rather sluggish when pushed. Handling on both the 250 and 350 models doesn't feel as sharp or responsive as with the BMW competition, owing in large part to an intrusive Vehicle Dynamics Integrated Management system that automatically eases up on the throttle during hard cornering. Emergency braking also isn't a confidence-builder. **Strong points:** More standard safety, performance, and convenience features than with the IS 300; the car is wider, longer, and more solid-looking; easy handling, and effective braking; an upgraded interior; optional navigation screen is user-friendly and easily read; pleasant riding; low beltline provides a great view; first-class workmanship; and a relatively quiet, high-quality interior. **Weak points:** Cramped rear seating. Insufficient front-corner crashworthiness. The car requires premium fuel and has outrageously high freight charges. *IS F:* A tiny cabin. **Safety:** NHTSA crash tested the 2013 IS 250 and 350 for rollover protection only, and both cars scored five stars. IIHS rated frontal offset and side crash protection as "Good"; roof strength and head-restraint merited an "Acceptable" score. Be wary of the high frontal offset score—subsequent tests produced worse results. **New for 2013:** Minor changes; 2014 model to be redesigned.

ALERT! The 2012 IS did miserably in July 2012 front-corner panel tests carried out by IIHS. It was rated "Poor." The IS F has lots of tire-smoking power and provides thrilling high-performance handling, but your thrills will come with a bone-jarring, teeth-chattering ride; a too-firm suspension; and no manual transmission option.

OVERVIEW: Targeting BMW's 3 Series, Lexus's entry-level IS 250 and IS 350 rear-drive sport-compact sedans come with either a 204 hp 2.5L V6 or a 306 hp 3.5L V6. The F version ups the ante considerably with its 416 hp 5.0L V8 powerplant, which is going into its fifth year on the market. Owner comments have been positive, and the car's residual value has been quite strong.

COST ANALYSIS: Lexus has lost a lot of its lustre after going through two years of safety-related recalls and increased competition from European and Japanese luxury carmakers. Look for prices to soften and discounts in the new year of about 15 percent, plus generous leasing deals by summer's end. **Best alternatives:** Try the Acura TL, BMW 3 Series, and Infiniti G37. Audi's A4 would be a contender, if it wasn't for its recent redesign and attendant glitches, coupled to a less than stellar quality-control history. Audi's quality shortcomings are borne out in *Consumer Reports*' annual member surveys and in independent European consumer publications. **Options:** Don't waste money on the sunroof, heated seats, or leather upholstery. **Rebates:** Expect $2,000–$3,000 discounts early in 2013, along with attractive financing and leasing deals as the European competition bounces back from its own economic woes. **Depreciation:** Much lower than average. **Insurance cost:** Higher than average. **Parts supply/cost:** Average availability, though parts may be quite expensive because of the lack of independent parts suppliers. **Annual maintenance cost:** Below average. **Warranty:** Bumper-to-bumper 4 years/80,000 km; powertrain 6 years/120,000 km; rust perforation 6 years/unlimited km. **Supplementary warranty:** Not necessary. **Highway/city fuel economy:** IS 250 man.: 7.5/11.4 L/100 km, 38/25 mpg. IS 250 auto.: 6.8/9.8 L/100 km, 42/29 mpg. IS 250 AWD: 7.6/10.5 L/100 km, 37/27 mpg. IS 350: 7.8/10.9 L/100 km, 37/27 mpg. IS 350C: 7.9/11.5 L/100 km, 36/25 mpg. IS F: 8.5/13.0 L/100 km, 33/22 mpg.

OWNER-REPORTED PROBLEMS: Sudden, unintended acceleration:

> On several occasions...the rpms increase randomly after the car has stopped and is stationary. The car inches forward and the driver has to apply more pressure on the brake pedal to make sure the car doesn't lurch forward and hit the car in front. The rpms go up almost 1000 rpms from idling. Happens in D and R. When turning on car, putting the gear [in] R, the car just lurches backwards unless the brake pedal is heavily [depressed]. This seems to be a software/ECM issue.

Many reports of premature brake wear and jerking the car to one side when the brakes are applied, and fit and finish imperfections. Poor instrument visibility:

> The visual displays on the center dashboard console indicating HVAC and audio information for the Lexus IS 250 C are so light as to be virtually invisible to the driver, particularly in bright sun and when the driver is wearing sunglasses.

Sunroof shattered while vehicle was underway; excessive window rattling when driving with the top down; loss of transmission fluid; and AC mildew odour (Lexus replaced the vehicle).

SERVICE BULLETIN-REPORTED PROBLEMS: Fuel gauge indicates Empty when there is gas in the tank. *2011–12:* Bubbled HID headlight housing.

GS 350, GS 450H, GS 460 ★★★

The Lexus GS 350.

RATING: Average. An exercise in passive driving—an abundance of electronic gadgetry cannot transform these luxury sedans into sports cars, and reliability reports tarnish some of the Lexus lustre. **Road performance:** Good high-performance powertrain set-up; pleasantly quiet ride; and acceptable handling and braking. **Strong points:** Average fuel economy, though premium fuel must be used. Good—no longer exceptional—quality control. **Weak points:** Primarily a four-seater with limited headroom for six-footers; the Audi A6 offers more rear legroom; middle-rear passengers, as usual in rear-drive sedans, get to ride the powertrain hump and thump the low roof with their heads; and some instruments are hidden by the steering wheel. **Safety:** No NHTSA crashworthiness data available. IIHS scores the 2013 models as "Good" for frontal, side, and rear protection and roof strength. The high window line impedes rear visibility. **New for 2013:** Nothing major.

ALERT! Lexus no longer has the quality moxie to demand higher prices than its competitors. Imagine, a discounted sticker price is now the Lexus calling card. Haggle hard when buying a GS.

OVERVIEW: The GS 350 luxury sedan comes with a 303 hp 3.5L V6 engine hooked to a 6-speed automatic transmission with sequential manual shift. The GS 460 and the GS 450h gas-electric hybrid are powered by a 342 hp V8 and a 340 hp V6, respectively. The GS 450h can run on one or both of its power sources, uses a CVT, and doesn't need plug-in charging. Standard safety features include traction/anti skid control, ABS, front knee airbags, front side airbags, side curtain airbags, a rear-view camera, and a Pre-Collision System designed to automatically cinch seat belts and apply the brakes if an unavoidable crash is detected. Other standard features include driver-adjustable shock absorbers (460 and 450h models), leather upholstery, and dual-zone climate controls, plus oodles of other safety, performance, and convenience features.

COST ANALYSIS: Since the 2013s are practically identical to last year's model, why not opt for a "leftover Lexus" and save thousands? **Best alternatives:** Granted, GS models are comfortable, polished luxury sedans, but sporty performers they are not. The Infiniti M, for example, allows for more driver input and is more satisfying to drive, owing mainly to smooth power delivery, crisper shifts, precise steering, more-predictable brakes, and a less-intrusive stability system. The Acura TL and BMW 5 Series are two other models you may consider. **Options:** Lexus has now packaged GS options so that it is almost impossible to get the essential without getting the frivolous or dangerous. Try to stay away from the in-dash navigator; it complicates the calibration of the sound system and climate controls. Other money-wasting options include a power sunshade, a moonroof, the Mark Levinson stereo, the XM radio, ventilated seats, a spoiler, Intuitive Park Assist parking sensors, and rain-sensing wipers with Adaptive Front Lighting swivelling headlights. Be wary of the Dynamic Radar Cruise Control that reduces your speed when cars cut you off; if it malfunctions, as other systems have, you're toast. **Rebates:** By early winter, expect $3,000 rebates, zero percent financing, attractive leasing terms, and discounting on the MSRP by about 10 percent. **Depreciation:** Slower than average. **Insurance cost:** Much higher than average. **Parts supply/cost:** Parts aren't easily found outside of the dealer network, and they're fairly pricey. **Annual maintenance cost:** Much less than average. **Warranty:** Bumper-to-bumper 4 years/80,000 km; powertrain 6 years/120,000 km; rust perforation 6 years/unlimited km. **Supplementary warranty:** Not necessary. **Highway/city fuel economy:** GS 350: 7.4/10.9 L/

KEY FACTS

Canadian Price (negotiable): *GS 350 AWD:* $54,650, *450h Hybrid:* $71,750 **U.S. Price:** *GS 350:* $46,900, *AWD:* $46,900, *450h:* $58,950, *460 RWD:* $55,370 **Canadian Freight:** $1,895 **U.S. Freight:** $875

POWERTRAIN (REAR-DRIVE/AWD)

Engines: 3.5L V6 (303 hp) • *Hybrid:* 3.5L V6 (340 hp) • 4.6L V8 (342 hp); Transmissions: 6-speed auto. • 8-speed auto. • CVT

DIMENSIONS/CAPACITY

Passengers: 2/3; Wheelbase: 112.2 in.; H: 56.1/L: 190/W: 71.7 in.; Headroom F/R: 2.0/2.0 in.; Legroom F/R: 41.5/28 in.; Cargo volume: 14.8 cu. ft.; Fuel tank: 70L/premium; Tow limit: N/A; Load capacity: 815 lb.; Turning circle: 37.1 ft.; Ground clearance: 5.0 in.; Weight: 3,685 lb.

100 km, 38/26 mpg. *GS 350 AWD:* 8.0/11.6 L/100 km, 35/24 mpg. *GS 450h:* 7.8/8.7 L/100 km, 35/23 mpg. *GS 460:* 8.1 /12.4 L/100 km, 36/32 mpg.

OWNER-REPORTED PROBLEMS: Car suddenly accelerated as it was being parked; vehicle wandering at highway speeds requires constant steering corrections; and brake failures.

SERVICE BULLETIN-REPORTED PROBLEMS: Front brake squeal or squeak; notchy steering feel.

RX 350, RX 450H ★★★★/★★★

The Lexus RX 350.

RATING: *RX 350:* Above Average. Lexus invented the luxury crossover segment with the RX series in 1998, and since then it has been a perennial bestseller. *RX 450h:* Average. Some fuel savings, but you will pay a heavy purchase price in Canada (in the States, the car costs much less). Buying the car in mid-2013 should save you about 15 percent in either country. Resale value for the hybrid will drop faster as you get closer to the battery pack's replacement time—around the eight-year mark. **Road performance:** Count on a smooth, car-like ride and a satisfying braking response and feel. Handling is not as positive; the car doesn't feel as agile as its competition. **Strong points:** Now in its third generation, the 2013 doesn't disappoint with its attractive styling, great safety ratings, lots of luxury in a spacious cabin, and adequate back-seat legroom. Also, the RX has excellent gas mileage for a luxury crossover. There's less steering feedback when compared to the RX 450h. **Weak points:** No third-seat option; expensive options packages; modest cargo capacity; and excessive road noise. *Hybrid:* Slow acceleration; takes more effort to turn; and the Remote Touch multifunction joystick and screen are distracting features. **Safety:** The 2013 models earned four-star crash scores from NHTSA for frontal and rollover crash resistance and five stars for side crash safety. IIHS gave the 2012 RX a "Good" ranking across the board. **New for 2013:** Nothing significant.

ALERT! During the test drive, pay careful attention to how the RX 450h 4×4 "On Demand" feature performs (see "Owner-Reported Problems").

OVERVIEW: Exterior styling is slightly different in the latest RX. Suspension is independent all around, and the progressive electronic power-steering system is speed-sensing for enhanced control. The front-drive and all-wheel-drive RX models come identically equipped. Rear cargo room has been increased slightly, and anti-lock brakes, stability control, traction control, and 10 airbags are standard.

COST ANALYSIS: Get the cheaper, practically identical 2012 model, but take 10 percent off the list price. **Best alternatives:** The BMW 5 Series, 2012 Hyundai Veracruz, and Lincoln MKX. **Options:** Stay away from the moonroof option. Not only is it nonessential and often failure-prone, but it also comes in packages that include other frivolous features. Be wary of the Adaptive Cruise Control; it may behave erratically. **Rebates:** Expect $3,000 rebates, zero percent financing, and good leasing terms. Discounting and rebates will become more attractive in the first quarter of 2013. **Depreciation:** Slower than average. **Insurance cost:** Much higher than average. **Parts supply/cost:** Parts are hard to find from independent sources; prices are on the high side. **Annual maintenance cost:** Less than average. **Warranty:** Bumper-to-bumper 4 years/80,000 km; powertrain 6 years/120,000 km; rust perforation 6 years/unlimited km. **Supplementary warranty:** Not needed. **Highway/city fuel economy:** RX 350: 8.2/11.6 L/100 km, 34/24 mpg. RX 450h: 7.2/6.6 L/100 km, 39/43 mpg.

OWNER-REPORTED PROBLEMS: Hybrid suddenly accelerated as it was being parked, brakes were ineffective, and the front tire exploded. Car surges forward when the brakes are applied. RX 450h brake failures are similar to those reported on the Prius:

> I wanted to alert you that other hybrid models that were manufactured with the same braking system as the Prius suffer the same issue. I have a 2010 Lexus 450h RX and its brakes disengage when I am driving on bumpy roads and over pot holes. I live in a

KEY FACTS

Canadian Price (negotiable): *RX 350:* $44,950, *Premium 1:* $48,000, *Premium 2:* $49,500, *RX 350 Touring:* $53,950, *RX 350 Sport:* $57,900, *Ultra Premium:* $59,450, *RX 450h:* $56,750, *Touring:* $60,850, *Ultra:* $67,050, *Ultra2:* $71,400 **U.S. Price:** *RX 350:* $39,310, *350 AWD:* $40,710, *450h FWD:* $45,910, *450h AWD:* $47,310 **Canadian Freight:** $1,950 **U.S. Freight:** $875
POWERTRAIN (FRONT-DRIVE/AWD)
Engines: 3.5L V6 (275 hp) • *Hybrid:* 3.5L V6 (295 hp); Transmissions: 6-speed auto. • CVT
DIMENSIONS/CAPACITY
Passengers: 2/3; Wheelbase: 108 in.; H: 67/L: 188/W: 74.2 in.; Headroom F/R: 3.0/4.5 in.; Legroom F/R: 41.5/28.5 in.; Cargo volume: 40 cu. ft.; Fuel tank: 70L/regular; Tow limit: 3,500 lb.; Load capacity: 825 lb.; Turning circle: 37.1 ft.; Ground clearance: 7.3 in.; Weight: 4,178 lb.

northeastern city with many bumps and my brakes stop working often and as a result I have to slam them on much more quickly.

The 4×4 system doesn't perform as advertised:

The RX450h is downright dangerous. The 4 wheel drive does not switch "on demand" as the advertising says. I live in snowy Massachusetts and do not need permanent 4 wheel drive, but it is essential when the roads are full of snow or ice. I was puzzled at first that the 4 wheel drive only actuated under 25 mph [40 km/h]. I tested it on sharp corners in the snow: the back slid out; and on faster, gradual corners: the car side slipped. Never did the 4 wheel drive switch on and correct the slide. I looked in the manual for the method to manually activate 4 wheel drive but couldn't find it. I contacted Lexus. They said that I should use the snow switch. This is a menu item which annoyingly [must] be switched on every time you drive. It didn't work, as it only changes the gear and acceleration characteristics like any other winter/summer switch. They also said that it should work at high speeds when more power is needed. I tried that and found that at 60 mph [95 km/h] if I absolutely floored the accelerator on a steep hill the 4 wheel drive would switch on briefly.

Audio system problems and poor fit and finish are other owner grievances. Owners also report excessive dust/powder blows from the AC vents; tire monitor system malfunctions; inoperative moonroof; the vehicle pulls to the right; and the original equipment Firestone Dueler H/L 400 tire having hairline splits along the side wall.

SERVICE BULLETIN-REPORTED PROBLEMS: *2011–12:* Inoperative smart key; insufficient charging.

Mazda

Mazda has lots to smile about. Four decades ago, it was a marginal automaker selling cheap, hard-to-service, here-today-gone-tomorrow rustbuckets. But during the past decade Mazda trimmed its Ford ties and improved the quality of its lineup, and it now specializes in peppy, fuel-sipping small cars, family sedans, a bestselling six-passenger mini-minivan, and a number of popular SUV crossovers.

The "Smiling" Automaker

Mazda's past is a story of missed opportunities. It snared the rights to the innovative Wankel rotary engine from GM (destined for the Vega and Astre) that had a reputation for being relatively small and powerful—but at the expense of poor fuel efficiency. Mazda put the Wankel in its RX-7 series of roadsters (1978–2002) and its RX-8 sports cars (2004–2010) and was fairly successful in marketing the cars to the high-performance crowd. But once North American fuel prices soared and gas station lineups stretched for blocks, Mazda switched gears, dropped the Wankel, and went back to building conventionally powered, nondescript econocars.

Ford saved Mazda from bankruptcy in 1994 by purchasing part of the company and sharing the production of their cars and trucks. Mazda soon turned profitable through better management and a popular new array of small cars and trucks made in partnership with Ford. The company's sole minivan, the MPV, was both a quality and performance boondoggle and never got any traction. It was put out of its misery in 2006.

Mazda went back to its small-car roots with last year's brand-new $13,995 Mazda2, a four-door hatchback powered by a 100 hp 1.5L 4-cylinder engine with a standard 5-speed manual transmission or optional 4-speed automatic. It gets 7.2 L/100 km (39 mpg) in the city and 5.6 L/100 km (50 mpg) on the highway.

Fast and Frugal

The slightly upscale Mazda3 does everything the Mazda2 doesn't. There's plenty of interior room, and the powertrain performs flawlessly. In fact, this little pocket rocket, marketed as an urban runabout, remains on back order, due to the performance crowd support since its debut as a 2004 model. This peppy and fuel-efficient compact takes Mazda back to its compact-car roots and adds some performance thrills to its fuel-saving powertrain. Recently the "3" was restyled, the suspension stiffened to enhance handling, and a third engine, a 155 hp 2.0L 4-cylinder, was added along with Mazda's new Skyactiv fuel-saving feature that was introduced last year and expanded to the 2013 models.

The Mazda5 minivan was revamped last year and has more innovative features to attract the minivan crowd to a smaller conveyance. The Mazda6 returns with a hatchback and a wagon to accompany its sedan version. In March 2012, Mazda launched the CX-5, its smallest SUV, equipped with a 148–155 hp 2.0L 4-cylinder engine. A 2.2L diesel version is planned for 2013. The CX-7 increases in size this year, as it replaces the larger CX-9. The Tribute (Ford's Escape SUV twin) was axed last year.

 MAZDA3 ★★★★★

RATING: Recommended. A fuel-efficient compact with a performance edge. **Road performance:** Good powertrain set-up, with plenty of reserve power for passing and merging; easy, predictable handling; good steering feedback; small turning radius; rear multi-link suspension gives the car great stability at higher speeds. **Strong points:** Spacious, easy-to-load trunk; user-friendly instruments and controls; and better-than-average workmanship. **Weak points:** The Mazda3 has a history of automatic transmission malfunctions (but no more than with Honda or Toyota models) and prematurely worn-out brake rotors and pads. A small trunk; limited rear footroom; excessive road noise intrudes into the cabin. **Safety:**

KEY FACTS

Canadian Price (negotiable): *GX sedan:* $16,295, *Auto.:* $17,495, *GX Sport:* $17,495, *Auto.:* $18,695, *GS sedan:* $19,595, *Auto.:* $20,795, *GS Luxury:* $21,690, *Auto.:* $22,890, *GT sedan:* $24,425, *Auto.:* $25,625, *MazdaSpeed:* $29,695 **U. S. Price:** *SV 4d:* $15,800, *Sport:* $16,705, *Touring:* $18,100, *s Sport:* $19,545, *s Grand Touring:* $22,510 **Canadian Freight:** $1,495 **U.S. Freight:** $795

POWERTRAIN (FRONT-DRIVE)

Engines: 2.0L 4-cyl. (148 hp) • 2.0L 4-cyl. (155 hp) • 2.5L 4-cyl. (167 hp); Transmissions: 5-speed man. • 6-speed man. • 5-speed auto. • 6-speed auto.

DIMENSIONS/CAPACITY (sedan)

Passengers: 2/3; Wheelbase: 104 in.; H: 58/L: 181/W: 69.1 in.; Headroom F/R: 4.5/3.0 in.; Legroom F/R: 41/25 in.; Cargo volume: 12 cu. ft.; Fuel tank: 55L/regular; Load capacity: 850 lb.; Turning circle (hatchback): 34.2 ft.; Ground clearance: 6.1 in.; Weight: 3,065 lb.

NHTSA's front-impact crashworthiness rating for the 2013 model is five stars, rollover resistance earned four stars, and side protection scored only three stars. IIHS gave the 2012 Mazda3 its top, "Good" score for frontal offset, head-restraint, and rear crash protection. Roof strength was also rated "Good." A high deck cuts rear visibility. **New for 2013:** Carried over unchanged.

ALERT! The Mazda3 is a theft magnet. Invest in an engine disabler and GPS tracker.

OVERVIEW: The Mazda3 is an econobox with flair that pleases commuters and "tuners" alike. The car offers spirited acceleration and smooth, sporty shifting. Handling is enhanced with a highly rigid body structure, front and rear stabilizer bars, a multi-link rear suspension, and four-wheel disc brakes. Interior room is quite ample with the car's relatively long wheelbase, extra width, and straight sides, which maximize headroom, legroom, and shoulder room.

COST ANALYSIS: There is an outrageously high $1,495 freight fee you shouldn't pay. Heck, just across the border Mazda charges Americans only $795. So, by driving 80 kilometres, smart shoppers can save $700, plus another $500 due to the lower price on the American side. The cheaper and virtually identical 2012 version is recommended but hard to find as higher gas prices stampede buyers toward anything that is fast and frugal. Hatchback models give you the most versatility. **Best alternatives:** A 2013 Honda Civic. **Options:** Don't accept the original Goodyear Eagle RS-A tires; go to *www.tirerack.com* to find some better tires for less money. The 5-speed automatic transmission with AC is a good start, although the 6-speed manual is lots more fun to drive. **Rebates:** Not likely. **Depreciation:** Much less than average. Consider this: A 2009 base Mazda3 sedan that sold for $14,895 is still worth $8,000. **Insurance cost:** Average. **Parts supply/cost:** Parts are easy to find. **Annual maintenance cost:** Less than average, so far. **Warranty:** Bumper-to-bumper 3 years/80,000 km; powertrain 5 years/100,000 km; rust perforation 5 years/unlimited km. **Supplementary warranty:** Not needed. **Highway/city fuel economy:** *2.0 man.:* 5.9/8.1 L/100 km, 48/35 mpg. *2.5 man.:* 6.9/10.2 L/100 km, 41/28 mpg.

OWNER-REPORTED PROBLEMS: The Mazda3 five-star rating hasn't changed mainly due to the absence of owner complaints and its superior highway performance. Nevertheless, some owners have reported premature wearout of brake pads and rotors, accompanied by an annoying grinding sound and pulling to one side when the brakes are applied; brake rotors are easily grooved; rear glass window may explode in chilly weather:

> Morning: 16 degrees F [−9°C]. Approached my car in the morning and heard a crackling noise. I thought the sound was ice. I started the car and the rear defogger. As I sat in my driveway…approximately 30 seconds after turning on the defogger…the rear glass exploded with a loud noise…. The car is 4 months old and under warranty…. I called Mazda and was told that this is due to outside influence (i.e. the same as if a tree branch fell on the car). He indicated that I should expect that this could happen in the cold weather. I cannot believe that I should expect that my rear window can explode in cold weather.

(Note: in the above-cited incident, the car owner could have easily sought restitution from small claims court on the grounds that the "balance of probabilities" points to a defective rear window.)

Front passenger-side airbag may be disabled even though an average-sized adult is seated; manual transmission clutch failure; and the rear sway bar link nut may loosen, causing a clunking sound to be heard coming from the rear undercarriage when the car passes over bumps or rough roads.

SERVICE BULLETIN-REPORTED PROBLEMS: *All Mazdas 2006–13:* Troubleshooting clunk, bang, or jolt from front of vehicle upon takeoff. *2001–13:* Excessive sulfur odours. *2004–11:* Intermittent no-starts in Park. *2004–12:* Brakes judder, or dragging troubleshooting tips. *2010–12:* Rust on bottom of rear door guide; Bluetooth hands-free diagnostic tips.

MAZDA5 ★★★

KEY FACTS

Canadian Price (negotiable): *GS:* $21,795, *Auto.:* $22,995, *GT:* $24,395, *Auto.:* $25,595 **U.S. Price:** *Sport:* $19,195, *Touring:* $21,185, *Grand Touring:* $23,875

Canadian Freight: $1,695 **U.S. Freight:** $795

POWERTRAIN (FRONT-DRIVE)

Engine: 2.5L 4-cyl. (157 hp); Transmissions: 6-speed man. • 5-speed auto.

DIMENSIONS/CAPACITY (2010)

Passengers: 2/2/2; Wheelbase: 108.2 in.; H: 64.1/L: 181.5/W: 68.7 in.; Headroom F/R1/R2: 4.5/4.5/2.0 in.; Legroom F/R1/R2: 41/29.5/22 in.; Cargo volume: 39 cu. ft.; Fuel tank: 60L/regular; Tow limit: No towing; Load capacity: 1,020 lb.; Turning circle: 37 ft.; Ground clearance: 5.9 in.; Weight: 3,408–3,465 lb.

RATING: Average. All the advantages of a small minivan, without the fuel penalty. **Road performance:** Agile, no-surprise handling. Drivers will find this Mazda a breeze to park and easy to manoeuvre with its tight turning radius and direct steering. The small 4-cylinder engine doesn't have much torque ("grunt," or pulling power) for heavy loads or hill climbing, and towing isn't recommended. Some body roll when cornering, and steering is somewhat vague. **Strong points:** Reasonably priced; decent fuel economy; a comfortable ride; dual sliding rear doors; an easy-access liftgate; and relatively quiet interior (except for omnipresent road noise—a common trait with small wagons). The cabin is roomy, and two wide-opening sliding doors make for easy access and are a great help when installing a child safety seat. **Weak points:** There isn't much room for passengers in the third-row seat, and the interior seats may be too firm for some. There's also a history of automatic transmission malfunctions (but no more than with Honda or Toyota vehicles), premature wearout of brake rotors and pads, and fit and finish deficiencies. **Safety:** NHTSA's front- and side-impact crashworthiness rating for the 2010 model is five stars, and rollover resistance scored four stars. **New for 2013:** Carried over without any significant changes.

ALERT! This little minivan is the perfect vehicle for servicing by cheaper independent garages. It hasn't changed much over the years, and its generic parts are available practically anywhere.

OVERVIEW: This small minivan is a relatively tall and narrow car—it looks like a long hatchback—with a thick, obtrusive front A-pillar. It's basically a compact miniwagon that's based broadly on the Mazda3 and carries six passengers in three rows of seats. Used mostly for urban errands and light commuting, the "5" employs a peppy, though fuel-frugal, 157 hp 2.5L 4-cylinder engine hooked to a standard 6-speed manual transmission or a 5-speed automatic.

COST ANALYSIS: Get a 15 percent cheaper, almost identical 2012. **Best alternatives:** The 2013 Honda Civic, Hyundai Tucson, and Toyota Corolla, Camry, or Matrix. **Options:** Any good tires, instead of Bridgestone or Firestone. **Rebates:** Look for $2,000 discounts as the new year approaches. **Depreciation:** Average. **Insurance cost:** Average. **Parts supply/cost:** Easy to find. **Annual maintenance cost:** Less than average, so far. **Warranty:** Bumper-to-bumper 3 years/80,000 km; powertrain 5 years/100,000 km; rust perforation 5 years/unlimited km. **Supplementary warranty:** Not needed. **Highway/city fuel economy:** Man.: 6.8/9.7 L/100 km, 42/29 mpg. Auto.: 6.7/9.5 L/100 km, 42/30 mpg.

OWNER-REPORTED PROBLEMS: Very few owner complaints recorded, except for the suspension, brakes, and fuel system (fuel pumps, mostly):

> The vehicle again suddenly shut down while driving on the highway. During this incident, not only was I about 80 miles [130 km] away from home, but I was traveling with 5 children in the vehicle! At this point, I became very concerned for the safety of my children in the car! The possibility that an accident could occur if my car lost power and another vehicle impacted the rear of the vehicle; or if I wasn't able to properly steer the vehicle was extremely high on such a busy highway!

Fit and finish glitches are quite common. Also, owners report a few automatic transmission failures; transmission gear hunting and fluid leaks; power-steering malfunctions; electrical system shorts; and rapid brake and tire wear. Airbag warning light and Traction Stability Control (TSC) light come on for no reason.

SERVICE BULLETIN-REPORTED PROBLEMS: *2008–12:* Bluetooth hands-free troubleshooting. *2011–12:* Headlights don't come on with parking lights. *2012–13:* Tips on getting rid of excessive sulfur odours.

MAZDA6 ★★★★

KEY FACTS

Canadian Price (negotiable): *GS I4:* $23,995, *Auto.:* $25,195, *GS V6:* $31,500, *GT I4:* $29,395, *GT V6:* $37,440 **U. S. Price:** *i SV:* $18,600, *i Sport:* $20,240, *i Touring:* $22,885, *i Touring Plus:* $24,490, *i Grand Touring:* $27,070, *s Touring Plus:* $27,330, *s Grand Touring:* $29,570

Canadian Freight: $1,695 **U.S. Freight:** $795

POWERTRAIN (FRONT-DRIVE)

Engines: 2.5L 4-cyl. (170 hp) • 3.7L V6 (272 hp); Transmissions: 6-speed man. • 5-speed auto. • 6-speed auto.

DIMENSIONS/CAPACITY

Passengers: 2/3; Wheelbase: 110 in.; H: 58/L: 194/W: 72.4 in.; Headroom F/R: 5/3 in.; Legroom F/R: 40.5/29.5 in.; Cargo volume: 16.5 cu. ft.; Fuel tank: 64L/regular; Tow limit: No towing; Load capacity: 850 lb.; Turning circle: 35.4 ft.; Ground clearance: 5.1 in.; Weight 3,185 lb.

RATING: Above Average. A car enthusiast's family sedan, although not as refined or as sporty as Honda's Accord. **Road performance:** Good powertrain set-up; very agile, with nice overall handling; responsive, precise steering; a tight turning circle; all-independent suspension; and impressive braking. **Strong points:** Comfortable seating, and acceptable workmanship. High prices can be easily bargained down as the model year plays out. **Weak points:** Excessive road noise intrudes into the cabin; unusually low roofline restricts access; and the V6 can increase your fuel consumption by almost 20 percent. Mazda has a history of automatic transmission and fit and finish deficiencies. **Safety:** NHTSA gives its top, five-star score to the 2013 Mazda6 for rollover protection, four stars for side crashworthiness, and three stars for frontal crash safety. Also, IIHS gives the 2012 its top, "Good" score for frontal offset and side occupant protection. Roof strength is rated "Acceptable," and head restraints get a "Marginal" score. **New for 2013:** Carried over unchanged.

ALERT! For most people, the 4-cylinder engine has power to spare for most driving needs. Don't opt for a more expensive, less fuel-efficient V6 before test-driving a model with the smaller engine.

OVERVIEW: This mid-sized sporty sedan offers a sweet combination of high performance, a roomy interior, and clean, aerodynamic styling.

COST ANALYSIS: There's no reason to spend more money with the identical 2013; shop for a cheaper 2012. **Best alternatives:** The Honda Accord, Hyundai Tucson, Nissan Altima, and Toyota Camry or Matrix. **Options:** The V6 engine is better-performing and more reliable; be wary of the Bridgestone and Firestone tires. **Rebates:** $3,000 sales incentives and low-cost leases and financing are most likely. **Depreciation:** Slower than average. A 2009 top-of-the-line GS V6 that sold for $27,695 is now worth $16,000. **Insurance cost:** Average. **Parts supply/cost:** Easy to find. **Annual maintenance cost:** Average. **Warranty:** Bumper-to-bumper 3 years/80,000 km; powertrain 5 years/100,000 km; rust perforation 5 years/unlimited km. **Supplementary warranty:** Not needed. **Highway/city fuel economy:** 2.5 man.: 6.6/9.8 L/100 km, 43/29 mpg. 2.5 auto.: 6.5/9.4 L/100 km, 43/30 mpg. 3.7: 7.9/11.9 L/100 km, 36/24 mpg.

OWNER-REPORTED PROBLEMS: Some minor problems with the transmission, electrical, and fuel systems. Many fit and finish deficiencies, particularly with paint delamination and peeling.

SERVICE BULLETIN-REPORTED PROBLEMS: Leather seat wrinkles. *2003–12:* Brake judder or dragging. *2003–13:* Tips on eliminating excessive sulfur odours. *2009–12:* Bluetooth hands-free troubleshooting; poor AC performance. *2011–12:* Headlights may not come on with the parking lights. *2012:* Water leak from left A-pillar/cowl area.

MX-5 ★★★★★

RATING: Recommended. A time-tested, reasonably priced, exceptional roadster. **Road performance:** Well-matched powertrain provides better-than-expected

KEY FACTS

Canadian Price (Firm): *GX:* $28,995, *Auto.:* $29,995, *GS:* $33,495, *Auto.:* $33,495, *GT:* $39,995, *Auto.:* $41,195 **U.S. Price:** *Sport:* $23,110, *Touring:* $24,450, *Grand Touring:* $26,710, *PRHT Touring:* $27,150, *PRHT Grand Touring:* $28,550 **Canadian Freight:** $1,695 **U.S. Freight:** $795

POWERTRAIN (REAR-DRIVE)

Engine: 2.0L 4-cyl. (167 hp); Transmissions: 5-speed man. • 6-speed man. • 6-speed auto.

DIMENSIONS/CAPACITY

Passengers: 2; Wheelbase: 92 in.; H: 49/L: 157/W: 68 in.; Headroom: 1.5 in.; Legroom: 40 in.; Cargo volume: 5.0 cu. ft.; Fuel tank: 48L/regular; Tow limit: N/A; Load capacity: 340 lb.; Turning circle: 30.8 ft.; Ground clearance: 4.6 in.; Weight: 2,458–2,632 lb.

acceleration and top-end power at the 7000 rpm range; classic sports car handling; perfectly weighted steering with plenty of road feedback; and a firm but comfortable suspension. **Strong points:** Impressive braking; mirrors are bigger and more effective than those found in most luxury sports cars; engine is fairly quiet, and little road noise intrudes into the cabin; instruments and controls are easy to read and access; good fuel economy; user-friendly trunk; manual top is easy to operate; very few safety- or performance-related defects; and a high resale value. **Weak points:** All the things that make roadsters so much "fun": a compact cabin, difficult entry and exit, and a can of tire sealant instead of a spare tire. **Safety:** The 2005 earned five stars for rollover protection, four stars for frontal crashworthiness, and three stars for side-impact protection, but NHTSA hasn't crash tested the MX-5 since then. No IIHS crash scores. Restricted rear visibility with the top up. **New for 2013:** Nothing important.

ALERT! Another neon sign saying "come and get me" to thieves. An engine disabler and GPS tracker are your best anti-theft devices. Forget about lights, alarms, and steering-wheel locks.

OVERVIEW: The MX-5 is a stubby, lightweight, rear-drive, two-seater convertible sports car that combines new technology with old British roadster styling reminiscent of the Triumph, the Austin-Healy, and the Lotus Elan. It comes in a variety of trim levels: The three convertibles are the Sport, Touring, and Grand Touring. The fourth model is the Touring (Power-Retractable) Hard Top. The lineup begins with the soft-top-only Sport; a removable hardtop is available as an option. All models come with a heated glass rear window.

It's amazing how well the MX-5 is put together, considering that it isn't particularly innovative and most parts are borrowed from Mazda's other models. For example, the engine is borrowed from the Mazda3 and Mazda6, and the suspension is taken from the RX-8. A 5-speed manual gearbox is standard fare, while the 6-speed manual and automatic are optional. The MX-5 is shorter than most other sports cars; nevertheless, this is a fun car to drive, costing much less than other vehicles in its class.

COST ANALYSIS: Get a discounted 2012, if you can find one; it's identical to the costlier 2013. **Best alternatives:** The BMW Z cars, Chevrolet Camaro, Infiniti G37 Coupe, Mercedes-Benz SLK, and Porsche Boxster. **Options:** The 6-speed manual transmission is a toss-up, since the 5-speed is so smooth. **Rebates:** Look for $1,500 discounts by year's end. **Depreciation:** Slower than average: A 2009

Miata GX convertible that sold for $28,495 is now worth $17,500. **Insurance cost:** Higher than average. **Parts supply/cost:** Parts are easy to find, but they often cost more than average. **Annual maintenance cost:** Much less than average, particularly when compared to other roadsters. **Warranty:** Bumper-to-bumper 3 years/80,000 km; powertrain 5 years/100,000 km; rust perforation 5 years/unlimited km. **Supplementary warranty:** Not needed. **Highway/city fuel economy:** *5-speed man.:* 7.1/9.2 L/100 km, 40/31 mpg. *6-speed man.:* 7.1/9.7 L/100 km, 40/29 mpg. *6-speed auto.:* 7.2/10.1 L/100 km, 39/28 mpg.

OWNER-REPORTED PROBLEMS: Some minor driveline, fuel system, and fit and finish complaints. Headlight beams blind oncoming drivers:

> I have to apply tape over the driver side headlight to "fix" the problem and now I get zero bright beam flashes from oncoming cars. Other auto manufacturers offer the same type of lighting for their products, but they also install a dial that is used to adjust the light beams up and down. This car does not have such a device. Affixing an ugly piece of tape to my car is not what I expected when I paid $34,000 for this automobile.

SERVICE BULLETIN-REPORTED PROBLEMS: *2006–12:* Brake judder or dragging. *2006–13:* Clunk, bang, jolt from front of vehicle at takeoff is considered "normal" by Mazda; excessive sulfur odours. *2007–12:* Hardtop rattles at windshield header. *2009–12:* Bluetooth hands-free troubleshooting tips. *2012–13:* Leather seat wrinkles.

CX-7, CX-9 ★ ★ ★

The Mazda CX-7.

RATING: Average. **Road performance:** *CX-7:* Well equipped; turbocharged engine has power to spare; and excellent handling, with a relatively tight turning radius and responsive steering. Base engine is a so-so performer, and the turbocharged version is hampered by considerable "turbo lag," which increases the response time from the throttle to the engine. Both engines are also relatively noisy, with

KEY FACTS

Canadian Price (Soft): *GX FWD:* $26,495, *GS AWD:* $29,995, *GT AWD:* $36,690, *CX-9 GS:* $36,395, *GS AWD:* $38,395, *GT:* $45,595 **U.S. Price:** *GX-7 i SV:* $21,990, *i Sport:* $22,795, *s Touring:* $26,255, *AWD:* $27,955, *s Grand Touring:* $31,640, *AWD:* $33,340, *CX-9 Sport:* $29,135, *AWD:* $30,525, *Touring:* $31,055, *AWD:* $32,445, *Grand Touring:* $33,145, *AWD:* $34,535 **Canadian Freight:** $1,695 **U.S. Freight:** $795

POWERTRAIN (FRONT-DRIVE/AWD)

Engines: *CX-7:* 2.5L 4-cyl. (161 hp) • 2.3L 4-cyl. (244 hp); *CX-9:* 3.7L V6 (273 hp); Transmissions: *CX-7:* 5-speed auto. • 6-speed auto.; *CX-9:* 6-speed auto.

DIMENSIONS/CAPACITY (CX-7 and CX-9)

Passengers: 2/3, 2/3/2; Wheelbase: 108.2 in., 113.2 in.; H: 52.7, 68.0/L: 184.3, 200.8/W: 73.7, 76.2 in.; Headroom: N/A; Legroom F/R: *CX-7:* 41.7/36.4 in.; *CX-9:* 41/39.3 in.; Cargo volume: 29.9 cu. ft., 37.5 cu. ft.; Fuel tank: 69L, 76L/regular or premium; Tow limit: 2,000 lb., 3,500 lb.; Load capacity: 1,190 lb.; Turning circle: 37.4 ft.; Ground clearance: 8.1 in., 8.0 in.; Weight: 3,500–4,007 lb., 4,265–4,585 lb.

the 2.5L producing a coarse drone and the turbo powerplant emitting an annoying whine. Irregular roadways give occupants a shaky ride. *CX-9:* The 273 hp 3.7L V6 delivers plenty of power with little noise or delay. Handling is better than average, and the ride is fairly smooth over irregular terrain. **Strong points:** *CX-7:* Plenty of cargo room, and good all-around visibility. *CX-9:* Even roomier, with more headroom, legroom, and storage space. Instruments and controls are nicely laid out and not hard to master. The CX-9 will be replaced by an enlarged CX-7 early in 2013. **Weak points:** *CX-7:* Ride comfort is so-so and may be a bit too firm for some; tall occupants may find headroom too limited; rear seating is a bit low and cramped; and interior garnishing seems a bit on the cheap side. Mediocre fuel economy; the turbo-equipped model requires premium fuel. *CX-9:* Third-row seating is mainly for children being punished, and gas consumption is relatively high. **Safety:** In NHTSA tests, the 2013 CX-5 side crashworthiness merited five stars, while frontal and rollover protection scored four stars each. Rear visibility is limited. The 2012 CX-7 and CX-9 rollover protection was rated four stars. **New for 2013:** 2012 is the CX-7's last model year; CX-9 to be slightly restyled.

ALERT! Owners say gauges on the instrument panel are hard to read at night and in bright sunlight.

OVERVIEW: *CX-7:* Essentially a small five-passenger front-drive and AWD SUV crossover, the car debuted as a 2007 model in Canada and has been one of Mazda's bestselling models ever since. Available safety features include ABS, traction control, an anti-skid system, side curtain airbags, and front side airbags. *CX-9:* The seven-passenger CX-9 is not an extended CX-7, yet. In fact, it shares its platform with the popular Ford Edge and adds a better interior in the process. Its Ford DNA makes the "9" a quieter-running and more agile performer than its smaller sibling.

COST ANALYSIS: There has been strong demand for these cars, and that may be their saving grace because the more CXs sold, the better servicing and supply should become. **Best alternatives:** The Chevrolet Equinox or Traverse, Ford Flex, GMC Acadia or Terrain, Honda Pilot, Hyundai Tucson or Santa Fe, and Toyota Highlander. **Options:** Nothing extra is needed. **Rebates:** Look for $2,500 discounts by year's end. **Depreciation:** Faster than average: A 2009 base CX-7 that once sold for $29,995 now sells for $15,500. The CX-9? Not much better. The base model first sold for $36,795, and now it's worth only $19,000. **Insurance cost:** Higher than average. **Parts supply/cost:** Parts are easy to find, but they often cost more than average. **Annual maintenance cost:** Average. **Warranty:** Bumper-to-bumper 3 years/80,000 km; powertrain 5 years/100,000 km; rust perforation 5 years/unlimited km. **Supplementary warranty:** Don't drive without one. **Highway/city fuel economy:** *CX-7 2.5L:* 7.2/10.4 L/100 km, 39/27 mpg. *CX-7 2.3L:* 8.7/12.2 L/100 km, 32/23 mpg. *CX-9 front-drive:* 9.1/13.4 L/100 km, 31/21 mpg. *AWD:* 9.6 /14.0 L/100 km, 29/20 mpg.

OWNER-REPORTED PROBLEMS: *CX-7:* Drivers have reported minor engine problems in addition to fuel system, brake, and fit and finish deficiencies. Excessive condensation in the front headlights; accelerator and brake pedals are mounted too close together; and persistent brake squeaking, groaning. *CX-9:* Among the few registered complaints, we find early brake wear, poor fit and finish, and audio system malfunctions.

SERVICE BULLETIN-REPORTED PROBLEMS: Bluetooth hands-free troubleshooting tips; silencing Bose speaker noise; combating excessive sulfur odours; wrinkled leather seats; remedy for excessive vibration from the floor or steering wheel during acceleration; front brake squeaking:

FRONT BRAKES SQUEAK ON BRAKE APPLICATION

BULLETIN NO.: 04-006/11   DATE: NOVERMBER 30, 2011

FRONT BRAKES SQUEAK WHEN APPLYING BRAKES

After parking in cold temperatures accompanied by a humid climate, some vehicles may exhibit a squeak from the front brakes during initial braking. This noise is caused due to deterioration of grease between the front disc pads, shims and the brake caliper. Customers having this concern should have their vehicle repaired using the following repair procedure.

REPAIR PROCEDURE

When you encounter a customer complaint, remove the disc pads (A) (right and left) and attache protectors to the original guide plates (B), then apply white grease to the location indicated on the caliper (C) and mounting support (D) according to the following procedures.

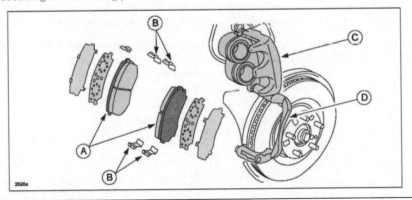

CX-7: *2007–12:* Fixing a partly detached rear spoiler. *2010–12:* Door armrest trim peeling.

Mitsubishi

Flying under the Radar

Mitsubishi has had a rocky road in Canada, particularly since 2003. This is mainly because of its practically nonexistent dealer network, maladministration, and the rise of many Japanese and South Korean makes that are more refined and better accepted by shoppers.

The 2013 Mitsubishi Eclipse.

Through June 2012, total year-to-date Mitsubishi sales in Canada were 10,310 vehicles. To put this in perspective, over that same period, 866,000 new automobiles were purchased or leased in Canada.

Nevertheless, Mitsubishi Canada's ensuing press release gushed over the good news:

Sales included a record 821 deliveries of the Mitsubishi RVR, while Mitsubishi's top-selling car, Lancer and its Sportback, Ralliart and Evolution models, notched 712 deliveries. The mid-size Outlander crossover saw 494 sales. Canada's most affordable four-passenger electric car, the Mitsubishi i-MiEV, hit 21 sales in June bringing total i-MiEV sales to 138 units. "Led by RVR's best month since launch and strong Outlander deliveries, we continue to build on the strength of our crossovers...," said Tony Laframboise, MMSCAN's Vice President, Sales and Marketing.

Mitsubishi crossovers may have helped, but natural disasters in Japan sidelining the competition is what led to Mitsubishi's sales upsurge in Canada. With Honda and Toyota on the ropes while they rebuilt their factories and renewed their supply lines, Mitsubishi got its best chance ever to increase sales worldwide.

MITSUBISHI SALES IN CANADA

RANK	MODEL	JUNE 2012 YTD	JUNE 2011 YTD	CHANGE
#56	Mitsubishi Lancer	3,922	3,330	+17.8%
#60	Mitsubishi RVR	3,522	3,945	−10.7%
#87	Mitsubishi Outlander	2,480	2,595	−4.4%
#93	Toyota Prius V	2,274	-----	-----
#110	Toyota Prius	1,619	1,047	+54.6%
#113	Toyota Prius C	1,521	-----	-----
#134	Smart Fortwo	957	1,025	−6.6%
#209	Mitsubishi Eclipse	171	323	−47.1%
#221	Nissan Leaf	137	-----	-----
#223	Mitsubishi i-MiEV	115	-----	-----
#225	Mitsubishi Endeavor	100	117	−14.5%

Despite Mitsubishi's optimism, smart money says its sales will fall as the Toyota and Honda competition heats up in the last quarter of 2013. As for Mitsubishi's bet that electric cars are the future, see the Chevrolet Volt sales chart, following.

ELECTRIC CAR SALES—OUT OF JUICE?

YEAR	CHEVROLET VOLT U.S. SALES	CHEVROLET VOLT CANADIAN SALES
2010	326	-----
2011	767	1275
2012 YTD*	10,666	600

* June 2011 through June 2012

Source: Automaker sales figures provided to Polk (*www.polk.com*)

GM predicted 10,000 Volt sales for 2011 and expects to sell 60,000 units in 2012. On a more positive side, May U.S. Volt sales beat out the Nissan Leaf and Toyota Prius Plug-in.

RVR Compact Crossover and Electric/Hybrids

Mitsubishi's RVR is a compact crossover that has been running on European and Japanese roads for some time. It has a pleasing, simple style and a rigid, lightweight body that's just over a foot shorter than the Outlander and shares the Outlander's stance and packaging while giving slightly better fuel economy. Sales of the RVR (or Outlander Sport, to Americans) are reasonably good, with ES pricing starting at $19,998.

Electric cars and hybrids, sprouting from the company's existing lineup, were Mitsubishi's main thrust for 2012 when Mitsubishi's first electric car arrived in November. Called the i-MiEV, the car is expected to sell 20,000 units annually and will be joined by three other electric car or plug-in hybrid vehicles by 2016. The first to follow the i-MiEV is the plug-in hybrid version of the Outlander crossover, launched last spring.

If all goes well, Mitsubishi says it should make a profit by March of 2013. But, that's a big "if."

The $32,998 i-MiEV sales may take off as fuel prices go higher, particularly now that the U.S. Environmental Protection Agency rates the i-MiEV as providing the equivalent of 128 mpg city and 99 mpg highway. (Curious as to how this conversion is done? See *http://physics.ucsd.edu/do-the-math/2011/08/mpg-for-electric-cars.*) But the car is facing stiff competition from other electric cars like the Nissan Leaf and Chevrolet Volt, two vehicles with limited sales in Canada that have failed to meet their own sales projections.

Mitsubishi also sells the following models in Canada: the compact Lancer ($15,998–$25,198 for the GT), the sporty Eclipse (ranging from $24,498 for the GS coupe manual to $30,498 for the Spyder manual), the Sportback ($19,998–$25,398), the Sportback Ralliart ($31,798), and the Outlander ($25,998).

Mitsubishi is giving $2,000–$3,000 rebates on leftover 2012 models bought with cash. Unfortunately, most of this rebate is eaten up by the company's clawback of its rebate through a $1,450 destination charge plus a $250 pre-delivery inspection fee. With these unjustified extra fees, Mitsubishi guarantees its place in the lower ranks of car sales in Canada.

Should You Buy a Mitsubishi?

Sure, if dealers drop the usurious extra fees noted above. Mitsubishis are reliable, good-performing vehicles that hold their value and are fairly durable. However, when you buy the product, you also buy the management, and that part is shaky and dispirited, especially now that the euphoria of last year's sales upturn is wearing off as sales slacken. The purchase of any Mitsubishi product is particularly risky for Canadians because of the company's weak dealer network and tenuous presence in Canada. Although insiders say that the automaker seriously considered leaving the North American market after going through two recessions in a row, it has decided to stay put—at least, for a while longer.

RATING: With the exception of the RVR (which is new to the market, though quite similar to the Outlander), all Mitsubishis are rated Average, with easily negotiated base prices. These cars are still fairly reliable; however, servicing continues to be a problem on models with complicated fuel-delivery systems or other high-tech features. Problems they all share include poor original-equipment tire traction; sudden loss of brakes; premature replacement of the brake pads and rotors; early clutch failures; and airbags that don't deploy when they should. NHTSA has given these vehicles mostly four- and five-star crash protection scores.

COST ANALYSIS: Although the Endeavor mid-sized SUV is the best of the lot, its maintenance is highly dealer-dependent. If Mitsubishi leaves town, repairs and parts will be hard to find. **Best alternatives:** The Honda Civic; Hyundai Accent, Elantra, or Tucson AWD; Mazda3; Nissan Sentra; and Toyota Yaris or Matrix. **Options:** Electronic stability control is recommended, but stay away from any of the models equipped with cash-gobbling turbocharged engines. Turbo repairs will devour your wallet. **Rebates:** Look for $2,500 discounts on the small cars and $4,000 on the SUVs. The Eclipse Spyder sportster, on the other hand, will continue to sell at its full retail price. **Depreciation:** Average. **Insurance cost:** Above average for the SUVs and Spyder. **Parts supply/cost:** Not always easy to find. **Annual maintenance cost:** Average. **Warranty:** Bumper-to-bumper 3 years/80,000 km; powertrain 5 years/100,000 km; rust perforation 5 years/unlimited km. **Supplementary warranty:** A good idea, if the warranty is sold by an insured independent company.

SERVICE BULLETIN-REPORTED PROBLEMS: Mitsubishi products have remarkably few serious defects. Thus, it's no surprise that most of the company's few service bulletins concern fit and finish deficiencies. Here are a few examples: 2011–12 Galant front suspension popping, rattling noise; exhaust-mounted heat shield rattling:

EXHAUST SYSTEM—HEAT SHIELD RATTLING NOISES

BULLETIN NO: TSB-11-15-001   DATE: MARCH, 2011

2004–11 Galant; 2004–11 Endeavor; 2006–12 Eclipse; and the 2007–12 Eclipse Spyder

PURPOSE: Customers of some affected may notice a rattle noise created by loose or corroded front exhaust pipe heat shields. This TSB advises the availability of heat shields as spare parts preventing the need to replace the front exhaust pipe.

PROCEDURE: Do not replace a front exhaust pipe to repair a heat shield rattle or other noise. Replace or remove only the affected heat shield(s).

Other service bulletins relate to an AC condensate sloshing noise coming from the dash, with water dripping onto the carpet, and another leak that wets the driver's side carpet:

A/C—WATER LEAKS ONTO DRIVER'S SIDE FLOOR

DULLETIN NO: TSD-11-55-003   DATE: AUGUST, 2011

2006–12 Eclipse; 2007–12 Eclipse Spyder; 2004–12 Galant; and the 2004–11 Endeavor

This is a new procedure to correct a condition of HVAC drainage re-entering the vehicle due to a deteriorated seal, without removing the HVAC unit (most vehicles).

PURPOSE: While being driven with the air conditioning on condensation created in the heater/ventilation/air conditioning unit (HVAC) drains through an outlet into the engine compartment. If the grommet that seals the HVAC case to the bulkhead deteriorates, air flow can force the drained condensation back into the vehicle's interior where it collects on the driver's floor. This TSB provides a procedure to add a 90°hose extension to the drain to correct this condition in most vehicles without removing the HVAC unit.

Nissan

Nissan, Honda, and Toyota were hurt the most by last year's Fukushima earthquake, tsunami, and nuclear plant meltdowns. Nevertheless, all three companies have returned to normal production, carrying a lineup of models that cover almost every marketing niche, with a few (like the small Cube and Juke) that are hard to pin down.

Judging by the last few years of complaints sent in by *Lemon-Aid* readers and reports received by government and private agencies, Nissan quality control has picked up considerably, though owners still complain about fuel-delivery systems, brake and original-equipment tire durability, climate controls, and fit and finish. The Altima, Murano, and Rogue models have the fewest complaints.

VERSA ★★★

KEY FACTS

Canadian Price (negotiable): *1.6 S Sedan:* $11,878, *SV:* $13,878, *SL:* $16,378, *1.8 S Hatchback:* $14,678, *SV:* $15,678, *Hatchback SL:* $17,678, *Auto.:* $18,978 **U.S. Price:** *Versa Sedan:* $10,990, *1.8 S:* $14,670, *1.8 SL:* $18,590 **Canadian Freight:** $1,567
U.S. Freight: $780
POWERTRAIN (FRONT-DRIVE)
Engines: 1.6L 4-cyl. (107 hp) • 1.8L 4-cyl. (122 hp); Transmissions: 5-speed man. • 6-speed man. • CVT • 4-speed auto.

DIMENSIONS/CAPACITY

Passengers: 2/3; Wheelbase: 102.4 in.; H: 60.4/L: 169.1/W: 66.7 in.; Headroom F/R: 5.0/3.5 in.; Legroom F/R: 40/30 in.; Cargo volume: 14.9 cu. ft.; Fuel tank: 50L/regular; Tow limit: N/A; Load capacity: 860 lb.; Turning circle: 37 ft.; Ground clearance: 5.0 in.; Weight: 2,538–2,758 lb.

RATING: Average. **Road performance:** Engine lacks "grunt" at higher rpms and produces an annoying drone when pushed; the manual 6-speed is a bit clunky; the suspension is tuned more to the soft side; the rear drum brakes are less effective; there is no stability control on some models; and a 6-speed manual transmission is available, whereas most small cars offer only a 4- or 5-speed gearbox. The car's larger wheelbase makes for a smooth ride. The 1.8L 4-cylinder engine provides plenty of power, and handling is responsive and predictable, thanks to the tight, power-assisted steering and independent front suspension. **Strong points:** Good-quality interior appointments; tilt steering column. As *Canadian Driver* columnist Paul Williams put it, the Versa is the "jumbo shrimp" of micro cars, offering a lot more interior room than what is found with other small cars in its class, thanks to a tall roofline that also makes for easy access. Visibility is first rate, and there's minimal road noise. The fuel tank dwarfs the mini-car field, where most tanks are 45L; standard 15-inch wheels are used, versus the competition's 14-inchers; and the Versa carries a 122 hp engine, while the other micro cars get by with 103–110 hp powerplants. **Weak points:** Owners say real-world fuel consumption is about 20 percent higher than what is represented. Mediocre defrosting. No illumination of the unlock/lock tabs on the inside panel of the front doors:

All the doors lock automatically once the car is driven, I believe that the unlock/lock tabs need to be illuminated [so] that driver and passenger can quickly see the unlock tabs so we can get out of the car. We are literally locked into our cars and in actually cannot see to get out of our car whenever it is dark.

Safety: NHTSA awarded the 2013 four-door Versa four stars for side and rollover crash protection and three stars for frontal occupant crash protection. IIHS gives the 2012 hatchback its top, "Good" score for frontal offset crash protection and head-restraint occupant protection, and "Acceptable" ratings for the car's roof strength and side crashworthiness. The hatchback version excelled in IIHS crash tests, earning a "Good" score in all categories. **New for 2013:** A sportier-looking redesigned hatchback.

ALERT! The 2013's slightly higher cost is justified by the car's added features and its relatively strong engine and roomy interior.

OVERVIEW: This year's model adds a stylish exterior design, well-appointed interior, more standard features that would cost extra on competing models, and exceptional room for five adults.

COST ANALYSIS: Get the 2013 hatchback coupled to a 6-speed manual transmission for the best overall performance and highest residual value. **Best alternatives:** Honda Fit and Hyundai Accent. **Options:** The 6-speed transmission is a much better performer than the CVT, and the hatchback has a better reliability record than the sedan. **Rebates:** Not likely. Expect a little discounting by early summer. **Depreciation:** Below average. **Insurance cost:** Average. **Parts supply/cost:** Parts aren't hard to find and are relatively inexpensive. **Annual maintenance cost:** Predicted to be much less than average. **Warranty:** Bumper-to-bumper 3 years/60,000 km; powertrain 5 years/100,000 km; rust perforation 5 years/ unlimited km. **Supplementary warranty:** Not needed. **Highway/city fuel economy:** *1.6L man.:* 5.4/7.5 L/100 km, 52/38 mpg. *1.8L man.:* 6.3/7.9 L/100 km, 45/36 mpg. *1.8L auto.:* 6.2/8.5 L/100 km, 46/33 mpg.

OWNER-REPORTED PROBLEMS: Very few owner complaints recorded. Some examples: Car can't be shifted into Reverse; car was parked on an incline, and it rolled backwards; sudden steering seizure; key sticks in the ignition, and car has to be turned off to unlock the doors; brake failures, reduced braking effectiveness, and many complaints of hard starting; speedometer can't be read in daylight; only the driver-side door can be unlocked from the outside. Owners also report problems with the fuel and climate systems, paint, and body integrity.

SERVICE BULLETIN-REPORTED PROBLEMS: Troubleshooting a rear hatch that is difficult to close in cold weather; diagnosing CVT oil leaks; rear brake squealing; front axle clicking; front-seat creaking; key sticking in the ignition, even though vehicle is in Park and shut off; drivebelt noise troubleshooting tips; and repair tips for a malfunctioning fuel gauge. There's also a voluntary service program (Campaign #PM053) involving the free replacement of the instrument panel cluster and a free correction for seatbacks that won't recline.

SENTRA ★★★

KEY FACTS

Canadian Price (negotiable): *2.0:* $15,478, *Auto.:* $16,778, *2.0 S:* $18,878, *Auto.:* $20,178, *2.0 SL:* $23,278, *2.0 SR:* $20,178, *2.0 SE-R Spec V:* $23,478 **U.S. Price:** *2.0:* $15,478, *2.0 S:* $18,878, *2.0 SL:* $23,278, *2.0 SR:* $20,178 **Canadian Freight:** $1,567 **U.S. Freight:** $780

POWERTRAIN (FRONT-DRIVE)

Engines: 2.0L 4-cyl. (140 hp) • 2.5L 4-cyl. (177 hp) • 2.5L 4-cyl. (200 hp); Transmissions: 6-speed man. • CVT

DIMENSIONS/CAPACITY

Passengers: 2/3; Wheelbase: 105.7 in.; H: 59.5/L: 179.8/W: 70.5 in.; Headroom F/R: 6.0/2.0 in.; Legroom F/R: 41/26.5 in.; Cargo volume: 13.1 cu. ft.; Fuel tank: 50L/regular/premium; Tow limit: 1,000 lb.; Load capacity: 850 lb.; Turning circle: 35.4 ft.; Ground clearance: 5.5 in.; Weight: 2,819–3,079 lb.

RATING: Average. **Road performance:** The 2.0L engine is underpowered, but the 2.5L engines provide lots of power; manual transmission shifter's location may be too high and forward for some drivers; some body lean when cornering under power; occupants are treated to a quiet, comfortable, "floaty" ride; easy handling if not pushed hard; the rear end tends to fishtail a bit; some road wander; and long braking distances, probably due to the use of rear drum brakes instead of the more-effective disc brakes. **Strong points:** Plenty of cabin space, and the rear seat cushion can be folded forward, permitting the split rear seatback to fold flat with the floor; a commodious trunk; the locking glove box could house a laptop; and good quality control, with few safety- or performance-related defects. **Weak points:** Body integrity and paint head the list of fit and finish complaints; a noisy rear suspension; and brake grinding. **Safety:** Not great crash protection scores. NHTSA gave the 2012 Sentra three stars for front and side crashworhiness, while rollover resistance garnered four stars. IIHS judged the 2012's frontal offset occupant protection to be "Good," while side, rear, and roof crashworthiness were rated "Acceptable." The front side pillar obstructs the view of what lies ahead, and tall drivers will need to lean back to have a clear view through the front windshield. Unlatched seat belt chime has been silenced. **New for 2013:** To be redesigned; details are sketchy.

ALERT! Mouseketeers' fast food:

The contact owns a 2012 Nissan Sentra. The contact stated that the vehicle was parked when he noticed that mice were building nests inside of the heater vents. As a result, the blower motor failed. The vehicle was taken to an authorized dealer and the nests were cleaned out from the vents, however, mice continued to enter the vehicle and build nests inside of the heater vents.

OVERVIEW: Unlike many bare-bones economy cars, entry-level Sentras offer dependable motoring with lots of safety, performance, and comfort. Besides making for a roomier interior, the large body produces a quieter, smoother ride. These entry-level small sedans come in three trim levels: a fuel-frugal base 140 hp 2.0L 4-cylinder engine and two 2.5L 4-bangers that produce 177 and 200 horses, respectively.

COST ANALYSIS: Get the practically identical and cheaper 2012. **Best alternatives:** Sentra's engine and body dimension improvements over the past few years have made it a good competitor for the Ford Focus, Honda Civic, Hyundai Elantra, and Mazda3. **Options:** Choose the 177 hp 2.5L 4-cylinder for the best power and fuel economy combination. Keep in mind that the sportier models don't handle much better than the base Sentra. **Rebates:** Expect $2,500 rebates in early 2013. **Depreciation:** Average. **Insurance cost:** Average for the base models. **Parts supply/cost:** Inexpensive parts can be found practically anywhere. Suspension parts and parts needed for recall campaigns are often back ordered. **Annual maintenance cost:** Less than average. **Warranty:** Bumper-to-bumper 3 years/60,000 km; powertrain 5 years/100,000 km; rust perforation 5 years/unlimited km. **Supplementary warranty:** Not needed. **Highway/city fuel economy:** 2.0L: 6.4/8.4 L/100 km, 44/34 mpg. 2.0L CVT: 5.8/7.5 L/100 km, 49/38 mpg. SE-R: 6.5/8.7 L/100 km, 43/32 mpg. Spec V: 7.0/9.8 L/100 km, 40/29 mpg. Many owners say they are getting about 30 percent higher fuel consumption than advertised.

OWNER-REPORTED PROBLEMS: Airbags failed to deploy; rear end of the car caught on fire; gas pedal is mounted too close to the brake pedal; sudden, unintended acceleration; defective computer module causes the vehicle to shut down; faulty oil-pressure sensor gasket; engine piston slap; blown engine head gasket; car was shifted into Drive but went into Reverse instead; early replacement of Bridgestone Turanza EL400 tires; premature wearout of rear tires due to factory misalignment of the rear suspension; sudden brake loss; brakes are hard to modulate, resulting in abrupt starts; power-steering failure; ABS clanks, grinds, and causes excessive vibration when it is active; car can be started without driver's foot on the brake, unlike most other cars; unstable front seats; seat belts snap back so quickly that they can cause injury; driver's sun visor obstructs the rear-view mirror; bottom of the windshield may be distorted; tire-pressure indicator malfunctions. Other problem areas include fuel, climate, electrical, and audio systems, in addition to horrendous fit and finish deficiencies (a misaligned trunk lid and malfunctioning trunk locks, for example) that produce excessive rattling and water leaks into the interior.

SERVICE BULLETIN-REPORTED PROBLEMS: *2007–12:* Front seats have a slight movement, won't adjust; there's the possibility of an oil leak from the upper end of the oil cooler:

ENGINE—OIL LEAK FROM UPPER END OF OIL COOLER

CLASSIFICATION: EM10-002A   DATE: SEPTEMBER 6, 2011

ALTIMA SEDAN AND COUPE, SENTRA, AND ROGUE WITH FOUR-CYLINDER ENGINE OIL LEAK

2007–12 Altima Sedan; 2008–12 Altima Coupe; 2007–12 Sentra; and the 2008–12 Rogue

IF YOU CONFIRM: Oil is leaking from the upper end of the engine oil cooler.

ACTION: Reseal the oil cooler

2011–12: Instrument cluster is too dim.

ALTIMA ★★★★

RATING: Above Average. **Road performance:** A powerful 4-cylinder engine delivers good fuel economy, and an even better V6 provides scintillating acceleration while sipping fuel; flawless automatic transmission shifting. The 2.5 S handles well and is relatively soft-sprung, whereas the pricier 3.5 SE models come equipped with a firmer suspension and wider tires. **Strong points:** Good braking; well laid-out instruments and controls; and better-than-average interior room. Quality problems have abated during the last three model years. **Weak points:** Limited rear headroom, and snug rear seating for three adults. **Safety:** NHTSA gave the 2013 two-door Altima five stars for rollover crash protection; the 2012 four-door was awarded five stars for side crashworthiness and four stars for front and rollover occupant protection. IIHS scored the 2012's frontal offset and side crash protection as "Good"; roof and rear crashworthiness were judged "Acceptable." **New for 2013:** Refreshed styling; a small horsepower boost (7); an upgraded continuously variable transmission (CVT) that decreases fuel consumption; a revised rear suspension; 79 fewer pounds; and a new infotainment feature.

ALERT! In your test drive, check out these three safety-related design deficiencies reported by other owners:

1. Painful front head restraints:

> The contact owns a 2013 Nissan Altima. The contact stated that the headrest caused the contact back pain, headaches and numbness in the arm. The contact took the vehicle back to the dealer where the dealer turned the headrest around. The contact stated that after the headrest was turned, there was no more pain.

2. A crooked driver's seat:

> The driver's seat is crooked—both across the back and across the seat. This means one's shoulders and torso are twisted and facing the center console, not the steering wheel. Hips are uneven with the right side significantly lower than the left. This is a very uncomfortable and painful position to be in. I have been informed by the dealership that all 2012 Altimas are like this and therefore it is not a warranty item! I have been able to determine the back of the seat is in fact crooked in the more than two dozen examples I have been able to check. However, the seat bottom is not supposed to sag or be uneven on either side. I've contacted Nissan North America and have been told the dealership is my only avenue to pursue a remedy. Due to the dealership's determination that the seat is supposed to be crooked, my choices are pay someone else or try myself to shim the entire seat or try to adjust the mechanism underneath to level the bottom. Nothing can be done about the seat back.

3. Brake and gas pedals that are mounted too close together:

> My husband complained of this a few weeks ago when he drove my car because his shoe got caught on the brake pedal as he was lifting his foot off the gas pedal. Then, yesterday, the same thing happened to me. I nearly drove my car through the front of the daycare where I was dropping off my son. I am now aware of how extra-cautious I have to be when driving my car so this doesn't happen again. This has never happened to me with any other car. I've been driving for 25 years!

OVERVIEW: Nissan's front-drive, mid-sized sedan stakes out territory occupied by the Honda Accord, Hyundai Sonata and Elantra, Mazda6, and Toyota Camry. The car's base 4-cylinder engine is almost as powerful as the competition's V6 powerplants, and the optional 270 hp 3.5L V6 has few equals among cars in this price and size class. And, when you consider that the Altima is much lighter than

KEY FACTS

Canadian Price: *2.5 S:* $23,998, *Auto.:* $25,298, *3.5 S:* $28,498, *3.5 SR:* $32,098, *2.5 S Coupe:* $27,698, *Auto.:* $28,998, *3.5 SR Coupe:* $35,298, *Auto.:* $36,598 **U.S. Price:** *2.5 S:* $20.410 **Canadian Freight:** $1,595 **U.S. Freight:** $760

POWERTRAIN (FRONT-DRIVE)
Engines: 2.5L 4-cyl. (182 hp) • 3.5L V6 (270 hp); Transmissions: 6-speed man. • CVT

DIMENSIONS/CAPACITY (2.5S)
Passengers: 2/3; Wheelbase: 109.3 in.; H: 57.9/L: 190.7/W: 70.7. in.; Headroom F/R: 4.5/2.0 in.; Legroom F/R: 41.5/29 in.; Cargo volume: 7.4–13.1 cu. ft.; Fuel tank: 76L/regular; Tow limit: 1,000 lb.; Load capacity: 900 lb.; Turning circle: 34.6 ft.; Ground clearance: 5.4 in.; Weight: 3,168–3,492 lb.

most of its competitors, it's obvious why this car produces sizzling acceleration with little fuel penalty. Four-wheel independent suspension strikes the right balance between a comfortable ride and sporty handling. The 3.5 S, 3.5 SE, and SR models add even more performance and luxury enhancements.

COST ANALYSIS: Buy the 2013 model for the small horsepower boost, added fuel efficiency, and more-refined rear suspension. Stay away from leftover Hybrid models. They are no longer built and are overall poor performers. **Best alternatives:** The Honda Accord, Hyundai Elantra, Mazda6, and Toyota Camry. **Options:** Watch out for option loading after you agree to a reasonable base price. Canny Nissan sales agents pretend that some options can't be bought without having others included. **Rebates:** $3,500 rebates or discounts and zero percent financing on fully loaded models. Attractive leasing deals will become more common in the new year. **Depreciation:** All Altimas depreciate quickly, making them poor new-car buys, but they're used-car bargains. For example, a 2006 SE-R high-performance model that sold new for $36,000 is now worth only $9,000. **Insurance cost:** Higher than average. **Parts supply/cost:** Slightly higher than average, but most parts are easily found. **Annual maintenance cost:** Average. **Warranty:** Bumper-to-bumper 3 years/60,000 km; powertrain 5 years/100,000 km; rust perforation 5 years/unlimited km. **Supplementary warranty:** Not needed. **Highway/city fuel economy:** 2.5: 6.2/8.8 L/100 km, 46/32 mpg. *CVT:* 6.0/8.7 L/100 km, 47/32 mpg. *Coupe:* 6.3/9.0 L/100 km, 45/31 mpg. *Auto.:* 6.2/8.9 L/100 km, 46/32 mpg. *3.5 sedan:* 7.2/10.2 L/100 km, 39/28 mpg. *Coupe:* 7.3/11.4 L/100 km, 39/25 mpg. *Auto.:* 7.3/10.2 L/100 km, 39/28 mpg. *Hybrid:* 5.9/5.6 L/100 km, 48/50 mpg.

OWNER-REPORTED PROBLEMS: Less than half (22) the number of complaints one would expect. Loss of brakes, and airbags failed to deploy; sudden, unintended acceleration when the car was started remotely:

> I used my automatic start...the car started and was warming up. As I approached my running car, I walked in front of the car to get around to the driver's side. I opened the driver's side door and the car accelerated and took off moving forward with nobody in it. I was holding onto the door chasing after my car trying to jump in and put my foot on the brake to stop the car. I was unsuccessful as the car ran into another car in the parking lot and came to an abrupt stop. My car was damaged and still running. The parked car that it hit was damaged. Upon impact, I was thrown against the open door and then onto the pavement on my back/right side. Many people were exiting church and gathered around.... It is fortunate that nobody was hit/run over by this "run-away" car.

Defective fuel-pump fuse makes it impossible to shut off the engine; vehicle may jerk when accelerating; while cruising, car suddenly veered to the right as the steering froze; transmission popped out of gear; premature clutch failure; loss of brakes; frequent AC, electrical, and fuel system failures; headlights don't cast a wide enough beam; and the ignition key may inadvertently start the car:

If you leave the key outside the vehicle and it is touching the vehicle the push-button ignition will acknowledge the key and start the vehicle. According to the manual the key must be with you (inside) in order for the vehicle to start. There is no warning stating otherwise.

SERVICE BULLETIN-REPORTED PROBLEMS: Oil may leak from the upper end of the engine oil cooler (see the Sentra profile); steering/suspension drift; sunroof water leak; rear end clunking, knocking on turns; brake master cylinder may slowly leak fluid:

BRAKE MASTER CYLINDER

BULLETIN NO.: NTB12-011A   DATE: APRIL 3, 2012

VOLUNTARY SERVICE CAMPAIGN
2007–12 Altima Sedan & Coupe Brake Master Cylinder
INTRODUCTION: Nissan is conducting a Voluntary Service Campaign on Model Year 2007–12 Nissan Altima Sedan and Coupe vehicles to inspect the brake systems in vehicles with an illuminated brake warning lamp. If no leak is present, the reservoir will be topped off. If a leak in the brake master cylinder is identified, the brake master cylinder will be replaced for free.

2007–12: Front seats bind, won't move fore or aft; inoperative driver power seat lumbar support. 2008–12: Buzzing wind noise from the A-pillar/mirror area.

MAXIMA ★★★★

RATING: Above Average. **Road performance:** The powerful V6 engine and smooth-shifting automatic transmission provide a comfortable, secure ride. Handling is compromised by steering that's overboosted at low speeds and then suddenly firms up. The 18-inch tires produce high-speed tire whine. **Strong points:** Good acceleration without much of a fuel penalty; a quiet cabin; and

KEY FACTS

Canadian Price (negotiable): *3.5 SV:* $39,800 **U.S. Price:** *3.5 S:* $31,750, *3.5 SV:* $34,450, *3.5 SV with Sport Package:* $36,550, *3.5 SV with Premium Package:* $37,750 **Canadian Freight:** $1,620 **U.S. Freight:** $760

POWERTRAIN (FRONT-DRIVE)
Engine: 3.5L V6 (290 hp); Transmission: CVT

DIMENSIONS/CAPACITY
Passengers: 2/3; Wheelbase: 109.3 in.; H: 57.8/L: 190.6/W: 73.2 in.; Headroom F/R: 4.0/2.0 in.; Legroom F/R: 42/30 in.; Cargo volume: 14.2 cu. ft.; Fuel tank: 70L/premium; Tow limit: 1,000 lb.; Load capacity: 900 lb.; Turning circle: 37.4 ft.; Ground clearance: 5.6 in.; Weight: 3,574 lb.

comfortable, supportive front seats. **Weak points:** Tall occupants may find rear seating a bit cramped; interior materials are rather basic; small trunk opening limits what luggage you can carry; many incidents of the SkyView roof suddenly shattering; and premium fuel required. **Safety:** The 2013 earned NHTSA's top, five-star crashworthiness rating for side and rollover crash protection. IIHS rates the 2012 as "Good" for frontal and side occupant protection, "Acceptable" for roof strength, and "Marginal" for head-restraint effectiveness. A low roofline complicates rear access and blocks visibility. **New for 2013:** Nothing significant.

ALERT! Only a small number of safety- and performance-related complaints have been reported to public and governmental agencies.

OVERVIEW: After its recent redesign, the front-drive, mid-sized Maxima soldiers on as Nissan's luxury flagship, a competent and roomy sedan that's a mini-step above the bestselling Altima. Its 290 hp 3.5L V6 is coupled to a continuously variable transmission, and the vehicle comes with an impressive array of standard equipment and a host of performance and safety features, such as large front brakes with full brake assist, a power driver's seat, xenon headlights, and 18-inch wheels. Granted, you get plenty of horsepower, comfort, and gadgets, but unfortunately the car isn't backed up with all the technical refinements and quality components provided by the competition.

COST ANALYSIS: The practically identical 2012 is a cheaper choice. **Best alternatives:** The Acura TSX, BMW 3 Series, and automatic versions of the Honda Accord V6, Lexus IS 5-speed, Mazda6 GT V6, and Toyota Camry V6. **Options:** Traction control wouldn't be a bad idea if you are lead-footed; otherwise, keep things simple. **Rebates:** $3,000 discounts and low-interest financing and leasing in early 2013. **Depreciation:** Average. Insurance cost: Higher than average. **Parts supply/cost:** Moderate parts prices, and some powertrain parts may be back ordered. **Annual maintenance cost:** Average. **Warranty:** Bumper-to-bumper 3 years/60,000 km; powertrain 5 years/100,000 km; rust perforation 5 years/unlimited km. **Supplementary warranty:** Not needed. **Highway/city fuel economy:** 7.7/10.9 L/100 km, 26/37 mpg.

OWNER-REPORTED PROBLEMS: Front airbags failed to deploy; passenger-side airbag is disabled when the seat is occupied; unstable driver's seat rocks back and forth; sometimes vehicle won't shift into Drive; engine surges when brakes are applied; drivers must constantly fight the steering wheel to keep from veering to the left or right; car would not shift out of First as the Check Engine warning light came on;

electrical problems knock out the interior lights, door locks, and other controls; headlights may provide insufficient illumination; head restraints obstruct rear visibility, particularly when backing up; and the adjustable steering wheel may stick in its highest position.

SERVICE BULLETIN-REPORTED PROBLEMS: Steering pull/drift; door panel looks faded, discoloured; rear-end squeak, clunk when driving over bumps; and driver's seat bottom shifts or rocks slightly. 2007–12: Loss of power between 0–70 km/h.

MURANO ★★★★

RATING: Above Average. **Road performance:** Nicely equipped with a refined, responsive powertrain that includes a smooth V6 coupled to a quiet CVT transmission; a comfortable, quiet ride; and no surprise, responsive, car-like handling. **Strong points:** A plush, easily accessed, comfortable, and roomy interior; good fuel economy; and better-than-average reliability. **Weak points:** There is less cargo space behind the second row than what is available in competing models; limited rear visibility; save your loonies for gassing up with premium fuel. **Safety:** NHTSA says the 2013 Murano merits five stars for side crash protection and four stars for frontal crashworthiness and rollover resistance. IIHS gives the 2012 Murano a "Good" rating for frontal offset, side, and head-restraint protection. Roof strength is considered "Marginal." The 2012 CrossCabriolet hasn't been crash tested yet. **New for 2013:** A minor restyling.

ALERT! The Murano is known for its "lag and lurch" acceleration when ascending small inclines:

KEY FACTS

Canadian Price (negotiable): *S:* $34,498, *SV AWD:* $37,548, *SL AWD:* $40,648, *LE:* $44,048 **U.S. Price:** *S:* $29,290, *SV:* $32,860, *SL:* $36,400, *LE:* $38,300
Canadian Freight: $1,650
U.S. Freight: $760
POWERTRAIN (FRONT-DRIVE/AWD)
Engine: 3.5L V6 (265 hp); Transmission: CVT
DIMENSIONS/CAPACITY
Passengers: 2/3; Wheelbase: 111.2 in.; H: 68.1/L: 188.5/W: 74.1 in.; Headroom F/R: 3.0/3.0 in.; Legroom F/R: 40.5/28 in.; Cargo volume: 31.6 cu. ft.; Fuel tank: 82L/premium; Tow limit: 3,500 lb.; Load capacity: 900 lb.; Turning circle: 39.4 ft.; Ground clearance: 6.5 in.; Weight: 4,034–4,153 lb.

At low speeds on a slight incline will not accelerate with input to gas pedal rpms will [increase but] vehicle will not respond then suddenly drivetrain will [respond] and engage (a slipping action) vehicle will suddenly launch forward with a slight bang and bucking.

OVERVIEW: The mid-sized Murano continues to be the car-based "ying" to the Pathfinder's truck-based "yang." Both vehicles embody strong, in-your-face styling and are loaded with many standard safety, performance, and convenience features.

COST ANALYSIS: The 2013 model isn't much different from the 2012 version, so pick up a discounted 2012. Delay your purchase until mid-2013 so as to take advantage of the inevitable discounts, rebates, and factory quality fixes. It would also be a good idea to buy the second-year Cabriolet to allow for prices to settle and the inevitable factory-related defects to get fixed. **Best alternatives:** The Buick Enclave, GMC Acadia, and Hyundai Santa Fe. **Options:** Don't buy the failure-prone, expensive, and back-ordered run-flat tires. **Rebates:** $4,000 rebate by early 2013. **Depreciation:** Average. **Insurance cost:** Higher than average. **Parts supply/ cost:** Parts are sometimes hard to find and can be costly. **Annual maintenance cost:** Higher than average. **Warranty:** Bumper-to-bumper 3 years/60,000 km; powertrain 5 years/100,000 km; rust perforation 5 years/unlimited km. **Supplementary warranty:** Not needed. **Highway/city fuel economy:** 8.7/11.8 L/100 km, 32/24 mpg.

OWNER-REPORTED PROBLEMS: Airbags failed to deploy when needed; passenger-side airbag may be disabled when an average-sized occupant is seated; frequent brake replacements (calipers and rotors) and poor body fit and finish, including paint defects and water/air leaks; Airbag warning light comes on continually, even after multiple resets by the dealer; vehicle rolls down incline when stopped in traffic; Check Engine light comes on after each fill-up (cap must be carefully resealed); faulty transmission body causes the powertrain to vibrate when cruising; headlights may suddenly shut off; the Start/Stop ignition button can be accidently pressed, and this can suddenly shut down the vehicle when it's underway; the tilt steering wheel may be unsafe in a crash; remote-controlled door locks operate erratically; sunroof may suddenly explode:

> Driving 30 mph [48 km/h] on open asphalt road, no cars ahead of me, no cars behind me, when I heard a loud explosion, similar to a shotgun blast. The moon roof had exploded. Appeared to be an upward explosion. Car taken to Nissan dealer for repairs. Damage was not caused from any flying objects. Has to be a defect.

Inoperative sunroof; faulty sun visors suddenly flop down, completely blocking visibility; and excessive vibration (fixed by reducing tire pressure from 41 psi to 36 psi).

SERVICE BULLETIN-REPORTED PROBLEMS: Intermittent power-steering noises; steering/suspension pull or drift diagnostics; Bluetooth voice recognition issues; there may be a grinding, knocking noise from the rear on turns (see the Rogue profile); defective navigation screen:

NAVIGATION SYSTEM—SCREEN GOES BLANK

BULLETIN NO.: EL12-010   DATE: MARCH 16, 2012

2010–12 370Z Coupe and Roadster; 2011–12 Murano and Cross Cabriolet; and the 2011–12 Quest.

IF YOU CONFIRM: The customer states the navigation display turns off, goes completely blank, or "blacks out" in DRIVE and REVERSE intermittently, and all functions of the audio system and heater/defroster/air conditioning work normally.

ACTION: Replace the AV display unit (also referred to as monitor or screen).

ROGUE ★★★★

RATING: Above Average. More car than truck. **Road performance:** The fuel-thrifty 2.5L 4-banger gets a bit noisy when pushed, but the fuel savings are worth it. The quiet-running CVT transmission smoothes out the power delivery. Handling is a pleasure. **Strong points:** Standard features abound, with stability control, curtain airbags, active head restraints, and anti-lock brakes. Well-crafted

KEY FACTS

Canadian Price (negotiable): *S FWD:* 23,648, *S AWD:* $26,448, *SV FWD:* $26,548, *SV AWD:* $28,548, *SL AWD:* $33,848 **U.S. Price:** *S FWD:* 21,460, *SV:* $23,900, *S Krome FWD:* $24,430

Canadian Freight: $1,650 **U.S. Freight:** $760

POWERTRAIN (FRONT-DRIVE/AWD)

Engine: 2.5L 4-cyl. (170 hp);

Transmission: CVT

DIMENSIONS/CAPACITY

Passengers: 2/3; Wheelbase: 105.9 in.; H: 65.3/L: 182.9/W: 70.9 in.; Headroom F/R: 3.5/4.0 in.; Legroom F/R: 42/30 in.; Cargo volume: 28.9 cu. ft.; Fuel tank: 60L/regular; Tow limit: 1,500 lb.; Load capacity: 953 lb.; *AWD:* 1,026 lb.; Turning circle: 37.4 ft.; Ground clearance: 8.3 in.; Weight: 3,315–3,469 lb.

interior, comfortable front seating, and impressive braking. Interestingly, fit and finish elicits few complaints, whereas this has been a chronic problem with Nissan's other models. **Weak points:** Some of the standard features are fairly basic, and those that are in the premium packages should be standard; engine sounds like a diesel when accelerating, and it could use a bit more "grunt"; lacks cargo space and rear-seat versatility. **Safety:** NHTSA gives the 2013 Rogue five stars for side crashworthiness and four stars for front-occupant crash protection and rollover resistance. The 2012 model got IIHS's top, "Good" rating for frontal offset, side, and head-restraint protection; roof strength was judged "Acceptable." Poor rearward visibility. **New for 2013:** Some minor trim changes.

ALERT! Owners say the sunroof doesn't open fully, and dealers say all Rogues are designed that way—check it out.

OVERVIEW: This compact SUV is based on the Sentra sedan and gives car-like handling and better fuel economy than the competition that's still wedded to truck platforms. Nevertheless, the Rogue's car DNA becomes all the more evident as the engine protests going through the upper reaches of the CVT when accelerating.

COST ANALYSIS: Go for an almost identical, cheaper 2012 version. **Best alternatives:** The Buick Enclave, GMC Acadia, and Ford Escape. **Options:** Consider getting the top-drawer Bose audio system, but stay away from the failure-prone, expensive, and back-ordered run-flat tires. **Rebates:** $2,500 by late 2012, in addition to low-cost financing and leasing. **Depreciation:** Slower than average: A first-year base 2009 Rogue that sold for $23,798 now goes for about $16,000. **Insurance cost:** Higher than average. **Parts supply/cost:** Parts are easily found in the Sentra bin and are reasonably priced. **Annual maintenance cost:** Average. **Warranty:** Bumper-to-bumper 3 years/60,000 km; powertrain 5 years/100,000 km; rust perforation 5 years/unlimited km. **Supplementary warranty:** Not needed. **Highway/city fuel economy:** *Front-drive:* 7.0/9.0 L/100 km, 40/31 mpg. *AWD:* 7.7/9.6 L/100 km, 37/29 mpg.

OWNER-REPORTED PROBLEMS: Only 11 complaints recorded over the past several years, but some are deadly serious, like the following:

> I was on my way to work and had entered our parking lot and was ready to pull into a parking space. As I pulled in and was at a stop, my car suddenly accelerated and I was unable to stop it. I started to turn the wheel to the right because there was a 2010

Ford Explorer that was parked in front but unfortunately I hit the back end of the car and pushed it at least 30 ft dead straight. My car continued going to the right and over an island and by the time I got it to stop, the air bag had gone off. I'm not sure how this happened since I was stopped. There were two witnesses that saw my vehicle stopped and the next thing it accelerated. I know my foot was on the brake because I was stopped and ready to exit the vehicle, but it would not stop.

Transmission, steering wheel, gear shifter, and brake failures (brakes may also suddenly lock up):

Nissan Rogue transmission failure at 16,000 miles [25,750 km]. Transmission began to make strange noises under load from the front end. Dealer replaced transmission and claimed there is no current recall. A check on the internet indicates the problem is pervasive.

Tire-pressure monitoring systems are so sensitive that they often give false alerts, so drivers end up ignoring them. Steering-wheel vibrations may numb your hands:

I think it's absurd my vehicle has 2,100 miles [3,380 km] on it and I've never owned a car that does this. You have to move your hands off the wheel because they go numb. I was told drive faster or take a different route to work.

Driver-side door handle broke, and it took over a month to get the part:

In the meantime, the only way to access my vehicle is by using the passenger side door and climb over the seats. If I were physically unable to climb over the seats, I would not be able to operate my vehicle. Fortunately, I am able, but if a person was not, they would either have to rent a vehicle or use some other means of transportation. I find this problem inexcusable. A simple door handle part must be sent from Japan to fix this problem.

SERVICE BULLETIN-REPORTED PROBLEMS: Steering/suspension pull or drift diagnosis; oil may leak from the upper end of the engine oil cooler (see Sentra profile); noise when turning the steering wheel; there may be a grinding, knocking noise from the rear on turns:

GRINDING/KNOCKING NOISE FROM REAR ON TURNS	
CLASSIFICATION: RA09-004A	DATE: OCTOBER 5, 2011

2003–12 Murano (Z50, Z51) AWD ONLY and 2008–12 Rogue (S35) AWD ONLY

IF YOU CONFIRM: There is a grinding or knocking noise or vibration from the rear of the vehicle:

ACTION: Remove the Rear Propeller Shaft and test drive the vehicle. If the noise/vibration DOES NOT stop: This bulletin DOES NOT APPLY. Refer to ASIST for further diagnostic assistance. If the noise/vibration DOES stop: Replace the Electrical Coupling Assy. (CPLG ASSY-ELEC) with the one from the Parts Information section of this bulletin.

2001–12: Troubleshooting water vapour in the exterior lights. 2007–12: Door locks inoperative with Keyless Entry. 2011–12: Inaccurate ambient display temperature; pull or drift diagnostic info.

FRONTIER ★★★★★

KEY FACTS

Canadian Price (negotiable): *King S 4×2:* $24,398, *SV 4×2:* $28,348, *4×4:* $30,348, *PRO-4X:* $33,298, *Crew SV 4×4:* $34,148, *PRO-4X:* $38,798 **U.S. Price:** *King S:* $18,200, *SV:* $21,380, *SV V6:* $21,970, *Pro-4X:* $26,620 **Canadian Freight:** $1,595 **U.S. Freight:** $820

POWERTRAIN (REAR-DRIVE/4×4)

Engines: 2.5L 4-cyl. (152 hp) • 4.0L V6 (261 hp); Transmissions: 5-speed man. • 6-speed man. • 5-speed auto.

DIMENSIONS/CAPACITY

Passengers: 2/3; Wheelbase: 126 in.; H: 70/L: 206/W: 73 in.; Headroom F/R: 3.0/3.5 in.; Legroom F/R: 40/27 in.; Cargo volume: 60 cu. ft.; Fuel tank: 80L/regular; Tow limit: 6,100 lb.; Load capacity: 1,160 lb.; Turning circle: 43.3 ft.; Ground clearance: 8.7 in.; Weight: 4,655 lb.

RATING: Recommended. **Road performance:** Carries a powerful V6, with towing horsepower to spare; the 4-cylinder engine is acceptable for light chores; and handling is quick and nimble. **Strong points:** Well equipped; an accommodating interior, especially with the Crew version; plenty of storage in the centre console; and outstanding reliability. **Weak points:** Ride is a bit stiff; stability control is optional; rear seatroom is tight in the Crew Cab; and you'll need to eat your Wheaties before attempting to lift the tailgate. **Safety:** NHTSA gives the Frontier four stars for rollover resistance, while the IIHS rates front, side, and roof crash protection as "Good." Head restraints were found to be "Acceptable." **New for 2013:** Nothing important.

ALERT! Delay your purchase until early 2013 so as to take advantage of the inevitable discounts, rebates, and manufacturing fixes. Be wary of the front head restraints:

The contact owns a 2012 Nissan Frontier. The contact stated that the front driver's seat headrest could not be adjusted. The headrest was positioned downward, causing the driver's head to be forced to look down. The dealer was made aware of the failure and advised the contact that the headrest was designed in that manner and they could not compromise the design of the vehicle.

OVERVIEW: These are gutsy, reliable pickups that are compact in name only. The PRO-4X model offers serious off-road features seldom found among compact trucks, like a locking rear differential, Bilstein dampers, and skid plates.

COST ANALYSIS: A cheaper 2012 Frontier will give almost everything that's offered with the 2013 version. **Best alternative:** A Toyota Tacoma. **Options:** Run away from the failure-prone, expensive, and back-ordered run-flat tires. **Rebates:** $2,000 by early 2013. **Depreciation:** Average. **Insurance cost:** Higher than average. **Parts supply/cost:** Parts are everywhere, and they don't cost much, since many parts are shared with the Pathfinder, Xterra, and Titan. **Annual maintenance cost:** Average. **Warranty:** Bumper-to-bumper 3 years/60,000 km; powertrain 5 years/100,000 km; rust perforation 5 years/unlimited km. **Supplementary warranty:** Not needed. **Maintenance/repair costs:** Less than average. **Highway/city fuel economy:** 2.5L man.: 8.7/10.7 L/100 km, 32/26 mpg. 2.5L auto.: 9.2/12.6 L/100 km, 31/22 mpg. 4.0L 4×2 auto.: 9.2/14.2 L/100 km, 31/20 mpg. 4.0L 4×4: 10.4/13.7 L/100 km, 27/21 mpg. 4.0L 4×4 auto.: 10.4/14.7 L/100 km, 27/19 mpg.

OWNER-REPORTED PROBLEMS: Passenger-side front airbag is disabled when an average-sized adult occupies the seat; airbags deploy for no reason:

> Myself and one passenger were off-roading in my 2012 Frontier PRO-4X going over a bumpy surface and without warning the side airbags went off! Luckily no one was injured, but we both got quite a scare due to the noise and lack of visibility. There is no damage to the front end nor were we at any degree of an angle. Yes it was bumpy but when you pay for a vehicle that states clearly off road and the side you expect it has the suspension to support the ride. The very last thing I was thinking of was the air bags, until they came out.

Delayed acceleration; faulty fuel-level sending unit sensor:

> I went online to *nissanhelp.com* after performing a search. I came across many others who have experienced the same problem. Apparently it has something to do with the fuel sending unit. A similar problem was found on the 2000–2004 Xterra models and a recall was performed when the vehicle would stop after not getting any fuel.

SERVICE BULLETIN-REPORTED PROBLEMS: Nothing important.

Subaru

An Extraordinary Ordinary Car

Even in these hard economic times, buyers are clamouring for Subaru's all-wheel-drive Forester, Impreza, and Legacy. And the company doesn't intend to risk its success with any dramatic changes. Except for a slight freshening of the Impreza, Subaru's overall product lineup this year stands pat, with most of the redesigns and styling changes scheduled for 2013.

Although all Subarus provide full-time AWD capability, studies show that most owners don't need the off-road prowess; only 5 percent will ever use their Subaru for off-roading. The other 95 percent just like knowing they have the option of going wherever they please, whenever they please—and they don't seem to care that an AWD burns about 2 percent more fuel. As one retired Quebec mechanic told me, "All-wheel drive simply means that you will get stuck deeper, further from home. It's no replacement for common sense."

FORESTER, IMPREZA, WRX, STI ★ ★ ★ ★ ★ / ★ ★ ★ ★ ★ / ★ ★ ★

The Subaru Forester.

KEY FACTS

Canadian Price (Forester: Firm; Impreza: negotiable):
Forester 2.5X: $25,995, *Convenience Package:* $28,295,
Convenience with PZEV: $28,995, *Touring Package:*
$29,095, *Limited Package:* $33,395, *XT Limited:*
$35,895; *Impreza 2.0i:* $19,995, *5d:* $20,895, *Touring
Package:* $21,695, *Touring Package 5d:* $22,595, *Sport
Package:* $23,895, *5d:* $24,795, *Limited Package:*
$26,895, *Limited Package 5d:* $27,795; *WRX Sedan:*
$32,495, *5d:* $33,395, *Limited 5d:* $36,395, *STI:*
$38,195, *5d:* $39,095, *Sport-Tech Package:* $41,795,
5d: $42,695

U.S. Price: *Forester 2.5X:* $21,295, *Premium:* $24,295,
Limited: $26,995; *XT Premium:* $27,295; *Touring:*
$29,995; *Impreza, 2.5i:* $17,495, *Premium:* $18,795,
*Sport Premium: $20,295, Sport Limited: $22,595; WRX
Sedan:* $25,595, *Premium:* $28,095, *Limited:* $29,095,
STI: $34,095, *STI Limited:* $37,445

Canadian Freight: $1,695
U.S. Freight: $750

POWERTRAIN (AWD)

Engines: *Forester:* 2.5L 4-cyl. (173 hp) • 2.5L 4-cyl.
Turbo (224 hp); *Impreza:* 2.0L 4-cyl. (148 hp); *WRX:*
2.5L 4-cyl. Turbo (265 hp); *WRX STI:* 2.5L 4-cyl. Turbo
(305 hp); Transmissions: 5-speed man. • 6-speed man.
• 4-speed auto. • CVT

DIMENSIONS/CAPACITY (FORESTER)

Passengers: 2/3; Wheelbase: 103 in.; H: 66/L: 180/W:
70 in.; Headroom F/R: 6.5/6.5 in.; Legroom F/R: 41/29.5
in.; Cargo volume: 35.5 cu. ft.; Fuel tank: 64L/regular/
premium; Tow limit: 2,400 lb.; Load capacity: 900 lb.;
Turning circle: 38 ft.; Ground clearance: 8.9 in.; Weight:
3,064–3,373 lb.

DIMENSIONS/CAPACITY (IMPREZA)

Passengers: 2/3; Wheelbase: 104.1 in.; H: 57.7/L:
180.3/W: 68.5 in.; Headroom F/R: 6.0/3.5 in.; Legroom
F/R: 43.5/35.4 in.; Cargo volume: 12 cu. ft.; Fuel tank:
64L/regular/premium; Tow limit: Not recommended;
Load capacity: 900 lb., *WRX, STI:* 850 lb.; Turning circle:
37 ft.; Ground clearance: 6.1 in.; Weight: 2,910–
3,384 lb.

RATING: *Forester:* Recommended. *Impreza:* Above Average. *WRX and STI:* Average.
Road performance: Good acceleration with the base 2.5L engine; however, the
WRX STI and STI Limited models have even more powerful 305 hp engines. But
with that power comes complexity—a complexity that requires good access to
parts and servicing. *Forester:* Acceptable acceleration without any torque steer; the
turbocharged engine is more robust, but fuel consumption increases and premium
fuel is required; the 4-speed transmission is Flintstone-dated; competent, agile,
and secure handling; and gives one of the smoothest rides in its class. *Impreza:*
Not impressive performance. The base Impreza has to split 148 horses between all
four wheels. (Yawn.) Some body roll when cornering, but the suspension
smoothes things out nicely; the outdated 4-speed automatic transmission shifts
roughly and wastes fuel, making the new CVT a must-have, though it augments
engine noise; lots of road noise, too. *WRX and STI:* Quick acceleration with some
turbo lag; solid handling; precise and responsive transmission, especially with the
optional short-throw shifter; easy riding over bumps; good steering feedback; and
some turbo whine at full throttle. **Strong points:** Full-time AWD; a roomy cabin;
spacious rear seating; lots of storage space with the wagons; a nice control layout;
good all-around visibility; and excellent quality control. **Weak points:**
Problematic entry and exit, some seats require additional lumbar bolstering and
more height; hatchbacks have more wind and road noise; high-mounted cabin
audio controls are hard to reach. Impreza interior materials look and feel cheap.

WRX and STI bucket seats also need more lumbar support, and both cars require premium fuel. **Safety:** Better than average. *Forester:* NHTSA gave the 2013 version four stars for front, side, and rollover crash protection. The 2012 Forester excelled in IIHS crash tests, getting the Institute's top, "Good" mark for frontal offset, side, roof, and head-restraint protection. *Impreza:* The 2012 Impreza got four stars for front and side occupant protection and five stars for rollover resistance from NHTSA; its IIHS scores were identical to the Forester's rating. *WRX and STI:* Tested for rollover resistance only, but they each got five stars. **New for 2013:** Carried over with minor changes.

ALERT! Keep in mind, there is nothing remarkable about Subaru's lineup except for the inclusion of AWD in all models. If you don't need the AWD capability, you're wasting your money.

OVERVIEW: The Forester is a cross between a wagon and a sport-utility. Based on the shorter Impreza, it uses the Legacy Outback's 2.5L engine or an optional turbocharged version of the same powerplant. Its road manners are more subdued, and its engine provides plenty of power and torque for off-roading. The two "Boxer" 4-cylinder engines are both competitive in terms of power and fuel economy, despite being coupled to an outmoded 4-speed automatic transmission.

The Impreza is essentially a shorter Legacy with additional convenience features. It comes as a four-door sedan, a wagon, and an Outback Sport wagon, all powered by a 173 hp 2.5L flat-four engine or a 224 hp turbocharged 2.5L. The rally-inspired WRX STI models have a more-powerful turbocharged engine (a 305 hp 2.5L variant), lots of standard performance features, sport suspension, an aluminum hood with functional scoop, and higher-quality instruments, controls, trim, and seats.

COST ANALYSIS: Buy a 2013 model. Subaru is holding the line on 2013 prices, with increases of only a few hundred dollars. Compare prices with dealers in the States; prices may be $10,000 less on some models bought south of the border. Be wary of Subaru's high-performance WRX and STI models. They require special parts and specialized mechanical know-how that may be hard to find in these troubled economic times. Remember, WRX versions are expensive, problematic Imprezas, but when they run right, they'll equal the sporty performance of most of the entry-level Audis and BMWs—cars that cost thousands of dollars more. STIs are just a notch up on the WRX and not worth the extra cash. **Best alternatives:** If you don't really need a 4×4, there are some front-drives worth considering, like the Hyundai Elantra, Mazda6, and Toyota Corolla or Matrix. **Rebates:** $2,500 rebates on the more-expensive models, and low-interest financing. **Options:** Larger tires to smooth out the ride, and the CVT automatic transmission to smooth out the gear changes. WRX and STI performance enthusiasts will want the short-throw shifter. **Depreciation:** Slower than average. A 2009 Forester 2.5X that originally sold for $25,795 is still worth half its original cost. WRX models hold their value just as well. A 2009 entry-level WRX that sold for $30,995 is now worth $16,000.

Insurance cost: Higher than average. **Parts supply/cost:** Parts aren't easy to find, and they can be costly. **Annual maintenance cost:** Average. Mediocre, expensive servicing is hard to overcome because independent garages can't service Subaru AWD powertrains and turbochargers. **Warranty:** Bumper-to-bumper 3 years/60,000 km; powertrain 5 years/100,000 km; rust perforation 5 years/unlimited km. **Supplementary warranty:** Protect yourself with an extended powertrain warranty. **Highway/city fuel economy:** *Forester:* 7.4/9.9 L/100 km, 38/29 mpg. *Auto.:* 7.5/9.9 L/100 km, 38/29 mpg. *Impreza:* 5.9/8.3 L/100 km, 48/34 mpg. *Auto.:* 5.5/7.5 L/100 km, 51/38 mpg. *WRX:* 8.0/11.1 L/100 km, 35/25 mpg. *STI:* 8.8/12.6 L/100 km, 32/22 mpg.

OWNER-REPORTED PROBLEMS: *Forester:* Sudden, unintended acceleration while the vehicle was cruising on the highway. *Impreza:* WRX models have had fewer owner complaints (mostly paint, trim, and body hardware) than the Impreza, which has been afflicted with similar fit and finish deficiencies, plus engine, exhaust, and fuel system complaints. Also, reports of sudden, unintended acceleration:

> While driving approximately 15 mph [24 km/h] on normal road conditions, there was sudden, aggressive, and forceful acceleration. The driver immediately depressed the brake pedal, but there was no response. The driver placed the gear shifter into Park, but the vehicle failed to slow down. The vehicle crashed into a brick wall. The failure occurred without warning. The police and ambulance were called to the scene and a police report was filed. The driver sustained severe back injuries. The vehicle was completely destroyed.

When accelerating, there's also a serious shift lag, then the vehicle surges ahead; defective engine had to be replaced; head restraints push head forward at an uncomfortable angle, causing neck strain and backache; and the moonroof system cavity allows debris and small animals to enter between the headliner and interior walls—the perfect place for fungi and mould to incubate.

SERVICE BULLETIN-REPORTED PROBLEMS: *Forester:* TCM computer reboot to cure harsh shifting; TSB #02-113-11R, published January 26, 2011, addresses cold-start engine noise and suggests that the timing chain tensioner be changed; excessive oil consumption, white exhaust smoke. *Impreza:* Highway speed, vibration, harshness, and noise diagnostic and correction tips.

LEGACY, OUTBACK ★★★★/★★★

RATING: *Legacy:* Above Average. *Outback:* Average; the car's greater number of safety complaints (related almost entirely to hesitation and stalling) shows sloppy assembly and the use of subpar components. Both cars are distinguished by their standard full-time all-wheel-drive drivetrain. This AWD feature handles difficult terrain without the fuel penalty or clumsiness of many truck-based SUVs. Without it, the Outback would be just a raised wagon variant that's well equipped but outclassed by most of the import competition. **Road performance:** A refined

The Subaru Legacy 3.6R Limited.

and reliable AWD system; a well-balanced 6-cylinder engine; precise, responsive handling, and a comfortable ride; the GT handles best and has power to spare. On the downside: the base 2.5L engine remains a sluggish, noisy performer, despite the engine's three extra horses added this year, and the more-powerful GT version is a fuel hog and available only with a manual gearbox. If you don't mind paying the fuel penalty, the 6-cylinder engine is quicker and quieter. *Outback:* This rugged SUV has all of the above and adds higher ground clearance. Handling degrades with extreme off-road use. **Strong points:** Interior materials and fit and finish

KEY FACTS

Canadian Price (negotiable): *Legacy 2.5i:* $23,495, *Convenience:* $25,995, *PZEV:* $26,695, *Touring:* $27,295, *Limited Package:* $32,495, *3.6R Limited:* $34,695, *Limited with Eyesight Option:* $36,195; *Outback 2.5i Convenience:* $28,495, *PZEV:* $30,495, *Touring Package:* $31,095, *Limited Package:* $36,295, *3.6R:* $34,495, *3.6R Limited:* $34,695, (2012) *GT navi.:* $38,595 **U.S. Price:** *Legacy 2.5i:* $20,295, *Premium:* $22,495, *Limited:* $25,895, *3.6R:* $25,395, *Limited:* $28,895; *Outback:* $23,495, *Premium:* $24,995, *Limited:* $29,095, *3.6R:* $28,495, *3.6R Limited:* $32,095

Canadian Freight: $1,695 **U.S. Freight:** $750

POWERTRAIN (AWD)

Engines: 2.5L 4-cyl. (173 hp) • 2.5L 4-cyl. Turbo (265 hp) • 3.6L V6 (256 hp); Transmissions: 5-speed man. • 6-speed man. • 5-speed auto. • CVT

DIMENSIONS/CAPACITY (LEGACY)

Passengers: 2/3; Wheelbase: 108.2 in.; H: 59.2/L: 186/W: 72 in.; Headroom F/R: 6.0/3.0 in.; Legroom F/R: 43/30 in.; Cargo volume: 15 cu. ft.; Fuel tank: 70L/regular/premium; Tow limit: 1,000 lb.; Load capacity: 850 lb.; Turning circle: 36.8 ft.; Ground clearance: 5.9 in.; Weight: 3,273–3,522 lb.

DIMENSIONS/CAPACITY (OUTBACK)

Passengers: 2/3; Wheelbase: 1,078 in.; H: 65.7/L: 188.1/W: 71.6 in.; Headroom F/R: 4.0/6.0 in.; Legroom F/R: 39.5/29 in.; Cargo volume: 36.5 cu. ft.; Fuel tank: 70L/regular; Tow limit: 2,700 lb.; Load capacity: 900 lb.; Turning circle: 39 ft.; Ground clearance: 8.7 in.; Weight: 3,540 lb.

have been substantially upgraded, and there's a spacious interior, with lots of cargo room (innovative under-floor, rear-car cargo storage area). *Outback:* An even roomier interior. **Weak points:** Fuel economy trails rivals like the Chevrolet Malibu, Ford Fusion, and Toyota Camry. Another mixed blessing: The stability control feature (VDC) adds exponential complexity to a vehicle that is already complicated to repair. Crosswinds require constant steering correction; excessive engine and road noise; limited rear access; front seats need more padding; interior garnishes look and feel cheap; the Mazda6 and Ford Fusion offer more cargo space; the V6 engine requires premium fuel; and these cars are very dealer-dependent for parts and servicing. God help you if you need parts when dealers are cutting back on inventory. **Safety:** NHTSA awarded the 2011 Legacy four stars for front and side protection and five stars for rollover resistance; the 2012 Outback got four stars across the board. The IIHS gave the 2012 Legacy and Outback its top, "Good," rating for frontal offset, side, roof, and rear crash protection. **New for 2013:** *Legacy:* Three more horses (173 hp), and greater low-end torque; brake/throttle override that combats sudden, unintended acceleration; chassis enhancements to improve ride quality; a restyled front end, including new headlights, grille, and front bumper; and the introduction of the brand-new EyeSight driver-assist system. *Outback:* A second-generation CVT transmission.

ALERT! During the test drive, remember that owners say the head restraints force the driver's head into a painful and unsafe chin-to-chest position (worse for short drivers), a problem plaguing all Subarus for several years. Running lights do not illuminate high or far enough, and headlights have a similar handicap. Owners have to pay up to $50 twice per year to have the federally mandated tire-pressure monitoring system reset when they change tires in the spring and fall.

OVERVIEW: The most fuel-efficient mid-size all-wheel-drive sedan in North America, the 2013 Legacy is better-equipped and cheaper (most models) than last year. A competent full-time 4×4 performer for drivers who want to move up in size, comfort, and features. Available as a four-door sedan or five-door wagon, the Legacy is cleanly and conventionally styled.

COST ANALYSIS: These are not cheap cars, but this year, Subaru offers substantial price reductions across all trim levels, so there's no reason to hold out for a leftover 2012 model. For example, the 2013 Legacy has many additions and upgrades, yet the well-equipped 2.5i is now offered at $23,495, which is $500 less than last year. The 3.6R Limited receives the greatest reduction, now offered for $1,000 less at its new price of $34,695. In addition to this, the MSRP of all CVT models has been reduced by $400. **Best alternatives:** The Honda CR-V, Hyundai Tucson or Santa Fe, and Toyota RAV4. **Options:** Base models hooked to an automatic transmission are performance-challenged. Stay away from the Firestone and Bridgestone original equipment tires. **Rebates:** $2,000 rebates and low-interest financing. **Depreciation:** Slower than average. **Insurance cost:** Average. **Parts supply/cost:** Parts aren't easily found, and they can be costly. **Annual maintenance cost:** Average. **Warranty:** Bumper-to-bumper 3 years/60,000 km; powertrain

5 years/100,000 km; rust perforation 5 years/unlimited km. **Supplementary warranty:** A good idea. **Highway/city fuel economy:** *Legacy 2.5:* 7.4/10.6 L/100 km, 38/27 mpg. *Auto.:* 6.5/9.2 L/100 km, 43/31 mpg. *GT:* 8.0/11.5 L/100 km, 35/25 mpg. *3.6R:* 8.2/11.8 L/100 km, 34/24 mpg. *Outback 2.5:* 7.4/10.6 L/100 km, 38/27 mpg. *Auto.:* 6.9/9.5 L/100 km, 41/30 mpg. *3.6:* 8.2/11.8 L/100 km, 34/24 mpg.

OWNER-REPORTED PROBLEMS: *Legacy:* Sudden, unintended acceleration when in Park:

> The vehicle was in Park when it accelerated in reverse through a yard, crashing into a retaining wall.

Long delay to get up to speed when accelerating; engine may default to very low idle, almost to the point of stalling out; cruise control and brake failures; steering shimmy and wobbles, and car sways from right to left (partially corrected by replacing the steering-column dampening spring and force-balancing the tires); excessive steering wheel, clutch, and brake vibration; Airbag warning light comes on for no reason; and driver-side floor mats may "creep" toward the accelerator pedal.

Outback: Sudden, unintended downshifting or accelerating:

> Situation: Travelling at 60 mph [97 km/h] up a steep hill in left passing lane. Cars following close, and cars in the right lane. For the first time (new car) I used the downshift paddle on the left side of the steering wheel to downshift to accelerate. I tapped it to downshift one gear. It instantly dropped to 1st gear. The engine rpms went to red line or above. The car decelerated dramatically, and I was tossed forward. I attempted to upshift using the right paddle but there was no response, and the car remained in first gear. The car behind nearly hit me. The only useful control that I had was the steering wheel (brakes or accelerator useless). Further, I assumed the brake lights were not lit. Due to the alertness of the driver behind and the drivers to my right as I slowed dramatically and got off the highway to the right shoulder, a serious accident was avoided.

> •

> Ever since purchasing the 2012 Outback we have had a serious issue when using the paddle shifters to slow down for a stop. When the tach slows to about 1100 rpm in first or second gear the engine then accelerates to up to 2500 rpm, slowing down and then speeding up again then repeating the cycle over even if you apply the brakes. Sometimes it would just run at 2500 rpm until you braked to a stop.

Faulty cruise control/traction control:

> Vehicle stopped cruise control & flashed Brakes & No Traction Control unexpectedly. Came close to a wreck shutting the vehicle down on the side of the road hitting various tire recaps & debris on the side of the road. Not told that this is a regular occurrence with this vehicle.

Passenger-side airbag may suddenly disable itself while vehicle is underway:

> Drove the car for approximately 45 minutes, made a quick stop with car turned off, when restarting car, air bag warning light came on and also the passenger side air bag light said it was off even though there was an adult passenger on that side of the car. Light stayed on even after restarting car, readjusting seatbelts, etc. Drove with warning light on for about an hour.

Transmission slipped from Neutral to Drive:

> I was setting the homelink mirror on my car to recognize a particular garage door opener. The mirror is powered so I needed to leave the car idling. I put the car in Neutral and began the programming process. The last step in the process is to engage the garage door opener from the motor head. To prepare to do this, I [exited] the car and moved on foot into the garage to look for a step ladder. As I was searching for a step ladder and after a period of at least one full minute, the automatic transmission slipped into "Drive" at which point the unoccupied car drove into the garage and hit the rear wall.

Chronic hesitation, stalling; steering shimmy, and wobble. Excessive wander over the roadway:

> When driving on the highway the vehicle exhibits very poor straight line stability. Vehicle wanders within the lane and requires excessive steering wheel correction to maintain straight direction. Vehicle 500 miles [800 km] on it (350 driven by owner) but is now sitting in driveway for fear of personal safety if emergency maneuver is necessary on the highway.

SERVICE BULLETIN-REPORTED PROBLEMS: Highway speed vibration, harshness, and noise countermeasures; and the sunroof binds when opening.

Suzuki

Suzuki builds reliable, fair-priced cars and SUVs, but no one knows, and that's why the company has done so poorly in North America. To be successful requires a large advertising budget and almost perfect timing in one's launches and promotion. Suzuki never put much money into advertising, and it has had a revolving door of incompetent executives who have run the company into the ground.

And forget about brand-name loyalty—most shoppers don't give the company a second thought, since many of its products were sold under GM's name. Then there was Suzuki's partnership with South Korean Daewoo—a fiasco that resulted in the entry of cheap, unreliable compacts that tarnished the Suzuki brand and has kept Suzuki sales in the basement.

In Canada, Suzuki sells three models: the SX4 and Grand Vitara compact SUVs and the Kizashi, a sporty all-wheel-drive, mid-sized sedan that retails for $30,000 (plus $1,495 freight and PDI) and carries a 180 hp 2.4L 4-cylinder engine coupled to a continuously variable transmission.

SX4 ★★★★

KEY FACTS

Canadian Price (Soft): *Sedan JE:* $15,495, *JA:* $17,835, *Sport:* $19,835 **U.S. Price:** *Sedan:* $13,849, *Sportback:* $16,949, *Crossover AWD:* $16,999 **Canadian Freight:** $1,450 **U.S. Freight:** $795 **POWERTRAIN (FRONT-DRIVE/AWD)** Engine: 2.0L 4-cyl. (150 hp); Transmissions: 6-speed man. • CVT **DIMENSIONS/CAPACITY (sedan)** Passengers: 2/3; Wheelbase: 98.4 in.; H: 60.8/L: 176,8/W: 68.1 in.; Headroom F/R: 4.5/3.5 in.; Legroom F/R: 40/25 in.; Cargo volume: 16 cu. ft.; Fuel tank: 50L/regular; Tow limit: No towing; Load capacity: 850 lb.; Turning circle: 34.8 ft.; Ground clearance: 6.5 in.; Weight: 2,744 lb.

RATING: Above Average. This roomy little car is a winner because of its better-than-average overall performance, low price, and versatile body styles that rival many wagons and hatchbacks. **Road performance:** The SX4 performs fairly well, as its lethargic, droning engine eventually reaches cruising speed; handling is reassuringly responsive; the automatic transmission shifts smoothly; the ride quality is acceptable, though sometimes jarring; and brakes are adequate, though a bit soft. **Strong points:** All models are bargain-priced, and they deliver a lot of content. The tall roofline ensures plenty of headroom for all passengers, makes for easy passenger access, and enhances overall visibility. There's a surprising amount of occupant and cargo room, and legroom is on par with or better than most of its competition. Lots of glass all around, making the cabin appear much larger than it is. ABS and front and side curtain airbags are standard. **Weak points:** Some engine and road noise, and fuel consumption is sharply increased with the extra weight of the AWD feature. Incidentally, deactivating the AWD won't save fuel, no matter what the sales agent tells you in the showroom. **Safety:** NHTSA gives the 2013 SX4 four stars for frontal and rollover crashworthiness and three stars for side-impact occupant protection. IIHS rates frontal offset and side-impact crashworthiness on the 2012 model as "Good," but roof crashworthiness and head-restraint protection get only a "Marginal" score. **New for 2013:** Hatchbacks get minor front-end styling changes, including a new grille and a revised front bumper.

ALERT! There are rumours that Suzuki will pull out of the North American market, where it has lost millions of dollars over the past decade. If Suzuki does leave, the car's higher-than-average resale value will fall a bit, but servicing shouldn't be a problem due to the car's simple design and easily found generic parts.

OVERVIEW: Available in both front-drive and all-wheel-drive trims, the SX4 crossover is a fun-to-drive, inexpensive small SUV-like hatchback with interior features and performance qualities that make it a great alternative to the top-ranked small cars. Practical dimensions, combined with a lengthy list of features and sporty dynamics, make the SX4 a good choice for anyone who's put off by the higher-priced competition. Reliability hasn't been a major issue, but a limited servicing network, less-than-average fuel economy with the AWD, and a cheap-looking plastic-wrapped cabin has turned away many buyers.

COST ANALYSIS: Most 2013 model prices have either been rolled back or increased only a few hundred dollars, making them the better buy than a 2012 leftover. **Best alternatives:** The Honda Fit or Civic, Hyundai Accent, Mazda3, Nissan Versa and Toyota Yaris or Matrix are affordable alternatives that have more-established reputations. **Options:** Stay away from the Firestone and Bridgestone original equipment tires. The Garmin GPS option looks like a real bargain. **Rebates:** $2,000 rebates and low-interest financing. **Depreciation:** Better than Average. A 2007 base SX4 that originally sold for $16,000 is still worth $6,500. **Insurance cost:** Average. **Parts supply/cost:** Parts aren't hard to find, and are moderately priced. **Annual maintenance cost:** Average. **Warranty:** Bumper-to-bumper 3 years/60,000 km; powertrain 5 years/100,000 km; rust perforation 5 years/unlimited km. **Supplementary warranty:** It's a good idea to get an extended powertrain warranty. **Highway/city fuel economy:** *Base sedan:* 6.0/9.0 L/100 km, 47/31 mpg. *CVT:* 6.1/8.0 L/100 km, 46/35 mpg. *SP sedan:* 6.2/9.1 L/100 km, 46/31 mpg. *Sport sedan CVT:* 6.7/8.9 L/100 km, 42/32. *Hatchback:* 6.3/9.1 L/100 km, 45/31 mpg. *Hatchback CVT:* 6.4/8.2 L/100 km, 44/34 mpg. *JX:* 6.6/9.3 L/100 km, 42/30 mpg. *JX CVT:* 6.9/8.9 L/100 km, 41/31 mpg.

OWNER-REPORTED PROBLEMS: There have been less than a dozen safety-related complaints registered by NHTSA during the past two years—50 complaints a year are the average for most cars. The headlights don't automatically turn on when the dash lights are lit; airbags fail to deploy; vehicle surges forward while cruising; stalling when underway; floor mats interfere with the accelerator and brake pedals; and the tire-valve-stem pressure sensors corrode and split. Other owner complaints mostly target the fuel system and fit and finish, where water leaks are common, paint is easily chipped, and the unprotected metal is quick to rust. These few complaints are all the more surprising because Suzuki is a small player in the automaker game and its vehicles are cheaper than most in the small-car category.

SERVICE BULLETIN-REPORTED PROBLEMS: Nothing significant.

Toyota

When Good Cars Go Bad

I have recommended Toyota models since the early '70s, when the company first came to Canada. Their vehicles were reliable and cheap (though rust-prone), and most disputed warranty claims were paid without forcing customers to file small claims court lawsuits.

All this came to an end over a decade ago when bean-counters took over the company and adopted the mantra that profit and market share trump quality and fair prices.

Let's look at prices. In my opinion, Toyota and its dealers used the Toyota Access program to keep retail prices artificially high in Canada. *Lemon-Aid* made a formal complaint to Ottawa, alleging Toyota price-fixing, and the next thing we knew, Toyota settled and agreed to give $2 million to a Canadian charity—without admitting guilt. Slick, eh? Price-fixing charges were never filed and Toyota prices have remained firm. Fast-forward to Toyota's sudden-acceleration woes over the past two years. Although NHTSA-logged complaints confirm that Toyota reps stonewalled thousands of Toyota car and truck owners, these same Toyota executives, claims managers, and lawyers said they were unaware that the vehicles would suddenly accelerate out of control. Toyota's president cried as he testified before the U.S. Congress in 2010 when confronted with complaint records. Shortly thereafter, Toyota recalled almost its entire lineup to change floor carpets and throttles.

There was no admission of guilt, nor any confirmation by Toyota that its own internal service bulletins (published in *Lemon-Aid*) confirmed that 2002 and 2003 Camrys can suddenly accelerate due to defective computer modules.

And get this: Apple Inc. co-founder Steve Wozniak repeatedly called Toyota over the course of several months to report brake failures with his Prius. Toyota officials ignored him. However, when he mentioned the problem in an aside during an Apple press conference, all hell broke loose. The company returned his call, apologized, fixed the car, and recalled thousands of others.

2011–12 ASIAN CAR SALES IN CANADA

RANK	AUTOMAKER	JULY 2012	% CHANGE	YEAR TO DATE	YTD % CHANGE
1	Toyota	14,028	+30.3	102,346	+26.3
2	Hyundai	12,850	+0.8	84,492	+3.7
3	Honda	9,604	+25.5	74,148	+57.1
4	Kia	7,683	+20.4	46,981	+19.0
5	Mazda	6,671	+1.2	44,278	+6.9
6	Nissan	4,635	-33.3	47,735	+0.9
7	Subaru	2,362	+23.3	17,061	+6.0
8	Acura	1,580	+35.7	8,870	+16.4
9	Mitsubishi	1,406	-16.4	11,716	-2.5
10	Lexus	1,107	+18.3	8,143	+9.6
11	Scion	684	+47.4	3,362	+22.3
12	Infiniti	681	+9.7	4,686	+22.9
13	Suzuki	505	+9.8	3,065	-7.3

Source: Automakers, and Automotive News

Toyota and Honda's July sales surge are "catch-up" sales following the Fukushimi earthquake production shutdown. Hyundai's and Kia's smaller increase reflects how well those companies did during the same period.

After the congressional hearings, the U.S. government fined Toyota $49 million for dragging its feet in implementing the above recalls. In the meantime, owners swear that electronic component failures are the real culprit and Toyota still ignores their pleas. Toyota responds that the problem isn't electronic-based, but just in case it's mistaken, a brake override feature has been added. European vehicles have had this safety device as a standard feature for years. Problem is, some motorists driving Toyota 2012 models, which should have the override feature added, say their cars still suddenly accelerate without warning.

Going into the 2013 model year, Toyota will likely continue with the same cost-cutting "decontenting" that caused a dramatic erosion of Toyota safety and quality. Why? Because it's easy to get away with and customer long-term loyalty is unaffected. Much of the cheapening of Toyota vehicles will go unnoticed in the showroom since lower-quality content and reduced performance isn't evident until you have lived with your car or truck for a few months. Honda, for example, cheapened its redesigned 2012 Civic, forcing *Consumer Reports* to change its "Recommended Buy" rating to "Not Recommended" in the space of a few months. Yet, look at Honda's latest sales figures, above: a whopping 57.1 percent increase in sales from July 2011 through July 2012.

Smart shoppers should wait until mid-2013 to ensure that the Yaris, Sienna, and Civic redesign errors are mostly corrected.

Toyota's Quality Decline

Toyota's image as a builder of quality vehicles has been legendary, with both J.D. Power and Associates and the Insurance Institute for Highway Safety giving the company high marks for building reliable, crashworthy vehicles. Not so, *Consumer Reports* and the U.S. Department of Transportation's National Highway Traffic and Safety Administration. They found that many Toyota models were unreliable and had serious throttle and brake defects. Read these NHTSA postings from angry 2012 Camry owners:

I want to bring to your attention a concern that is primarily one of safety but which also involved poor and misleading information by Toyota related to the Blu-Logic cell-phone connection system included as a feature on my new 2012 Camry Hybrid. My concern stems from the fact that the Blu-Logic system, obviously coined to sound like Bluetooth, and even listed on some dealer websites as a Bluetooth connection, is misleadingly described as handsfree communication and a handsfree solution in the separate brochure provided by Toyota. In actuality, the system is at best only 50%? handsfree. Only incoming calls may be engaged in without cell phone in hand. Outgoing calls may be initiated handsfree only if one's cell phone itself is equipped with voice-activated dialing, a 4G-type feature I would estimate only a fairly small minority currently possess. So the de facto reality of the Blu-Logic system is that it forces most drivers into the unsafe practice of manually initiating outgoing calls by manually dialing with cell phones in hand. But in a deceptive omission, the Toyota guides do not even mention the possibility of making calls in this manner. Indeed, the phone-bank rep I spoke to told me, presumably with a straight face, that it was not possible to do so, even though I have accomplished it on several occasions. It is hard not to see this omission of both service and information as a cynical evasion by Toyota, part of a cost-cutting effort to appear to offer handsfree in-car cell-phone service, a la Bluetooth, while actually providing an unsafe system which forces a driver to use hands to make calls. And part of this evasion appears to include a cover-up when a customer raises the issue.

•

Entering a driveway at 2 mph the car accelerated to approximately 30 mph and struck a brick wall. The air bags deployed causing injury and the car was totaled.

•

On April 30th 2012 my Camry 2012 was hit as I was making a U-turn to pick up my son from school. 35 mph. Upon impact the car did not stop, went over the median, into the bush area. In the meantime I tried to put the car in Park. The car did not stop. [I] turned off the engine. The car did not stop, the car did not pick up speed. The whole time I was braking but the car would not stop. It finally came to full stop upon impact [with] a tree.

•

The contact owns a 2012 Toyota Camry SE. The contact stated that while driving approximately 40 mph, there was a delayed response when the accelerator pedal was engaged and within seconds the vehicle abruptly accelerated. The failure occurred intermittently. The vehicle was taken to an authorized dealer three different times for the identical failure. The technician was unable to duplicate the failure.

•

I entered into a parking lot behind a cluster of homes, a car was behind me and the driver indicated that I was going at less than 3–5 miles per hour. I park the car and all of a sudden the car accelerated, went over the parking bump and over a wood safety wall, over some bushes and landed 2 feet down, damaging the homes and a couple of heating units. I pressed the brake but the car kept on accelerating. This car should not be on the market.

•

It sometimes will not shift into normal Reverse. On these occasions, when you shift into Reverse, it will not move or creep slowly back as it normally does. It feels like a brake is on and you must push hard on the gas to get the car to back up at all. The car then lunges backward until you take your foot off the gas and it will jerk to a stop without you even touching the brakes. This is scary when you are in a parking space at a retail store, restaurant, etc. and have someone parked on both sides of you. You can't back up slowly, only can lurch out of your parking spot and hope not pedestrians or vehicles are coming by.

•

The contact owns a 2012 Toyota Camry. The contact stated that another vehicle drove in front of her and she crashed into the side of that vehicle while driving 40 mph. None of the air bags deployed during the crash.

•

I was driving approx 30 mph when a Ford F150 truck ran a stop sign and I T-boned them. None of the airbags deployed. It hit hard enough to break the windshield.

In the late '90s, Toyota's reputation took a battering when angry owners refused to pay $6,000–$9,000 to repair the sludged-up engines used on many Toyota and Lexus models. After first blaming the problem on poor owner maintenance, the automaker relented and quietly settled most claims (see *www.oilgelsettlement.com*).

One would think Toyota has learned to fess up when it messes up, but recent developments show the contrary. Remember the case of Mark Saylor, a California Highway Patrol officer who was loaned a Lexus ES350 by a San Diego dealer? The Lexus accelerated, flipped, and burst into flames. As the car careened out of control, the occupants dialed 911 and you can hear them screaming in terror.

The dispatcher asks where they are passing, and Lastrella is heard asking someone in the car where they are. He exclaims: "We're going 120 [mph]! Mission Gorge! We're in trouble—we can't—there's no brakes, Mission Gorge...end freeway half mile."

The dispatcher asks if they can turn the car off.

Lastrella doesn't answer and says repeatedly, "We are now approaching the intersection, we're approaching the intersection, we're approaching the intersection."

The last sounds heard on the tape are someone saying "hold on" and "pray." Lastrella says: "Oh shoot...oh...oh." Then a woman screams.

Saylor, 45, his wife, their 13-year-old daughter, and Saylor's brother-in-law, Lastrella, died in the crash on August 28, 2009.

Toyota blamed the driver, denied knowledge of similar incidents reported by other Toyota and Lexus owners, and refused to support its dealer, who claimed Toyota electronics were to blame for the crash. (The dealer was sued separately.) Bowing to public pressure, the company finally paid $10 million to the officer's estate on February 25, 2011, in an out-of-court settlement. The automaker asked that a gag order be issued to prevent disclosure of the settlement sum. This was refused (*John Saylor v. Toyota Motor Corp.*, 37-2010-00086718, California Superior Court, San Diego County).

But the story doesn't end there.

Toyota rejected a petition from Phillip Pretty, the owner of a Ford Explorer that was hit by the above-mentioned out-of-control Lexus speeding behind him at more than 160 km/h. Pretty was hospitalized with a concussion and injuries to a shoulder and knee. Toyota denied all responsibility—in the same accident it had paid $10 million a few months earlier to settle.

Oh, what a feeling! Toyota!

Lemon-Aid is skeptical of Toyota's claim that sudden acceleration is no longer a problem with its vehicles. There are too many complaints coming from owners of 2012 models and service bulletins that point to an electronic failure in the throttle system.

U.S. Senator Charles Grassley believes that the government investigation of "runaway" Toyotas may have wrongly ruled out electronic glitches as the cause triggering some vehicles to unexpectedly speed out of control.

Investigators from NHTSA and NASA engineers ruled out a malfunction in Toyota's electronic throttle control system as a possible cause. This conclusion has been contested by many independent engineers, safety advocates, and other critics who insist the analyses were flawed. They point to Toyota out-of-court settlements and requests for judicial gag orders as proof the company doesn't want the real facts to come out.

Senator Grassley asked if NASA engineers considered the presence of "tin whiskers," ultra-thin crystalline which can collect on tin and tin-coated surfaces, creating electrical shorts and leakage paths that cause electronic malfunction.

A recent independent study by the University of Maryland's Center for Advanced Life Cycle Engineering (CALCE) concluded that an electronic cause for the sudden unintended acceleration problem in Toyota vehicles was highly likely. Researchers pointed to the presence of tin whiskers, which have been found on Toyota circuitry, as the likely culprit behind sudden acceleration events.

The Department of Transportation replied that it did not believe tin whiskers were a plausible explanation for runaway incidents. The agency did admit, however, that the tin whiskers phenomenon could cause a "jumpy" throttle.

Toyota has also systematically rejected owner complaints over dangerously defective drivetrains that possibly affect all of its 1999–2011 lineup. A look at NHTSA's safety complaint database shows a ton of complaints alleging these vehicles have an electronic module glitch that causes a "lag and lurch" when accelerating, decelerating, or turning.

Toyota knows that if it confirms the defect is electronic in nature, the company re-opens the sudden acceleration polemic and could be forced to replace electronic control modules on millions of vehicles—modules that cost far more than a floormat anchor.

Also, perusal of *Lemon-Aid* readers' letters and emails, as well as NHTSA reports, shows that recent-model Toyotas have been plagued by engineering mistakes that put occupants' lives in jeopardy. These include Corollas that wander all over the road, Prius hybrids that temporarily lose braking ability, and trucks with rear ends that bounce uncontrollably over even the smoothest roadways. Other safety failures include engine and transmission malfunctions; fuel spewing out of cracked gas tanks; sudden, unintended acceleration; gauge lights that can't be seen in daylight; and electrical system glitches that can transform a power door into a guillotine.

A quick glance at NHTSA's 2010 safety defects complaint log shows that the Camry, Corolla, and Prius are runaway bestsellers—"runaway" in the sense that you may find yourself an unwilling hostage in a car careening out of control with a stuck accelerator, no brakes, and limited steering.

When running properly, Toyotas do hold up very well over the years, are especially forgiving of owner neglect, and cost very little to service at independent garages.

But the kicker for most buyers is how little most Toyotas depreciate: It's not unusual to see a five-year-old Camry or Avalon selling for over half its original selling price (most Detroit Three vehicles sell for half their price after only three years). But this is not the case with Toyota trucks, hybrids, and the Sienna minivan, which depreciate quite rapidly. Evidently word has gotten out that, first, these vehicles have serious performance and quality deficiencies, and second, hybrid fuel economy is not all that impressive when one considers that a $3,000 (U.S.) battery pack replacement can buy a lot of gas.

YARIS ★★★

RATING: Average. Yaris is a function-over-form classic commuter car, where practicality trumps style and driving pleasure. Not a sporty performer by any stretch. **Road performance:** Car feels underpowered, especially when equipped with the automatic transmission, which often doesn't downshift quickly or smoothly. A tall profile and light weight make the car vulnerable to side-wind buffeting and the base tires provide poor traction in wet conditions. Still, the Yaris passes over uneven terrain with less jarring movements than do other minicompacts, and is quite nimble when cornering. Better road feel with SE models, thanks to electric power steering. **Strong points:** Lots of interior space up front; a nice array of storage areas, including a huge trunk and standard 60/40 split-folding rear seats; well-designed instruments and controls don't look as cheap as before; comfortable, high front seating; easy rear access; surprisingly quiet for a small car; and excellent visibility fore and aft. **Weak points:** Not overly generous with standard features. Interior ergonomics are not the best; interior materials look and feel cheap; and rear seating is cramped. There's also excessive torque steer (sudden pulling to one side when accelerating); some wind noise from the base of the windshield; the steering wheel is mounted too far away for some drivers; and gas mileage doesn't match the competition. **Safety:** NHTSA gives the

2013 Yaris liftback five stars for side crash safety and four stars for frontal and rollover crash protection. IIHS rates frontal offset and side crashworthiness protection as "Good," but says the 2012 hatchback head-restraint protection is only "Marginal." **New for 2013:** Only an upgraded stereo.

ALERT! Steer clear of the poor-performing original equipment tires. MSRP includes an "administration fee"; don't pay it.

OVERVIEW: Positioned just below the Corolla, the Yaris manages to offer about the same amount of passenger space, thanks to a tall roof, low floor height, and upright seating position. The car also has a more-modern look with its large windows, additional legroom, and high-quality trim and seats that give it the allure of a much more expensive car.

COST ANALYSIS: Get the identical, cheaper 2012 model. **Best alternatives:** The Honda Fit is the best of the competition—it's got more room and is a lot more fun to drive. Nevertheless, the Hyundai Accent, Kia Soul, Rio, or Forte hatchback, Mazda2 or Mazda3, Nissan Versa, and Suzuki SX4 are all worthwhile candidates. **Options:** Beware of option loading, where you have to buy a host of overpriced, nonessential, impractical features in order to get the one or two amenities you require. **Rebates:** 2013 models will get $1,000 rebates early in the new year. **Depreciation:** Much slower than average. **Insurance cost:** Below average. **Parts supply/cost:** Easily found and reasonably priced. **Annual maintenance cost:** Costs over the long term are predicted to be low. **Warranty:** Bumper-to-bumper 3 years/60,000 km; powertrain 5 years/100,000 km; rust perforation 5 years/unlimited km. **Supplementary warranty:** Not needed. **Highway/city fuel economy:** *Man.:* 5.5/6.9 L/100 km, 51/41 mpg. *Auto.:* 5.7/7.0 L/100 km, 50/40 mpg.

OWNER COMPLAINTS: Airbags did not deploy in a high-speed frontal collision; vehicle wanders all over the road, requiring constant steering corrections; driver-side window spontaneously shattered.

SERVICE BULLETIN-REPORTED PROBLEMS: Passenger-side airbag OFF light will come on even though the seat is unoccupied.

KEY FACTS

Canadian Price (negotiable): *Hatchback CE 3DR.:* $13,990, *LE 5DR.:* $14,890, *SE 5DR.:* $18,990, *Sedan:* $14,400, *Convenience:* $15,990, *Enchanted:* $16,520 **U.S. Price:** *L:* $14,115, *SE:* $17,200 **Canadian Freight:** $1,425 **U.S. Freight:** $760

POWERTRAIN (FRONT-DRIVE)
Engine: 1.5L 4-cyl. (106 hp); Transmissions: 5-speed man. • 4-speed auto.

DIMENSIONS/CAPACITY
Passengers: 2/3; Wheelbase: 100.4 in.; H: 57.5/L: 169.3/W: 66.7 in.; Headroom F/R: 3.5/1.5 in.; Legroom F/R: 40.5/27 in.; Cargo volume: 13.7 cu. ft.; Fuel tank: 42L/regular; Tow limit: 700 lb.; Load capacity: 845 lb.; Turning circle: 30.8 ft.; Ground clearance: 5.5 in.; Weight: 2,315–2,355 lb.

COROLLA ★ ★

KEY FACTS

Canadian Price (negotiable): *CE:* $15,450, *S:* $20,605, *XRS:* $24,840 (2012) **U.S. Price:** *L:* $17,025, *LE:* $18,975, *S:* $19,855 **Canadian Freight:** $1,425 **U.S. Freight:** $825

POWERTRAIN (FRONT-DRIVE)
Engine: 1.8L 4-cyl. (132 hp); Transmissions: 5-speed man. • 4-speed auto.

DIMENSIONS/CAPACITY
Passengers: 2/3; Wheelbase: 102.4 in.; H: 57.7/L: 178.7/W: 69.3 in.; Headroom F/R: 4.0/2.0 in.; Legroom F/R: 41/28 in.; Cargo volume: 12.3 cu. ft.; Fuel tank: 50L/regular; Tow limit: 1,500 lb.; Load capacity: 825 lb.; Turning circle: 37.1 ft.; Ground clearance: 5.8 in., *XRS:* 5.3 in.; Weight: 2,722 lb.

RATING: Below Average. The Corolla has dropped two notches in *Lemon-Aid's* rating due to a number of serious safety-related complaints. **Road performance:** Average acceleration requires constant shifting to keep in the pack; automatic-transmission-equipped versions are slower still; clumsy emergency handling; and poor steering performance:

> The problem is the steering is dangerous over 65+ mph! The front end of the car feels like it floats at highway speeds. I have zero feeling of the road from my hands to the wheels. The car tracks and never stays true on the road. This is constant and not intermittent which means I am focusing more on the steering issue then on the traffic. I am either overcompensating for any slight movement of the steering wheel to barely touching the wheel to keep this car remotely driving straight in the center of the lane, and that doesn't help! It worsens at speeds of 75+ mph. Someone is going to get hurt! Please recall this EPS system now!!!

Strong points: The user-friendly interior ergonomics are enhanced by the flat rear floor, which provides more room. A high resale value is another plus. **Weak points:** Lots of high-speed wind and road noise; limited front legroom; and plastic interior panels and trim look cheap. Overall reliability is average to below average. **Safety:** NHTSA says the 2013 Corolla merits five stars for side crashworthiness and four stars for frontal and rollover occupant protection.

Interestingly, the 2011 model earned only two stars for side crash safety. IIHS rates the 2012 Corolla as "good" in all categories tested. Reports of airbags deploying inadvertently or failing to deploy. **New for 2013:** An exterior/interior redesign and more fuel-efficient transmissions.

ALERT! During the test-drive, check for excessive steering wander, or swaying. Also, look for distracting glare from the interior chrome trim panels near the gear shift console.

OVERVIEW: A step up from the Yaris, the Corolla has long been Toyota's conservative standard-bearer in the compact sedan class. Over the years, however, the car has grown in size and price, to the point where it can now be considered a small family sedan. All Corollas ride on a front-drive platform with independent suspension on all wheels. There are three variants: the value-leader CE base version and the more-upscale S and XRS models. Power is supplied by a torquey 132 hp 1.8L twin-cam 4-cylinder teamed with a standard 5-speed manual gearbox or optional 4-speed automatic.

COST ANALYSIS: Selling prices are firming up as the market turns to smaller cars. **Best alternatives:** Other small cars that are good investments include the Hyundai Elantra and Mazda3 or Mazda6. **Options:** For better steering response and additional high-speed stability, order the optional 185/65R14 tires. **Rebates:** $1,500 rebates, low-interest financing, and modest discounting early in 2013. **Depreciation:** Much slower than average. **Insurance cost:** Average. **Parts supply/cost:** Parts are easily found and reasonably priced. **Annual maintenance cost:** Lower than average. **Warranty:** Bumper-to-bumper 3 years/60,000 km; powertrain 5 years/100,000 km; rust perforation 5 years/unlimited km. **Supplementary warranty:** Not needed. **Highway/city fuel economy:** *1.8 man.:* 5.6/7.4 L/100 km, 50/38 mpg. *Auto.:* 5.7/7.8 L/100 km, 50/36 mpg. *2.4 man.:* 6.7/9.4 L/100 km, 42/30 mpg. *2.4 auto.:* 6.5/9.4 L/100 km, 43/30 mpg.

OWNER-REPORTED PROBLEMS: Owners report a major steering defect that makes the Corolla unsafe to drive. Steering tends to allow the vehicle to wander all over the road; car cannot track a straight line on a flat road (alignments and a new steering rack don't help):

> It is very difficult to keep the vehicle within the lane. If it deviates (which is normal) and a correction is made, the car over-reacts and the vehicle veers to the other side of the lane. Another correction puts the vehicle back to the other side. So the vehicle moves side to side.

Sudden acceleration accompanied by total brake failure:

> While driving 50 mph [80 km/h] the vehicle suddenly accelerated. As the vehicle is accelerating, the contact is trying to slow the vehicle down by applying the brakes. At this time the brakes are malfunctioning and increasing in speed. The contact was unable to slow the vehicle down and crashed into another vehicle.

Car speeds up or slows down on its own:

> I see variations of about 500 rpm on the tachometer. Sometimes when letting off the throttle pedal, the car keeps going and doesn't get the message it's supposed to slow down. This is scary, it's almost like the car thinks it's on cruise control when it's not at all (here is a link to a forum where owners of 2011 Toyota Corollas describe exactly the same safety issue with the car: *www.corollaforum.com/showthread.php?p=285#post285*).

Sudden brake failure:

> I went over a dip in the road at about 40 mph [64 km/h] and went to hit the brakes while taking a turn that was approaching a stoplight when the brakes would not let me push them down and would give me feedback as if ABS was active. After a couple seconds I was able to reapply pressure to the brakes to stop. This happened a total of eight times in 2,100 miles [3,380 km]. The car has been in some close calls, and all the incidents happened after hitting a dip while trying to reduce my speed from over 50 mph [80 km/h] to the time of hitting the dips.

Airbags fail to deploy:

> The driver fell asleep at the wheel, awoke and tried to correct his lane position. Upon his attempt, the car could not be stabilized or controlled. This was a front end crash at speed of approximately 50–55 mph going through a chain link fence, hitting hundreds of stacked lobster crates (like hitting a brick wall). The car was completely totaled, the driver had seat belt on. Not one air bag deployed. The driver side mirror smashed through the driver side window and a piece of wooden lobster crate with nails came through the front windshield and into the vehicle. This caused serious injury to the driver, severe facial and elbow lacerations, and major amounts of glass fragments in his body.

Driver cannot open the rear window with the other windows closed, as it produces a dramatic vibration and shaking inside the vehicle; car parked on a small hill and with the parking brake applied will still roll away; harsh downshift when stopping; seat belt warning alarm isn't loud enough; instrument-panel rattling; front-seat squeaking, and the front power seat grinds and groans.

SERVICE BULLETIN-REPORTED PROBLEMS: N/A.

CAMRY, CAMRY HYBRID   ★★★

RATING: Average. The Camry is another example of one of Toyota's "good" cars gone "bad." Nevertheless, Camry's rating has been upgraded one star for 2013 mainly because safety-related failures have declined, although there are some serious ones that remain. Another positive change is the addition of a brake/throttle override to combat sudden, unintended acceleration. **Road performance:** Last year's redesign corrected most of the Camry's performance gaps, however vague steering causing excessive road wander remains a problem:

Steering is vague and not predictable. Never had a car with elec. steering. Car follows its own course. It takes a lot of attention to keep it on the road.

A retuned SE trim level delivers sporty handling; the base 4-cylinder is a competent, responsive performer; surprisingly, the 3.5L V6 powertrain set-up delivers fuel economy figures that are almost as good as the base 4-banger; although the ride has smoothed out, the SE suspension is a bit stiff. The 6-speed automatic transmission has a taller final drive ratio, which saves fuel, but slows acceleration. **Strong points:** There's a nice array of standard safety and convenience features that include a telescoping steering column, 10 airbags, stability control, antilock brakes, and four-wheel disc brakes that are larger than those on the 2011 models. The cabin is quieter; instruments and controls are well laid-out in an interior that has a richer look and feel; and passenger and storage space is better than average. **Weak points:** Paint on the lower plastic bumper is easily chipped. Hybrid fuel economy is overstated by almost 30 percent, says *Consumer Reports* and almost everyone else. **Safety:** The same safety-related failures are reported year after year and will likely increase with the 2013 redesign. These defects can be especially lethal to older drivers with slower reflexes. Indeed, probably few Camry drivers have the necessary driving skills to confront excessive steering wander caused by the new

KEY FACTS

Canadian Price (negotiable): *LE:* $25,310, *Convenience:* $26,700, *SE:* $27,755, *LE V6:* $29,020, *XLE:* $31,235, *SE V6:* $34,255, *XLE V6:* $36,410, *Hybrid:* $31,310 **U.S. Price:** *LE:* $22,500, *SE:* $24,500, *XLE:* $27,500, *Hybrid:* $26,000 **Canadian Freight:** $1,490 **U.S. Freight:** $760

POWERTRAIN (FRONT-DRIVE)

Engines: 2.5L 4-cyl. Hybrid (200 hp) • 2.5L 4-cyl. (178 hp) • 3.5L V6 (268 hp); Transmissions: 6-speed auto. • CVT

DIMENSIONS/CAPACITY

Passengers: 2/3; Wheelbase: 109.3 in.; H: *Camry:* 57.9, *Hybrid:* 57.9/L: 189.2/ W: 71.7 in.; Headroom F/R: 5.0/2.0 in.; Legroom F/R: 42/29 in.; Cargo volume: *Camry:* 15 cu. ft., *Hybrid:* 10.6 cu. ft.; Fuel tank: *Camry:* 66L, *Hybrid:* 65L/ regular/premium; Tow limit: *Camry:* 1,000 lb., *Hybrid:* Not advised; Load capacity: 900 lb.; Turning circle: 36.1 ft.; Ground clearance: *Camry:* 5.3 in., *Hybrid:* 5.9 in.; Weight: *Camry:* 3,190 lb., *Hybrid:* 3,638 lb.

electric steering feature, or sudden engine surging or delayed transmission engagement when accelerating, merging, passing, or turning. NHTSA gives the Camry and its Hybrid variant four stars for side crashworthiness and rollover resistance and three stars for frontal crash protection. IIHS also gives the Camry its top rating for frontal offset, side, and roof crash protection. IIHS rates head-restraint effectiveness as only "Marginal." **New for 2013:** Carried over with no significant changes.

ALERT! Many owners say their Hybrid's real-world fuel consumption is much more than Natural Resources Canada estimates. Can you endure the severe wind buffeting if driving with one window open?

> The wind buffeting that occurs in this car is unbearable. This causes an unsupportable pressure that you feel in your ears and head. Speaking while one of the rear windows is open is also impossible because our voices will echo.

Make sure there's no rear window defroster line reflection at night:

> The rear window reflects all the defroster lines when a car is behind you. So when looking out the rear window and there is 1 car you see 20 lines of lights and if there [are] 2 cars you see 40 lines of lights and so on.

•

> The contact owns a 2012 Toyota Camry. The contact stated that when looking out of the rear window, the defrost lines going across the window and the tint caused the contact to see multiple headlights. The contact stated that one headlight would appear as twenty various headlights, disorientating the driver. The contact took the vehicle to multiple dealers and was told that the design was normal.

Also, be wary of the factory-ordered window tinting. Check out the tint in the day and at night before purchase:

> The contact stated that she was unable to see out of the factory rear window tint. The vehicle was taken to the dealer. The dealer confirmed the failure was with the factory window tint.

OVERVIEW: The Camry is based on the Avalon platform and is available as a four-door sedan only. Power is supplied by a peppy 178 hp 2.5L 4-cylinder engine, a 200 hp 2.4L gas-electric hybrid 4-cylinder, or a 268 hp 3.5L V6. The non-hybrid engines use a 6-speed automatic transmission, while the hybrid model employs a CVT tranny. There are many standard features available on all Camrys: side airbags, side curtain airbags, a driver's knee airbag, and anti-lock, four-wheel disc brakes; stability and traction control (traction/anti-skid control) can be found on the higher-end models and the Hybrid. Rear seats have shoulder belts for the middle passenger; low-beam lights are quite bright; and the headlights switch on and off automatically as conditions change.

COST ANALYSIS: Both the Camry and its main rival, the Honda Accord, have lost considerable sales traction to the Hyundai Sonata, Ford Fusion, and Nissan Altima. Through the first half of last year, Camry sales in Canada were down 38.8 percent due to the earthquake and tsunami in Japan and press reports in North America that Toyotas were unsafe and had lost their quality edge. Now shoppers are looking for the deal that best suits their pocketbook and are returning to Toyota and Honda. In an effort to attract buyers, Toyota says it will continue to hold the line on prices and plans to offer substantial price reductions and rebates before year's end through the fall of 2013. **Best alternatives:** The Honda Accord, Hyundai Elantra, Mazda5 or Mazda6, and Nissan Sentra or Altima. **Options:** Toyota's new Entune system, which integrates smartphones and apps into a handy package, forces you to buy $1,000+ in options that bundles more features than needed. Another wasteful expenditure is the Leather Package, it includes a $1,000 sunroof, $200 carpeted floor mats, a $75 cargo net and a $75 rear bumper appliqué. Stay away from the optional moonroof: It robs you of much-needed headroom and exposes you to deafening wind roar, rattling, and leaks. Original equipment Firestone and Bridgestone tires should be shunned in favour of better-performing tires recommended by *thetirerack.com*:

> The car has Bridgestone Turanza EL 400-02 tires, which had 689 miles [1,109 km] on them. The rear driver-side tire failed at 60 mph [96 km/h] when the tread split. After reading all the similar complaints by other Toyota car owners, I believe these tires are dangerous. After a very ugly discussion with the dealership, the one tire was replaced, but Toyota would not replace the remaining three.

Rebates: $3,000 rebates, plus low-interest financing and very attractive leasing deals in late 2012. **Depreciation:** Lower than average; in Canada, safety complaints and slow sales haven't affected the Camry's resale value. For example, a 2007 entry-level Camry LE that sold for $25,800 is still worth $12,000. Most Detroit vehicles lose half their value two years earlier. **Insurance cost:** Higher than average. **Parts supply/cost:** Owners report long service waits for their Hybrids. Parts are generally moderately priced. **Annual maintenance cost:** Average. **Warranty:** Bumper-to-bumper 3 years/60,000 km; powertrain 5 years/100,000 km; rust perforation 5 years/unlimited km. **Supplementary warranty:** Not needed. **Highway/city fuel economy:** *Hybrid:* 4.9/4.5 L/100 km, 58/63 mpg. *XLE:* 5.1/4.7 L/100 km, 55/60 mpg. *2.5:* 5.6/8.2 L/100 km, 50/34 mpg. *3.5 V6:* 6.4/9.7 L/100 km, 44/29 mpg. Owners say fuel-economy figures are much lower than advertised.

OWNER-REPORTED PROBLEMS: As seen with other Toyota models (like the 2010 Prius, which has received 1,700 complaints), sudden, unintended acceleration without any brakes has been the top reported problem for Camrys, with an added twist: They still speed out of control after having recall work done:

> Entering a driveway at 2 mph the car accelerated to approximately 30 mph and struck a brick wall. The air bags deployed causing injury and the car was totaled.

Other safety problems reported: Airbags fail to deploy; when accelerating from a stop, the vehicle hesitates, sometimes to a count of three, before suddenly accelerating; and when decelerating, the vehicle speeds up, as if the cruise control were engaged. The close placement of the brake and accelerator pedals also causes unwanted acceleration due to driver error; however, this cannot explain the large number of incidences of sudden acceleration reported. Hybrid owners report the car pulls sharply to the left when braking. Frequent failures of the engine cam head, which is often back ordered; transmission shift lever can be inadvertently knocked into Reverse or Neutral when the vehicle is underway; harsh shifting; vehicle may roll backwards when parked on an incline; and electronic power steering operates erratically and is sometimes unresponsive.

There have also been reports that the steering constantly pulls the car to the left, into oncoming traffic, no matter how many alignments you get; one car caught fire after being plugged into a block heater; the centre console below the gear shift becomes extremely hot; Hybrid's lower beam lights are inadequate for lighting the highway; excessively bright LED tail/brake lights will impair the vision of drivers in trailing vehicles; inaccurate speedometer readings; gasoline in the fuel tank hits the tank baffle with a loud bang; wheels locked up; driver-seat lumbar support may be painful for some drivers; a strong "out-gassing" odour may permeate the cabin; windows often stick in the up position; rear windshield distortion when viewed through the rear-view mirror during night driving; and head restraints obstruct driver's rearward vision. Reports of the front windshield cracking from the driver-side upper left corner and gradually extended toward the middle of the windshield. Glass sunroof implodes and in one incident the rear window exploded while the vehicle was stopped in traffic.

Trunk lid "beans" people when the weak struts fail:

> A short time after I took delivery of the car and I parked it on my driveway which has a small climb to the garage. The car was parked with the rear end lower than the front. When I opened the trunk to unload it and released the trunk lid it came down and hit me in the head. It happens every time when the trunk is opened under the same conditions and sometimes when the car is level. Obviously the trunk lid needs a tighter spring.

Passenger-side window fell out; front windshield distortion looks like little bubbles are embedded in the glass; rear window-defrosting wires don't clear the upper top of the windshield; a number of Hybrid AC failures have also been reported. Owners say the Camry is a "rat-hostel":

> While driving 40 mph [64 km/h], the driver noticed a rat crawled from under the passenger seat into the glove compartment and into the air conditioner. The [sight] of the rat almost caused the driver to crash. The contact was able to get the rat out of the vehicle. Two days later the contact took the vehicle to the dealer to repair the back seat and the seat belt that the rat has chewed through and also clean the air conditioner.

SERVICE BULLETIN-REPORTED PROBLEMS: A Toyota secret warranty (Campaign # (LSC) 90K) will cover the cost to replace the VVT-I oil hose in some V6-equipped Camrys. When the oil hose fails, it will cause unusual engine noise and make the engine run hot. This campaign will expire March 31, 2013. Passenger-side airbag OFF light will come on even though the seat is unoccupied. Uneven rear brake wear; insufficient alternator charging may be corrected with an updated pulley assembly. Remedy for a front/rear suspension noise that occurs when passing over bumps in the road; a front door trim panel rattle; underbody rattling; and troubleshooting a windshield back glass ticking noise.

PRIUS, PRIUS C ★★

The Toyota Prius C.

RATING: *Prius:* Below Average. We know the problems: Sudden acceleration, no brakes or weak brakes, and a cruise control that doesn't turn off are scary enough. But what about a steering column that becomes unhinged? *Prius C:* Below Average. Hope springs eternal. We expect the c model to be a better-built *petite* Prius, but the jury's still out. The best priced hybrid around, this little hybrid is Not Recommended until it shows us more after its first year on the market. **Road performance:** Slow-steering, has lots of body roll when cornering, and is prone to stalling. Braking isn't very precise or responsive, and the car is very unstable when hit by crosswinds. Highway rescuers are wary of the car's 500-volt electrical system, and take special courses to prevent electrocution and avoid toxic battery components. **Strong points:** Good fuel economy and acceleration in most situations with only little cabin noise. **Weak points:** The car is too darn dangerous to drive; owners are still reporting that the brakes give out when they pass over a bump in the road. Poor performance in cold weather; battery pack will eventually cost about $3,000 (U.S.) to replace; fuel consumption may be 20 percent higher than advertised; 50 percent depreciation after five years; higher-than-average insurance premiums; dealer-dependent servicing means higher servicing costs; rear seating is cramped for three adults; sales and servicing may

KEY FACTS

Canadian Price (negotiable): *Prius C: $20,950, Prius C Technology: $23,160, Base Prius: $25,995, Moonroof Upgrade Package: $29,295, Touring Package: $29,550, Technology Package: $34,080* **U.S. Price:** *Prius II: $22,800, Prius III: $23,800, Prius IV: $26,600, Prius V: $28,070* **Canadian Freight:** $1,490
U.S. Freight: $760
POWERTRAIN (FRONT-DRIVE)
Engine: 1.8L 4-cyl. (134 hp);
Transmission: CVT
DIMENSIONS/CAPACITY
Passengers: 2/3; Wheelbase: 106.3 in.; H: 58.3/L: 175.6/W: 68.7 in.; Headroom F/R: 4.0/2.0 in.; Legroom F/R: 40.5/30 in.; Cargo volume: 15.7 cu. ft.; Fuel tank: 45L/regular; Tow limit: No towing; Load capacity: 810 lb.; Turning circle: 34.2 ft.; Ground clearance: 5.5 in.; Weight: 3,042 lb.

not be available outside large urban areas; and the CVT cannot be easily repaired by independent agencies. Reliability is subpar and performance is summed up quite well by Ontario-based car columnist and editor of *Straight-Six.com* John LeBlanc, who calls the Prius "the worst car of the last decade." **Safety:** NHTSA gave the 2013 Prius a five-star rating for side crash protection, and four stars for front-impact and rollover crashworthiness. *Prius, Prius V,* and *C:* IIHS gave all three 2012 models its top, "Good," rating for frontal offset, side, roof, and head-restraint protection. Sun reflects into the driver's eyes:

My 2012 Prius V has a serious reflection in the point of view of the side view mirrors, when the front windows are rolled up, and the sun is high noon (+-5 hours) position. This is caused by the white dash trim that the sun hits.

Also, the low driver's seat impedes visibility:

The drivers seat does not raise far enough to allow shorter drivers to see over the dash board, base of windshield and rear of hood. This prevents shorter drivers from being able to see the ground anywhere near the car. Giving the drivers a 2 dimensional view of the traffic and objects between 3 and 5 feet high. Anything below 3 [feet] tall is not visible for 30 to 50 feet in front of the car. The raised belt line is also causing this problem of 2 dimensional views versus 3 dimensional views. This is a serious safety issue. It could be fixed with increased travel height for the driver's seat. As I have had to offer several friends chair cushions to prop them up so they could see.

New for 2013: A Prius plug-in is on its way. Hold off buying one until it has at least a one-year track record.

ALERT! Okay, the fuel savings are exaggerated, but how about running out of gas?

When driving, dashboard [reads] "Hybrid system not working. Pull over..." This was 7/3/2012. It had run out of gas even though there were 2 bars out of 10 still present on gas gauge. On 7/30/12 later this happened again with 4 bars showing. Got the fuel sensor and gauge replaced on 7/30/12. 8/14/12 with 3 bars showing, cruising range of 60 miles and having gone 480 miles the same warning "Hybrid system not working...." I was able to get to a gas station before running out of gas. The Prius manual states the tank holds 9.5 gallons. Filling up the tank took 9.91 gallons. There is clearly something wrong.

During the test drive, verify if you can drive safely with the car's blind-spots:

There are very dangerous blind spots on both rear driver and passenger sides of the Prius V. Vehicles located near the mid to rear of the car cannot be seen in mirrors or by glancing over the shoulder when changing lanes. I have had numerous near collisions due to this design defect.

Finally, check that your child's safety seat can be safely installed in the Prius V—some can't:

> The latch system design on the seats on the new Prius V is flawed. Instead of having four latch points, one set of two for the left seat and one set of two for the right seat, they have only three latch points, one in the middle of the left seat, one in the middle of the right seat and one in the middle of the car. Our child safety seat has three buckles designed to work with the latch system, one on the left, one on the right and a top tether. The left and right buckles cannot attach to the same latch point because then the child safety seat will pivot.

OVERVIEW: Toyota sells four Prius models in Canada: the base Prius, Prius V wagon, Prius C subcompact (set on the Yaris platform), and the incoming Prius Plug-in Hybrid. This year's third-generation Prius contains a 1.8L DOHC 16-valve 4-cylinder engine. It may sound hard to believe, but the bigger engine doesn't have to work as hard. So at highway speeds, the lower rpms save about 1.3 km/L (3 mpg). With the debut of the Prius V five-door wagon, Prius is now approaching the Camry in size, and its powerplant is more sophisticated, powerful, and efficient than what you get with similar vehicles in the marketplace. Interestingly, because the car relies primarily on electrical energy, fuel economy is better in the city than on the highway—the opposite of what one finds with gasoline-powered vehicles.

An electric motor is the main power source, and it uses an innovative and fairly reliable CVT for smooth and efficient shifting. The motor is used mainly for acceleration, with the gasoline engine kicking in when needed to provide power. Braking automatically shuts off the engine, as the electric motor acts as a generator to replenish the environmentally unfriendly NiMH battery pack. The Solar Panel option uses solar energy to keep the vehicle cool when it's parked.

COST ANALYSIS: Do the math: You will spend a lot of money upfront to save a little money later on. After two decades you may break even. One surprising statistic comes from R.L. Polk, an automotive marketing research company based in the United States. Polk's August 2012 study found only 35 percent of hybrid owners purchased another gas-electric vehicle when trading in during 2011. Repurchase rates varied across hybrid models, with the highest percentage of hybrid loyalty going to the Toyota Prius. Removing Prius from the mix shows a repurchase rate under 25 percent. Prices are relatively firm due to the 2012 improvements. Wait until the new year to allow prices to settle down a bit. **Best alternatives:** Honda Fit or Insight, Hyundai Accent, and Nissan Versa. In a Prius-versus-Insight matchup, the Prius gets better fuel economy but is more expensive; the Insight, despite its fewer horses, is more fun to drive, though it's not as fast as the Prius.

On the other hand, the Insight won't abduct you at high speed, or send you head-on into a guardrail with no brakes. **Options:** Stability control and the 17-inch wheels will make for quicker steering response and better road feedback. **Rebates:** The Prius's popularity rises and falls in tandem with fuel prices and safety defect horror stories, so $1,500 (maximum) rebates will quickly come and go. **Depreciation:** Unbelievably fast. A 2007 Prius that sold for $31,280 is now worth barely $12,000. **Insurance cost:** Higher than average. **Parts supply/cost:** Parts aren't easily found, and they can be costly. **Annual maintenance cost:** Average, so far. **Warranty:** Bumper-to-bumper 3 years/60,000 km; powertrain 5 years/100,000 km; hybrid-related components (battery, battery-control module, inverter with converter) 8 years/unlimited km; major emissions components 8 years/130,000 km; rust perforation 5 years/unlimited km. **Supplementary warranty:** Not needed. **Highway/city fuel economy:** 4.0/3.7 L/100 km, 71/76 mpg.

OWNER-REPORTED PROBLEMS: Only 15 safety-related complaints have been posted against the 2012 Prius, while over 1,800 incidents were reported on the 2010 model; 50 reports would be average. Almost all of the earlier complaints concern sudden acceleration, loss of brakes, and cruise control failures.

A major complaint with the 2012s is the sudden loss of Drive or Reverse:

> Car becomes immobile – will not shift into Reverse or Drive. Computer keeps sending the message to put it in Park and depress brake, but once that is done, any attempt to shift into Reverse or Drive triggers the message, endlessly. The problem is apparently intermittent. Occurred for two hours yesterday, after occurring to a lesser extent in preceding days (in the days preceding the total breakdown, I was able to shift after a slight delay and a few attempts). The dealership to which I had it towed said it was fine today. Everything checks out. This is a safety hazard because the car can be in an unsafe position when it becomes immobile. I was partly out of a parking space, somewhat blocking traffic. The problem involves the computer and the transmission – at least.

The car is also extremely vulnerable to side winds, and light steering doesn't help much, causing the vehicle to wander all over the road and require constant steering corrections. Owners of 2012 models continue to report brake failures as the car continues accelerating. This occurs despite Toyota's much-vaunted brake/throttle override:

> As I was approaching a turn I began to brake and the brakes failed. I tried pressing the brake pedal harder and making sure that I had proper foot placement and It felt like the car accelerated at that point. Since the car was not slowing down I was unable to make the turn and ended up crossing the road diagonally and going up onto the curb. Once the car was over the curb and in the grass the brakes finally engaged and the vehicle came to a stop.

Car lurches forward when brakes are applied; many reports of loss of braking even after having the recalled ECU replaced:

Since Toyota updated the software for the recall, I still experience the same problem multiple times, and it is not only [happening] during slow and steady application of brakes, also [happening] when I use the brake in more sudden fashion even at moderate speed (30–40 mph [48–64 km/h]).

Cruise control doesn't disengage quickly enough:

I have to press the brake harder than any prior vehicles I have owned to kill the cruise control and if I release the brake before the cruise control is released then the car lurches forward. Many other people have experienced this issue and have documented their experiences on the forum *priuschat.com*. They have even fixed the problem themselves by moving the cruise control disengagement closer to the top of the brake pedal.

The steering column may fall out of its mount:

My wife and 2 daughters were driving on Interstate 90/94 when the entire steering column slowly dropped. I double checked the lever underneath to adjust it, but that was tight. I could see wires and bolts where the column had been dropped several inches. I lifted the column up and thought it would lock in or click back in place. When I did this, the entire column collapsed in my lap. An alarm sounded and I had no control of the steering while going 110 [km/h].

Inaccurate fuel readings; hands-free phone system is inordinately complicated to use; transmission sometimes goes into Reverse when shifted into Drive, or goes into Drive when Reverse is selected; traction control engages when it shouldn't; airbags failed to deploy; headlights go on and off intermittently; musty AC smell; noisy rear brakes; and the driver-side seat can't be adjusted away from the steering wheel.

SERVICE BULLETIN-REPORTED PROBLEMS: An extended warranty (Limited Service Campaign) covers repairs to the Lane-Keeping Assist feature until May 31, 2015. *2012 Prius V:* Under SC-C0F1204241-002, Toyota will replace free of charge the exhaust gas control actuator which may leak coolant. This Service Campaign will apply until May 31, 2015. Abnormal noise when brake pedal is released and excessive roof sun shade noise. Cleaning tips to keep the HV battery cooling fan at peak efficiency; and troubleshooting rear windshield ticking.

AVALON ★★★★

RATING: Above Average. The 2013 Avalon is a relatively reliable luxury sedan that returns this year with more compact dimensions, a lighter curb weight and a Camry Hybrid powerplant. **Road performance:** A smooth and responsive powertrain that provides quick acceleration combined with good fuel economy; acceptable handling and the ride is both comfy and quiet. Some negatives: a mushy brake pedal and ultra-light steering that can degrade handling. **Strong points:** A roomy, limousine-like interior with reclining backrests and plenty of

KEY FACTS

Canadian Price (negotiable): *Base:* $42,000 **U.S. Price:** *Base:* $33,955, *Limited:* $35,685 **Canadian Freight:** $1,650 **U.S. Freight:** $800

POWERTRAIN (FRONT-DRIVE)

Engine: 3.5L V6 (268 hp), *Hybrid:* 2.5L 4-cyl. (200 hp); Transmissions: 6-speed auto. • CVT auto.

DIMENSIONS/CAPACITY

Passengers: 2/3; Wheelbase: 111 in.; H: 57/L: 195/W: 72 in.; Cargo volume: 16 cu. ft.; Fuel tank: 70L/regular; Headroom F/R: 3.0/2.5 in.; Legroom F/R: 41/31 in.; Tow limit: 1,003 lbs; Load capacity: 875 lb.; Turning circle: 36.9 ft.; Ground clearance: 5.3 in.; Weight: 3,497 lb.

rear seat room and storage space; large doors make for easy front- and rear-seat access; comfortable seats; user-friendly controls; exceptional reliability; and good resale value. **Weak points:** Rear-corner blind spots, and some options are standard on competing models. **Safety:** NHTSA gave the 2005–10 Avalon five stars for front and side crash protection and four stars for rollover resistance. IIHS rates the 2009–12 Avalon as "Good" for frontal offset, side, roof, and rear (head restraint) crash protection. **New for 2013:** Returns restyled with cleaner lines like those of the Audi A7. The interior has been reworked to increase headroom and trunk capacity, make controls easily accessible, add more supportive seats, and give the cabin a high-end look. The suspension has been stiffened to reduce cabin noise and improve handling. *Hybrid:* This fuel-efficient Camry cloned powerplant employs a 2.5L 4-cylinder engine that's teamed with nickel-metal hydride batteries and two motors. Driver can choose any one of three driving modes: EV, ECO, and SPORT. EV runs on battery power alone up to 25 mph; ECO reduces throttle response and AC/ventilation output; and SPORT mode produces a quicker throttle and transmission response.

OVERVIEW: This five-passenger, near-luxury, front-engine, front-drive, mid-sized sedan offers more value and reliability than do other, more expensive cars in its class. The Camry-tested Hybrid components should be relatively trouble-free, having served the Camry well since 2007.

ALERT! Toyota has promised to improve the electric power steering to make it firmer and provide better driver feedback. Check it out during your test-drive.

COST ANALYSIS: Buying an Avalon means you are getting the equivalent of an entry-level Lexus: It performs well, is loaded with safety, comfort, and convenience features, and costs thousands of dollars less than a Lexus. **Best alternatives:** The Honda Accord V6, Hyundai Genesis, Mazda6, and Nissan Altima. **Options:** The engine-immobilizing anti-theft system and dealer-installed towing package are worthwhile items. Stay away from the navigation control system: It's still a pain to program. **Rebates:** $4,000+ on the 2012 models, plus low-interest financing. **Depreciation:** Average. **Insurance cost:** Higher than average. **Parts supply/ cost:** Parts are relatively inexpensive and easily found. **Annual maintenance cost:** Less than average. **Warranty:** Bumper-to-bumper 3 years/60,000 km; powertrain 5 years/100,000 km; rust perforation 5 years/unlimited km. **Supplementary warranty:** Not needed. **Highway/city fuel economy:** 7.0/10.7 L/100 km, 40/27 mpg. Expect actual fuel consumption to be about 20 percent higher than advertised.

OWNER-REPORTED PROBLEMS: There have been no safety-related complaints logged by NHTSA on the 2012 Avalon (50 complaints would be expected). Here are some of the 32 failures reported on the 2011 version (100 reports would be normal): "lag and lurch" when accelerating; when cruise control is engaged, applying the brake slows the car, but as soon as the foot is taken off the brake, the car surges back to its former speed; vehicle rolls backward when parked on an incline; "chin-to-chest" head restraints; a defective telescopic steering-wheel lever may cause the steering wheel to collapse towards the dash when the vehicle is underway; steering column is unusually loose; "outgassing" produces an interior film that coats the inside of the windows, seriously distorting visibility; newly designed high-intensity discharged headlights only partially illuminate the highway; and electrical shorts may suddenly shut down dash lights.

Practically all owner complaints unrelated to safety concern poor fit and finish and water leaking into the cabin through the headliner. Other concerns include engine and rear windshield/window ticking; a front power-seat grinding, groaning noise; transmission control module (TCM) updates needed to improve shifting; problems with the trunk opener; and sunshade switches that are located too close together.

SERVICE BULLETIN-REPORTED PROBLEMS: N/A.

SIENNA ★★★

KEY FACTS

Canadian Price (negotiable): *Base:* $28,140, *V6:* $29,140, *LE 8-pass.:* $32,905, *LE AWD 7-pass.:* $35,730, *SE V6 8-pass.:* $37,205, *XLE V6:* $39,740, *Limited AWD:* $41,425 **U.S. Price:** *Base:* $26,435, *SE:* $33,575, *XLE:* $33,360, *Limited AWD:* $39,955 **Canadian Freight:** $1,635 **U.S. Freight:** $810

POWERTRAIN (FRONT-DRIVE/AWD)
Engine: 3.5L V6 (266 hp); Transmission: 6-speed auto.

DIMENSIONS/CAPACITY
Passengers: 2/3/2; 2/3/3; Wheelbase: 119.3 in.; H: 69.5/L: 200.2/W: 78.2 in.; Headroom F/R1/R2: 3.5/4.0/2.5 in.; Legroom F/R1/R2: 40.5/31.5/2.5 in.; Cargo volume: 39.1 cu. ft.; Fuel tank: 79L/regular; Tow limit: 3,500 lb.; Load capacity: 1,120 lb.; Turning circle: 36.7 ft.; Ground clearance: 6.2 in.; Weight: 4,189–4,735 lb.

RATING: Average. Serious safety complaints involving injuries to children and adults combined with an unproven redesigned model adds up to this year's low grade. That said, the Sienna's 2011 redesign is worrisome because reworked Siennas have a history of being glitch-prone for the year or two following each redesign—hence, the Average designation for the 2012 and 2013 versions. **Road performance:** Smooth (most of the time) 3.5L V6 powertrain performance; and optional full-time AWD; standard stability control. Handling isn't as sharp and secure as some of the competing vans. Sienna is in the top of its class when all systems are working correctly, but when they don't:

Joining highway in a situation where vehicles giving way … braking then acceleration repeatedly, transmission refused to downshift on kick down, vehicle would not accelerate, actually slowed significantly forcing following vehicles to brake. Vehicle eventually began to pick up speed. Generally poor response from transmission in all modes. Transmission drops out of drive at low speeds causing engine to race before taking up Drive, very hard to operate vehicle smoothly. Excessive engine vibration and noise.

Strong points: Nicely restyled; plenty of standard safety, performance, and convenience features; a fourth door; a tight turning circle; and a good amount of passenger and cargo room. **Weak points:** Recommended options are bundled with costly gadgets; an unusually large number of body rattles and assorted other noises. The 2013s aren't as versatile or as reasonably priced as Chrysler's vans. How's this for "spin control"? Toyota says slimmer seats and controls add to the feeling of "roominess." No matter how they spin it, the interior looks less luxurious than before, cabin noise levels are higher, and fit and finish is far from acceptable. **Safety:** NHTSA says the 2012 Sienna merits four stars for frontal and rollover crash protection and five stars for side crashworthiness. IIHS gives the car its top, "Good," rating for frontal offset, side, roof, and head restraint protection. **New for 2013:** The under-powered, noisy, 4-cylinder engine is gone. Other small improvements include an eight-way power adjustable driver's seat, a four-way power adjustment for the front passenger's seat, enhanced climate controls, and a cabin air filter.

ALERT! Be wary of the fast-wearing and expensive-to-replace run-flat tires. There have also been many owner reports that the brake and accelerator pedals are mounted too close together; see if this affects your driving during the dealership test-drive:

> The contact owns a 2012 Toyota Sienna. The contact stated that when attempting to brake or accelerate, both pedals would be depressed simultaneously. The contact stated that the two pedals were too close in proximity. The manufacturer and the dealer were notified of the failure, but denied any assistance with repairs to the vehicle. The vehicle was not repaired. The failure mileage was 60 miles and the current mileage is 1,300 miles.

OVERVIEW: Toyota's redesigned, third-generation Sienna has become more car-like than ever in its highway handling and comfort, while offering a larger, restyled interior. It is sold in a broad range of models, and stands out as the only van with an all-wheel-drive option (though this is not recommended). It's available only with a 6-cylinder engine and as a seven- or eight-passenger carrier.

Toyota built the Sienna for comfort and convenience. If you want more performance and driver interaction, get a Honda Odyssey. Sienna's V6 turns in respectable acceleration times, and the handling is also more car-like, but not as agile as with the Odyssey. However, the spacious interior accommodates up to eight passengers. All models come with standard four-wheel disc brakes, and all-wheel drive is available.

COST ANALYSIS: Toyota is keeping 2013 prices near last year's levels, making this year's model a better buy from a price perspective. As far as quality is concerned, it would be wise to delay your purchase another year to take advantage of more-generous summer and fall 2013 sales incentives. **Best alternatives:** The Honda Odyssey and Mazda5 (a mini-minivan). Chrysler's minivans bring up the rear of the pack due primarily to their Pentastar V6 and automatic transmission failures.

Why not Nissan's Quest? Its serious powertrain and fit and finish deficiencies over the past five years preclude its purchase until we see if the upcoming redesign removes or exacerbates present design flaws. **Options:** Power windows and door locks, rear heater, and AC unit. Be wary of the power-sliding door and power-assisted rear liftgate. The doors can crush children and pose unnecessary risks to other occupants, while the liftgate can seriously injure anyone standing under it. Go for Michelin or Pirelli original-equipment tires; don't buy Bridgestone or Dunlop run-flats. **Rebates:** *2012:* $3,000; *2013:* $2,000 in the new year. **Depreciation:** Faster than average and expected to lose much more value as the aggressively discounted 2012 and 2013 models drive prices down. For example, a 2009 LE seven-passenger AWD Sienna that sold for $37,420 now sells for $17,500. **Insurance cost:** Higher than average. **Parts supply/cost:** Excellent supply of reasonably priced parts taken from the Camry's parts bin, but run-flat tire replacements are expensive and hard to find. **Annual maintenance cost:** Less than average. **Warranty:** Bumper-to-bumper 3 years/60,000 km; powertrain 5 years/100,000 km; rust perforation 5 years/unlimited km. **Supplementary warranty:** An extended warranty isn't necessary. **Highway/city fuel economy:** *(2012)* 2.7L: 7.5/10.4 L/100 km, 38/27 mpg. 3.5L: 8.1/11.5 L/100 km, 35/25 mpg. *AWD:* 9.0/12.8 L/100 km, 31/22 mpg. The 2.7L 4-cylinder engine burns almost as much fuel as the V6.

OWNER-REPORTED PROBLEMS: Believe it or not, 2012 Siennas *continue* to suddenly accelerate and lose braking capability, in spite of Toyota's brake/throttle override phased in last year:

> The contact owns a 2012 Toyota Sienna. The contact was driving 15 mph when the vehicle suddenly accelerated. The contact attempted to stop the vehicle but the brakes would not respond. The contact had to shut the vehicle off while it was moving to stop the vehicle from accelerating and avoiding a possible crash. The failure mileage was 2,800 miles.

•

> The contact stated that as he approached a stop light, he suddenly experienced sudden acceleration and there was an increase in the engine rpms up to 8,000 rpms. The contact forcefully applied the brakes and shifted into Neutral. The vehicle then decelerated and the contact drove home slowly. The dealer was notified and towed the vehicle in for a diagnostic test. They were unable to diagnose a failure and attributed it to a driver's error. The manufacturer was notified and offered no assistance. The failure mileage was 900 miles.

When the brakes *do* work, and are applied, the driver's seat moves forward; cruise control won't turn off; brake failure:

> At around 5 pm on a clear Monday evening I went to turn left into a parking spot. I stepped on the gas and nothing happened, I let up a bit and stepped again and my Sienna shot forward. I slammed on the brake halfway into the parking spot and ran into the tree in front of the van.

Airbags don't deploy when needed; power-sliding rear doors and power rear hatch are two options known more for their dangerous malfunctions than their utility:

> My 17 month old's head got jammed between the right rear wheel and the right rear door panel while the electric door slid open. Even though my wife pulled on the door handle the door kept sliding open. My baby's head was crushed between the tire and door panel. This is a very unsafe design as my wife tried to stop the door from sliding back and the door kept moving.

•

> My 2 year old daughter got her leg caught in the back part of the sliding door of a 2011 Toyota Sienna. She was inside the car. The door was opened. Her leg fell into the space while the door was opening. The door opened as far as it could and constricted her leg. Her leg was so constricted we could not reposition her body to open the door…. She was trapped (screaming) for 20–25 minutes. Her leg was cold and turning blue before it was freed…. I'm very concerned about the design of the door. I've looked at other minivans (even the same make and model but different year) and they don't have the gap in the back part of the door like the 2011 Toyota Sienna.

•

> Couple of months after I got the car, there were several incidents [in which] me and family members were hit on our heads and shoulders by self closing liftgate [and we] didn't know what the cause was. After researching about this problem, Toyota had recalled Sienna in the past about this same problem for older models for faulty strut used for power liftgates.

In another reported incident, a driver accelerated to pass another car, and his Sienna suddenly accelerated out of control, while the brakes were useless. Brakes can take a couple of seconds before they engage; the slightest touch of the gear shifter causes a shift into Neutral or Reverse; airbags fail to deploy; multiple warning lights come on, and the vehicle cannot shift; engine ticking; more ticking from the windshield/back glass; transfer-case fluid leaks; sunroof may spontaneously explode; front windshield distortion:

> I noticed a distortion across the lower 3" of the windshield. It is very distracting, as the paint stripes on the road "bend" towards the driver. It's worse at night.

Excessive rear-view mirror vibration; factory-installed TV screen obstructs the field of vision through the rear-view mirror; rear tires quickly wear out; front passenger seatback tilts forward when braking and second-row seats may be unstable; water puddles in the van's rear storage area near the back door.

SERVICE BULLETIN-REPORTED PROBLEMS: Insufficient alternator charging may require an updated pulley assembly.

RAV4 ★★★★

KEY FACTS

Canadian Price (negotiable): *Base:* $24,865, *Base 4WD:* $27,500, *Base 4WD V6:* $30,115, *Sport 4WD:* $30,810, *Sport 4WD V6:* $32,565, *Limited 4WD:* $35,045, *Limited 4WD V6:* $37,300 **U.S. Price:** *Base:* $22,650, *Base 4WD:* $23,875, *Base V6:* $24,510, *Base 4WD V6:* $25,910, *Sport:* $24,175, *Sport V6:* $26,105, *Sport 4WD:* $25,575, *Sport 4WD V6:* $27,505, *Limited:* $25,465, *Limited V6:* $27,385, *Limited 4WD:* $26,855, *Limited 4WD V6:* $28,785 **Canadian Freight:** $1,635 **U.S. Freight:** $825 **POWERTRAIN (FRONT-DRIVE/AWD)** Engines: 2.5L 4-cyl. (179 hp) • 3.5L V6 (269 hp); Transmissions: 4-speed auto. • 5-speed auto.

DIMENSIONS/CAPACITY

Passengers: 2/3; 2/3/2; Wheelbase: 105 in.; H: 66/L: 181/W: 72 in.; Cargo volume: 39 cu. ft.; Fuel tank: 70L/regular; Headroom F/R: 6.55/4.0 in.; Legroom F/R: 41.5/29 in.; Tow limit: 1,500 lb.; Load capacity: 825 lb.; Turning circle: 37.4 ft.; Ground clearance: 7.5 in.; Weight: 3,590 lb.

RATING: Above Average. **Road performance:** 4-cylinder acceleration from a stop is acceptable with a full load; excellent V6 powertrain performance; transmission is hesitant to shift to a lower gear when under load, and sometimes produces jerky low-speed shifts; some noseplow and body lean when cornering under power; and some road and wind noise. Good handling and a comfortable, and a relatively quiet ride are big improvements over earlier, more firmly sprung models; **Strong points:** Base models offer a nice array of standard safety, performance, and convenience features, including electronic stability control and standard brake override; RAV4 seats five, but an optional third-row bench on Base and Limited models increases capacity to seven; comfortable seats; a quiet interior; cabin gauges and controls are easy to access and read; exceptional reliability; and good fuel economy with the 4-cylinder engine (the V6 is almost as fuel-frugal). **Weak points:** Resale value is only average, which is good news for smart used-car shoppers only. **Safety:** NHTSA gives the RAV4 five stars for side crashworthiness and four stars for frontal and rollover protection. IIHS says head-restraint protection, frontal offset, side, and roof crashworthiness are "Good." **New for 2013:** This year's model is mostly a carryover of the 2012 version.

ALERT! 2013 marks the return of the Marquis de Sade-designed front head restraints. Try them during your test drive.

OVERVIEW: This SUV crossover combines a car-type unibody platform with elevated seating and optional all-wheel drive. Although classed as a compact SUV, the RAV4 is large enough to carry a kid-sized third-row bench seat, giving it seven-passenger capacity. A powerful V6 makes this downsized SUV one of the fastest crossovers on the market.

COST ANALYSIS: If you can find a substantially discounted (ten percent, or more) 2012, buy it. The 2013s don't offer much more. **Best alternatives:** The Honda CR-V, Hyundai Tucson, and Nissan X-Trail. **Options:** The engine-immobilizing anti-theft system and dealer-installed towing package are worthwhile items. The Sport model has an option that uses run-flat tires and dispenses with the tailgate-mounted spare tire. Stick with the regular tire: It's cheaper and less problematic. **Rebates:** $2,000+ on the 2012s and $1,000 on the 2013s, plus low-interest financing and leasing. **Depreciation:** Average; a 2007 Base 4WD that sold for $29,300 is now worth about $11,500. **Insurance cost:** Higher than average. **Parts supply/cost:** Parts are relatively inexpensive and easily found. **Annual maintenance cost:** Less than average. **Warranty:** Bumper-to-bumper 3 years/60,000 km; powertrain 5 years/100,000 km; rust perforation 5 years/unlimited km. **Supplementary warranty:** A waste of money. **Highway/city fuel economy:** *2.5L:* 6.9/9.4 L/100 km, 41/30 mpg. *2.5L AWD:* 7.2/9.7 L/100 km, 39/29 mpg. *3.5L:* 7.4/10.7 L/100 km, 38/26 mpg. *3.5L AWD:* 7.7/11.7 L/100 km, 37/25 mpg. Owners say fuel economy figures are too high by 20 percent.

OWNER-REPORTED PROBLEMS: The 2012 RAV4 has elicited only seven safety-related complaints, which is impressive for such a popular SUV. Among the incidents reported, we see the return of sudden, unintended acceleration (even after recall repairs were done) and loss of braking:

> After attempting to drive in reverse out of a parking space with the brake pedal engaged, the vehicle suddenly accelerated and crashed into a parked vehicle. A police report was filed. The driver sustained bruises to her leg. The vehicle was taken to the dealer who was unable to diagnose the failure. The failure and current mileage was 4,620 miles. The consumer stated the vehicle changed gears on its own, and the gas pedal went to the floor on its own as well.

•

> The contact owns a 2012 Toyota RAV4. The contact stated that upon shifting into Drive, there was a rapid increase in the engine rpms and the vehicle began to surge forward. The contact applied excessive pressure to the brake pedal, but the engine continued to rev. Another individual opened the doors and turned off the ignition.

•

My 2012 has done this virtually from day 1. When braking, there is a sudden acceleration for 1/4 to 1/2 second at the time the transmission downshifts. I also notice it while driving at high speeds and braking. It is more dangerous at slower speeds especially when braking at a light with someone in front of you. It feels like you are pressing both the brake and accelerator at the same time. It does not do this all the time. Maybe once or twice a day. I think it has to do with how hard you brake and what speed you are going. It is most noticeable just before you come to a stop. It always happens just as the transmission automatically downshifts and most noticeable when it downshifts to Second or First. I notice it when braking say from 65 to 55 mph as well, but the sudden acceleration at that speed has no or minimal affect and is not that noticeable.

Other reports: Fire erupted in the engine compartment; steering angle sensor malfunction causes the vehicle to stall out; a "thumping" rear suspension noise; cracking front windshields:

Vehicle is only a few weeks old and the windshield began developing a crack from the passenger side spreading towards the center of and down towards the bottom of the passenger side.

Original-equipment Yokohama tires may blow out their side walls; and the defroster/air circulation system is weak.

Practically all of the owner complaints unrelated to safety concern poor fit and finish and audio system malfunctions. Some drivers say they are sickened by a sulphur smell that invades the interior. Owners also deride the flimsy glove box lid, loose sun visor, constantly flickering traction control light, sticking ignition key, uncomfortable head restraints, squeaks and rattles from the dashboard and rear-seat area, and wide rear roof pillars that obstruct visibility. And, the mice are back! Rodents routinely enter the vehicle at will through the clean-air filter. One dealer suggested owners buy mouse traps or adopt a cat:

Check Engine light indicated. The car was taken to the dealer, where the dealer mentioned, "Evidence of rodent/small animal has chewed wiring harness at connector completely through." The car will need wiring harness.

SERVICE BULLETIN-REPORTED PROBLEMS: N/A.

VENZA

RATING: Above Average. This combination of a small SUV and a wagon has proven itself to be relatively problem-free and a good highway performer. **Road performance:** Powerful and efficient engines; pleasant riding though the ride is stiff at times; and handling is acceptable, though there isn't much steering feedback. **Strong points:** Roomy interior; innovative cabin storage areas; an automatic headlight dimmer; easy entry and exit; and a low rear loading height. **Weak points:** No third-row seat; radio station indicator washes out in sunlight;

and high-intensity discharge headlights are annoying to other drivers, are often stolen, and are expensive to replace. Resale value is lower than one would expect for a Toyota SUV. **Safety:** NHTSA gave the 2012 Venza a three-star rating for front crashworthiness, five stars for side protection, and four stars for rollover resistance. IIHS rated the vehicle as "Good" for frontal offset, side, roof, and rear occupant protection. **New for 2013:** Minor trim changes.

ALERT! Yikes! Not the poorly designed head restraints, again!

> The headrest for the front seats on the Venza makes these seats the most uncomfortable I have ever sat in, let alone drive. I am only 5'4" tall and the way the headrest lands, it pushes my head forward when I drive. I end up with both a headache and a neck ache whenever I drive. It appears this vehicle was designed for someone taller, perhaps a man. The headrest needs to be redesigned for someone of my stature. I would gladly pay for another headrest if one was available. But the bottom line here is that once again the needs of women (shorter than men) are not what is driving the design. I expect more from all car manufacturers. It is time to recognize that women make up 51% of the population.

KEY FACTS

Canadian Price (negotiable): *Base front-drive:* $29,310, *AWD:* $30,760, *V6:* $30,800, *AWD:* $32,250 **U.S. Price:** *Base front-drive:* $27,700, *V6 front-drive:* $29,520, *AWD:* $30,970, *XLE:* $31,360, *AWD:* $32,810 **Canadian Freight:** $1,635 **U.S. Freight:** $810

POWERTRAIN (FRONT-DRIVE/AWD)
Engines: 2.7L 4 cyl. (182 hp) • 3.5L V6 (268 hp); Transmission: 6-speed auto.

DIMENSIONS/CAPACITY
Passengers: 2/3; Wheelbase: 109.3 in.; H: 63.4/L: 189/W: 75 in.; Cargo volume: 33 cu. ft.; Fuel tank: 67L/regular; Headroom F/R: 5.0/4.5 in.; Legroom F/R: 41.0/30 in.; Tow limit: 2,500–3,500 lb.; Load capacity: 825 lb.; Turning circle: 39.1 ft.; Ground clearance: 8.1 in.; Weight: 4,125 lb.

OVERVIEW: Toyota's Venza is a five-passenger wagon sold in two trim levels that match the two available engines. Going into its fourth year, the car offers the styling and comfort of a passenger car with the flexibility of a small SUV. A perfect alternative for Toyota customers who need more vehicle than what the Camry offers but not as much as the Highlander.

COST ANALYSIS: Most of the 2012s have been sold; expect to pay almost full list price for a 2013, until competition heats up at year's end. **Best alternatives:** The Ford Edge, Nissan Murano, and Toyota Highlander. **Options:** Stay away from the panoramic roof option and backup camera: both are expensive gadgets of doubtful utility. **Rebates:** $2,000 on the 2013s later in the new year, plus low-interest financing. **Depreciation:** Faster than average, especially for a Toyota; for example, a 2009 entry-level Venza that sold new for $28,270 is now worth only $15,000. **Insurance cost:** Average. **Parts supply/cost:** Parts are average-priced and easily found. **Annual maintenance cost:** Less than average. **Warranty:** Bumper-to-bumper 3 years/60,000 km; powertrain 5 years/100,000 km; rust perforation 5 years/unlimited km. **Supplementary warranty:** Not needed. **Highway/city fuel economy:** *2.7L:* 6.8/10.0 L/100 km, 42/28 mpg. *AWD:* 7.1/10.2 L/100 km, 40/28 mpg. *3.5L:* 7.6/11.0L/100 km, 37/26 mpg. *AWD:* 7.9/11.5 L/100 km, 36/25 mpg.

OWNER-REPORTED PROBLEMS: Not a single safety-related incident reported with the 2012 Venza; only seven complaints were filed against the 2011 model. Sudden, unintended acceleration being the most life-threatening:

> We accelerated our Venza to match ongoing traffic speeds, when the throttle stuck wide open and was increasing in speed. I stepped on the brakes, which failed to respond. I then checked the cruise control, to see if I had inadvertently engaged it, but I had not. I then started to pump the accelerator pedal with extreme force, and after numerous pumps, the throttle disengaged.

Transmission would not go into Reverse; the Hill-Start Assist feature doesn't prevent the car from rolling back when stopped on a hill in traffic:

> I feel Toyota should immediately send out a safety notice requiring all employees be briefed about the Hill-Start Assist feature, how it doesn't activate automatically, and how to activate the feature when stopped on an uphill slope.

Airbags failed to deploy; brakes don't immediately work when slow and steady pressure is applied; sometimes, after the brakes are applied, the car won't accelerate; automatic rear hatch can crush a hand if it is caught when the hatch is closing; seat belt began strangling a three-year-old, who had to be cut free; sunroof exploded for no reason; the radio overheated up to 63 degrees C (145 degrees F); and chin-to-chest head restraints:

> The head rest on my vehicle pushes my neck forward into an extremely uncomfortable position. This cannot be adjusted. As a 5'4" female, I was having to seek medical treatment for neck and shoulder pain following long trips. I have reversed the head rest so that I can continue to drive my car. I am now concerned about the safety of this in

the event of an accident (whiplash), but feel like I have no choice. Severe neck pain was interfering with ability to turn my head while driving.

SERVICE BULLETIN-REPORTED PROBLEMS: N/A.

HIGHLANDER ★★★

RATING: Average. Highlander has been downgraded one star this year due to the resurgence of brake failures and complaints of sudden, unintended acceleration. **Road performance:** Powerful engines and a smooth, refined powertrain; the Hybrid can propel itself on electric power alone; a quiet interior enhances the comfortable ride; and responsive handling. **Strong points:** Roomy second-row seating is fairly versatile. **Weak points:** The third-row seat is a bit tight and doesn't fold in a 50/50 split. **Safety:** NHTSA gives the 2013 Highlander and its Hybrid variant four stars for frontal crashworthiness and rollover resistance; five stars were awarded for side impact protection. IIHS rates the vehicle as "Good" for frontal offset, side, roof, and rear occupant protection. **New for 2013:** Minor styling revisions; 2014 model will use an upgraded Camry platform.

ALERT! V6-equipped models best represent the Highlander's attributes, as the Hybrid models' higher prices will take years to offset in fuel savings.

OVERVIEW: A crossover alternative to a minivan, this competent, refined, family-friendly SUV puts function ahead of style and provides cargo and passenger versatility along with a high level of quality.

COST ANALYSIS: Look for an identical 2012 model discounted by about 10 percent. **Best alternatives:** From the Detroit SUV side: the Buick Enclave, Chevrolet Traverse, Ford Flex, and GMC Acadia. A good Asian SUV is the Honda Pilot. The Honda Odyssey is the only suitable Asian minivan choice. **Options:** Say yes to the

KEY FACTS

Canadian Price (negotiable): *Base: $31,675, V6 4WD: $35,925, Limited V6 4WD: $45,075, Hybrid: $42,990, Hybrid Limited: $51,950* **U.S. Price:** *Base: $28,090, Limited 4WD: $37,045, Hybrid: $38,140, Hybrid Limited: $43,795*
Canadian Freight: $1,635 **U.S. Freight:** $810

POWERTRAIN (FRONT-DRIVE/AWD)
Engines: 2.7L 4-cyl. (187 hp) • 3.3L V6 (270 hp) • 3.5L V6 (270 hp); Transmissions: 5-speed auto. • 6-speed auto. • CVT

DIMENSIONS/CAPACITY
Passengers: 2/3/2, *Hybrid: 2/3;* Wheelbase: 110 in.; H: 69.3/L: 188.4/W: 75.2 in.; Cargo volume: 37.5 cu. ft.; Fuel tank: 72.5L/regular; Headroom F/R1/R2: 3.5/5.0/0.0 in. (Ouch! Third-row seat is for only the very young or very short.); Legroom F/R1/R2: 41.5/32/23.5 in.; Tow limit: 3,500–5,000 lb.; Load capacity: 1,200 lb.; Turning circle: 38.7 ft.; Ground clearance: 8.1 in.; Weight: 4,050–4,641 lb.

engine-immobilizing anti-theft system, amd no to the failure-prone and costly-to-maintain tire-pressure monitoring system. **Rebates:** $2,500+ on the 2012s; $1,500+ on the 2013s, plus low-interest financing and leasing. **Depreciation:** Faster than average; a Base 2009 AWD version that originally sold for $37,150 can now be picked up for $19,500. **Insurance cost:** Higher than average. **Parts supply/cost:** Parts are relatively inexpensive and easily found. **Annual maintenance cost:** Average. **Warranty:** Bumper-to-bumper 3 years/60,000 km; powertrain 5 years/100,000 km; rust perforation 5 years/unlimited km. **Supplementary warranty:** Not needed. **Highway/city fuel economy:** 7.3/10.4 L/100 km, 39/27, mpg. *V6:* 8.8/12.3 L/100 km, 32/23 mpg. *Hybrid:* 8.0/7.4 L/100 km, 35/38 mpg.

OWNER-REPORTED PROBLEMS: NHTSA's safety-defect log sheet shows only 14 complaints registered against the 2012 Highlander. Again, sudden, unintended acceleration and brake failures were front and centre:

The contact owns a 2012 Toyota Highlander. The contact stated that while attempting to park with the brake pedal depressed, the vehicle suddenly accelerated and went over the curb. The contact applied the brake with both feet and shifted into Park in order to bring the vehicle to a complete stop.

•

The contact owns a 2012 Toyota Highlander. The contact stated that while driving at 40 mph, she attempted to brake but the vehicle accelerated rapidly instead. She attempted to apply the brake, however the brake pedal had become very stiff. She had to apply extreme pressure to the brake and the vehicle stopped 15 feet later. She shifted into Neutral and turned the vehicle off. The vehicle was taken to the dealer for diagnosis where the contract was informed that there was an idle up clutch defect, which occurred at low speeds and when the air conditioner was activated. The dealer would not repair the vehicle. The manufacturer was notified but offered no assistance. The vehicle had not been repaired. The current mileage is 6,800 miles.

•

My Highlander was at the airport for three days parked. When I was leaving the lot I was driving slow in the lot to pay my parking. When I got out of the lot to mainstream traffic I tried to accelerate and the car would only go slow as I kept pushing the throttle. There were cars on both sides of me with no one in front and then the car just took off. It did startle me because I was not expecting this. Thank god no one was in front of me because I am sure I would not have reacted fast enough to stop because of the rapid acceleration. Something is wrong with the throttle in these vehicles. I did not take it in because I am sure they would not have been able to reproduce the problem. This has only happened once and I hope it doesn't happen again.

•

While pulling into parking space in private shopping mall at slow rate of speed the vehicle suddenly and without warning rapidly accelerated forward into vehicle parked directly in front of my vehicle. My vehicle went up and over parked vehicle causing damage to both vehicles. No one was hurt in this accident and no police report was made as it was on private property. Complaint was made to Toyota who investigated and Toyota determined that no vehicle defect or design existed and refused to offer any assistance. My wife who was driving the vehicle has never had an accident and swears as to the fact. She did not contribute at all to this accident. Toyota is marketing a defective vehicle which will eventually and unfortunately result in death or serious injury if they are not now held accountable.

Other incidents: Airbag failed to deploy; transmission will not hold car parked on an incline; speedometer overstates the car's true speed by about 3 mph; sudden brake failure; brake and steering both went out as driver was making a turn; engine replaced after overheating, due to road debris damaging the radiator; engine loses power in turns; and Bridgestone Dueler HL400 original equipment tire blowouts due to cracks in the sidewall.

SERVICE BULLETIN-REPORTED PROBLEMS: Insufficient alternator charging may require an updated pulley assembly; procedures needed to fix a loose roof drip moulding.

TACOMA ★★★

KEY FACTS

Canadian Price (negotiable): *Access Cab 4x2:* $22,100, *4x2 SR5:* $24,125, *4x4:* $26,450, *4x4 SR5:* $28,325, *4x4 V6:* $26,900, *4x4 V6 SR5:* $29,200, *V6 TRD offroad:* $31,950, *Double Cab V6:* $28,500, *Double Cab V6 TRD Sport:* $31,950 **U.S. Price:** *Access Cab 4x2:* $20,315, *4x4:* $21,375, *4x4 V6:* $25,705, *Double Cab V6:* $26,705

Canadian Freight: $1,635

U.S. Freight: $825

POWERTRAIN (REAR-DRIVE/AWD)

Engines: 2.7L 4-cyl. (159 hp) • 4.0L V6 (236 hp); Transmissions: 5-speed man. • 6-speed man. • 4-speed auto. • 5-speed auto.

DIMENSIONS/CAPACITY

Passengers: 2/2; Wheelbase: 127.8 in.; H: 70/L: 208.1/W: 75 in.; Fuel tank: 80L/regular; Headroom F/R: 4.0/3.0 in.; Legroom F/R: 42.5/28 in.; Cargo volume: N/A; Tow limit: 3,500–6,500 lb.; Load capacity: 1,100 lb.; Turning circle: 44.6 ft.; Ground clearance: 8.1 in.; Weight: 4,115 lb.

RATING: Average. This cheap and reliable light-duty truck would have been rated higher if it weren't for owner reports that Toyota's infamous, decade-old lag and lurch transmission and sudden acceleration problems have spilled over into the 2012 lineup. **Road performance:** Well-chosen powertrain and steering set-up; standard electronic stability control; ideal for off-road work with the optional suspension; good acceleration, although delayed transmission engagement is still present. Very responsive handling over smooth roads; over rough roads, the ride can be jolting and degrade steering control. The driving position also seems low when compared with the competition. **Strong points:** A well-garnished, roomy interior; plenty of storage space; and good reliability. **Weak points:** Depreciation during the first three years takes a big bite out of the Tacoma's resale value. **Safety:** 2013 model gets three stars from NHTSA for frontal crashworthiness, five stars for side protection, and four stars for rollover resistance. IIHS rates front, side, roof, and head-restraint protection as "Good." **New for 2013:** New hood, grille, headlights, and bumpers, in addition to various interior trim changes.

ALERT! Payload capacity may be overly optimistic:

My 2012 Toyota Tacoma TRD Off Road does not meet its payload capacity. It has a limit of 1240 lbs and routinely bottoms out with 300–500 lbs in the bed of the truck. Toyota knows about the issue [and] has issued TSBs on the leaf springs but refuses to solve the issue on the new 2012 trucks.

OVERVIEW: Toyota's entry-level pickup isn't as utilitarian as its predecessors or some of the competition, but it has sufficient power and is relatively inexpensive if not too gussied up. If you decide to go for the optional off-road suspension, you will quickly notice the firmer ride and increased road feedback.

COST ANALYSIS: Look for a nearly identical (except for the bumper, grille, hood, and headlights) 2012 models discounted by about 15 percent. **Best alternatives:** The Nissan Frontier. **Options:** The stiffer suspension for off-roading, an engine-immobilizing anti-theft system, and the dealer-installed towing package are all worthwhile items. **Rebates:** $2,000+ on the 2012s, plus low-interest financing and leasing. **Depreciation:** Faster than average for both front-drives and four-wheel drives; a 2007 front-drive Access Cab that originally sold for $22,635 now fetches barely $7,500. An entry-level 2007 4WD V6 that sold for $29,660 is now worth $11,500. **Insurance cost:** Average. **Parts supply/cost:** Inexpensive and easily found. **Annual maintenance cost:** Average. **Warranty:** Bumper-to-bumper 3 years/60,000 km; powertrain 5 years/100,000 km; rust perforation 5 years/unlimited km. **Supplementary warranty:** Not needed. **Highway/city fuel economy:** *2.7:* 7.8/10.5 L/100 km, 36/27 mpg. *Auto.:* 7.9/11.0 L/100 km, 36/26 mpg. *AWD:* 9.1/12.0 L/100 km, 31/24/ mpg. *4.0 4×4:* 10.8/14.7 L/100 km, 26/19 mpg. *Auto.:* 9.9/13.4 L/100 km, 29/21 mpg.

OWNER-REPORTED PROBLEMS: Only seven complaints registered on the 2012 model where 50 reports would be the average. Some examples: touted payload capacity cannot be met; suspension bottoms out at 300–500 lbs.; truck surges forward when stopped; AC malfunctions; and some fit and finish complaints.

SERVICE BULLETIN-REPORTED PROBLEMS: Bouncy rear suspension ride with a heavy load can be corrected by installing free upgraded rear spring assemblies up to 3 years/36,000 miles; 2005–12 models may produce a steering shaft rattle when driven over rough road surfaces.

EUROPEAN VEHICLES

Europe's in a financial meltdown, and its automobile industry reflects this.

On both sides of the Atlantic, European automakers are having their worst sales year in a decade. Germany is the major exception. BMW and Daimler remain profitable in part because they are taking market share from the other manufacturers by offering luxury vehicles at a middle-class price. Volkswagen/Audi is also a major winner after holding the line on prices and discounting its high-end models.

Hard times in Europe impacts Canadian new car buyers in the following ways:

- **Price-gouging**—Initially, some European automakers will take advantage of Canada's strong dollar by charging up to 20 percent more for their vehicles in Canada than what they sell them for in the States. Prices will subsequently fall as Canadians take their business elsewhere.
- **Deeper discounts**—Other European manufacturers will offer deeper cuts to Canadians in the new year through the use of low-cost financing, dealer discounts, and manufacturer rebates. Volvo will likely join the Daimler, BMW, and VW parade to lower prices, while Audi, Land Rover, Jaguar, and Porsche will likely both gouge and cut. Fiat, on the other hand, is riding a wave of fuel-economy minded buyers and will either stand pat on prices or increase them only slightly.
- **More cross-border shopping**—Cross-border shopping will surge as buyers of high-end cars and SUVs flock to the States to take advantage of cheaper prices. This is already happening, says Statistics Canada in a cross-border travel report issued August, 2012, which found Canadian residents took nearly 2.8 million overnight trips abroad in June, the highest monthly figure since record keeping began in 1972.

European "Orphans"

Orphans are those vehicles that have been sold by their parent builder, or, as in Volvo's case, sold twice to different automobile manufacturers. Usually when this occurs, the purchased companies dwindle into bankruptcy or irrelevancy after a few years. It happened with American Motors, Bricklin, Chrysler, DeLorean, and Saab, and may also bring down Volvo.

There are many problems with buying orphan models. First, there's the high cost of servicing, due to increased costs for parts that become rarer and rarer. Second, it's incredibly difficult to find mechanics who can spot the likely causes of some common failures; there isn't a large pool of them who work on those vehicles all the time, and those who can work on them don't have current service bulletins to

EUROPEAN VEHICLE SALES IN CANADA

RANK	VEHICLE	JULY 2012 YTD	JULY 2011 YTD	%	RANK	VEHICLE	JULY 2012 YTD	JULY 2011 YTD	%
1	VW Jetta	14,482	16,391	−11.6	36	Porsche Cayenne	813	804	+1.15
2	VW Golf	7,974	8,306	−4.0	37	BMW 1 Series	737	1,082	−31.9
3	Mercedes C-Class	6,605	5,178	+27.6	38	Audi A6	559	271	+106
4	BMW 3 Series	5,822	6,915	−15.8	39	Volvo XC70	508	498	+2.0
5	Fiat 500	5,686	3,240	+75.5	40	Audi A7	507	323	+57.0
6	Fiat 500C	1,600	175	+814	41	BMW X6	502	619	−18.9
7	VW Passat	4,561	1,025	+345	42	Volvo C30	494	443	+11.5
8	BMW X1	3,716	1,215	+206	43	VW Eos	451	510	−11.6
9	Mercedes M-Class	3,577	1,819	+96.6	44	Porsche 911	434	361	+20.2
10	Audi A4	3,539	3,362	+5.3	45	Mercedes SLK-Class	393	235	+67.2
11	Toyota Highlander	3,433	3,288	+4.4	46	VW Routan	392	577	−32.1
12	Toyota Hylander	559	518	+7.9	47	Mercedes S-Class & CL-Class	376	438	−14.2
13	Hyundai Veloster	3,425	-----	-----	48	Volvo XC90	330	474	−28.9
14	VW Tiguan	3,400	3,430	−0.9	49	BMW 7 Series	322	277	+16.2
15	Audi Q5	3,342	2,696	+24.0	50	Land Rover LR4	317	374	−15.2
16	Mercedes GLK-Class	3,069	3,172	−3.2	51	Audi TT	314	274	+14.6
17	Mini Cooper	2,868	2,129	+34.7	52	Mercedes R-Class	284	312	−9.0
18	Mercedes E-Class & CLS-Class	2,510	2,110	+19.0	53	Porsche Panamera	245	234	+4.7
19	BMW X3	2,493	2,588	−3.7	54	BMW 6 Series	244	77	+217
20	Nissan Juke	2,478	2,277	+8.8	55	Jaguar XF	239	246	−2.8
21	Lincoln MKX	2,300	2,398	−4.1	56	BMW Z4	235	250	−6.0
22	BMW X5	2,115	2,184	−3.2	57	Land Rover, Range Rover	230	232	−0.9
23	BMW 5 Series	1,663	1,651	+0.7	58	Mercedes SL-Class	178	134	+32.8
24	Volkswagen Beetle	1,384	196	+606	59	Land Rover LR2	172	220	−21.8
25	Smart Fortwo	1,196	1,163	+2.8	60	Volvo S80	170	283	−39.9
26	Volvo XC60	1,196	1,162	+2.9	61	Porsche Boxster	149	120	+24.2
27	Audi A5	1,182	1,362	−13.2	62	Audi A8	137	128	+7.0
28	Volvo S60	1,078	868	+24.2	63	Volvo C70	107	125	−14.4
29	Mercedes GL-Class & G-Class	1,062	894	+18.8	64	Jaguar XJ	105	137	−23.4
30	VW Touareg	1,025	1,029	−0.4	65	Audi R8	83	90	−7.8
31	Audi Q7	1,015	930	+9.1	66	Porsche Cayman	82	77	+6.5
32	Audi A3	939	753	+24.7	67	Mercedes SLS	75	81	−7.4
33	Land Rover, Range Rover	916	801	+14.4	68	Jaguar XK	71	88	−19.3
34	Mini Cooper Countryman	853	774	+10.2	69	Saab 9-3	15	73	−79.5
35	Land Rover, Range Rover Evoque	828	-----	-----	70	Saab 9-5	6	35	−82.9
					71	Mercedes B-Class	1	2,099	−99.9

Source: *Automotive News*; sales figures from Polk

guide them. There's also an absence of secret ("goodwill") warranties to pay for work outside of the warranty period, because the automaker will have dropped the warranty extensions along with the models. Finally, most of these unwanted cars suffer from plummeting resale values.

Saab

Saab is no more.

Saab's bankruptcy was like a train wreck in slow motion.

GM sold Saab in February 2010 to Spyker, a small Dutch company that made its name by building luxury high-performance cars that typically sold for $1 million apiece. Spyker never made a dime in sales, and the Saab car plant was shut down on April 2011, a year before declaring bankruptcy. Since then, GM has stepped in and assured Saab owners that anyone who bought the car with a GM/Saab warranty would have that warranty honoured by GM.

Volvo

Volvo is on shaky ground now that it is owned by Geely, a Chinese truck manufacturer that has limited experience in automobile manufacturing and marketing and no experience in North America. The 16-year-old company faces the formidable task of integrating the Swedish and Chinese corporate cultures, with a little Ford thrown into the mix. Its greatest challenge, though, will be to make a profit from what had been a perennial money pit for Ford. Ford even lost money in selling off the dying brand to Geely: Originally purchased for $6.45 billion in 1999, Volvo was sold by Ford for a measly $1.5 billion (U.S.). Having lost its quality edge after the Ford purchase over a decade ago, car shoppers are leery of the company's products, which many feel are outrageously overpriced in Canada.

The 2013 Volvo S80 (above) sells for $38,950, plus a $895 freight fee in the States. In Canada, the same car costs $49,100, plus a $1,095 destination charge. Surprise! Canadian S80 sales are down 39.9% through July 2012.

Jaguar Land Rover

Tata-owned Jaguar Land Rover is the exception; it is making money—$372 million in the second quarter of 2012, thanks to better sales in India, Asia, and North America. Buoyed by the popular Land Rover Evoque, a Ford-conceived model, Tata has also improved quality control and continued to build its models in England, where it leaves most product decisions up to Jaguar Land Rover. Tata Motors plans to soon launch a redesigned Range Rover and an F-Type Jaguar roadster to replace the E-Type that dates back to 1961.

Luxury Lemons

European vehicles are generally a driver's delight and a frugal consumer's nightmare. They're noted for having a high level of performance combined with a full array of standard comfort and convenience features. They're fun to drive, well-appointed, and attractively styled. On the other hand, you can forget the myth about all European luxury vehicles holding their value; most don't. They're also unreliable, overpriced, and a pain in the butt to service.

LUXURY DEPRECIATION: FROM RICHES TO RAGS

2010 MODEL	SELLING PRICE	PRICE AFTER THREE YEARS
Audi A8 Quattro	$100,000	$46,000
BMW 7 Series	$113,000	$48,000
Jaguar XK Convertible	$103,200	$60,000
Mercedes S-Class Hybrid	$105,900	$61,000
Range Rover HSE	$93,830	$58,000
Volvo XC90 AWD	$52,000	$35,000
VW Routan	$28,075	$15,000

This last point is important to remember because in hard economic times such as these, cash-strapped dealers do not invest in a large parts inventories or mechanic training to adequately service what they sell. For them, the present is chaotic and the future is unknown and threatening, so you should buy a model that's been sold in relatively large quantities for years and has parts that are available from independent suppliers. If you insist on buying a European make, be sure you know where it can be serviced by independent mechanics in case the dealership's service falters or servicing costs are too high. Interestingly, in my travels across Canada, independent BMW, Mercedes, Volkswagen, and Volvo garages seem to be fairly well distributed, while Jaguar, Saab, and Smart repairers are found mostly in the larger cities, if at all.

So what's wrong with European cars? First, they can't compare to cheaper Asian competitors in terms of performance and durability. Who wants a Mercedes when offered a Lexus? Why get a dealer-dependent VW Passat when you can have more fun with a Mazda3 Sport (even with its stupid grin on the front grille)? Second, when times get tough, European automakers get out of town or go belly up. Remember ARO, Dacia, Fiat, Peugeot, Renault, Saab, Skoda, and Yugo? Asian automakers, like Mitsubishi and Suzuki, tough it out. Finally, European vehicles aren't that dependable and tend to be poorly serviced, with maintenance bills that rival the cost of a week in Cannes. Shoppers understandably balk at these outrageously high prices, and European automakers respond by adding complicated, failure-prone electronics that drive up servicing costs even more.

Here are some typical factory-related defects addressed in various Audi, Mercedes, and Volkswagen service bulletins:

2012 AUDI A4 QUATTRO SEDAN L4 2.0L TURBO

Technical Service Bulletins

NUMBER	DATE	TITLE
701227	04/13/2012	Trunk Lining Handle Incorrectly Positioned
371246	04/13/2012	No Speed Signal From ECU
571264	03/30/2012	Door Can Be Opened from Inside, Not Outside
271213	03/22/2012	No-Start Due to Discharged Battery
371243	03/16/2012	Transmission Warning Lamp On
941269	03/15/2012	LED Daytime Running Lamp Diagnostic Tips
371242	03/15/2012	Vehicle Doesn't Move, Moves after Key Cycle
001233	03/14/2012	Electrical Malfunctions after Window Tint
391210	03/07/2012	Drivetrain—Squeal or Howl at Low Speeds When Cold
371240	02/28/2012	Rough Gear Changes When Accelerating and Decelerating
271212	02/28/2012	Low Battery Diagnosis Tips/TAC Instructions
371238	02/22/2012	A/T Key Stuck, Vehicle Won't Lock
551221	02/15/2012	Fuel Door Doesn't Open/Close Properly
691223	02/13/2012	Airbag Control Module Can't Be Coded
691222	02/13/2012	Comfort Control Unit (BCM2) Can't Be Coded
911232	01/24/2012	Instruments—MMI Screen Appears to Flicker
171226	01/20/2012	Distance to Empty Display Info
571262	01/09/2012	Trunk Can't Be Unlocked with Remote
601117	01/05/2012	Noises from the Sunroof Area
461116	12/09/2011	Disc Brake Squeal
301111	12/09/2011	No-Start or Only Starts When Clutch Firmly Applied
261107	11/04/2011	Exhaust System—Noises from Rear Silencer
371128	11/02/2011	Campaign 37G1—Hesitation/Harshness
571161	10/31/2011	Outer Door Seals Are Loose
011132	10/26/2011	Fuel System—MIL ON/DTCs P0087/P0192/P119A
911121	10/24/2011	Poor Bluetooth Call Quality
911120	10/21/2011	Rattling/Humming Noise from Speakers
571160	10/21/2011	Key Memory Settings Are Not Available
571159	10/21/2011	Outer Door Seals Are Loose/Detached
941152	10/05/2011	Moisture Accumulation in Exterior Lamps
911116	10/05/2011	Cell Phone—Poor Voice Recognition/Hard to Hear Call
911109	09/20/2011	Cannot Pair Bluetooth Phone to Vehicle
571155	08/22/2011	Remote Key Is Inoperative
571153	08/18/2011	Door Handle Touch Sensors Inoperative
571151	08/15/2011	Exterior Trunk Handle Is Inoperative
911188	06/20/2011	Nonstandard CD Playback Problems
911189	06/20/2011	No Rear-View Backup Camera Display
691115	03/08/2011	Can't Code Replaced Comfort Control Module
911180	01/31/2011	Voice Recognition Inoperative
571142	01/21/2011	Interior/Audio—Interior Noises with Heavy Bass
701122	01/10/2011	Sound Is Distorted or Completely Inoperative

NUMBER	DATE	TITLE
281013	12/01/2010	Key Won't Stay in Ignition Lock
911068	10/26/2010	Navigation Joystick Is Loose or Fallen Off
911060	09/28/2010	Parking Assist System—False Warnings Set
101002	09/14/2010	Engine—Inspect for Debris in Transferred Assemblies
691009	09/10/2010	Airbag/Pyrotechnic Deployment Inquiries
971010	07/01/2010	Electrical—Harness Damage from Animal Bites
941014	05/24/2010	Lighting—One or More DRL LEDs Inoperative
571022	05/19/2010	Alarm Sounds for No Apparent Reason

2012 MERCEDES-BENZ E350 BLUETEC SEDAN 3.0L V6 DSL TURBO

Technical Service Bulletins

NUMBER	DATE	TITLE
LI54-10_P-051049	04/05/2012	Consumer Shutoff Intermittently Active
LI27-57_P-053496	04/05/2012	Auxiliary Oil Pump
LI27-50_P-049710	04/03/2012	Switches to Limp Home Mode
S-54_65-252	02/07/2012	Parking Assist—Malfunction and Fault Scenarios
S-54_65-251	02/07/2012	Parking Assist—Parktronic Sensor Return Policy
S 82_00-701	01/03/2012	Repair of Wiring Harnesses
S-32_25-82B	12/21/2011	Strut/Shock Absorber Replacement Guidelines
LI32-25_P-051123	12/20/2011	Noises from Front Axle Suspension Struts
S-88_30-87	10/28/2011	Body—License Plate Bracket Omission
S-54_21-244A	07/20/2011	Engine Control Module Flashing
P-88_60-85	07/12/2011	Fuel Filler Door
LI28-10_P-051935	05/25/2011	Oil Leak Between A/T and Transfer Case
LI27-60_P-051470	03/23/2011	Hard 2–3 Upshift or Slips, No 3rd Gear

2012 VOLKSWAGEN JETTA SEDAN 2.5L

Technical Service Bulletins

NUMBER	DATE	TITLE
9212-02	04/05/2012	Windshield Wipers Streak or Smear
8712-03	04/04/2012	Unpleasant Odors Coming from Vents
0012-02	03/26/2012	Squeak and Rattle Kit
9112-04	02/10/2012	Multimedia Interface (MDI)—iPod Tagging Overview
9212-01	01/17/2012	Wipers/Washers—Damage Evaluation
3811-03	12/21/2011	Harsh Shifting in Low Gear
9111-41	12/19/2011	Cell Phone—Bluetooth, Voice Recognition Buttons Inoperative
2711-05	12/15/2011	Diagnosis for Excessive Static Current Draw
9111-39	12/07/2011	Bluetooth—Inoperative, No Communication to Module
9111-37	12/06/2011	Bluetooth—Various Concerns

NUMBER	DATE	TITLE
9411-04	11/14/2011	Exterior Light Moisture Accumulation
9111-35	11/08/2011	Bluetooth Inoperative, Calls Dropped
9111-34	10/18/2011	Cell Phone—Bluetooth Software Update
1911-01	09/08/2011	Cooling System—Cooling Fans Run with Ignition Off
4611-06	04/18/2011	Brake Vibration/Pulsation upon Application
4611-05	04/15/2011	Abnormal Vibration When Braking
5711-03	04/06/2011	Remote Key Inoperative
9111-08	03/29/2011	Bluetooth—Voice Recognition Language Incorrect

British independent automotive journalist Robert Farago, former editor of the *Truth About Cars* website (*www.thetruthaboutcars.com*), writes:

> Once upon a time, a company called Mercedes-Benz built luxury cars. Not elk aversive city runabouts. [An allusion to the Smart Car.] Not German taxis. Not teeny tiny hairdressers' playthings. And definitely not off-roaders…. In the process, the Mercedes brand lost its reputation for quality and exclusivity. In fact, the brand has become so devalued that Mercedes themselves abandoned it, reviving the Nazi-friendly Maybach marque for its top-of-the-range limo. Now that Mercedes has morphed with Chrysler, the company is busy proving that the average of something good and something bad is something mediocre.

You won't read this kind of straight reporting from the cowering North American motoring press, as they fawn over any new techno-gadget-laden vehicle hailing from England, Germany, or Sweden. It's easy for them; they get their cars and press junkets for free.

Lemon-Aid readers who own pricey European imports invariably tell me of powertrains that stall, transmissions that jump out of gear, nightmarish electrical glitches that run the gamut from annoying to life-threatening, and computer malfunctions that are difficult to diagnose and hard to fix. Other problems noted by owners include premature brake wear, excessive brake noise, AC failures, poor driveability, hard starts, loss of power, and faulty computer modules leading to erratic shifting. Plus, servicing diesels will get costlier and more complicated in the future, now that your diesel's urea tank has to be refilled regularly—only by the dealer. Yikes!

Service with a Shrug

Have you visited a European automaker's dealership lately? Although poor servicing is usually more acute with vehicles that are new on the market, it has long been the Achilles' heel of European importers. Owners give European dealerships low ratings for mishandling complaints, for inadequately training their service representatives, and for hiring an insufficient number of mechanics—not to mention for the abrasive, arrogant attitude typified by some automakers and dealers who bully customers because they have a virtual monopoly on sales and servicing in their regions. Look at their dealer networks, and you'll see that most European automakers are crowded in Ontario and on the West Coast, leaving their customers in eastern Canada or the Prairies to fend for themselves.

Not Recommended European Models

Lemon-Aid doesn't give a "Recommended" rating to vehicles built by Audi, Jaguar, Land Rover, Saab (now bankrupt), Smart, or Volvo because the costs of owning and servicing them are too great. Moreover, buyers risk owning vehicles with plummeting resale values that cannot be serviced due to a shortage of skilled mechanics or underfunded parts inventories. Most of these brands have been disowned by their parent manufacturers and sold for barely a third of their value to Indian, Dutch, and Chinese interests. Their former owners couldn't support the cost of ownership, and neither can you.

Audi

Saddled in the early '80s with a reputation for making poor-quality cars that would suddenly accelerate out of control, Audi fought back for two decades and staged a spectacular comeback with well-built, moderately priced front-drive and AWD Quattro sedans and wagons that spelled "Performance" with a capital "P." Through an expanded lineup of sedans, coupes, and Cabriolets during the last decade, Audi gained a reputation for making sure-footed all-wheel-drive luxury cars loaded with lots of high-tech bells and whistles—and they look drop-dead gorgeous.

Sure, Audi and VW are seeing profitable times, but many Audi lovers say this has been done through the "gentrification" of the Audi spirit.

Audi's quality control, servicing, and warranty support remain problematic and are not expected to get much better as the company rebounds from the recession. It's no secret that reliability in most Audis declines quickly after a few years of use, causing many owners to walk away when their lease or warranty expires. As used Audis pile up in dealer inventories, resale values take a beating, even among the models that have a relatively clean record. Take, for example, the TT: A 2008 TT Quattro Coupe that originally sold for $50,600 is now worth barely $23,500 after four years—a boon for used-car buyers with independent garage connections, but a bust for owners who bought new. The fact that Audi powertrains are covered under warranty only up to 4 years/80,000 km is far from reassuring, since engines and transmissions have traditionally been Audi's weakest components and many other automakers cover their vehicles up to 5 years/100,000 km. This worry is backed up by *Consumer Reports* surveys showing serious powertrain problems with the entire Audi lineup, including the recently launched Q7 SUV, the entry-level A3, and the long-standing A4. The 2012 $68,600 A7 (now worth $15,000 less) is rated Not Recommended until it proves its worth.

Audi launches four new 2013 models: the RS 5, S6, S7, and S8. The Q7 gains a new engine with new power figures. The 2013 Q7 3.0L TDI gets a slight power increase to 240 hp. The Q5 will be out in the late fall with a 3.0L engine and a hybrid option.

No more Europe envy—additional diesel models are on their way to North America. The TDI should follow in the new year in both the Q5 and A6. Then, the A6, A8, and Q5 will gain a 3.0L TDI option in the 2014 models, which will debut sometime in mid to late 2013. It's expected there will be a diesel-powered A4 for 2015 and that the 2014 TT could include a diesel option, as well.

A3 ★★★★

RATING: Above Average, but only if you find good servicing and can keep the car six years or more to offset the high buy-in and depreciation loss. **Road performance:** The car's a superb highway performer, thanks to its powerful and smooth-running engines and transmissions. Handling is crisp, steering is accurate, and cornering is accomplished with minimal body roll. **Strong points:** Lots of safety, performance, and convenience features. Audi rates the A3 as capable of carrying five passengers; however, the three back-seat passengers had better be friends. **Weak points:** Fairly expensive for an entry-level Audi; on top of that, depreciation will likely be much faster than average, which doubles your losses. Also, a freight fee that nudges $2,000 should be made a felony. Premium gas is required, and insurance premiums are higher than average. Numerous factory-related problems affecting primarily the electrical system, powertrain, brakes, and accessories. Fit and finish are not up to luxury-car standards, either. **Safety:** No NHTSA crashworthiness data. IIHS rates the 2012 A3 as "Good" for head-restraint and roof protection and in protecting occupants in frontal offset and side crashes. **New for 2013:** Returns relatively unchanged. A new sedan arrives in 2014.

ALERT! Canadian Audi dealers have had a very good sales year and are willing to haggle over prices to keep their inventory moving. Just be wary of bloated costs from bundled options, specious "administrative" fees, and usurious delivery charges.

OVERVIEW: Based on the redesigned Volkswagen Golf, the A3 is Audi's entry-level, compact, four-door hatchback. It's a well-appointed, generously powered vehicle that arrived in the summer of 2005. The A3 comes in Standard and Premium trim levels, with a choice of two engines: 2.0 T versions have a 200 hp 2.0L turbocharged 4-cylinder engine, available with a 6-speed manual or 6-speed automatic transmission; the 2.0 TDI has a 140 hp 4-cylinder turbodiesel with the automatic only. All A3s are available in front-drive, and Audi's Quattro all-wheel drive is available on automatic transmission 2.0 Ts. Standard safety features include ABS, traction control, an anti-skid system, front side airbags, rear side airbags, and side curtain airbags.

COST ANALYSIS: This four-door hatchback is smaller and less costly than Audi's A4 compacts, and is just as much fun to drive. Since the 2013 cars are mostly carryovers from the 2012s, their prices haven't increased by more than a few hundred dollars, and some models have been heavily discounted. **Best alternatives:** Acura TSX, BMW 3 Series, and a fully loaded VW Jetta TDI. **Rebates:** Not likely, though prices will soften in late winter. **Depreciation:** Faster than average. A $33,800 entry-level 2008 A3 is now worth only $14,500. Audi values usually nosedive when the base warranty expires. **Insurance cost:** Higher than average. **Parts supply/cost:** Frustrating. Owners report months-long waits for fuel system, powertrain, and electronic components. Independent suppliers scratch their heads when you ask about Audi parts. **Annual maintenance cost:** A bit higher than average. **Warranty:** Bumper-to-bumper 4 years/80,000 km; rust perforation 10 years/unlimited km. **Supplementary warranty:** Don't leave the dealership without getting at least five-year coverage for the powertrain. **Highway/city fuel economy:** 2.0 *front-drive man.:* 6.7/10.4 L/100 km, 42/27 mpg. 2.0 *front-drive auto.:* 6.9/9.4 L/100 km, 41/30 mpg. 2.0 *AWD:* 7.5/9.6 L/100 km, 38/29 mpg. *TDI:* 4.7/6.7 L/100 km, 60/42 mpg.

OWNER-REPORTED PROBLEMS: Sudden loss of diesel power when accelerating; the transmission engages and then disengages when accelerating from a stop or when parking:

KEY FACTS

Canadian Price (negotiable): *2.0:* $34,100, *S tronic:* $35,700, *Quattro:* $37,500, *TDI:* $37,100 **U.S. Price:** *2.0 Premium:* $27,270, *Premium S tronic:* $28,750, *Premium Plus:* $29,270, *Premium Quattro:* $30,850, *Premium Plus Quattro:* $32,850, *TDI Premium:* $30,250, *Premium Plus:* $32,250 **Canadian Freight:** $1,995 **U.S. Freight:** $895

Powertrain (front-drive/AWD)

Engines: 2.0L 4-cyl. Turbo (200 hp) • 2.0L 4-cyl. Diesel (140 hp); Transmissions: 6-speed man. • 6-speed auto.

Dimensions/capacity

Passengers: 2/3; Wheelbase: 101.5 in.; H: 56/L: 169/W: 69 in.; Headroom F/R: 4.5/2.0 in.; Legroom F/R: 42.0/25.5 in.; Cargo volume: 19.5 cu. ft.; Fuel tank: 55L and 60L/premium/diesel; Tow limit: Not recommended; Load capacity: 990 lb.; Turning circle: 35 ft.; Ground clearance: 4.3 in.; Weight: 3,219 lb.

While pulling out into an intersection the DSG transmission briefly went into neutral and I saw the tachometer needle shoot up and heard the engine whine. I was in manual mode at the time. I down shifted and let off the gas and it re-engaged. The following day...the same thing happened again. This time I was also in manual mode and was again pulling out into traffic from an almost complete stop. I have since learned that this is an ongoing and known issue with VW/Audi DSG transmissions.

Engine failures and oil burning, transmission, climate control, fuel pump, and electrical system glitches, as well as fit and finish deficiencies. Owners also report blinking headlights and interior lights when the brakes are applied; premature brake replacements (rotors and calipers); and bad original equipment tires that are shredded by the tire rim.

SERVICE BULLETIN-REPORTED PROBLEMS: Bose Radio erratic sound volume; no-start due to discharged battery; electrical malfunctions after window tint; and excessive engine noise:

RATTLING/JARRING NOISE FROM ENGINE

BULLETIN NO.: 2027585/2   DATE: MARCH 6, 2012

Model(s)	Year	VIN Range	Vehicle-Specific Equipment
TT	2008–2012	All	2.0 TFSI (EA888)
A3			

CONDITION: Rattling/jarring noises from the engine compartment/exhaust system between 1800–2900 rpm.
TECHNICAL BACKGROUND: Because of exhaust gas pulsations, the wastegate flap and rods vibrate at the start of the boost air control. This leads to rattling or jarring noises. **SOLUTION:** Fit a spring clip on the wastegate adjustment.

Tiptronic DSG transmission malfunctions can be corrected via a software upgrade; Parking Assist System false warnings; front window binds or is noisy during operation; inaccurate "distance to empty" display; noises from the sunroof area; disc brake squeal; can't eject navigation DVD; rattling, humming noise from speakers; radio turns on/off, locks self-activate; inoperative Remote key; dash cluster lighting appears to flicker; fuel system malfunction warning; moisture accumulation in exterior lights; cannot pair Bluetooth phone to vehicle; poor cell phone voice recognition; and expensive harness damage caused by rodent bites:

Model(s)	Year	VIN Range	Vehicle-Specific Equipment
All Audi	2007–2010 2012–2015	All	
R8	2011	All	
A3	2011	All	
A4, S4	2011	All	
A4 Cabriolet	2011	All	Not Applicable
A5, S5	2011	All	
A5 Cabriolet	2011	All	
A6	2011	All	
Q5	2011	All	
Audi Q7	2011	All	

CONDITION: The customer may report:

- Engine warning light illuminated in IP cluster
- Reduced driving performance
- Engine does not start
- Coolant warning light illuminated.
- ABS warning light illuminated
- Parking system warning illuminated in IP cluster
- Cable or rubber hose damages in the engine compartment.

TECHNICAL BACKGROUND: Animal damage primarily occurs on easily accessible, exposed cables and on thin cables. To avoid future animal bites, advise the customer to clean the engine compartment. Electrical deterrents and cable protection have proven effective, but 100% protection cannot be guaranteed.

WARRANTY: This damage is due to outside influence and is not covered by any Audi warranty.

RECOMMENDED ANIMAL PROTECTION MEASURES: Electric deterrents. Similar to electric fences, these deterrents ensure effective and sustainable protection. Animals are driven away by harmless electric shocks.

A4, S4, A5, S5 ★★★

RATING: Average. Quality has improved measurably over the past several years. Servicing is still spotty. On the positive side, so many of these vehicles have been sold for so long that sustained digging will usually find you the part and a mechanic who can service the vehicle competently. Plus, there has been a dramatic reduction in safety-related problems reported by owners. This series of cars should be kept at least six years to compensate for their high initial cost and depreciation losses. **Road performance:** The base 2.0L engine provides gobs of low-end torque and accelerates as well with the automatic transmission as it does

The Audi A4.

KEY FACTS

Canadian Price (negotiable): *2.0 TFSI:* $37,800, *Quattro:* $39,700, *Quattro Tiptronic:* $41,300, *allroad Quattro:* $45,100, *Premium:* $49,700, *Premium Plus:* $51,900, *S4 3.0 Quattro:* $53,000, *S4 Quattro S tronic:* $54,600, *Premium:* $57,800 **U.S. Price:** *2.0 TFSI:* $32,500, *Quattro Premium:* $33,300, *Premium Plus:* $36,700, *Quattro Premium Plus:* $37,600, *Quattro Premium:* $33,400, *Quattro Prestige:* $43,150, *S4 Premium Plus Quattro:* $47,600, *S4 Premium Plus Quattro 7-speed:* $49,000, *S4 Prestige Quattro:* $53,850, *S4 Prestige Quattro 7-speed:* $55,250, *S5 Premium Plus Quattro 6-speed man.:* $50,900, *7-speed man.:* $52,300, *S5 Prestige Quattro 6-speed man.:* $57,550, *7-speed man.:* $58,950 **Canadian Freight:** $1,995 **U.S. Freight:** $895

POWERTRAIN (FRONT-DRIVE/AWD)
Engines: 2.0L 4-cyl. (211 hp) • 3.0L SC V6 (333 hp); Transmissions: 6-speed man. • 8-speed auto. • 7-speed auto. • CVT

DIMENSIONS/CAPACITY (A4 SEDAN)
Passengers: 2/3; Wheelbase: 110.5 in.; H: 56.2/L: 169.5/W: 71.8 in.; Headroom F/R: 3.5/2.5 in.; Legroom F/R: 41.5/24.5 in.; Cargo volume: 16.9 cu. ft.; Fuel tank: 62L/premium; Tow limit: Not recommended; Load capacity: 1,060 lb.; Turning circle: 37.4 ft.; Ground clearance: 4.2 in.; Weight: 3,665 lb.

with the manual. The turbocharger works well, with no turbo delay or torque steer. The manual gearbox, Tiptronic automatic transmission, and CVT all work flawlessly. Comfortable ride; exceptional handling, though not as sporty as Acura's TSX; acceptable braking performance. Not as fast as rivals; the ride is stiff at low speeds, and a bit firm at other times; some body roll and brake dive under extreme conditions; braking can be a bit twitchy. **Strong points:** Loaded with safety, performance, and convenience features, and you get lots of cargo room in the wagon. Safety-related complaints have dropped considerably. The new allroad Quattro offers more ground clearance than the A4 wagon (Avant) it replaces. **Weak points:** Limited rear seatroom (the front seatbacks press against rear occupants' knees); some tire drumming and engine noise; and overpriced, with an outrageously high $2,000 freight charge and depreciation that is a wallet-buster.

Another expense to consider is the car's high maintenance cost, especially because of its costly servicing. **Safety:** NHTSA gave both the 2013 A4 and S4 five stars for side and rollover protection; 2012 models received four stars for frontal protection. IIHS awarded even better scores, giving the 2012 models a "Good" rating for frontal offset, side, roof, and head-restraint protection. **New for 2013:** Minor trim upgrades; a more aggressively styled rear end; Premium and Prestige packages remain unchanged; and the allroad Quattro replaces the A4 Avant wagon. *S5 Coupe and Cabriolet:* A horsepower downgrade with the replacement of the 354 hp 4.2L 8-cylinder engine with a 333 hp 3.0L 6-cylinder. Also new: the 7-speed S tronic transmission; 18-inch five-parallel-spoke S-design wheels with 245/40 summer tires; and a three-spoke flat-bottom steering wheel.

ALERT! Models where the 8-cylinder engine has been replaced with the weaker 6-cylinder are discounted by $5,000. Dealers have an extra $2,000 to put in the pot.

OVERVIEW: This is Audi's bread-and-butter model, probably because it comes in so many variations, including sedans, Avant wagons, and convertibles; the lineup also includes high-performance models that are sold under the S4 and S5 labels. The A4 bills itself as Audi's family sports sedan and targets the BMW 3 Series and Mercedes E-Class customer by featuring a roomy interior, an 8-speed automatic transmission, all-wheel drive, independent suspension, low-speed traction enhancement, automatic climate control, and more airbags than you can imagine.

The 2013 Audi A4 lineup also includes a recently restyled and upgraded supercharged S4 sedan model, along with four-door sedans and Avant wagons. The Cabriolet convertible has been redesigned and is sold as part of Audi's A5 and S5 lineup. Sedans and wagons continue to offer Audi's Quattro all-wheel drive, and some versions of the sedan are available as front-drives. Sedans and Avants come as the 2.0 T and feature a turbocharged 211 hp 2.0L 4-cylinder engine. A continuously variable automatic transmission is standard on front-drive 2.0 Ts. The S4 sedan and S5 convertible are powered by a powerful 333 hp 3.0L supercharged V6 mated to either a 6-speed manual or an 8-speed automatic. This setup provides impressive torque that kicks in at just 2500 rpm and remains constant through 4850 rpm, making the car especially responsive in everyday driving. All models are loaded with standard high-tech safety and performance features that add to the car's complexity and price.

COST ANALYSIS: Buy a 2013 model, and profit from Audi's decision to cut prices on this year's models. Better yet, buy one used, and save $10,000 and additional money when servicing it at an independent garage. S5 convertibles cost about $10,000 more than A5 convertibles mainly due to the V8 engine used by the S5. This is too much to pay for what is only a slightly better performer. **Best alternatives:** If you like the S4 or S5 tire-burners, also consider the BMW M3 convertible or 5 Series and the Porsche 911 Carrera. A4 alternatives are the Acura TL or TSX, BMW 3 Series, Hyundai Genesis, Infiniti G37, and Lexus ES 350 or IS series. **Options:** An automatic transmission and all-wheel drive. Think twice about getting the power moonroof if you're a tall driver. **Rebates:** $4,000–$7,000 rebates, and a variety of dealer incentive plans and low-interest financing programs. **Depreciation:** Incredibly fast; a 2008 A4 that sold for $35,350 is now worth $15,500; a 2008 S4 that once cost $70,400 now barely fetches $28,500. Not even high-performance S5 variants can escape value-robbing depreciation: The 2008 V8-equipped S5 coupe that originally sold for $66,000 is now worth $28,500. Worse yet, convertibles are no longer a safe haven: A 2010 S5 convertible that once sold for about $69,000 is now worth $39,000. **Insurance cost:** Higher than average. **Parts supply/cost:** Often back ordered and expensive. Forget about saving money by getting parts from independent suppliers; they carry few Audi parts. **Annual maintenance cost:** Higher than average, but not exorbitant. **Warranty:** Bumper-to-bumper 4 years/80,000 km; rust perforation 10 years/ unlimited km. **Supplementary warranty:** Don't leave the dealership without it. **Highway/city fuel economy:** *2.0 front-drive man.:* 6.5/8.9 L/100 km, 43/31 mpg. *2.0 front-drive auto.:* 7.0/10.0 L/100 km, 43/30 mpg. *2.0 Quattro man.:* 6.5/9.5 L/100 km, 38/28 mpg. *2.0 Quattro auto.:* 7.0/10.0 L/100 km, 38/28 mpg. *A5 convertible:* 7.0/10.0 L/100 km, 35/23 mpg. *A5 coupe man.:* 6.5/9.5 L/100 km, 36/23 mpg. *S4 man.:* 8.1/12.2 L/100 km, 35/23 mpg. *Auto.:* 7.9/12.1 L/100 km, 36/23 mpg. *S5 convertible:* 8.1/12.9 L/100 km, 35/23 mpg. *Coupe man.:* 9.4/15.1 L/100 km, 36/23 mpg. *Auto.:* 9.8/12.8 L/100 km, 36/23 mpg. New 3.0L engines have not been tested yet. Remember, AWD models exert a heavy fuel economy penalty for better traction.

OWNER-REPORTED PROBLEMS: NHTSA logs show only 73 safety-related complaints going back to the 2008s and no incidents for the 2011 models. The smattering of reports show continued acceleration while braking; acceleration lag and engine surge; vehicle lunging every time the Tiptronic transmission is downshifted; stalling caused by faulty fuel injectors; CVT allows the vehicle to roll down an incline when stopped; secondary radiator is easily damaged from road debris; sudden water pump failure; and the windshield wipers stop working when the vehicle comes to a stop. The following problems have all taken these cars out of service for extended periods in the past: airbag fails to deploy; excessive steering shake due to a faulty lower control arm; engine, fuel-system (fuel-injectors, principally), and powertrain component failures; defective brakes; electrical shorts; and abysmal fit and finish. The electrical system is the car's weakest link, and it has plagued Audi's entire lineup for the past decade. Normally, this wouldn't be catastrophic; however, as the cars become more electronically complex and competent mechanics are fired as dealerships open and close, you're looking at a greater chance of poor-quality servicing, long waits for service, and unacceptably high maintenance and repair costs.

SERVICE BULLETIN-REPORTED PROBLEMS: (See the service bulletin summary on page 446.)

The Audi R8.

RATING: Average. The A6 would have been rated higher if its build quality was better and its residual value didn't drop so much. Stick with Audi's simpler models. **Road performance:** A potent base engine that produces incredible acceleration times and gives excellent gas mileage; predictable handling; and good braking. A6's Servotronic steering is improved, but it is still the car's weakest feature. It is both over-boosted and uncommunicative in "Comfort" mode and ponderous and numb in its "Dynamic" setting. The V8 is a bit "growly" when pushed, and the firm suspension can make for a jittery ride. **Strong points:** Comfortable seating; interior includes a user-friendly navigations system and an analog/digital instrument panel that is a joy to behold and use; plenty of passenger and cargo room (it beats out both BMW and Mercedes in this area); easy front and rear access; and very good build quality. Dropping the failure-prone DSG automatic

KEY FACTS

Canadian Price (negotiable): *A6 2.0 Quattro:* $52,500, *Premium:* $58,500, *3.0:* $59,800, *R8 4.2:* $134,000
U.S. Price: *A6 2.0 Premium: $42,000, 8-speed Quattro: $44,400, 2.0 Premium Plus: $46,500, 8-speed Quattro: $48,700, 3.0: $50,400, 3.0 Premium Plus Quattro: $54,700, 3.0 Prestige Quattro: $56,95, S5 3.0 Quattro: $50,900, S5 Convertible: $50,300, Prestige 7-speed: $58,950, S6 4.0L Quattro: $71,900, R8 Quattro: $114,200* **Canadian Freight:** $1,995 **U.S. Freight:** $895
POWERTRAIN (FRONT-DRIVE/AWD)
Engines: 2.0L 4-cyl. (211 hp) • 3.0L V6 (310 hp) • 4.0L V8 (420 hp) • 5.2L V10 (550 hp) • Transmissions: 7-speed S tronic • 8-speed auto. • 6-speed man. and S tronic • CVT

DIMENSIONS/CAPACITY
Passengers: 2/3; Wheelbase: 114.7 in.; H: 57.8/L: 193.9/W: 73.8 in.; Headroom F/R: 3.0/3.0 in.; Legroom F/R: 41.3/37.4 in.; Cargo volume: 14.1 cu. ft.; Fuel tank: 75L/premium; Tow limit: Not recommended; Load capacity: 1,100 lb.; *R8:* 551 lb.; Turning circle: 39 ft.; R8: 38.7 ft.; Ground clearance: *A6:* 4.6 in.; *S6:* 4.6 in.; *R8:* 4.5 in.; Weight: 3,891 lb.

transmission in favour of the 8-speed automatic on the A6 was smart. The Avant wagon performs like a sport-utility, with side airbags, high-intensity discharge xenon headlights, and excellent outward visibility. **Weak points:** The restyling looks limp and dated: overdone lights, ho-hum grille, and a painfully boring interior. Some tire thumping and highway wind noise; uncomfortable centre-rear seating; the wagon's two-place rear seat is rather small; and servicing can be problematic. And, if high servicing costs aren't enough, at the end of four years you may find your Audi is worth only a third of its original value. **Safety:** No NHTSA crashworthiness ratings. IIHS considers the 2012s crashworthiness to be "Good" in all crash categories. **New for 2013:** *A6:* There is a new 8-speed Auto Tiptronic Quattro option. *S6:* All-new for 2013, the sporty version of the A6 sedan boasts more power, exclusive styling, and a level of technological sophistication few cars offer. The V10 is replaced by a 420 hp 4.0L twin-turbocharged V8, hooked to a 7-speed S-tronic automatic. It posts a 0–60 mph time of 4.8 seconds and a top speed of 250 km/h (155 mph). Other refinements: upgraded adaptive air suspension, larger disc brakes, and better tires. *R8:* Returns with its V10 boosted to 560 hp.

ALERT! The multi-tasking joystick control for all the entertainment, navigation, and climate-control functions can be confusing. It's similar in function to BMW's iDrive system, which has been roundly criticized as being dangerously distracting.

OVERVIEW: The A6 is a comfortable, spacious front-drive luxury vehicle that comes as a sedan or wagon and offers standard dual front side airbags and head-protecting side curtain airbags; torso side airbags are optional. Also standard are ABS, an anti-skid system, and xenon headlights (thieves love 'em). The A6 sedan comes with a base 211 hp 2.0L four or an optional 310 hp 3.0L V6. Both engines are mated to a CVT or an 8-speed automatic transmission with manual-shift capability; Audi's Quattro all-wheel drive is also available.

The Audi R8 is an all-wheel-drive, two-seat coupe with a mid-mounted engine. The entry-level 4.0L has a 420 hp V8 engine, but the 5.2L has a 550 hp V10. Both models are available with a new 7-speed S tronic automatic transmission or a 6-speed manual. As with other Audis, depreciation is a value-killer. A 2008 (its debut year) top-of-the-line R8 that sold new for $139,000 is now worth about $68,000—$71,000 less—in not quite three years.

COST ANALYSIS: Audi has never been a major player in the global mid-size luxury sedan market. For every A6 sold in 2010, Mercedes sold seven E-Series models and BMW moved five 5 Series sedans. This means you can haggle to your heart's delight because Audi dealers have a substantial profit margin to share, and they'll do almost anything to poach buyers from their competitors. **Best alternatives:** Although the base A6 2.0T models are cheaper and more fuel-efficient than many competitors, they are also the least powerful cars in the segment. *A6 4-cylinder:* This base model rivals the more-powerful BMW 528i. On the downside, the 528i's gas consumption can't match the A6. *A6 3.0T:* Infiniti's M37x is worth test driving. Other vehicles worth taking a look at are the Hyundai Genesis and Lexus GS.

Options: Think twice about getting the power moonroof if you're a tall driver. **Rebates:** $8,000 rebates and low-interest financing. **Depreciation:** Lightspeed fast: A 2008 A6 Quattro that sold new for $63,600 sells used for one-third that price. **Insurance cost:** Higher than average. **Parts supply/cost:** Very dealer-dependent and expensive. Independent suppliers carry few Audi parts. **Annual maintenance cost:** Low during the warranty period, and then it climbs steadily. **Warranty:** Bumper-to-bumper 4 years/80,000 km; powertrain 4 years/80,000 km; rust perforation 10 years/unlimited km. **Supplementary warranty:** A prerequisite to Audi ownership, and it guarantees a good resale price. **Highway/city fuel economy:** *3.0:* 8.0/12.0 L/100 km, 35/24 mpg. *4.2 Quattro:* 8.6/13.0 L/100 km, 33/22 mpg. *3.0 Avant Quattro:* 8.6/13.0 L/100 km, 33/22 mpg. *R8 4.2 Coupe man.:* 10.2/16.3 L/100 km, 28/17 mpg. *Auto:* 11.4/17.0 L/100 km, 25/15 mpg. *S6 5.2:* 10.0/15.2 L/100 km, 27/19 mpg.

OWNER-REPORTED PROBLEMS: Very few safety-related complaints recorded over the past two model years. Among the reports: sudden, unintended acceleration; brakes barely stop the car at low speeds; power brake failure; and the brake and accelerator pedal are mounted too close together. Non-safety related problems concern mostly the electrical and fuel delivery systems, in addition to scads of fit and finish deficiencies.

SERVICE BULLETIN-REPORTED PROBLEMS: Not much to report, except for electrical harness damage caused by animal chewing.

The Audi TT.

RATING: Above Average, due to its nice balance of agility and comfort. Be prepared for a surprisingly low resale value and handling that's not the equal of a Hyundai Genesis, Mazda RX8, or Porsche Boxster. **Road performance:** The TT and TTS both come exclusively with the less reliable dual-clutch manumatic 6-speed transmission. The TT RS is available with a 6-speed manual transmission only. **Strong points:** A very well-appointed and tastefully designed interior; comfortable, supportive seats; plenty of passenger and cargo space (especially with the rear seatbacks folded); standard ABS; "smart" dual front airbags; and standard stability control. **Weak points:** Poor rear and side visibility; a useless back seat; difficult rear-seat access; awkward navigation system interface; and lots of engine and road noise. The hatch is heavy to raise, and a rear windshield wiper would be nice. **Safety:** No recent NHTSA or IIHS crashworthiness tests. NHTSA awarded the 2006 TT convertible five stars for side occupant protection and rollover resistance. **New for 2013:** Nothing significant.

ALERT! Again, Audi dealers are discounting some of their models, like the TT, that haven't changed much this year. Haggle for a 10 percent cut in the MSRP.

OVERVIEW: These cars, like most Audis, don't hold their value well. Used bargains abound if you are a savvy Audi mechanic or have access to a competent independent repairer. The TT Coupe Quattro debuted in the spring of 1999 as a $49,000 sporty front-drive hatchback with 2+2 seating, set on the same platform used by the A4 and the VW Golf, Jetta, and New Beetle. The TT's engines are coupled to a manual 6-speed front-drive gearbox. A spoiler and anti-skid system are also standard. Audi's TTS version is an upgraded, more powerful version of the standard car.

More beautifully styled and with better handling than most sporty cars, the TT comes with lots of high-tech standard features that include four-wheel disc brakes, airbags everywhere, stability and traction control, a power top (Quattro), a heated-glass rear window, and a power-retractable glass windbreak between the roll bars (convertible). An alarm system employs a pulse radar system to catch prying hands invading the cockpit area.

TT Coupes carry two variations of the same 2.0L 4-cylinder engine: a 211 hp 2.0L 4-banger and a 265 hp turbocharged version of the same engine. On the safety front, all of the cars have self-supporting run-flat tires, a tire-pressure warning system, full-sized two-stage front airbags, and side (head/thorax) and knee airbags. There's also a connection located in the glove box for playing and charging your iPod, which you can control via the radio or the multi-function steering wheel. A

Bluetooth mobile telephone feature allows for hands-free operation with voice-controlled capabilities.

TT RS

The series' most powerful model, the RS is powered by a 360 hp 2.5L 5-cylinder turbocharged engine hooked to a revised 6-speed manual transmission (there is no automatic). This little rocket goes from 0 to 60 mph in just 4.3 seconds, with a top speed of 174 mph [280 km/h].

COST ANALYSIS: Buy a discounted 2012 TTS, priced thousands of dollars less and powered by a torquier small engine. **Best alternatives:** The BMW Z Series, Hyundai Genesis Coupe, Infiniti G37 Coupe, and Mazda Miata. **Options:** Think twice about getting the power moonroof if you're a tall driver. On the other hand, the Audi Magnetic Ride option truly personalizes suspension performance, but its high price ($1,900) is an unexpected jolt. **Rebates:** $6,000 rebates and low-interest financing. **Depreciation:** Surprisingly fast, but slower than other Audi models, like the A5 and A6. **Insurance cost:** Higher than average. **Parts supply/cost:** Very dealer-dependent and expensive. Independent suppliers carry few Audi parts. **Annual maintenance cost:** Low during the warranty period, and then it climbs steadily. **Warranty:** Bumper-to-bumper 4 years/80,000 km; powertrain 4 years/80,000 km; rust perforation 10 years/unlimited km. **Supplementary warranty:** A prerequisite to Audi ownership, and it guarantees a good resale price. **Highway/city fuel economy:** *TT Coupe Quattro 2.0:* 6.4/9.1 L/100 km, 44/31 mpg. *Roadster:* 6.4/9.1 L/100 km, 44/31 mpg. *TTS Coupe:* 7.4/10.7 L/100 km, 38/26 mpg. *Roadster:* 7.4/10.1 L/100 km, 38/28 mpg.

OWNER-REPORTED PROBLEMS: No safety-related incidents reported for the last two model years.

SERVICE BULLETIN-REPORTED PROBLEMS: Rattling, jarring engine noise; disc brake squeal remedy; door can be opened from the inside only; no-starts due to dead battery; window tint causes electrical malfunctions; inaccurate Distance to Empty display; false warnings from the parking-assist system; radio turns on/off, locks self-activate; DSG transmission software update; fuel-system malfunction alert; dash cluster lighting flickers; moisture accumulation in exterior lights, and possible harness damage from animal bites (see page 453).

BMW

There are many things about cars and computers that are similar. Both cars and computers are very complex systems, and there are lots of useless specs that some car nuts THINK have a lot of value—like horsepower. Two identical cars, with different horsepower, will have different results—but there are many, many other factors as well. Like torque and weight of the car. A [Cadillac DeVille] may have a monster motor, but it ain't going to out power or out handle a car with a little less HP and a lot less weight. RPMs are useless for performance or power, though most people think MHz are valuable—yet they mean roughly the same thing. What matters doesn't fit into a single spec…just like computers. People know that benchmarks are nice small indicators, but not to take them too seriously (individually)…. I think the [Audis] were probably a better value (at least they didn't charge you $500 for split rear seats)—but it was better if you were only looking at features (it was a more luxurious car, that handled worse and wasn't as powerful). Many American cars were better values if you were looking at cost (but most handled much worse, had worse repair records and so on).

DAVID K. EVERY
WWW.MACKIDO.COM/MYTHS/BMW.HTML

BMW Strengths

Despite the hard economic times, and unlike Toyota and Honda, BMW has resisted the temptation to keep prices down by decontenting its vehicles. In fact, the company is expected to hold the line on the cost of its 2013s by offering an array of discounts, rebates, and other incentives in the new year to keep its number-one spot in Canada's pantheon of luxury cars. Consumers haven't balked at BMW's high prices, yet, inasmuch as they are more attracted by the automaker's reputation for offering well-built, nicely appointed cars with excellent handling and superior driving comfort. No matter if fuel prices rise or fall, BMW has a product that will be appropriate for the times. Entry-level shoppers have the 1 and 3 Series; families with more disposable income may opt for the 5 and 6 Series; and for those who have the cash to buy loads of cachet, there's always the flagship 7 Series. Sport-utility fans also have four vehicles to choose from: the X1 "baby SUV," the compact X3, and the larger X5 and X6.

Although they may not offer the same cachet and superb driving performance, there are plenty of other cars that cost less, offer more interior room, have fewer defects, and don't cost as much to service.

BMW's X5 has the worst reliability history of all the company's recent production. Engine, fuel, electrical system, and brake deficiencies abound.

BMW Shortcomings

BMWs have excellent road manners and shout "I got mine!" Unfortunately, there's barely a whisper to warn you of factory-related defects that are far more frequent than Audi's but typical of what we find in most European cars and SUVs. Owner surveys show, and internal service bulletins confirm, the cars are afflicted with chronic fuel and electrical system and powertrain deficiencies that can be quite expensive to troubleshoot and repair. Surprisingly, coming from a country that extols its

German craftsmanship, BMW fit and finish is embarrassingly bad. Germany is also famous for its top electronics firms, but BMW electronic components head the list of parts most likely to cause owners grief. Three authoritative websites that list BMW problems and fixes are *alldata.com*, *safercar.gov*, and *www.roadfly.com*.

Remember, the entry-level versions of these little status symbols are more show than go, and just a few options can blow your budget. Adding to that, the larger, better-performing high-end models are much more expensive and don't give you the same standard features as many Japanese and South Korean imports do. Also, be prepared to endure long servicing waits and body and trim glitches.

3 SERIES   ★★★/★

RATING: Average. Many competitors deliver more interior room and standard features for less money. Smart BMW buyers will stick with the simple, large-volume, entry-level models until the recession blows over. *M3*: Not Recommended; the transmission hesitation on acceleration or deceleration is too risky. **Road performance:** Good acceleration; the 6-cylinder engines and the transmissions are the essence of harmonious cooperation, even when coupled to an automatic transmission—there's not actually that much difference between the manual and the automatic from a performance perspective. Light and precise gear shifting with easy clutch and shift action; competent and predictable handling on dry surfaces; no-surprise suspension and steering make for crisp high-speed and emergency handling; a somewhat harsh ride (but the M3 is harsher than most); lots of road feedback, which enhances rear-end stability; smooth, efficient braking that produces short stopping distances; and top-notch quality control. **Strong points:** Very well-appointed. **Weak points:** Seriously overpriced; depreciation is only slightly slower than with Audi's lineup; insufficient front headroom and seat lumbar support for tall occupants; limited rear seatroom and cargo area; tricky entry and exit, even on sedans; confusing navigation system controls; excessive tire noise, especially with the M3; radio buzz; and requires premium fuel. **Safety:**

KEY FACTS

Canadian Price (Firm): *328i Coupe:* $44,300, *328i Convertible:* $57,300, *328i xDrive Sedan:* $46,200, *328i xDrive Coupe:* $46,800, *335i Coupe:* $53,400, *335i Convertible:* $68,900, *M3 Coupe:* $71,700, *M3 Convertible:* $82,300, *M5 Sedan:* $101,500, *M6 Coupe:* $124,900, *M6 Convertible:* $128,900 **U.S. Price:** *328i Sedan:* $36,500, *Convertible:* $47,600, *335i Coupe:* $45,100, *335is Convertible:* $60,800, *335i Sedan:* $42,800, *335i xDrive Sedan:* $44,800, *335i xDrive Coupe:* $46,800, *M3 Coupe:* $60,100, *M3 Convertible:* $68,750 **Canadian Freight:** $1,995 **U.S. Freight:** $895

POWERTRAIN (REAR-DRIVE/AWD)

Engines: 2.0L 4-cyl. (240 hp) • 3.0L 6-cyl. (230 hp) • 3.0L 6-cyl. Turbo (300 hp) • 3.0L 6-cyl. Diesel (265 hp) • 4.0L V8 (414 hp); Transmissions: 6-speed man. • 8-speed auto.

DIMENSIONS/CAPACITY

Passengers: 2/3; Wheelbase: 109 in.; H: 56/L: 178/W: 72 in.; Headroom F/R: 3.5/2.5 in.; Legroom F/R: 40.5/27.5 in.; Cargo volume: 11 cu. ft.; Fuel tank: 63L/ premium; Tow limit: No towing; Load capacity: 1,060 lb.; Turning circle: 19.4 ft.; Ground clearance: 5.5 in.; Weight: 3,485 lb.

NHTSA gives the 2013 328i four-door its top crashworthiness score—five stars—for side protection and rollover resistance; frontal crash protection garnered four stars. IIHS frontal, side, roof strength, and rear crashworthiness merited a "Good" rating, while front-quarter protection was rated "Marginal." **New for 2013:** The 3 Series wagon is fully redesigned, taking its cues from the all-new sedan launched last year. Styling has been updated; occupants are treated to a more spacious interior; and a new engine/transmission package cuts fuel consumption. The liftgate still features a separately opening window, but it is now power operated. The new-generation sedan and wagon are larger but weigh less, thanks to the use of lighter metals and the electrically driven steering feature, which also saves gas but doesn't communicate road feel very well. Another fuel-saving device used by both the sedan and wagon is Driving Dynamics Control, a feature that allows drivers to select the best driving modes to maximize fuel savings.

ALERT! Short drivers report the head restraints are uncomfortable; check this out during the test-drive. Be wary of the diesel power option; the system is relatively new and much more complicated to service and repair than earlier versions.

OVERVIEW: With BMW's recent mechanical upgrades, styling changes, and increased exterior and interior dimensions, the 3 Series has come to resemble its more-expensive big brothers, with super-smooth powertrain performance and enhanced handling.

COST ANALYSIS: Buy the improved 2013 models. **Best alternatives:** Other cars worth considering are the Hyundai Genesis Coupe or Sedan and the Lexus IS series. **Options:** If you buy a convertible, invest $1,800 in the rollover protection system that pops up from behind the rear seat. The optional Sport suspension does enhance handling and steering, but it also produces an overly harsh, jiggly ride on rough pavement. Wider tires compromise traction in snow. Stay away from the Turanza run-flats and Bridgestone tires:

> Bridgestone tire exhibits unsafe characteristics in wet weather, with noticeable drift and hydroplaning in any amount of standing water, even as little as 1/16 inch [1.5 mm]. In heavy rains, even with no standing water present, the tire seems incapable of dispersing water as quickly as it falls, again leading to vehicle instability. From a ride quality point of view the tire is also unsatisfactory in that it flat spots every morning, especially in cool

weather, but even in warmer weather as well, leading to vibrations in the initial miles of any drive. It is also especially harsh over roadway expansion joints, and is so loud on concrete pavement that it poses a safety hazard due to driver fatigue induced by the continuous noise. I also understand that there may be an issue regarding the rating as an "all season tire" with many owners reporting that this tire is virtually useless in any kind of snow conditions.

Rebates: Not likely. Instead, dealers will push generous leases and low-interest financing. **Depreciation:** The entry-level models keep their value reasonably well, but as you get into the pricier BMWs, the depreciation is mind-spinning. For example, a 2008 BMW 323i that once sold for $35,900 is still worth about $16,500, but a 2008 750i that sold for $108,500 is now worth only $32,500. Ouch! **Insurance cost:** Higher than average. **Parts supply/cost:** Parts are less expensive than those for other cars in this class. Unfortunately, they aren't easily found outside of the dealer network, where they're often back ordered. That said, parts and repairs are far easier to find than with Audi, Jaguar, Mini, Porsche, and Saab. **Annual maintenance cost:** Average—until the warranty runs out. Then your mechanic starts sharing your paycheque. **Warranty:** Bumper-to-bumper 4 years/80,000 km; rust perforation 6 years/unlimited km. **Supplementary warranty:** Not needed. **Highway/city fuel economy (2011 models):** 323i: 6.9/11.1 L/100 km, 41/25 mpg. *Auto.:* 6.7/11.2 L/100 km, 42/25 mph. *328i:* 7.0/10.9 L/100 km, 40/26 mpg. *Auto.:* 6.9/11.3 L/100 km, 41/25 mpg. *328i xDrive:* 7.6/12.2 L/100 km, 37/23 mpg. *Auto.:* 7.8/11.9 L/100 km, 36/24 mpg. *335i:* 7.9/11.9 L/100 km, 36/24 mpg. *Auto.:* 7.6/11.9 L/100 km, 37/24 mpg. *335i xDrive:* 7.9/12.2 L/100 km, 36/23 mpg. *Auto.:* 7.9/12.2 L/100 km, 36/23 mpg. *335d:* 5.4/9.0 L/100 km, 52/31 mpg. *M3:* 9.7/15.3 L/100 km, 29/18 mpg. *M3 Cabrio:* 10.1/15.7 L/100 km, 28/18 mpg.

OWNER-REPORTED PROBLEMS: Fire originated in the fog light socket; engines, brakes, electrical system (telematics), and some body trim and accessories are the most failure-prone components; engine overheating is a serious problem; noisy run-flat tires; and premature tire wear—and owners are forced to pay for tire failures. *325i:* Excessive hesitation on acceleration:

> When the driver demands a sudden increase in acceleration, the car hesitates anywhere from 1.5 to 3 seconds. This is a dangerous condition when someone is making a left turn in traffic, or getting onto a highway, or passing on a 2 lane country road, etc. Other cars traveling at 60 mph [96.5 km/h] are moving at 88 ft./sec. [27 m/s]. The amount of leeway this car needs is much too excessive.

Bridgestone tire-tread separation and side wall buckling:

> Bridgestone Potenza RE050A run-flat tires. The tires buckled on the side wall after less than 8,000 miles [12,870 km]. Out of curiosity I checked the Bimmerfest (*www. bimmerfest.com/forums/showthread.php?t=146728*) forum and discovered this is a widespread problem among BMW owners.

328: Very few 2010 and 2011 model safety-related incidences recorded by NHTSA (12). Some of the failures reported during the past few years: Airbags fail to deploy; underhood fire ignited while car was parked; premature tire failure (bubbles in the tread); sudden acceleration; engine slow surge while idling at a stoplight; when accelerating, engine cuts out and then surges forward (suspected failure of the throttle assembly); severe engine vibrations after a cold start as Check Engine light comes on; poor rain handling; First gear and Reverse are positioned too close together, as are the brake and gas pedals; sunroof spontaneously shattered; a rear-quarter blind spot with the convertibles; seat rails that project a bit into the foot area could catch the driver's feet; and the front passenger head restraint won't go down far enough to protect short passengers. 330i: Side airbag deployed when vehicle hit a pothole; vehicle overheats in low gears; and vehicle slips out of Second gear when accelerating. 335i: Delay in throttle engagement when slowing to a roll and then accelerating; frequent false brake safety alerts; sunroof suddenly exploded; tires lose air due to defective tire rims; faulty fuel injectors; and engine stalling and loss of power, which was fixed by replacing the fuel pump—now exhaust is booming, fuel economy has dropped, and there's considerable "turbo lag" when accelerating. Many other cases of loss of power on the highway, or the high-pressure fuel pump failing, with some owners having to replace the pump four times. 335d: After a short downpour, engine started sputtering. Dealer and BMW said there was water in the fuel and held the car owner responsible for the full cost of the repairs. M3: Tail light socket overheats, blowing the bulb and shorting other lights—costs $600 to rewire; vehicle loses power due to faulty fuel pumps; transmission hesitates when accelerating in Second gear (see *www.roadfly.com*).

SERVICE BULLETIN-REPORTED PROBLEMS: Reduced engine power; buttons on iDrive controller don't work; inoperative keyless system; erratic operation of the wiper rain-light feature; brake pedal squeaks; troubleshooting tips to correct electrical failures that are often caused by a shorted fuel-sender harness; intermittently inoperative cell phone; odometer reading can't be recovered; various audio system complaints; radio continues to play after ignition is turned off; "door open" displayed when door is properly closed; key doesn't stay in ignition; BMW Assist doesn't work properly; AC howling or rough-running noise; deteriorated headlight wiring; headlight nozzle doesn't fully retract; interior door handle paint peeling; steering wheel leather peels from the rear; and engine whistling, hooting, or squealing:

ENGINE WHISTLING, HOOTING, OR SQUEALING NOISE	
BULLETIN NO.: SI B11 03 11	DATE: SEPTEMBER 2011

1 Series; 3 Series; 5 Series; 6 Series; X3; X5; X6; and Gran Turismo.
SITUATION: The customer states that a noise described as whistling, hooting or squealing can be heard from the engine compartment while the engine is running. The noise may be more apparent after the engine has reached operating temperature.
CAUSE: The noise is due to a manufacturing error in the rear crankshaft oil seal.

The BMW X3.

RATING: *X3 and X6:* Average. *X5:* Below Average. Overpriced vehicles that depreciate quickly. *X3:* A small crossover that has swelled to the size of the previous-generation X5. There is plenty of room for front passengers, while rear legroom is generous and well-paired with comfortable seating, making this one of the most family-friendly SUVs in its class. *X5:* BMW's first crossover SUV has been on the market since 1999. It's a mid-sized seven-seater that is quick to depreciate and has a poor reliability record that is worse than what owners have reported on the X1, X3, and X6. *X6:* An X5 spin-off that gives you many of the X5 advantages and fewer of the disadvantages, but in a larger box. **Road performance:** *X3:* A potent 6-cylinder engine; an efficient 4-cylinder engine; crisp handling; precise, predictable steering. Last year's changes provide a more-forgiving suspension; a softer, less choppy ride; and more power-steering assistance. Unfortunately, the car's old nemesis—accelerator lag—is still present. Kickdown response suffers from a similar delay. Some help, though, is offered by leaving the transmission setting in Sport mode, which keeps the transmission in lower gear longer. Jerky stops, caused by the transmission's inherent imprecise shifting, compounded by the standard Brake Energy Regeneration system. *X5:* Engines deliver plenty of power, and there's a turbocharged diesel option; smooth, responsive power delivery; secure handling; and good steering feedback. *X6:* Billed as BMW's "sports activity" coupe because it's loaded with high-performance features. It carries a turbocharged 3.0L 6-cylinder engine or a powerful optional 4.4L V8 and is a bit taller than most coupes. Capable handling—the AWD system can vary the torque from side to side to minimize under-steer. Delayed throttle response continues to be a problem, and the 8-speed automatic transmission makes

KEY FACTS

X3

Canadian Price (Soft): *28i:* $42,450, *35i:* $47,400 **U.S. Price:** *28i xDrive:* $36,750, *35i:* $41,050 **Canadian Freight:** $1,995 **U.S. Freight:** $875

POWERTRAIN (REAR-DRIVE/AWD)

Engines: 2.0L 4-cyl. (240 hp) • 3.0L 6-cyl. (240 hp) • 3.0L Turbo. 6-cyl. (300 hp) Transmission: 8-speed auto.

DIMENSIONS/CAPACITY

Passengers: 2/3; Wheelbase: 110.6 in.; H: 67/L: 182.8/W: 74 in.; Headroom F/R: 4.0/3.0 in.; Legroom F/R: 41.5/27.5 in.; Cargo volume: 63.3 cu. ft.; Fuel tank: 67L/premium; Tow limit: 3.500 lb.; Load capacity: 905lb.; Turning circle: 38.4 ft.; Ground clearance: 8.5 in.; Weight: 4,067 lb.

X5

Canadian Price (negotiable): *35d xDrive:* $61,800, *50i xDrive:* $75,700 **U.S. Price:** *35i xDrive:* $47,200, *35i xDrive Premium:* $54,800, *35i xDrive Sport Activity:* $57,300, *35d xDrive:* $51,800, *50i xDrive:* $63,800 **Canadian Freight:** $1,995 **U.S. Freight:** $875

POWERTRAIN (REAR-DRIVE/AWD)

Engines (Turbo): 2.0L 4-cyl. (240 hp) • 3.0L 6-cyl. (300 hp) • 4.4L V8 (400 hp); Transmission: 8-speed auto.

DIMENSIONS/CAPACITY

Passengers: 2/3/2; Wheelbase: 116 in.; H: 70/L: 191/W: 76.1 in.; Headroom F/R: 3.5/3.0 in.; Legroom F/R: 40.5/26.5 in.; Cargo volume: 36 cu. ft.; Fuel tank: 93L/premium; Tow limit: 6,500 lb.; Load capacity: 1,290 lb.; Turning circle: 42 ft.; Ground clearance: 8.3 in.; Weight: 5,265 lb.

X6

Canadian Price (negotiable): *35i xDrive:* $66,800, *50i xDrive:* $82,200, **U.S. Price:** *35i xDrive:* $43,600, *50i xDrive:* $69,500 **Canadian Freight:** $1,995 **U.S. Freight:** $895

POWERTRAIN (REAR-DRIVE/AWD)

Engines (Turbo): 3.0L 6-cyl. (240 hp) • 4.4L 8-cyl. (400 hp) • 4.4L 8-cyl. (555 hp) • 4.4L 8-cyl. Hybrid (480 hp); Transmissions: 6-speed auto. • 7-speed auto. • 8-speed auto.

DIMENSIONS/CAPACITY

Passengers: 2/2; Wheelbase: 116 in.; H: 67/L: 192/W: 78 in.; Headroom F/R: 3.5/2.5 in.; Legroom F/R: 40/27.5 in.; Cargo volume: N/A; Fuel tank: 85L/premium; Tow limit: No towing; Load capacity: 935 lb.; Turning circle: 42 ft.; Ground clearance: 8.5 in.; Weight: 4,895–5,687 lb.

gearshifts less than luxurious. **Strong points:** *X3:* Abundant cargo space; good cabin access; and a quiet, nicely appointed interior, with a better integrated centre screen. The second-row seats have good leg and elbow room, and rear seating is relatively comfortable. *X5:* Comfortable first- and second-row seating; and a high-quality cabin. Suspension improvements have smoothed out the ride. *X6:* Comfortable front seats and solid construction. **Weak points:** *X3:* This little SUV with its somewhat narrow interior is way overpriced; options are a minefield of inflated charges; and mind-spinning depreciation makes Wall Street look tame. Reliability is compromised by powertrain deficiencies, serious fit and finish problems, audio system malfunctions, power equipment failures, and electrical system glitches. Although backseat legroom is adequate, the seat cushions are too low, forcing your knees to your chin. *X5:* A smallish cargo area; bundled options can be pricey; and there have been long-standing quality control issues with the fuel system, brakes, powertrain, electrical components, climate control, body integrity, and fit and finish. The complicated shifter and iDrive controls can also be hard to master without a lot of patience and frustration; and the third-row seats are a bit cramped. *X6:* Insufficient back seat headroom with no adjustments; a small cargo area; hefty price; heftier weight; fit and finish glitches; and seats only four. **Safety:** The X3 and X6 haven't yet been crash tested, but NHTSA gave the 2010 X5 five stars for front and side crash protection and four stars for rollover resistance. X6: Poor rearward visibility. **New for 2013:** X3: The naturally aspirated inline-six base engine has been dropped in favor of a high-tech, turbocharged 6-cylinder with equal power and more torque, with the bonus of significantly improved fuel economy. Two other new fuel-saving features are the stop/start feature, which kills the engine when the vehicle comes to a stop, and an Eco Pro setting that optimizes the engine, transmission, heating, AC, and electrical functions for optimum fuel efficiency. X5: New M Performance Package adds 15 hp to the 6-cylinder, 40 hp to V8. X6: Comfortable front seats; solid construction.

ALERT! The smaller X3's high buy-in puts it at a disadvantage against larger, mid-size luxury crossover SUVs like the Acura MDX and Lexus RX 350. But the X3 has a generous amount of passenger and cargo room, which outshines "compact" competitors like the Audi Q5 and Mercedes-Benz GLK350.

OVERVIEW: Here is where BMW took on the Asian automakers and came out second best. Despite BMW's recent sophisticated (and complicated) engineering, mechanical upgrades, styling changes, and increased exterior and interior dimensions, the X3, X5, and X6 SUVs are not very impressive from either a performance or a comfort/convenience perspective. Despite tax credits and superior gas mileage figures, BMW is reportedly having a tough time selling its new diesel-equipped X5 35d xDrive. Last year's X6 35i xDrive and 50i xDrive gasoline engines are rated at 15/21 mpg (15.7/11.2 L/100 km) and 13/18 mpg (18.1/13.1 L/100/km), respectively. As for replacing the 6-speed transmissions with 8-speeds, BMW says fuel economy is increased by 7 percent and 0–60 mph times are shaved by one- to two-tenths of 1 percent. Big deal, eh?

COST ANALYSIS: X3: Buy the more fuel-efficient 2013 if that's your main concern, but wait until the second-series model's arrival in March to make sure the electronics are less glitch-prone. Or, pick up a less-expensive 2012 V6-equipped X3, sans the latest changes. The money saved could buy a lot of fuel. X5: If the reports of poor quality don't faze you, get an almost identical, cheaper 2012 version. X6: The X6? A big, brash, and beautiful barge—for potentates and poseurs. **Best alternatives:** Acura RDX and Honda's recently redesigned CR-V. Other worthy contenders: the GM Acadia, Enclave, Escalade, Terrain, or Traverse, and the Lexus RX Series. **Rebates:** $4,000–$7,000 discounts along with low-rate financing and generous leasing terms. Remember, slow sales with the X Series models has created a buyer's market; patience is your ally. **Depreciation:** Faster than a speeding bullet. A 2010 X3 that once sold for $39,000 is now worth only $25,000. Hold on, it gets worse: a 2007 X5 sold for $61,900 new, yet its used value is now barely $22,000—a loss of almost $40,000 in five years. Incidentally, the 2008 X6 (its debut year), sold new for $64,000, may eventually take the crown for "treasure turning to trash." Its value five years later: $26,000. **Insurance cost:** Higher than average. **Parts supply/cost:** Moderately expensive, often on dealer back order, and they aren't easily found outside the dealer network. **Annual maintenance cost:** Average until the warranty runs out, and then your mechanic gets to know you real well. **Warranty:** Bumper-to-bumper 4 years/80,000 km; rust perforation 6 years/unlimited km. **Supplementary warranty:** A wise decision. **Highway/city fuel economy:** *X3 28i:* 8.3/12.2 L/100 km, 34/23 mpg. *X3 30i:* 8.2/12.5 L/100 km, 34/23 mpg. *X5 30i:* 9.3/13.6 L/100 km, 30/21 mpg. *Diesel:* 7.5/10.7 L/100 km, 38/26 mpg. *X5 48i:* 10.2/15.6 L/100 km, 28/18 mpg. *X5 M:* 11.9/17.2 L/100 km, 24/16 mpg. *X6 35i:* 10.0/14.4 L/100 km, 28/20 mpg. *X6 50i:* 11.0/17.1 L/100 km, 26/17 mpg. *X6 M:* 11.9/17.2 L/100 km, 24/16 mpg. *X6 Hybrid:* 10.3/12.6 L/100 km, 27/22 mpg.

OWNER-REPORTED PROBLEMS: Parts are scarce outside of major metropolitan areas, and independent mechanics who can service these vehicles are rare. Servicing deficiencies are accentuated by a weak dealer network and unreliable suppliers. *X3:* Only 22 safety complaints sent to NHTSA during the past two years: Steering wheel seized while car was parked; acceleration lag, and when the car does get up to speed, it veers to the right:

> Car veering to the right, increased on sudden stops; happens at various speeds. The prominent and dangerous condition is lag in acceleration. Sent the following e-mail to dealer & BMW along with 3 service reports from dealer attempts to address: "This X3 3.5i with all [its] electronic engine/drive train controls is a nightmare. It's a huge design flaw that is going to kill someone eventually. Yet again, yesterday, I felt unsafe due to the hesitation. The car didn't move for about a second or two when I tried to make a left turn in an intersection and then again when I was on the highway changing lanes. There were cars heading towards me but the initial distance was quite comfortable and safe. With the hesitation of the X3, I was actually in a panic and stepped really hard on the gas pedal to avoid a potential collision. And since then I have been stepping on the gas pedal much harder, guzzling gas, not to mention rough starts off of a full stop. I have seen countless Internet threads of people complaining about the same thing with the X3 model, both versions, however equipped. I would strongly suggest someone look at how this car's software is failing to function and fix this thing. I will report the problem to the appropriate governmental agencies. The veering is still there and eventually I will come to pass the issue with the low tread life run-flats.

Rear main crankcase seal failure; car will roll backwards even if in Park; total shutdown of the electrical system:

> The windshield wipers don't work, the headlights operate sporadically, the power door locks and power windows do not operate, the A/C doesn't work, the horn honks periodically, the tailgate won't open to facilitate replacement of fuses. The fuel gauge is inoperative and the cruise control doesn't work. Windshield wipers are a crucial safety item in the Pacific NW as are headlights.

Run-flat tires are noted for their short tread life; chronic stalling; vehicle rolls away in Park; steering failures on vehicles not included in prior steering recall;

and car veers to the right with sudden stops. General complaints target the fit and finish, power equipment, audio system, fuel system, and transmission as most in need of special attention. X5: Engine surges and stalls:

> The vehicle sporadically suffers from engine failure when executing a sharp turn. This has happened so far on three separate and distinct instances during its first 1,000 miles [1,609 km] of service, under the operation of two different drivers, with several passenger witnesses on one occasion. When these failures happen, the vehicle engine stalls or otherwise shuts itself off, which leads to loss of power steering in mid-turn and loss of braking. The only way to recover control of the vehicle is to let it coast to a stop, then put the vehicle in Park, then push the ignition button to re-start the car.

•

> I leased my 2012 BMW X5 35I in May 2011. I was driving on the interstate with 2 toddlers at around 65 mph [105 km/h], when the car suddenly lost power and the message displayed "Engine Malfunction, Reduced Power". I pulled over on the shoulder, and tried to re-start the car, but it won't start. When it did start after multiple attempts, the car shook vigorously and then turned off. I initiated the SOS call via the BMW Assist feature in the car. For some reason, the call failed multiple times, and the data could not be transferred. When the call did go through, the car could not send my exact coordinates to the reps to help me get a tow truck. After trying for about 30 min to get help from the BMW Assist, I tried to restart the car, which started normally as if nothing ever happened. The in-built diagnosis said "All Systems OK". I got on the interstate, and as I reached around 60 mph [97 km/h], the engine stalled again with the same message.... For the next 1.5 hours, I tried to call the BMW Assist over my phone to get help. They said the tow truck should come in the next hour. For about 2 hours, the 2 toddlers and 3 adults were sitting by the interstate. When the tow truck did not show up, I called the BMW Assist reps again, to be told that the truck shall take another 45 minutes to reach us. I then called my friend to take everybody home, and I stayed with the car. I then tried to drive at about 40 mph [64 km/h] and take the car to the dealer, only to be pulled over by the highway patrol. He said I was violating the law by driving at 40 mph in a 70 mph zone. I then called my insurance company to get a tow truck, which arrived in 30 min. The next day my wife took the car to the dealer, and the report sheet they provided said that the high pressure pump was faulty.

Owners also complain that the transmission shifts abruptly; the car is very hard-riding; there is no air from the AC; the exhaust system rusts; the leather indents easily and stays indented; and the rear tailgate doesn't always open with key fob. Other problem areas concern the powertrain, electrical system, climate controls, inadequate braking, audio system, body integrity, and fit and finish. The four overhead reading lights don't have protective covers and can seriously burn a child's hand or finger. X6: No significant complaints reported.

OIL LEAK FROM TRANSFER CASE

BULLETIN NO.: SI B27 01 12

DATE: APRIL 2012

MODEL: X3, X5, and X6.

SITUATION: Oil is leaking from the transmission area, or oil seepage is noticed from the transmission/transfer case area during a service.

CAUSE: The leak can be misdiagnosed as a transmission fluid leak from either the mechatronics sleeve or transmission oil pan. The leak is actually coming from the transfer case (input or output shaft seal).

PROCEDURE: Before attempting to perform any repairs, check the fluid level in both the transmission and transfer case. If the level is low in the transfer case, repair as necessary.

Delay in engine response may require recalibration of the software; engine whistling, hooting, or squealing; intermittent engine rattle upon cold start; noise from the transmission bell housing area; faulty various electrical/computer malfunctions; inoperative front window; free replacement of the right front window regulator under Service Action #214, published in March 2012; whistle noise from rearview mirror; humming noise from front of car; AC blows warm air; wipers/washers self-activate, can't be shut off; revised sun visor repair instructions; Check Gas Cap alert; excessive door mirror vibration; inoperative cell phone; and leather peeling from the steering wheel.

Mercedes-Benz

Daimler AG, Mercedes' governing company, made a healthy profit in 2011—mostly generated by strong sales of the lucrative E-Class and S-Class models, a drop in costly sales incentives, and a surprisingly sharp rebound in demand from Chinese and U.S. car buyers. But all that may be coming to an end.

The money is drying up. North America, Europe, and Asia are in the midst of a recession where only the strongest brands (mostly German automakers) survive. Shoppers want luxury, but they also want powerful, fuel-efficient, comfortable vehicles with a high-performance edge. Automobile alchemists capable of creating fast, fancy, and frugal cars will be the winners of 2013

Mercedes is doing just this. The company has pulled off an amazing sales turnaround by successfully marketing smaller and less-expensive cars, after stumbling badly with econocars nobody wanted, like the failure-prone 190E, bare-bones C-Class, toy-like Smart Car, and overpriced B-Class. Mercedes also managed to sell larger and more expensive models in Europe and Asia, until the recession cut into those sales this year. No surprise, we'll soon see more compacts, light hybrids, electrics, crossovers, and a return to turbocharged 4- and 6-cylinder engines that haven't been offered in years. Daimler's 2013 A/B platform is ready-made to accommodate gasoline-, diesel-, and hybrid-powered cars.

Mercedes' Small-Car Flops

Mercedes hasn't been very good at making reliable or well-performing small cars over the past few decades. Its first efforts were disappointing, and the jury is still out on the 2013 compact B-Class entrants.

190E
(1982–93)

Smart Car
(2004–13)

C-Class
(1982–2013)

B-Class
(2005–13)

Mercedes' first effort, called the "Baby Benz" was the Mercedes 190. The A-Class rolled over in a 1997 test run called the "moose test," a performance exercise used for decades in Sweden that calls for the driver to suddenly change lanes while going 70–80 km/h (45–50 mph), as though trying to avoid hitting a moose. What shocked most of the West German Daimler dignitaries was that the Trabant—a much older, widely mocked car from Eastern Germany—passed the test with flying colours.

New Products

Except for its small-car B-Class revamp this year, Mercedes is saving most of its new products for 2014. Some 2013 models are getting more-powerful V6 engines hooked to a fuel-efficient 7-speed gearbox. The popular fuel-saving ECO stop/start feature is also extended over the entire lineup.

Quality Concerns

Although Mercedes quality is improving, some models continue to do much worse than others. For example, the C-Class, E-Class, and GLK-Class have few quality shortcomings, except for fit and finish, but other models like the CLK, GL-Class, and M-Class SUV can make your life miserable. Most ironic of all, in the Mercedes lineup the most expensive models like the S-Class are also the most troublesome. Selling for $91,850 to $210,900 (U.S.), the S-Class has the worst Mercedes reliability rating as measured by *Consumer Reports*' annual million-plus member survey.

Way before *Consumer Reports* got involved, everyone (except for some clueless buyers) knew that Mercedes' 1998 M-Class sport-utilities were abysmally bad. You couldn't have made a worse vehicle, judging by the unending stream of desperate-sounding service bulletins sent from head office to dealers after the vehicles' official launch. Two bulletins stand out in my mind. One was an authorization for dry-cleaning payouts to dealers whose customers' clothing had been stained by the dye from the burgundy-coloured leather seats. The other was a lengthy scientific explanation (which the Germans compose so well) as to why drivers were "tasered" by static electricity when entering or exiting their vehicles.

Car columnists have always known that Mercedes has made some bad cars and SUVs, but it took business reporters (not auto beat writers) from the gutsy *Wall Street Journal* to spill the beans. In a February 2, 2002, article titled "An Engineering Icon Slips," the *WSJ* cited several confidential industry-initiated surveys that showed that Mercedes' quality and customer satisfaction had fallen dramatically since 1999—to a level below that of GM's Opel, a brand that had one of the worst reputations for poor quality in Europe.

Industry insiders give different reasons for why Mercedes-Benz quality isn't world class. They say quality control has been diluted by M-B doubling its product lineup since 1997. Helpful, too, were the company's aggressive PR campaigns and the company mindset that blamed the driver rather than the product—both spectacularly successful in keeping the quality myth alive in the media until the *Wall Street Journal* broke its story. Neither mindset nor PR worked to mitigate owners' displeasure over M-B's engine sludge stonewalling, though. It cost Mercedes $32 million (U.S.) to settle with owners of 1998–2001 models after the company denied that there was a factory-related problem.

Although Mercedes sales are on the upswing, its vehicles' residual values have fallen dramatically. At the top end, a 2007 65 AMG that cost $248,000 new is now worth barely $67,000. Even the entry-level B-Class models feel the depreciation bite: A 2008 B-Class 200 that originally sold for $30,000 is now worth only $13,500, and a 2009 E-Class E320 BlueTEC sedan, once priced at $68,100, can now be bought for $27,000.

B-CLASS ★★

RATING: Below Average. Not up to the level of the all-new Audi A3 and the recently introduced BMW X1. This is the first year of the car's redesign, and most reworked Mercedes models do poorly integrating electronics and hardware during the first few years after a redesign. Further complicating the reliability and servicing is the B250's absence from the United States market. This means servicing waits can be long in the States (a problem also facing Mercedes Smart owners), forcing prudent owners to plan Canada-only driving vacations. Audi, BMW, and VW competitors have nationwide servicing networks throughout the States. **Road performance:** Considering its small size, the "B" has an unusually large turning circle, which cuts its urban usefulness. The new 7-speed dual-clutch transmission, which replaces the previous year's inadequate CVT gearworks, delivers power smoothly

and quietly. **Strong points:** More powerful, with greater fuel efficiency this year, thanks to turbocharging and the advent of an ECO stop/start feature that saves on gas in stop-and-go traffic. Occupant ingress and egress is much improved, and rear-seat passengers can sit in relative comfort. Roomy, with lots of storage space, and feature-laden, with four-wheel disc brakes, stability control, seven standard airbags, upgraded suspension and steering, and a classier, more user-friendly interior. Impressive fuel economy. **Weak points:** The retail price could be trimmed by at least $5,000, making the car more competitive. Furthermore, shoppers would be wise to consider the equivalent Mazda or other Japanese or European compacts that can cost less and be serviced everywhere. **Safety:** Crashworthiness hasn't yet been tested. The turn signal and cruise control stalks have been repositioned to prevent misapplication. Other safety enhancements: collision avoidance, drowsy driver alert, Adaptive Brake Assist, Lane Keeping Assist, Attention Assist, Collision Prevention Assist, and Blind Spot Assist. **New for 2013:** A new engine and transmission; a revised platform that can house an upcoming diesel or hybrid powerplant; and more-muscular styling. This year's B250 is wider and longer, and has a stretched wheelbase, but it's actually shorter height-wise.

ALERT! The paddle shifters take getting used to and may discourage spirited driving. Check out the left side-view mirror's blind spot.

OVERVIEW: First launched as a 2006 model, the B-Class is Mercedes' second-smallest car, following the Smart. It is sold mainly in Canada and Europe. Power is provided by a 4-cylinder gasoline engine (why not the European diesel, as well?) hooked to a 7-speed gearbox. There's also a fuel-saving automatic stop/start

KEY FACTS

Canadian Price (Negotiable): *B250:* $29,900 **Canadian Freight:** Price includes $1,995 freight fee

POWERTRAIN (FRONT-DRIVE)
Engine: 2.0L Turbo 4-cyl. (208 hp); Transmission: 7-speed auto.

DIMENSIONS/CAPACITY
Passengers: 2/3; Wheelbase: 106 in.; H: 61.7/L: 172/W: 79 in.; Headroom: N/A; Legroom F/R: 43.0/38.4 in.; Cargo volume: 23.5 cu. ft.; Fuel tank: 50L/premium; Tow limit: 3,307 lb.; Turning circle: 39.2 ft.; Ground clearance: N/A; Weight: 3,252 lb.

feature. The front seats are set lower and sit more upright than before, while the lengthened wheelbase provides more rear-seat legroom and luggage space.

COST ANALYSIS: The B-Class complements the C-Class lineup in the same way that the A3 and A4 models draw less demanding Audi shoppers and the 1 Series and 3 Series bring BMW cars within reach of buyers with fewer dollars to spare. Without the Mercedes cachet, this is an ordinary, middle-of-the-pack, overpriced subcompact. M-B is selling the 2013 entry-level B-Class for the same price that it sold the 2011, so there is no price advantage to buying a leftover 2012. **Best alternatives:** Take a look at the BMW 1 Series, Kia Rondo, Mazda5, and Toyota Matrix. **Options:** Nothing much worth buying; the car comes well-quipped. **Depreciation:** Faster than average; a $30,000 2008 B-Class 200 is now barely worth $13,500. **Insurance cost:** Average. **Parts supply/cost:** Remember, these are Canada-only cars, so parts may not be easily found. Parts are moderately expensive. **Annual maintenance cost:** Average. **Warranty:** Bumper-to-bumper 4 years/80,000 km; powertrain 5 years/120,000 km; rust perforation 5 years/120,000 km. **Supplementary warranty:** A good idea for the new powertrain. **Highway/city fuel economy:** 4.9/8.8 L/100 km, 48/27 mpg.

OWNER-REPORTED PROBLEMS: Mostly fit and finish problems, electrical system shorts, and premature brake wear gripes.

C-CLASS ★★★

RATING: Average. These little entry-level cars lack the simplicity and popular pricing found with the Japanese luxury competition; save up for an E-Class or a Hyundai Genesis. **Road performance:** A big improvement in power and handling with this year's adoption of V6 power. The ride is generally comfortable, though sometimes choppy, and braking is first-class. The light steering requires constant correction, and there's some tire thumping and engine and wind noise in the cabin. **Strong points:** Additional V6 power, and smoother shifting with the 7-speed automatic transmission. Plenty of high-tech performance and safety features; a good V6 powertrain matchup; available AWD; and an innovative anti-theft system. **Weak points:** Higher prices than are reasonable when compared with competitors; complicated controls; limited rear-seat and cargo room; and tight entry and exit. Also, the cars are noted for their weak resale value and for being very dealer-dependent for parts and servicing—a problem likely to worsen with this year's new powertrains. **Safety:** NHTSA awarded the 2011 C-Class four-door five stars for side-impact occupant protection, four stars for rollover protection, and three stars for frontal crashworthiness. IIHS crash tests gave top marks ("Good") for frontal offset, side, roof, and head-restraint crash protection. However, the cars were rated "Poor" in front-corner crashes. Standard safety features include stability and traction control systems, four-wheel ABS disc brakes with brake assist, active anti-whiplash front head restraints, nine airbags, and driver drowsiness detection. Optional safety features: Adaptive Highbeam Assist, Park Assist, Lane Keeping Assist, and Blind Spot Assist. **New for 2013:** C300 and C350 models now have 3.5L engines with ECO start/stop technology.

KEY FACTS

Canadian Price (Negotiable): *C250:* $37,300, *C300 4Matic:* $39,990, *C350 Sedan:* $44,750, *350 4Matic:* $47,700, *C63 AMG:* $65,300 **U.S. Price:** *C250 Sport:* $35,350, *C250 Luxury:* $35,770, *C300 4Matic Sport:* $38,950, *4Matic Luxury:* $39,360, *C350 Sport Sedan:* $41,400, *C63 AMG:* $59,800 **Canadian Freight:** Price includes $1,995 freight fee **U.S. Freight:** Price includes $875 freight charge

POWERTRAIN (REAR-DRIVE/AWD)

Engines: 1.8L 4-cyl. (201 hp) • 3.5L V6 (248 hp) • 3.5L V6 (302 hp) • 6.3L V8 (451 hp); Transmission: 7-speed auto.

DIMENSIONS/CAPACITY

Passengers: 2/3; Wheelbase: 108.7 in.; H: 56.9/L: 182/W: 70.0 in.; Headroom F/R: 2.5/1.5 in.; Legroom F/R: 42/26 in.; Cargo volume: 12.4 cu. ft.; Fuel tank: 62L/premium; Tow limit: Not recommended; Load capacity: 835 lb.; Turning circle: 35.3 ft.; Ground clearance: 4.2 in.; Weight: 3,565 lb.

ALERT! Average reliability, and unlike the B-Class B250, entry-level C-Class cars can be repaired anywhere.

OVERVIEW: The C-Class comprises three rear-drive sedan and coupe configurations—C250, C350, and C63 AMG—as well as a C300 4Matic AWD sedan or C350 4Matic AWD coupe. C250 and C300 sedans are sold in either Sport or Luxury trim levels. Here's how they vary: The C250 is powered by a 201 hp 1.8L turbocharged 4-cylinder engine (7 horses less than the small B250), while the C300 is equipped with a 248 hp 3.5L V6, and the C350 uses a 302 hp 3.5L V6. The high-performance C63 AMG comes with a hand-built 451 hp 6.3L V8 engine. A more fuel-efficient and smoother 7-speed automatic transmission with manual shift mode is standard, and steering-wheel-mounted paddle shifters are available. The C250 and C300 are well-appointed with a power sunroof, 17-inch aluminum wheels, MB-Tex upholstery, dual-zone climate control, HD radio and a USB port, plus Bluetooth communications. The C350 piles on more features of dubious utility, like a rear spoiler, heated front seats, and satellite radio. C63 AMG models add 18-inch aluminum wheels, AMG seats, and leather/simulated suede upholstery. Four-passenger coupe models provide high-end sport seats and a Panorama sunroof.

COST ANALYSIS: Take a pass on this year's models until mid-2013, when prices will surely tumble and the new engines will be tweaked to perform better. **Best alternatives:** Take a look at the BMW 3 Series, or a Hyundai Genesis Coupe. **Options:** The Bose sound system is a good investment. **Rebates:** $5,000 rebates, generous leasing deals, and low-interest financing. **Depreciation:** Faster than average: a $41,000 2008 C300 Sedan is now barely worth $17,500. **Insurance cost:** Higher than average. **Parts supply/cost:** Limited availability, and parts are expensive. **Annual maintenance cost:** Average. **Warranty:** Bumper-to-bumper 4 years/80,000 km; powertrain 5 years/120,000 km; rust perforation 5 years/120,000 km. **Supplementary warranty:** Extra powertrain coverage would be a good idea. **Highway/city fuel economy (2012):** *C250, 1.8L:* 6.3/9.6 L/100 km, 45/29 mpg. *2.5L:* 8.3/12.4 L/100 km, 34/23 mpg. *Coupe:* 6.4/9.7 L/100 km, 44/29 mpg. *C300:* 7.9/11.8 L/100 km, 36/24 mpg. *4Matic:* 10.8/16.3 L/100 km, 26/17 mpg. *C350:* 7.0/10.8 L/100 km, 40/26 mpg. *4Matic:* 7.0/10.7 L/100 km, 40/26 mpg. *4Matic Coupe:* 7.1/10.8 L/100 km, 40/26 mpg. *63 AMG:* 10.4/16 L/100 km, 27/18 mpg. *Coupe:* 10.4/16.1 L/100 km, 27/18 mpg. *CL550:* 8.8/13.8 L/100 km, 32/20 mpg. *CL600:* 11.2/18.1 L/100 km, 25/16 mpg. *CL 63 AMG:* 9.3/13.8 L/100 km, 30/20 mpg. *CL 65 AMG:* 10.9/17.4 L/100 km, 26/16 mpg. *CLS 550 4Matic:* 8.2/12.7 L/100 km, 34/22 mpg. *CLS 63 AMG:* 8.6/13.6 L/100 km, 33/21 mpg.

OWNER-REPORTED PROBLEMS: *C250:* Turn-signal control light is barely visible in daylight, and steering-column-mounted levers (cruise control, for instance) are hard to see behind the steering wheel. *C300:* Owners complain of severe noise invading the cabin when the window is rolled down while driving (which seems unusual for a luxury German-made car):

> The contact owns a 2012 Mercedes Benz C300. The contact stated that while driving 35 mph [56 km/h], the rear passenger side window exhibited a loud, abnormal noise when opened. As a result, the contact experienced a temporary loss of hearing from the high pitch of the noise. The vehicle was taken to the dealer who stated that the loud noise was common for the vehicle.

Lemon-Aid readers and *Consumer Reports* subscribers have also reported problems with the climate control systems, body hardware and paint, and fit and finish.

SERVICE BULLETIN-REPORTED PROBLEMS: *C250:* Oil leakage at the seam between the automatic transmission and the transfer case housing; suspension noise from front axle suspension struts on vehicles equipped with a 1.8L engine; and automatic transmission hard 2–3 upshift or slipping, no Third gear. *C300, C350, C63 AMG, and CL550:* Vehicle doesn't perform automatic engine stop; repair tips for engine cylinder head cover leaks; consumer electrical shutoff intermittently active; automatic transmission switches to "limp home" mode; automatic transmission hard 2–3 upshifts, slipping, or no Third gear; oil leakage at the seam

COMPLAINT: Hard shift operation 2–3 upshift or transmission slips (3rd gear may not be reached).
CAUSE: K1 piston damaged (adaptation data of shift operation 2–3 on positive/negative end stop, +20/–20 and/or +2000/–2000). **REMEDY:** If the complaint can only be reproduced for the upshift from gear 2 to gear 3 or if the 3rd gear cannot be reached, there is a defect in the K1 piston. Replace the multidisk clutch Ki as per EPC. Then readapt the vehicle.

between the automatic transmission and the transfer case housing; front suspension noise; and Parking Assist malfunctions.

E-CLASS   ★ ★ ★

RATING: Average. Redesigned only a few times during the past decade, these family sedans, wagons, and convertibles manage to hold five people in relative comfort while performing acceptably well. **Road performance:** Solid acceleration in the higher gear ranges; 4Matic all-wheel drive operates flawlessly; good handling, though not quite as crisp as with the BMW 5 Series; impressive braking with little brake fade after successive stops; and an acceptable ride, although the Sport model may feel too stiff for some. The car feels much slower than it actually is. **Strong points:** Well-appointed with many safety, performance, and convenience features; good engine and transmission combo; a relatively roomy interior (except for front headroom); lots of cargo room (with the 4Matic wagon); plush, comfortable seats; an innovative anti-theft system; and average quality control, though the AWD version generates more owner complaints. **Weak points:** Complicated electronic control centre, and navigation system controls are a pain to use; diesel engine cabin noise; a surprisingly small trunk; and tall drivers may be bothered by the knee bolsters and limited headroom. **Safety:** NHTSA awarded the 2010 models four stars for driver and passenger frontal crash protection, and five stars for rollover resistance and side protection; IIHS designated the 2012

KEY FACTS

Canadian Price (Negotiable): *E300 4Matic Sedan: $58,300, E350 BlueTEC Sedan: $65,600, Coupe: $61,400, E350 4Matic Sedan: $66,300, 4Matic Coupe: $62,400, 4Matic Wagon: $70,400, 4Matic BlueTEC Diesel: $62,500, E350 Cabriolet: $69,200, E550 Coupe: $72,900, 4Matic: $74,900, E550 Cabriolet: $79,900, E63 AMG: $99,700, E63 AMG Wagon: $102,300* **U.S. Price:** *E350 Coupe: $51,120, Sedan: $51,000, Cabriolet: $59,070, 4Matic Wagon: $57,700, E550 Coupe: $57,960, E550 4Matic: $60,400, E550 BlueTEC Sedan: $50,900, E550 Cabriolet: $66,220, E63 AMG: $89,800, Wagon: $92,400* **Canadian Freight:** Price includes $1,995 freight fee **U.S. Freight:** Price includes $875 freight charge

POWERTRAIN (REAR-DRIVE/AWD)

Engines: 3.0L V6 turbodiesel (210 hp) • 3.5L V6 (302 hp) • 4.7L V8 (402 hp) • 5.5L V8 (518 and 550 hp); Transmission: 7-speed auto.

DIMENSIONS/CAPACITY

Passengers: 2/3; Wheelbase: 113.1 in.; H: 57.7/L: 191.7/W: 71.9 in.; Headroom F/R: 3.0/3.0 in.; Legroom F/R: 44/28.5 in.; Cargo volume: 16 cu. ft.; Fuel tank: 80L/premium; Tow limit: N/A; Load capacity: 960 lb.; Turning circle: 36.2 ft.; Ground clearance: 4.1 in.; Weight: 4,020 lb.

model as "Good" for offset crashworthiness, side-impact protection, roof strength, and head-restraint effectiveness. **New for 2013:** The E-Class models will continue unchanged through the 2013 model year, but the 2014s will also be completely revised, with a new front end, the 3.5L V6 powering the E350 and the 4.7L twin-turbo V8 going into the E500 and E550. AMG's powerful 458 hp V8 will remain the same. Other goodies rumoured to be coming next year are Congestion Assist, a feature that lets you follow another car through traffic, and a camera-based detection system that automatically adjusts the car's suspension for potholes only the camera sees.

ALERT! During your test drive, look for distracting side mirror reflections coming from the cabin and check out the front seat and seat belts for comfort:

The 2012 EC50 interior dash vents (shiny items) are reflected onto the side mirrors making it dangerous when changing lanes because one cannot be sure what one is seeing in those lanes because the reflection is very pronounced. These vents and other dash items are also reflected on the windshield, almost like an obstruction when one is driving. In addition, the adjustable front seats are so uncomfortable that one is constantly adjusting the seat setting while driving. These issues can cause quite a distraction and are obviously dangerous. The dealer's product expert's solution to the reflection problem was to roll down the windows when driving. The individual who sold us the car tells me, now, that he notices this reflection on all these cars. The dealership is indifferent about these items brought to their attention.

•

The owner of a 2012 Mercedes-Benz E350 stated that the front driver and passenger seat belts became inoperable while driving 35 mph [56 km/h] and above. The contact stated that the [seat] belt would continuously vibrate against his shoulder. The seat belt would vibrate so uncontrollably that the contact would have to tuck the belt under his arm to drive safely. The vehicle was taken to an authorized dealer three times, and they were unable to repair it.

OVERVIEW: Mercedes' E-Class cars have improved incrementally over the years, but they have also suffered from unreasonably high base prices, some content-cutting, overly complex electronics and fuel-delivery systems, and poor quality control relative to the automatic transmission, brakes, fuel pump, and electronics. This year, we again rate the E-Class as Average, and shoppers are cautioned to be wary of the latest diesel-equipped models, which may require costly periodic urea fill-ups at the dealership. Try to get your urea off the shelf, and pour it yourself.

A few years ago, *Consumer Reports* took its own diesel-powered Mercedes-Benz GL320 BlueTEC to a dealer because a warning light indicated that the SUV was low on AdBlue urea. The fill-up cost? $316.99! The GL needed 7.5 gallons, which accounted for $241.50 of the total bill ($32.20/gallon). Labour (twisting a cap and pouring) and tax accounted for the remaining $75.49. It took *CR* about 26,660 kilometres (16,565 miles) to run low on AdBlue, which means they'll be spending $1,457.80 on the stuff over 160,935 kilometres (100,000 miles). BMW covers this cost for its diesel-powered vehicles up to 80,470 kilometres (50,000 miles).

COST ANALYSIS: A discounted 2012 is your best bet. Again, diesel owners be wary: Diesels have radically changed since 2007, and it is much more difficult to find competent, inexpensive servicing by independent agencies. **Best alternatives:** The Hyundai Genesis sedan or high-performance coupe. They both have lower price tags, fantastic interiors, rear-drive power delivery, and powerful V8s. Other choices include the Acura RL, BMW 5 Series, Infiniti M35x, and Lexus GS AWD. Why no Volvo S80? We are waiting for the dust to settle around Geely, Volvo's new China-based owner, to see which models are dropped and which new models will debut. **Options:** Nothing is needed. **Rebates:** $5,000+ rebates/discounts, generous leasing deals, and low-interest financing. **Depreciation:** Faster than average. Forget those myths about E-Class high resale values: A $74,300 2006 E350 entry-level model is now worth $14,000—great news if you are buying used, but depressing if the car was purchased new. **Insurance cost:** Higher than average. **Parts supply/cost:** Hard to find outside the dealer network, and they can be expensive at times (body and electronic parts, especially). **Annual maintenance cost:** Higher than average. **Warranty:** Bumper-to-bumper 4 years/80,000 km; powertrain 5 years/120,000 km; rust perforation 5 years/120,000 km. **Supplementary warranty:** Not needed. **Highway/city fuel economy:** *E350:* 8.3/12.7 L/100 km, 34/22 mpg. *E550:* 8.6/13.8 L/100 km, 33/20 mpg. *E63:* 10.2/16.5 L/100 km, 28/17 mpg.

OWNER-REPORTED PROBLEMS: Only six safety-related incidences have been reported to NHTSA relative to the 2012s; 50 complaints would have been normal.

SERVICE BULLETIN-REPORTED PROBLEMS: *E350 Sedan and BlueTEC Diesel:* Automatic transmission switches to "limp home" mode; hard 2–3 upshifts, slipping, or no Third gear; and oil leakage at the seam between the automatic transmission and the transfer case housing. Also the vehicle doesn't perform automatic engine stop; the front suspension may be noisy; and repair tips for Parking Assist malfunctions.

Volkswagen

A Recession Winner

Volkswagen is one of the few automakers that have increased market share during the present worldwide recession. It has done this through a combination of diesel popularity, less exposure to the slumping American market than other automakers, the right mix of vehicles that responds well to up-and-down fuel prices, and a solid international footing. It has profitable operations in Latin America; an expanding presence in China, Russia, and India; and a dominant role in Western Europe, where it also markets its Seat and Skoda brands.

VW's small, fuel-efficient cars and diesel-equipped lineup has touched a nerve with Canadian shoppers in much the same way as the company's first Beetle captured the imagination and support of consumers in the mid-'60s. Building on that support, over the past few years Volkswagen has cut prices and features to keep its small cars affordable.

But quality has always been the company's Achilles' heel, from the first Beetle's no-heat heaters that your mom and dad will probably never forget, to gear-hopping, car-stopping DSG transmissions afflicting Volkswagen's 2007–11 models:

> I own a 2009 Jetta TDI with a DSG transmission. I feel like I am going to get hit when I start from a stop. The transmission jumps and hesitates. It has been to the dealer without being fixed. It is terrifying to drive a car that may or may not accelerate, which also jumps in and out of gear!

We can all agree that Volkswagens are practical drivers' cars that offer excellent handling and great fuel economy without sacrificing interior comfort. But overall reliability goes downhill after the fifth year of ownership and servicing is often more competent and cheaper at independent garages, which have grown increasingly popular as owners flee more expensive VW dealerships. Unfortunately, parts are fairly expensive, but they aren't that hard to find, except for electronic components.

With rare candor Volkswagen now admits that car buyers see its products as failure-prone, and the automaker vows to change that perception by building a more reliable, durable product and providing timely, no-return servicing.

Taking a page out of Toyota's sudden, unintended acceleration/brake failure Congressional testimony several years back, Volkswagen says it is now paying more attention, sooner, to problems reported by fleet customers and dealers in order to find and fix problems before they become widespread among individual customers.

A check of the NHTSA owner complaints log at *safercar.gov* does show safety-related incidents have dropped during the last three years, probably as a result of the recall of the DSG transmission and subsequent warranty extension to address DSG claims. Nevertheless, automatic transmission-related problems are still the number-one failure reported to NHTSA's safety complaint website.

Two years ago, *Lemon-Aid* exposed the DSG problem and rated Audi and VW models equipped with DSG transmissions as Not Recommended. Since then, VW and Audi have recalled the tranny several times and extended the warranty to 10 years/100,000 miles on 2007–10 models.

For a copy of VW's extended warranty, go to *www.dsgproblems.co.uk/Volkswagen%20 of%20America%20Inc.pdf.*

Now there is fresh evidence that tranny failures have spread to the 2012 models. Therefore, be wary.

New Products

Except for the introduction of a Hybrid Jetta this fall, Volkswagen is saving its big changes for 2014.

- The Jetta Hybrid will combine best-in-class performance with an estimated combined fuel consumption of 5.2 L/100 km (45 mpg)—it goes on sale in late fall.
- Jetta models get interior upgrades; the GLI now has a launch-control feature.
- The manual Beetle TDI Coupe and Beetle TDI Convertible will achieve EPA-estimated fuel economy ratings of 5.7 L/100 km (41 mpg) on the highway.
- An all-new Beetle Convertible launches late in 2012 in Turbo, 2.5L, and TDI Clean Diesel forms.
- The Beetle Fender Edition will be on sale late in 2012.
- The CC, which went on sale as a 2013 model in March, will add a new R-Line version at the end of 2012.
- The Eos gets a new Sport trim level, and there will be upgrades to the Lux and Executive models.
- The Touareg TDI engine's output will be raised from 225 hp to 240 hp.

"Green" Diesels

During the past few years, diesel emissions have been cleaned up to the point that environmentalists and economists alike see the increased use of diesel engines as the only way to gain time for the development of cleaner-burning fuel alternatives.

Just don't look for big fuel savings in the interim.

Keep in mind that, unless you travel more than 30,000 km a year, diesel cost savings may be illusory. Granted, there are usually fewer things that go wrong with diesel engines, and their fuel economy is high, but gasoline-powered Asian compacts are much more reliable, their parts are cheaper and more easily found, and they're almost as fuel-frugal. And here's the biggest drawback with recently redesigned diesels: They have been completely changed to be as emissions-free as possible. Mechanics aren't yet familiar with them. Backup parts are still "in the pipeline," supposedly, and dealers aren't rushing to buy replacement parts until they can sell their old stock. Therefore, wise shoppers will steer clear of VW's diesel-equipped vehicles, at least until late next year when we can hope that servicing know-how and parts distribution will have improved.

GOLF, JETTA, CC ★ / ★ / ★ ★

The Volkswagen Golf.

RATING: *All gasoline- and diesel-powered models equipped with the DSG automatic transmission:* Not Recommended, due to reports of serious, life-threatening powertrain and fuel-delivery defects. *Manual transmission-equipped vehicles:* Below Average. **Road performance:** Drivetrain problems aside, these cars are good all-around front-drive performers when coupled to a manual shifter and adequate engine. The DSG's shifts are unreliable and soft in full-auto mode. The sporty GLI, with its turbocharged 200 hp 2.0L 4-cylinder engine, delivers high-performance thrills without much of a fuel penalty, and the 170 hp 2.5L 5-cylinder engine is well suited for city driving and most leisurely highway cruising, thanks mainly to the car's light weight and handling prowess. Be wary of models equipped with the wimpy 115 hp 2.0L 4-cylinder engine. **Strong points:** A comfortable ride; plenty of headroom, legroom, and cargo space; standard tilt/telescope steering column; a low load floor; and good fuel economy. **Weak points:** Powertrains on the 2011s and 2012s are showing failures similar to the recalled 2007–10 models'. Base Jettas come with a 115 hp 4-cylinder engine that is the runt of the litter. It fails to meet the driving expectations of most Jetta buyers, who want both good fuel economy and an engine with plenty of low-end torque and cruising power. Diesel-equipped

Canadian Price (Negotiable): *Golf 3d:* $19,975, *5d:* $21,475, *Sportline:* $23,300, *Highline:* $23,980, *2.0 TDI:* $25,275, *2.5 Sportline Tiptronic:* $25,300, *2.5 Highline:* $26,475, *DSG:* $26,675, *2.5 Highline Tiptronic:* $27,875, *2.0 TDI Highline:* $28,775, *2.0 TDI Highline DSG:* $30,175, *GTI:* $29,375, *R:* $39,675, *Jetta:* $15,875, *2.5 Trendline:* $22,175, *Jetta TDI Trendline:* $24,475, *Jetta 2.5 Comfortline:* $24,875, *Jetta TDI Comfortline:* $27,175, *Jetta 2.0 Highline:* $29,075, *Jetta TDI Highline:* $30,875, *Jetta Wolfsburg:* $27,275, *GLI:* $27,475, *CC:* $35,125 **U.S. Price:** *Golf 2d:* $17,995, *Golf 4d:* $19,795, *GTI:* $23,995, *R:* $33,990, *TDI 2d:* $24,235, *TDI 4d:* $24,935, *Jetta S:* $16,495, *Jetta SE:* $18,495, *Jetta SEL:* $23,195, *SportWagen:* $20,395 *GTI:* $23,995, *TDI 2d:* $24,235, *TDI 4d:* $24,935, *Jetta GLI:* $23,945, *Autobahn:* $26,195, *CC Sport:* $30,610, *Sport*

Plus: $32,850, *Lux:* $35,355, *V6:* $37,730, *VR6 4Motion Executive:* $41,420

Canadian Freight: $1,395 **U.S. Freight:** $825

POWERTRAIN (FRONT-DRIVE/AWD)

Engines: 2.0L 4-cyl. (115 hp) • 2.0L TDI 4-cyl. (140 hp) • 2.0L Turbo 4-cyl. (200 hp) • 2.0L Turbo 4-cyl. (256 hp) • 2.5L 5-cyl. (170 hp) • 3.6L V6 (280 hp); Transmissions: 5-speed man. • 6-speed man. • 6-speed auto • 7-speed auto • 4Motion all-wheel drive

DIMENSIONS/CAPACITY (JETTA)

Passengers: 2/3; Wheelbase: 104.4 in.; H: 57.2/L: 182.2/W: 70 in.; Headroom F/R: 4.5/2.5 in.; Legroom F/R: 43/30 in.; Cargo volume: 15 cu. ft.; Fuel tank: 55L/regular; Tow limit: 1,500 lb.; Load capacity: 1,070 lb.; Turning circle: 35.7 ft.; Ground clearance: 5.5 in.; Weight: 3,090 lb.

models with cruise control can't handle small hills very well, and often slow down by 10–15 km/h. Excessive engine and road noise; difficult entry and exit; and restricted rear visibility. Folding rear seats don't lie flat. Maintenance costs increase after the fifth year of ownership. **Safety:** NHTSA gave the 2013 CC and Golf four stars for rollover resistance; other types of crashes weren't tested. The 2013 Jetta scored five stars for side crash protection and four stars for frontal crashworthiness and rollover resistance. IIHS awarded top marks to all three models for the traditional crash scenarios. However, in a new quarter-frontal IIHS crash-test category, the CC was given a "Marginal" rating. The test is designed to replicate what happens when the front corner of a car collides with another vehicle or an object like a tree or utility pole. There's also a high number of NHTSA-registered safety-related complaints on two-year-old or older models involving DSG and other powertrain failures. **New for 2013:** CC: LED tail lights will resemble units used on the Jetta and Passat, and new headlights adopt a boxier design that incorporates LED running lights. There's also a larger grille that copies Volkswagen's European-market Phaeton sedan, a restyled sedan trunk, and a more aggressive-looking front bumper. Inside, we find optional seating for five, made possible by the addition of an extra seat belt and a flat middle cushion to the sedan's rear bench seat. Revised interior amenities include a new analog clock in the centre of the sedan's dashboard and redesigned climate controls. The sedan will also feature new standard equipment, like bi-xenon headlights with Volkswagen's adaptive front lighting system, a fatigue-detection system that alerts drivers when they become drowsy, stainless steel door sill plates, and front headrests with a longitudinal adjustment. Early in 2013, we will see the introduction of a new sporty trim level called the R-Line, equipped with a 200 hp turbocharged 4-cylinder engine and several sporty exterior and interior modifications. *Golf and GTI:* Mostly minor trim changes, except for the addition of the Golf R, a sportier version of the GTI, equipped with a 256 hp 4-cylinder (Europe gets a 270 hp version) and a 6-speed manual transmission. It's available as a three- and five-door and uses larger brakes with 18-inch wheels. *Jetta/ SportWagen:* Sedans get updated interior appointments and a backup camera. A launch-control feature for smoother acceleration will be standard with GLI models equipped with the DSG transmission, and a hybrid version will debut by year's end. It is VW's second-ever hybrid model and the first hybrid in the world to use a 7-speed DSG dual-clutch automatic transmission.

ALERT! Before opting for the cheapest 2013 Jetta with its glacial 115 hp 4-cylinder engine, take it for a test drive and see if the reduced power is acceptable. Also, be wary of last-minute $375 dealer "administration" or "processing" fees; they're scams.

OVERVIEW: "Practical and fun to drive" pretty well sums up why these VWs continue to be so popular—at least for the first couple of years. True, they offer an accommodating interior, plenty of power with the higher-end models, responsive handling, and great fuel economy. Jetta S models use a 115 hp 2.0L 4-cylinder engine. The SE and SEL are powered by the same 170 hp 2.5L 5-cylinder engine from the previous-generation Jetta. The TDI continues with its 140 hp 2.0L turbodiesel 4-cylinder. Interestingly, the GLI will keep its 200 hp turbocharged 2.0L 4-cylinder—the same engine that produces 265 horses in the Audi TTS. A 5-speed manual transmission is standard on the S, SE, and SEL. A 6-speed manual is standard on the TDI and GLI. Optional on the S, SE, and SEL is a 6-speed automatic. The GLI and TDI offer a 6-speed dual-clutch automated manual that behaves much like an automatic…when it's not hesitating, falling into Neutral, or simply falling apart.

Again, we raise the caveat that VW's relatively new diesel design will likely have higher servicing costs and parts availability problems. That said, auto analysts say diesel is the best alternative to paying high fuel prices at the moment. *Autoweek* magazine concluded, "For comfort, quiet, and highway handling, our drivers found the TDI had significant advantages over every other car in the test. It would have been our choice, in other words, for an easy daytrip on the interstates, regardless of fuel economy. And we topped the hybrids by driving with just a little attention to fuel economy, not making it an obsession."

COST ANALYSIS: VW has kept a lid on 2013 entry-level model prices, so there's no advantage in buying a 2012. Price increases on 2013 higher-end versions may top a few thousand dollars. **Best alternatives:** Other cars worth considering are the Honda Civic and Civic Si or Accord, Hyundai Elantra, Kia Forte, Mazda6, Nissan Sentra, Suzuki Kizashi, and Toyota Corolla or Matrix. **Options:** Stay away from the electric sunroof; it costs a bundle to repair and offers not much more than the well-designed manual sunroof. On top of that, you lose too much headroom. **Rebates:** $1,000 rebates on non-diesels, low-interest financing, and attractive leases. **Depreciation:** About average. However, as you approach the end of the four-year warranty, the value drops sharply, even with the popular Jetta. For example, a 2008 Jetta 2.0L sedan that first sold for $27,475 is now worth $12,500. **Insurance cost:** Higher than average. **Parts supply/cost:** Not hard to find, but parts can be more expensive than for most other cars in this class. Diesel parts may be expensive and harder to find. **Annual maintenance cost:** Less than average while under warranty. After that, repair costs start to climb dramatically. Just replacing a fuse can be a head-scratcher:

> Volkswagen of America fails to provide their customers with a fuse diagram, making it impossible to safely identify and replace a simple blown fuse. Without a basic fuse diagram, the only choice for VW owners needing to replace a fuse is to pull fuses one-by-one as they search for the blown fuse. With many unused slots, should a fuse be inadvertently replaced in the incorrect slot, a critical safety system such as brake lights, tail lights, headlights, ABS brake control, windshield wipers, horn, etc. can be accidentally disabled without any immediate knowledge on the part of the owner.

Warranty: Bumper-to-bumper 4 years/80,000 km; powertrain 5 years/100,000 km; rust perforation 12 years/unlimited km. **Supplementary warranty:** A good idea. **Highway/city fuel economy:** *Golf City 2.0L:* 7.0/9.8 L/100 km, 40/28 mpg. *Golf 2.5L:* 7.0/10.4 L/100 km, 40/27 mpg. *Auto.:* 6.9/9.2 L/100 km, 41/31 mpg. *TDI:* 4.7/6.7 L/100 km, 60/42 mpg. *Auto.:* 4.6/6.7 L/100 km, 61/42 mpg. Jetta fuel economy should be similar.

OWNER-REPORTED PROBLEMS: The numbers of reported safety-related incidents range from fewer than normal to about average. Still, those that are mentioned are definitely life-threatening, and many of the same failures have been reported since 2007. Premature brake wear, electrical and electronic failures, and fit and finish defects are the top problems reported by the owners of the 2012 model. Fender sound system rattles (covered by a special service campaign). Water leaks are commonplace. *CC:* When coming to a stop, the car still inches forward; factory-installed GPS tells the driver to turn just moments before the turn must be made; the horn doesn't sound immediately; Low Tire Pressure warning indicator malfunctions; and the wheel rim may suddenly self-destruct:

> The right front wheel on my 2012 VW CC shattered. My concern is focused on the safety of the wheel design and my belief that the overinflation of the tires contribute to rim failure.... There were no visible defects in the road... While driving in the middle lane the car clearly came in contact with an irregularity, one that every car before and after was able to transverse without a problem. In my case the rim shattered and separated from the car causing a loss of control. I was able to pull to the side of the road. The car that was behind me pulled over after seeing what he described as an explosion on the right front side. I have attached pictures of the rim. Clearly showing product failure. When the tow truck arrived, he commented that he has never witnessed rim failure like that. The dealer upon review of the damage concurred. My concern is twofold. One, the safety of the design and construction of the rim and the overinflation upon delivery of the tires which contributed to the weakness of the design. I am requesting an inquiry into the safety of this design, the training of the

staff on proper inflation guidelines and the reimbursement for costs associated with this failure.

Golf: Failure of the high-pressure fuel pump on diesel models is one cause of chronic stalling and unbelievably high repair bills reported for the past several model years:

At 6,519 miles [10,490 km], while about to enter the on-ramp of a local highway, the Check Engine light and glow plug indicator light began to flash. I was able to veer off the entrance ramp and continue down…to the nearest safe parking lot area; as I pulled into the parking lot area, the vehicle shuddered and suddenly shut off. It would not re-start, and we had to arrange for a tow to a family members house through our insurance company. In the morning we had a tow to our dealer set up through Volkswagen roadside service, who would not cover the entire cost of the tow to our preferred dealer, so we paid the difference out of our own pocket. I was notified by the dealer that the fuel pump (commonly referred to as HPFP) basically imploded and sent metal throughout the entire fuel system, which now needs to be replaced. We own two Volkswagen diesel (TDI) vehicles; this one, a 2012 Golf TDI, and a 2010 Jetta TDI. They are both filled up at the exact same pump from the exact same station about 99% of the time. At the time this incident occurred, the Golf had 281 miles [452 km] on the current tank of diesel which was filled up on 08/03/2012. I filled up my Jetta TDI at the same pump on 08/06/2012, currently have over 230 miles [370 km] on that tank of diesel, and have not experienced any problems. We keep meticulous documentation of our diesel usage, cost, etc. with receipts and other logs, and can safely state that this was not due to a mistake on our part. Rather, this is a design failure and/or oversight on the part of both Volkswagen and Bosch, the HPFP manufacturer. I am a veteran member of the TDIClub VW Diesel online community, and there is extensive information and documentation there of these repeated failures.

DSG automatic transmission failures have returned to haunt the 2011–12 models:

Leaving a parking lot in my 2012 Golf, put the gear into Reverse and was going forward. Put the gear in Parking 3X and back to Reverse 3X, but still going forward. Couldn't turn off the engine. Opened the door, and after maybe 10 minutes was able to turn off the engine, gave it a minute and then use the Reverse gear and it worked.

GTI: DSG transmission won't shift into gear, and sometimes the engine suddenly surges or stalls, accompanied by total brake failure:

During rush hour traffic, I had to slow down a little in order to allow the car next to me to pass so I could change lanes without hitting the car in front of me. The car seemed to shift into Neutral and did not respond when I hit the accelerator. The accelerator pedal actually sunk down to the floor with no response. After a few seconds, the transmission did shift into gear and took off too fast. In the meantime, I was almost rear-ended. This happens almost every day that I drive in heavy traffic. I can't control it so I have to make sure there is not a car within ¼ mile behind me when I change lanes because the car frequently almost stalls. This also happens sometimes when I make a turn—again, I have to make sure there isn't a car within about ¼ mile because I may end up practically stopped right in front of an oncoming car. It generally happens when I decelerate and then accelerate and the transmission is in Drive. I took the car to the dealer for its 3-month checkup and told them about this. They had a DSG software upgrade which they installed. Neither VW nor the dealer had notified me of this upgrade even though it applied to my car. Unfortunately, the problem still occurs on an almost daily basis. The dealership told me to let them know if I still have the problem when I come back for the 10,000-mile service. This is a safety issue which should be addressed now, not in 7000 miles. I understand that this problem has been reported in GTIs with DSG transmissions since 2009, but VW still has not corrected it.

•

My 2012 6-speed has had two incidents – first, the car wouldn't engage into Reverse from a stop until the vehicle's ignition was turned off and on several times. Car operated normally for about 2 weeks. Second incident, car wouldn't engage into any gear while moving 10–15 mph [16–24 km/h] uphill while in First gear. During loss of powertrain, the engine revved in the 4000–5000 rpm range, smoke was visibly coming out of the engine bay and there was complete loss of brakes, including the emergency brake. The vehicle started to roll backward downhill and was stopped by turning the vehicle into the sidewalk. After 2 days of diagnostics, the technicians were not able to replicate the issue and concluded that the vehicle was operating within manufacturer specifications.

•

I was driving down the road and was coming to a stop sign. I had the clutch all of the way in and shifted into Neutral while slowing down, I put it into 1st gear with the clutch all the way in and the clutch engaged, causing the car to jerk violently. It went from 2200 rpm to over 6000 immediately. After getting stopped and in Neutral I released the clutch pedal for it to stay slammed to the floor. It would not go into First easily with the clutch all the way in.

Jetta: Starter/electrical fires due to starter overheating during attempts to start locked engine; chronic shudder and stalling upon acceleration or deceleration, often with no brakes:

After less than 3 minutes of operation, my 2012 Jetta will stall under a specific set of circumstances. The incidences (13 and counting in 2 months) always occur when in Second or Third gear at ~30–35 [mph]. The driver is slowing down (as to stop at a red light) and then accelerates (light changes to green). About 2–3 seconds after acceleration begins the engine stalls and must be restarted. The engine just cuts out during acceleration.

•

Purchased a VW Jetta SE on 7/20/12 and almost 1 month after the purchase I was driving on a local highway at apx. 50 mph [80 km/h] around 5:30 pm when car headlights blinked and car died (stalled). Attempted to re-start a car without any success. Since VW dealer was closed already—called a local auto shop and they towed [the] car to a shop to find [the] issue. Mechanic could not see anything obvious so he re-set a computer in my car and he was able to start it. Drove home. Later in the evening—drove to pick up some food and on the way home (inside a development)— while making a left turn at apx. 15–18 mph [24–29 km/h]—pressed brakes and realized I had none and at the same time car stalled and since it was raining and I was already slightly turning left—car slid in the direction on my turn and right rear tire hit the curb, tire fall off, car hit a street sign and an electric pool (both fell to the ground) and brought me to a complete stop on the grass.

Sudden, unintended acceleration; complete loss of braking capability; high-pressure fuel pump failures; Reverse lights don't work; fuel filler leaks because some gas pump handles don't fit into the fuel nozzle; left outside mirror blind spot cannot be adjusted; many complaints of a cracked fuel line from the common rail on diesel-equipped models; drivers complain of both sudden, unintended acceleration and chronic stalling:

Without warning, the engine shut down while driving down a busy road. Check Engine and Glow Plug warning light came on. Was just able to coast to the shoulder of the road. Car would turn over, but engine would not start. Car towed to dealer. Was told there was a catastrophic failure of the high pressure fuel pump, and metal shards were found throughout the fuel system. VW replaced the entire fuel supply system (including fuel tank) and fuel injection system.

Vehicle was idling on an incline with the brakes depressed, and it started rolling backwards, even though brakes were continuously applied; when stopped on an incline, the automatic transmission holds the car for only a few seconds before the vehicle starts rolling backwards; while attempting to start the vehicle, the steering wheel locked; premature replacement of the rear brakes; windshield distortion; roof design sends excess rainwater to the front windshield, and the wipers push large amounts of water into the driver's viewing range; wipers slow down as engine speed decreases; inoperative wiper motor; delayed horn response; premature original-equipment tire failures; bubbling in the side wall of Continental original equipment tires; the muffler extends too far out from the underbody—one woman was burned on the leg while unloading groceries; and heated seats can catch on fire and give occupants much more than a "hot foot," as one owner so succinctly wrote to government investigators:

My heated seats caught fire and burnt my ass...

SERVICE BULLETIN-REPORTED PROBLEMS: *1995–2013:* Squeak and rattle kit available. *1999–2013 (except Routan):* Abnormal vibration when braking caused by excess corrosion or an out-of-round rotor; tackling unpleasant odours coming from the AC vents, and reducing exterior light moisture accumulation, headlight lens blemishes; the cooling fan runs with the ignition turned off. *2008–12:* Engine rattling noise. *2011–12:* If the heater doesn't blow hot enough, reboot the system with upgraded software. *Golf:* Tips on preventing windshield wipers from smearing the windshield. *Turbo diesels:* Engine hesitation; harsh shifting in low gear; cold weather no-starts:

NO START IN COLD WEATHER

BULLETIN NO.: 21 12 01 **DATE: MARCH 12, 2012**

Model(s)	Year	Eng. Code	Trans. Code	VIN Range From	VIN Range To
Jetta, Jetta Wagon	2009	2.0L TDI (CBEA)	All	All	All
Jetta	2010	2.0L TDI (CJAA)	All	All	All
Golf, Jetta SportWagen, Golf Wagon	2010–2013	2.0L TDI (CJAA)	All	All	All
Jetta	2011–2013	2.0L TDI (CJAA)	All	All	All

CONDITION: Frozen Charge Air Cooler. Engine will not start after standing in cold weather below 0°C (32°F), MIL may be illuminated with various induction and/or boost system faults stored in ECM.

TECHNICAL BACKGROUND: Moisture from the intake air condenses and collects in the charge air cooler. At cold temperatures this moisture can freeze causing blockage of the intake air system.

PRODUCTION SOLUTION: None.

SERVICE: Install revised charge air cooler kit P/N 1K0 198 803B to avoid the formation of this moisture in the boost system.

PASSAT, PASSAT CC

RATING: Below Average. Not recommend for driving or parking over hilly terrain (see the "Alert!" section) or for drivers or passengers who are tortured by the poorly designed head restraints:

Recently I drove several new cars (the latest being the 2012 Passat) and found one common complaint: The headrests on these cars are tilted forward way too much with no adjustments available. My understanding is that NHTSA requires vehicles' headrests to be higher and close to the head to reduce whiplash injuries. How do you improve safety if it's impossible to find a comfortable driving position? The new headrest regulation forces the driver to slouch forward (and looking down) while driving, causing fatigue to set quickly. For me, the only way to find a comfortable position while driving these new Passats are by reclining the seat back excessively

The Volkswagen Passat.

(so my head won't tilt forward). This, in my opinion, isn't safe since this position reduces the driver's alertness. With the active headrest technology, in my opinion the new headrest regulation is an easy and lazy way to reduce whiplash injury without proper research (i.e. only based on measurements with no regards to driver's comfort).

The fault isn't with government regulation, however. It's with VW's design engineers who picked the cheapest, most uncomfortable restraints possible—ones that would make the Marquis de Sade scream with joy (and pain). Ford had a similar inhumane design with its 2011 models until buyer protests forced the company to bring out versatile and comfortable head restraints later that year. **Road performance:** Impressive acceleration with the turbocharged engine hooked to the smooth-performing manual gearbox. The sophisticated, user-friendly 4Motion full-time all-wheel drive shifts effortlessly into gear; refined road manners; no turbo lag; better-than-average emergency handling; quick and predictable steering; handling outclasses most of the competition's; and the suspension is both firm and comfortable. Some negatives: engine/automatic transmission hesitates when accelerating; excessive brake fade after successive stops; and you can't trust the speedometer reading:

> Vehicle does not show the true speed of the car. Speedometer is off by 7–8 kmh. @ 100 kms. VW does not accept that there is any problem and will not fix the problem.

Strong points: Well-appointed and holds its value fairly well. Quiet-running; plenty of passenger and cargo room; impressive interior fit and finish; and exceptional driving comfort. **Weak points:** Function sacrificed to style with rear-corner blind spots and rear head restraints that impede rear visibility; many safety and performance complaints after the two-year mark (faulty airbags and transmissions, distorted windshields, and chronic stalling); plus, these models are expensive to purchase and service. **Safety:** Good crashworthiness scores from both

NHTSA and IIHS. NHTSA gave the 2013 Passat five stars for frontal and side crash protection and four stars for rollover protection. IIHS gave the 2012 Passat a "Good" rating for frontal offset crashworthiness, side crash protection, roof protection, and head-restraint effectiveness. Power windows freeze shut in cold weather. **New for 2013:** A backup camera is standard on all SEL-trimmed models.

ALERT! Volkswagen says the redesigned 2012 Passat has tackled the company's well-known quality problems. True, owner safety-related complaints are down significantly; however, the failures reported relative to the powertrain are just as hair-raising as ever. In the 2011 J.D. Power Initial Quality Survey, VW tied with Mini for 29th among 32 brands. In your test drive, check out the car's ability to parallel park on a hill, after first making sure there are no cars parked nearby that you might hit:

> Our new Passat has problem controlling the car while using Reverse on a hill. It appears that VW has tied the accelerator and braking function together in a way that the driver may lose control of the vehicle while in Reverse. If the brake is pressed, the accelerator is disengaged thus allowing the engine [to] fall to an idle and not develop any thrust. If the driver is using both feet to control the vehicle, left foot on the brake, right foot on the accelerator while depressing the brake, the engine develops no power even if the accelerator is depressed fully. By releasing the brake while the accelerator is depressed fully, the vehicle will lurch at full throttle in Reverse in an out of control condition until the driver realizes what is happening and removes their foot from the accelerator. It was fortunate that no one was behind the car when this happened to me or there might have been an injury or even a fatality. It is clear that the VW engineering staff has never tried parallel parking the Passat on a hill in San Francisco. VW engineers should remove the software code that ties the accelerator and brake function together while in Reverse or at least activate it when the speed is greater than 5 miles an hour. If you don't use two feet and only use one, then the hill hold will be effective and generally you can control the vehicle. There is no warning that this implementation exists and when parking on a steep hill, in a very tight spot, you almost always use two feet to have total control. Volkswagen engineers, in good faith, implemented the NHTSA recommendation for "brake throttle override". Docket No. NHTSA-2012-0038. Page 16 has specific comments on intentional "two footed use". The VW dealer investigated and offered us a full return and refund. We are hoping the NHTSA will work with VW to help reconcile this software anomaly.

KEY FACTS

Canadian Price (Negotiable): *Trendline 2.5L:* $23,975, *Plus 2.5L:* $24,875, *Comfortline 2.5L:* $27,975, *Highline 2.5L:* $31,475; *Comfortline 3.6L:* $33,575, *Highline 3.6L:* $37,475, *CC:* $33,375, *VR6:* $46,375, *Trendline diesel:* $27,475, *Comfortline diesel:* $30,575, *Highline diesel:* $33,775 **U.S. Price:** *S 2.5L:* $20,845, *SE 2.5L:* $23,945, *SEL 2.5L:* $28,925, *V6 SE:* $29,235, *CC:* $30,610, *VR6:* $41,420, *SE diesel:* $26,225, *SEL diesel:* $32,915 **Canadian Freight:** $1,395 **U.S. Freight:** $825

POWERTRAIN (FRONT-DRIVE/AWD)

Engines: 2.0L 4-cyl. diesel (140 hp) • 2.5L 5-cyl. (170 hp) • 3.6L V6 (280 hp); Transmissions: 5-speed man. • 6-speed man. • 6-speed auto. • 6-speed manumatic.

DIMENSIONS/CAPACITY

Passengers: 2/3; CC: 2/2; Wheelbase: 106.6 in.; H: 55.9/L: 188.8/W: 73 in.; Headroom F/R: 4.0/3.0 in.; Legroom F/R: 43/29 in.; Cargo volume: 14.2 cu. ft.; Fuel tank: 70L/premium; Tow limit: 2,000 lb.; Turning circle: 38 ft.; Ground clearance: 4.5 in.; Weight: 3,853 lb.

OVERVIEW: The Passat is an attractive mid-sized car that rides on the same platform as the Audi A4. It has a more stylish design than the Golf or Jetta, but it still provides a comfortable, roomy interior and gives good all-around performance for highway and city driving. The car's large wheelbase and squat appearance give it a massive, solid feeling, while its aerodynamic styling makes it look sleek and clean. Base Passats come with a 170 hp 2.5L 5-cylinder engine and front-drive, while the 3.6L models use a 280 hp V6 harnessed to a front-drive or 4Motion all-wheel-drive powertrain. Passats come fully loaded with anti-lock four-wheel disc brakes, traction and anti-skid control, front side and side curtain airbags, tinted glass, front and rear stabilizer bars, and full instrumentation. In addition to the standard 6-speed manual transmission found on 4-cylinder models, an optional, problem-prone 6-speed Direct Shift Gearbox (DSG) automated manual transmission is available.

COST ANALYSIS: Get an identical 2012 model with a sizeable discount (at least 15 percent), and tell the dealer to take a hike if you are asked to pay a $300–$400 "administration" or "processing" fee. **Best alternatives:** The BMW 3 Series, Ford Fusion, Honda Accord, Hyundai Genesis, and Toyota Camry. **Options:** The AWD will give you the extra sure-footedness and traction when you want it. **Rebates:** $3,000–$5,000. **Depreciation:** Faster than average. How'd you like to lose over half the car's value after barely three years? That's what would happen if you had bought a new 2009 Passat sedan for $29,976. **Insurance cost:** Higher than average. These cars are a favourite among thieves—whether for stealing radios, wheels, VW badges, or entire cars. (No, the delayed tranny shifts and fire-prone fuel system are *not* anti-theft measures.) **Parts supply/cost:** Parts are getting harder to find as dealers and suppliers close. **Annual maintenance cost:** Higher than average. **Warranty:** Bumper-to-bumper 4 years/80,000 km; powertrain 5 years/100,000 km; rust perforation 12 years/unlimited km. **Supplementary warranty:** A must. Maintenance costs are higher than average once the warranty expires. **Highway/city fuel economy:** 2.5L: 6.5/10.1 L/100 km, 43/28 mpg. *Auto.:* 6.7/9.6 L/100 km, 42/29 mpg. *3.6L:* 7.4/10.9 L/100 km, 38/26 mpg. *TDI diesel:* 4.4/6.8 L/100 km, 64/42 mpg. *Auto:* 4.9/6.9 L/100 km, 58/41 mpg.

OWNER-REPORTED PROBLEMS: Traditional deficiencies dating back to the 2006 model year include failure of the powertrain, fuel, and electrical systems, and various fit and finish flaws. Nevertheless, fewer (15) safety related defects have been reported to NHTSA by 2012 model owners; 50 complaints are the average. Some of the transmission failures reported on the 2012s are eerily similar to complaints heard from owners five years ago. For example, delayed shifts and transmission fluid leaks that require a transmission transplant:

> The vehicle has a significant delay/hesitation upon initial acceleration (2.5L). This is dangerous when pulling into or across traffic. This issue is known to others and is reported elsewhere on the Web.

> •

> As I was driving my new 2012 Volkswagen Passat from my house to my destination, my transmission fluid began to leak out onto the street. I had purchased the car

eight days earlier which was a new car from the dealership which only had 2 miles on the car. The amount of miles I had put on the car was 500 miles [800 km] and the transmission fluid leaked because of a malfunction inside of it. The car was under warranty and the dealership had to put a new transmission into my car because the old one had defective parts inside.

Fuel leaks within the first few months of ownership are also common:

I unlocked my 2012 Passat and opened the door to get some items from the car. Again, the sound of draining fluid could be heard and a strong odor of gasoline emitted from the vehicle. I checked underneath the car again, and a fresh pool of gasoline has formed. The gas is dripping from the passenger side, near the rear wheel. Needless to say, this is very disappointing, as the vehicle has only been driven for a little more than 1,000 miles [1,600 km].

SERVICE BULLETIN-REPORTED PROBLEMS: Implausible transmission whistle or whine at highway speeds requires the installation of an updated shifter cable bracket. A harsh engagement from Park to Drive or Reverse (requires a software update).

Appendix I

2013–2014 MINI-REVIEWS AND PREVIEWS

The following mini-reviews and previews represent vehicles that are relatively new to the market or scheduled to be introduced next year as 2014 models. We also look at the slow sellers that haven't yet built up a reliable track record. There are a number of cars and trucks not reviewed in this year's guide due to time and page constraints. If there is a model you are considering that's not here, write me at *lemonaid@earthlink.net* and I'll be glad to send you some updated info.

New car prices generally rise in the fall and drop in the winter. Popular vehicles maintain their original value well into the summer, while the average car or truck is discounted by about 10–15 percent in early winter after auto show and media hoopla has subsided and showroom traffic has gone south.

Two factors that have a huge impact on prices are production delays and the cost of fuel. The first factor affects particular companies, while the second impacts specific models. Honda, Nissan, and Toyota, for example, have been hurt by a series of natural disasters over the past few years that forced them to curb production by 50 percent. Now their plants have re-opened, and supplier lines are rebuilt. And, they are breaking with tradition by using generous rebates, low-interest leases, and special financing programs to capture sales in all model niches.

The price of fuel is another wild card that affects new vehicle prices, depending upon how much fuel each model burns. As gasoline becomes more expensive, large trucks and SUVs become cheaper to buy as compacts and mini-compacts sell at a premium. However, once a barrel of oil goes below $90 U.S., small car sales wane and large car, truck, and SUV sales surge.

Yes, these are volatile times; car and truck prices fluctuate dramatically and fuel costs change every day. Still, take your time before choosing a new vehicle. Usually, the longer you wait, the less you will pay. You don't want the economic burden of buying a car that's on the market for the first time or one that has been radically changed this model year—the value of these vehicles is yet unproven. Nor should you invest in a vehicle that merely looks nice or is cheap if it doesn't have a positive reliability history. And you certainly don't want to overpay for a car or truck simply to be the first in your town with something "different" (remember the Chrysler PT Cruiser?). The uniqueness will pass; the repairs will remain constant.

Consider these tips:

1. If you really want to save money, try to buy a vehicle that's leased by a family member. You'll likely get a good buy for half what the vehicle originally cost and with some warranty coverage left. Plus, there won't be any secrets; everyone will know how the vehicle was driven and maintained, and you can use the same repair facilities that have been repairing your family's vehicles for years.

2. Get a fuel-efficient car. Be wary of diesel-equipped or hybrid cars that may require more-expensive dealer servicing that could wipe out any fuel consumption savings. Don't trust hybrid fuel economy hype—sometimes it can be off by 40 percent. Also, don't buy a "lemon" simply because it's touted as being fuel-efficient; a failure-prone Chrysler Sebring/Avenger may cost you more to repair than to fuel, and a 4-cylinder pickup like GM's Canyon and Colorado—though cheap to run—can make highway merging a white-knuckle affair.

UPCOMING 2012–2014 ELECTRICS

MANUFACTURER	MODEL	CLASS	DATE AVAILABLE*
Audi	A4	Small Car	2014
BMW	i8 EV	Small Car	2013–2014
BMW	i3 EV	Small Car	2013–2014
Cadillac	ELR	Large Car	2013–2014
Chevrolet	Spark	Small Car	2012–2013
Ford	C-Max	Minivan	2013 2014
Ford	Focus EV	Small Car	2012–2013
Ford	Fusion Energi	Midsize Car	2012–2013
Honda	Accord	Small Car	2012–2013
Infiniti	LE	Large Car	2014
Mercedes	S500	Large Car	2013–2014
Porsche	918 Spyder	Sports Car	2012–2013
Tesla	S	Roadster	2012–2013
Volkswagen	Golf EV	Small Car	2013–2014

*Availability dates typically indicate calendar year rather than model year.

UPCOMING 2013–2014 DIESELS

MANUFACTURER	MODEL	CLASS	DATE AVAILABLE*
Mercedes-Benz	GLK350	SUV	2012
Audi	A4	Small Car	2013
Audi	A6	Midsize Car	2013
Audi	A8	Midsize Car	2013
Audi	Q5	SUV	2013
BMW	3 Series	Sedan	2013
BMW	7 Series	Sedan	2013
Chevrolet	Cruze	Midsize Car	2013
Jeep	Grand Cherokee	SUV	2013
Mazda	Mazda6	Midsize Car	2013
Porsche	Cajun	SUV	2013
Porsche**	Cayenne	SUV	2014

*Availability dates typically indicate calendar year rather than model year.
**Preliminary EPA fuel economy figures show Cayenne Diesel trumps the hybrid version.

3. Use *www.insurancehotline.com* to find out which cars are the cheapest to insure. Remember, having an additional licensed driver in the family places your policy in a higher risk category, with accompanying higher premiums. Not giving that extra driver permission to use the car has little bearing on your rates—you'll still pay more.

4. Crashworthiness *is* important and has nothing to do with how much you paid. Many entry-level vehicles have high crash protection scores given out by both the National Highway Traffic and Safety Administration and the Insurance Institute for Highway Safety. Imports unrated by American agencies will likely have been tested in Europe or Australia (see *www.crashtest.com*).

5. Delay buying a new car until early 2013, when automaker and dealer clearance rebates bring down new prices and lots of inexpensive trade-ins reduce used prices. Also, refuse all preparation charges, wear and tear insurance, and $375+ "administration" or "processing" fees. It's uncanny how automakers and dealers create problems and then sell you the solution. For example, extended warranties are bought because the car industry rejects so many valid warranty claims. The solution? Buy a reliable vehicle recommended by *Lemon-Aid* that doesn't need costly extra protection.

6. Buy an entry-level Asian model or Asian/American co-venture like the small Korean-built Chevrolet Spark.

7. Stay away from superflous fancy options like failure-prone manumatic transmissions; hard-to-replace, overpriced "run-flat" tires; leak-prone, headroom-robbing sunroofs; and tone-deaf, distracting, and confusing voice-controlled electronic systems. The worst of these infotainment options are Toyota's distracting Entune; Ford's MyFord Touch, which has a cluttered layout, small on-screen type, and a sluggish performance; and the BMW

iDrive system, which is not only distracting, but can take six steps and 10 seconds to manually tune the radio.

8. Be wary of all European models. Even the venerable *Consumer Reports* now agrees with *Lemon-Aid:* European makes are way overpriced, depreciation is head-spinning, parts and servicing can be a problem, and poor quality control will drive you to "speak in tongues"—and not necessarily French, German, or Italian.

9. Don't buy "nostalgia" cars; they aren't as good as the memories they evoke. This includes the resurrected Dodge Challenger.

10. Buy in the States, or use lower American prices as leverage with Canadian dealers. It's easy to find fully loaded trucks, sports cars, and luxury vehicles for up to $20,000 less than what you would pay in Canada. Look in Part Three of this guide and compare costs between the two countries.

Best Vehicles for Students

Young drivers feel they are invulnerable to accidents and would never admit that they are poor drivers, or that they are more responsive to peer pressure than parental admonition. That's why you want to buy a car that gets top marks in crashworthiness and reliability, sips gas, and doesn't look like a Flintstone retread. Advanced safety features such as electronic stability control and full-torso side-curtain airbags are a plus. Large pickups or SUVs can be rollover-prone, hard to control on the highway, and carry too many distracting passengers. Sports cars beg to be driven too fast and inspire a false sense of confidence.

Acura TSX	Honda Civic	Mazda3
Chevrolet Camaro	Hyundai Accent	Mazda Miata
Ford Focus	Hyundai Elantra	Nissan Rogue
Ford Mustang (auto.)	Hyundai Tucson	Subaru Impreza/Outback
Honda Fit	Kia Soul	Toyota Matrix

Best Vehicles for Families and Seniors

Vehicles that are recommended for families and seniors have much in common: a reasonable price, good crashworthiness ratings, and dependable reliability are paramount. Electronic stability control, full- torso side-curtain airbags, and no-hassle child safety seat installation are also a plus. Appearance is not as important as access. Good visibility, maximum seat and head restraint comfort, a comfortable driving position, a spacious interior, and intuitive, easily operated controls are key factors worth consideration. For more details as to what makes the ideal car for seniors, see page 48.

Acura RDX	Honda Odyssey	Hyundai Santa Fe
Ford F-150	Honda Pilot	Mazda5
Ford Fusion	Honda Ridgeline	Nissan Altima
Honda Accord	Hyundai Azera	Subaru Forester
Honda CR-V	Hyundai Elantra	Toyota Camry
Honda Element	Hyundai Genesis	Toyota Corolla

2013–2014 Model Changes

Here are the new cars and trucks that will undergo the most change, mechanical and stylistic, this year and next. Some models are totally "first-timers," others incorporate major redesigns,

Redesigns are carried out every three years. Remember, never purchase new or redesigned models during the first six months they are on the market. The second series that comes out in late spring will have fewer defects, thanks to assembly-line fixes or a change of suppliers. As for a car or truck that has been dropped, don't automatically draw an X across its name; some can be outstanding buys. It all depends upon which vehicles have a good reliability reputation and whether parts are available from similar models still being built.

Acura ILX

Acura ILX—Not Recommended. Acura's smallest sedan ($27,790). Competitors have better performance, gas mileage, and cargo space. The sluggish base engine perks up only through the addition of the manual transmission. If you want more fuel economy, you'll have even less power to work with. Not a people-hauler. Crashworthiness not tested yet. No changes expected for the 2014 model. The Buick Verano is a good alternative.

Acura RL—The Above Average $69,690 flagship of the Acura fleet, the RL is loaded with intuitive (Hello, Ford?) high-tech gadgetry and premium luxury features that don't confound or distract the average driver. Except for some minor sound system glitches, the RL is flawless. NHTSA crash-tested the 2012 RL for rollover protection and gave it a five-star rating.

Acura RLX (2014)—Not Recommended during its first year on the market. Nevertheless, the advance showing of this impressive hybrid confirms the matchup of a solid V6 engine with electric motors and AWD. The untested powertrain hookup means prudent buyers should wait well into 2014 for early production problems to be corrected.

Acura NSX (2014)—Predicted to arrive in mid-2014, the resurrected NSX (it was dropped in 2005) is estimated to cost $150,000 and will be offered as a hybrid. It will employ a mid-mounted 3.7L V6 hooked to a twin-clutch 7-speed transmission, and an electric motor driving the rear wheels. Two more electric motors will spin the front wheels independently, delivering exceptional torque-vectoring to help pull the car around corners as well as the original NSX did. The Sports Hybrid AWD system claims to deliver V8 performance with "better-than-four-cylinder" fuel economy (don't believe it).

Audi A4 Allroad—A Below Average buy. This is a comfortable and versatile $45,100 wagon that offers mediocre highway performance with its turbocharged four-banger and extra height. It also has a seemingly small interior, and an unjustifiably high retail price. Since this is an all-new model, wait for the improved 2014 version that will offer today's options as standard features. No crash data. The Acura TSX Sports Wagon and BMW 3-Series Sports Wagon are worthy alternatives.

Audi Q5—An Average buy. Audi's history of factory-related glitches (engine and fit and finish) and its "lag and lurch" powertrain are immediate turnoffs. Sales of the smaller models and 3.2 Standard upgrade have been quite good. That's probably why prices haven't increased much this year: *2.0 TFSI Premium: $41,200; 2.0 TFSI Premium Plus: $45,300; 3.2 FSI Standard: $45,500; 3.2 FSI Premium: $49,900.* The Q7's smaller brother debuted in 2009 as a stylish five-passenger luxury crossover compact full of high-tech gadgetry, including an adaptive suspension that allows for firm, sporty handling, if so desired. The Q5 power comes by way of a 270 hp 3.2L V6 and the latest rear-biased version of AWD. These models are stylish with many luxury appointments. They are noted for good acceleration; excellent handling; and lots of nifty safety, performance, and convenience goodies. The negatives aren't many. Owners say the cars are overpriced; there's limited rear seat room and cargo space; and, in the best German tradition, controls are needlessly complicated. Servicing is highly dependent upon a weak dealer network and parts are problematic. Furthermore, powertain performance is less than stellar. Owners report hard and delayed upshifts and downshifts between First and Second gear; sometimes, when coming to a stop, the transmission downshifts just as the engine suddenly surges. Excessive wind noise. NHTSA awarded five stars for front and side crashworthiness and four stars for rollover protection. IIHS gave its top, "Good," rating for frontal offset and side protection. Head restraint effectiveness is also rated "Good."

Audi Q7—An Average buy. These are complicated five- or seven-passenger machines that are made from bits and pieces of VW's other models. The Q7 offers both gasoline and diesel powertrains hooked to an 8-speed automatic transmission. Past reliability has been poor, the ride is stiff, and handling is mediocre. Prices have remained steady: *3.0 TFSI: $53,900; 3.0 TFSI Premium: $59,000; 3.0 TFSI Sport: $69,200; 3.0 TDI: $58,900; 3.0 TDI Premium: $64,000.* The new 3.0T Premium and 3.0T Prestige are powered by a supercharged 3.0L V6 engine, putting out 272 and 333 horses, respectively. The 3.0 TDI Premium carries a 225 hp 3.0L turbodiesel V6. Maximum towing capacity is 6,600 pounds. The Q7 is a VW Touareg/Porsche Cayenne combo with an Audi badge and new powertrains that so far have presented a few reliability concerns. Off-road prowess is not as great as the Touareg's or Cayenne's; fuel economy is not impressive; ride quality is ho-hum; rear visibility is limited; and the third-row entry/exit is problematic. Early owner feedback indicates that this large crossover AWD wagon has some factory-related defects affecting the fuel and electrical systems, powertrain components, and fit and finish—exactly the problems owners find with Porsche and VW models. Poor servicing and recurring factory glitches are to be expected. NHTSA gives the Q7 five stars for front and side crash protection and four stars for rollover resistance. IIHS gives its top, "Good," score for frontal offset, side, and head-restraint protection.

BMW ActiveHybrid3—Not Recommended. This BMW is a hybrid in name only. Actually, you get a $49,200 (U.S.) high-performance luxury hybrid that accelerates from 0 to 60 in 5.2 seconds and gives you just a bit better gas mileage than the BMW335i. If you must have a hybrid, pick up a $39,970 Toyota Highlander.

BMW I Series—An Average buy. This little Bimmer is a joy to drive—when the powertrain, fuel, and electrical systems aren't acting up. Fit and finish isn't first-class, either, and servicing requires sustained dealer support. BMW's entry-level 128i and 135i include either a two-door coupe or convertible with a power-folding softtop. A standard 3.0L inline 6-cylinder is shared with the 3-Series. The 128i has 230 hp, while the 135i is turbocharged and has 300 hp. All models carry a 6-speed manual transmission, though the 128i offers an optional 6-speed automatic. The top-end 135i offers an optional 7-speed automated manual transmission; in the past, this has been a problematic transmission. Prices are a bit high: *128i Coupe:* $35,800; *128i Convertible:* $41,200; *135i Coupe:* $43,000; *135i Convertible:* $48,500. These cars can be counted on for excellent acceleration, steering, and handling; good outward visibility (coupes); and average depreciation. Some critics say the styling is too "unique" for their taste; the cars are harsh riding—you feel every bump in the road; there's poor outward visibility with the convertible top up; and fuel consumption is a big letdown. Owners also report chronic fuel pump failures covered by a 10-year secret warranty; ABS malfunctions; early ignition coil, clutch plate, and DTC traction failures; run-flat tire alerts that come on for no reason; a cramped interior that makes for awkward entry and exit; and few storage spaces. No crashworthiness data is available.

BMW i3 (2014)—Not Recommended. The BMW i3 is an urban electric car that will be launched as a 2014 model by the end of 2013. It will likely sell in the $43,000–$50,000 (U.S.) range.

BMW X1—An Average buy. This rear-drive, small luxury SUV starts at $38,500 ($30,650 U.S.) and is powered by either a base 240 hp 2.0L turbocharged 4-cylinder or an optional 300 hp 3.0L V6. The Buick Encore is an alternative worth considering.

BMW X4 (2014)—Not Recommended during its first year on the market. The X4 shares powertrains with the X3, including four- and six-cylinder gasoline and diesel engines. Best alternatives include the Land Rover Evoque, Porsche Macan, and future Audi Q6. Six-speed and 7-speed dual-clutch transmissions will be standard; an 8-speed Steptronic transmission will be optional.

BMW 5 Series GT—Launched just a few years ago, this BMW has misjudged its market, which wants conservatively styled sedans that don't have an ungainly liftback or a high load floor. Mercedes laughs all the way to the bank.

BMW X6—A "sports activity coupe" (SAC?) that answers a question no one asked. The more traditional and cheaper X5 outsells this $100,000 turbocharged trans-something almost eight to one. An endangered species.

Buick Encore—Too early to recommend. The 2013 Encore is a small luxury SUV that is only slightly larger than the Chevrolet Sonic with which it shares its platform. Touted as a five-passenger SUV, the Encore can sit only four comfortably. Powered by the Sonic's optional 140 hp 1.6L turbocharged four, the Encore stresses fuel economy over speed.

Buick Verano—An Average buy; doesn't have the luxury look or feel of some of its rivals. The $23,000 entry-level Verano returns with few changes, except for a new turbocharged 250 hp version. Buick has outfitted the Verano with many of the suspension and body components used by the Chevrolet Cruze, but the Verano is much more than a warmed-over Cruze. Its style (please, get rid of the portholes on the hood), engine, and luxury features set it apart. However, this is not a quick car: the base 180 hp 2.4L 4–cylinder engine will do 0–60 mph in about nine seconds, but the responsive 6–speed automatic tranny makes those extra seconds uneventful. The suspension is softly sprung without degrading handling. You also are treated to a quiet and luxurious cabin and generous standard features. Only two owner complaints have been posted by NHTSA for the 2012 Verano: a rattling suspension noise when passing over uneven terrain and chronic stalling. No crash data has been compiled yet.

Cadillac CTS (2014)—An Average buy. The current, second-generation Cadillac CTS sedan is the backbone of the GM luxury division's sales. The next model should be significantly more stylish, feature the CUE touchscreen driver interface, and have a more elegant interior. The next CTS will be easier on fuel with no loss of performance with a twin-turbocharged 3.0L V6 coupled to a new 7-speed automatic and/or manual transmission. The CTS-V will follow in 2015 and incorporate whatever high-output engine GM uses in the upgraded Corvette.

Cadillac SRX—A Below Average buy. Base models are front-drive, while Luxury versions include all-wheel drive; both are powered by a 308 hp 3.6L V6 hooked to a 6-speed automatic transmission, with a maximum towing capacity of 3,500 pounds. Available safety features include ABS, traction control, an anti-skid system, side curtain airbags, and front side airbags. Optional safety features include steering-linked headlights and adjustable pedals. Alternative vehicles are the Lexus RX or Acura RDX. Prices: *Base FWD:* $41,780; *AWD (entry-level):* $48,000. Prices are negotiable. The SRX has sporty handling when the tranny and engine are in sync (which has been a problem). Other observations: the car is overpriced; it quickly loses resale value; the AWD model is slower to accelerate than the rear-drive, and the transmission often hesitates before downshifting. There's insufficient rear passenger room; poor fit and finish; costly, dealer-dependent servicing; and suspension may be too firm for some. Owners report the following safety related glitches, no doubt related to the SRX's redesign: chronic stalling (the vehicle then proceeds to roll downhill); electrical malfunctions that knock out instruments and gauges as the car automatically switches to Neutral; an automatic transmission that sticks in low gear (vehicle has to be brought to a stop and restarted); the hood release is located too close to driver's left foot; brakes grind as pressure is slowly lifted off the brake pedal; and it's hard to get a spare tire. NHTSA has given its five-star rating for front and side crash protection; rollover resistance received four stars.

Chevrolet Colorado/GMC Canyon—Below Average buys. Not quite as cheap as they first appear, the Colorado/Canyon pickups have a base price of $24,045 minus a cash credit of $7,000. But you have to add in about $2,200 for freight and administration fees, boosting the real price to about $19,000. Main drawbacks are wimpy engines, poor handling, so-so reliability, and sloppy fit and finish. The upcoming reworked 2014 model will likely be a better buy. If you can't wait, pick up a 2010 Honda Ridgeline for $21,000.

Chevrolet Express and Savana—A Recommended buy. These full-sized, rear-drive vans have been around forever. They're not that expensive, either, with the 2013 Express selling for $31,465 and the Savana costing only a few hundred dollars more. These are easily accessed, capacious vans. And the good news doesn't stop there. With fuel prices going higher and the economy softening, these vehicles are turning into "blue-light specials" and are discounted by up to 25 percent at different times during the year, like in the dead of winter and just prior to the arrival of new models. Both vans are perfect recession buys because any independent garage can repair them and most of their reliability issues aren't expensive to correct. Some weak areas: they are fuel-thirsty, ponderous performers, and are frequent prey to water leaks. NHTSA gives the Express 1500 cargo van five stars for frontal protection; the 1500 passenger van gets five stars for frontal protection and three stars for rollover resistance. The 2500 and 3500 12-passenger vans and the 3500 15-passenger van earned three stars each for rollover resistance. But, as *Lemon-Aid* has reported before, 15-passenger vans can be killers due to their high propensity to roll over.

Chevrolet Orlando—An Average buy. This Opel-inspired seven-seater combines reasonable fuel economy with a minivan passenger load in much the same way as the Mazda5, Kia Rondo, and my old favourite, the long-gone, greatly lamented Nissan Axxess. Thanks to its European DNA, the $20,000 Orlando rides and handles well and is reasonably fuel-efficient. Merging and hill-climbing with a full load are patience-building exercises due to the Orlando's sluggish 6–speed automatic transmission. Also, the third-row seats are suitable for children only. Reliability has been average. No crashworthiness data yet available.

Chevrolet Spark—A Below Average buy, the Spark engine has only 85 horses, yet doesn't get any better gas mileage than the 150 hp Honda Civic or 140 hp Chevy Cruze. This front-drive four-door hatchback is smaller than Chevy's Aveo subcompact. Since it's built by GM Daewoo, think of it as the Aveo's smaller brother. Light, direct steering is useful in the city and the car's $13,495 base price is quite reasonable. Accept the fact that this is a slow four-passenger urban econocar and you won't be disappointed. Five TV's *Fifth Gear* clocked the acceleration time for 0–100 km/h (0–62 mph) with the 1.0L and 1.2L engines. The results? 15.5 and 12.1 seconds, respectively, so bring along a good book and an hourglass. Some other faults: the steering is a bit light for highway driving; gear shifts are a bit clunky; the steering column doesn't telescope; the ride is harsh when going over uneven terrain; and refinement isn't what the Spark is best known for. No crash tests have been done in North America.

Chevrolet plans to launch a Spark electric vehicle next year as a 2014 model. Smart shoppers will stay away during the car's first year on the market.

Chevrolet SS (2014)—Too early to rate, this sedan is a product of GM's Australian Holden division and is essentially a reworked version of the current Caprice police cruiser. The SS will use a slightly shorter wheelbase than the Caprice police car. Power will be supplied by a direct-injection 3.6L V6, making about 323 hp, with the Camaro's 426 hp 6.2L V8 optional.

Chevrolet Volt—Not Recommended. Not an Electric Edsel, but close. Volt is GM's two-year-old electric compact four-seater. It was rolled out in Canada as a 2012 model with an astoundingly high starting price of $41,545. Disappointing sales forced GM to discount the car by $10,000 last August in addition to a provincial tax credit of up to $7,500. These two factors have led to a surge in Volt sales going into the last quarter of 2012. Also helpful is NHTSA's five-star crashworthiness rating for the 2013 Volt's side and rollover crash protection; frontal protection scored four stars.

So why isn't the car Recommended?

Here are some reasons: The car costs $7,000 more than the Leaf, and $15,000 above a well-equipped compact with a gas engine. Canadian shoppers also say they are not seeing the promised discounts. Furthermore, owners of the 2012 are angry that they paid the full $41,000 price and they get practically apoplectic over their car's $25,000 current (October 2012) value. Wait until they have to replace the battery.

Buying a Volt means you become the "captive customer" of a limited number of Chevrolet dealers; God help you if the car has an electrical short away from a large urban area. Also, according to *safercar.org*, owners of 2011 and 2012 models report these safety flaws: front suspension may collapse; rear Reverse lights are too dim; rear windshield distorts the view; rear end "slips" when accelerating; and the charging system may overheat and short out. Also, if one leaves the car without powering down, it may keep running silently.

Bottom line: Consider the cheaper Nissan Leaf or buy a well-equipped compact car.

Chrysler 100 (2014)—Derived from the Dodge Dart platform and produced in Illinois, the 100 hatchback takes the place of the PT Cruiser. Expect the 100 to be smaller and lighter than the Dart.

Chrysler 200 (2014)—The 2014 Chrysler 200 mid-size arrives early next year as a 2014 model. Essentially a lengthened and retuned Dodge Dart, the 200 boasts much more passenger and trunk space. The engine is a 3.2L Pentastar V6 hooked to a 9-speed automatic transmission. Buyers wanting a little more power can get the optional 3.6L Pentastar V6.

Dodge Grand Caravan and Chrysler Town & Country (2014)—Chrysler's large minivan changes completely for the 2014 model year. It gets a new 9-speed automatic transmission that should enhance acceleration and gas mileage (hopefully, it will also improve reliability, as well). It will use a new E-EVO platform and a 3.2L Pentastar V6 as the sole engine choice. While horsepower is down somewhat from the 3.6, gas mileage is up, and the 9-speed provides superior acceleration. The Lancia version will offer a standard diesel engine.

Dodge Dart—An Above Average buy that's reasonably-priced: *SE*: $15,995; *SXT*: $18,595; *Rallaye*: $19,495; *Limited*: $23,245. The Dodge Dart is a much better performer than the Caliber it replaces. Buyers have the choice of one of three 4-cylinder engines: a 160 hp turbo 1.4L; a 160 hp 2.0L; or an 184 hp 2.4L. There are three choices of 6-speed gearboxes: one manual, one automatic, and one dual-clutch variant. The interior has some nice features, like a central seat cushion that flips up to open a huge storage area for handbags, etc., and the user-friendly Uconnect media screen.

Driving the Dart is a breeze, although the base 1.4L engine's turbo takes a bit of time to get the car up to speed. Going head-to-head with the Chevy Cruze, Ford Focus, Honda Civic, and Toyota Corolla, the Dart leads the pack for highway performance, especially with a manual transmission. Building on this advantage, 2014 Darts will offer a high-performance 300 hp SRT package complete with a 9-speed gearbox (okay, you can get up off the floor, now). No crashworthiness data yet.

Fiat 500—An Average buy. Fiat's back in Canada after walking out on its U.S. and Canadian owners in 1984 and leaving them high and dry with worthless warranties and rust-cankered vehicles. The automaker now heralds its triumphant return to North America as Chrysler's saviour (actually, Chrysler may save Fiat's beleaguered European operations). When Fiat pulled out of North America, I was in the trenches as president of the Automobile Protection Association and remember only too well the many Fiat owners who were stunned that their rusty, unreliable, and unwanted pieces of crap would never be fixed. Fiats are reasonably priced in Canada at $14,995 (POP); $17,595 (Sport); $18,795 (Lounge); and $23,995 (500 Abarth). These minicars have adequate acceleration; are fuel frugal; handle well; and have good outward visibility. Quality is still a big question that has yet to be answered. The May 2009 J.D. Power quality survey put Fiat at the bottom—28th of 28—in U.K. satisfaction rankings. Seating is for four only and parts availability and mechanic competency will be built up slowly. Other minuses include a small interior, a "sit-straight" driving position, a harsh ride, and wind buffeting. NHTSA gives the 2013 hatchback four stars for frontal and rollover crash protection; the 2012 scored similarly, except side crashworthiness scored three stars. IIHS found the 500 Cabrio "Good" in all safety categories.

Ford C-MAX Hybrid Energi—Not Recommended during its first year on the market; buy a Mazda5 instead. Part hatchback, wagon, and micro- van, the C-MAX Hybrid is a tall five-seater powered by an electric motor and a 2.0L 4-cylinder gas engine. It is barely larger than a Ford Focus, but boasts more passenger volume than the Prius (a Ford two mountain bikes can fit inside). C-MAX will operate electrically up to 100 km/h, allowing the electric traction motor to power the vehicle, providing maximum fuel- efficiency. The car comes with two electronic features that may not yet be ready for prime time: the Microsoft-conceived Ford Sync voice command suite and the MyFord Touch infotainment system with touch-screen controls for audio, climate, and navigation. C-MAX Prices: *SE*: $28,849; *SEL*: $31,849; and *SEL Energi*: $38,649.

Ford Econoline E-Series—An Average buy. These gas-guzzling full-sized vans haven't changed much over the years and quickly lose their value, making them a better deal used. *Commercial van*: $31,299; *Passenger van*: $36,399. Parts are plentiful and repairs aren't dealer-dependent, but like most large vans, the Econolines are vulnerable to side winds and rapid brake wear. Owners also complain about poor-quality original equipment tires; electrical system shorts; excessive steering wander; and surging, power loss, or black/white smoke (6.0L engines); and harsh automatic transmission shifts and automatic transmission converter clutch lockup, causing hesitation and/or lack of power when shifting. NHTSA gives the van three stars for rollover protection.

Ford Edge/Lincoln MKX—Below Average buys; the $46,500 Lincoln MKX is the luxury-laden spin-off of the $28,000 Edge. Some worthy alternatives: the Mazda CX-9, Nissan Murano, or Toyota Highlander. The Edge is stylish and gives good gas mileage, but like its Lincoln Twin, it is also problem-plagued with serious safety- and performance-related defects. A five-passenger wagon/SUV crossover based on the same platform as the Fusion sedan, the Edge comes in either all-wheel drive (without low-range gearing) or front-drive. The turbocharged four, 285 hp 3.5L V6, and optional 305 hp 3.7L V6 are hooked to a fuel-efficient 6-speed automatic transmission. Owners report good acceleration and handling that is better than average for a crossover. There is also plenty of passenger and cargo room. NHTSA gives the 2013 Edge and MKX five stars for side protection, four stars for rollover resistance, and only three stars for frontal crashworthiness. IIHS rated the 2013 Edge "Good" in front offset, side, roof, and rear crashworthiness.

Some of the Edge negatives: some hesitation and gear-hunting when downshifting; mediocre fuel economy; lots of engine noise; spongy brakes; and though softly sprung, the ride is jittery. Parts are a bit scarce and repairs are highly dealer-dependent. Optional equipment you don't need: Ford's Vista Roof (a glass roof with a sliding glass sunroof over the front seats), a navigation system, a DVD entertainment system, leather upholstery, and larger wheels. Edge owner complaints according to NHTSA: drivetrain failures; sudden stalling and unintended acceleration; windshield shatters for no reason; excessive torque steer; poorly designed head restraints:

> The consumer stated forward tilted head rests produce a lot of neck pain which may force consumers to look for different alternatives that may alter safety specifications. The consumer is looking for a way to replace the head rest.

Fit and finish flaws; tire TPMS system becomes brittle and breaks when you check the air in the tire; excessive road noise; confusing, distracting controls; and a complicated MyFord Touch and Sync infotainment system. It's also easy for drivers to confuse the accelerator with the brake pedal.

MKX failings generally track the Edge complaints except for some safety-related incidents: rear passenger-side door ajar and warning light didn't activate; navigation and other electronic system malfunctions and distractions; fuel tank cannot be filled to capacity; and reflections from the chrome air vents reflect onto both the driver- and passenger-side mirrors.

Ford Expedition—Below Average. This gas-guzzling, overpriced full-sized SUV quickly loses its value and, like Ford trucks, is a better deal bought used. For example, an XLT sells for $49,049; the Limited costs $60,949; and a Limited Max goes for $63,449. Expeditions come with standard Trailer Sway Control that works with Ford's AdvanceTrac and Roll Stability Control to enhance safety while towing. An SOS Post-Crash Alert System activates the horn and emergency flashers should the airbags deploy. And, like the rest of Ford's lineup, Sync with available voice-activated navigation features, HD Radio, and Sirius Travel Link offers Expedition customers more choices in information and entertainment, if the features don't fail and you can figure them out—many owners can't. The Expedition comes with a 310 hp 5.4L V8 housed in a truck-based chassis. Extended-length versions have more cargo space and seating for up to nine passengers. GM's Suburban, Acadia, Tahoe, and Yukon represent credible alternatives.

The Expedition has adequate passing/merging power and can tow up to 9,200 pounds. Occupants have a comfortable ride, and interior appointments are exceptional. Most large SUVs have heavy third-row seats that must be manually removed for more cargo space; however, the Expedition has second- and third-row seats that automatically fold flat into the floor. Both seat rows offer plenty of room, and the seats are nicely bolstered. Repairs aren't dealer-dependent and parts can be easily found at discount suppliers. On the other hand, powertrain performance is seriously deficient, base trim is Spartan, and the interior feels cheap. Owners also say the V8 engine is sluggish and noisy. Ponderous handling is outclassed by GM's Tahoe and Yukon. Rapid depreciation: The $61,899 2010 King Ranch 4×4 model is now worth about $30,000. NHTSA safety-related logs report few complaints. Owners have mentioned chronic stalling; rapid brake wear; transmission failures; harsh automatic transmission shifts; blown fuses; poorly-designed head restraints; water leaks; electrical malfunctions; and overheated seats. NHTSA gives the 2013 Expedition five stars for side crash protection and four stars for frontal crashworthiness and AWD rollover resistance. Only three stars were given for front drive rollover resistance. IIHS hasn't crash tested the Expedition.

Ford Flex—Above Average. This $29,999 boxy front-drive or AWD four-door wagon seats either six or seven passengers in three rows of seats. Power comes from a 285 hp 3.5L V6 mated to a 6-speed automatic transmission and an optional turbocharged 3.5L that unleashes 355 horses while mated to the same gearbox. Safety features include ABS, traction control, an anti-skid system, front side airbags, and curtain side airbags. Some of the Flex's other features include a rear-view camera, power liftgate, voice-activated navigation system with real-time traffic and weather updates, four-panel glass roof, and refrigerated centre console. Another available feature is Ford's Sync, which is a voice-activated system that controls navigation, communication, and entertainment features. Other vehicles worth considering: the Chevrolet Traverse, GMC Acadia, Honda Pilot, Hyundai Santa Fe, Mazda CX-9, and Toyota Highlander.

The 2013 Flex has acceptable acceleration and handling; improved brakes, a roomy interior; comfortable third-row seating; easy entry/exit; a quiet cabin; a soft, compliant suspension that provides a comfortable ride for seven with car-like handling; and good overall visibility. But, this pricey wagon loses value quickly and is a gas-burner. It's relatively new to the market, so servicing is very dealer-dependent. Steering is a bit too light; there's excessive nose dive upon hard braking; moderate engine noise when accelerating; a harsh, uneven idle; and power locks that cycle on their own. Owners have also complained of airbags that fail to deploy in a head-on collision; sudden brake failure; and chronic stalling. NHTSA gave the 2013 Flex four stars for rollover resistance. IIHS awarded the 2013 Flex its top, "Good," score in all categories.

Ford Taurus—An Average buy. Restyled 2013 entry-level versions sell for $28,000 and offer a more-powerful 237 hp turbocharged 2.0L four to accompany the base 290 hp 3.5L V6. The SHO (super high-output) returns with an EcoBoost turbocharged 365 hp 3.5L V6 engine, 6-speed automatic transmission, and AWD. SHO models have performance-oriented steering, suspension tuning, better-performing brakes, and 20-inch summer performance tires.

Highway performance has been cranked up several notches, and the interior is more user-friendly, with better-quality materials and more attention paid to ensuring proper fit and finish. Excellent overall reliability. Good acceleration and steering/handling with the SHO version; the base Taurus does reasonably well. Owners say the automatic transmission performance is degraded by frequent gear-hunting (non-SHO), and the SHO ride can be uncomfortably firm. Owner complaints centre on electrical and suspension glitches and roof pillars that obstruct rearward vision. The interior feels closed-in and there's not much rear-seat room. NHTSA gives the 2013 Taurus five stars for frontal and side crash protection; four stars for rollover resistance. IIHS has awarded the car its top, "Good," rating for front offset, side, roof, and rear crash protection.

Ford Transit Connect—An Average buy. Only three years on the market and sales volume is low. This $28,200–$29,500 compact van returns this year with versions capable of running on batteries, compressed natural gas, or liquid petroleum gas. Sold worldwide for over a decade, it can seat two, four, or five passengers. It has minivan-like sliding rear side doors and two rear "barn doors," similar to a commercial van. Powered by a puny 136 hp 2.0L 4-cylinder engine and a rather primitive, fuel-thirsty 4-speed automatic transmission, the Transit is longer, wider, and heavier than a Focus. This vehicle is aimed at the small-business commercial market and fits between the discontinued compact Chevrolet HHR and the problematic Dodge Sprinter. Essentially an easily accessed, capacious rolling box with traction control, the Connect offers an anti-skid system; a vehicle tracking device; and an Internet connection. Handling is fairly good, though fuel economy is only acceptable. Its weak areas include lethargic acceleration caused by a sluggish, uncertain transmission (a deal-breaker, for sure); side wind vulnerability; cheap interior materials; tall head restraints and closed rear quarter panels that limit visibility; drivetrain pedals that are too close to each other for such a wide interior; and excessive engine and road noise. Owners can expect problems with premature brake wear and powertrain glitches due to the Transit's heft. NHTSA gives the 2013 Connect three stars for protection from frontal or rollover injury and only two stars for side crashworthiness. IIHS has yet to test the van.

Honda Insight—An Average buy. One of the least expensive hybrids available in North America. The first hybrid had such a checkered reliability and performance history that Honda took it off the market for a few years. Now that it has returned, Honda marketing gurus are learning to their dismay that car buyers have long memories. Toyota sells seven Prius hybrids for every Insight that makes it out of the showroom.

Hyundai Veloster—The Veloster is an Average buy that is going into its third year. This $19,499 sporty hatchback is instantly recognizable by its three doors, with the passenger-side rear door offering easy access to the rear seats. Equipped with a base 1.6L 138 hp 4-cylinder engine, or the optional 201 hp turbocharged version, coupled to a 6-speed manual or manumatic, the Velostar provides plenty of power, a sports car–stiff ride, and nimble handling. NHTSA-posted safety complaints include the sunroof shattering for no reason:

Airbags failing to deploy; stalling when accelerating; lag and lurch acceleration; loss of power steering; brake caliper sticking to the rotor (see *www.veloster.org*); incorrect speedometer readings; and the passenger side mirror can't be adjusted sufficiently to see blind spots. Neither NHTSA nor IIHS have crash-tested this car.

Jaguar F-Type Roadster (2014)—Jaguar makes a play to save its own soul with the introduction of the all-new 2014 F-Type Roadster. It's a pure two-seater, powered by a new supercharged V6 that should make around 380 hp. With its small size, 8-speed ZF transmission, and open cockpit, it's more Porsche 911 steak and potatoes than a high-end exotic. So expect it to be priced in the 80k range.

Jeep Liberty (2014)—Not Recommended. This orphan ended its model-run in August 2012 and the redesigned 2014 model won't be sold until May 2013. That version will use the Fiat/Chrysler platform, be available in front- and all-wheel-drive configurations, and use a 9 speed automatic transmission. Engineers are also shooting for a much-improved fuel-economy rating by switching to front-wheel drive.

Lexus CT 200h—An Above Average, $31,450 luxury sporty car, the CT 200h returns this year with an upgraded lateral performance damper system to minimize body vibration and increase overall ride comfort; an updated version of Lexus' Enform infotainment system meant to enhance the navigation system; and assorted interior improvements. Powered by Lexus' advanced Hybrid Drive, the CT gives you superior fuel efficiency in four option packages, including the F Sport package. No crash data, yet; no safety-related incidences logged by NHTSA.

Mercedes-Benz R-Class—An Average buy. Mercedes first called this low-riding minivan a "sports cruiser" and when that was met with underwhelming enthusiasm, changed the name to "family cruiser" (anything to avoid the dreaded "minivan" moniker). Somber styling, awkward long rear doors, poor reliability, and a 7-speed transmission that "hunts" for the right gear.

Mini Cooper—An Average buy. This eye-catching classic British-*cum*-German car is a good highway performer, but high maintenance bills makes "cute" costly. Although the base Mini has an average reliability rating, the Cooper S has been much less reliable. This is a driver's car, especially when equipped with the 181–208 hp 1.6L turbo four. The car handles well and has exceptionally responsive steering. There is sufficient front legroom but back seat room is limited. Stability and traction control are standard. You will find the base engine adequate, but the Cooper S is more spirited. Expect a high freight/PDI fee; mediocre fuel economy; a choppy ride; and limited front and rear visibility. IIHS rates the 2012 Cooper as "Good" for offset crash protection and head-restraint effectiveness; side and roof crashworthiness were given an "Average" score. NHTSA says the 2013 Cooper merits a five-star rating for its resistance to rollovers; other crash categories weren't tested.

Nissan Titan—A Below Average buy; buy a Ford F-150 or Dodge Ram instead. The Titan is a full-sized truck that hasn't been updated in over a decade. It is outclassed by the competition, which offers more safety, performance, and convenience features, in addition to a more upscale interior. NHTSA gives the 2013 Titan three stars for rollover protection; no other tests were carried out. Prices: *King Cab S 4×2*: $33,898; *Crew Cab S 4×4*: $39,898.

Subaru Tribeca—A Subaru version of the ugly and unpopular Pontiac Aztek, the Tribeca's odd, rounded styling and triangular grille have turned off buyers since the car was first launched in 2005. Now the car has a new look, but it, too, is failing to catch on with an unimpressed public.

Smart Fortwo—Not Recommended. Buyers want more than a cute, toy-like mini-compact. American megadealer Roger Penske has dumped the brand, which seals Smart's fate in North America. Canadian dealers are desperately looking for a "Smart" move from Mercedes that will reduce the car's price and add more safety and convenience features.

Volkswagen Eos—An Average buy, as long as you stay away from the unpredictable, failure-prone DSG automated manual transmission. The Jetta-based Eos is a four-seater convertible equipped with a retractable roof and powered by a more-than-adequate 200 hp 2.0L turbocharged 4-cylinder engine coupled to either a standard 6-speed manual or an optional 6-speed automatic transmission. The car is agile, handles well, and provides a comfortable, taut ride. Braking is smooth and easy to modulate. Instruments and controls are intuitive and easily accessed. Front seats are supportive; rear seats are a bit firmer. Some negatives include limited rear interior access, legroom, and headroom, and excessive cabin engine/road noise. Owners give the Eos a below-average reliability score with most complaints targeting the AC, electrical, and fuel system. Transmission failures and poor fit and finish are also common complaints. IIHS gives the 2012 Eos its top, "Good" rating in all crash categories.

Prices are a bit high: *Comfortline*: $39,875, *Highline*: $45,775, plus a $1,395 delivery fee. On the higher-end models, get an identical 2012 version and seek a 10 percent discount. Don't pay any $300–$400 dealer "administration" or "processing" fees. Depreciation is unusually steep for a convertible; a 2009 Eos Trendline that sold for $36,000 is now worth only $19,500. Two good alternatives are the BMW 3 Series Cabriolet and the Mazda Miata.

Volkswagen Tiguan—An Above Average small SUV that's based on the Golf platform, the Tiguan has been a sales success story mainly because it is well positioned between moderately priced small SUVs, like the Honda CR-V, and more upscale offerings, like the Acura RDX. Powered by a competent and fuel-efficient 200 hp 4-cylinder turbocharged engine, the car is well-equipped; handles nicely; gives a comfortable, though stiff, ride; and offers plenty of room in the rear.

Reliability is outstanding. Nevertheless, 2012–13 VW service bulletins note there have been many Bluetooth and other infotainment electronic malfunctions. Make verifying the performance of these systems a key part of your test drive. Fuel system failures and AC malfunctions have been other problem areas. But only nine 2012 safety-related complaints are registered with NHTSA where 50 would be the norm. They include reports of the transmission transfer case falling out, loss of braking, and false low tire pressure alerts. This small SUV has also earned excellent crash scores from both NHTSA and IIHS.

Tiguans are pricey compared to the competition: a Trendline will cost $27,875, while the Comfortline base price is $31,275. Shave costs by getting the practically identical 2012 version. Again, watch out for phony dealer fees plus an unbelievable $1,580 freight charge. Another surprising expense is a faster than average depreciation rate. For example, a 2009 Highline AWD that once sold for $38,375 is now worth only $16,500. Two good alternatives: a Honda CR-V or Hyundai Tucson.

Appendix II
INTERNET INFO

Recent surveys show that close to 80 percent of car buyers get reliability and pricing information from the Internet before visiting a dealer or private seller. This trend has resulted in easier access to confidential price margins, secret warranties, and lower prices—if you know where to look.

Getting the Transaction Costs

If you want a low price and abhor dealership visits and haggling, search out a reliable new- or used-car broker. For years, *Lemon-Aid* has recommended Dealfinder, an Ottawa-based auto broker that helps clients across Canada. Go to *www.dealfinder.org/about.htm*.

For those readers who feel comfortable negotiating all of the transaction details with the dealer, here's what to do: First, compare a new vehicle's "discounted" MSRP published on the automaker's website with invoices downloaded from the Automobile Protection Association (*www.apa.ca*), Car Help Canada, Car Cost Canada, the Canadian Automobile Association (*www.caa.ca*), and a host of other agencies. Second, check the prices you find against the ones listed in this book. Third, pay particular attention to the prices charged in the States by accessing the automaker's U.S. website—just type the company name into Google and add "USA." For example, "GM USA" will take you directly to the automaker's American website, whereas "GM Canada" gives you the Canadian headquarters, models, and prices. If you find the U.S. price is substantially lower than what Canadian dealers charge, take your U.S. printout to the Canadian dealers and ask them to come closer to the American price. There is no reason why you should pay more in Canada. And this includes freight and pre-delivery inspection fees.

Free Online Trade-in Values

If you have a trade-in, it's important to find out its true value to decide whether selling it privately would put more money in your pocket than selling it to the dealer.

Right now, there is a shortage of good three- to five-year-old used cars on the market and private buyers are paying a premium for them.

Problem is, how do you find how much your trade-in is worth? In the past, dealers had a monopoly on this information because only they could afford the hundreds of dollars in annual subscription fees charged by the "Black Book" and "Red Book" publishers. That has now changed with the advent of the Internet and the free online values for used cars given out by VMR Canada at *www.vmrcanada.com/canada_makes.htm*.

Free Confidential Reliability Info

Unearthing reliability information from independent sources on the Internet takes a bit more patience. You should first wade through the thousands of consumer complaints logged in the NHTSA database at www.safercar.org. Next, use the NHTSA and ALLDATA service bulletin databases to confirm a specific problem's existence, find out if it's caused by a manufacturing defect, and learn how to correct it. Augment this information with tips found on car forums and protest/information sites. *Lemon-Aid* does this for you in its guides, but you can stay current about your vehicle's problems or research a particular failure in greater depth on your own by using the above search methods.

Automobile companies have helpful—though self-serving—websites, most of which feature detailed sections on their vehicles' histories and research and development, as well as all sorts of information of interest to auto enthusiasts and bargain hunters. For example, you can often find out the freight fee before you even get to the dealership; sales agents generally prefer to hit you with this charge at the end of the transaction when your guard is down. Manufacturers can easily be accessed through a search engine like Google or by typing the automaker's name into your Internet browser's address bar followed by ".com" or ".ca". Or, for extra fun and a more balanced presentation, type the vehicle model or manufacturer's name into a search engine, followed by "lemon," "problems," or "lawsuits."

CROSS-BORDER SHOPPING

Who would have thought that, once again, the Canadian loonie would be worth more than the American dollar? Certainly not automakers. They have been ripping us off for years with car prices 15 to 20 percent higher than the American price.

But Canadians are fighting back by shopping in the States, where vehicles are much cheaper. For example, in July 2008, what was a trickle of buyers from Canada turned into a tsunami of 240,000 vehicles imported from the United States into Canada. Now with the Canadian dollar's value once again flying high, Canadian buyers of high-end, fully-loaded vehicles are again flocking to dealer showrooms in the States.

Dealers on both sides of the border are hungry for sales and aren't likely to knuckle under automaker pressure to refuse warranty repairs or service on cars purchased in the States, as they attempted to do a few years ago. Also, Transport Canada has made it easier to import new and used cars from the States, and businesses on both sides of the border have sprung up to facilitate purchases for Canadians. It's clear that getting a cross-border bargain is easier than ever. Especially since most of us live within an hour's drive of the border.

Shopping Tips

Reported savings range from around 10 percent for subcompact and compact vehicles, compact SUVs, and small vans, to over 20 percent in the luxury vehicle segment. Most manufacturers honour the warranty, and many dealers and independent garages will modify cars to Canadian standards, including speedometer and odometer labels, child tether anchorage, daytime running lights, French airbag labels, and anti-theft immobilization devices. Some will complete the import paperwork for you. Again, whether it's worthwhile importing a car from the U.S. depends upon how much of a discount you can get. Usually a 10 percent cut makes the cross-border purchase worthwhile. A listing of Canadian border crossing spots where you can bring in a just-purchased new or used car can be found at *www.ucanimport.com/Border_Crossing_Info.aspx*.

The Montreal-based Automobile Protection Association (*www.apa.ca*) says buying a car in the States as part of your vacation trip and driving it back to Canada or using an auto broker is a sure money-saver and easy to do. Canadian dealers claim the practice is unpatriotic and not fair to dealers, and that U.S. cars have softer paint and weaker batteries.

Canadian independent new- and used-car dealers aren't buying that argument; they are some of the biggest buyers of used cars in the States. For example, Advantage Trading Ltd. in Burnaby, B.C. (one of the largest importers on the West Coast) says they can get U.S. cars so cheaply that they can offer discounts to Canadians and still make a handsome profit. The only downside is that there is a shortage of some popular makes and models.

If you do decide to import a vehicle on your own, Transport Canada suggests you use the Registrar of Imported Vehicles' comprehensive and easy-to-follow check-lists (*www.riv.ca/ImportingAVehicle.aspx*), which outline

- What to do before importing a vehicle
- What to do at the border,
- What to do after the vehicle enters Canada,
- What RIV fees will be applied, and
- Who to contact for vehicle import questions, including contact information for the Canada Border Services Agency (CBSA)

These lists are all you need to import almost any car and get big savings. There are also independent resources listed at *www.riv.ca/HelpfulLinks.aspx* and *www.import-cartocanada.info/category/faq*.

MODEL INDEX